The Indian Army and the E

The partition of British India in 1947 resulted in the establishment of the independent states of India and Pakistan and the end of the British Raj. The decision to divide British India along religious lines caused widespread upheaval and communal violence in the period leading up to and following the official day of independence, 15 August 1947. In this book, Daniel Marston provides a unique examination of the role of the Indian Army in post-Second World War India. He draws upon extensive research into primary source documents and interviews with veterans of the events of 1947 to provide fresh insight into the vital part that the Indian Army played in preserving law and order in the region. This rigorous book fills a significant gap in the historiography of the British in India and will be invaluable to those studying the British Empire and South Asia more generally.

DANIEL MARSTON is Professor of Military Studies in the Strategic and Defence Studies Centre at the Australian National University. He is also the Principal of the Military and Defence Studies Program at the Australian Command and Staff College in Canberra, Australia. He has been a Visiting Fellow with the Oxford Leverhulme Programme on the Changing Character of War. His first book *Phoenix from the Ashes*, an in-depth assessment of how the British/Indian Army turned defeat into victory in the Burma campaign of the Second World War, won the Templer Medal in 2003. He completed his doctorate in the history of war at Balliol College, Oxford University, and is a Fellow of the Royal Historical Society.

Cambridge Studies in Indian History and Society 23

Cambridge Studies in Indian History and Society will publish monographs on the history and anthropology of modern India. In addition to its primary scholarly focus, the series will include work of an interdisciplinary nature which will contribute to contemporary social and cultural debates about Indian history and society. In this way, the series will further the general development of historical and anthropological knowledge and attract a wider readership than that concerned with India alone.

A list of titles which have been published in the series can be found at the end of the book.

The Indian Army and the End of the Raj

Daniel Marston

The Australian National University

CAMBRIDGE
UNIVERSITY PRESS

CAMBRIDGE
UNIVERSITY PRESS

32 Avenue of the Americas, New York NY 10013-2473, USA

Cambridge University Press is part of the University of Cambridge.

It furthers the University's mission by disseminating knowledge in the pursuit of education, learning and research at the highest international levels of excellence.

www.cambridge.org
Information on this title: www.cambridge.org/9780521899758

© Daniel Marston 2014

First published 2014

A catalogue record for this publication is available from the British Library

Library of Congress Cataloguing in Publication data
Marston, Daniel.
The Indian Army and the end of the Raj/ Daniel Marston.
    pages cm. – (Cambridge studies in Indian history and society)
Includes bibliographical references and index.
ISBN 978-0-521-89975-8 (Hardback)
1. India. Army–History–20th century.   2. India–History–1947–   3. India–History–British occupation, 1765–1947.   4. Decolonization–Social aspects–India–History.   5. Social conflict–India–History–20th century.   6. Internal security–India–History–20th century.   7. Civil–military relations–India–History–20th century.   8. India–History, Military.   I. Title.
UA842.M325 2014
355.00954´09044–dc23
2013036444

ISBN 978-0-521-89975-8 Hardback

For Nancy and Bronwen

Contents

Illustrations

Maps

Acknowledgements

There are many people to thank in support of this book. The first group includes three of my key mentors, Professor Robert O'Neill, Professor Raymond Callahan, and Professor Judith Brown. All three have been instrumental in the preparation and production of this book, going back to 2001, when the first foundations of the book were laid out. I would like to thank Professor Sir Hew Strachan for his support and mentorship in earlier iterations of the book and for accepting an article framing the book for publication in his *War in History* series. I would also like to thank Professors Ayesha Jalal and Ian Talbot for feedback in the early stages of the research and shaping of the book.

I would also like to thank Dr Carter Malkasian for his thoughts and edits; we have worked together on many projects going back to our time at Oxford as doctoral students, and as always, Carter took the time to provide advice and criticism. I wish to thank Professor Peter Dennis, who kindly took time to read the chapter dealing with the Indian Army's involvement in French Indo-China and the Netherlands East Indies. Cambridge University Press has been great to work with over the last few years. Marigold Acland originally agreed to commission the book and shepherded the project through the early stages. Lucy Rhymer took over the contract and has provided excellent support through the latter stages. I would also like to thank Claire Poole for all her contributions in the final production of the book. It has been a pleasure working with everyone at the Press. Thank you to Karen Anderson Howes for her excellent copy-editing.

I would like to thank all my colleagues at the Strategic and Defence Studies Centre (SDSC), The Australian National University for their support, particularly the Head of Centre, Dr Brendan Taylor. Brendan helped organize a seminar to hone various themes and, importantly, provided funding for the photos and maps. Kay Dancey and Jennifer Sheehan from the ANU Digital Hub created the maps for the book; and I thank them for all their support and hard work. I would also like to thank my former colleagues at the Royal Military Academy Sandhurst (RMAS) and the US Army Command and General Staff College (CGSC) at Fort Leavenworth for their input and support, especially Dr Nick Murray and Dr Mark Hull.

My students at RMAS, CGSC, and SDSC are all owed a thank you as well. As I corrected and edited their work, I relearned quite a bit, and it made my manuscript a stronger product. I would especially like to thank my Art of War students at CGSC: Ken, Mac, Matt, Carrie, Karsten, Mike, Travis, Jesse, Nate, Mark, Rob, Rick, Ben, Dustin, Aaron, Tom, Mike, Stew, Eric, Marcus, Darrell, Wil, Chris, Tom, Kevin, Mark, Darrell, and Chuck, all of whom made me a better historian and a critical thinker. Finally, I would like to thank the Australian Command and Staff College Class of 2013. It has been an honour and pleasure to have taught all of these students; their thirst for knowledge and motivation to apply it have challenged me to focus my own work.

I would like to thank all the librarians and archivists at the various libraries throughout the United Kingdom, the United States, and Australia who have aided my search for obscure records of the final phase of the British Indian Army. In particular I would like to thank the National Archives in the UK, the Oriental and India Office Reading Room at the British Library, the Liddle Hart Centre at Kings College London, the National Army Museum, Imperial War Museum, and the John Rylands Library at the University of Manchester. Grateful acknowledgement is also made to these archives, cited throughout the book, for their kind permission to quote extensively from documents held in their collections.

The final group to whom I owe a debt of gratitude are the Indian Army veterans whom I had the honour of interviewing, and who have generously shared their stories and memories with me over the last fifteen years. They were fundamental to my first work on the Indian Army, *Phoenix from the Ashes*, and their contributions and insights helped lay the foundation for this, the final chapter of the story of the British Indian Army.

Last but not least: Nancy, thank you for all your support and editing.

While many people have supported this work, any errors are my responsibility.

Introduction

Provided that they [the Indian Army or IA] do their duty, armed insurrection in India would not be an insoluble problem. If however the IA were to go the other way, the picture would be very different.[1]

We do not have the military force to hold India against a widespread guerrilla movement or to reconquer India ... It is doubtful if we could keep the Indian troops loyal.[2]

The two quotes above highlight a fundamental, but largely unconsidered, aspect of the last days of the British Raj. Throughout complex processes of diplomatic negotiation and large-scale planning in British India and the United Kingdom, one critical element on which the success of the entire endeavour rested was the ongoing loyalty and stability of the British Indian Army. However, despite thousands of books, monographs, and articles which consider one aspect or another of this most difficult and complicated period of history for India, Pakistan, and the United Kingdom, the role and conduct of the Indian Army have gone largely unexamined.

When the Indian Army is discussed in relation to this period, it is often in an offhand or simplistic manner. Perry Anderson described the Indian Army in 1946 as 'composed of veterans of domestic repression and overseas aggression fresh from Imperial services in Saigon and Surabaya'.[3] Kirpal Singh, discussing events in the Punjab during the harrowing summer of 1947, claimed that 'the Punjab Boundary Force [PBF] did its best to quell ever increasing lawlessness but with little success ... because the military force under General Rees was infected with communalism'.[4]

---

[1] Nicholas Mansergh, ed., *The Transfer of Power, 1942–1947*, 12 vols. (London: HMSO, 1970–83) (henceforth *TOP*), vol. VI, Prime Minister Clement Attlee to Secretary of State for India, Lord Pethick-Lawrence, 6 Dec. 1945, 271, p. 616.

[2] Attlee to Chiefs of Staff, *TOP*, XI, p. 68.

[3] Perry Anderson, 'After Nehru', *London Review of Books*, 34, 15 (2 Aug. 2012), pp. 21–36 (quotation p. 22).

[4] Kirpal Singh, ed., *Select Documents on the Partition of the Punjab 1947* (New Delhi: National Book Shop, 1991), p. xxviii. By contrast, a veteran of the civil war, Brigadier

The fact that the Indian Army, as an institution, did *not* collapse is a real and lasting testament to the professionalism of the force. As the events of 1947 will clearly show, there were concerted efforts to undermine its integrity from many of the same people who would later claim that its performance was unsatisfactory. The Indian Army went through a period of instability that could have destroyed any military organisation. Its experience in the events surrounding independence and partition is unique in the annals of military history and decolonisation. No other force has had to deal with such extreme and varied pressures. The Indian Army was essentially asked to prevent, or to attempt to contain, a civil war erupting among the various ethnic and religious groups from which its own soldiers, officers, and viceroy commissioned officers (VCOs) were drawn. The fact that there were isolated incidents where bias was demonstrated by army personnel is surprising only because they were not more widespread. Any military force confronted with the carnage of the Punjab would been hard pressed indeed trying not only to stop the killings, but also to prevent its own units from becoming emotionally, if not physically, involved in the situation.

No one could have predicted the level of violence that erupted or the fact that the police and the civil administration, already under incredible communal pressure, ceased, for all intents and purposes, to operate with any cohesion across much of northern India. This breakdown of law and order left the Indian Army to handle situations as best it could, operating under strength and in a situation of unprecedented social disruption. Lieutenant General Sir Francis Tuker commented that 'Many people were encouraged to kill that summer [1947] by the almost total collapse, in the Punjab, of the legal sanctions which normally operate in civil society to inhibit such behaviour.' 'It appears as if there is not Government ruling over this area', wrote a jemadar of the Indian Army on leave at Jullundur, 'everybody [at] present [is] at liberty to kill as many [people] as he likes.'[5]

This book is an attempt to fill a significant gap – not only in the history of the Indian Army, but also in British imperial history, the history of

---

R. C. B. Bristow, who was engaged in the Punjab operations during August 1947, summarised thus the gap in which the PBF found itself stranded, with doctrine and history on one side, and the realities of the Punjab on the other: 'The normal internal security role of the army was to support the civil power in maintaining law and order, but we faced a crisis in which the civil power was ineffective, law and order had completely broken down, and the reliability of the troops varied' (Bristow, *Memories of the British Raj: A Soldier in India* (London: Johnson, 1974), p. 164).

[5] Both quoted in Ian Copland, 'The Master and the Maharajas: The Sikh Princes and the East Punjab Massacres of 1947', *Modern Asian Studies*, 36, 3 (2002), p. 697.

partition, and the histories of India and Pakistan. It will present key aspects of the Indian Army's own history – such as background, decision-making, and ethnic and officer make-up over the century preceding the Second World War – that contributed to the structure and functioning of the Indian Army as it stood in 1945. The army emerged from the Second World War triumphant, but still something of an enigma beyond its own ranks, and poorly understood by both its incumbent political masters in London, and its future political masters in South Asia. This book aims to provide a much deeper analysis of the army than has been undertaken previously, and in particular a more critical assessment of its performance during the final days of its existence.

The Indian Army's evolution and performance in the Second World War are factors that have not been fully evaluated in considering its role in the post-war landscape. The initial, crushing defeats that the Indian Army suffered in 1942 made clear the fact that extensive reforms, both tactical and social, were badly needed. The crucial political correlation to the defeats in Burma and Malaya was the chilling realisation for many Indian soldiers that, with the arrival of the Japanese Army on their borders, they were fighting for the defence of India itself, regardless of under whose command they fought. As social reforms, particularly increased commissioning of Indian officers and expansion of recruitment practices, as well as tactical training for fighting in the hills and valleys of Assam and Burma, took hold from 1943 and defeats were turned into victories, morale and discipline improved, and the rate of desertions dropped.[6] Improvements in officer relations, spurred on by war-time Indianisation of the officer corps and performance of Indian commissioned officers, also helped to dispel the last vestiges of belief that Indian officers were second-class citizens. The fact that the Indian Army not only recovered from crushing defeats early in the war, but also emerged successful and victorious, was a significant contributor to its morale, its *esprit de corps*, and its continued professional performance. The army's image of itself as professional and successful, as cohesive and, perhaps most essentially, *non-communal*, was critical to the performance of thousands of individual men during the difficult days of 1946 and 1947.

---

[6] It was reported that by March 1943 there had been 3,000 desertions in the Punjab: Ian Talbot, *Khizr Tiwana: The Punjab Unionist Party and the Partition of India* (London: Curzon Press, 1996), p. 100. The reasons for these desertions cannot be blamed entirely on political issues; one alternative explanation that has been offered is the signing bonus given to men by the Indian Army upon joining up, which could have led to multiple registrations under different names. Another focuses upon the potential communal issues in the Punjab, as described earlier. Whatever the reasons, desertions dropped significantly after 1943.

The Indian Army's renaissance during the Second World War was directed and supported by a cast of innovative commanders, including Field Marshal Claude Auchinleck, Gen. Sir William Slim, and Gen. Sir Reginald Savory, among others. Their efforts to garner Indian support for the war effort, along with their revolutionary efforts to dismantle the last vestiges of pre-war prejudice against Indian commissioned officers commanding 'British white officers', were critical in shaping the Indian Army's perceptions of itself during and after the war. The officers and other ranks of the Indian Army emerged from the Second World War knowing that major changes lay ahead for India, and were committed to helping the subcontinent to prepare for independence with an army that was professional and capable.

In examining the Indian Army's role, this book will consider a number of themes relevant to the Indian Army's political and social relationships to its homeland during the war-time and post-war periods. Chapter 1 deals with the 'foundations' of the Indian Army on the eve of the Second World War – its organisation, recruitment, and evolving command structures. The second chapter provides an overview of the Indian Army's battlefield experience during the Second World War, along with the dramatic changes to the officer corps and recruitment practices during this period.

The Indian Army's experience in the Second World War also involved grappling with the military and cultural implications of a Japanese-sponsored collaborationist force, the Indian National Army. Chapter 3 focuses on the impact of this force and the trials that occurred after the war. Chapter 4 examines one of the most contentious political and strategic decisions of the post-war period: the use of Indian Army forces to re-impose French and Dutch colonial rule in their respective Asian colonies. This episode highlights how the relationship between India and the United Kingdom was changing more quickly than most British politicians could grasp.

Chapter 5 deals with the rise of a new form of communal violence – one that was well organised and orchestrated by the various political and religious parties in the areas that would become independent India and Pakistan. Chapter 6 focuses on the massive, rapid demobilisation of the army in the post-war period; the political debates that surrounded its implementation; and its impact on the volatile political and social environment of the post-war period. This chapter also examines the difficulties arising from plans to partition the subcontinent, and the ramifications of that decision for the Indian Army. The seventh and final chapter discusses the civil war that erupted in northern India in 1947 in the immediate aftermath of independence and partition, and the Indian Army's role in that conflict.

Major General J. C. Bruce, commander of Lahore area, speaking at a press conference on 3 June 1947, may have provided the best and most succinct summary of the Indian Army's position, responsibilities, and beliefs during this period:

The Army is not an inferior organization, we do not take sides, we do not fight for one community against another. Unfortunately in all countries and amongst all communities there are wicked and selfish men who are only too ready to stir up trouble and to seek personal gain from the misery of others ... [T]he enemies against which we have now to be prepared to operate, are, therefore, brutality and chaos in whatever form these threats may present themselves and I am confident that all ranks will not only recognize their clear duty in this respect, but will be proud to show once again that forces of goodwill and sound commonsense always prevail ... [W]hen you see fellow countrymen, perhaps even your own friends or relations, either the victims of brutal assaults, or else guided by thoughtless or evil agitation into unworthy acts or violence, you must not give way to your personal feeling for one moment. You must remember that you are on the spot as the impartial instrument of justice and truth ... You must restrain the evil doers. You must protect and secure those who have suffered or are in danger. You must not be overcome by any desire for revenge ... In this way you will have shown yourself a worthy member of the great Indian Army to which you belong and will have held up the noble tradition of your unit.[7]

This book will examine the performance of the Indian Army during the most testing period of its history – from the end of the Second World War, in 1945, through to independence and partition, in 1947 – and the role it played in the tumultuous events of that period. By assessing its performance across many lines of operation during this period, this book will demonstrate that the Indian Army's experiences in the Second World War were central to the role it played in post-war India, and that the importance of its involvement in preventing total societal break-down during the transfer of power has been generally overlooked or underestimated.

---

[7] 'Firm Action to Suppress Lawlessness', *Civil Military Gazette*, 3 Jun. 1947, quoted in Kirpal Singh, ed., *Partition of the Punjab*, pp. 99–100.

1   The bedrock of the Raj: the Indian Army before 1939

This chapter will outline some of the key themes that played a significant role in the final years of the British Raj and the Indian Army. In order to understand the strains that became evident when India and Pakistan were preparing for independence, it is first necessary to see how the Indian Army had developed since the late eighteenth century and how it was recruited, trained, and organised on the eve of the Second World War.

The recruitment practices of the British authorities, and how these changed throughout the nineteenth and early twentieth centuries, are of critical importance to events on the eve of the Second World War. This chapter will consider the political implications of these practices in some depth, particularly the army's over-reliance on the Punjab and northern India as a recruitment base and its relation to the Unionist Party of Punjab. Another key theme is the expansion during this period of the officer corps, which began to recruit from the Indian population, and the British authorities' slow and somewhat resistant recognition of the necessity of this action. The practical changes in the organisation and leadership of the Indian Army will be considered, especially in the early to mid twentieth century. Finally, the army's traditional role in carrying out internal security (IS) or 'Aid to the Civil Power' duties throughout the nineteenth and early twentieth centuries will be discussed, along with the factors involved in its apparent breakdown in the summer of 1947.

Recruitment and organisation of the Indian Army before 1914

The recruitment structure of the old English East India Company (EIC)[1] during the eighteenth and early nineteenth centuries was notably different from that of the twentieth-century Indian Army.

---

[1] See the following works for more detail for this period of the EIC: Douglas Peers, *Between Mars and Mammon: Colonial Armies and the Garrison State in Early Nineteenth Century India*

The company was divided into the three presidencies of Bombay, Bengal, and Madras, each of which fielded its own units. By the late 1750s, the British had adopted the French practice of recruiting local Indians as sepoys[2] and training them in 'continental' or traditional linear warfare style. However, as the nineteenth century progressed and the English East India Company became dominant, the recruiting practices of the various presidencies changed. Madras tended to recruit from the Madras region, from all classes,[3] which meant that no one class dominated the army. The Bombay Army followed a similar process.

The army of the Bengal presidency was different. At the beginning of the 1760s, many of the soldiers came from the Rajput and Brahmin castes. Over the next fifty years, the Bengal Army chose to recruit almost exclusively from the high-caste members of the Awadh region.[4] By the early 1800s the Bengal Army was the dominant army of the three presidencies, but there were those who felt that it had become too segregated. Restricted recruitment of high-caste soldiers created problems for the Bengal Army officers: high-caste soldiers would not take orders from a low-caste native officer or non-commissioned officer

---

(London: Tauris, 1995); Channa Wickremesekera, *'Best Black Troops in the World': British Perceptions and the Making of the Sepoy, 1746–1805* (New Delhi: Manohar, 2002); Raymond Callahan, *The East India Company and Army Reform* (Cambridge, MA: Harvard University Press, 1972); Amiya Barat, *The Bengal Native Infantry: Its Organisation and Discipline, 1796–1852* (Calcutta: Firma K. L. Mukhopadhyay, 1962); V. Longer, *Red Coats to Olive Green: A History of the Indian Army, 1600–1974* (Bombay: Allied Publishers, 1974); Kaushik Roy, 'The Armed Expansion of the English East India Company: 1740s–1849', in Daniel Marston and Chandar Sundaram, eds., *A Military History of India and South Asia: From the East India Company to the Nuclear Era* (Bloomington: Indiana University Press, 2008), pp. 1–15; Nile Green, *Islam and the Army in Colonial India: Sepoy Religion in the Service of Empire* (Cambridge University Press, 2009); and Seema Alavi, *The Sepoys and the Company: Tradition and Transition in Northern India, 1770–1830* (New Delhi: Oxford University Press, 1995).

[2] From the Persian word *sipah*, meaning army.

[3] See Heather Streets, *Martial Races: The Military, Race, and Masculinity in British Imperial Culture, 1857–1914* (Manchester University Press, 2004); Tan Tai Yong, *The Garrison State: The Military, Government and Society in Colonial Punjab, 1849–1947* (New Delhi: Sage Publications, 2005); Susan Bayly, 'Caste and Race in the Colonial Ethnography of India', in Peter Robb, ed., *The Concept of Race in South Asia* (Oxford University Press, 1997), pp. 165–218; Stephen Cohen, 'The Untouchable Soldier: Caste, Politics, and the Indian Army', *Journal of Asian Studies*, 28 (1969), pp. 453–68; Douglas Peers, 'The Martial Races and the Indian Army in the Victorian Era', in Marston and Sundaram, eds., *Military History of India and South Asia*, pp. 34–52; and David Omissi, *The Sepoy and the Raj: The Indian Army, 1860–1940* (Basingstoke: Macmillan, 1994). It is interesting to compare their definitions and discussion of 'classes', 'castes', martial races, and the central role of the Punjab in recruitment with Lt Gen. Sir George MacMunn, *The Martial Races of India* (London: Sampson Low, 1933).

[4] Alavi, *Sepoys and the Company*, pp. 292–5.

(NCO),[5] and insisted on food being prepared to strict standards in accordance with their religious prescriptions.[6] The Bengal Army's deployment to war in Afghanistan in 1838 also raised religious issues. As Subedar Sita Ram noted: 'The sepoys dreaded crossing the Indus because it was beyond Hindustan; this is forbidden by our religion and the very act means loss of caste.'[7] Many soldiers deserted or discharged themselves from duty rather than undertake this act.

After the First and Second Anglo-Sikh Wars of the 1840s, the Bengal Army began to recruit from the Punjab region. The Sikhs had created a reputable army of Muslims, Hindus, and Sikhs who had been drilled in the European fashion. After the wars had ended, the British recruited some of the defeated army into the Punjab Irregular Force,[8] later the Punjab Frontier Force, and some recruitment was allowed within the Bengal infantry units stationed in the Punjab. For the most part, however, opposition to opening up the regular regiments of the Bengal Army to former soldiers of the Sikh army persisted for a variety of reasons: professional jealousy, suspicion of Sikhs, and ongoing assertions from some British authorities on the necessity of demilitarising the Punjab.[9] The sepoys of the Bengal Army also resented this incursion into their ranks by the peoples of the Punjab. Subedar Ram noted: 'This annoyed the sepoys exceedingly, for the Sikhs were disliked by Hindustanis who considered them to be unclean and were not permitted to associate with them.'[10]

The reluctance to recruit from the Punjab changed with the Indian Mutiny of 1857.[11] During the Mutiny, eighteen new regiments had

---

[5] The Gurkha battalions raised both during and after the Nepal wars of 1815 and 1819 from the independent kingdom of Nepal seemed to be separate from these issues. While they were part of the Bengal Army establishment, they seemed not to have any of the caste issues that affected parts of the Bengal Army (*ibid.*, pp. 274–81). As the martial race theory dominated the composition of the Indian Army during the later stages of the nineteenth century, the Gurkhas were included in the list. However, within Nepal men were specifically recruited from certain regions, while other areas were excluded. There have been many books and articles written about the Gurkhas; some historians feel that the best comprehensive account is Tony Gould's *Imperial Warriors: Britain and the Gurkhas* (London: Granta Books, 1999).

[6] By 1855, lower castes were formally excluded from the Bengal Army: Omissi, *The Sepoy and the Raj*, p. 5; see also Streets, *Martial Races*, pp. 26–7.

[7] James Lunt, ed., *From Sepoy to Subedar* (London: Papermac, 1988), p. 85. (Questions have been raised regarding the provenance and authenticity of Sita Ram's memoirs. However, issues of service outside Hindustan and dissension between Bengalis and peoples of northern India are well documented.)

[8] Close to 14,000 men.   [9] Yong, *Garrison State*, pp. 37–9.

[10] Lunt, *From Sepoy to Subedar*, p. 159, and Yong, *Garrison State*, pp. 42–3.

[11] As with many of the themes covered in this chapter, the Indian Mutiny has been the topic of hundreds of books and articles since 1857. The following books are a good starting point for understanding the complexities of this event: G. B. Malleson, ed., *Kaye's and Malleson's History of the Indian Mutiny of 1857–1858*, 6 vols. (London: Allen, 1898);

been raised from the Punjab which remained loyal throughout the crisis, in both the Punjab and the United Provinces. With the Punjab Irregular Force and the new regiments, this meant that there were more than 50,000 men under arms in the Punjab who were loyal to the British suppression of the mutinous Bengal Army regiments in northern India.[12]

The military recruitment of the Bengal Army did not change dramatically in the immediate aftermath of the Mutiny, but over the next twenty-five years some significant reforms were put in place. Most of the Bengal Army was reorganised under the Peel Commission findings of 1859;[13] however, this reform left unresolved the question of what to do with the new Punjab-raised irregulars. Ultimately a decision was made to open up the recruitment for the Bengal Army along regional lines: the Bengal Army would still recruit from across northern and central India, but would consist of many classes and races. Many on the commission felt it was best to create a system that fostered the concept of 'divide and rule' to avoid re-creating the environment that had existed prior to the Mutiny. The recruitment of high-caste Brahmins and Rajputs was decreased in response to their perceived involvement in the Mutiny, while the recruitment of Gurkhas from Nepal was expanded in recognition of their perceived loyalty and performance during the same period. Also, regiments were to recruit and serve in their local areas, which meant that henceforth only Punjab-raised regiments would serve in the Punjab and the Frontier regions. This meant that, by 1870, only 35 per cent of the Bengal Army was recruited from the Punjab.[14] Many of the irregular

---

Philip Mason, *A Matter of Honour: An Account of the Indian Army, Its Officers and Men* (London: Cape, 1974); S. N. Sen, *Eighteen Fifty-Seven* (New Delhi: Government of India, 1957); C. A. Bayly and Eric Stokes, *The Peasant Armed: The Indian Revolt of 1857* (Oxford University Press, 1986); Saul David, *The Indian Mutiny: 1857* (London: Viking, 2002); J. A. B. Palmer, *Mutiny Outbreak at Meerut* (Cambridge University Press, 1966); Rudrangshu Mukherjee, *Mangal Pandy: Brave Martyr or Accidental Hero?* (New Delhi: Penguin Books, 2005); Peter Stanley, *The White Mutiny: British Military Culture in India 1825–1875* (New York: C. Hurst, 1998); and Raymond Callahan, 'The Great Sepoy Mutiny', in Marston and Sundaram, eds., *Military History of India and South Asia*, pp. 16–33.

[12] Yong, *Garrison State*, p. 48.

[13] See Great Britain Organization of the Indian Army Committee, 'Report of the Commissioners Appointed to Inquire into the Organization of the Indian Army' (London: Eyre & Spottiswoode, 1859), together with Minutes of Evidence and Appendix, multiple volumes, for more specific details.

[14] The Bengal Army in 1870 had forty-nine infantry regiments, of which the Gurkhas and other 'hill people' made up four and the Punjab sixteen; the rest came from outside the Punjab and Nepal: Yong, *Garrison State*, pp. 54–5.

regiments raised in the Punjab during the crisis were taken into the Bengal Army line.[15]

The anticipated threat presented by Russia and the Second Afghan War (1879–81) changed recruitment for the Indian Army again, and in particular began a shift towards the northern and north-western regions as the main recruiting area. The changes began with the findings of the 1879 Eden Commission Report, which recommended some significant reforms. Among these were the creation of an army corps that would fall under the command of a single commander-in-chief (CinC), which would obviate the need for the three separate CinC positions in existence at that time. Other suggestions included formally bringing the Punjab Frontier Force under army command, further recruitment of troops from the Punjab region, and scaling down the Madras Army.

There was considerable opposition to this plan from within the Indian Army, including from Sir Frederick Haines, then CinCI.[16] The opposition to the Eden Commission's findings would be overcome with appointment of Field Marshal Lord Roberts of Kandahar[17] as CinCI in 1885. Lord Roberts stated: 'I have no hesitation myself in stating that except Gurkhas, Dogras, Sikhs, the pick of Punjabi Muhammadans, Hindustanis of the Jat and Ranghur casts … [and] certain classes of Pathans, there are no Native soldiers in our service whom we could venture with safety to place in the field against the Russians.'[18] The recruitment drive to bring more northern Indians into the Bengal Army, later expanded to the army as a whole, was the product of what became known as the martial race theory.[19] This assertion – that some groups

---

[15] A number of famous irregular cavalry regiments were raised during the Mutiny: among them Hodson's Horse, Wale's or Probyn's Horse, and 2nd Sikh Irregular Cavalry were among those formally listed as Bengal Cavalry. See Lt Gen. Sir George MacMunn, *The Armies of India* (London: A & C Black, 1911), pp. 111–12, and Maj. A. E. Barstow, *Handbooks for the Indian Army: Sikhs* (Calcutta: Government of India, 1928), p. 17.

[16] Streets, *Martial Races*, p. 97.

[17] Commander-in-chief of the Madras Army, 1880–5; commander-in-chief of the Bengal Army (hence unofficial commander-in-chief of all three presidencies), 1885–93.

[18] See C. H. Philips, ed., *Select Documents on the History of India and Pakistan, IV: The Evolution of India and Pakistan, 1858–1947* (Oxford University Press, 1964), p. 517. For an interesting perspective, see also Roberts' comments in his book, *Forty One Years in India* (London: Bentley Brothers, 1898), pp. 531–2.

[19] Between the circumstances of the Mutiny and the influence of opinions of officers who had served in the Punjab, peoples such as the Bengalis and Madrassis came to be widely considered non-martial. As Thomas Metcalf noted, 'whether defined by race, climate, or personality, martial races were those who most closely resembled what the British imagined themselves to be … they were what the Bengali was not' (*Ideologies of the Raj* (Cambridge University Press, 1995), p. 127). See also Omissi, *The Sepoy and the Raj*, Streets, *Martial Races*, MacMunn, *Martial Races*, Yong, *Garrison State*, and Roberts, *Forty One Years*, for more discussion of the concept of 'martial races'.

were martial and others non-martial – was to have lasting repercussions in India. Many classes[20] of Indians, such as Bengalis and numerous groups from southern India, were deemed 'non-martial' and, as a result, were excluded from the army.[21] The northern areas of India, especially the Punjab, were favoured as the main recruiting grounds. The bias towards northerners was partially a physical one: Punjabi Musalmans (PMs),[22] Sikhs, and Pathans tended to be taller and stronger than their southern counterparts, as well as lighter-skinned. Physical distinctions such as these led some British officers to believe, for example, that the Pathans of the North-West Frontier region were descended from the armies of Alexander. Even so, not all northern classes or peoples were acceptable. People who lived in cities and towns were not considered to be of the correct stock – only those from the countryside. Within a given class of people, caste also played a role: Jat Sikhs, for example, were considered best suited for the infantry, while other castes, such as the Mazbhi and Ramdasia Sikhs, were recruited for the Pioneers.[23]

Most units of the Bombay and Madras presidencies had remained loyal during the Indian Mutiny, and so were not greatly affected by removal of units from the *Army List*. The feeling in the British government, as well as among those serving on the Peel Commission, was that those units which had remained loyal during the Mutiny deserved to remain in service.[24] The poor performance of the Madras regiments in the Third Burma War of 1885 reinforced the notion that the Madrassi soldiers had lost their fighting abilities. Roberts has been quoted as saying: 'I tried hard to discover in them those fighting qualities which had distinguished their forefathers during the wars of the last and beginning of the present century. But long years of peace and security and

---

[20] 'Class' was used to denote a given tribe or ethnic grouping within the army.

[21] As noted by Maj. Gen. D. K. Palit, despite his Bengali family's belonging to the warrior caste and having a long tradition of military service, adherence to martial race theory resulted in his family slowly being stripped of its martial traditions (author's interview with Palit, 4 Nov. 2000).

[22] A term formerly used to refer to Muslims; either it or its abbreviation PM will be used throughout.

[23] This issue will be considered further when discussing the re-raising of Mazbhi and Ramdasia Sikhs (M and R Sikhs) as infantry during the Second World War (Sikh Light Infantry). Pioneers were units of infantry who were also capable of engineering tasks. After the First World War they turned more and more to engineering, but when financial considerations were brought to bear this also meant their demise, since the tasks of engineering were already carried out by units called sappers and miners. Pioneers became redundant, although they were re-raised during the Second World War.

[24] The Madras Army had fifty-two battalions; Bombay thirty battalions; the Bengal had eighteen pre-Mutiny regiments, thirteen new Punjabi regiments, six low-caste Hindu regiments, plus various other Sikh, Gurkha, and Punjabi units raised during the war. See Omissi, *The Sepoy and the Raj*, pp. 8–9, and Streets, *Martial Races*, p. 93.

prosperity attending it had evidently had upon them, as they always seem to Asiatics, a softening and deteriorating effect.'[25]

There were those who criticised Roberts' comments as oversimplification, and blamed the Madras Army's poor performance instead on the fighting capabilities and leadership of the British and native officers of that army. Many officers, upon appointment to the Indian Army, preferred service with the newly constituted Bengal Army or the Punjab Frontier Force. Their reasoning was that the likelihood of seeing action was greater in the Bengal and Punjab units, due to their involvement on the Afghan frontier, and that the Bengal and Punjab regiments were increasingly considered to be 'elite'.[26]

Military critics of this trend noted not only that some of the blame for poor troops should be placed on the lack of good officers, but also that relying on a given area or class for the majority of the army's recruitment was bound to have dire consequences in the long run,[27] especially in the event of a major war. The practice continued, however, and by 1891 twenty-one battalions of Madras infantry had been disbanded. By 1893, 44 per cent of the Indian Army was drawing recruits from the martial races.[28] The Madras units remaining on the *Army List* had been opened to recruitment from the northern areas of India and, by 1900, only twenty-five regiments still recruited from the Madras region. Some units completely lost their connection to the old Madras Army in the 1903 reorganisation[29] and, by 1910, the number of regiments still recruiting from Madras was eleven. The rest of the regiments of the old Madras Army were made up of troops from North India, mostly the Punjab.[30]

The Bombay Army also found itself in a difficult position when its recruiting grounds were expanded to include some of the northern regions. By 1903, just 54 of the 208 companies of the army were recruited from the old Bombay recruiting grounds. The rest of the companies were from the Punjab, North-West Frontier region, and Rajputana.[31] On the

[25] Mason, *A Matter of Honour*, p. 345.
[26] See Streets, *Martial Races*, Yong, *Garrison State*, Mason, *A Matter of Honour*, Omissi, *The Sepoy and the Raj*, Roberts, *Forty One Years*, and MacMunn, *Martial Races*, for more details and comments from serving officers.
[27] This issue was raised during the First World War, as traditional recruiting grounds were drying up by 1916. The recruitment policy favoured a small regular army, and would continue to be tested in any conflict where large numbers of men were needed.
[28] Streets, *Martial Races*, p. 100.
[29] The 2/1st Punjab is an example of this tendency: it was originally raised in 1761 in Madras, and served throughout the southern campaigns of the 1700s and early 1800s. However, it became 'Punjabised' and was designated the 66th Punjab Regiment in 1903. This change severed the link with Madras entirely, except for the early Battle Honours.
[30] Omissi, *The Sepoy and the Raj*, p. 19, and Yong, *Garrison State*, p. 71.
[31] Omissi, *The Sepoy and the Raj*, p. 19, and Yong, *Garrison State*, pp. 71–2.

eve of the First World War, of the 552 infantry companies in the Indian Army as a whole, 211 were composed of men from the Punjab, 121 were from the Frontier region, 80 companies were Gurkhas, and the remaining troops came from the other regions of acceptable classes.[32] Overall, by 1914, 75 per cent of the Indian Army was recruited from the martial races.[33]

As mentioned above, the Indian Army had been divided into the three major presidency armies of Bombay, Bengal, and Madras since the eighteenth century, while the Punjab region was essentially treated as a separate entity in the Punjab Frontier Force.[34] In 1903,[35] Lord Kitchener,[36] CinC of the Indian Army, abolished the old structures and created a more centralised organisation for the army.[37] All of the infantry regiments (battalions) and cavalry regiments were renumbered in sequential order, and units of the Punjab Frontier Force were formally integrated as part of the army.[38] Gurkha regiments were given their own

---

[32] The reason for the breakdown in the companies list is that most infantry battalions and cavalry regiments were composed of various class companies or squadrons. This practice, which had been started before the Mutiny, was reinforced afterwards, in the belief that if a battalion had a three- or four-company mixture of classes, it would be more difficult for the unit to unify in a common revolt. However, during the Mutiny, whole units of Muslims and Hindus did join together in open revolt. Not all regiments followed the practice of creating companies of different classes (the 14th and 15th Sikh were entirely composed of Jat Sikhs and the Gurkha regiments were all Hindu): Omissi, *The Sepoy and the Raj*, p. 19.

[33] Streets, *Martial Races*, p. 100. See also Yong, *Garrison State*, ch. 2, 'Recruiting in the Punjab: "Martial Races" and the Military Districts', pp. 70–97, for more detail on the specific recruiting grounds as well as motivating factors for the various recruits and the beginning of the 'garrison state' concept in the Punjab.

[34] This force was formed in 1846 and re-embodied in 1849. It was independent of the presidency armies and was accountable to the governor of the Punjab. In 1886, the Punjab Frontier Force was transferred to the direct control of the commander-in-chief, India.

[35] In 1893, the Bombay and Madras commander-in-chief positions were abolished. See the Madras and Bombay Armies Act of 5 December 1893, in Philips, ed., *Select Documents, IV*, p. 517. The process of abolishing the old presidency armies continued, and Lord Kitchener formally ended the naming of regiments and any associations with the old presidencies in 1903.

[36] Horatio Herbert Kitchener, First Earl of Khartoum and Broome, was commander-in-chief, India, from 1902 to 1909.

[37] The move towards reorganisation had begun in 1880, but it took twenty years for the formal unified command structure to be put in place under Kitchener.

[38] The old Bengal Army list started the numbering process first, e.g. 1st Brahman Infantry remained the 1st Brahmans; 30th Punjab Infantry became the 30th Punjabis. The Punjab Frontier Force regiments came in the numbering in the 50s, so that 2nd Sikh Infantry became 52nd Sikhs. The Madras line came next and also repeated the 'Punjabisation' of the Madras line: for example, 6th Madras Infantry became 66th Punjabis, 16th Madras Infantry became 76th Punjabis, and so forth. The Bombay line came last: 5th Bombay Light Infantry became 105th Mahratta Light Infantry, 25th Bombay Rifles became 125th Napier's Rifles. See John Gaylor, *Sons of John Company: The Indian and Pakistan Armies, 1903–1991* (Tunbridge Wells, UK: Spellmount, 1992), for more detail.

regimental numbering system from 1 to 10. While the infantry regiments (each consisting of one battalion) were listed in sequential order, they were also grouped in loose federations of units of two to five battalions, and given a regimental centre to which recruits would report. By the beginning of the First World War, there were 43 such regimental groupings. This number rapidly expanded to 115 with the onset of war.[39]

Impact of the First World War

During the First World War, the old system of recruitment, with heavy emphasis on the Punjab, continued for at least the first years.[40] This system, which had a specific battalion send out officers to recruiting areas to find replacements, worked well initially. As the war expanded and there was more need for Indian troops, the structure suffered increasing strain, reaching a crisis point in 1915.[41] As a result, much of the pre-war class recruitment system was abandoned, and in the Punjab other areas were opened up: twenty-two new classes were added to the recruitment list, and in 1917 a new system of territorial recruitment began.[42] Regimental officers and depots were established in regions where no recruitment had ever happened. In doing so, Army High Command noted that there were numerous classes which had not previously been recruited who were suitable candidates for army service. As one Indian civil servant noted: 'there was also considerable exclusiveness on the part of the army; certain tribes capable of providing excellent material were barred by reason of some real or fancied social objection'.[43] Whole regions of the Punjab were opened to recruitment from a variety of regiments, not just steered into specific units. By the end of the First World War, the Punjab had supplied more than 40 per cent of all recruits for the combat arms of the Indian Army. It came down to 1 soldier out of every 26 men, compared to the rest of India with 1 soldier of every 150 men

---

[39] See Gaylor, *Sons of John Company*, pp. 8–9, for more detail.

[40] For a general narrative of the professional performance of the Indian Army in the First World War, see Mason, *A Matter of Honour*, as well as Charles Chenevix Trench, *The Indian Army and the King's Enemies, 1900–1947* (London: Thames and Hudson, 1988); and G. Corrigan, *Sepoys in the Trenches: The Indian Corps on the Western Front: 1914–1915* (London: Spellmount, 1996). An important perspective from the 'ranks' is available in David Omissi's *Indian Voices of the Great War: Soldiers' Letters, 1914–1918* (London: Macmillan, 1999); and Nikolas Gardner, *Trial by Fire: Command and Control and the British Expeditionary Force in 1914* (Westport, CT: Praeger, 2003).

[41] Indian Army formations were on the western front, East Africa, Gallipoli, Mesopotamia, and Palestine, as well as in normal IS duties in India.

[42] Yong, *Garrison State*, pp. 108–17.

[43] M. S. Leigh, *The Punjab and the War* (Lahore: Government of the Punjab, 1922), p. 34.

mobilised.[44] If percentages from the Punjab and the recruiting grounds of the United Province are combined, three-quarters of all Indian Army recruits from this period came from these regions.[45] Even with this dominance, other peoples from across India who had previously been dropped from the *Army List*[46] were once again considered eligible. The performance of some of the non-martial races in the First World War sparked some debate and attempts to bolster support for the martial race theory, but the controversy was short-lived.

The civil authorities, led by the Punjab governor, Sir Michael O'Dwyer, also worked closely with military authorities to streamline the recruitment process.[47] O'Dwyer sought the involvement of local landed elites from across the Punjab in mobilising communities for recruits, offering compensation for this co-operation in the form of major land grants and formal titles.[48] This centralisation of recruitment efforts during the First World War, the involvement of military and civil authorities, and the co-opting of the rural elite were to lay the foundations of a heavily militarised province and a structure that would have significant ramifications for the political situation in 1947. As Tan Tai Yong stated:

> The process of mobilization brought about a close association between the military and the provincial civil administration, laying the foundations of a militarized bureaucracy in colonial Punjab. From 1916 to 1919 the Punjab 'home front' was in effect governed by a military bureaucracy, whose administrative/military tentacles reached into every level of society and the economy. The direct assumption of a military function by the Punjab government, and its intrusion into society on behalf of the military during the war, was to mark the beginning of a quasi-military state in the Punjab.[49]

Recruitment for the Indian Army in the inter-war period followed pre-war practices. Initially the Government of India wished for a large post-war standing army that would encompass many of the newly raised units and expanded classes of people. The idea behind this was that it

[44] *Ibid.*, p. 41. See also pp. 59–62 for complete lists of the recruits from the different districts in the Punjab.

[45] 'The Simon Commission on Army Recruitment, 1930', in Philips, ed., *Select Documents, IV*, p. 533.

[46] Coorgs, Mahars, Mappilas, and 51,000 men from Madras: Omissi, *The Sepoy and the Raj*, p. 38.

[47] See Leigh, *The Punjab and the War*, for a very comprehensive study of the impact of the Punjab on the campaign in terms of recruitment as well as the many land grants given in various areas for 'service in the war'. See also Yong, *Garrison State*, ch. 3, 'Garrison Province at Work: Punjab and the First World War', pp. 98–140, for more details.

[48] See Leigh, *The Punjab and the War*, pp. 140–75 (Appendix B), for specific lists of land grants, as well as other gifts to specific regions for their service. See also Yong, *Garrison State*, pp. 125–38, for additional detail.

[49] Yong, *Garrison State*, pp. 139–40.

would be easy to recruit and maintain reserves for any future conflict. Unfortunately, the Government of India had to cut back due to the financial constraints of the 1920s and 1930s, and when the axe fell the first units to suffer were those that had been newly raised. Under pressure, the government followed the old line of sticking to pre-war martial race theory.[50] As the Indian Army reorganised into large regimental units, the 3rd Madras Regiment was set at four regular battalions and one training battalion.[51] The class composition of the Madras Regiment was Tamils, Madrassi Musalmans, Paraiyahs, and Christians. By the end of the 1920s, however, the regular and training battalions had been disbanded in response to economic pressures.[52] Senior members of the government made their feelings on the Madras infantry known,[53] and only territorial units survived. Interestingly, the 3rd Madras Regiment was never struck from the *Indian Army List*, but was considered in a state of hiatus until 1941.

The findings of the Simon Commission on Army Recruitment in 1930 further reinforced the bias towards the martial race recruitment practice. It openly stated, 'broadly speaking, one may say that those races [martial] which furnish the best sepoys are emphatically not those which exhibit the greatest accomplishments of mind in an examination'.[54] It also highlighted that in 1930 the Punjab provided 54% of all recruits for the army (and if one were not to include the Gurkha regiments, this number rose to 62%). The report went on to elaborate that, due to economic conditions, it was desirable to recruit from the best groups to ensure professionalism and fighting ability. It also stated that, while Indian politicians wished for more Indian unity as embodied in the army, the politicians did not understand the role of the army and that such a vision

---

[50] Within other units the class compositions were streamlined, with an overwhelming focus on the Punjab and northern India. See the make-up of the following battalions and regiments to clarify: 2/1st Punjab Regiment was designated to have two companies of Punjabi Musalmans, one of Jat Sikhs, and one of Rajputs. The Jats who had been part of the battalion were sent to other regiments or were disbanded. Cavalry regiments also followed suit. The 5th Probyn's Horse was designated to have only three squadrons: one of Hindustani Musalmans and Musalman Rajputs, one of Rajputs, and one of Jats. The 7th Light Cavalry, again a former Madras-based regiment, was restructured to comprise one squadron of Punjabi Musalmans, one of Sikhs, and one of Dogras. The other two pre-war battalions followed their previous rules. The 1/11th Sikh recruited only Jat Sikhs and the 4/12th FFR and 2/13th Frontier Force Rifles (FFRifles) all had one company each of PMs, Sikhs, Dogras and Pathans: No. A-8552-1, L/MIL/7/5483, India Office Papers, British Library (henceforth OIOC, BL) and *Indian Army List* 1930.
[51] *Indian Army List* 1923.   [52] Gaylor, *Sons of John Company*, pp. 138–9.
[53] Omissi quotes Sir Claud Jacob saying that the Madras infantry was of no military value: *The Sepoy and the Raj*, p. 40.
[54] 'Simon Commission', in Philips, ed., *Select Documents*, IV, p. 532.

would take years to achieve, due to the competing religions and racial tensions that existed. It clearly stated that defence problems in India were quite complex, and that the political push for self-government did not fully take this complexity into account.[55] In short, these findings preview the disconnect between the army and the developing political leadership of the Indian nationalist movement: a disconnect that was the source of numerous problems in the post-Second World War period and which exacerbated communal conflicts in 1947.

The final economic measure that affected recruitment practices in the Indian Army before the Second World War occurred in February 1933, when the Pioneer battalions were disbanded. While this decision may not appear to be comparable with the others described, it had a significant effect upon those classes of peoples who were recruited exclusively for the pioneers. Within the Sikh community, the Jats were recruited for the infantry, and the Mazbhi and Ramdasia Sikhs for the Sikh Pioneers.[56] As noted in the *Handbooks for the Indian Army: Sikhs*, 'their extraordinary bravery, endurance ... soon won them a high reputation as soldiers ... in the numerous campaigns on the Frontier ... and during the Great War'.[57] Notwithstanding such a praiseworthy record, this decision meant that the Mazbhi and Ramdasia Sikhs were effectively denied the opportunities offered by military service until the Second World War.

By 1939, the composition of the Indian Army was similar to its 1914 counterpart, relying heavily on a select group of classes of Indians, mostly from the Punjab, for all its recruitment needs. As had occurred in the First World War, the exhaustion of the limited recruiting pool became a problem early in the Second World War, especially in the Punjab.

Nationalist political influence and questions of loyalty

At the end of the First World War, as in the United Kingdom, the Government of India had to contend with thousands of demobilised soldiers.[58] Indian Soldier Boards were established in all the provinces

---

[55] *Ibid.* See the Indian Statutory Commission, Government of India, Cmd 3568 (1930), vol. I, for more details.

[56] J. D. Hookway, ed., *M and R: A Regimental History of the Sikh Light Infantry 1941–1947* (Radley, UK: Reesprint, 1999), pp. 1–2.

[57] Barstow, *Handbooks for the Indian Army: Sikhs*, p. 77.

[58] The authorities had censored and monitored mail from the Indian soldiers serving in the First World War. There had been fears, largely unwarranted, of nationalist politics somehow infiltrating the ranks. Morale issues arose during the early phases of the war; however, as with their British counterparts on the western front, these were mostly the result of gruelling battlefield conditions. The Ottoman Empire's entry into the war sparked additional fears that Muslim soldiers would refuse to wage war against their

of India,[59] and District Soldier Boards (DSBs) were established at the district level, to reintegrate demobilised soldiers back into civil society and provide support in the form of employment and financial subsidy, and land and service rewards,[60] as well as safeguarding the interests of soldiers and their dependants. Soldiers returning to the Punjab and India in general had to deal with massive inflation, especially of food goods. Many veterans also sought 'land grants', not all of which the Government of India was able to honour.[61]

Demobilisation was further complicated by riots and political agitation across India.[62] The inter-war period was one of significant political upheaval for India, characterised by the growing influence of political discussion and protest on national thought. This was largely a result of the efforts of the Indian National Congress Party and the Muslim League. Of particular importance was the policy of civil disobedience introduced by M. K. Gandhi. Gandhi understood that British rule in India depended upon the co-operation of the Indian population, especially those involved in civil departments, the police, and the army. Civil disobedience was an attempt to break down the ingrained response of co-operation, without openly advocating insubordination within the army.

To counter the threats from a large mass of demobilised soldiers and their potential indoctrination by various Indian nationalist parties, the Punjab Provincial Government had their DSBs carry out a counter-propaganda mission in the villages that still served as a recruiting base for the army. The civil–military cohesion that was organised in the First World War to improve recruitment practices was reorganised to influence the countryside and attempt to block any influence from the nationalist parties. Many commanders in the Indian Army, as well

co-religionists. There was a mutiny of the 5th Light Infantry in Singapore, traced to outside influence from a local mosque and rumours spread in the battalion by German prisoners. While issues of Islam played a part in the mutiny, ultimately the culprit was poor leadership by the British officers. Notwithstanding this, and the ongoing anxiety it generated, the Indian Army, including many Muslims, fought well against Turkish forces in Gallipoli, Sinai, Palestine, and Mesopotamia. See Mason, *A Matter of Honour*, pp. 422–7, as well as Omissi, *Indian Voices*, for more details.

[59] Except for Bengal.

[60] More than 420,000 acres of Colony Land was distributed to 6,000 commissioned and non-commissioned army officers: Talbot, *Khizr Tiwana*, p. 56.

[61] See Yong, *Garrison State*, pp. 141–52.

[62] Some 400 unarmed civilians were killed at Jallianwalla Bagh in Amritsar in April 1919. See vols. VI and VII of V. N. Datta, ed., *New Light on the Disturbances in 1919* (Simla: Indian Institute of Advanced Study, 1975), as well as N. A. Collet, *The Butcher of Amritsar: General Reginald Dyer* (London: Palgrave Macmillan, 2005), for more detail.

as in the Indian Civil Service (ICS), understood that the 'loyalty' of the soldiers when they were on leave was paramount, especially during the inter-war years. The DSBs served to reinforce the 'imperial narrative' that was considered essential to guarantee the loyalty of the martial races in the countryside during the political upheaval of the 1920s and 1930s.[63]

The small size and restricted recruitment practices of the Indian Army during this period ensured that nationalist influence was minimal, especially within the rank and file. As David Omissi noted: 'Nationalism had little impact on the ranks, and attempts by Congress to subvert the army got nowhere.'[64] There were members of the Indian commissioned officer corps who had leanings towards an independent India, but these were the exception rather than the rule.[65]

The education level of the average *jawan* (sepoy) of the 1920s and 1930s was not particularly high, nor was his political awareness likely to be highly developed when he was recruited, generally in his late teens. The Indian Army recruited from selected areas of India that had provided generations of soldiers to particular regiments, and both veterans and potential recruits viewed service within the Indian Army as a tradition, a noble profession that also paid a very good wage. A career in the army enabled many *jawan*s to buy property in their villages, marking them as successful in the opinions of the village elders.

The structure of the Indian Army, like the British Army, promoted the development of regimental *esprit de corps*. This was furthered by ex-servicemen who went back to live in rural villages and reminisced about their army service. With the establishment of the DSBs, this was better organised and reinforced. Regiments went back to the same families and villages that had provided good and loyal soldiers in the past, and recruited from the same sources again and again. By the inter-war period, it was not unusual for a *jawan* arriving at a regimental centre to be the fifth generation of his family to serve in the army. *Jawan*s dismissed from service for disobedience or political agitation were shamed before not only their families but also the village elders, and were considered to have dishonoured the family and village. This was a harsh judgement, but not an unrealistic one: such a black mark could worsen the chances for the family and village to supply recruits to the army in the future.

---

[63] See Yong, *Garrison State*, ch. 4, 'Maintaining the Military Districts: Civil–Military Integration and District Soldiers' Boards', pp. 141–86, for more detail.

[64] Omissi, *The Sepoy and the Raj*, p. 151.

[65] Author's interviews with Indian officers, 1999–2009.

The recruitment base for the Indian Army was so restricted that the British authorities had the luxury of being very selective in ensuring a minimum of political agitation within its ranks. Even so, one instance of Indian troops disobeying orders in the face of a political protest demonstrates the complexities of the situation. In April 1930, the 2/18th Garhwal Regiment stationed in Peshawar had two platoons refuse to take up arms and deal with a nationalist protest. On 23 April, two platoons from the battalion were deployed across a road as a crowd approached. They were under orders not to fire, orders which were not countermanded when they were set upon with stones and other missiles. Many men were wounded, and firing commenced after a soldier's rifle was seized by protesters. The following day, when two more platoons were ordered to move out to deal with a second protest, they refused. A number of observers within the nationalist community, as well as opposition members of the British Parliament (MPs), claimed that this refusal was politically motivated, that the men were refusing specifically to disperse political protests. The majority opinion, however, was that the men had been 'subjected to treatment which no soldier should be asked to stand without retaliation' and had reacted appropriately.[66]

The Indian National Congress was interested in the policies and practices of the Indian Army during the 1930s. In the last years of the decade there were frequent debates in the Indian Legislative Assembly on the potential broadening of Indian Army recruitment policies, expansion of the Indianisation of the officer corps,[67] and modernisation of the army.[68] As a general rule, however, Congress's interest was not reciprocated, or at least not openly. As Yong stated:

The general failure of the Congress to create an impression in the military districts of the Punjab could be attributed to the fact that the majority of villages in these districts possessed large numbers of pensioners who depended on the government for their pensions and welfare generally ... the continued existence of the boards [DSBs] and committees formed a ready channel for representation for the ex-soldiers' communities ... the soldier knew his interests would be looked after and there was little incentive for him to turn to agitation.[69]

---

[66] Court of Enquiry, 28 Apr. to 7 May 1930, L/MIL/7/7282, OIOC, BL, as quoted in Omissi, *The Sepoy and the Raj*, p. 139.

[67] See below for more details.

[68] Dorothy Norman, ed., *Nehru: The First Sixty Years* (London: Bodley Head, 1965), p. 22.

[69] Yong, *Garrison State*, p. 181. The Punjab had one of the lowest rates of disturbances of any province in the early 1930s. See Judith Brown, *Gandhi and Civil Disobedience: The Mahatma in Indian Politics, 1928–1934* (Cambridge University Press, 1975), pp. 284–5.

With the ending of the First World War, the British government and the Government of India recognised the need for some devolution of power at the provincial level to maintain moderate support for the Raj.[70] The Montagu–Chelmsford Report of 1918 attempted to address this need by allowing a certain level of enfranchisement within the various provinces, where selection of certain ministers would be decided by voting.[71] However, key positions such as law and order, revenue, and justice remained in the hands of the ICS and the provincial government. The Provincial Government also had the right to fire elected officials if they were deemed unfit. In retrospect, the report was clearly the first step towards a gradual change to self-government.[72]

Lt Governor Sir Michael O'Dwyer of the Punjab opposed the reforms in general and the report in particular.[73] He feared that the 'urban' elites would destroy his hard work in the First World War and dominate the rural districts from which came the bulk of recruits for the Indian Army. For the first few years, he was in vocal opposition to any political reform in the province, but over time he realised that a significant change was happening, and set out to, as he perceived it, 'protect' the rural population by manipulating enfranchisement practices in the Punjab. He favoured rural elites, former soldiers, and small landholders, essentially setting up veterans and serving soldiers as a counter-balance to the urban nationalist voting block. From 1920 to 1923, this group set out to establish and oppose various enfranchisement practices.[74] Formally created as the Punjab National Unionist Party[75] in 1923, this political bloc dominated the Punjabi political process from 1923 until the Second World War,[76] effectively undermining the influence of both the Indian National Congress and the Muslim League throughout the province. As a senior British official

---

[70] See Judith Brown, *Modern India: The Origins of an Asian Democracy*, 2nd edn (Oxford University Press, 1994), for more detail.

[71] See 'Report on Constitutional Reforms' (Montagu Report), 1918, in Philips, ed., *Select Documents, IV*, pp. 265–85, for much more detail.

[72] Yong, *Garrison State*, pp. 123–5.

[73] He was relieved of his post following the Jallianwala Bagh massacre in Amritsar in 1919.

[74] See Yong, *Garrison State*, ch. 6, 'Securing the Reins of Power: Politics and the Punjab's Rural-Military Elites', pp. 240–80, for detail of the process.

[75] The Unionist Party was unusual in India at that time in that, although it had quite a large landowner block, it received broad support from people from a diverse assortment of class and community backgrounds: Talbot, *Khizr Tiwana*, p. 51.

[76] See *ibid.*, ch. 3, 'The Unionist Party', pp. 51–64, as well as Talbot, *Punjab and the Raj, 1849–1947* (Delhi: Oxford University Press, 1988), for more detail.

stated: 'it was the best instance of the right kind of provincial government, based broadly on the landlords, peasants and soldiers'.[77]

Indianisation of the officer corps

The Indian Army was officered for more than 100 years by a system of British officers and native (later viceroy) commissioned officers.[78] Indians were not allowed to receive commissions from Addiscombe, the East India Company officer training academy, or, later, from the Royal Military College, Sandhurst, or the Royal Military Academy, Woolwich.[79] Only white British officers were put in charge of battalions or regiments. The reasons given for these decisions were fear of a lack of loyalty, and that Indians were not considered capable of leading battalions or regiments in the field – a myth that was perpetuated for many years.[80] Even in the nineteenth century, this position sparked debate and discussion, most of which fell on deaf ears, especially during the tenure of Gen. Sir Frederick Roberts as commander-in-chief of the Bengal Army. He was against any proposal that allowed the possibility of native officers having command over their British counterparts, and the system had been designed to ensure that British officers would not be commanded by Indian officers, no matter how junior in age or experience the former might be.[81] Native officers were considered able to command many different classes of Indians without getting caught up in the men's

---

[77] Quoted in Yong, *Garrison State*, p. 269.

[78] Native and later viceroy commissioned officers were Indian sepoys who had risen through the ranks of a unit based upon seniority instead of merit. The ranks of the native officers were jemadar, subedar, and subedar major (infantry) and jemadar, risaldar, and risaldar (cavalry). So a senior Indian VCO, subedar major, or risaldar major would most likely have served for twenty years before attaining the rank. However, a subedar major still had to accept orders from a young subaltern just out from Addiscombe or Sandhurst. There is no exact rank equivalent in the British Army: VCOs commanded platoons, as did lieutenants. For a wider discussion of the debates of the nineteenth century, see Chandar Sundaram, 'Grudging Concessions: The Officer Corps and Its Indianization, 1817–1940', in Marston and Sundaram, eds., *Military History of India and South Asia*, pp. 88–101.

[79] Officers for the infantry and cavalry regiments of the British Army and later the Indian Army were trained at Sandhurst, while officers for the artillery and engineers were trained at Woolwich.

[80] See Chandar Sundaram, 'Reviving a Dead Letter: Military Indianization and the Ideology of Anglo-India, 1885–1891', in P. S. Gupta and A. Deshpande, eds., *The British Raj and Its Armed Forces, 1857–1939* (Delhi: Oxford University Press, 2002), pp. 45–97, and 'Grudging Concessions'.

[81] While this is true, all of the Indian and British officers interviewed noted that the VCOs were the backbone of the battalion or regiment and were respected at all levels, and especially by officers just arrived from Sandhurst or Dehra Dun. The VCOs were the link between the men and the British officers.

religious or class issues;[82] but Indian native officers were considered incapable of rising above these controversies.[83]

Despite these prejudices, in reality native officers regularly commanded companies of men during the days of the East India Company and the early years of the British Government's control of India, because the numbers of British officers were quite low in any given unit, especially the irregular corps.[84] The performance of native officers serving with irregular units during the Mutiny of 1857 demonstrated that Indians, when given the responsibility, could perform well in the field.[85] Many in the establishment believed that native officers should rise through the ranks on the basis of merit, but conservative elements decided that men would be awarded VCO ranks by seniority instead. This system ensured that VCOs were old and trusted soldiers. By 1914 the numbers of British officers had risen to twelve to fifteen men per infantry battalion or cavalry regiment, while VCOs numbered around eighteen to twenty men. The VCOs were in command of platoons, while the British officers served as company commanders and company officers.

Some in the British establishment felt that the commissioned officer class should be opened to Indians,[86] but this development was not to take place for several more years.[87] A significant reason for this delay was

[82] This was an issue with the VCOs. VCOs were of the same class as the company to which they were assigned. The VCOs from a Sikh or Pathan company commanded platoons of the same class. The idea was that sepoys would follow the orders and commands of VCOs due to the fact they were of the same class. This system led to preferential treatment in certain companies, as the VCO would favour men from his own village.

[83] This was eventually proved to be false. Indian commissioned officers were found generally not to prefer any one class over another even if one of the classes was their own. Sepoys also did not have difficulty in following the commands of Indian commissioned officers even if they were not of the same class or if the officer originated from a non-martial race class.

[84] The irregular forces were mostly cavalry regiments. The units raised during the Indian Mutiny, such as Hodson's Horse and Fane's Horse, are examples of these. The Punjab Irregular Force also had different officering levels due to the fact it was seen as an irregular force for a number of years.

[85] See Henry Lawrence, 'Military Defence of Our Empire in the East', *Calcutta Review 2*, no. 3 (1844), pp. 32–72, which discusses the efforts of Gen. Sir George Chesney as a member of the Viceroy's Executive Council.

[86] General O'Moore Creagh (commander-in-chief, India, 1909–14): Omissi, *The Sepoy and the Raj*, p. 160.

[87] The Imperial Cadet Corps (ICC) was begun in 1901 to open a form of commissions for Indians. However, it was doomed to failure by the decision that its officers were not given the same rights as a formally commissioned Sandhurst or Woolwich graduate. They had no power of command over a British or Indian soldier in the Army in India. Most of the officers were placed in the Princely State Forces or Imperial Service Troop formations. Gen. Creagh, CinC, India, pushed for the ICC to be expanded to have powers of command in the Indian Army in 1912, but this reform was blocked by the

loyalty: it was widely believed that if Indian commissioned officers took over, they would be susceptible to class loyalties and thus be potentially disloyal to the army. Alternatively, as India's political consciousness developed, the contention shifted to become the claim that educated Indians would seek commissions only to undermine the authority of the British by turning the battalions or regiments into bastions of Indian nationalism.

The First World War and the sacrifices made by the Indian Army finally opened the door for Indian commissions,[88] but only by a little. A select few VCOs were given King's Commissions; the majority had served most of their lives and would retire shortly before they reached the higher ranks.[89] An Indian Cadet College was established in Indore[90] in 1918 and closed in 1919, to give commissions to men who had served in the war. Many were men of VCO rank, but few of them had received any significant level of education. Maj. Gen. A. A. Rudra was an exception: he had served as a private, and later sergeant, in the Royal Fusiliers. He had been at Cambridge University when war broke out and was not allowed to receive a commission although, strangely, he was allowed to serve as a ranker with a British unit. He felt that many of the soldiers sent to Indore were not of the best quality and that in fact they had been sent there by senior British officers expressly to fail, thus reinforcing the pre-war prejudices about Indians' inability to command.[91]

The attempt to broaden commission eligibility was part of an overall British policy in India which included devolution of far greater power to elected Indian politicians, particularly at the provincial level through the Montagu–Chelmsford Reforms[92] of 1918, and more rapid Indianisation of a broad range of civilian services. The Government of India Act of

viceroy and the War Office in the UK. The ICC experiment was ended in 1914. See Sundaram, 'Grudging Concessions', p. 93.

[88] Indians had received commissions as medical officers during the war. An estimated 700 men were commissioned into the Indian Medical Services, but not as fighting soldiers. See Trench, *The Indian Army and the King's Enemies*, p. 116.

[89] There was only one feature that differentiated British king's commissioned officers from king's commissioned Indian officers, and this would later affect the Indian commissioned officers from Dehra Dun. British officers, upon appointment to the Indian Army, were paid an extra wage because they were serving far from home. As the Indian cadets graduated, they were not granted this extra wage since they were serving at home. While the Government of India had imposed this as a cost-saving measure, it caused bitter resentment among the Indian cadets, who felt that they had been shunted aside in some way and were not considered of the same quality. This issue would not be properly addressed until 1945.

[90] Cadets were then sent to Sandhurst.

[91] D. K. Palit, *Major General A. A. Rudra* (Dehra Dun: Lancer Publishing, 1993), pp. 7–9.

[92] Sir Edwin Montagu, the India secretary, had stated in 1917: 'The Government have decided that the bar which has hitherto precluded the admission of Indians to

1919[93] created a Legislative Assembly for India, composed of both elected and appointed officials at the provincial level. Issues such as recruitment and further Indianisation of the officer corps were debated by the assembly and relevant questions forwarded to the Government of India.

Beginning in 1920, ten places at Sandhurst were reserved for Indians. At first, most of those selected came from the martial races, and were either themselves VCOs or the sons of VCOs; some university-educated men were also chosen. The first cadets from both Sandhurst and Indore received King's Commissions, which meant that in theory they held the same powers of command and punishment as any white officer in the Indian Army, and underwent the same training process as white officers had done since the Mutiny. They were posted for a year as platoon commanders with a British battalion in India; after that they were posted to any regiment they chose, provided a vacancy was available.[94] At first there appeared to be no issues of racial discrimination, although some senior officers expressed reservations, fearing that junior British officers might end up serving under an Indian. For many British officers in the Indian Army, this possibility was still inconceivable.[95]

Maj. G. A. A. Rudra joined the 28th Punjab in 1920.[96] He noted in his memoirs that, when he first arrived, the commanding officer (CO) and adjutant did not take much notice of him. He later learned from a VCO that, upon arrival, subalterns generally were introduced to all the VCOs of the regiment by the colonel, a courtesy that had not been observed for him. Rudra was fortunate in that he had been at Cambridge University and was a keen sportsman, so the officers did warm to him after a few days, and he was posted to the various companies as a company officer.[97]

Eight-unit scheme

Following these first Indianisation initiatives, issues arose over how the process would continue. One scheme, which was rejected, proposed that Indianisation be instituted in three phases, with the army fully Indianised over the course of forty-five years. Attempts to move the process

---

commissioned rank in His Majesty's Army should be removed' (quoted in Sundaram, 'Grudging Concessions', p. 94).

[93] Reforms originated in Monatgu–Chelmsford Report, 1918, were published within this act.

[94] Gurkha regiments were not part of the process. They were still open only to British cadets. This would not change until Indian independence in 1947.

[95] Mason, *A Matter of Honour*, p. 454.

[96] After 1922 it became the 4/15th Punjab Regiment.   [97] Palit, *Rudra*, pp. 80–90.

forward were hindered by the concern that British men would not join the Indian Army if they thought there was a possibility that they would be commanded by an Indian.[98] Some in the Indian military still wished to end the process altogether, but by this point it was no longer possible to turn back.

Field Marshal Henry Rawlinson, commander-in-chief of the Indian Army, announced an eight-unit scheme in 1923, which earmarked designated units for Indianisation.[99] Only those British officers already serving would continue to do so and complete their time, so that there would be no possibility of an Indian commanding a British officer.[100] The eight-unit scheme was a scaled-back version of an earlier proposal (which had called for twenty units); this was necessary because the failure rate of Indian cadets at Sandhurst at this time was about 30 per cent,[101] and Rawlinson feared it would prove difficult to get the required number of Indian officers to implement the first proposal.

Interestingly, most of the eight units selected for Indianisation[102] were not so-called elite units. The two cavalry units were old Madras non-silladar units; elite cavalry units such as Probyn's or Hodson's Horse were not included. There were also no infantry units of the old Punjab Frontier Force in the list.[103]

The scheme called for cadets to be sought from all over India, but the feeling persisted that only cadets from the martial races were suitable.[104]

---

[98] This was further confirmed in a lecture given in 1931 at the Imperial Defence College, London. It was stated that there was 'clear evidence that British cadets were reluctant to face prospect of coming under the command of Indian officers' (L/MIL/5/857, OIOC, BL).

[99] He had actually envisioned a different Indianisation process, in which 25 per cent of all Indian Army commissions would go to Indians, allowing the Indianisation of the officer corps to occur much more quickly: Omissi, *The Sepoy and the Raj*, pp. 166–72.

[100] A British graduate of Sandhurst in 1936 remembers a lecture by the commandant which stated that, while Indians were being commissioned, the system in place would never allow Indians to command British officers: author's interview with Lt Col M. Wilcox, 1st Battalion 13th FFRifles, 12 Nov. 1999.

[101] One reason for the failure rate was the intense discipline of the regime at Sandhurst. Many British cadets had some experience of this sort of discipline from having attended public schools, but the Indians who were sent to Sandhurst had not previously encountered it. The Prince of Wales Royal Military College was founded in 1922 to rectify this and prepare Indian cadets for Sandhurst. Another important issue was the distance that Indian cadets travelled from home to attend: author's interview with Brig. C. S. Mehta, 28 Oct. 2000.

[102] 7th Light Cavalry, 16th Light Cavalry, 2/1st Punjab, 5/5th Mahratta Light Infantry, 1/7th Rajput, 1/14th Punjab, 4/19th Hyderabad, 2/1st Madras Pioneers.

[103] These would appear in the second list of units in 1933, although none of the elite cavalry units was ever earmarked for Indianisation.

[104] The Punjab provided 42%; United Provinces 10.5%; and Bombay 14%. Interestingly, Bengal provided 10.5% of the cadets for Royal Military College Sandhurst between

This prejudice was propagated by the belief that the martial race troops – such as Sikhs, PMs, and Dogras – would not consent to being led by officers who were Bengali or Madrassi. Recruiting cadets from the preferred martial races initially posed some problems, as candidates often lacked the educational requirements stipulated by the selection process, forcing the army to recruit from other classes as well. To complicate matters still further, the establishment was also concerned that VCOs would not respect newly commissioned Indian officers.

After the eight units had been designated, Army Headquarters (AHQ) India called for all previously commissioned Indian officers to leave the regiments where they were stationed and choose one of the eight units. Three Indian officers opted not leave their regiments;[105] one of these was Maj. Gen. Rudra. The impetus for this decision was actually Rudra's subedar major, who refused to permit him to leave the regiment and went to the colonel himself to state that the men and the VCOs did not wish Rudra to be released. The request was dropped and Rudra remained with the battalion until the Second World War, in the process helping to debunk several of the myths described above. As was indicated by the subedar major's actions, as a king's Indian commissioned officer he was clearly not resented by the VCOs. Over the course of fifteen years, he commanded British officers, provoking no controversy or even comment. Finally, the men were content to be led by Rudra, although he was not of a northern martial class.[106]

Indian cadets who were commissioned continued to be sent to British units for a year of training, then were posted to one of the eight Indianised units. Like their predecessors, the men held King's Commissions and were referred to as king's Indian commissioned officers (KCIOs). In theory, they still had the right of command over British officers, but the capacity for actually carrying this out was limited by their placement in Indianised units.

Over the course of the 1920s, the number of Indian men seeking officers' commissions dropped. Sandhurst was one stumbling-block;

1919 and 1925. See Pradeep Barua, *Gentlemen of the Raj: The Indian Army Officer Corps, 1817–1949* (Westport, CT: Praeger, 2003), p. 154. Officer recruitment from both Bengal and Bombay had dropped dramatically by the 1930s (see below).

[105] Many felt that the eight-unit scheme was a system of segregation and that the rest of the army units would look down upon them (which turned out to be true); thus these three men opted to remain with their parent units. Even Sir George MacMunn, a military author who is considered quite conservative, had issues with the segregation; he wrote in his *Martial Races* in 1933 that 'if the British Dominion is to remain on sound lines the less separation takes place the better it will be' (p. 350).

[106] Author's interview with Brig. N. K. Chatterji, nephew of Maj. Gen. Rudra, 25 Oct. 2000.

the amount of money required for fees, and the distance that most cadets would be required to travel, were daunting for many prospective candidates.[107] According to the Indian Sandhurst Committee's Report from 1927, the limiting 'eight unit scheme' was another reason why the number of applicants had not increased. As it stated: 'it is necessary to widen the field of opportunity'.[108]

Indian Military Academy

Following the demand by the Indian legislature for more Indians to be commissioned at Sandhurst, and the subsequent lack of response from potential cadets, the decision was made to create an Indian Military Academy (IMA) at Dehra Dun. The academy was formally opened on 10 December 1932; cadets who completed the required course of training would henceforth achieve the designation of Indian commissioned officer (ICO), and they would only be eligible to command Indian soldiers,[109] unlike their predecessors, the king's commissioned Indian officers, who had been eligible for positions of command over both British and Indian troops.[110] A precedent for this decision did already exist, in that Dominion officers experienced a similar fate. The cases were not generally considered equivalent, however, since on the whole few British troops or officers were present throughout the Dominions, while Indian commissioned officers regularly had to contend with the reality of British Army troops and British officers in their country. This decision was to cause bitter resentment among the officers,[111] and to create significant friction between KCIOs and ICOs.[112]

---

[107] Omissi, *The Sepoy and the Raj*, pp. 172–6.

[108] See 'The Indian Sandhurst Committee's Report, November 1926', in Philips, ed., *Select Documents, IV*, pp. 531–2.

[109] This was similar to the graduates of the Canadian and Australian Military Academies (Kingston and Duntroon) who held commissions only within their own Dominion forces.

[110] Realistically, the possibility of a KCIO commanding a British officer had been limited by the eight-unit scheme.

[111] This perception of ICOs as 'second class' was considered a contributing factor to the decision by some ICO prisoners of war to switch sides and participate in the formation of the Indian National Army. Captain Mohan Singh, an ICO who graduated from IMA, was one of the first officers to join the INA. See Chapter 2 for more discussion on the INA and its impact in the Second World War and Chapter 3 which will deal with the INA trials in late 1945 and early 1946.

[112] Brig. R. B. Chopra, a graduate of IMA Dehra Dun in July 1936, noted a speech from an Indian major who was a KCIO. He paraded the men and said that he was different from them (because he was a graduate of Sandhurst) and that they must always remember that point: author's interview with Brig. Chopra, 22 Oct. 2000.

The course at the IMA was designed to last two and half years, the extra year of instruction having been added to instruct cadets in British customs which might be unfamiliar to them.[113] There were two terms a year, and forty cadets were accepted for each term. Fifteen cadets were selected from the Indian Army, ten from the Princely States, and fifteen from open competition.[114] Even with such quotas established, selection continued to be made primarily from the designated martial races.[115] Lt Gen. K. P. Candeth noted that, of his entering class in 1934, 40% were Musalmans, 30% were Sikhs, and the rest were Dogras, Jats, and Mahrattas. He, as a Madrassi,[116] was the only cadet who could be considered non-martial.[117]

Although the initiatives undertaken by the Indian Army could be construed as attempts to limit or undermine the success of the Indianisation process and segregate the cadets into specific units, there were those who clearly did not want the scheme to fail. One piece of evidence for this is the calibre of the training officers selected for the IMA. Many officers have noted that the British training officers were first class; Lt Gen. Harbarkash Singh even claimed that British officers selected for the IMA 'were known for their sympathy for the Indian cause'.[118] While this statement may seem an exaggeration, other officers have noted that the British officers respected the Indian cadets and did not perpetuate a colour bar. One of the first officers posted to the IMA was Maj. Reginald Savory[119] of the 1/11th Sikh, and many Indian officers later commented on his open-mindedness.[120] Lt Gen. K. S.

---

[113] Many Indian officers felt that the extra year's instruction gave them an advantage over officers coming from Sandhurst: author's interviews in Pakistan and India, 1999–2009.

[114] Omissi, *The Sepoy and the Raj*, p. 184.

[115] Three Indian officers that I interviewed came from the martial races. Their fathers had served either in the Indian Civil Service or in the army as subedars.

[116] Author's interview with Lt Gen. K. P. Candeth, 28 Oct. 2000.

[117] The Punjab was listed as having provided 41% of the cadets at IMA from 1932 to 1936, with the North-West Frontier Province and the United Provinces providing an additional 24% of the total intake. Madras and Bengal provided only 1.5% and 1% respectively. See Pradeep Barua, *The Army Officer Corps and Military Modernisation in Late Colonial India* (University of Hull Press, 1999), p. 155.

[118] Mss Eur T95/2 Lt Gen. Harbarkash Singh, OIOC, BL.

[119] Savory was later to command the 23rd Indian Division during 1942–3 and played a considerable role in the tactical reform of the Indian Army to improve its fighting potential in the jungles of Burma. He became the director of infantry, India, in 1943 and remained so until the end of the war. During the post-war period, he became the adjutant general of the Indian Army.

[120] Col John Maling of the 1st Sikh Light Infantry was a pre-war officer. While at Sandhurst in 1934, he met Savory, who discussed the Indianisation process and his full support of it. Maling joined the 1/11th Sikh Regiment while Savory was the CO in the late 1930s. He noted that Savory made all British officers aware of the Indianisation process and made his positive feelings known: author's correspondence with Col John Maling.

Katoch described how his company commander, Maj. David 'Punch' Cowan,[121] set the tone for the training company with the attitude that, if the cadets were good enough for the king, they were good enough for the rest of the Indian Army.[122]

Once the IMA was operational and accepting a full complement of candidates, the need for more units in which to place the cadets became apparent. By 1933, a further seven infantry battalions, one cavalry regiment, and ancillary units had been selected for Indianisation, with the idea of forming a division entirely of Indianised units, although the time when an ICO would attain the rank of lieutenant colonel was still far in the future. This second round of Indianisation included elite infantry units,[123] but the elite cavalry formations were still not on the list and would not accept Indian officers until the outbreak of the Second World War.[124] The British officer instructors encouraged their cadets to join their own regiments; Lt Gen. Harbarkash Singh was encouraged by Savory to join the 11th Sikh,[125] and Maj. Gen. Prasad was encouraged to join the 12th Frontier Force Regiment (FFR) by his training officer, who reinforced his argument by pointing out that other Indian cadets had joined.[126]

ICOs continued to spend a year with a British regiment stationed in India before proceeding to their chosen Indian regiment. On the whole, ICOs felt that they were well received by their British regiments; they occasionally encountered officers who were a bit standoffish, but overall British officers did not feel threatened by Indian officers, since they did not fear being replaced. Most Indian officers found it easier to fit in if they were good at sport.[127]

Following their induction year, ICOs were posted to their selected Indianised battalions. All of the officers that I was able to speak with mentioned that upon their arrival they were greeted as would any officer being welcomed to his new unit, and that it was entirely up to the CO to

[121] As with Savory, Punch Cowan was to command a division during the Burma campaign. He commanded the 17th Indian Division from the Battle of Sittang in March 1942 until 1945. He was also instrumental in the tactical reform of the army to fight in the jungles and open plains of Burma.

[122] Author's interview with Lt Gen. Katoch, 4 Nov. 2000.

[123] 5/6th Rajputana Rifles, 5/11th Sikh, 4/12th FFR, and 6/13th FFRifles; the rest were 5/2nd Punjab, 5/8th Punjab, 5/10th Baluch: L/MIL/17/5/1800, OIOC, BL.

[124] 3rd Cavalry was selected.

[125] Mss Eur T95/2 Lt Gen. Harbarkash Singh, OIOC, BL.

[126] Including one Lt S. H. J. F. Manekshaw, who later became a field marshal in the Indian Army: author's interview with Maj. Gen. N. Prasad, 28 Oct. 2000.

[127] Brig. Chopra took nine wickets for his British Battalion, the 22nd Cheshire Regiment, which helped them to adjust to him.

set the tone within his unit. Most COs seem to have made protecting their men in all types of situations a priority; while this was not always true, when a unit was first listed to be Indianised, it seems in most cases that within a year or two most of the men who wanted to leave had been posted out and others brought in for the transition period.[128] Maj. Gen. Prasad mentioned an incident concerning a British major of the 4/12th FFR who had made it clear that he was not happy about the situation, and for his pains was called up in front of the CO and given a talking-to in front of the Indian officers.[129]

The last controversy of the Indianisation scheme before the start of Second World War was the platoonisation of infantry units. While issues of the rates of pay and apparent segregation into specific units were significant concerns, the implementation of the platoon system was a major grievance of Indian officers, who saw it as definitive proof that they were being assigned second-class status in comparison to their British counterparts.[130]

With the increase in Indian officers in the late 1920s, proposals were made to change the organisation of the Indianised infantry battalions,[131] but no initiatives were formally undertaken until January 1935.[132] At this point the number of ICOs sent to each battalion was set at around twenty to twenty-four officers, who would command platoons. The old VCOs would gradually be sent to other units of the given regiments and the VCO ranks would be abolished,[133] with the ICOs taking over their positions. The British Army had a similar system in place, with lieutenants commanding platoons, but the Indian Army had not adopted this practice.

Maj. Gen. D. K. Palit contends that the main reason for this policy was to make the process of Indian officers going up the rank ladder take longer. He was convinced that he himself would never rise above the rank of major.[134] AHQ contended that since both officers and men were now Indian, they no longer needed the added support buffer of the VCO ranks. However, some Indian officers had more in common with their British counterparts than with their men, and this decision therefore created friction. Overall, the Indian officers felt

---

[128] All seven pre-war Indian commissioned officers noted this in the interviews.
[129] Author's interview with Maj. Gen. Prasad, 28 Oct. 2000.
[130] Many ICOs from the pre-war period highlighted these issues during the initial interview period. There was a silver lining to this argument, ironically: when war broke out in 1939, there was a demand for more Indian officers to help expand the army.
[131] IAO No. 174 (1934); 386 (1935), OIOC, BL.
[132] Omissi, *The Sepoy and the Raj*, p. 182.   [133] L/MIL/17/5/1800, OIOC, BL.
[134] Author's interview with Maj. Gen. Palit, 4 Nov. 2000.

that they had been insulted and were looked down upon by the rest of the army;[135] one Indian Army officer mentioned that when an Indianised battalion was stationed in a cantonment with other Indian Army regiments there was frequently a sense of inferiority among the Indian officers.[136] Significantly, Indian officers did make a distinction between the orders and directives handed down by AHQ, and on the whole did not blame the British officers for the directives.[137]

The drop in Indian officer candidates as the decade drew to a close was attributed to the various aspects of Indianisation. The general sentiment was, why join a segregated unit to get paid a lower wage, or command at a lower level than British officers? An attempt to rectify this was made in 1938, when it was formally recognised that ICOs could command British officers in the Indian land forces who were of a rank equivalent to or below their own, based upon seniority. There was one major omission: ICOs had similar powers to KCOs, but did not have power of punishment over British other ranks.[138] This was to cause problems, and provoke further changes, during the first years of the war.[139]

The 1920s and 1930s had marked slow progress for the Indianisation system, but the foundations for the future had been laid. The myths that men and VCOs of the martial classes would not want to be led or commanded by Indian officers (of either the martial or non-martial classes) were in the process of being dispelled as Indian officers and men served together in operations on the frontier and during Aid to the

---

[135] This issue was among those brought forward when interrogation of ex-officers who had joined the INA began in 1945 and the reasons for their switching sides were discussed.

[136] Brig. Gubrux Singh related an incident at a club dance, where the Indian junior officers all stayed on one side and the British junior officers stayed on the other. He noted that the Indians felt that they were as good as the British, but feared that the British would shun them: author's interview with Maj. Gen. Gubrux Singh, 23 Oct. 2000.

[137] Author's interviews with Lt Gen. Candeth, 29 Oct. 2000, Lt Gen. Katoch, 4 Nov. 2000, Maj. Gen. Prasad, 28 Oct. 2000, Maj. Gen. L. Singh, 26 Oct. 2000, Brig. Chopra, 22 Oct. 2000.

[138] L/MIL/17/5/1800, OIOC, BL.

[139] The final significant development of pre-war Indianisation was the formal raising of an Indian field artillery unit in 1935. Previously, all field artillery units had been exclusively British Royal Artillery from the time of the Indian Mutiny. As a result of that event, the widespread feeling was that Indians could not be trusted with large artillery pieces, although they were allowed to serve in mountain artillery units. On 15 January 1935 the 1st Field Brigade was formed at Bangalore, with four batteries made up of Madrassis, PMs, Rajputana Rajputs, and Ranghars: L/MIL/7/19154, OIOC, BL. All officers posted to this unit were to be Indians; they would serve one year's attachment to a Royal Artillery unit in India and then move to the 1st Field Brigade. This system laid the foundation for proper Indian Field regiments to be raised during the Second World War: author's interview with Lt Gen. Candeth, 25 Oct. 2000, one of the first Indian officers of the brigade.

Civil Power exercises. The growing numbers of Indian officers, as well as their performance, helped to enhance their reputation to some degree with British officers serving outside the Indianised units.[140] Senior Indian Army officers who felt there should be no colour bar helped to set the tone within their own battalions and regiments, or trained future Indian officers at the IMA. Maj. Gen. E. H. W. Grimshaw, a Sandhurst cadet in 1931, recalled similar sentiments. He was the son of the former colonel of the 62nd Punjab Regiment (1/1st Punjab Regiment) and attended Sandhurst with three Indian cadets in his company. He did not feel that there were any colour issues among the cadets. The Indian cadets performed as well as the British, and the general feeling in his company was, why not have Indian officers in the Indian Army? Grimshaw later led the 1/1st Punjab in the Burma campaign with an ICO[141] as his second-in-command and, when he relinquished command, he recommended the Indian officer to replace him. His recommendation was carried forward, and Lt Col Sher Ali Khan led the battalion during Operation Extended Capital in 1945; he received high marks from all in the 1st Punjab Regiment, as well as from Field Marshal Auchinleck.[142]

Many ICOs followed the British military tradition of not talking about politics in the mess. Etiquette in the mess of course did not mean that officers were lacking political feelings or ideas during the inter-war period. While many Indian officers were drawn from sons of the VCOs and soldiers, who were generally expected to hold traditional political opinions, there were others who were sons of officers in the ICS and other civil departments. Those who came from ICS families were more likely to be politically aware, and might be considered more likely to support nationalist policies. Some of these men had joined the army when Indianisation was initiated, because they had always wished to but military service had traditionally been denied to their family since they were not of the martial races. Maj. Gen. G. J. Hamilton, Guides Infantry (5/12th FFR), noted that 'we all knew, even in the '20s, that independence for India could not be long delayed and it was our duty to

---

[140] Lt Col Michael Willcox, 1/13th FFRifles, mentioned that when he left Sandhurst in 1937 he knew something of the system. By 1939 he had heard positive things about Indian officers serving in the 6/13th FFRifles: author's interview, 23 Nov. 1999.

[141] Maj. Sher Ali Khan originally joined the 7th Light Cavalry, but was posted out as a result of problems in the regiment during the war. Gen. Auchinleck sent him to the 1/1st Punjab Regiment as second in command: author's interview with Maj. Gen. E. H. W. Grimshaw, CB, CBE, DSO, 6 Dec. 2000.

[142] Author's interview with Maj. Gen. Grimshaw, 6 Dec. 2000.

see that our Indian successors, both in the services and civil administration, were properly trained'.[143]

Most officers, whatever their political leanings, recognised that India
would reach either Dominion status or full independence in the near
future and that there would be a need for Indian officers for the Indian
Army.[144] As Jawaharlal Nehru noted when discussing the Indianisation
of the ICS: 'There were some members of this civil army [the ICS] who
were able and patriotic and nationalistically inclined but like the soldier,
who also may be patriotic in his individual capacity, they were bound up
by the army code and discipline and the price of disobedience, desertion
and revolt was heavy.'[145]

Many officers who may have had nationalist inclinations felt that their
service to the Indian Army, and more particularly their regiment, was
their priority and therefore chose not to upset the balance by overt
demonstration of political leanings. There were officers who had become
bitter through mistreatment at the hands of some British officers and
civilians and relegation to second-class status as soldiers. This mistreatment was a major reason for some Indian officers' decision to break their
oaths of allegiance and join the Japanese-sponsored Indian National
Army (INA) after the defeats in Malaya and Burma in 1942.[146]

A young subaltern, Robin Hastings, arriving in India to be posted to
his British regiment (the Rifle Brigade) in February 1939, recorded one
of his earliest observations of interaction between the Indian Army and
India. An Indian gentleman (and officer), sent by Government House to
fetch him at Bombay, was subjected to an onslaught of racist abuse by the
British disembarkation officer. The Indian officer was unruffled, but
the subaltern never forgot it, commenting that the incident was
'an example of how the worst type of Englishman could alienate a whole
nation'. He found it even more striking when compared to his subsequent exposure to his own and other Indian Army regiments, where he
never witnessed any such behaviour towards Indian officers from either
officers or men.[147]

The Government of India Act of 1935 had devolved significant power to
the provinces, in an effort to appease nationalist sentiments. As the two
major nationalist parties, Congress and the League, began to win seats in

---

[143] Gaylor, *Sons of John Company*, p. 29.
[144] Author's interviews with Indian officers, 1999–2009.
[145] Jawaharlal Nehru, *The Discovery of India* (London: Meridien Books, 1956), p. 329.
[146] The INA falls outside the scope of this chapter but will be discussed in greater detail in
Chapter 3.
[147] He served in India for a year: Robin Hastings, *An Undergraduate's War* (London:
Bellhouse, 1997), pp. 31–2.

the provincial assemblies, parties which won a majority were entitled to appoint a chief minister, who worked with the governor from the ICS. However, law and order were still vested in the hands of the Government of India. The governors of each of the provinces were to take the advice of the provincial assemblies, but they could disregard any advice at their discretion if security was at risk. The ICS and Indian Police (IP) also remained under the control of the governor-general (viceroy).[148]

Organisation and roles of the army in the inter-war period

The First World War also demonstrated significant deficiencies in the army's supply network, training practices, and general organisation. The regimental groupings were not highly organised, and the establishment of individual centres meant that each one requested materiel and weapons from AHQ separately, frequently overwhelming the supply network. Each centre was also responsible for finding its own recruits from the local populations that traditionally served in each of the battalions, an unwieldy system that created numerous breakdowns in management and processing reinforcements for overseas duty. Perhaps most important, nothing had been done to establish formal training procedures, and recruits had to be ready to go overseas quickly. This meant that training of the recruits was generally of a low standard.[149]

The cavalry units, with similar organisation, faced similar problems. The old silladar system[150] of most of the cavalry units[151] of the Indian

---

[148] See Government of India Act, pp. 164–6; also in Philips, ed., *Select Documents, IV*, pp. 320–35.

[149] Gaylor, *Sons of John Company*, p. 18.

[150] Under the silladar system, new recruits to many of the Indian cavalry regiments paid for their horses and equipment when they arrived. Upon leaving the regiment, they would sell the horses and equipment back to the regiment. This was an old cavalry practice, dating from before the British Indian Army existed and actually originating with the Mahratta and Mughal cavalry units. There had been a division of irregular and regular cavalry units under the East India Company, with many of the irregular cavalry originating from the locally raised Sikh and Punjabi Musalman units. However, since many Bengal Army units participated in the Mutiny, the irregular cavalry units were taken into the line. With the abolition of the East India Company, the Indian Army cavalry units all became silladar units except the units of the Madras presidency. The clear advantage for the British government in India to adopt this policy was that it cost them less than to outfit cavalry regiments, since it would only have to provide for them during war-time. The rates of pay for soldiers in the silladar system were also higher. By the turn of the century the silladar system had changed a little; the recruits no longer bought horses, but paid fees for their upkeep instead. See Maj. Gen. S. S. Hamid, *So They Rode and Fought* (Tunbridge Wells, UK: Midas Books, 1983), pp. 33–4.

[151] The 26th, 27th (later 7th Light Cavalry), and 28th Madras Lancers did not operate under the silladar system. They were equipped with horses and other supplies by the government.

Army finally broke down under the pressures of war. The ability of units to acquire and ship replacement horses to the various fronts was seriously compromised, as was the quality of horses acquired as demand increased throughout the war. The system of processing recruits for both the infantry and cavalry also ran into difficulties. Recruits originally earmarked for one regiment were sent to others, in response to wherever the demand for reinforcements was greatest. This caused morale issues, and created an additional complication when assamis[152] could not be collected, creating further financial problems. Regiments felt that they could not ask men for assamis before they left when there was a strong possibility that they might be posted to another regiment upon arrival overseas.

In the face of an increasingly chaotic situation, the Government of India was forced during the First World War to take over the many regimental systems providing horses and equipment to the troops. This in turn provoked a major governmental reorganisation of the army after the war ended, driven primarily by the need to increase economic efficiency. The first major reform was the amalgamation of the old thirty-eight cavalry units into twenty-one cavalry regiments.[153] In conjunction with this change, the silladar system was abandoned and the Government of India assumed responsibility for providing all of the necessary horses, equipment, and food. The peace-time establishment of the Indian Cavalry Regiment was set at 14 British officers, 18 VCOs,[154] and 504 NCOs[155] and men. The cavalry regiments were grouped into a unit of three regiments, to facilitate the easier recruitment process of the various classes.[156]

---

[152] The fee that was paid to the cavalry regiment was called the assami. Each regiment had a stud farm where horses were reared for operational units; these were then leased out to regiments. The assami was also thought to compel loyalty from soldiers; if a soldier was discharged with a good record, he would receive most of his assami in return. If he was dishonourably discharged, however, he received nothing. See Omissi, *The Sepoy and the Raj*, pp. 72–3.

[153] Regiments: 1st Skinner's, 2nd Lancers (Gardner's Horse), 3rd Cavalry, 4th Hodson's Horse, 5th Probyn's Horse, 6th Duke of Connaught's Own Lancers (Watson's Horse), 7th Light Cavalry, 8th King George V's Own Light Cavalry, 9th Royal Deccan Horse, 10th Guides Cavalry (Frontier Force), 11th Prince Albert Victor's Own Cavalry (Frontier Force), 12th Cavalry (Frontier Force), 13th Duke of Connaught's Own Lancers, 14th Scinde Horse, 15th Lancers, 16th Light Cavalry, 17th Poona Horse, 18th King Edward's Own Cavalry, 19th King George V's Own Lancers, 20th Lancers, Central India Horse (21st King George V's Own Cavalry). See Gaylor, *Sons of John Company*, pp. 333–5.

[154] Jemadar, subedar, and subedar major.

[155] Lance naik (lance corporal), naik (corporal), dafadar (sergeant).

[156] See section on recruitment for full explanation of classes.

The Indian infantry was formally grouped together, with the various battalions reorganised into twenty large regiments.[157] The idea was that each regiment would be made up of four or five battalions, plus a formal training battalion.[158] (Gurkha battalions were organised differently.)[159] All recruits would proceed to the training battalion at the regimental centre and then pass on to a specific unit. Each regiment would recruit from a specific class and the men would be liable for posting to any unit in that regiment. There were exceptions to this rule.[160] The authorised strengths of battalions were formalised and standardised, eliminating the five different authorised battalion strengths that had existed before the war. Indian infantry battalions were assigned 12 British officers, 20 VCOs, and 742 Indian NCOs and other ranks. Training battalions had 9 British officers, 14 VCOs, and 636 Indian NCOs and other ranks.[161] By 1929 the specific organisation of an infantry battalion changed to an HQ wing, a machine gun company, and three rifle companies,[162] which affected the class composition[163] of the various regiments.[164] This was the last major reorganisation until 1938.[165]

The three chief roles of the Indian Army during the period between the end of the First World War and 1939 were providing Aid to the

---

[157] Regiments: 1st Punjab, 2nd Punjab, 3rd Madras, 4th Bombay Grenadiers, 5th Mahratta Light Infantry, 6th Rajputana Rifles, 7th Rajput, 8th Punjab, 9th Jat, 10th Baluch, 11th Sikh, 12th FFR, 13th FFRifles, 14th Punjab, 15th Punjab, 16th Punjab, 17th Dogra, 18th Royal Garhwal Rifles, 19th Hyderabad, 20th Burma Rifles (left Indian Army establishment in 1937). See Army Instructions No. 58 (1922), L/MIL/7/5483, OIOC, BL. Some examples: 2/1st Punjab – old 66th Punjab Regiment; 1/11th Sikh – old 14th King George's Own Ferozepore Sikh; 4/12th FFR – old 54th Sikh (Frontier Force). The numbering is represented thus: 2/1st Punjab is the 2nd battalion 1st Punjab Regiment. Another example: 1/11th Sikh is 1st battalion, 11th Sikh Regiment.

[158] On the whole most regiments had five regular battalions, numbered 1–5, and one training battalion, numbered the 10th battalion. There were exceptions to this rule.

[159] Gurkha regiments numbered ten. As noted previously, they had been grouped into ten regiments in 1903, with two battalions per regiment. Each battalion had four active companies and one training company: 15 Apr. 1926, L/MIL/7/5483, OIOC, BL.

[160] The 1st, 2nd, and 3rd Battalions of the 11th Sikh Regiment were single-class battalions made up of Jat Sikhs, whereas the 4th, 5th, and 10th Battalions were a mixed unit of two companies of Jat Sikhs and two companies of Punjabi Musalmans. The 17th Dogras were made up of all one class of Dogra Rajputs.

[161] Gaylor, *Sons of John Company*, pp. 18–19.

[162] Previous to 1929, battalions had four double companies, which meant that different classes would be represented in a single company. By 1929 there was a desire to have one class for each company. Depending upon the regiment, some units had all the same class in the battalion, while others (the majority) had mixed battalions of various companies.

[163] See section on recruitment for definition of class composition.

[164] Maj. Mahommed Ibrahim Qureshi, *The First Punjabis: History of the 1st Punjab Regiment* (Aldershot: Gale & Polden, 1958), pp. 258–9.

[165] See section on the Chatfield Committee.

Civil Power[166] (IS garrison), and carrying out policing duties on the North-West Frontier[167] (Covering Troops) and conventional warfare (Field Army).[168] It did not seem likely that the Indian Army would fight a European power again, although conventional training remained a centrepiece of tactical training.

As a result of the Amritsar Massacre of 1919,[169] the Indian and British Army units were given clear instructions: 'Your troops should be kept in a position to make use of the weapons at their disposal

---

[166] To many in the army as well as in the Government of India, this was considered to be the most important mission. Aid to the Civil Power was defined by minimum use of force, civil–military co-operation, and deterrence of unrest. There are many accounts by British and Indian Army officers of difficult experiences with IS. One of the best and most accessible is by Field Marshal Sir William Slim, *Unofficial History* (London: Cassell, 1959); see pp. 75–98. Many of the key principles taught and developed for the Indian Army in this role – human intelligence, civil–military relations, and minimum force – are still discussed to this day within various militaries.

[167] Units of the Indian Army had been carrying out countless small- and large-scale campaigns in the North-West Frontier region since the mid 1800s. The tribes (commonly referred to as Pathans) living in the region periodically came down from the hills to attack civil and military outposts in the region for various reasons. The army continuously maintained troops in the area as a buffer between the tribal regions and the plains below. Units were regularly called upon to 'open' tracks or roads to relieve pressure on a post under tribal attack. Over the course of many years the Indian Army had developed various tactics to deal with these incursions. During the 1930s there were two major frontier operations, each of which involved a large amount of troops. These were the Mohmand operation, Aug.–Sep. 1935, and the Waziristan operations of 1936–7. For a very detailed analysis of the doctrine and various major actions of the time and region, see Timothy Moreman's *The Army in India and the Development of Frontier Warfare, 1849–1947* (London: Macmillan, 1998). For specific details of operations, see 'Report on the Mohmand Operations', pp. 18–19, L/MIL/7/16968, OIOC, BL, and 'Report of the 1st Phase of Operations', L/MIL/7/16971, OIOC, BL.

[168] The Army in India (Indian Army and British Army units) of 1931 was deployed as follows:

British Army units: five cavalry regiments, four in the Field Army and one on IS duty; British Infantry battalions: five battalions on Frontier duty (Covering Troops); twelve in the Field Army; four on IS duty; two in Burma.

Indian Army units: five cavalry regiments on Frontier duty; seven attached to the Field Army; seven lines of communication duties; two on IS duties; Indian Infantry battalions: thirty-seven on Frontier duty; thirty-six in the Field Army; twelve lines of communication duties; eleven on IS duty; and two in Burma.

The Field Army units were trained and organised for conventional defence of any invasion by a neighbouring country (chiefly Afghanistan), while the covering troops were stationed in the NWFP and Baluchistan on frontier duties. See L/MIL/17/5/1793, OIOC, BL.

[169] See Report of the Committee appointed by the Government of India to investigate the disturbances in the Punjab, L/MIL/17/1/12/42, OIOC, BL; 'Statement by Brigadier R. E. Dyer' in Evidence Taken before the Disorders Inquiry Committee, Vol. III, Amritsar, V/26/262/5, OIOC, BL; Collett, *Butcher of Amritsar*, Alfred Draper, *Amritsar: The Massacre That Ended the Raj* (London: Cassell, 1981); and Charles Gwynn, *Imperial Policing* (London: Macmillan, 1934), for more information.

and they should not be committed to a hand to hand struggle with the mob.' The orders also stated that, in a case where it was necessary to open fire, verbal warning should be given or bugles used to get the crowd's attention; the number of rounds fired should be named and noted; and fire should be directed at the front of the crowd or at conspicuous ringleaders.[170]

The Indian Army was called out many times during the 1920s and 1930s as an Aid to the Civil Power. Omissi noted that in 1922, over a four-month period, the army was called out on sixty-two occasions.[171] Usually they were summoned to disperse crowds who were engaged in communal violence, political agitation, trade union protests, and general *dacoit* behaviour.[172] There was only one serious incident involving the army in a major episode of civil unrest; this took place in the North-West Frontier in the city of Peshawar in 1930.[173]

In the end, success in IS[174] rested with the ability of the ICS, IP, and Indian Army collaborating on many levels to truly create civil–military co-operation and to make sure that all individuals were working within the confines of civil and military law and utilising correct and actionable intelligence, usually from the ICS and IP, who understood the area. The district magistrate usually represented the ICS, while the commissioner of police and usually the general officer commanding (GOC) represented the security line. By the 1930s the three services had instructions, doctrine,[175] and training[176] in the various roles of IS. The troops and police tended to work together when they were called in. The military would

---

[170] L/MIL/17/5/4252, OIOC, BL. For an account of the development of the IS doctrine for the Indian Army during the inter-war period, see Srinath Raghavan, 'Protecting the Raj: The Army in India and Internal Security, 1919–1939', *Small Wars and Insurgencies*, 16, 3 (Dec. 2005), pp. 253–79, and for more details see Gyanesh Kudaisya, '"In Aid of Civil Power": The Colonial Army in Northern India, 1919–1942', *Journal of Imperial and Commonwealth History*, 32, 1 (Jan. 2004), pp. 41–68.

[171] Omissi, *The Sepoy and the Raj*, p. 219.

[172] *Dacoit* behaviour, defined legally, referred to an armed robbery involving five or more people. The British authorities expanded the definition to include any civil or guerrilla activity. See *ibid.*, p. 220.

[173] See Francis Ingall, *The Last of the Bengal Lancers* (London: Leo Cooper, 1988), 'Red Shirts and Afridis', pp. 47–51, for a practitioner's view of the Aid to the Civil Power.

[174] See Chapter 5 for a much more detailed discussion of IS duties and the development of doctrine and actual performance in the field.

[175] Several manuals were developed specifically to focus on IS. The starting points were *Manual of Indian Military Law*, *Manual of Military Law*, *Regulations for the Army in India*, followed by more directive works including *Security Instructions, India*, 1937, as well as the War Office publications *Duties in the Aid of the Civil Power*.

[176] Officers were instructed in IS at both the British Army Staff College, Camberley, and the Indian Army Staff College, Quetta, as well as the Senior Officer's School, India. Regiments and battalions also carried out various Tactical Exercises Without Troops (TEWTS): Raghavan, 'Protecting the Raj', pp. 272–3.

provide lectures to the civilian agencies on IS. The overall emphasis in all of this was the ability to gather timely, and disseminate actionable, intelligence on potential 'troublemakers' within the community. Overall, the system worked well, although there were numerous instances of friction due to personality clashes and differing interpretations of manuals, directives, and the like.[177]

Following the violence at Amritsar, drills and training were stepped up, especially within the army, to avoid any recurrence of violence on that scale. To give an overview of the system, Brigadier R. C. B. Bristow, a veteran who had served from the 1920s to the middle of the Punjab violence of 1947, stated:

Responsibility for calling out the troops rested with the civil authority. If the police were unable to control a rioting mob, threatening life and property, a magistrate would ask the officer commanding the troops on the spot to disperse them, which he confirmed in writing by signing a form. If possible, the troops would run out barbed wire to their front so as to avoid a hand to hand encounter. A red banner was unfurled between two poles warning the mob to disperse, or else the troops would fire ... If the mob still refused to withdraw, the officer had the duty to disperse them by using minimum force. Warnings were seldom ignored, but if they were the officer would normally order one man to fire one round at the ringleader. If that failed to disperse the mob, fire would be gradually increased by a few rounds at a time, and stopped immediately the mob showed signs of moving away. Empty cartridge cases would be collected and counted to prove the use of minimum force, for a court of enquiry would certainly follow. As soon as possible the wounded would be given first aid.[178]

While this sequence may appear fairly formalised and straightforward, in action things were more complicated. The future field marshal Sir William Slim noted in his discussion of Aid to the Civil Power that instructions such as the Indian Army's IAF D908 (*Instructions to Officers Acting in the Aid of the Civil Power for Dispersal of Unlawful Assemblies*) '[were] a useful thing to have about'. He felt that the four pages helped effectively summarise the many legal volumes on what he could and could not do in the IS role, including the need for the magistrate to sign the fourth detachable page. As he stated, when he found himself in the middle of a disturbance: 'keep your troops in a position to make use of their weapons ... do not commit them to hand to hand struggle ... act in the closest co-operation with the civil authorities ... get the magistrate to fill in the card'.[179]

[177] *Ibid.*, p. 262.   [178] Bristow, *Memories*, p. 28.

[179] Slim, *Unofficial History*, pp. 77–81. As stated above, the chapter 'Aid to the Civil Power', pp. 75–98, in the *Unofficial History* provides a succinct understanding of the tensions and the issues that can arise in this role.

This formalised structure during the inter-war period worked fairly well in containing communal violence as well as political agitation that sometimes became violent. Troops were called out regularly, but frequently were not required to use force to dispel a crowd. The ability of the ICS and IP to provide accurate intelligence and other important information allowed for the troops to quell disturbances quite easily. The bedrock of order, the civil–military team during this period, would encounter major problems during the post-Second World War period, as will be discussed later. For the inter-war period, as Gyanesh Kudaisya noted: 'Though the "in the aid to the civil power" function experienced routinisation in the 1920 contraction and partial withdrawal[180] in the late 1930s ... the internal security troops remained extraordinarily effective.'[181]

The effectiveness of the army in India's ability to deal with IS was further reinforced by the findings of a series of reorganisation committees that were formed in both India and the United Kingdom in the late 1930s. Maj. Gen. Claude Auchinleck[182] was made deputy chief of the General Staff, India, in 1936. The commander-in-chief of the Indian Army at this time was Gen. Sir Robert Cassels, and he instructed Auchinleck to form a committee to assess the capability of the Indian Army to modernise for war.[183] The specific roles of the army were to be clearly defined for all to understand.

Auchinleck's findings outlined several roles for the army. The first designation was the Frontier Defence Troops, which would encompass most of the army's strength. The second grade was the IS Troops, reflecting the continuing need for troops to be ready to give service in Aid to the Civil Power. The last three categories indicate the changing focus of the army's priorities at the end of the 1930s. Coast Defence Troops were established to guard the ports of Bombay (Mumbai), Madras (Chennai), Calcutta (Kolkatta), and Karachi from foreign

---

[180] See below, pp. 42–3, for discussion of the Chatfield Committee.

[181] Kudaiysa, '"In Aid of Civil Power"', p. 63.

[182] Auchinleck served with the 62nd Punjab Regiment, later the 1/1st Punjab Regiment, and won a Distinguished Service Order (DSO) in the First World War. He served as an instructor at the Indian Staff College, Quetta, and commanded the Peshawar Brigade during the Mohmand operations of 1935. He later became commander-in-chief of the Indian Army on two occasions during the Second World War, and was considered a man of reforming ideals by many ex-Indian officers and men. He was a champion of the Indian officer, disliked the pre-war segregation system, and was not inclined to believe that there were only specific martial races in the country. More of his reforming ideas will be dealt with later. He is a large figure in this work both for his ability and desire to reform the army and for his position as the commander-in-chief, India, from mid 1943 until the end of the Raj in August 1947.

[183] Known as the Modernisation Committee.

invasion. The General Reserve was made up of units prepared to reinforce all of the categories listed above. The External Defence Troops, the last and smallest contingent, were to be a rapid reaction force to defend outposts vital to India's security (e.g. Aden). All of these recommendations were accepted by the commander-in-chief without any changes.[184]

The British government formed a committee to assess how to bring about the modernisation of the Indian armed forces, and to report on the overall expenditure that would be needed to achieve the necessary improvements.[185] This report was initiated after a similar committee had met to determine the modernisation of the British armed forces in the UK. The Indian committee was chaired by Admiral of the Fleet Lord Chatfield,[186] and included other senior officers of the services. Because Auchinleck had recently completed his own report, he was made a member of the committee,[187] which held seventy-eight meetings and consulted sixty-three witnesses. It convened in London in January 1939 to finalise the report, which reached almost the same conclusions as Auchinleck's earlier report. The frontier, IS, and coastal defence troops were retained as the top three priorities, but the external defence troops disappeared and were replaced with air defence troops to guard India against air attack. The General Reserve became the fifth role for the Indian Army and was designated to deal with any unforeseen emergency and to reinforce any of the troops listed above. In peace-time, the highest formation would be a brigade.[188]

While Auchinleck was a member of the Chatfield Committee, he did not fully agree with its final report. His two major criticisms concerned the proposals to disband units and to deploy troops in Western Command.[189] The Chatfield report proposed to disband two Indian cavalry

---

[184] Mason, *A Matter of Honour*, p. 467, and Connell, *Auchinleck*, pp. 68–9.

[185] The Expert Committee on the Defence of India, 1938–9.

[186] It was subsequently referred to as the Chatfield Committee, L/MIL/5/886, OIOC, BL.

[187] No. 2, 24 Oct. 1938, Letter from India Office, Whitehall to Auchinleck, in the Field Marshal Sir Claude Auchinleck Papers at the University of Manchester.

[188] Brigade HQ, three infantry battalions, and one cavalry regiment: L/MIL/17/5/1805, OIOC, BL.

[189] India had been divided into four commands since the reorganisations of 1895. The terms used were Southern, Central, Northern, and Eastern Commands. During the Second World War, the commands changed their names into 'armies' and the Northern and Western Commands were amalgamated into Northwestern. In 1945, the commands were reorganised and relisted as Northern, Eastern, Central and Southern Commands and then specific 'city' designations. Northern Command covered the Punjab to the NWFP. Eastern Command stretched from Delhi to the Burma frontier, including Calcutta and as far south as Central Command, constituting the vast central provinces. Southern Command covered all areas south of the Central Provinces, including Bombay and Madras.

regiments and fourteen infantry battalions, and to withdraw two British
cavalry regiments and six battalions of infantry. Auchinleck felt that this
would cause major disruption in India.[190] The report went further in
terms of IS: it called for a major reduction of both British and Indian
army forces to support the mission of IS.[191] Auchinleck believed that,
with growing tensions in Europe, there was likely to be a need for Indian
Army regiments and battalions – troops that needed to be able to contend with any modern European power, not just Pathan tribesmen.

Conclusion

The Indian Army of 1939 appeared prepared to carry out its chief
missions: duty on the North-West Frontier and IS. It was a professional
force that could cope with most of the pressures of the 1930s. Its soldiers,
NCOs, VCOs, and officers were loyal to their regiments. Due partly to its
restricted recruitment processes, it had been able to carry out its missions
with professionalism in a largely apolitical atmosphere. The political
upheaval of the 1920s and 1930s further insulated the army from the
rest of India's experience; this isolation provoked various Indian nationalist politicians, who came to consider the Indian Army a purely mercenary force – nothing more than the 'sword of the Raj'. This disconnect and
suspicion between the army and the future leaders of both India and
Pakistan were significant contributors to the problems that flared in the
post-Second World War period, and the resulting manipulations and
distrust that characterised relations among the various parties.

The questions of recruitment and the Indianisation process became
points of contention between the Indian nationalists and the British
authorities that would not be overcome until the advent of the Second
World War. The process of Indianisation, although slow and segregated,
proved to be useful as the starting point for the rapidly expanding Indian
Army during the first years of the Second World War. The Indianisation
process had support from the higher and lower echelons of the Indian
Army, and the Second World War was the excuse required to disband
the pre-war system and promote the need for Indian officers. War-time
requirements also provided the opportunity to open up the recruitment
process. This was an especially significant development because, unlike

---

[190] Because the Second World War broke out soon after the report was submitted, no units
were disbanded.
[191] British units were to be reduced from twenty-six to twenty-one and Indian Army units
were to be reduced from twenty to eleven. See Kudaisya, "'In Aid of Civil Power'",
p. 58, and L/MIL/5/886, OIOC, BL.

the First World War, many of the new classes recruited would have a role to play in the post-war army and thus in the future of independent India.

The Indian Army was on the verge of becoming fully modernised, but the advent of war in Europe and Asia constrained its ability to expand and deploy for war. The war years would be bumpy ones for the Indian Army, but it was already demonstrating the flexibility and innovative thinking that would make the crucial difference in the Second World War. While the Indian Army would expand beyond all expectations and include more Indians in both the ranks and the officer corps, its prospects were marred by a lack of strategic planning on the part of both Indian nationalists and British authorities as the war came to an end in 1945.

2 The performance of the Indian Army in the Second World War

> As the tanks burst away down the road to Rangoon ... [the Fourteenth Army] took possession of the empire we had built ... Twenty races, a dozen religions, a score of languages passed in those trucks and tanks. When my great-great-grandfather first went to India there had been as many nations; now there was one – India ... It was all summed up in the voice of an Indian colonel of artillery. Now the Indian, bending close to an English colonel over a map, straightened and said with a smile, 'OK, George. Thanks. I've got it. We'll take over all tasks at 1800. What about a beer?'[1]

It would be difficult to overstate how far-reaching and fundamental were the changes that the Indian Army went through in the Second World War. In 1945, it was a highly professional and modern force that included in its ranks representatives of ethnic groups that had traditionally been ignored as 'non-martial' as well as Indian commissioned officers (ICOs) in positions of command on the battlefield, and was bonded by a hard-won *esprit de corps*. It had played the leading role in the destruction of the Imperial Japanese Army in Burma, as well as significant supporting roles in the defeats of the Italian and German forces in North and East Africa and Italy. Throughout all of these engagements, the Indian Army also continued to maintain its traditional duties of frontier defence on the North-West Frontier and Aid to the Civil Power in India. In almost every way, the Indian Army of 1945 – battle-seasoned, imbued with regimental *esprit de corps*, and above all victorious – was a different force from the one that suffered crippling defeats in the difficult early days of the Second World War.

Through all the upheaval of the war years, the Indian Army's officers and men kept focused on the need to learn from the mistakes that were inevitable for any force finding itself in new situations and environments with inexperienced personnel. The army had a number of teething

---

[1] John Masters, *The Road Past Mandalay: A Personal Narrative* (London: Michael Joseph, 1961), pp. 312–13.

troubles as it grew in strength and experience, but it was always able to point with pride to its ability to learn from mistakes and adapt to conditions. The Indian Army of 1944–5 had answered the question Gen. Sir Phillip Chetwode posed, in 1934, at the Indian Army Staff College:

[A]m I altogether wrong in thinking that, to many Englishmen, to be independent in thought, to have imagination, to go outside the obvious, to be different to others, is to be almost un-English, or even that more frightful crime, 'not sound'?[2]

The Indian Army's formations, units, soldiers, NCOs, viceroy commissioned officers (VCOs), and officers, in the North African, East African, Italian, and Burma campaigns, could claim to be independent in thought, imaginative, willing to go outside the obvious, different – and very possibly un-English.[3]

By the beginning of 1944, the Indian Army had reached a level of performance characterised by consistent and reliable professionalism in an impressive variety of types and theatres of warfare.[4] This success, particularly in contrast to earlier defeats in Malaya and Burma, reinforced the army's perceptions of itself as a truly professional force, and bolstered *esprit de corps* throughout the war and into the post-war period, even in the face of impending national independence and change.[5]

The 'fusion' of battle in bonding combat veterans and veteran identity in general have not been well understood or considered by historians in the post-war period. Gen. Archibald Wavell, speaking as viceroy in 1945, stated that 'the Indian Army had done splendidly during the war and had enhanced its own and India's reputation'.[6] The emotional bonds and sense of pride forged in combat were to be important factors in India's move towards independence and the army's role in that transition, particularly in relation to how Indian politicians perceived their involvement in the political process.[7]

---

[2] Raymond Callahan, *Churchill's Generals* (Lawrence: University of Kansas Press, 2007), p. 19.

[3] See Timothy Harrison Place, *Military Training in the British Army, 1940–1944* (London: Frank Cass, 2000), David French, *Raising Churchill's Army* (Oxford University Press, 2000), and Stephen Hart, *Montgomery and the 'Colossal Cracks': The 21st Army Group in Northwest Europe, 1944–1945* (Westport, CT: Praeger, 2000), for a wider discussion of the issues that plagued the British Army during the same time period and that may provide a useful comparison with the Indian Army's performance and issues of reform.

[4] The performance of the Indian divisions in the North African campaign remains largely unexamined. A comparative analysis with other Commonwealth forces is needed.

[5] This image of the Indian Army in Indian society had significant political weight, as even members of the Indian National Congress came to recognise.

[6] Cabinet Paper, 18 Jul. 1945, *TOP*, V, 624, p. 1272.

[7] Author's interviews with close to 200 retired Indian Army officers in the UK, Pakistan, and India, 1999–2009.

Many of the themes that emerged in Chapter 1 remained relevant during the war and carried on into the post-war period and the transition to independence. These include: professional status and perceptions thereof; Indianisation; recruitment; Aid to the Civil Power; and issues of loyalty.

Opening phase

The inception of international hostilities in 1939 sparked a major political problem for India. In 1935, the Government of India Act had secured more domestic autonomy for India, the first steps on the road to independence. New Delhi had given more power to the provincial governments, but the country had yet to achieve even Dominion status. This meant that when the United Kingdom declared war on Germany, India was at war as well. The viceroy[8] proclaimed a state of war without consulting either the Indian National Congress Party, which controlled eight provincial governments, or the Muslim League. While constitutionally he was not required to do so, many observers felt that it would have been politic for him to have undertaken some sort of consultation with the provincial governments before making the proclamation. His decision underscored that India was still – increasingly unwillingly – a UK dependency, especially since it was motivated by the possibility that Congress could choose to embarrass the Government of India by deciding not to support the war.

Following the proclamation, the eight Congress-led provincial governments of India resigned.[9] This was part of a continuing trend of deteriorating relations between the Government of India and the Indian Congress Party, which was eventually to culminate in the Quit India movement of August 1942.[10] By contrast, the two Muslim League-controlled provinces, Bengal and Sind, offered their support for the war effort. The Punjab, traditionally strongly connected to the army, was controlled by the Punjab Unionist Party[11] and also offered its support.

In the first months of the war, the British government in London did not expect to need to use the Indian Army. Offers of troops were

---

[8] Lord Linlithgow, Viceroy of India, 1936–43.

[9] Not all Congress party members supported their party in this issue; an official mentioned in a letter to the viceroy that Thakor Todar Singh, a Congressman, was offering his services and his ability to recruit members for the army: L/WS/1/136, OIOC, BL.

[10] The Quit India movement had a bearing on the army as troops were called out in Aid to the Civil Power.

[11] See Talbot, *Khizr Tiwana*, for more detail.

declined by Neville Chamberlain and his government,[12] who considered Indian troops in a European war unnecessary (apparently forgetting the Indian troops who had served with the British Army in the First World War;[13] see Chapter 1 for more detail). Initially, the Indian Army's focus was expected to be contending with any potential threat to the North-West Frontier Province (NWFP), as well as to deal with any specific Aid to the Civil Power duties that might arise.[14] This assumption on the part of the British government would prove to be a serious error.

The British government's initial refusal of troops meant there was no major expansion of the army from September 1939 to May 1940,[15] despite calls throughout India to start recruitment drives for the army. The call was loudest in the Punjab, which was not surprising because of the recruitment practices of the previous hundred years and the links with the Unionist Party.[16] As stated in a memo to the viceroy, 'Everybody is keenly interested in the possibility of recruitment and there seems little doubt that if it becomes necessary, we should be able to obtain large numbers of recruits in this district.'[17] Lord Linlithgow, however, believed that men from more than just the Punjab should be brought in, possibly recognising that a broader recruitment drive could offset political pressure from the Congress Party's anti-war stance.[18] He also recognised that recruitment had come from a variety of provinces and classes in the First World War, and that those recruits had proved their worth. Regardless, an official report stated that by 30 June 1940 only

[12] Lord Linlithgow to H. G. Haig, Governor of the Punjab, L/WS/1/136, OIOC, BL.

[13] Two Indian divisions, Lahore and Meerut, arrived in France in October 1914, and other formations were raised and fought in Mesopotamia and the Middle East. As stated earlier, the Indian Army played a major role in specific campaigns in the First World War. More than 1.5 million Indians served and some 50,000 died.

[14] Two major formations, the 5th and 11th Brigade Groups (which formed the basis of the 4th Indian Division), which had enough modern equipment and weapons, had been shipped to Egypt in August–September 1939 as a strategic Imperial Reserve to the area. See Trench, *The Indian Army and the King's Enemies*, p. 138.

[15] The regular units of the army were organised into formal division structures. See Bisheshwar Prasad, *Official History of the Indian Armed Forces in the Second World War: Expansion of the Armed Forces and Defence Organisation* (New Delhi: Orient Longmans, 1956), for more details.

[16] The governor of the Punjab, H. G. Haig, made the contention that the best soldiers could be found only in the Punjab, and that it was unnecessary to go anywhere else. He said that the villages were calling up young men and offering their services for the war: Haig to Lord Linlithgow, 17 Sep. 1939, and Marsden to Haig, 29 Sep. 1939, L/WS/1/136, OIOC, BL.

[17] Sir Henry Craik to Linlithgow, 16 Sep. 1939, L/WS/1/136, OIOC, BL.

[18] He specifically said to the commander-in-chief, Gen. Cassels, that recruitment must encompass other provinces as well. He did not mention non-martial areas but he did not speak against them either: Linlithgow to Commander-in-Chief Cassels, 24 Sep. 1939, L/WS/1/136, OIOC, BL.

20,029 men had been recruited, mostly from the martial races, although Madrassis and Ahirs[19] were also represented.[20]

The 'phoney war' period (September 1939–April 1940) marked a series of equipment and organisational changes in Indian Army units, which were limited in their ability to re-equip with modern weapons. The British Army units in Europe were also having problems preparing for war, as re-armament programmes had begun only a few years earlier.[21] As a result, only a few Indian formations were equipped to deal with mechanised warfare as they prepared to move to North Africa. These units were organised into the 5th and 11th Indian Infantry Brigade groups, and deployed in August and September 1939 to safeguard the defence of Egypt. The 7th Indian Infantry Brigade group followed in 1940, and the three brigades formed the nucleus of the 4th Indian Division, which was the first Indian Army unit to see active service in the Second World War.[22]

North/East Africa and the Middle East

General Headquarters (GHQ) India envisioned only the possibility of deployment in a Middle East war. In the event, both the 4th and 5th Divisions fought in Eritrea (Italian East African region) against the Italians in very difficult mountainous terrain, where many of the lessons of fighting on the North-West Frontier came to the fore.[23] Both units performed well against the Italians, earning a good reputation. Both

---

[19] A northern Indian Hindu caste.

[20] The official list is as follows: 1,259 Pathans; 5,961 PMS; 3,002 Sikhs; 1,726 Dogras; 18 Gurkhas, 949 Garhwalis; 718 Kumaonis; 1060 Rajputs; 1,469 Jats; 425 Ahirs; 1,278 Mahrattas; 2,164 Madrassis (WS 1680, L/WS/1/136, OIOC, BL).

[21] As a result, India and Burma had to be given low priority for new weapons and equipment, a policy that all in India agreed with, understanding that the British Army in Europe should receive precedence, given the greater threat.

[22] See Gen. Sir Francis Tuker Papers in the Imperial War Museum, London (henceforth Tuker Papers, IWM), for a very detailed picture of this division. See also G. R. Stevens, *Red Eagle: The Fourth Indian Division* (London: McLaren & Sons, 1948).

[23] The first phase of the battle for Keren was an attempt to dislodge the Italians from the west; the focus then switched to the east, and then back to the west side of the gorge. Most of the fighting centred on the western side, along what became known as Cameron Ridge. After the first attacks of 4–12 February, the 5th Indian Division withdrew to the rear to resupply and undertake further training in mountain warfare. The second attack, on 15 March, involved both divisions in attacks along the ridges, trying to find a breakthrough. Bitter fighting ensued; the Indian divisions seized the vital ridges and held on against an Italian counter-attack. By 27 March, the Italians were withdrawing from their defences, and Keren fell without a fight. The two Indian divisions followed up the Italian withdrawal and captured the vital port of Massawa on 8 April. See Gen. Sir Geoffrey Evans, *The Desert and the Jungle* (London: Kimber, 1959), as well as Evans, *Tiger Kills* (London: HMSO, 1944), for more details on the fighting in Eritrea.

Figure 2.1 Victorious soldiers in the North African campaign
© Imperial War Museums (Image No. E 6940)

formations returned to North Africa. Maj. (later Gen. Sir) Geoffrey
Evans, then brigade major in the 11th Indian Infantry Brigade, recalled:
'we were sent out into the desert ... and since our training for desert
warfare had been hard and continuous, we were fit, we were tough and
we were ready for battle'.[24]

The defeat of France in 1940, along with Italy's entry into the war,
changed the strategic map, and the British government reversed its
decision and called for the Indian Army's expansion. Six new units were
raised from summer 1940 to summer 1941: the 6th, 7th, 8th, 9th, 10th,

---

[24] Evans, *Desert and Jungle*, p. 17.

and 11th Indian divisions.[25] By the end of 1941, the 14th, 17th, 19th, 20th, and 34th Indian Infantry and 32nd Armoured Divisions were also forming.[26] The Indian Army expanded from about 200,000 men and officers to more than 1 million between 1939 and 1941. As a result of this rapid growth, many units lacked properly trained officers[27] and men, which was to play a major impact on the formations and units that deployed to the Far East – chiefly, Malaya and Burma.[28]

The rapid expansion of the Indian Army was driven by the need to have an Imperial Reserve, and the deployments of 1941 truly highlighted this demand on the Indian Army. The various deployments are not examined here in depth, but an overview demonstrates that the Indian Army was being overstretched as a result of the expansion policy. The expansion also had a negative impact on training officers, with minimal training and experience, to effectively command in the field. This led to small mutinies and command-and-control issues in the early campaigns.[29]

The fear of a Russian attack in the NWFP kept large numbers of troops stationed in the area, while German meddling in the internal affairs of Iraq prompted the mobilisation of the 8th Indian Division.[30] The 8th

---

[25] The divisional structure was to follow the British system: three brigades, with three battalions of infantry. However, over the course of the next two years, each brigade was restructured to have two Indian battalions and one British battalion. The British battalion was there as the 'backbone' for the brigade. As will be demonstrated by subsequent events, the perceived need for a British backbone was outdated and unnecessary.

[26] Prasad, *Official History: Expansion*, pp. 212–30.

[27] See pp. 22–5 for a discussion of the ending of the pre-war Indianisation process.

[28] Author's interview with Brig. J. Randle, 10 Apr. 2000; Lt C. R. L. Coubrough, 27 Mar. 2000, 7/10th Baluch; and Maj. T. Kirkwood, 15 Mar. 2000, 1/11th Sikh.

[29] This was highlighted by many officers I interviewed both for this book and for *Phoenix from the Ashes: The Indian Army in the Burma Campaign* (Westport, CT: Praeger, 2003). See also Bristow, *Memories*, p. 117. He emphasises the lack of language ability of many new officers who joined his battalion.

[30] Iraq, which had become an independent state in 1930, suffered a military *coup d'état* in March 1941. The British government considered the Iraqi Army pro-German, and this situation, combined with threats in North Africa and the Balkans, motivated London and GHQ India to act. The 20th Indian Brigade, 10th Indian Division, was earmarked to land at Basra in April. One junior officer described the advance into Basra: 'in the event there was no opposition. As we approached Basra I remember clearly passing an Iraqi Army barracks with a parade ground. A medium machine gun unit with its British-made Vickers was on parade. The guns were lined up with their locks open, as if to show there was not hostile intent.' This was important, as he noted that 'fortunately we were not called up to defend the place [the RAF base at Shaiba] because the battalion were woefully inexperienced' (Ken Ross, 'With the 2/8th Gurkhas in Iraq 1941–1942', *Red Flash*, no. 22, p. 55). The 21st and 25th Brigades arrived in Basra shortly thereafter, and the 10th Division, once completed, moved towards Baghdad. They struck north, seizing the valuable oilfields in and around Mosul. The 21st Indian Brigade then moved into

division landed in Kuwait and pushed north, through Basra and then on to the capital, Baghdad. It seized Baghdad and was followed by the 10th Indian Division,[31] sent to the region to protect British interests in the area from any internal rebellion. Later, in mid 1942, Iran was invaded by both divisions, under the pretext that the Persian government could not protect itself from a possible German attack. This operation required the creation of Persia and Iraq Force (PAIFORCE).[32]

In retrospect, the period from 1941 to 1943 was one of the most difficult in the history of the Indian Army. While lack of equipment was generally considered its greatest weakness, the over-expansion of officer and other ranks played a major role in the army's poor perform-ance early in the war. Existing regular units were 'milked'[33] of cadres of men and officers to bolster newly established units,[34] providing a core of experience for the new unit but also weakening the older one.[35] A slow

western Syria to support British efforts there. At the same time the campaign in Iraq was getting under way, the 5th Indian Brigade, 4th Indian Division, had been sent to Palestine to aid in the capture of Vichy Syria. The attack into Syria began in May, and ended within three weeks with the capture of Damascus. Still one of the best sources for the reasons and the operations in both Iraq and Persia (Iran) was written in 1948. See *Paiforce: The Official Story of the Persia and Iraq Command, 1941–1946* (London: HMSO, 1948), as well as John Connell, *Auchinleck: A Critical Biography* (London: Cassell, 1959), pp. 180–233, and the Auchinleck Papers, University of Manchester, for more details, including specific correspondence between Gen. Auchinleck and senior command in London.

[31] This division was commanded by Maj. Gen. William Slim, who played a large role during the war. He is widely considered to be the best British general since the Duke of Wellington, even though he was in the Indian Army. See Callahan, *Churchill's Generals*, as well as Slim's own memoir, *Defeat into Victory* (London: Cassell, 1956), for more detail. *Defeat into Victory* is one of the best memoirs written by a senior officer, due to its self-criticism and honesty; not many generals admit making mistakes in battle.

[32] The oilfields of Persia (Iran) also became a strategic consideration during the summer of 1941. The Germans had placed agents in Tehran, as they had done in Iraq the previous spring. The British and the Soviets decided to mount a joint invasion of Persia, to begin on 25 August 1941, in the hope of safeguarding the oilfields and potentially establishing supply routes through Persia. The Soviets planned to invade the northern regions, along with the 8th and 10th Indian Divisions from Iraq. The British, meanwhile, seized Tehran, effectively completing the invasion. One veteran described the reasons for the invasion as 'justifiable only on the grounds of war-necessity'. See Trench, *The Indian Army and the King's Enemies*, p. 159. To safeguard the conquests of Persia, men equivalent to nearly two and a half Indian divisions performed internal security duties in the occupied territories over the remainder of the war. Both the 8th and 10th Indian Divisions would eventually be shifted to the Middle East fighting.

[33] The process of 'milking' was detrimental to many units due to lack of cohesion that ensued. However, with the impetus to expand quickly, there was no obvious alternative.

[34] By the end of the war, some regiments would have close to twenty numbered battalions in their organisation. See Gaylor, *Sons of John Company*, and Prasad, *Official History: Expansion*, for more detailed descriptions.

[35] An example is of an order dated 29 November 1940 that states that it was necessary to raise sixty-three battalions. However, only 30 per cent of units still stationed in

expansion could allow for the regular unit to absorb new emergency commissioned officers (ECOs) and new enlisted men to replace those sent off to new units, but the pace of expansion meant that regular units were being drawn on more than once to fill the new units, and the reserves of the small professional force dried up rapidly.[36] Newly raised units themselves were even 'milked' for the higher-numbered battalions within a given regiment, which caused problems when units were posted with minimal training.[37] While the 4th and 5th Indian Divisions performed well in the North African campaign,[38] the issues caused by too-rapid expansion affected the Malaya and Burma campaigns more noticeably.[39]

The early successes of late 1940 and early 1941 in East and North Africa were short-lived for British and Commonwealth forces. The Italians reinforced their Libyan army, and the Germans intervened when Gen. Erwin Rommel arrived with the Afrikakorps in February 1941. Rommel launched a major counteroffensive on 24 March, not long after the 3rd Indian Motor Brigade arrived in North Africa.[40] Some of the best troops of the British forces had been redeployed elsewhere, principally Greece and East Africa. The Germans and the Italians smashed into the British forces left in the region and pushed them back across Libya.[41] Gen. Sir Archibald Wavell,[42] commander-in-chief, North Africa, waited

India were regular units. The rest had been sent overseas as part of the 4th and 5th Indian Divisions. See Adj. Generals Branch: Indian Infantry Expansion, L/WS/1/394, OIOC, BL.

[36] In 1939, the Army in India (British and Indian units) numbered around 200,000 men.

[37] It was specifically stated that raw recruits should not be sent overseas. However, as demands on the army increased over the next year, this order could not always be followed: L/WS/1/394, OIOC, BL.

[38] They comprised regular formations and units and were not 'milked' as heavily as the army expanded.

[39] See pp. 64–76 for more discussion.

[40] The experience of this brigade highlights the heavy fighting in North Africa, as it was over-run and re-formed on two occasions. In the end, it was withdrawn in late 1942 to Iraq where it was once again re-formed and renumbered as the 43rd Indian Infantry Brigade (Lorried). All the cavalry regiments were replaced with Gurkha battalions. The brigade went on to serve with distinction in the Italian campaign.

[41] The performance of the Indian divisions in the North African campaign remains largely unexamined. Alan Jeffries is writing a major work that will add needed depth of knowledge. A comparative analysis with other Commonwealth forces is required as well, although Callahan's *Churchill's Generals* covers some of the important debates. There are many reasons for British tactical and operational shortcomings in the North African campaign. Two very good books that focus on these issues are French, *Raising Churchill's Army*, and Niall Barr, *Pendulum of War: The Three Battles of El Alamein* (London: Jonathan Cape, 2004).

[42] Gen. Wavell later played a large role in the Indian Army during the late war and the post-war periods, in his capacities of commander-in-chief, India, and viceroy of India.

for the remainder of the 4th Indian Division to arrive, as well as replacement tanks for the 7th Armoured Division, before launching the British counter-attack, Operation Battleaxe, on 15 June. The offensive failed, and units of the 4th Indian and supporting tanks from the 7th Armoured Division were forced back to their original positions. In July 1941, Wavell was replaced as commander-in-chief for the Middle East by Gen. Sir Claude Auchinleck.[43] Meanwhile, the Afrikakorps and British and Commonwealth forces licked their wounds and prepared for the autumn offensives. The British Western Desert Force was renamed the Eighth Army as planning for the campaign got under way.

Gen. Auchinleck waited for reinforcements to arrive before he ordered another offensive in North Africa. Operation Crusader was scheduled to begin in November. The 4th Indian Division, commanded by Maj. Gen. Frank Messervy,[44] was part of XIII Corps, who were ordered to attack the major enemy defensive positions (known as the 'Omars') to support the main drive of XXX Corps.

Units of the 4th Indian Division had been reconnoitring the area since September.[45] Lessons from earlier campaigns had been compiled and disseminated via the Army in India Training Memoranda (AITM). Reports from the 4th and, later, the 5th Indian Divisions were regularly disseminated throughout the army for training purposes.[46]

The general offensive began on the night of 18/19 November. XXX Corps crossed the frontier and headed north-west, hoping to destroy Axis forces between Tobruk and the frontier. By 22 November, XXX Corps and the rest of XIII Corps were pushing hard to reach their objectives. The attack by XXX Corps was being heavily engaged by the Germans and Italians. A large gap had opened between XXX and XIII corps, which Gen. Rommel made haste to exploit. Auchinleck sacked the Eighth Army commander, Gen. Sir Alan Cunningham, and replaced him with Gen. Neil Ritchie. Confusion reigned within the British and

---

[43] See Connell, *Auchinleck*, pp. 237–653 (Book III), for a more detailed discussion of Auchinleck's tenure as CinC Middle East. Book III has much personal correspondence between Auchinleck and other members of senior command in both India and London. See also Auchinleck Papers, University of Manchester, for more details.

[44] He would go on to command the 7th Indian Division in the second Arakan campaign of 1944 and a corps in Burma. In the post-war period, he would command Northern Command and, upon India's independence, he became chief of staff in the Pakistan Army.

[45] The professionalism of the two formations was noted.

[46] See War Diary entries, 'Defence Notes', WO 169/3289, National Archives (NA) as well as AITM, nos. 2–9. The future commander of 4th Indian, Maj. Gen. Tuker, created more than forty 'training instructions' for his units during his two years as commander. See 71/12/2, Tuker Papers, IWM.

Commonwealth forces as reports circulated about German movements along the front. The 4th Indian Division, supported by both the 5th and 11th Brigades, decided to hold their lines and build up their defensive positions in the Omars. The field artillery of the 4th Indian, with supporting infantry, held their lines and thwarted various German attacks for more than two days. The German attack to link up with the Omar positions and force the British back from Tobruk failed.[47]

On 25 November, the Allies counter-attacked. The 2nd New Zealand Division moved towards Tobruk, while the 4th Indian continued the attacks against the last remnants of the German and Italian defenders in the Omars. By 30 November, the Omars had been cleared, and the Axis forces began to retreat on all fronts. The Germans and Italians withdrew across Cyrenaica once again. This time the retreat was orderly, allowing them to inflict substantial damage upon the British forces on their heels. The Central India Horse seized Benghazi before Christmas, followed closely by the rest of the 4th Indian Division.[48]

While units of the 4th Indian Division, under the command of Maj. Gen. F. I. S. Tuker,[49] were stationed in western Cyrenaica in late 1941, Rommel struck.[50] With Rommel moving towards Benghazi, confusion reigned. Reports indicated German tanks to the north and east of Benghazi; it became apparent that the Germans had created a large gap between the 1st Armoured and the 4th Indian in Benghazi. On 27 January, Tuker and his command staff left Benghazi, and the 7th Brigade was ordered to hold on in the town. The 5th Brigade was ordered to withdraw further to the east to avoid the German advance. The 7th was encircled and cut off from the roads to the north. Brig. Harold Briggs,[51]

---

[47] Refer to *Tiger Strikes* (HMSO, 1942), pp. 27–46; and 4th Indian Division, Dec. 1941, WO 169/3289, NA.

[48] *Tiger Strikes*, pp. 46–7; and Dec. 1941, WO 169/3289, NA.

[49] Tuker led the 4th Indian for the next two years and instituted a process of 'lessons learned' and training directives: 71/12/2, Tuker Papers, IWM. He also played a large role in the post-war period, as he commanded Eastern Command in 1946–7 and debated with Auchinleck on key issues dealing with the post-war period. See Chapters 6 and 7 for more details. See Tuker Papers, IWM, and Tuker, *While Memory Serves* (London: Cassell, 1950), for more details. Tuker wrote his book immediately after the events of 1947. The book draws upon many letters from other officers, VCOs, and soldiers who served throughout India, as well as operational orders of the day.

[50] The professionalism of the 4th Indian Division continued under Tuker's leadership. He specifically stated that training must continue. See 14 Jan. 1942, Subject: Training: 'it is unfortunately true that the standard of individual training in the division has shown signs of deterioration and this must be put right' (71/12/2, Tuker MSS, IWM). The 4th Indian Division had been split up, 7th Brigade was in Benghazi, the 5th was in the rear in Barce, and the 11th was in Tobruk.

[51] Gen. Briggs went on to command the 5th Indian Division from May 1942. He led the division during the hectic fighting in North Africa and, later, the important fighting in

in a bold stroke, decided to break out. He divided his brigade into three groups, and they cut behind the Germans and Italians, before striking into the open desert and making their way to the British lines at El Mechili.[52] The rest of the 4th Indian Division had already met up with units of the 5th Indian Division[53] in Barce. Serious fighting ensued as the German and Italian forces came up against the British forces withdrawing towards Tobruk. They arrived at Acroma, south-west of Tobruk, on 4 February 1942, and began digging defences to hold the line.

March to May 1942 was a stalemate in North Africa. The 4th Indian Division was relieved,[54] and the three brigades were shipped to Cyprus, Palestine, and the Suez Canal Zone for rest. The 5th Indian Division, under the command of the recently promoted Maj. Gen. Briggs, took over their positions. The 10th Indian Division, under the command of Maj. Gen. T. W. (Pete) Rees,[55] was also sent to North Africa from PAIFORCE to support the British and Commonwealth defences.

On 27 May 1942, Rommel struck once again, hitting the British positions along the Gazala defence lines. On 20 June 1942, Tobruk[56] fell to the Germans, and the British began to retreat back into Egypt. Elements of the 10th Indian Division put up a stalwart defence at Mersa Matruh, only to have their flanks exposed and then receive orders on 28 June to break out to the east. By the end of June, the British had withdrawn to the final defence lines west of El Alamein. The 18th Indian Brigade put up a valiant defence against Rommel's advance at the foot of the strategically important Ruweisat Ridge, stopping the advance in early July.

On 14 July, the 5th Indian Brigade, 5th Indian Division, successfully attacked in and around the Ruweisat Ridge, which formed a centrepiece to the defensive lines at El Alamein. Rommel counter-attacked almost

---

the Arakan and Imphal regions in Assam in 1944. He also became director of operations in 1950 during the Malayan Emergency, where he created the 'Briggs Plan' for which he remains famous.

[52] 4th Indian Division, Jan. and Feb. 1942, WO 169/7529, NA; and *Tiger Strikes*.

[53] After Eritrea, it had gone to Iraq and Cyprus.

[54] Even while the division was being split up, Tuker carried out lesson discussions with his officers and created training instructions. As he stated on 13 March, 'as future moves of this division have not been settled, division command has decided that individual training will begin'. Later, in April, he wrote: 'battle group training will be continued and two months of training will begin' (71/12/2, Tuker MSS, IWM).

[55] Slim had relinquished command to go to Burma and head up Burma Corps (Burcorps). The division was taken over by Maj. Gen. Rees, who would later command the 19th Indian Division in Burma and, more pertinently, the 4th Indian Division and the Punjab Boundary Force in 1947.

[56] The 11th Indian Brigade, 4th Indian Division, was part of the garrison. Some units continued to fight for 36 hours after the capitulation.

immediately, but failed to gain any ground. Over the course of the month, the rest of the 5th Indian Division reinforced the area. Rommel attempted another attack on 30 August, but called it off after two days. The front had been stabilised, and more troops, along with new tanks, artillery, and supplies, began to arrive in Egypt.[57]

On 13 August 1942, Gen. Harold Alexander replaced Auchinleck as commander-in-chief, Middle East,[58] and Gen. Bernard Montgomery became Eighth Army commander. The 4th Indian Division relieved the 5th Indian Division on the ridge; the 5th left North Africa for Iraq and was later ordered to India to undergo jungle warfare training for deployment to Burma in 1943.[59] The 10th Indian Division was withdrawn for garrison duty in Cyprus for close to two years. The 4th Indian was the sole Indian formation present for the Allied victory in North Africa. Gen. Tuker carried on with compiling lessons learned in battle and training instructions for his division throughout.[60]

Following the heavy fighting of the spring and summer of 1942, the 4th Indian Division and other formations in the Eighth Army were resupplied and rested for an offensive planned for October. The 4th Indian Division carried out lesson discussions and training.[61] The role of the 4th Indian Division was to provide support to the main effort; they were stationed in the southern area of the defensive line and ordered to carry out raids and tie down the Axis forces in the area. As Gen. Tuker noted to his officers and men on the first day of the battle (23 October), 'this is to be a hard fight and prolonged battle. None of us thinks it will be otherwise ... [N]o position will be given up. Surrender is shameful.'[62]

For ten days, as battle ebbed and flowed to the north, the 4th Indian Division applied pressure along their defensive lines. With Rommel's

---

[57] See Callahan, *Churchill's Generals*, and Barr, *Pendulum of War*, for more detail.

[58] Auchinleck would return to India without portfolio, until the summer of 1943, when he took up his final and most important post, commander-in-chief, India, where he remained until independence in 1947. See letter from Amery to Linlithgow, 4 Dec. 1942, *TOP*, III, 251, p. 340, for a detailed discussion of the need for Auchinleck to be made CinC once again; as Amery stated: 'Like myself, he [CIGS, Alanbrooke] feels that it is really very hard that Auchinleck, who was ideal as CinC and had every expectation of a full term of office, should now be stranded.'

[59] See pp. 71–6 for more discussion of the Burma campaign and the role of the 5th Indian Division.

[60] See 71/12/2, Tuker MSS, IWM.

[61] The 7th Indian Brigade was not optimistic: 'D-Day – what is to be the outcome? I do not expect too much but keep this to myself' (Personal Diary, 23 Oct. 1942, 91/40/2, Maj. Gen. A. W. Holworthy MSS, Imperial War Museum (henceforth Holworthy MSS, IWM)).

[62] Personal Diary, 23 Oct. 1942, Tuker Papers, IWM.

tanks cornered towards the coast, orders came on 1 November for Operation Supercharge. The 5th Indian Brigade was ordered to cut a line in the Axis defences, to allow the 7th Armoured and 2nd New Zealand Divisions to strike out. The brigade achieved its goal, and the Allied divisions thrust forward to destroy the Afrikakorps. The 4th Indian Division began to round up Axis soldiers in and around the defensive positions, but pursuit of the Afrikakorps was carried out by other troops. Gen. Tuker was outraged at plans to use the 4th Indian Division as a mop-up force, and sent his objections to XXX Corps. Lt Gen. Brian Horrocks agreed and passed along his thoughts to Gen. Montgomery, emphasising that 'There is no doubt that this [4th Indian] is an experienced division, more experienced probably than any other division in the Middle East.'[63] This availed nothing.[64]

The Afrikakorps withdrew towards Tunisia, pursued by the Eighth Army. The terrain in Tunisia was dramatically different from the open desert, and specialist skills were required to overcome the Axis defensive line positions at the Mareth Line.[65] The 4th Indian Division was moved forward in March 1943, and its units conducted raids and reconnaissance patrols assessing the German and Italian defences. Following a series of unsuccessful attacks by the 50th Division, a revised battle plan was called for. By the end of March, with valuable support from the 4th Indian, the 2nd New Zealand Division had enveloped the Mareth Line from the west, forcing the Axis to withdraw to a series of hills to the north.

In April, the 4th Indian was assigned a diversionary role in the clearance of the Wadi Akarit positions. The attack involved two brigades, and the fighting was bitter.[66] Eventually the British succeeded in turning the Axis forces from their defences,[67] and the Germans and Italians withdrew again as Allied forces (First Army) entered the battle from the west. On 11 May 1943, the German commander of the Afrikakorps and Italian

---

[63] See *Tiger Kills*, pp. 150–60; Trench, *The Indian Army and the King's Enemies*, p. 223; and Tuker MSS, IWM. Tuker created a system of 'Patrol Master', which continued in the division for the remainder of the war.

[64] Tuker referred to Montgomery as 'self-confident, conceited, very persistent and tenacious, unimaginative'. See Callahan, *Churchill's Generals*, p. 145.

[65] Tuker recognised this fact and had ordered a training directive to deal with mountains as the division moved across Libya. See Box 71/21/2/7, Tuker MSS, IWM.

[66] Denis Blomfield-Smith, ed., *Fourth Indian Reflections* (privately published, 1987), p. 38.

[67] An officer from the 4/16th Punjabis described the scene: 'After a while I saw the platoon advancing across the valley, turn west across a road, then in open formation, return to attack another strongly held feature. I could not stop them … [A]ll we could do was provide supporting fire. What a sight! Twenty-five men attacking a high hill, studded with enemy trenches … [The enemy] threw down their arms and surrendered – 300 or more of them' (*ibid.*, p. 39).

troops surrendered to Lt Col L. C. J. Showers of the 1/2nd Gurkhas, ending the war in North Africa. Montgomery's comment on the Indian Army's performance in North Africa was succinct. 'I sent the First Army my best', he said, '7th Armoured and 4th Indian.'[68]

The Italian campaign

Some senior officers and politicians expected that a campaign in Italy would be easy, referring to it as 'the soft under-belly of the Axis'. In July 1943, the Allies landed on Sicily, with the Indian Army providing a few battalions as 'beachhead' units.[69] The campaign ended quickly; in early September the Allies crossed to mainland Italy, and the Italians surrendered shortly thereafter. The Germans and a hard-core group of fascist Italian forces decided to defend the peninsula themselves. Italy's mountainous terrain, numerous rivers, and fortified villages were perfect for defence, and the Germans knew that they could tie down many Allied forces with relatively few troops. The Italian topography, combined with the skill of the German defenders, made the conquest of Italy a long and bloody campaign that ended only with the surrender of the German forces in other regions.

The 8th Indian Division landed at Taranto in September 1943. The Eighth Army, meanwhile, was moving north along the Adriatic coast. The Germans began to fall back towards their first major defensive position, the Gustav Line, north of Naples. In early November, the 8th Indian Division began its first major action, crossing the Trigno River. It took three days of fighting to clear the Germans from their positions, after which the division moved forward to confront the Sangro River defences. The division crossed the Sangro on 25 November and began to fight its way through a series of fortified villages en route to join up with other divisions and cross the next river, the Moro. The crossing was successful, and on the other side the units were involved in more heavy fighting in the villages. By the time the Allies had cleared the area, winter had set in, slowing the campaign to a series of raids on both sides of the front. The 8th Indian Division spent the winter months snowbound.[70]

---

[68] Trench, *The Indian Army and the King's Enemies*, p. 229.

[69] No major comparative analysis has been done regarding the performance of Indian Army formations in the Italian campaign. Alan Jeffreys is intending to write about this significant gap in our understanding in his upcoming monograph.

[70] See *Tiger Triumphs* (London: HMSO, 1946), as well as 8th Indian Division GS, Mar.– Dec. 1943, WO 169/14766, NA.

Figure 2.2 Indian troops on the move in Italy © Imperial War
Museums (Image No. NA 9807)

The 4th Indian Division had left North Africa for Palestine in the
summer of 1943 for rest and training.[71] In early December, the division
was ordered to Italy also. Arriving in the Adriatic sector of the front, they
immediately set out to learn from the formations around them. Tuker
called for a series of lectures and training packages focusing on better
armoured co-operation and the important 'Town and Village
Fighting'.[72]

Early in February 1944, the division was sent, with the 2nd New
Zealand Division, to serve under the command of the US Fifth Army

---

[71] During this six-month period, Tuker and his commanders set out to create training
exercises emphasising the lessons learned from the recent North Africa campaigns:
Jun.–Dec. 1943, WO 169/14735, NA.
[72] See Tuker MSS, IWM, and Jun.–Dec. 1943, WO 169/14735, NA.

and to seize the town of Cassino and the surrounding hills. This action would involve the two divisions in a prolonged, bloody, and attritional battle for just one section of the Gustav Line. The fight for Cassino encompassed four major battles.[73] The US troops had failed in the first attack in January. The Indians and New Zealanders took part in the defeats of the second and third battles. The German troops in and around Cassino were some of the best troops in the German order of battle and had the advantage of excellent defensive arrangements, centred around Cassino itself, the mountains, and the monastery over-looking the town.[74] Tuker was replaced, due to illness, just before the division went into battle. The 4th Indian Division took over positions from the US troops in the area. The first battles for the 4th centred around the fighting en route to the monastery. As with Keren in East Africa, only a brigade could be maintained in the area, due to the mountainous terrain. Two battalions were thrown at the ridge over the course of four days. All the attacks failed; no ground was taken. The New Zealanders, in the town, fared no better.[75]

The third offensive was called for 15 March. The 4th Indian attempted to seize the monastery and the northern part of town from a different direction. The fighting centred around Castle Hill, which the 4th Indian had taken over from the 2nd New Zealand Division, and the heroic efforts of the 1/9th Gurkhas, who succeeded in reaching Hangman's Hill, just below the monastery. Realising the danger they were in, the Germans attacked the Gurkha positions, and heavy fighting ensued. By 23 March, a stalemate had developed once again. The two major battles had cost the division more than 4,000 dead and wounded.[76]

The fourth and final battle for Cassino involved the 8th Indian Division, along with other formations from the Eighth Army that took part in two major flank attacks. The 4th Indian Division had returned to the Adriatic sector, and the 8th Indian and 4th British Divisions were to breach the German defences along the Gari River to the south of Cassino. The attack began on the evening of 11/12 May, as Allied

---

[73] There are many books on the battles in and around Cassino. Three of the best are John Ellis, *Cassino: The Hollow Victory* (London: Andre Deutsch, 1994); E. D. Smith, *Battles for Cassino* (London: Scribner, 1975); and Fred Majdalany, *Cassino: Portrait of a Battle*, 3rd edn (London: Orion, 1999).

[74] The formations included the veteran 1st Fallschirmjäger (Parachute) Division.

[75] See *Tiger Triumphs* as well as 'Attack on Cassino: NZ Corps and 4th Indian Operation Instructions', WO 204/7275, and Mar.–Jun. 1944, WO 169/18776, NA.

[76] The General Staff Officer (Grade) 1 for the division, Col J. K. Shepheard, noted that 'morale is very low in many units' ('23 March Situation of the 4th Ind. Div.', 99/69/1, Maj. Gen. J. K. Shepheard MSS, IWM).

artillery pounded the German defences. The crossing was a bitter struggle, but by midday on 12 May various toeholds had been created. The Germans put up a stiff resistance in and around the town of St Angelo. After a few days of fierce fighting, it was finally cleared.[77]

The formations that crossed after a series of heavy fights were able to pierce the Gustav defences, opening the road to Rome. Allied troops successfully completed the link-up with the Anzio beachhead, and Rome fell on 4 June 1944. The 8th Indian Division continued to pursue the Germans towards Perugia; they had advanced more than 200 miles since crossing the Gari River.[78]

The 10th Indian Division arrived in the Adriatic sector of Italy in March 1944.[79] Maj. Gen. Denys Reid, commander of the 10th, was, like many of his counterparts in the Indian Army of 1944, convinced of the need for training directives based upon lessons learned in combat. When the division arrived in Italy, their sector was quiet, enabling units to undertake further training and patrolling activities, to learn different styles of fighting, and to hone their skills. In May, after the bloody battles of Cassino, the 4th Indian relieved the 10th Indian, allowing the 10th to carry out higher-level exercises in mountain warfare. This continued until the division was ordered to move on 10 June to relieve the 8th Indian Division outside Perugia.[80]

On 30 June the 10th Indian Division began to push towards Florence. The fighting in northern Italy was similar to earlier campaigns – countless river crossings; the taking of hills, mountains, and fortified villages; and ferocious fighting all the way. The Germans had been busy building a second major defensive line, called the Gothic Line, to the north of Florence. This line, like the Gustav Line, ran right across the Italian peninsula. By August, the 8th Indian Division had joined the 10th, and the two formations reached Florence in mid August. They pressed on to the Gothic Line positions in early September, when the 10th was moved

---

[77] See *Tiger Triumphs* and May–Jun. 1944, WO 169/18797, NA.

[78] See *Tiger Triumphs*.

[79] Before their deployment, the formation had been carrying out training, using lessons from the gruelling fighting in North Africa and Italy. The commander of the 25th Indian Brigade recalled that 'in Cyprus our training was chiefly on elementary and individual standard ... We ... returned to Lebanon to complete a mountain warfare course before going out to Italy' (97/7/1, Brig. E. A. Ardene MSS, IWM).

[80] See PP MCR 06 Reel 7, Maj. Gen. Denys Reid MSS, IWM. The general theme after each operation was a system of 'General Tactical Lessons', all listed after the narrative of an operation. See also 10th Indian Division, 1944, WO 169/18813, NA: 'Much information regarding combat experience has been gained in the Italian theatre of operations ... all commanders must apply the lessons to training.'

back to the Adriatic sector to support the 4th Indian against German defences in the Foglia valley.[81]

Overall, the Allied effort in Italy was suffering a manpower shortage in late 1944. Men equivalent to nearly seven divisions had already been withdrawn to fight in France,[82] and in late September the 4th Indian Division followed suit, redeployed to Greece to intervene in the civil war erupting there in the wake of the German withdrawal.[83]

The remaining Indian divisions continued the advance and constant attritional fighting of patrols and raids throughout the rest of 1944 and into 1945 in the Adriatic sector of the front. Allied commanders recognised the abilities of the Indian divisions; the 8th Indian Division served as a fire brigade, and at one point moved in to replace the US 92nd Division when it encountered problems holding the front. The secretary of state, India, Leopold Amery, visited the Indian divisions and formations in Italy in late summer 1944. He commented. 'I was immensely proud [of] their fine spirit, discipline, and all I heard of their good behaviour.'[84]

The final offensives in Italy began in April 1945. The 8th and 10th divisions were involved with the crossing of the Senio River. The attack began on 9 April, when the 8th crossed the river. As with all the previous river crossings, the fighting was bitter as the Germans made the Allies pay. When the Germans finally began to give ground, the 10th Indian Division and 43rd Gurkha Lorried Brigade took part in the pursuit. The 10th was ordered to storm the Idice River, the last river crossing before the Po. After yet more ferocious fighting, the Indian units managed to hold on to their small bridgeheads, while other formations stormed through. The Germans withdrew, the Po valley opened up, and the war in Italy came to an end.[85]

The Indian Army's increasing professionalism and successes in the North and East African as well as the Italian campaigns were duly noted

[81] The 8th Indian Division carried out lessons and training exercises during this respite. 'Record in convenient form knowledge acquired ... attention will be called to incidents from which valuable lessons can be learnt.' See 'Training Instructions 2, 7, and 8', Aug.–Dec. 1944, WO 204/7570, and Jul.–Sep. 1944, WO 169/18798, NA.

[82] See *Tiger Triumphs* for more details.

[83] Without Gen. Tuker in command, the division carried on with lessons and training directives under the command of Maj. Gen. Holworthy. See 91/40/1, Holworthy MSS, IWM, and Jul.–Sep. 1944, WO 169/18777, NA. The division was complimented highly by senior officers for their efforts in Italy as well as North Africa. See letters of 9 and 29 Sep. and 5 Oct. 1944, 91/40/1, Holworthy MSS, IWM.

[84] Amery to Wavell, 28 Sep. 1944, *TOP*, V, 24, p. 50.

[85] See *Tiger Triumphs* and Mar.–Apr. 1945, 10th Indian Division, WO 169/22249, NA.

by many Allied commanders.[86] While the various formations and units served as part of a wider war effort, the Indian Army formations were at times in the forefront of the campaigns. Throughout this period, the units and formations included new recruits and new ICOs and emergency Indian commissioned officers (EICOs) who gained in professionalism through the seasoning of battle; many went on to play roles in the post-war period as members of a professional and victorious force.

Far East campaigns (Malaya and Burma)

The Indian Army's campaign in the Far East also contributed a chapter of growth in its professionalisation. Along with their counterparts in the Middle East and Africa, the formations in the Far East went through significant growing pains. As with the army as a whole, these units recruited from ethnic and religious groups from across India, who consistently performed well and contributed to the army's success and growth. The formations in the Far East also benefited from the expansion of the officer corps to include more Indians, who proved themselves in combat and were in some cases leading battalions in battle by 1945.[87]

The Indian Army sent two Indian battalions to Hong Kong in 1940, who would later be captured by the Japanese alongside their Canadian and British allies. Over the course of 1941 government leaders decided to reinforce Malaya and Burma in the face of the threat of Japanese aggression. The 9th and 11th Indian Divisions were sent to Malaya, but they lacked equipment and training, and their units were newly raised and had already been heavily 'milked'. Thus hampered, they failed to tackle the tactical problems of fighting in the jungles and rubber-tree plantations of the area, and their ability to carry out traditional war fighting functions was similarly limited.[88] To compound this problem, any training and planning that was undertaken by Indian troops at depots in India emphasised the type of fighting that was typical of North Africa – open spaces

---

[86] See Tuker Papers, IWM, and 91/40/1, Holworthy MSS, IWM, letters of 9 and 29 Sep. and 5 Oct. 1944. As noted previously, Indian units were used at times to back up other Allied units, including British units. One example was noted by a British officer from the Rifle Brigade. He stated, 'a private told me [about] an unfortunate county battalion ... brigaded with Indian troops. The whole battalion had cut and run from a German tank attack. The Indians recaptured the ground. The brigadier formed both battalions into a square, the Indians on the outside with their weapons, the county regiment on the inside, without their weapons. He then told them what he thought of them' (quoted in Callahan, *Churchill's Generals*, p. 291, n. 23).

[87] See pp. 76–99 for discussions on the recruitment policy and expansion of the Indianisation process of the officer corps.

[88] See Marston, *Phoenix*, pp. 41–7, as an example.

Figure 2.3 Indian troops in central Burma © Imperial War Museums
(Image No. SE 3271)

and large mechanised formations – and did not envision the complexities
of terrain that existed in both Malaya and Burma.[89]

Under the circumstances, it is perhaps not surprising that the 1941
campaign in Malaya ended in unequivocal defeat.[90] Many of the reasons

---

[89] See Marston, *Phoenix*, and Tim Moreman, *The Jungle, the Japanese and the British
Commonwealth Armies at War, 1941–1945: Fighting Methods, Doctrine and Training for
Jungle Warfare* (London: Frank Cass, 2005), for an exhaustive discussion of the
complexities of the campaigns in the Far East and the ability of the Indian Army to
reform to deal with the Imperial Japanese Army.

[90] For more details on the Malayan campaign at the strategic, operational, and tactical
levels, see Moreman, *Jungle*; Brian Farrell, *Defence and Fall of Singapore* (Stroud:
Tempus Publishing, 2005); Garth Pratten, *Australian Battalion Commanders in the*

for the defeat were beyond the control of the troops themselves, and in many cases they rested on decisions made by strategic planners in the 1920s and 1930s. Their performance was conclusively undermined by their lack of training in general, and lack of training in jungle warfare techniques in particular, as well as rapid expansion of the Indian Army ranks, NCO, VCO, and officer corps. As Tim Moreman stated: 'The British garrison of Malaya, however, was still far from ready in December 1941 for war ... [They] paid a heavy penalty in northern Malaya for the limitations of their organisation and equipment and the failure of pre-war training to fit them for the war in the jungle.'[91]

The III Indian Corps, comprising the 9th and 11th Indian Divisions and supporting brigades, formed the main defensive line in northern Malaya. On 8 December 1941, the Imperial Japanese Army landed veteran troops along the coast, and struck hard at the Indian troops. The Japanese, while not jungle experts, were able to use the terrain to their advantage and constantly outflank III Corps. Within days, Indian troops were in retreat, spending most of their time trying to forestall the Japanese advance. To make matters worse, units in Malaya received very few replacements, and those who did arrive were generally half-trained officers and men who did not know how to fight in the terrain. The campaign was over in seven weeks, when Singapore surrendered on 15 February 1942. The Japanese captured more than 100,000 Australian, Indian, and British officers and men during the campaign.

The Japanese offensive into Burma (first Burma campaign) began on 11 December 1941.[92] As with Malaya, the Indian forces in Burma were

Second World War (Melbourne: Cambridge University Press, 2009); Raymond Callahan, *The Worst Disaster: The Fall of Singapore* (Newark: University of Delaware Press, 1977); Tomoyuki Ishizu and Raymond Callahan, 'The Rising Sun Strikes', pp. 47–62, and Callahan, 'Coping with Disaster', pp. 63–78, both in Daniel Marston, ed., *Pacific War Companion* (Oxford: Osprey Publishing, 2005).

[91] There were exceptions: the 2nd Argyll and Sutherland Highlanders and the 12th Indian Brigade carried out numerous exercises without much direction from Malaya Command. See Moreman, *Jungle*, pp. 12–28 (quotations pp. 24, 28).

[92] Many books cover the war in Burma from the strategic, operational, and tactical levels. Useful titles include Raymond Callahan, *Burma, 1942–1945* (London: Davis-Poynter, 1978); Louis Allen, *Burma, the Longest War, 1941–1945* (London: Dent, 1984); Slim, *Defeat into Victory*; Marston, *Phoenix*; Moreman, *Jungle*; Alan Jeffreys, *The British Army in the Far East, 1941–1945* (Oxford: Osprey Publishing, 2005); Bristow, *Memories*; Michael Calvert, *Prisoners of Hope* (London: Leo Cooper, 1996); K. W. Cooper, *The Little Men* (London: Hale, 1985); Raymond Cooper, *'B' Company, 9th Battalion the Border Regiment: One Man's War in Burma* (London: Dobson, 1978); C. R. L. Coubrough, *Memories of a Perpetual Second Lieutenant* (York: Wilton 65, 1999); Patrick Davis, *A Child at Arms* (London: Buchan & Enright, 1985); Evans, *Desert and Jungle*; George MacDonald Fraser, *Quartered Safe Out Here* (London: Harvill, 1992); Scott Gilmore, *A Connecticut Yankee in the 8th Gurkha Rifles* (Washington, DC: Brassey's, 1995); Tom

heavily 'milked', and any training was very limited and geared for the open areas of North Africa.[93] The collective training for the two divisions, the 1st Burma and 17th Indian, had been minimal as well.

The first Burma campaign can be divided into two significant parts: first, the fighting to the Sittang Bridge and loss of Rangoon; and, second, the retreat to Assam. The Japanese were able to outflank their road-bound and half-trained enemy during the first phase. Burma had been reinforced first by the 13th and later by the 16th Indian Brigades. Following the Japanese attack on Pearl Harbor, the 46th Indian Brigade and the Divisional HQ of the 17th Indian Division arrived in Rangoon in January 1942. The 17th Indian Division was below 40 per cent strength after the heavy fighting to the Sittang River during January and February. Following the loss of defences along the river, changes were made within the campaign command structure. Lt Gen. William Slim, as Burma Corps (Burcorps) commander, and Maj. Gen. Cowan arrived to take over the 17th Indian Division. The last reinforcements arrived in Rangoon as Japanese forces set out to destroy the British, Burmese, and Indian units. Rangoon fell on 9 March, cutting off Burcorps from the outside world. Burcorps was forced to retreat north as the Japanese were reinforced and increased the pressure to entrap and completely destroy the British and Indian formations, as well as the Nationalist Chinese forces that had intervened in the eastern Shan states. As the units were forced relentlessly north, Burcorps finally decided on 28 April to formally abandon Burma and withdraw to Assam. The last troops entered the Imphal Plain by late May.[94]

This was the longest retreat in British military history, more than 900 miles. The Japanese had failed to completely destroy Burcorps. Unlike Malaya, many veterans from the Burma campaign escaped to Assam,

---

Grounds, *Some Letters from Burma: Story of the 25th Dragoons at War* (Tunbridge Wells, UK: Parapress, 1994); John Hill, *China Dragons: A Rifle Company at War* (London: Blandford, 1991); M. A. Lowry, *An Infantry Company in Arakan and Kohima* (Aldershot: Gale & Polden, 1950); Tony Mains, *The Retreat from Burma: An Intelligence Officer's Personal Story* (London: Foulsham, 1973); Masters, *Road Past Mandalay*; John Prendergast, *Prender's Progress: A Soldier in India* (London: Cassell, 1979); Robin Schlaefli, *Emergency Sahib* (London: Leach, 1992); John Smyth, *Before the Dawn: A Story of Two Historic Retreats* (London: Cassell, 1957); John Randle, *Battle Tales from Burma* (Stroud: Leo Cooper, 2004); and James Lunt, *Hell of a Licking: The Retreat from Burma, 1941–1942* (London: Collins, 1986).

[93] One junior officer remembered his CO asking a staff officer about training; the reply was 'training – you can't do any training because it is bloody jungle' (author's interview with Brig. John Randle, 7/10th Baluch Regiment, 10 April 2000); see also Randle's own account of the war, *Battle Tales from Burma*.

[94] For a more detailed discussion of the first Burma campaign, see Allen, *Burma*; Callahan, *Burma 1942–1945*; Slim, *Defeat into Victory*; Marston, *Phoenix*; and Moreman, *Jungle*.

taking with them valuable experiences and lessons.[95] The Indian Army was castigated for its performance in both the Malaya and the first Burma campaigns by Prime Minister Winston Churchill,[96] but it must be remembered that British units served alongside the Indian Army troops and shared the defeat. None of the units and formations that served in Malaya and Burma were prepared for the sort of warfare that the Japanese unleashed upon them. It is a tribute to both Indian and British Army units that they learned from their defeats, using them as a tool to retrain and eventually inflict a far worse defeat upon the Japanese Army.

Assessment and reform

The period following the defeats in Malaya and Burma was a trying one for the Indian Army. During the summer of 1942, the Indian National Congress Party initiated the Quit India movement.[97] The movement caused considerable disruption for the Indian Army, as more than sixty battalions were called out to act as Aid to the Civil Power.[98] Many units continued to assess and teach the valuable lessons learned in the fighting in both Malaya and Burma, but there was still no centralised system to co-ordinate such efforts.[99] Around this time, the 14th Indian Division was ordered to begin an operation to clear the Japanese from the Arakan region of Burma. The division had carried out some jungle warfare training and had several veteran officers with jungle warfare experience, but it was not sufficiently trained to undertake this mission. And, because no centralised training system had been established, any reinforcements that arrived had not received any jungle warfare

---

[95] Some Malaya veterans were able to escape from the debacle as well, but many more men and officers from the Burma campaign escaped to influence subsequent reforms. *The Fighting Cock: Being the History of the 23rd Indian Division, 1942–1947* (Aldershot: Gale & Polden, 1951), by Lt Col A. J. R. Doulton, as well as works by Randle, *Battle Tales from Burma*, Slim, *Defeat into Victory*, and Lunt, *Hell of a Licking*, offer very interesting insights into the arrival of the retreating Burcorps, as the 23rd was shipped into Assam to receive the survivors of Burcorps and prepare the defences of the area.

[96] See Auchinleck to CIGS 9 Sep. 1941, Auchinleck Papers, University of Manchester; Connell, *Auchinleck*, pp. 755–7; Churchill to Gen. Ismay, in Connell, *Auchinleck*, p. 771, to see Churchill's outdated views on the Indian Army and his lack of confidence in the organisation. See also Michael Roberts' comments in Callahan, *Churchill's Generals*, pp. 192, 226.

[97] See pp. 99–110 for more discussion.

[98] There will be more discussion of the Indian Army in the role of the Aid to the Civil Power, pp. 99–110.

[99] For in-depth discussions of this period, see Marston, *Phoenix*, pp. 79–110, and Moreman, *Jungle*, pp. 46–76.

training. The division advanced slowly, but by the end of 1942 it was close to the end of the peninsula.[100]

The advance ended outside Donbaik and Rathedaung near the end of January 1943, and from there the British launched numerous unsuccessful attacks against the Japanese positions. A battle of attrition ensued, and more and more British and Indian brigades were sent into battle. The Japanese, meanwhile, built up their reserves in the area, preparatory to launching a counter-attack in mid March. The British and Indian units, caught off guard, were forced to retreat once again. By the end of April, British and Indian units had been forced to withdraw all the way to their original starting positions.[101] Gen. Wavell, CinC India, reflecting on the campaign, commented that 'we still have a great deal to learn about jungle fighting'.[102]

The defeat in the Arakan convinced GHQ India to confront the Indian Army's tactical limitations in the terrain of the Far East.[103] The Infantry Committee, formed in June 1943 to assess the situation, criticised the practice of 'milking' regiments, which had left many units below strength and deprived of their best officers and men. The Infantry Committee called for a centralised doctrine and training system. They also addressed a number of other issues which are outside the scope of this chapter.[104]

As a result of the Infantry Committee's recommendations, the 14th and 39th Indian Divisions were organised as jungle warfare training divisions. Doctrine, in the form of the *Jungle Book*, was created and disseminated to enable officers and men to understand the tactics of jungle warfare. Initiatives and practices relevant to training, operational lessons, and constant performance assessment began to permeate the whole of the Indian Army from mid 1943. The army's war in the Far East was also reorganised. South East Asia Command[105] was created in

---

[100] S. Woodburn Kirby, *War Against Japan*, vols. I–V (London: HMSO, 1957–69), II, pp. 260–2.

[101] See the actions of the 2/1st Punjab to understand the environment and the limitations of the army at the time: Marston, *Phoenix*, pp. 86–91.

[102] See *ibid.*, p. 88.

[103] This book will not deal with the efforts of Maj. Gen. Orde Wingate and his Chindits. They have been the subject of many debates since 1943. For a quick overview, see Callahan, *Churchill's Generals*, and for a very deep and excellent analysis that covers a wider period of Wingate's career, see Simon Anglim, *Orde Wingate and the British Army, 1922–1944* (London: Pickering & Chatto, 2010).

[104] See Moreman, *Jungle*, Marston, *Phoenix*, and Jeffreys, *British Army in the Far East*, for more information.

[105] See Vice-Admiral Lord Louis Mountbatten, *Report to the Combined Chiefs of Staff by the Supreme Allied Commander, South East Asia, 1943–1945* (London: HMSO, 1951), for details on the history and the set-up of this command as well as a general narrative of the campaign in Burma and Malaya.

August 1943 under the command of Admiral Lord Louis Mount-batten;[106] Fourteenth Army was the land component, led by Gen. Slim, while Gen. Auchinleck[107] headed up India Command. More formations arrived to bolster the war effort in the east.

Slim considered Auchinleck's appointment to India Command as one of the most important contributions to the Indian Army's progress towards eventual victory in Burma. He opined that

> Luckily, General Auchinleck was the man to do it. There was a considerable and prompt injection of ginger into the Indian administrative machine, military and civil. Even at the beginning of 1944 the results of Auchinleck's drive began to show ... It was good for us when he took command of India ... [W]ithout him and what he and the Army in India did for us we could not have existed, let alone conquered.[108]

The Indian Army's training transformation was under way: by the end of 1943, the 17th and 23rd Indian Divisions, both of which had instituted assessment and jungle warfare programmes, were holding the line in the Imphal region of Assam.[109] The 5th[110] and 7th Indian Divisions were sent to the Arakan region to start another offensive along the Mayu Range.[111] The Imperial Japanese Army, for their part, failed to notice

---

[106] He would serve as the last viceroy of India and play a prominent role in the decisions made in 1947.

[107] Auchinleck became commander-in-chief of the Indian Army on 20 June 1943. See Callahan, *Churchill's Generals*, pp. 194–8, as well.

[108] Slim, *Defeat into Victory*, pp. 175–6; see also Linlithgow's letter of 1 Jun. 1943, *TOP*, III, 755, p. 1034: 'My own judgment is that so far as India and the training and improvement of morale of the Indian Army is concerned, Auchinleck is much the best man we can get ... [H]is excellent qualities are primarily the qualities of the fighting soldier, and a soldier's general.' Note also Linlithgow's letter to Amery on 10 Jun. 1943, *TOP*, III, 769, p. 1053: 'His [Auchinleck's] value, as you and I both recognize, is in terms of the effects of his employment on Indian Army morale, and our being able to use his great experience with the Indian soldier in connection with training, etc.'

[109] See 17 Ind. Div., 1943, WO 172/1960, NA, as well as Marston, *Phoenix*.

[110] The 5th was a veteran division, having served in East and North Africa; however, it had undergone further training in jungle warfare. See Antony Brett-James, *Ball of Fire: The Fifth Indian Division in the Second World War* (Aldershot: Gale & Polden, 1951), for more details.

[111] See 5 Ind. Div., WO 172/1936, and 7th Ind. Div., 1943, WO 172/1943, NA. See also Lt Gen. Frank Messervy Papers, MSS (7 Ind. Div.) and Maj Gen. Sir Douglas Gracey Papers, MSS (20th Indian Division), for more evidence of training and lessons work being done by the units. They are located at the Liddell Hart Centre for Military Archives, King's College London (henceforth Liddle Hart Centre, KCL). See also Marston, *Phoenix*, and Moreman, *Jungle*. The Mayu Range was a line of mountains that ran north to south, almost equally dividing the Mayu peninsula. They were jungle-clad and thought impenetrable, as there were not many tracks.

that the forces arrayed against them in late 1943 and 1944 were not the same as those they had faced in the past.

Rise of the phoenix

In 1944, the formations that fought in the Fourteenth Army had been transformed. In early 1944, the Japanese decided to launch Operation Ha-Go in the Arakan to offset British advances in the area and distract attention from their major offensive in the Imphal region. By early February, the Japanese 55th Division was on the move, intending to destroy the 5th and 7th Indian Divisions, XV Corps. But these British and Indian units did not break and run as their predecessors had; they stood and fought their ground. This was a transformed army, ensconced in their new box formations and patrol bases and refusing to budge.[112]

The fighting was vicious.[113] Some mistakes[114] were made during the opening phase of battle, but British and Indian units were able to correct the situation, and within a few weeks they had neutralised the Japanese threat. By early March, the Indian Army in the Arakan was on the counteroffensive. It slowly started to destroy the Japanese Army, as formations from the north closed in and provided support to the 5th and 7th Indian Divisions. The Japanese units, caught in a vice, were slowly and systematically destroyed.[115]

Around the same time, Gen. Slim began to receive reports that the Japanese were on the move in the Assam region. IV Corps – the 17th, 20th, and 23rd Indian Divisions and various brigades – were stationed in and around the Imphal region. The Japanese had amassed more than three divisions, with orders to destroy IV Corps and seize the important supply depots in the area. Operation U-Go began on 9 March, when the 17th Indian Division made contact along the Tiddim Road. The 17th and 20th Indian Divisions were ordered to withdraw to the Imphal Plain.

---

[112] See Allen, *Burma*, Kirby, *War Against Japan*, Slim, *Defeat into Victory*, Callahan, *Churchill's Generals*, and Geoffrey Evans, *Slim as a Military Commander* (London: Batsford, 1969), for more detailed analyses of the 1944 campaign.

[113] One account, of an action by the 1/11th Sikhs, is indicative: 'C coy was hit hard in the flank from unseen Japanese trenches ... A naik [corporal] named Nand Singh crawled forward and attacked three Japanese trenches in intense hand to hand fighting. He single-handedly cleared all three trenches, allowing the rest of the platoon to come forward.' Nand Singh was awarded the Victoria Cross for his actions. See Marston, *Phoenix*, p. 133.

[114] There was some criticism surrounding the 'pull-back' to Admin Box and the surrounding areas. However, after the initial issues, the units learned quickly and settled into using effective tactics to hold their lines and destroy the Japanese forces.

[115] Due to space considerations, a detailed discussion of the fighting in Burma is not possible. Please consult the books listed in n. 92 for more detail.

Figure 2.4 Defeat into victory © Imperial War Museums (Image No. IND 4901)

The 17th Indian found it more difficult to extricate itself from the Japanese advance, but eventually succeeded in withdrawing to the south of the plain. The 20th Indian's withdrawal was more orderly.[116]

At the end of March, British and Indian units returned to Imphal. The road network to the north, via Kohima, had been cut off by the Japanese advance. Elements of the Indian National Army (INA) were also involved in the attacks upon the Indian formations and units in and around Kohima and Imphal. Overall they did not perform well, with large numbers deserting to the Indian Army upon contact.[117]

---

[116] Some units became so adept at jungle warfare and patrolling that they were able to cause considerable damage to the Japanese advance. See 14/13th FFRifles fighting in Marston, *Phoenix*, pp. 142–5.

[117] See Chandar Sundaram, 'A Paper Tiger: The Indian National Army in Battle, 1944–1945', *War and Society*, 13, 1 (May 1995), pp. 35–54; Sundaram, 'The Indian National Army, 1942–1946: A Circumstantial Force', in Marston and Sundaram, eds., *Military History of India and South Asia*, pp. 123–40; and references to the INA in C. A. Bayly and T. N. Harper, *Forgotten Armies: The Fall of British Asia, 1941–1945* (Cambridge, MA: Belknap, 2005). See also Chapter 3.

The fight for Imphal and Kohima became a battle of attrition as British and Indian units held their ground against countless Japanese attacks. Maj. R. S. Noronha, an ICO, in a situation characteristic of the campaign, was ordered to hold an area to the 'last man, last round'. A company of 4/3rd Madras Regiment, under Noronha's command, was repeatedly attacked by Japanese along its positions at Sita for seven days and nights. The company held its ground against every assault.[118]

Troops in such situations were reinforced with air-dropped and air-landed supplies and troops.[119] The British/Indian counteroffensive began from the north, as elements of the 5th and 7th Indian (recently flown in from the fighting in the Arakan), along with the 2nd British Division, fought and destroyed the Japanese forces in and around Kohima, linking up with the Imphal garrison on 22 June. The Japanese refused to accept defeat until 9 July, when they ordered a withdrawal to Burma. By that time, however, it was too late, and IV Corps, seizing the advantage, carried on with a counteroffensive and started to destroy the Japanese forces in the region and push south towards the Chindwin River.

The rest of the Fourteenth Army had not been idle either. As the 5th Indian and 11th East African divisions continued the advance to destroy the Japanese withdrawal during the monsoon season, other formations sat down to assess lessons from the operations of 1944 and make improvements in training and deployment accordingly. Assessment also identified the fact that, when the army advanced into Burma, the terrain would change, offering new challenges that would need to be examined and discussed. The divisional commanders, as their counterparts in North Africa and Italy had done, expected officers and men to write down experiences, identify lessons, and assess mistakes. These assessments were incorporated in divisional lessons and training exercises, as well as in the official doctrine written by GHQ India and embodied in the AITM and Military Training Pamphlets (MTPs), with lessons that were shared among the various theatres of operation.[120]

Operations Capital and Extended Capital brought about the final destruction of the Imperial Japanese Burma Area Army.[121] Slim and

---

[118] Noronha received the Military Cross. See Marston, *Phoenix*, p. 146.

[119] Both the 5th and 7th Indian Divisions were flown into the fighting in Kohima and Imphal to reinforce the garrisons.

[120] See Marston, *Phoenix*, pp. 170–9, and Moreman, *Jungle*, pp. 146–60, as well as the countless MTPs and AITMs that are available at the British Library, National Army Museum (henceforth NAM), and Imperial War Museum.

[121] The XV Corps, 25th, 26th Indian, 81st and 82nd West African Divisions, continued its advance down the Arakan region of Burma and were successful in tying down Japanese forces in the area. Ramree Island was seized by February 1945. Airfields were seized on the island that would prove pivotal to support the campaign in central Burma.

his commanders began the advance into Burma in November 1944. The offensive began in early December, when the 19th and 20th Indian Divisions crossed the Chindwin River and advanced on Japanese forces stationed on the other side, hoping to trap the latter on the Shwebo Plain and seek the decisive battle. However, the Japanese had placed only rear-guard troops on the Shwebo Plain; most of their forces had withdrawn to the east and south, back across to the far side of the Irrawaddy River. Their defensive line followed the river from north of Mandalay south towards Nyaungo.

Realising that his original plan, Operation Capital, was not going to work, Slim altered it accordingly. Under the revised plan, Operation Extended Capital, IV Corps was earmarked to carry out a secret route march that would end up opposite the thinly defended river area near Nyaungo. There they would cross and strike towards the important Japanese supply network based at Meiktila. Meanwhile, XXXIII Corps was ordered to cross the Shwebo Plain and draw the Japanese into a decisive battle in and around Mandalay. Gen. Slim theorised that 'If we took Meiktila while Kimura [Kimura Heitaro, Japanese commander] was deeply engaged along the Irrawaddy about Mandalay, he would be compelled to detach large forces to clear his vital communications. This would give me not only the major battle I desired, but the chance to repeat the hammer and anvil tactics [used previously at Imphal and Kohima] ... [with] XXXIII Corps the hammer from the north against the anvil of IV Corps at Meiktila and the Japanese between.'[122]

The apparently newly reformed and professional army had impressed even members of the British War Cabinet, who had previously had a rather low opinion of it. Members of the War Cabinet who met with elements of the Fourteenth Army commented favourably and, as they noted in March 1944, 'the morale of the Indian troops in Burma was remarkably high, and impressed visitors from the UK who had seen them. In quality, the Indian Army were more than a match for the Japanese.'[123]

Slim's plan worked, but fighting in the bridgeheads was ferocious. The 1/11th Sikhs, as part of the 7th Indian Division's bridgehead, encountered Japanese and INA forces determined to destroy their positions before the division could launch a strike towards Meiktila. The Japanese launched repeated attacks, and the brutal conditions are indicated by the story of 1/11th Sikhs' Jemadar Parkash Singh, who rallied his men repeatedly and carried ammunition between posts. He was wounded three times

---

[122] Slim, *Defeat into Victory*, p. 327.
[123] War Cabinet, 26 Mar. 1945, *TOP*, V, 339, p. 734.

before a grenade killed him, and died in the arms of his company commander. He was later awarded the Victoria Cross.[124] As the 7th Indian Division held the bridgehead, the 17th Indian Division crossed and pushed out, in a charge for Meiktila. The best efforts of the Japanese and the INA to destroy the advance were to no avail. Meiktila was in British hands by early March 1945, and the Japanese were regrouping to defend against the British and Indian bridgeheads in and around Mandalay.

Fierce fighting ensued in and around Mandalay and Meiktila and along the Irrawaddy River. One machine gun company noted more than 250 dead Japanese outside their perimeter after three nights of fighting.[125] The Japanese began to withdraw from the Irrawaddy River, Mandalay, and Meiktila on 24 March, unable to hold their positions against the aggressive British and Indian forces. A Japanese commander commented that 'since 2[8]th of February allied tanks [thrust] deep into our positions every day ... [I]n this fighting the co-operation among allied infantry, artillery and tanks was made admirably.'[126]

With the area firmly under British and Indian control, the race to Rangoon began. The Indian Army's professionalism was demonstrated as its units quickly adapted to new conditions; some units executed open-style and mechanised warfare, while others reverted to jungle tactics, as the Japanese were systematically destroyed along the banks of the southern reaches of the Irrawaddy and the road to Rangoon. The pre-war notion that British units were needed to 'prop up' the Indian units was effectively debunked;[127] British units were underperforming (many soldiers and officers wishing to be demobbed), and at the end of the campaign the British contribution represented only 13 per cent of the effort. The army that marched to Rangoon was in all important respects the Indian Army.[128] Rangoon fell to an amphibious and airborne assault on 3 May, ending the war in Burma for all intents and purposes.

---

[124] See Marston, *Phoenix*, p. 211; and author's interview with Maj. G. C. Coppen, 1 Nov. 1999.

[125] 9/13th FFRifles, interviews with Majs. D. Lamond, 27 Oct. 1999, and D. Wright, 20 Dec. 1999.

[126] Lt Gen. Tadashi Hanaya, 'Story of the Japanese 33rd Division', Gen. Evans Papers, IWM.

[127] By October 1944, the British units in Burma were short 10,000 men and Slim had to fill the gap with more Indian Army units: Callahan, *Churchill's Generals*, p. 227. See also letter from Auchinleck to Wavell, 22 Aug. 1945, Auchinleck Papers, University of Manchester, stating: 'Recently in Burma higher commanders have definitely preferred to use Indian units rather than British and have actually asked that British units should be replaced by Indian.'

[128] See Raymond Callahan, 'The Indian Army, Total War, and the Dog That Didn't Bark in the Night', in Jane Hathaway, ed., *Rebellion Repression Reinvention: Mutiny in Comparative Perspective* (Westport, CT: Praeger, 2002), p. 126.

The Burma campaign, which had begun as the longest retreat in British military history, ended as the Imperial Japanese Army's most conclusive defeat, with the Indian Army playing the central role. It was a spectacular reversal of the events of 1942. The Indian Army's successes in Africa, the Middle East, Italy, and particularly the Far East could not have occurred without fundamental reforms, notably expanding recruitment of ethnic groups and classes far beyond traditional limitations and restructuring the officer corps to admit more ICOs, and allow Indians to command and sit on courts martial of white soldiers and officers. These reforms went hand in hand with the tactical and operational level reforms that occurred on the battlefields of the Second World War.

The main engine for such radical changes was ultimately senior Indian Army leadership, led by officers such as Auchinleck, Slim, and Savory. As Raymond Callahan noted:

The rebuilding of the Indian Army and Slim's Arakan and Imphal victories were demonstrations of the aggressive determination and imaginative leadership Churchill had always called for and so frequently lamented. But those qualities were being displayed by an army he had always undervalued and in a campaign he had never wanted to fight ... It is doubtful if either man [Churchill and chief of the Imperial General Staff [CIGS] Alanbrooke] ever fully realized that the greatest British feat of operational manoeuvre, not only for the war but of the twentieth century, had not been the work of Monty [Eighth and later Second Army] or Alex [Eighth Army in Italy] but of Slim ... [The Indian Army] had remade itself by 1944 and 1945, perhaps in some ways aided by the quasi autonomy that allowed Auchinleck, Savory, Slim, and many others to get on with the business of forging a battleworthy weapon, with few interventions from above ... [T]he war in Burma was the war the Indian Army had, and it got on with preparing to win it, accepting whatever new structures or doctrines were necessary. It seems safe to predict that Slim's campaigns will be deemed examples of the military art far longer than any of Monty's victories.[129]

Recruitment and Indianisation of the army during the Second World War

The Second World War precipitated a period of unprecedented expansion for the Indian Army. Between 1939 and 1945, the army expanded from 200,000 to more than 2.5 million men and officers, even though conscription was never imposed. The Indian Army began the war as the

---

[129] Callahan, *Churchill's Generals*, pp. 211 and 239; see also Callahan, 'Were the Sepoy Generals Any Good? A Re-Appraisal of the British–Indian Army's High Command in the Second World War', in Kaushik Roy, ed., *War and Society in Colonial India* (New Delhi: Oxford University Press, 2006), pp. 305–29.

'Imperial Reserve' for the British government, and by its end had lost 24,000 killed, 64,000 wounded, 60,000 captured,[130] and 11,000 missing on active service.[131]

Throughout the Second World War the Indian Army also faced fundamental questions about its existence, size, and composition.[132] The Indianisation of the officer corps reached new heights during this period, signalling the end of the traditional all-British officer corps. Recruitment also expanded to include South Asian ethnic groups that had long been dismissed as being 'non-martial'.[133] The army's rapid expansion in response to the needs of the war raised additional questions concerning the quality of troops and officers.

Recruitment of the army during the Second World War

The rapid expansion of the Indian Army placed a significant strain on the areas from which recruits were traditionally drawn, especially in the Punjab. One key issue that arose early in the war was the recruitment of Jat Sikhs.[134] The political and ethnic tensions of the 1920s and 1930s were exacerbated in 1940 by discussions of a future Pakistan. There were two small mutinies during this period that included Jat Sikhs; their involvement led them to be labelled as 'troublesome' and created a reluctance to recruit them. By 1942, the recruitment numbers of Jat Sikhs had dropped to all-time lows. The British perpetuated this trend, recruiting non-Jat Sikhs as well as more Muslims from the Punjab. As Jat Sikh numbers dropped,[135] the numbers of Muslims (or PMs) quadrupled. By 1943, with the Punjab providing 37% of all soldiers recruited into the army, the Jat Sikhs represented 7% of the total, Hindu Jats 5%, and PMs and Pathans accounted for more than 25%.[136]

---

[130] Most of these men were captured early in the war in the Malayan and first Burma campaigns of 1941–2.

[131] S. L. Menezes, *Fidelity and Honour: The Indian Army from the Seventeenth to the Twenty-First Century* (New Delhi: Viking, 1993), p. 370.

[132] Questions were raised in certain quarters about whether the Indian Army needed to be expanded. Churchill in particular denigrated the efforts of the Indian Army throughout the war, even after it had undertaken significant reforms, conclusively defeated the Imperial Japanese Army, and played an important supporting role in the successful East African, North African, and Italian campaigns. See Callahan's work in *Churchill's Generals* for a detailed discussion of the tensions between Churchill and his Indian Army commanders, chiefly Gens. Auchinleck and Slim.

[133] See Chapter 1 for background to the issues surrounding martial races and the Indianisation of the officer corps before 1939.

[134] See Yong, *Garrison State*, pp. 286–90, for a detailed description of the issues.

[135] Although they still represented a large proportion of the Jat Sikh male community, as noted by the final tally of 88 per cent. See L/MIL/17/5/2153, OIOC, BL.

[136] Yong, *Garrison State*, pp. 290–1.

Rapid expansion placed noticeable strain upon the resources of the traditional recruitment areas, and GHQ India realised that recruitment must be broadened to other areas and groups. This decision was undertaken tentatively at first, by taking Madrassis and others into the expanding service corps of the army. Following Auchinleck's appointment as commander-in-chief, recruitment reform became more decisive. Auchinleck stated that: 'as regards to recruitment of the rank and file I have no doubt at all that apart from political considerations we must broaden our basis and this was already in hand before I arrived. I propose to continue and hasten the process. There is plenty of good untouched material which we can and should use.'[137]

Nor did Auchinleck intend to confine recruitment from non-martial races to the service corps. He specifically suggested that the old 3rd Madras Regiment should be re-raised, and that new infantry units should be raised to represent the other provinces.[138] He asserted that these units were not to be for show only, but would be used alongside other units in fighting the war. He recognised the political dimensions of this move, stating that 'it will greatly help in meeting the political demand for the wider representation in the army'.[139] Amery, as secretary of state for India, recognised and accepted these proposals, and was disappointed when Auchinleck was chosen as commander-in-chief of the Middle East in June 1941, taking him away from the opportunity to implement them personally.[140]

The recruitment of non-martial races had been stepped up between 1940 and 1942, but there was still a faction in GHQ India which doubted their potential as fighting troops. Many of the new recruits were sent to non-infantry or cavalry services within the army, as well as to the Indian Army Service Corps, signals, engineers, and artillery.[141] A report published in February 1942 documents 38,000 recruits from non-martial

---

[137] Auchinleck to Amery, 17 Mar. 1941, Auchinleck Papers, University of Manchester.
[138] When he was commander-in-chief, Middle East, the Assam, Bihar, Chamar, and Afidi Regiments were raised.
[139] Auchinleck to Amery, 17 Mar. 1941, Auchinleck Papers, University of Manchester.
[140] Amery stated that he was sad to lose Auchinleck because of his great work for the Indian war effort and his point of view on certain issues relevant to the Army. See Amery to Auchinleck, 25 Jun. 1941, Auchinleck Papers, University of Manchester.
[141] There were other infantry units besides the Sikh Light Infantry and the Madras Regiment raised from the new classes: four battalions of the Bihar Regiment, of which the 1st Battalion saw active service in Burma; three battalions of the Assam Regiment, of which the 1st Battalion saw service in Burma; five battalions of the Mahar Regiment although none saw active service; four battalions of the Ajmer Regiment; and two battalions of the Chamar Regiment, of which one served in Burma. See Gaylor, *Sons of John Company*, pp. 207–13. None of these units saw active service until 1944 and 1945; prior to this they were all held in reserve.

races enlisted, of whom 33,000 were stationed in India. Meanwhile, 'martial races' such as Jat Sikhs and Punjabi Musalmans reported numbers at 50% stationed in India and 50% overseas.[142] In response to an Indian politician's questions during debates in the Council of State, GHQ India wrote a note stating that 'other classes are not yet battle tried so it will be a while before their martial qualities are assessed'.[143]

A report by the adjutant general's office in late 1942 argued for recruitment from non-martial races by making the claim that the performance of PMs, Dogras, and Jat Sikhs in the field was declining. The report stated that 'the general quality of the recruit [pre-war classes] is tending to decline both physically and in terms of intelligence and this is when guts and brains are needed'.[144] The report by the adjutant general's office also documented how many of the units, including both the Madras and Sikh Light Infantry, were lacking in junior leaders, and recommended that this be remedied quickly, noting, however, that 'foreign' VCOs or British NCOs were not the answer.[145] On the other hand, at least one witness considered that the Madras Regiment's turn-out and abilities improved when it received British Guardsmen as drill instructors. Maj. T. A. J. Barton, in an interview, commented that in his opinion the Guardsmen had filled a vacuum created by the pre-war neglect of these units.[146]

In a War Staff communiqué to London, GHQ India formally announced that 'the former distinction of martial and non martial race has been removed'.[147] By mid 1943 there were still those within the Indian Army who were willing to concede that the recruitment of non-martial races was necessary, but continued to assert that it should not be done too quickly. Gen. G. N. Molesworth commented, in support of this argument, that 'the Northwest groups are virile and that the rest of India had lost its appetite for war'.[148]

The arrival of Auchinleck as commander-in-chief, India, in late June 1943 brought a strong supporter of expanding recruitment and training of non-martial race troops for battle. His arrival coincided with the aftermath of the first Arakan defeat, when the British government was calling for the Indian Army to be shrunk. Churchill stated clearly what he felt the problems were, but he failed to recognise the significance of the

---

[142] 1 Feb. 1942, L/WS/1/456, OIOC, BL.   [143] 25 Sep. 1942, L/WS/1/136, OIOC, BL.
[144] 3 Nov. 1942, L/WS/1/968, OIOC, BL.   [145] *Ibid.*
[146] Author's interview with Maj. T. A. J. Barton, Madras Regimental Centre and 4/3rd Madras, 5 Jul. 2000.
[147] 17 Feb. 1943, L/WS/1/136, OIOC, BL.
[148] 21 Jul. 1943, L/WS/1/136, OIOC, BL. Molesworth was the secretary, Military Department, India Office, London.

tactical errors that were committed in battle and that were subsequently rectified. He was also apparently unaware that non-martial race units had not seen active service in the campaigns.[149] They had all been stationed in India or near the front on lines of communication duties. Churchill stated to Leo Amery, 'It [the Indian Army in 1943] bears no relation to the splendid old time Indian units.'[150] Issues of insubordination arose with troops from the martial races in the field and not the non-martial races.[151] During the summer of 1943, the British government called upon the Indian Army to reduce the numbers of units and formations. Auchinleck viewed this as a signal that the British government had lost confidence in the Indian Army and that this loss was partly due to the expanded recruitment of non-martial races. In a letter of response to the viceroy, Field Marshal Wavell, Auchinleck described in some detail his thoughts and feelings on the topic of non-martial races and the government's attitude. He bluntly stated: 'the idea underlying the demand for reduction seems to be based upon the idea that the Indian Army is now composed to a large extent of men who because they belong to classes previously untried as soldiers are unreliable and unsuitable'.[152]

Auchinleck went on to comment that the Madrassis comprised about half of the new recruits and noted that 'from all accounts the Madrassis are doing very well'. He further stressed that 'the recruitment of the old classes has been pushed to such lengths that the recruits now coming forward are often of poor quality and it is time to say that it is preferable to secure good specimens of new classes which can be maintained'. A further example of his commitment to the new classes is highlighted at the end of the letter when he stated, in no uncertain terms, 'there is little doubt that [the] new classes must continue to have their place in the Indian Army of the future'.[153]

A speech given in the Indian Assembly in November 1943 highlighted GHQ India's attempts to deal with the issues of recruitment. The officer speaking stated that the Indian Army was open to all of the classes of India. The only parameters for officers and other ranks were sufficient education and physical attributes. The officer ended his speech by

---

[149] Even Amery stated, in a letter to Linlithgow on 27 August 1942: 'Congress has nothing in common with the fighting races of India of whom well over a million have volunteered for the Army during the present war' (*TOP*, II, 637, p. 830).

[150] Quoted in Callahan, *Churchill's Generals*, p. 202.

[151] There were a few examples of restlessness among Sikh troops for religious issues or fear of the formation of the state of Pakistan and the division of the Punjab: L/WS/1/707, OIOC, BL.

[152] Auchinleck to Wavell, 'Size and Composition of the India Army', 2 Aug. 1943, Auchinleck Papers, University of Manchester.

[153] *Ibid.*

stating: 'Sir I assure the house that there is no discrimination at present against scheduled classes and there will be none.'[154]

Auchinleck's commitment resulted in two significant achievements. First, he was able to forestall the vast cuts proposed to the numbers of the Indian Army.[155] Some units were disbanded, but this was because units from the North-West Frontier and PAIFORCE were brought back to serve in the Burma campaign. Second, he had some of the non-martial race infantry units committed to battle to gain experience and, if possible, to make a name for themselves and quiet critics.[156]

By the end of the war, the recruitment totals from all classes clearly indicate a preference for the pre-war classes, but this is partly attributable to the recruitment bias which was still extant during the early part of the war. The numbers of the new class recruits[157] rose steadily towards the end of the war; the numbers listed represent the percentages of the total numbers of each male population who were eligible for military service: Jat Sikhs 88%;[158] Kumaonis 50%; Pathans 50%; Jats (Hindus) 46%; Sikhs (others, including Mazbhis and Ramdasias) 40%; Garhwalis 38%; Dogras 32%; PMs 30%; Ranghars 27%; Gujars 24%; Brahmins 23%; Rajputs 22%; Rajputana Musalmans 18%; Mahrattas 16%; Coorgs 15%; Madrassis 14%; Baluchis 10%; Mahars 8%; Ahirs 7%; Assamese 3%; and Chamars 3%.[159] The Punjab was still heavily represented, and this fact would have a major impact in the post-war period as demobilised soldiers returned home.

The Indian Army's recruitment history during the Second World War highlights the reforms and expansions that its recruitment policies underwent. 5th Probyn's Horse saw a drop in the numbers of available Dogra Rajputs early in the war; as a result, the regiment was ordered to accept Dogra Hindus for the Dogra Squadron. Officers of the 5th Probyn's stated that the Dogra Hindus proved themselves excellent soldiers over the course of the war.[160] The battalions of the 13th Frontier Force Rifles

---

[154] No. 1175/1/LB, Nov. 1943, L/WS/1/136, OIOC, BL.

[155] This was to prove crucially important later, when British Army units in the Burma campaign in 1945 were being forced to withdraw due to lack of reinforcements, and their places being filled by Indian units.

[156] L/WS/1/707, OIOC, BL.

[157] 'New class' implies units raised during the Second World War. Many of the peoples had served in either the East India Company Army or the Indian Army but had fallen out of favour at different periods.

[158] Most of this represented recruitment from the early part of the war.

[159] L/MIL/17/5/2153, OIOC, BL. See also Cohen, 'The Untouchable Soldier', for more details.

[160] Author's interview with Maj. H. E. I. C. Stewart, 11 Jul. 2000, and Probyn's Newsletter 1945, p. 2.

(FFRifles), who also saw a drop in their traditional pool of recruits, introduced two additional classes, one of which was new. The problems of securing enough Jat Sikhs for the Sikh Company led to the recruitment of Jat Hindus, including VCOs.[161] Captain J. R. Wallis, 14/13th FFRifles, noted in an interview that he was sent on a recruiting drive in 1943, which included seeking out non-Jat Sikhs, Mazbhis and Ramdasias included.[162] The FFRifles also recruited Ahirs to bring their battalions up to strength.[163] Capt. Hank Howlett, a training officer at the regimental centre, Abbottabad, noted that the new classes of men 'smoothly slotted into the training company ranks'.[164]

The FFRifles were not alone in broadening their base of recruitment. Low numbers drove the 1st Punjab Regiment to open up its recruitment to include Jat Hindus for the Sikh companies. The Baluch Regiment began accepting Brahmins from non-Dogra areas to bring the Dogra companies up to strength. The FFR accepted Kumaonis into its battalions to fill up the spaces created by the drop in Dogras and Jat Sikhs.[165] Officers from various units noted that recruits from the new classes performed as well as the pre-war classes already serving in the battalions.[166] The battlefield performances of the Indian Army in North and East Africa, Italy, Iraq, and Burma, previously described, demonstrate the ability of battalions and classes to mesh and perform as cohesive units.

The new classes also provided significant numbers of men and officers for the supporting combat and non-combat services. Failure to expand recruitment would have resulted in a shortage of supplies for the forward units, brought on by a shortage of troops in the Indian Army Services Corps. The supporting services provided by the engineers and artillery paid huge dividends for the army during operations in North and East Africa, Italy, and Burma.

Indianisation

With the expansion of the Indian Army in April/May 1940, Indianisation of the officer corps took on a new importance, since the army would need

[161] Author's interview with Maj. A. Delafield, 2/13th FFRifles, 23 Jan. 2001.
[162] Author's interview with Capt. J. R. Wallis, 2 Feb. 2000.
[163] Army Reorganisation Committee (henceforth Willcox Report), Part II, L/WS/1/1030, OIOC, BL.
[164] Author's interview with Capt. Hank Howlett, 31 May 2001.
[165] Willcox Report, Part II, L/WS/1/1030, OIOC, BL.
[166] Author's interviews with officers of the 1st Punjab, Baluch, FFR, FFRifles, and Probyn's.

more officers to make up the war establishment.[167] By 1945, there were 7,546 Indian officers in the combat arms of the Indian Army. Counting the non-combat arms, the number was closer to 13,000 officers. The total, British and Indian, for the Indian Army, including all arms and services, was close to 40,000 officers. Indian officers in the combat arms represented 25% of the number, compared with 10% in 1939.[168]

In *Nationalisation of the Indian Army*, Lt Col Gautum Sharma draws several conclusions at the end of his chapter on Indianisation during the war, most of which are oversimplifications of what actually occurred during the period. He claims that 'discrimination was practised on a liberal scale during the war against the Emergency Indian Commissioned Officers (EICOs) by the British Emergency Commissioned Officers (ECOs)'. He asserts that there were instances 'when the son of a British tailor or shoe-maker was considered superior and better for the grant of a King's commission than an Indian even of the martial classes'.[169] While there were indisputably instances of discrimination, my research indicates that by 1945 they were practised by only a small minority of British officers. Evidence compiled in interviewing officers for *Phoenix from the Ashes* and this book presents a somewhat different picture from that given by Sharma.[170]

Many Indian officers felt that there were three important changes which brought about the transformation of opinion.[171] First, the vast majority of ECOs came from the UK, and so had no preconceived notions about what relations between Indian officers and Britons should be. Moreover, most knew nothing of the pre-war Indianised system, so did not consider the idea of serving with or under the command of Indians as foreign or unacceptable. Second, by 1943 Indians and EICOs had proven themselves in battle alongside their British counterparts, and this was widely acknowledged and commended. Third, during

---

[167] In cavalry units, the establishment was doubled. The British and Indian officers (ECOs and EICOs) would command troops. In infantry battalions the numbers also doubled; extra officers were not platoon leaders but extra company officers. VCOs remained in all units.

[168] Prasad, *Official History: Expansion*, p. 182, and Lt Col Gautum Sharma, *Nationalisation of the Indian Army* (New Delhi: Allied Publishers, 1996), p. 194.

[169] Sharma, *Nationalisation of the Indian Army*, p. 196.

[170] The perspective that these officers present is supported by the fact that UK officers have continued to maintain contact with their Indian counterparts since 1945. British and Indian/Pakistani regimental associations do likewise. It was this close relationship that enabled me to meet with so many Indian officers and visit regiments in both India and Pakistan; in most cases, it was British officers and associations who provided introductions to their colleagues.

[171] Author's interviews and correspondence with retired Indian officers, 1999–2009.

Auchinleck's second tenure as commander-in-chief, many ECOs and regular officers looked to him as a leader and shared his views.[172] Many Indian officers, from both the pre-war and war years, expressed the opinion that it was the CO who set the tone, either negative or positive, within the regiment or battalion. It appears that a majority of COs sought to emulate Auchinleck, and as a result a majority of units accepted Indianisation.[173]

The process of change

In 1939 there were 577 Indian officers serving in the Indian Army.[174] As early as 22 September of that year, Army Headquarters in India contacted London about the possible need to expand the Indian officer corps, noting that many Indians had asked to join up as officers but that under current conditions they were barred from doing so. The Army Headquarters had been contemplating Emergency Commissions for Indians,[175] but it is unclear who in the headquarters actually began the process of expanding the Indian officer corps. Auchinleck was still the deputy chief of the General Staff when war broke out. His relationship with the then commander-in-chief, Gen. Sir Robert Cassels, was very good. Cassels may have shared Auchinleck's views[176] or eventually been swayed by him when the need presented itself with the outbreak of war. However, there are no records in the British Library or the University of Manchester that specifically state that he was the main instrument of the change. Also, Auchinleck was posted to the UK and European fronts in early 1940 for several months when some of the major changes began to occur. However, the secretary of state for India, Leo Amery, specifically stated in his diary entry of 19 June 1940, 'He [Auchinleck] is keen on general Indianisation in the Indian

---

[172] See comments by C. A. Bayly and Harper in *Forgotten Armies*, p. 74.

[173] I have interviewed more than 200 officers since 1999 and this was the majority sentiment that came across.

[174] There were 274 Hindus, 138 Muslims, 75 Sikhs, and 70 others: Sharma, *Nationalisation of the Indian Army*, p. 174.

[175] A series of letters in late 1939 and early 1940: Emergency Commissions for Indians, L/MIL/7/19157, OIOC, BL.

[176] Auchinleck took a keen interest during the pre-war years in the careers of some of the ICOs. He persuaded his Indian friends to have their sons join up as officers, notably in two instances. Maj. Gen. D. K. Palit's father served with Auchinleck as the Indian Medical Officer of the 1/1st Punjab. Auchinleck was present at the selection board for D. K. Palit in the 1930s. He sat in the back of the room (author's interview with Maj. Gen. Palit, 4 Nov. 2000). During the first years of the war he influenced his old *munshi* (language teacher) to have his son Ibrahim Quereshi join as an ECIO in the 1st Punjab Regiment (author's interview with Brig. Quereshi, 10 Oct. 2000).

Army',[177] which gives credence to the theory that he was an instrument for change in Army Headquarters. Others in Headquarters took it upon themselves to help change the system, but Auchinleck spent most of the war attempting to destroy any barriers left in the system. The war and the need for expansion of the officer corps offered a chance to end the old system of Indianisation, and the Indian Army took the lead. When Auchinleck was commander-in-chief in 1941, and later in 1943, he made it clear that he intended to overcome any obstacles to placing Indian officers on par with their British counterparts.

A press communiqué dated 17 June 1940, sent from the Government of India Defence Department at Simla to the secretary of state for India, signalled the end to the pre-war Indianisation process. Due to expansion, the Defence Department stated that all units of the Indian Army would be opened to ICOs.[178] This communiqué meant that from then on all emergency Indian commissioned officers could be posted anywhere in the army, not just to designated pre-war Indianised battalions and regiments. The old VCO rank structure was brought back to the Indianised units affected by 'platoonisation' in the 1930s.[179] The Defence Department then tried to tackle the differences in pay for ICOs who were posted to non-Indianised units, noting that ICOs needed more money, since non-Indianised units generally had higher mess bills.[180]

Government of India staff also expressed concern about two potential problems: first, the financial side of the proposal, specifically having ICOs paid at the same rate as KCIOs. Second, they were worried that the reinstatement of the VCO rank to the Indianised units would undermine the earlier justification for installing ICOs, which was that they were needed to command platoons. Moreover, they were surprised that the whole system had been abandoned without official notification to the secretary of state for India.[181] Lt Gen. Auchinleck did, however, send a letter[182] to the secretary of state for India, Leopold Amery, in October 1940, which was very critical of the pre-war system of Indianisation. He specifically stated that 'we have been playing a losing hand from the start in this matter of Indianisation ... and held the following views for many

---

[177] John Barnes, ed., *Empire at Bay: The Leo Amery Diaries, 1929–1945* (London: Hutchinson, 1988), p. 626. He went on to say, '[Auchinleck,] who struck me as a real good fighting soldier, all for getting rid of unnecessary trimmings and creating an offensive spirit.'

[178] The official order was published as File No. B/59865/AG-1 (6) of 3 August 1940.

[179] L/MIL/7/19156, OIOC, BL.

[180] Defence Dept to Sec. of State, India, Sep. 1940, L/MIL/7/19156, OIOC, BL.

[181] Mr Turnbull to A. W. Thompson, 20 Sep. 1940, L/MIL/7/19156, OIOC, BL.

[182] He was responding to Amery's questions regarding Indianisation.

years'. He also gave it as his opinion that platoonisation was wrong, and that VCOs should command platoons within the Indianised battalions. He even raised the issue of pay discrepancies, stating that 'pay of all officers British and Indian should be the same and the present invidious distinctions should be removed'. He commented that British regulars and ECOs could be part of the expanding Indian Army 'provided they refuse to acquire the racial prejudices which have soured the whole course of Indianisation'. Finally, he stated that 'the only logical corollary is equal treatment, regardless of colour'.[183] This last statement made clear his intention that all new British emergency commissioned officers were to be posted throughout the army, with the possibility that they would be commanded by ICOs. Auchinleck was aware that his opinions were not widely shared; he made clear that his views were personal and that at the time 'they [were] far from being accepted widely in India ... [and] some may look on them as dangerous and unworkable'.[184] As units expanded, many ICOs were posted to new units where British officers might serve under them.[185]

There were teething problems during the expansion of the Indian officer corps,[186] but Commander-in-Chief Gen. Cassels and the Indian Army opened the door in the summer of 1940. It is interesting to note that Amery may have taken an interest in Auchinleck's opinions. A month after his communications with Amery, Auchinleck was appointed commander-in-chief, India,[187] for the first of two tenures, partly due to the fact that Amery believed that Auchinleck could mobilise the war effort in India.[188]

While Auchinleck was commander-in-chief in 1941, the order ending the old Indianised system was formally listed.[189] The last group of regular ICOs graduated in June 1941, and the Indian Military Academy, Dehra Dun, was re-opened as an 'emergency' Officer Training School (OTS), initially for Indian cadets. Auchinleck, as CinC, tried to deal with

---

[183] Auchinleck to Amery, 12 Oct. 1940, L/MIL/7/19156, OIOC, BL.   [184] *Ibid.*

[185] In the 4/12th FFR, Captain S. H. J. F. Manekshaw was the commander of A Company with various British ECOs junior to him. He went on to win the Military Cross during the campaign: 29 Jan. 1942, War Diary, WO 172/932, NA. The 7/10th Baluch provides a further two examples: Capt. Siri Kanth Korla, commander of C Company, was awarded the DSO during the campaign. The second-in-command of the 7/10th Baluch was an Anglo-Indian named Maj. Dunn: Jan. 1942, War Diary, WO 172/928, NA.

[186] The issues of the power of punishment of British personnel would not be resolved until early 1943.

[187] 21 Nov. 1940.

[188] Philip Warner, *Auchinleck: The Lonely Soldier* (London: Buchan & Enright, 1981), p. 70; see also letters of Amery to Linlithgow, 4 Dec. 1942, *TOP*, III, 251, pp. 340–5, and 351, p. 516.

[189] Army Instruction (India) No. 76 of 1941, L/MIL/17/5/531, OIOC, BL.

the differences of pay of Indian and British officers within the first few months of his taking command. In a letter to Amery he stated:

I am not happy about our system for the recruitment of Indians for Emergency Commissions. We are getting some good stuff but I feel we are losing many of the best of them. I have this in hand of one thing I am quite sure we can no longer differentiate between Englishmen and Indians in the matter of pay . . . when both are doing the same job side by side. There are many anomalies which need adjusting and I am hoping to be able to do this.[190]

Officer cadets had been coming out from the UK to take up positions in the Indian Army; however, Auchinleck did not want to see the numbers of British Emergency Commissions stay high while the numbers of Indians dropped. Further on in the letter to Amery, Auchinleck went on to say that while good officer material was coming out from the UK, 'all the same we must at our end see that we get an adequate supply of Indians both as regards quantity and quality'.[191] By the end of 1941, the ratio of Indian officers to British officers had risen by 4 percentage points,[192] an upward trend that continued throughout the war.[193] The training time given to ECOs, both British and Indian, was drastically shortened from the normal schedule as a result of war-time expansion. Regular pre-war British commissioned officers received eighteen months' training at Sandhurst and pre-war ICOs thirty months at Dehra Dun. Both then received a year's further training in a battalion before being posted to take up their own commissions. In war-time circumstances, ECOs, both British and Indian, received only four to six months of tactical training at the various OTSs set up in India.[194] Then, when an officer was posted to a battalion or regiment, his instruction continued, at least in theory.

Shortening the training time also affected the way that officers, both British and Indian, generally learned Urdu, the language of the army.[195]

---

[190] Auchinleck to Amery, 17 Mar. 1941, Auchinleck Papers, University of Manchester.
[191] *Ibid.*
[192] In 1940 it was 25%–75%. By 1941 it had risen to 29%–71%: Sharma, *Nationalisation of the Indian Army*, p. 180.
[193] There were some within the Indian Army as well as the British government who did not want to see the numbers of British cadets dry up. Other senior Indian Army officers, such as Auchinleck, Savory, and Maj. Gen. Punch Cowan, supported dismantling the pre-war model.
[194] OTSs Mhow, Bangalore, and Belgaum. The IMA was opened for Indian emergency commissions on 19 June 1941 after the last regular commissions ended their term: author's interview with Brig. Mehta, 30 Oct. 2000.
[195] Except in Gurkha units, where the language of command was Gurkhali. Officers joining Gurkha units had to learn Urdu first and then were instructed in Gurkhali. ECOs joining Gurkha units were further hampered by a lack of formal instruction in Gurkhali. Regardless of this, officers were expected to learn it quickly and through the period of

All verbal commands to the VCOs and men were traditionally given in Urdu, and pre-war instruction for officers encompassed a year's training with a personal *munshi*, or language teacher. At the end of this time, the officer was expected to pass an exam in Urdu and receive his certificate. War-time conditions meant that the instruction was seriously curtailed, which in practice meant that, at least at first, neither British nor Indian officers had sufficient knowledge of the language of command to give orders and caused many issues in the opening stages of the Second World War, especially in the Far East.

The pre-war Indianisation process officially came to an end in 1941 with Army Instruction (I) No. 76.[196] Of course this did not mean that prejudices disappeared overnight among officers, and the important question is when and how the prejudices were for the most part eradicated.[197] From January 1940, all Indian and British officer candidates who joined the Indian Army were ECOs.[198] The first batch of EICOs was sent to Dehra Dun for a shortened emergency commission course, while an OTS was set up at Belgaum to accept British cadets only. By summer 1940 two more OTS units were set up at Bangalore (British) and Mhow (Indian/British). During this early period, many British cadets and other ranks were sought for commissions, and by January 1941, the ratio of British to Indian officers had risen from 10:1 to 12:1. The trend peaked there, however: from 1941 on, the numbers of British cadets dropped significantly, while the numbers of Indian cadets rose.[199]

commanding troops: author's interviews with British officers of the 4/4th and 4/8th Gurkha Battalions.

[196] It had been provisionally ended the previous year with File No. B/59865/AG-1 (6) of 3 August 1940.

[197] Some Indian officers felt that there were British officers in Gurkha units who still felt superior to Indian officers because they did not have any Indian officers in their units. When I interviewed officers from the 4/4th and 4/8th Gurkhas, they did not express this feeling. They did note, however, that they came into contact with few Indian officers, since the Burma campaign was mostly very small unit fighting. The one prejudice that all officers, British and Indian, did express was that they considered the class of soldier that they commanded – Pathan, PM, Dogra, Madrassi, or Gurkha, etc. – to be the best soldiers in the Indian Army.

[198] As with pre-war Indian cadets, these came from both martial and non-martial race backgrounds. There tended not to be distinctions made regarding the Indian cadets' background. British cadets also represented many different classes of their society, including NCOs promoted to the officer ranks. Some British cadets felt that they would not have been welcomed by the pre-war Indian Army officer class, as they came from working- or lower middle-class backgrounds.

[199] There are a few reasons for this. First, the British Army, both at home and abroad, also needed to fill officer positions. A programme was begun to recruit NCOs from British battalions in India, but this was a failure and was admitted as such by the War Office. Another effort was launched to attract 'white' cadets from the Commonwealth, but demand in their home countries limited these as well. Americans were also sought from

By January 1945, the rate was 4.2 British officers for every 1 Indian officer throughout the Indian Army.[200] By 1945, there were 36,438 British officers and 15,747 Indian officers (including medical officers).[201] Additionally, by the end of the war, all of the OTSs, except Bangalore, were accepting both British and Indian cadets, including the IMA. Mixing training companies of Indian and British officer cadets had been happening since 1943, and many of the officers who participated in this, both Indian and British, felt that this integration had helped to break down any remaining barriers.[202]

A pamphlet listed as 'Lectures for Officers Joining the Indian Army', intended for British officers from the UK joining the Indian Army, was published in 1942. The pamphlet discusses the various fighting 'classes' targeted for recruitment into the army, including the new ones, and makes clear that there were already ICOs in the Indian Army. Old designations, such as KCIO and ICO, were to be done away with. All officers were to be classified as BOs, British officers. The pamphlet stresses that the British must 'get to know' their fellow Indian officers and 'pull together', and points out that, in an expansion, there will be good and bad officers, both Indian and British. The author, a brigadier, stressed the equality of all officers by commenting, '[as for] one of my ICOs I could not wish for a better leader British or Indian'.[203] Another pamphlet, 'Notes for Guidance of Commanding Officers, Staff and Regimental Officers', published in January 1943, also highlighted an important point regarding Indian officers. It still divided the Indian officers into KCIOs, ICOs, and VCOs. In discussing ICOs, which included the emergency Indian commissioned officers, it stated that 'they wear the same badges of ranks as British officer

---

the American Field Service Corps. These efforts netted twenty to thirty Americans: author's interviews with three 'American' Indian Army officers, Scott Gilmore, 4/8th Gurkhas, 22 Jul. 1999; Pat Pattullo, 13th FFRifles, 26 Jul. 1999; and Wendell Nichols, 18th Garhwal Rifles, 18 Jul. 1999. It became clear that Indians were needed to fill the spots: L/WS/1/799, OIOC, BL.

[200] Prasad, *Official History: Expansion*, pp. 181–2, and Sharma, *Nationalisation of the Indian Army*, pp. 183–4. However, by 1945 there were problems attracting enough Indian officers of 'sufficient quality'. (There were also problems attracting British officers of 'sufficient quality'.) This was an issue that Auchinleck felt was going to create major headaches unless confronted: Secret Telegram from Viceroy to Sec. of State for India, 21 Dec. 1944, L/WS/1/799, OIOC, BL.

[201] Telegram from India Command to the War Office London, 1 May 1945, L/WS/1/707, OIOC, BL.

[202] Some officers noted that many of the participants mixed socially, at the OTSs and during leave periods as well. Some British officers spent time at the family homes of Indian officers: author's interviews with officers, 1999–2009.

[203] L/MIL/17/5/2225, OIOC, BL.

and should be treated in exactly the same way'.[204] While information was disseminated to new British officers, there were still some issues with officers who did not want to serve in India; however, for many officers their primary motivation was the belief that they were needed to fight in Europe and did not want to miss the 'show'.[205] This is why the findings of the Infantry Committee later in the year were so important.[206]

Expansion of the Indian Army and Indianisation of the officer corps raised organisational as well as racial issues. Two of these were rates of pay for Indian officers and powers of punishment over British soldiers. The principal grievance raised by Indian officers was that they had traditionally not been paid at the same rate as British officers. This discrepancy was eliminated for the most part early in 1942, when pay for all regular commissioned officers and ECOs was standardised.[207] This was a step in the right direction, but one inequality remained: British personnel serving overseas were eligible for bonus pay. This issue was not resolved until April 1945, but Auchinleck, as commander-in-chief, was able to alter the rates of pay to mitigate this imbalance.[208] The Indian CO of the 1st Bihar Regiment wrote to Auchinleck to thank him for his conscientiousness:

I know who is behind all these moves ... and the ICOs thank you for your kindness you have showed them during your command ... [I]t seems that the welfare of the ICOs is constantly in your mind ... [Y]ou have removed the last worry for the ICOs and the many conscientious British Officers ... [I] thank you for all this and all you have done for us.[209]

Power of punishment over British soldiers at this time was a more controversial issue, for obvious reasons.[210] Once the war had begun, Indians were given equal command rights but were denied 'powers of punishment' as outlined in paragraph 193 of the King's Regulations,

---

[204] L/MIL/17/5/2330, OIOC, BL.

[205] Author's interviews with British officers, 1999–2009; and see also Adjutant General in India's Committee on Morale, Report of the Fourth Meeting, 15 Jul.–15 Oct. 1943, L/WS/2/71, OIOC, BL, for more detail as well as Kaushik Roy, 'Military Loyalty in the Colonial Context: A Case Study of the Indian Army During World War II', *Journal of Military History*, 73 (Apr. 2009), p. 510.

[206] See below, pp. 69–70.

[207] Sharma, *Nationalisation of the Indian Army*, pp. 176–7.

[208] See Wavell to Amery, 19 Oct. 1944, *TOP*, V, 57, 100, p. 210, n. 1; 120, p. 254; 134, p. 270, for earlier discussion of the pay issues.

[209] Indian CO of 1st Bihar Regiment to Auchinleck, 13 Apr. 1945, Auchinleck Papers, University of Manchester.

[210] The central question was whether an Indian officer could sit on a court martial and pass judgement on an accused British soldier.

1940.[211] This issue was not confronted until 1942[212] when the Right Honourable Leo Amery, representing the Government of India, stated in a letter that Indian officers should be allowed to sit on courts martial of British soldiers. The Government of India felt that to do otherwise was detrimental to the morale of Indian officers.[213] Both the viceroy, Lord Linlithgow, and the commander-in-chief, India, Gen. Sir Archibald Wavell, shared this view. The letter was sent to the secretary of state for war in London requesting an appropriate resolution of this question. A response, sent in early July 1942, clearly illustrates the British government's opinion. The letter stated unequivocally 'that ICOs should not have power of punishment over white men', commenting that 'Gandhi is on the verge of breaking out again.' The absurdity of this statement is magnified by the further assertion that 'while India Command agree with making it easier I expect their predecessors were saying the same kind of thing on the eve of the [Indian] Mutiny'.[214] Amery stated to Linthligow, 'Winston at Cabinet last night supremely unreasonable. Says demand for power of punishment just sop to please your executive and publicise further appeasement in India, last humiliation to poor British soldier, etc.'[215] These letters made their way to the Army Council, London, in August 1942, commenting that 'events in Malaya and Burma [defeats] have undoubtedly seriously affected the prestige of the white man in the east and we do not want to do anything that will make matters worse'.[216] This debate – and the responses from London – clearly demonstrates the limited understanding of the Indian Army on the part of His Majesty's Government (HMG), and was later to play a role in the post-war period, when decisions were made regarding the Indian Army without any context and awareness of the force.

---

[211] Powers of Punishment, WO 172/10685, NA.

[212] Part of the reasoning for this might have been that GHQ India failed to recognise the immediate likelihood of Indian officers being in the position of commanding British personnel. This did not happen in the cavalry, infantry, or artillery but in other services such as Signals and Engineering. A case of an Indian Officer in Signals in the Middle East was brought forward as an example of the need to deal with the problem. Another reason may have been that GHQ India was receiving reports of the beginnings of the Indian National Army by May 1942. They may have recognised that this last vestige of pre-war Indianisation must be eradicated. See WO 172/10685 and L/MIL/7/19158, OIOC, BL.

[213] L/MIL/7/19158, OIOC, BL.

[214] Sec. of State for War, London, to Rt Hon. Amery, MP, 13 Jul. 1942, L/MIL/7/19158, OIOC, BL. There were those in GHQ India who shared London's views. A secret document, published in February 1942, declares that a British officer is the surest guardian against any soldier unrest: L/WS/1/456, OIOC, BL.

[215] Amery to Linlithgow, *TOP*, II, 350, p. 480.   [216] WO 172/10685, NA.

Amery drafted further letters, with the support of Wavell and Linlithgow, stating that he did not understand the reasoning behind the refusal, as Indian officers had been deemed capable of exercising powers of command. The replies that he received stated only that 'while we might ultimately have to concede the power of punishment to Indian officers it would be most inexpedient to make this concession at the present time'.[217] The British government maintained this position for another six months, but the issue was formally resolved by Indian Army Orders 237–8, January 1943,[218] followed by an official communiqué on 5 June 1943 stating that Indian officers were to have powers of punishment over British Army personnel.[219] The official communiqué stressed that

it would be a poor response to the magnificent achievements of Indian officers and men in this war if we were to delay ... in according these powers ... [A]n Indian officer who is felt able to exercise command is obviously to be trusted to exercise powers of punishment and if he is deprived of such powers just because he is an Indian, not only will it have a bad effect on his morale but may cause issues with the men.[220]

Necessity was initially the prime motivation for the rapid expansion of the Indian officer corps. When Auchinleck returned for his second stint as commander-in-chief of the Indian Army in the summer of 1943, he took on the role of champion of the abilities of the Indian officers and their capacity for command. Auchinleck had inherited an army that had been soundly defeated in two campaigns in Burma as well as Malaya. The report produced by the Infantry Committee, India, in June 1943 also considered the calibre of officers serving in the Indian Army, noting that leadership in the Indian battalions left much to be desired, and that both British and Indian officers were lacking in this respect.[221] Reports had come in that some British officers were complaining about serving in India, and the recommendation was to ship these men home as soon as possible, as the need for their physical presence was outweighed by the

---

[217] Extracts from War Cabinet Conclusions, Jul.–Aug. 1942, L/MIL/7/19158, OIOC, BL; see also Amery to Linthligow, 1/9/42, TOP, II, 673, pp. 874–8, for more detail.

[218] Paragraph 193 of the 1940 regulations was deleted and rephrased to include powers of punishment: WO 172/10685, NA.

[219] It was resolved when the Military Department in London finally recognised the need for the change, and significantly after the Quit India movement had been decisively suppressed in the autumn of 1942.

[220] Sec. of State, Military Department, India, 5 Jun. 1943, L/MIL/7/19158, OIOC, BL.

[221] This was the same report that recommended the formation of the training divisions and tactical reforms for the Indian Army. It also included a section on morale which dealt with officers: L/WS/1/1371, OIOC, BL.

demoralising effect of their negative attitude. The report also made reference to what were apparently unresolved issues between Indian and British officers, stressing that 'no discrimination must be allowed' by or among officers.[222]

In July 1943, Gen. G. N. Molesworth was tasked with answering a series of questions drawn up by the India Office, London, concerning the Indian Army, particularly the Indianisation process up to that point.[223] Although there is no proof, it is very likely that Auchinleck had prior knowledge of Molesworth's answers, which endorsed views that he himself had expressed earlier in the war. The document firmly states that: 'the pre-war system amounted to segregation . . . [I]t was so segregated to ensure the Indians would not command British officers . . . [T]here is a school of thought in which I include myself which considers the segregation policy a mistake.'[224] It goes on to say that, at the time of writing, Indians were in command of British officers and no significant problems had been reported.

Gen. Auchinleck brought Lt Col (later Maj. Gen.) Rudra to GHQ India in the autumn of 1943, in part to 'keep in touch with promotions and appointments for Indian officers'. Auchinleck had heard reports that Indian officers believed they were being denied access to higher command.[225] In August 1943 there were ninety-seven Indian lieutenant colonels, of which only six were in command of fighting units. The vast majority were in the Indian Medical Services, with a few in staff positions. There were six lieutenant colonels at General Staff Officer (GSO) (Grade) 1 level, nine majors at GSO 2, and three captains at GSO 3,[226] so obviously Indian officers were under-represented at high levels of command at this juncture. However, the casualty rates of 1940–3 were not that high, so many COs had not been replaced and one cannot rapidly promote officers who have not been trained and educated for their positions. This would happen later, in 1944 and 1945, and as a result more Indians took command at the company, battalion, and even

---

[222] The rest of the report considered other, more specific problems. One issue raised was that the war in Burma required younger and fitter COs to command battalions. The committee recommended, as a general rule, that commanding officers should be replaced after two years' service, as remaining with any one battalion for too long made them stale. In reality, most COs did not spend this long with their units. The officers were either promoted or sent to other units, and probably did not have the opportunity to become stale: L/WS/1/1371, OIOC, BL.

[223] This was the basis of a report that was to be sent to the US government to provide background information on the Indian Army.

[224] 9 Jul. 1943, L/WS/1/1366, OIOC, BL.   [225] Palit, *Rudra*, pp. 269–72.

[226] Sharma, *Nationalisation of the Indian Army*, p. 180.

brigade levels. Nevertheless, Rudra stated that Auchinleck 'was determined to do something to redress the grievances'.[227]

The numbers of Indian COs of regiments and battalions had risen by 1945, and three Indian brigadiers had been rewarded for their service with the Distinguished Service Order (DSO). This was not good enough for some supporters of independence, but it demonstrates how hard Auchinleck had pushed to get many officers promoted.[228] Lt Col Gautum Sharma notes, in his conclusion to *Nationalisation of the Indian Army*, that 'in spite of the changed scenario during the war, Indian officers were given command most reluctantly'.[229] This is partially true, but it fails to consider the whole picture, and particularly to recognise Auchinleck's efforts from mid 1943 through the end of the war.[230]

In December 1944, Auchinleck clearly stated his intentions for the future of the Indian Army:

I propose as a principle that the three services [Indian Army, Air Force, and Navy] after the war shall be officered entirely by Indian officers so far as this is possible and that the number of European officers shall be limited to that required to fill positions which cannot be held by Indians owing to their lack of experience or training.[231]

Auchinleck's intent in formulating this proposal was partially to determine the post-war demand for British personnel. By the end of 1944 there were only a handful of Indians capable of brigade-level commands.

---

[227] Palit, *Rudra*, p. 274. One example of the continued persistence of discrimination that existed in some places also shows the efforts of some senior commanders to stamp it out. It involves Captain M. Nair, who had been serving with the 16th Light Cavalry. When he was posted to Fourteenth Army HQ as GSO 3, the staff was expecting an Irishman after hearing his name and his accent when he spoke on the phone. Captain Nair was not Irish but an Indian, and his arrival astonished the HQ, which promptly sent him back to Delhi with excuses. Upon hearing of these, Auchinleck immediately signalled Gen. Slim, who had not been present, to register his complaint about such behaviour. Slim agreed with Auchinleck and immediately advised all units and formations within the Fourteenth Army that this type of incident would not be tolerated again. See Palit, *Rudra*, pp. 279–84.

[228] Auchinleck personally promoted Lt Col M. R. Dutt to command the 7/10th Baluch in the 1945 campaigns. The battalion's officers objected to this decision, not because Dutt was Indian but because they preferred that Maj. Korla (also Indian) should be in command: author's interviews with officers of the 7th Baluch. Auchinleck also posted Maj. Sher Ali Khan from 7th Light Cavalry to his old battalion, the 1/1st Punjab. Sher Ali took over command of the battalion during the 1945 campaign.

[229] Sharma, *Nationalisation of the Indian Army*, p. 196.

[230] As noted in a letter previously described, from the Indian CO of the 1st Bihar Regiment, Auchinleck was different from his predecessors. This sentiment was reiterated by more than fifty retired Indian/Pakistani officers, who felt that Auchinleck was very perceptive and did as much as was humanly possible to redress past imbalances.

[231] Auchinleck to Wavell, 19 Dec. 1944, L/WS/1/924, OIOC, BL.

It was improbable to believe that senior Indian officers would be able to hold command positions at the division or corps level by the end of 1945, due to natural wastage and the need for proper training and education for senior command. Officers, both British and Indian, would not be promoted without the necessary battlefield experience and attendance at Staff College. Auchinleck had set the system in motion: one need only look at the attendance figures at the Staff College at Quetta to see this.

Attendance at Quetta was the precursor to higher command positions during the pre-war and war periods, and during Auchinleck's tenure the admission of Indian officers increased significantly. The Staff College class of 1940 at Quetta listed sixty-two officers, of whom four were Indian. The staff of this period included eleven instructors, of whom none was Indian.[232] The last time that students were listed by name at the Staff College was January 1942; in this class, there were 140 officers, of whom 21 were Indians. The staff of twenty-three instructors included only one Indian.[233] For the remainder of the war, students were not listed, only instructors. The 1944 list showed twenty-five instructors, including three Indian officers,[234] indicating a slow but steady trend.

Lt Gen Candeth was a student at Quetta in 1944. He noted that, of the 140 students, nearly 30 per cent were Indian officers. He also commented that relations among staff and Indian and British officers were very cordial. He felt that this was attributable to two factors: first, Indian officers had proven themselves in the field; and, second, Auchinleck firmly supported Indian officers. This attitude filtered down to all levels.[235] Brig. R. B. Chopra, a graduate of the class of 1945 Staff College, mentioned that five of the forty instructors were Indian. His class numbered some 180 officers, of whom nearly 40 were Indian. He agreed with Lt Gen. Candeth's comment that relations were good between officers and instructors, regardless of ethnicity.[236]

The trend outlasted the end of the war. The first peace-time Staff College course at Quetta was set for 1947. The number of students was established at 200, of which 62 were Indian officers. Additionally, another nine Indian officers were selected to complete the course at the British Army Staff College, Camberley. Auchinleck was still the commander-in-chief of the Indian Army when these plans were made.[237]

---

[232] *Indian Army List*, 1940.   [233] *Indian Army List*, 1942.
[234] *Indian Army List*, 1944.
[235] Author's interview with Lt Gen. Candeth, 29 Oct. 2000.
[236] Author's interview with Brig. Chopra, 22 Oct. 2000.
[237] L/WS/1/824, OIOC, BL.

Wider spectrum of Indianisation

Due to the bottom-up process of Indianisation, I have found that the best source of information for assessing the impact of the changes is the series of interviews that I have conducted over the last ten years. Data from these interviews, with officers who served at the battalion level and below, were at the heart of my first work focusing on the Indian Army in the Burma campaign, *Phoenix from the Ashes*.[238] Later interviews expanded to veterans of other Second World War campaigns, to broaden the scope of the research picture. This section incorporates information from interviews with Indian officers to ascertain whether the feelings and attitudes they experienced are consistent with those presented here.

In the autumn of 1944, Leo Amery went on a tour visiting with Indian Army units and formations in Italy. In the course of his visits, he observed in his diary that: 'relations everywhere between British and Indian officers seem natural and happy and there is great comradeship'.[239]

Brig. H. N. Shingal of the 9/13th FFRifles went to OTS Bangalore and was part of a mixed company of British and Indian cadets. In his opinion, most of the men related well. He felt that issues arose among officers, whether at OTS or at the regiment, only as a result of personality, not ethnic, conflicts.[240] Brig. C. S. Mehta and Mr P. L. Roy joined the army together, and both felt that the regular officers seemed aloof when they first arrived at the 2nd Punjab Regimental Centre in 1942. Brig. Mehta pointed out that this aloofness extended to the new British ECO arrivals as well. Both men felt that early in the war there was a 'regular' versus ECO rivalry among the officers, rather than any racial division.[241] Brig. Mehta did comment that he felt that his CO was suspicious of him when he was posted to an active battalion in late 1942 during the height of the Quit India movement. He perceived that this disappeared as the war continued, and overall he had good relations with most of the British

---

[238] Space considerations prevent the listing of officers of other regiments; names of all the British and Indian officers interviewed are listed in the Bibliography. Many British officers felt that, by the end of the war, instances of ethnic prejudice in their units had decreased considerably. Some did note that there was still an 'old guard' in existence at the Regimental Centres, but their view was gradually overshadowed by the performance of Indians at the front. Significant statements from British officers included the following: 'he [Indian company commander] was greatly respected by all the British officers' – correspondence with Maj. R. Schlaefli; 'he [Lt Col Sher Ali Khan, 1/1st Punjab] was popular and efficient ... excellent relationships [with Indian officers]' (author's correspondence with Maj. D. H. Pailthorpe).

[239] Barnes, ed., *Empire at Bay*, p. 1000.

[240] Author's interview with Brig. C. S. Shingal, 21 Oct. 2000.

[241] Author's interviews with Mr P. L. Roy, 25 Nov. 1999, and Brig. Mehta, 30 Oct. 2000.

officers with whom he came into contact.[242] Maj. Gen. A. K. Luthera of the 1/1st Punjab, an EICO, found relations in his battalion very good, including those with his CO, Maj. Gen. Grimshaw, who was a pre-war regular.[243] Brig. Gupta also joined the 1/1st Punjab.[244] Both men felt that as the war progressed the attitudes shifted more and more in favour of Indian officers.[245]

The Indian officers who were part of the pre-war Indianised process – Lt Gen. Candeth, Lt Gen. Katoch, Maj. Gen. Palit, and Brig. Chopra – all noted that relationships among officers progressed well beyond expectations. They all felt that this was due both to the open-mindedness of the British ECOs and to the reform-minded regular officers, especially Auchinleck.[246] All of the Indian and British officers interviewed expressed their admiration for Auchinleck and for all that he did for Indian officers during the war.

The popular image is that there must have been some sort of friction between British and Indian officers, but according to the survivors of some of the units this was not really the case, especially after 1943.[247] Some may say that time and age have mellowed memories, or that the fact that these men fought and died together may have overshadowed any prejudices either group might have had. There was a commonly held opinion that the views of the old guard persisted at the regimental centres,[248] which is not surprising since most of the staff would not have the bond of active service. As documented in many previous conflicts, the shared experience of the battlefield tends to break down prejudices that may exist in peace-time or in barracks.[249]

---

[242] Author's interview with Brig. Mehta, 30 Oct. 2000.

[243] Author's interview with Maj. Gen. A. K. Luthera, 28 Oct. 2000.

[244] Author's interview with Brig. Gupta, 27 Oct. 2000.

[245] This observation was reiterated in interviews with Brig. Chatterji, 10th Baluch, 24 Oct. 2000, Brig. Lachiman Singh, Indian Engineers, and Maj. Gen. Sinha, 50th Parachute Brigade, 26 Oct. 2000.

[246] Author's interviews with Lt Gen. Candeth, 29 Oct. 2000, Lt Gen. Katoch, 4 Nov. 2000, Maj. Gen. Palit, 3 Nov. 2000, and Brig. Chopra, 22 Oct. 2000.

[247] See Marston, *Phoenix*, for a detailed discussion of the Indianisation process at the battalion and regimental level.

[248] By 1943, the 13th FFRifles' regimental centre at Abbottabad appeared to be experiencing less controversy concerning Indian officers. Capt. Hank Howlett served on staff at the centre from 1943 to 1946. He noted that, when he arrived, there were some senior Indian officers. Many had served overseas and a few had been decorated. He served under the command of Maj. (later Lt Gen.) K. S. Katoch. Capt. Howlett, as an ECO, had no concerns about serving under Maj. Katoch's command, considering him a 'top-class officer': author's interview with Capt. Howlett, 31 May 2001.

[249] This was not true just for the Indian Army; it also occurred with black American troops in the Second World War and the Korean War, as well as with African and European soldiers in the 'bush wars' of the 1970s and 1980s.

End of the beginning: Indianisation

In the spring of 1945,[250] Auchinleck, Wavell, and Amery began the process of full Indianisation of the Indian Army.[251] Anticipating that either Dominion status or outright independence was imminent for India, the three men agreed on the need for planning ahead. In one of the first memoranda written on this topic, Wavell outlined three areas of focus: first, the need to maintain the efficiency of the army during whatever transition period would be necessary; second, the need to convince Indian political leaders and the population that the intent was ultimately to hand over full control of the Indian Army to them; and, third, the need to safeguard the interests of British officers who would remain during the interim period.

To attain these goals it was understood that many EICOs would need to be offered regular commissions. The Government of India began the final process of Indianisation with this document.[252] Further deliberations continued; members of the War Cabinet (as well as others) were aware that British officers would need to remain in some positions, especially at the highest levels, due to the lack of Indian officers at and above the brigadier rank. It was estimated that it would take a decade for the Indian Army to educate and train enough senior Indian officers to take over the higher levels of command from British officers, and twenty years for complete Indianisation to occur.[253] By early April, Amery and Auchinleck were moving to end the entry of any British officers to the

---

[250] Auchinleck ordered a committee to report on the future size and needs of the Indian Army in early 1945. It was named the Army in India Reorganisation Committee (Willcox Committee). The section dealing with the future size of the officer corps was largely drafted by Brig. Enoch Powell (later the Rt Hon. Enoch Powell, who gave the infamous 'rivers of blood' speech in 1968). It stated that, considering future needs and problems with recruitment of Indian officers, the Indian Army would need to recruit British officers for the next twenty-five years. The secretary of the Chiefs of Staff Committee, India, Philip Mason noted that Powell had based this conclusion on certain axioms, completely failing to recognise the human aspect and reality of the political situation in India in 1945. As Mason noted, 'Auchinleck dismissed this chapter as altogether off the mark': Mason, *A Shaft of Sunlight* (London: Andre Deutsch, 1978), pp. 197–8.

[251] See 'Future Provision of officers for the Indian Armed Services, Memo by sec of state for India', 24 Apr. 1945, *TOP*, V, 407, pp. 943–5, for clear direction for the ending of entry of British officers and the further Indianisation of the army.

[252] Wavell to Amery, 5 Mar. 1945, *TOP*, V, 297, pp. 649–56. See also 298, pp. 656–60, which highlights the initial debates, but also reinforces the notion that the army performed well during the war, even during the Quit India movement.

[253] War Cabinet, 27 Mar. 1945, *TOP*, V, 346; see pp. 775–6 for specific numbers. However, in a later memo, the time period was decreased to ten to fifteen years; see War Cabinet, 23 Apr. 1945, *TOP*, V, 405, p. 933.

army at the lowest levels.[254] This move caused much political tension for the coalition government in London. As stated by Sir J. Grigg, Secretary of State for War,

the proposal to recruit no more British officers into the Indian Army is fundamental and the more I think of it the further does it seem to lead us. As you [Amery] point out it can only be decided by the War Cabinet but surely the India Committee must consider it before we make any final recommendation to the Cabinet in regard to the Viceroy's interim political proposals.[255]

Following deliberations, the War Cabinet and the India Committee released their findings on the proposal on 25 April. They stated, in part:

The Secretary of State for War said that he was ready, if that was the general sense of the Committee, to say that in view of the pledges of the past and the way the Indians had fought in this war, he regarded as inescapable the Indianisation of the Indian Army along the lines proposed ... The Committee accepted the view of the Secretary of State for War and agreed that the report should state in [no uncertain] terms that in their view this was the inevitable and inescapable conclusion which must be announced at the same time as any political announcement.[256]

It was all formally agreed in War Cabinet on 27 April 1945, with Churchill's acquiescence.[257]

Auchinleck reinforced the trend towards complete Indianisation throughout the summer of 1945. His actions were noted during the Army Commanders Conference in 1945: 'relationships between British and Indian officers must be kept constantly in mind by Army commanders. He had laid down the policy of complete integration between the two types and COs and others (Indian as well as British) who did not do all they could to complete that policy would be removed.'[258]

Loyalty of the Indian Army

The importance of keeping the Indian Army apolitical throughout the war period is highlighted in the following quote, taken from a report of a conversation between Gen. Wavell, the viceroy, and Mohandas Gandhi on 24 June 1945:

---

[254] War Cabinet, 2 Apr. 1945, *TOP*, V, 363, pp. 805–7, paragraph 10.
[255] Sir J. Grigg to Amery, 23 Apr. 1945, *TOP*, V, 403, p. 928; see also Wavell to Amery, 26 Apr. 1945, *TOP*, V, 419, p. 975.
[256] War Cabinet, 25 Apr. 1945, *TOP*, V, 413, p. 967; see also 422, pp. 977–8.
[257] See War Cabinet, 27 Apr. 1945, *TOP*, V, 423, p. 983.
[258] L/WS/1/1523, OIOC, BL.

[Gandhi] then digressed into a long story about members of the Indian Army who had wished to see him but had been compelled to come to him by night and in mufti. I said the one thing which was disastrous for any Government was if the Army became political; that the Indian Army had a CinC [Auchinleck] in whom they had their full trust; that their reputation never stood higher and that I could assure him that the Indian Army was on the whole a thoroughly contented body. He agreed to all these statements.[259]

The political loyalty of the Indian Army during the Second World War was never threatened on a large scale, but this did not mean that individual soldiers or officers did not have political opinions or sympathies with the nationalist movement or that there were not small mutinies.[260] The traditional attractions of *esprit de corps*, family and village connections, *izzat* for some communities,[261] and a wage[262] still enticed many men to join during the war. As recruitment was expanded and new classes were accepted, many recruits flocked to the army as a way to ensure their status.[263] Many Indian men who joined as officers felt it was their duty to join to fight the fascist threat, and considered that the issue of the British presence in India could wait until the end of the war.[264] Issues of morale were noted, especially in the early campaigns, due to over-expansion of the ranks and officer corps and lack of training. This trend was reversed by 1943, as the Indian Army began to reform training and officer selection. As Tarak Barkawi stated: 'The Indian Army should have encountered some serious difficulties for cohesion and fighting spirit … yet by and large, it remained loyal and fought effectively during the war.'[265]

[259] Penderel Moon, ed., *Wavell: The Viceroy's Journal* (London: Oxford University Press, 1973), p. 145.
[260] See Callahan, 'The Indian Army, Total War'; Roy, 'Military Loyalty'; Tarak Barkawi, 'Culture and Combat in the Colonies: The Indian Army in the Second World War', *Journal of Contemporary History* 41 (2006), pp. 325–55; and Yong, *Garrison State*, pp. 282–6, for more detail.
[261] It was seen as an honour to fight, especially as viewed by some communities in northern India; this is referred to as *izzat*. See D. F. Karaka, *With the 14th Army* (Bombay: Thacker & Co., 1944), pp. 34–6.
[262] There was lack of employment in rural India throughout this period. See S. C. Aggarwal, *History of the Supply Department: 1939–1945* (New Delhi: Government Publications, 1947), and Roy, 'Military Loyalty', for more detail.
[263] Many of the officers interviewed noted the troops' lack of political sophistication when the war came to an end and thoughts turned to the future of India: author's interviews and correspondence with officers, 1999–2009. Roy also stated: 'Despite the food problem and the somewhat muted anti-Raj activities by political parties, the Indian soldiery remained loyal, and recruits continued to flow into the army between late 1943 and mid 1945' ('Military Loyalty', p. 517).
[264] See L/WS/2/71, OIOC, BL. See especially the reports dealing with November and December 1944 and January 1945 for more detail.
[265] Barkawi, 'Culture and Combat', p. 328.

There were two significant incidents of 'mutiny' or disobedience by the rank and file of some units during the early years of the war that were thought to have been influenced by political considerations.[266] Interestingly, both involved members of the traditional recruitment groups – the martial races – rather than newly recruited classes. The first incident occurred early in December 1939 and involved troops of the Royal Indian Army Service Corps (RIASC) stationed in Egypt. Thirty-four men (twenty-two Jat Sikhs, eleven PMs, and one Hindu) were arrested after refusing to be used as porters and loaders of supplies. The men were reservists called up for duty as drivers. They regarded the orders as 'coolie work' and considered being seen to do it as a loss of face. The Indian Army took the incident very seriously, and launched an investigation in both Egypt and the Punjab to track down any potential political causes for the disturbance. Three official causes were eventually given for the incident: first, that British and Indian officers were not applying themselves appropriately in their duty as officers; second, subversive propaganda; and, third, the issue raised by the soldiers themselves, the potential loss of face brought about by doing the work ordered.[267] The Kirti Lehar group was cited as the main political agitator.[268] In the end, despite the fact that a political element was considered to be part of the problem, GHQ India felt that the best way to resolve the problem was for the officers to make more of an effort to get to know their men and to perform their duties in a more professional fashion.[269]

---

[266] Another incident occurred in April 1940: an ICO from the 4/19th Hyderabad Regiment, while stationed in Singapore, wrote a letter to India that was picked up by the censors. The letter talked about the need for the Second World War to last for such a long time that it would exhaust the British Empire and make it easier for Indians to turn them out of the country. The officer in question, Lt Mohammed Zahir-ud-Din, had already been monitored by the army's intelligence section for seditious letters. The officer admitted his offence, and the authorities moved to ship him back to India to face a court martial. However, due to the 'milking' of the army that was happening at the time, officer turnover within the battalion was high, and this played a role in the unit's response: the battalion's Ahir company called for the lieutenant to be reinstated. When this failed, they protested, and were disarmed as a result; they then proceeded to go on a hunger strike. Other ICOs and KCIOs were called in by senior command to come up with a strategy, and these officers were able to meet with the strikers and convince them of the impropriety of Lt Zahir-ud-Din's actions. The company was reformed and the situation ended. See Chandar Sundaram, 'Seditious Letters and Steel Helmets: Disaffection Among Indian Troops in Singapore and Hong Kong, 1940–1941, and the Formation of the Indian National Army', in Roy, ed., *War and Society in Colonial India*, pp. 126–60.

[267] Commander-in-Chief, Egypt, to Commander-in-Chief, India, 16 Jan. 1940, L/WS/1/303, OIOC, BL.

[268] Report by J. P. Worton, Indian Police, 2 Feb. 1940, L/WS/1/303, OIOC, BL. The Kirti Lehar was a Sikh Communist organisation.

[269] Commander-in-Chief, India, to Commander-in-Chief, Egypt 13 Feb. 1940, L/WS/1/303, OIOC, BL.

Another incident concerned the Sikh squadron of the Central India Horse Regiment (CIH). In July 1940, when the regiment was ordered to embark from Bombay to Egypt, the Sikh squadron refused the order. The whole squadron was immediately removed and sent to Bolarum without incident,[270] while the rest of the regiment sailed.[271] Upon investigation, many of the same issues were uncovered as had been revealed in the RIASC case. The most important point made was that the officers were not in touch with their men and the 'state of discipline left much to be desired'.[272] Political influence was also listed as a cause of the problems. The main reason why the Kirti Lehar had gained influence was the fact that reservists had been called up to both units and thus had been exposed to the organisation's political opinions. Another point raised by GHQ India was that there appeared to be rising communal agitation over the possibility of an independent Pakistan and the partition of the Punjab. Some recruiting officers noted that able-bodied men of the Sikh, Dogra, and PM communities wished to remain with their villages in case of violence. The commander-in-chief, India, at the time, Gen. Sir Robert Cassels, recommended several changes to avoid the problem recurring. Most important, the CIH would no longer have a Sikh Squadron, and all Sikh recruits and reservists would be discharged. No more Jat Sikhs would be sent to the RIASC. Expansion of Jat Sikh recruitment to the army as a whole would be decreased, and newer classes such as Mazbhi and Ramdasia Sikhs would be sought instead.[273] The Intelligence Bureau Indian Army released a report stating that, while political agitation might contribute to incidents of insubordination, its effects could be countered with good discipline and morale.[274]

Overall political influence as a distinct factor on the behaviour of Indian Army troops and officers is harder to gauge. However, the lack of mutinies, combined with the army's documented ability to function in Aid to the Civil Power[275] against the Indian National Congress indicates

---

[270] Viceroy to Sec. of State for India, 2 Aug. 1940, L/WS/1/303, OIOC, BL.

[271] A Sikh squadron from the 19th Lancers petitioned to be sent as the replacement squadron of the CIH: Mason, *Matter of Honour*, p. 514.

[272] Viceroy to Sec. of State, India, 9 Aug. 1940, L/WS/1/303, OIOC, BL.

[273] Viceroy to Sec. of State, India, 10 Sep. 1940, L/WS/1/303, OIOC, BL.

[274] Note by Intelligence Bureau, 5 Sep. 1940, L/WS/1/303, OIOC, BL.

[275] Training in the Aid to the Civil Power during the early war years was difficult as units were expanded and shipped to other areas of the world to fight. The Indian Army still felt that this was a major role that it needed to fulfil. In 1941, it published an updated version of doctrine for the Indian Army, *MTP No. 11 (India) Notes on Training for Duties in the Aid of the Civil Power*, L/MIL/17/5/2252, OIOC, BL. It reinforced earlier doctrine: 'Army in India will be called upon in suppressing disturbances when disorder in a locality develops beyond the power of the civil police ... [T]he instructions in this

that political influence was not significant.[276] Writing on this topic in 1994, Judith Brown noted that 'despite the temporary losses of control [during the Quit India movement] the overall security of the Raj was never endangered by the movement. After its destruction the British proved capable of putting Indian politics on ice until the end of the war ... It was after the war that the loyalty of the police and troops came to be seriously doubted or displayed.'[277]

The onset of war was confusing for men and officers who may have been nationalist, since there were differing views even within the nationalist movement as to what the response to the war should be. As noted earlier, the Indian National Congress Party was not in favour of men joining the Indian Army, but there was dissension in the party ranks, as many members felt that Congress should support the war effort. Also, Congress' opposition to the war focused chiefly on the fact that the viceroy had declared war without the courtesy of first consulting the Indian nationalist parties, rather than any specific reason why India should not be involved. Gandhi wrote an article in April 1942 and later articles, after the defeats in Malaya and Burma, discussing the role of 'foreign soldiers in India' and the need for the British to Quit India. Many within the Government of India felt this was an attempt to stir things up among British, American, and Indian soldiers. It explicitly claimed that the Indian Army was maintained to hold India in subjection and called for its dissolution.[278] Such articles created problems for the Government of India. At one point in London, Leo Amery was asked by the Soviet ambassador if the Indian Army was still firm in support of the war effort. Amery responded, 'the Army was entirely indifferent to Congress and either hostile to it or contemptuous of its pretensions'.[279]

By August 1942, some army personnel were expressing suspicion about the opinions of various ICOs and KCIOs. In early August, Gandhi went on a hunger strike and the viceroy, Linlithgow, asked GHQ India

---

training pamphlet confer no new powers on military commanders. They are a mere guide as to the way in which certain operations can be carried out.'

[276] The Punjab Unionist Party, which controlled the Punjab for most of the war, supported the war effort. As Yong noted: 'Until 1945 ... the Unionist government fully backed the mobilization process, by which some 800,000 combatants were recruited from the Punjab and 250,000,000 rupees gathered through war loans' (*Garrison State*, p. 301).

[277] Brown, *Modern India*, pp. 324–5.

[278] Sir M. Hallet to Linlithgow, 4 May 1942, MSS Eur F125/110, OIOC, BL; also in *TOP*, II, p. 24; see also letter from Sir H. Twynam to Linlithgow, 25 May 1942, *TOP*, II, pp. 117–18, and Linlithgow to Amery, 15 Jun. 1942, *TOP*, II, pp. 205–6, for more details on Gandhi's rhetoric.

[279] Note by Amery, 22 Jul. 1942, *TOP*, II, 305, pp. 429–30.

for an assessment of sentiment in the army if he were to die. It was reported as follows: 'No effect on Moslem rank and file. Possibly some effect on Hindu rank and file ... [T]he broadening of the basis recruitment of officers has increased chance of definite reactions. I feel little doubt that whole of the officer class would give vent to very violent criticism [of Gandhi].'[280]

Gandhi went on another hunger strike in early 1943, and the Government of India again attempted to assess the army's feelings in the event of his death. In the same vein as the earlier intelligence reports, no major change in attitudes was anticipated; if anything, the Government of India expressed less concern about the possibility of future tension. As Wavell reported to Linlithgow,

> So far we have had no indication that the attitude of the VCOs, NCOs, and men of the 'fighting' portion ... will be any different from that hitherto consistently adopted in these matters ... [A]s regards ICOs, so far we have only had one case of the officer in Ambala, who after the August disturbances, indicated that his political views made it impossible for him to carry out orders involving actions against Congress activities. We have seen nothing to indicate that ICOs as a class have been affected, or are likely to allow the political situation to affect their attitude.[281]

The vast and rapid expansion of the Indian Army meant an influx of recruits and officers with minimal experience. This was a factor in the army's Far East losses in 1942, and was also a catalyst for dramatic shifts in army policy and culture. The defeats at the hands of the Japanese destroyed the long-standing belief that the British were invincible. The overall performance of the army during this period was very poor and morale was at an all-time low. Paradoxically, however, the Japanese conquest of Burma threatened the frontier of India. Many nationalist-inclined youths who had not previously seen the point of joining the Indian Army to fight in the Middle East suddenly found themselves signing up to enrol as officers to defeat a more direct and deadly threat to the future of India.[282]

The two major political events of the war period – the Quit India movement of August 1942 and the Bengal famine of 1943 – caused tension for the Government of India, and many within the government worried about how the Indian Army would react to the two crises. The Quit India movement began in August 1942, and some considered it the

[280] Linlithgow to Amery, 2 Aug. 1942, *TOP*, II, 479, p. 636.
[281] Wavell to Linlithgow, 24 Feb. 1943, *TOP*, III, 533, pp. 726–7.
[282] Author's interviews with Indian officers, 1999–2009; see also Roy, 'Military Loyalty'.

greatest threat to British rule since the Indian Mutiny of 1857.[283] However, no Indian Army units mutinied.[284] A detailed discussion of the Cripps Mission in March 1942 and the reasoning behind the Indian National Congress Party, seeking to create a non-cooperation campaign, calling for a resolution by Congress for the British to Quit India and to start a mass struggle on non-violent lines, falls outside the scope of this book.[285] (In the end, it was not all non-violent; there were incidents of violence, and people were killed.) The relevance of the movement to this book lies in considering the Indian Army's ability to contain the major disruptions which resulted from the arrests of many senior and mid-level leaders of the Indian National Congress Party on 9 August.[286]

The Government of India (GOI) recognised that the Indian National Congress party was organising a non-violent campaign that could have major repercussions. They moved first: they arrested some 66,000 people, outlawed their committees, imposed a blackout on the press, and arrested the senior leadership of Congress. Rioting broke out following news of the arrests: more than 200 police stations were attacked and burned; telephone and railway lines were cut; revenue offices and court houses were destroyed. The attacks on the railways (with more than 300 stations affected) were considered the most daring and dangerous, due to the need to reinforce the eastern provinces, particularly as the Japanese Army stood at the gates to India.[287] The GOI and senior command in the Indian Army viewed this outburst not simply as a

---

[283] 'By far the most serious since that of 1857': Linlithgow to Churchill, 31 Aug. 1942, in Barnes, ed., *Empire at Bay*, p. 808; however, he contradicts this in various other memos of this period which state that the situation was under control, etc. C. A. Bayly and Harper specifically stated in *Forgotten Armies*: 'convulsed by the biggest revolt against British rule since 1857' (p. 239).

[284] C. A. Bayly and Harper, *Forgotten Armies*, p. 249: 'The army and police had, despite all the fears, remained solid.'

[285] See Nicholas Owen, 'The Cripps Mission of 1942: A Reinterpretation', *Journal of Imperial and Commonwealth History*, 30, 1 (2002), pp. 61–98, and *TOP*, II, for much more detail; see also Barnes, ed., *Empire at Bay*, pp. 805–51, as a detailed primer on the background and viewpoint from Amery. See C. A. Bayly and Harper, *Forgotten Armies*, pp. 281–91 and 295–8, for a short synopsis. As stated in a variety of sources and confirmed by the author, see the 'India intelligence summaries', Aug.–Oct. 1942, L/WS/1/1433, OIOC, BL, for the best primary source narratives of the episode.

[286] More than 30,000 members of the Indian National Congress were arrested. See Linlithgow to Amery, 3 Oct. 1942, *TOP*, III, 57, pp. 75–86, for a more detailed discussion of the role of Congress in the August violence; for a counter-argument, see a report written by a BBC official, *TOP*, III, enclosure to 138, pp. 196–200, as well as C. A. Bayly and Harper, *Forgotten Armies*, pp. 247–8.

[287] Rob Johnson, 'The Indian Army and Internal Security: 1919–1946', in Kaushik Roy, *The Indian Army in the Two World Wars* (Leiden: Brill, 2012), p. 383.

political protest, but as one that sought to destroy the ability of the Raj to protect the country from Japanese aggression.[288]

The Indian Army was called out immediately in support, and tasked with taking over areas that the police had been forced to abandon or that were in need of reinforcement. Air assets were used to cover the rail lines, and there were discussions about the possibility of strafing people found on the lines. The need to protect the rail lines raised the issue of minimum force.[289] The Indian Army and the Indian Police opened fire more than 300 times during this period, killing 1,000 people and wounding another 2,000.[290]

The insurrection occurred at the same time as the Indian and British Armies were 'licking their wounds' and preparing to defend India against a possible Japanese invasion. Most of the disturbances took place in the eastern part of the United Provinces (UP) and Bihar Province, as well as some of the urban districts. There was relatively little disruption in the Punjab, NWFP, Sind, and Assam, where Muslim opinion was opposed to the campaign. Units defending Assam in the east were cut off for a period of time in August, as the movement carried out a series of attacks, especially in Bihar[291] and eastern parts of the UP.[292] By 11 August, Linlithgow stated to Amery that the 'situation was not too bad ... taken over the country as a whole, the total casualties hardly exceed, indeed hardly approach, those that result from a severe communal riot in Bombay or Ahmeddabad'.[293]

By the end of August, the situation appeared to be under control; the War Cabinet in London stated as much in their minutes.[294] The Quit India movement was dealt with swiftly, and appeared to have had little

---

[288] See the various letters from the viceroy, Linlithgow, to Churchill, *TOP*, II. Linlithgow specifically called it the 'most serious rebellion since that of 1857' (see pp. 853–4).

[289] See comments in Johnson, 'The Indian Army and Internal Security', and the open debates in Parliament for the use of the Royal Air Force to strafe the people on the railway lines.

[290] *TOP*, II, p. 933.

[291] See War Cabinet conclusions, 17 Aug. 1942, *TOP*, II, 575, pp. 736–9, and 24 Aug. 1942, 621, pp. 800–2, for more details.

[292] Barnes, ed., *Empire at Bay*, pp. 807–8; see also Linlithgow to Amery, 17 Aug. 1942, *TOP*, II, 577, pp. 739–45, for more detail.

[293] Linlithgow to Amery, 11 Aug. 1942, *TOP*, II, 509, p. 662: see also *TOP*, III, 51, pp. 67–8, for a full list of casualties.

[294] 'The PM expressed gratification at the firmness with which the government of India had dealt with the situation in India'; it went on, perhaps prematurely: 'the limited response to the revolutionary campaign of the Congress Party had provided a practical demonstration that Congress did not represent the masses of the Indian people' (War Cabinet Minutes, 31 Aug. 1942, *TOP*, II, 664, p. 855).

impact on the army's loyalty.[295] The Indian Army appeared to have fulfilled its duties in the Aid to the Civil Power effectively, despite fears for their lack of resolve.[296] In one report, Amery asserted that 'The soldiers regard Congress as contemptible politicians (Army has been untouched by these events).'[297] Many Indian and British officers who supported the future independence of India nevertheless felt that the Quit India movement's timing was inappropriate,[298] considering that the threat of Japanese invasion outweighed internal political consider-ations.[299] Lord Linlithgow, summing up the efforts of the Indian Army during the difficult days of August, wrote 'The army has come through the recent trouble untouched and loyal. It has given us the fullest backing in the restoration of order.'[300] Despite this praise, Churchill remained unconvinced. On 24 June 1943 Gen. Wavell recorded in his journal that

He [Churchill] found another subject for criticism in the loyalty of the Indian Army. Amery had sent a paper to the War Cabinet calling attention to obvious dangers arising from the expansion of the Indian Army. It was a result of some papers I had sent home as C-in-C. We realized the dangers in India, were keeping a close watch on them, but were not in least alarmed and convinced of the general soundness of the Indian Army. The PM, however, chose to read into Amery's note the impression that the Indian Army was liable to rise at any moment; and he accused me of creating a Frankenstein by putting modern weapons in the hands of the sepoys, spoke of 1857, and was really childish about it.[301]

The Bengal famine of 1943 placed considerable strain on the Govern-ment of India and raised concerns in London about its potential impact

---

[295] There was one incident involving an officer who refused to undertake action against Congress, which was attributed to his Parsee ethnic background. Congress' actions were worrying for some Indians working within the system, but most considered them merely a nuisance. See Linlithgow to Amery, 1 Sep. 1942, *TOP*, II, 672, pp. 872–3, as well as Amery to Linlithgow, 5 Oct. 1942, *TOP*, III, 69, p. 99, for more debate regarding the officer in question. There was also a report written by a member of the BBC that made its way to Linlithgow and Amery, highlighting that there was much tension in the countryside against the British and comments regarding the Indian Army, such as 'I was given the most absolute assurance in the Punjab that the peoples from whom the Indian Army is recruited are absolutely loyal to us. Young Indians who came in contact with Indian soldiers on trains told me they were as full of their own prowess as they were of contempt for the British Army.'
[296] See Sir T. Stewart to Linlithgow, 22 Aug. 1942, *TOP*, II, 612, pp. 787–91, for evidence of the Indian and British troops carrying on with their missions. See Amery to Linlithgow, 3 Nov. 1942, *TOP*, III, enclosure to 138, pp. 196–200.
[297] Amery to Linlithgow, 24 Aug. 1942, *TOP*, II, 618, p. 7.
[298] Even Gen. Auchinleck commented to Linlithgow that the effects on the Army were 'loss of six to eight week's training ... and close to 57 battalions used on Internal Security duties': Linlithgow to Amery, 10 Sep. 1942, *TOP*, II, 722.
[299] Author's interviews with British and Indian officers, 1999–2009.
[300] Linlithgow to Viscount Halifax, 22 Sep. 1942, *TOP*, III, 9, p. 17.
[301] Moon, ed., *Wavell: The Viceroy's Journal*, pp. 3–4.

on the Indian Army.[302] Before the Second World War, India had ceased to be capable of producing sufficient grain to feed its population. The vast majority of food imports came from Burma and Malaya. The Japanese occupation of both countries meant that India was cut off from some of its important sources of rice and other food grains. While rationing was imposed, a shortage arose in 1943, at least partially due to human error.[303] Responding to this, merchants in Bombay, Madras, and Bengal began to hoard stocks, and prices for all food goods rose sharply.

Although Bengal was the worst-affected area, the Bengal Provincial Government was reluctant to ask for help or advice. By July, large numbers of starving rural peasants had come to Calcutta seeking relief. The Provincial Government did nothing in the way of providing relief, shelter, or supplies. It is estimated that 3–3.5 million people died by the end of 1943,[304] with deaths averaging more than 2,000 per week at one point. The Government of India was alerted to the scope of the problem primarily by the many war correspondents who were based in Calcutta, reporting on the misery.[305]

Over the next six months, the Government of India attempted to consolidate the rationing system throughout the country, and called for other provinces to ship their surplus stocks to Bengal.[306] Linlithgow sent a note to Amery stating that the army would most likely have to be involved, especially in transport of relief goods.[307] Amery was also aware that, if the famine spread to other areas, many sepoys, NCOs, VCOs, and ICOs would be fearful for their families, and that this would be detrimental to morale.[308]

---

[302] See extensive coverage of the famine in *TOP*, IV, where many letters are covered showing the awareness and attempts to deal with the growing food shortages. C. A. Bayly and Harper have a short synopsis in their *Forgotten Armies*, pp. 281–91 and 295–8.

[303] Amery states on 7 Dec. 1943 that there was evidence that the Bengal administration had started to see signs of crop failure by April 1943; Barnes, ed., *Empire at Bay*, p. 954. Also, when the Government of India requested that the British government help deal with the shortfall, they could not promise much support due to shipping concerns. See Yong, *Garrison State*, p. 292. See also Sir Lumley to Linlithgow, 30 Dec. 1942, *TOP*, III, 302, pp. 436–7, for an early discussion of the issues of lack of food supplies; War Cabinet Paper, 31 Jul. 1943, *TOP*, IV, 67, pp. 139–41, for specific details forecasting potential famine; and C. A. Bayly and Harper, *Forgotten Armies*, p. 251.

[304] Yong estimates that 3.5 million people died (*Garrison State*, p. 291).

[305] Barnes, ed., *Empire at Bay*, pp. 909–13.

[306] This would cause some tensions for the Government of India and the 'loyal' Unionist government in the Punjab. See Yong, *Garrison State*, pp. 292–5.

[307] Linlithgow to Amery, 20 Sep. 1943, *TOP*, IV, 125, pp. 284–5.

[308] Economic Situation in India, 22 Sep. 1943, *TOP*, IV, 132, p. 306: 'sight of famine conditions cannot but cause distress to European troops and anxiety to the Indian troops as to the condition of their families in other parts of India'.

London was not taking the crisis seriously; as Leo Amery noted in his diary entry of 24 September 1943: 'Winston [Churchill] may be right in saying that the starvation of anyhow under-fed Bengalis is less serious than sturdy Greeks, at any rate from the war point of view, but he makes no sufficient allowance for the sense of Empire responsibility in this country.'[309] Wavell became viceroy on 20 October 1943 and moved quickly to try to apply military capabilities and planning to deal with the crisis. Preliminary moves to use the resources of the Indian Army in support of relief efforts began at the end of October.[310] On 1 November, Auchinleck approved a scheme to employ emergency resources. The army was to raise and utilise every available kind of transport – rail, road, and water – to release supplies to the correct people and places. A brigade and its supporting elements were earmarked to carry out these important duties. As Wavell stated to Amery, 'troops are being located throughout the worst affected districts to assist the civil authorities in movement and escorting allotted quotas to villages … [T]roops are being drafted into Bengal from other parts of India to give assistance.'[311] Within a fortnight, the relief effort doubled;[312] the army seized 'hoarded' stocks and distributed them,[313] and the price of food goods began to drop. Auchinleck and the army were praised by the viceroy and Amery for their huge efforts and effectiveness, within a few weeks of formally becoming involved.[314] The Indian Army continued to support relief efforts through the end of 1943 and into early 1944, even as various divisions began the counteroffensives in the Arakan and Assam regions of the India/Burma frontier.[315]

---

[309] Amery, 24 Sep. 1943, Barnes, ed., *Empire at Bay*, p. 943. It was noted earlier in the entry that Winston admitted something should be done, however, 'the Indians are not the only people who are starving in this war' (*ibid.*). See also C. A. Bayly and Harper, *Forgotten Armies*, pp. 286–7.

[310] Wavell to Amery, 30 Oct. 1943, *TOP*, IV, 193, p. 415: 'this is now definitely a military as well as a charity problem since the army must have a stable base'.

[311] Wavell to Amery, 2 Nov. 1943, *TOP*, IV, 200, p. 443.

[312] Connell, *Auchinleck*, pp. 758–9: see also Wavell to Amery, 1 Nov. 1943, *TOP*, IV, 199, pp. 431–48, especially enclosure 4, for more details of the army's preparedness to support the relief effort.

[313] One Indian Army officer, who wishes to remain anonymous, reported that some of the merchants who were found to be 'hoarding' were 'despatched' by some sepoys. The army was commended for their efforts within days of deploying. Wavell stated to Amery, 'Army got going with commendable speed' (8 Nov. 1943, *TOP*, IV, 213, p. 456).

[314] See letters from viceroy to Auchinleck, 2 Nov. 1943, and Amery to Auchinleck, 11 Nov. 1943, Auchinleck Papers, University of Manchester.

[315] Government of India, Food Department to Sec. of State, 6 Jan. 1944, *TOP*, IV, 299; see pp. 598–9.

As late as March 1944, Government of India officials were expressing concern that the crisis was not fully resolved.[316] There were signs of improvement, however, as evidenced by the decision to shift army support units from Bengal to the fronts in the Arakan and Imphal Plain as the fighting in those regions intensified.[317]

Morale reports

Examining the secret documents housed in the Oriental and India Office Collections, British Libraries, compiled to assess the overall morale of all units (British, African, and Indian) within South East Asia Command (SEAC) and India Command shows an increase in morale from 1943, peaking during the 1945 campaigns. The report from October 1943 indicates that the majority of desertions came from the ranks of recruits, and cites non-payment of signing bonuses as the primary reason. It also notes that many PMs and Sikhs were wary of the future role of the Indian Army under an Indian Congress government, fearing a drastic cutback in numbers and loss of money for the men.[318]

The report for October 1944 indicates a dramatic improvement in attitudes in the Indian Army. The Japanese offensives of 1944 had been decisively defeated; desertions had significantly decreased; and the reasons for desertions still occurring continued to centre on signing bonuses. One concern raised by Indian other ranks was about the future, but this focused mostly on demobilisation and jobs after the war's end. This was another cause for desertions in the Indian engineers and other service-related units, as men deserted to gain lucrative jobs in the civil sector. Many Indian officers took offence to a letter published in 1944 by the American special envoy to New Delhi, William Phillips, in which he stated that the Indian Army was a mercenary army and that the morale of

---

[316] Barnes, ed., *Empire at Bay*, pp. 913–14. See also Amery's entry for 26 Jun. 1944, 'India now calculates that there is a shortage of two million tons of food all over and that something like a million tons of wheat must be imported by next April to hold the situation' (*ibid.*, p. 989). A second famine was seen as a potential strategic issue for the future. As stated in the War Cabinet, 'a second famine might have serious effect on the morale of the Indian Army and on the security of India as a whole ... the provision of wheat for India is therefore a military requirement of great strategical importance' (18 Mar. 1944, *TOP*, IV, 432, p. 817).

[317] Wavell to Amery, 18 Apr. 1944, *TOP*, IV, 465, p. 896. Wavell would still emphasise in later letters the need to avoid a second famine for fear of morale issues for the army throughout the summer of 1944, as the Indian Army followed up their recent success in the Arakan and Imphal and started to push the Japanese back into central Burma.

[318] October 1943 Report, L/WS/2/71, OIOC, BL.

the Indian officers was low.[319] An Indian officer's letter of rebuttal was included in the report. In response to the comment about a mercenary army, he stated: 'I have not yet met a soldier of any rank of any nationality who is doing work without accepting any money in return.'[320]

The morale report of February 1945 confirms that desertion was lower than in previous reports. It also states that the successful advance in Burma 'ha[d] raised the already high morale of Indian troops yet higher and it [was] generally considered by unit commanders that morale [was] ... at its peak'. A letter from an Indian captain was included in the report, exhorting, 'Wake up young men of India. Sacrifice everything for your country and save your country from the hands of the Japanese.'[321] Lord Wavell characterised sentiment in the army towards the end of war in a report to the War Cabinet:

[Wavell] thought there was no question of any spread of political ideas among the troops. As regards the Officers, we had taken in a very large number of temporary officers from all classes, some of whom might be politically minded. There was, however, no sign in the Army as a whole of any sort of political movement. There had been in connection with the August 1942 disturbances a single case of a temporary officer who had resigned because he did not agree with the Army being used in those disturbances, but his case, Lord Wavell thought was unique. He doubted very much if the majority of the Army ever thought of the Pakistan issue. An officer, whatever his religion, had Hindus and Muslims alike serving under him. In Arakan there had been one Indian Brigadier with three Indian commanding officers, and this had worked without any difficulty.[322]

Congress' view of the Indian Army in July 1945 may confirm Wavell's assessment. An official from Congress, Dr Abul Kalam Azad, regarded the make-up of the Indian Army as separate from normal Indian society, specifically stating to Wavell that 'the character of the Indian Army ... [was] divorced from the Indian people'.[323] However, as Wavell made clear during the Simla Conference in July 1945, keeping the Indian Army separate from politics was part and parcel of its successes:

No government could permit its army to take part in politics. The Indian Army had done splendidly during the war and had enhanced its own and India's reputation. He [Wavell] believed it to be a contented army and he thought the delegates did not realize what rapid progress had been made with Indianisation during the war. He would certainly oppose any suggestion that the Indian Army

---

[319] Author's interviews with Indian officers (1999–2009) and Oct. 1944, L/WS/2/71, OIOC, BL.

[320] October 1944 Report, L/WS/2/71, OIOC, BL.

[321] February 1945 Report, L/WS/2/71, OIOC, BL.

[322] War Cabinet, 26 Mar. 1945, *TOP*, V, 339, p. 740.

[323] Amery to Wavell, 16 Jul. 1945, *TOP*, V, 620, p. 1265.

should be brought into politics. On the other hand he wished it to be a truly national army, efficient and contented.[324]

Conclusion

The Indian Army entered the post-war period as a major victor. It had defeated the Imperial Japanese Army and the German and Italian Armies. It was seen by many as a very professional force, due to the many reforms that took place as well as the performance in battle. The ending of the war also saw the Indian Army as a changed force, one that would not return to the pre-Second World War days and one that saw its future in a different light, due to the rise in the Indian nationalist movement. The army also had to contend with the future officer make-up as recruitment of British officers came to an end, as well as war-time recruitment practices. It was a professional force; however, the make-up of the officer corps and the *jawan*s was slowly changing.

In a letter written not long after the end of the Second World War, Auchinleck articulated two important points about the future of the Indian Army. The first was that a place must be found in the Indian Army of the future for the new infantry regiments raised during the war.[325] The second was that 'the [Indian] army [of 1945] recognises no difference of caste or creed or race and I hope that it never will'.[326] This second point is particularly poignant when considering how the army cut back in the post-war period, setting precedents which have largely continued up to the present and are evident in contemporary recruitment methods of the Indian and Pakistan Armies.[327] Unlike what had happened at the end of the First World War, however, some of the new classes were kept within the Indian Army on a level appropriate to the reductions made by a peace-time army, although recruitment in the Punjab would still remain high in the post-war period.[328]

---

[324] Cabinet Paper, 18 Jul. 1945, *TOP*, V, 624, p. 1272.

[325] Two battalions from the Assam and Bihar Regiments were commended for their performance during the Burma campaign. Contrast this with two battalions of the Chamar and Ajmer Regiments, who also saw service but were reported not to have done particularly well. The findings also reported that failings in these units were due to weak junior leaders, rather than poor fighting capability of the men. See Willcox Report, Part II, Library of Field Marshal Sir John Chapple, London.

[326] Auchinleck to National Defence Council, 13 Oct. 1945, Auchinleck Papers, University of Manchester.

[327] Interestingly, this was confirmed by many Indian and Pakistani officers during the interviews and visits with various regiments in 2000: author's interviews with Indian and Pakistani officers, 1999–2009.

[328] For example, the 16th Light Cavalry, originally raised in Madras in the late 1700s, reverted to a one-class Madrassi regiment in 1946: Gaylor, *Sons of John Company*, p. 93.

Many senior British officers remained in post; the plan was a gradual transition as more Indian officers were prepared for higher command. There no longer seemed any argument against their ascendancy in the face of the Indian Army's uniformly successful performance against German, Italian, and particularly Imperial Japanese forces. The expansion of the Indian Army, more than 2 million men and thousands of officers for the war effort, was critical to this success, and reforming the pre-war Indianisation process as well as the recruitment practices of the pre-war period was critical to effective expansion. The Indian Army's performance in 1945 made it clear to many detractors, including Prime Minister Winston Churchill, that it was a different army from the one that had entered the war six years earlier. The records of Indian officers provided further proof that, contrary to prejudiced expectations, Indians were more than capable of commanding not just other Indians but also British officers in combat. In fact, it is not far-fetched to claim that the Indian Army of 1945 might not have been as successful without these changes.

Many of the pre-war ills of the Indianisation process were rectified by late 1942. In the meantime, however, Japanese victories had seriously damaged the Indian Army's morale. It was clear that extensive reforms, both tactical and social, were badly needed. The crucial political correlation to the defeats in Burma and Malaya was that, with the arrival of the Japanese Army on the borders of India, many Indian officers felt that they were fighting for the defence of India, regardless of whether that might mean fighting under the command of the British.

After the first Arakan campaign, the Indian Army was prepared to tackle the Burma campaign. Its performance during the 1944 and 1945 campaigns was testament to the effect of the recently implemented reforms. The attendant rise in morale lowered the rate of desertions,[329] and the improved performance of officers helped to increase discipline and morale. Improvements in officer relations and performance also helped to dispel the last vestiges of belief that Indian officers were second-class citizens. The performance of Indian Army units in Italy and Greece reinforced *esprit de corps*, and they also benefited from recruitment and Indianisation reforms within India Command.

The creation of the Indian National Army[330] and reports of desertion in the field during 1942 and 1943 in Burma were mostly the result of poor morale and leadership, as well as military setbacks. Gen.

---

[329] Talbot, *Punjab and the Raj*, p. 100.

[330] See Chapter 3 for a more in-depth discussion of the INA and its impact on the post-war period.

Figure 2.5 Announcement of the Japanese surrender in Singapore
© Imperial War Museums (Image No. CF720)

Auchinleck, commenting on the motives of captured INA soldiers and
officers, pointed out bluntly that 'it is quite wrong to adopt the attitude
that because these men had been in service in a British controlled Indian
Army that therefore their loyalty must be the same as British soldiers. As
I have tried to explain, they had no real loyalty towards Britain as Britain,
not as we understand loyalty.'[331] The successful performance of Indian
Army formations in Africa and the Middle East during the same period
serves to underscore this point. As social and tactical reforms took hold
in 1943 and defeats were turned into victories, both morale and discipline improved, and the INA became less of a factor.

Officers and recruits were drawn to the army for many reasons: relatively lucrative wages, *izzat*, regimental pride and *esprit de corps*, the
opportunity to serve as an officer, and the desire to fight against fascism.
Many officers considered themselves nationalist at heart but believed
regardless that joining up was the best option available, both to enable

---

[331] Gen. Auchinleck, 'Strictly personal and secret', quoted in Gajendra Singh, 'Breaking
the Chains with Which We Were Bound: The Interrogation Chamber, the Indian
National Army and the Negation of Military Identities', in Roy, ed., *The Indian Army
in the Two World Wars*, p. 518.

them to take part in the defence of India and to secure a good position for themselves in the eventual creation of the independent Indian state. Some officers came from families that had nationalist sympathies and personal connections to senior Congress officials.

The contention that the army was primarily 'apolitical' is perhaps best supported by considering its performance during the trying days of the Quit India movement and the Bengal famine, as described earlier. Even in these situations, they were not shamed or criticised by their families when they joined the army. On the contrary, many officers pointed out that the general feeling was that an independent India would need these men as the core of its army.[332] The defeat of the Japanese Imperial Army, Nazi Germany, and fascist Italy, and the role played therein by Indian soldiers and officers, instilled in the army and its men a newfound sense of self-confidence that political leaders could not ignore and soon recognised as an advantage for the independent India to come.

The Indian Army was taxed throughout the coming years, as the INA trials occurred, it was deployed to South East Asia, and communal violence in India exploded to unprecedented heights. The professionalisation and *esprit de corps* that were reborn through battlefield exploits in the Second World War helped the army to steer a fairly clear path in the coming years. Their loyalty was tested; however, the Indian Army could claim that the institution remained loyal during the tumultuous post-war period.

---

[332] Author's interviews with Indian officers, 1999–2009.

3   Question of loyalty? The Indian National Army and the Royal Indian Navy mutiny

Map 3.1 India 1945–1947

There is, however, one silver lining in the cloud that has overtaken us, and that is, the British Indian Army of today is not the British Indian Army of the last war. Soldiers of the Azad Hind Fauj [Indian National Army] have had numerous opportunities of coming in close contact with members of the British Indian Army ... There is no doubt that at the heart large sections of the British Indian Army sympathize with Azad Hind Fauj and its fight for freedom. But the British Indian Army is not yet prepared to take the risk and line up with the revolutionaries.

Subhas Chandra Bose, 21 May 1945[1]

Some historians feel that the Indian National Army can be considered proof, of an unorthodox kind, of latent political sentiment within the Indian Army.[2] As mentioned in Chapter 2, the INA was raised during the Second World War, with the support of the IJA;[3] lasted less than three years; and went through two different configurations during that period. In total, it numbered some 40,000 men and women, half of whom are estimated to have been recruited from Indian Army prisoners of war (POWs).[4] The INA's battlefield performance was quite poor when assessed either alongside the IJA or against the reformed Fourteenth Army on the battlefields of Assam and Burma. Reports of its creation in 1942/3 caused consternation among the political and military leadership

---

[1] Quoted in Sugata Bose, *His Majesty's Opponent: Subhas Chandra Bose and India's Struggle Against Empire* (Cambridge, MA: Harvard University Press, 2011), p. 295.

[2] This chapter will focus only on the formation of the INA under the auspices of the Imperial Japanese Army. It will not deal with the German-raised Free India Legion, which was raised from Indian prisoners of war from the North Africa campaign and numbered close to 3,000 men. For more information on the Free India Legion, see Milan Hauner, *India in Axis Strategy: Germany, Japan and Indian Nationalists in the Second World War* (Stuttgart: Klett-Cotta, 1981). For a wider discussion on the INA, see the following sources in the OIOC, BL: L/WS/1/1433, L/WS/1/1576, L/WS/1/1771, L/WS/2/45, L/WS/ 2/46, L/WS/1/1506. See K. K. Ghosh, *The Indian National Army* (New Delhi: Meenakshi Prakashan, 1969); Joyce Lebra, *Jungle Alliance: Japan and the Indian National Army* (Singapore: Asia Pacific Press, 1971); Gerrard Corr, *War of the Springing Tiger* (London: Osprey, 1975); Hugh Toye, *The Springing Tiger. A Study of a Revolutionary: Subhas Chandra Bose* (London: Cassell, 1959); Peter Ward Fay, *The Forgotten Army: India's Armed Struggle for Independence* (Ann Arbor: University of Michigan Press, 1993); Bose, *His Majesty's Opponent*; Leonard Gordon, *Brothers Against the Raj: A Biography of Indian Nationalists Sarat and Subhas Chandra Bose* (New York: Columbia University Press, 1990); Mohan Singh, *Soldier's Contribution to Indian Independence* (New Delhi, 1974); Shah Nawaz Khan, *My Memories of the INA and Its Netaji* (Delhi, 1946); K. S. Giani, *Indian Independence Movement in Asia* (Lahore, 1947); Stephen Cohen, 'Subhas Chandra Bose and the Indian National Army', *Pacific Affairs*, 36, 4 (Winter, 1963–4), pp. 411–29; Sundaram, 'The Indian National Army'; Sundaram, 'Paper Tiger'; Chandar Sundaram, 'Soldier Disaffection and the Creation of the Indian National Army', *Indo-British Review*, 19, 1 (1990), pp. 155–62; Sundaram, 'Seditious Letters and Steel Helmets'; and Gajendra Singh, 'Breaking the Chains'.

[3] They were referred to as 'Jiffs' (Japanese Indian Forces) by many within the Indian Army.

[4] See Gajenda Singh, 'Breaking the Chains'.

of the GOI, but in the end its formation did not constitute a legitimate mutiny, and its presence had a negligible impact on the Indian Army.[5]

The INA's dubious battlefield performance notwithstanding, political fallout from INA recruits after the Second World War was considerable. Chandar Sundaram describes them as 'paper tigers'; Christopher Bayly summed it up thus: '[The] INA was to become a much more powerful enemy of the British Empire in defeat than it had been during its ill-fated triumphal march on Delhi.'[6]

Many Indian National Congress and Muslim League politicians did not support the INA during the war;[7] Nehru was quoted on 19 August 1945 as saying that: 'I was of the opinion and am still of the opinion that the leaders and others of this Army [INA] had been misguided in many ways and had failed to appreciate the larger consequences of their unfortunate association with the Japanese ... Therefore, whatever the motive behind these people, they had to be resisted in India or outside.'[8]

However, after the war, the Indian National Congress party, and Jawaharlal Nehru in particular, used the INA as a political card in an attempt to further destabilise British rule. After the war ended, the Indian Army had to decide how much of a threat these people were, and what should be done with them. The situation was politically fraught; the Indian Army generally considered INA members despicable traitors, but Nehru and other politicians were lauding them as freedom fighters striving to liberate India from the yoke of British colonial oppression. This pulled at the conflicting loyalties felt by many in the Indian Army – professional loyalty to the regiment and the army, against personal loyalty to India and, often, a longing for independence.

After a lengthy and rigorous assessment process, the decision was made to court-martial a representative selection of the 20,000 Indian Army personnel identified as members of the INA.[9] Ultimately the number sent for trial was quite small, since Gen. Auchinleck was concerned with the state of the Indian Army's morale and thought it best to put the whole matter behind them as quickly as possible.[10]

INA members were to have another unforeseen and damaging role in the chaos of partition. Released due to political pressure from both

---

[5] See Callahan, 'The Indian Army, Total War ... ', p. 127.

[6] C. A. Bayly and Harper, *Forgotten Armies*, p. 402.

[7] See comments by Cohen in 'Subhas Chandra Bose', pp. 420–2.

[8] Quoted in Connell, *Auchinleck*, p. 798 and Toye, *The Springing Tiger*, p. 171.

[9] Cohen, 'Subhas Chandra Bose', p. 413.

[10] See letter of 26 Nov. 1945, Auchinleck to Wavell, No. 1119, Auchinleck Papers, University of Manchester, on his reasons why leniency was the best way forward. This was a controversial position, but so would its opposite have been; the best way to handle this matter was a subject of considerable controversy in the Indian Army. See also Connell, *Auchinleck*, specifically the chapter on the INA trials (pp. 794–819).

Indian and British political leaders, many of these men sought employment as 'military advisers' to the growing number of paramilitary
political volunteer groups forming in 1946 and 1947, including the
Congress Volunteer Corps, Rashtrya Swayam Sewak Sangh (RSS
Sangh), Revolutionary Socialist Party of India Army, Muslim League
National Guards, and Sikh Jathas (legion). INA veterans provided
advice in military tactics, weapons, and organisation, and many went
on to command and lead various 'gangs' in their pursuit of killing rival
political or communal groups, wreaking havoc not just in the Punjab
but also in Bengal and the United Provinces.[11]

Raising of the first INA

The INA was created from Indian POWs who were convinced or coerced
to fight for the Japanese, generally in the expectation of helping a victorious Japanese Army to liberate India from British imperial rule and, not
incidentally, betray their oaths to the king-emperor.[12] The first phase of
its creation occurred under the leadership and planning of Giani Pritam
Singh of the Independent League, with the assistance of a recently
captured Indian Army officer, Captain Mohan Singh, and a Japanese
Army officer, Maj. Fujiwara Iwaichi, from Japanese Imperial General
Headquarters (IGHQ). Two days after the fall of Singapore, 15 February
1942, Mohan Singh and Maj. Fujiwara briefed the 40,000 captured
Indian officers, VCOs, NCOs, and soldiers from the 9th and 11th Indian
Divisions. As stated in Chapter 2, the units and formations that had been
sent to Malaya in 1940 and 1941 had been heavily 'milked'. The basic
training of the soldiers, NCOs, VCOs, and officers had been lacklustre.
The ability of the EICOs and ECOs had been wanting due to the lack of
training and familiarity with their soldiers. All these issues came to a head

---

[11] See Ayesha Jalal, *Self and Sovereignty: Individual and Community in South Asian Islam
Since 1850* (London: Routledge, 2000), pp. 526, 534. Jalal also highlights a very
dangerous trend of former Gurkha soldiers being hired to train some of the volunteer
groups as well (*ibid.*, p. 531). See also Tuker, *Memory*, p. 447, and Swarna Aiyar,
'August Anarchy', in D. A. Low and Howard Brasted, eds., *Freedom, Trauma,
Continuities: Northern India and Independence* (London: Sage Publications, 1998),
pp. 28–32.

[12] The actual raising of the force was down to the efforts of the Japanese Imperial General
Headquarters and the Indian Independent League, a violent Indian nationalist
movement headquartered in Thailand. The Independent League viewed the INA as its
military wing: Sundaram, 'Paper Tiger', pp. 35–7. See also Sundaram, 'Seditious Letters
and Steel Helmets', for more details regarding the disaffection in the Indian Army units
serving in Hong Kong in 1941. As Sundaram pointed out: 'the two incidents discussed
in this article [Hong Kong and Singapore] did not, by themselves, lead to the formation
of the INA. That occurred only with the conjunction of the political situation in India
and the unmitigated disaster of the British Far Eastern strategy' (*ibid.*, p. 149).

as soldiers, NCOs, VCOs, and some ICOs questioned their loyalty to the Indian Army from the perspective of captivity. By April 1942, close to 15,000 were reported to have joined the INA; it appears that of the fifty ICOs who surrendered, thirty-five joined the INA, along with nearly one hundred VCOs.[13]

The reasons for joining the INA have been debated since the end of the war.[14] Possible explanations offered have included: nationalism; soldiers following the lead of officers, VCOs, or NCOs;[15] preferential treatment from the Japanese;[16] monetary incentives; attempts to protect Indian soldiers from harsh treatment at the hands of the IJA; attempts to deploy to the battlefront to surrender as soon as possible and rejoin the ranks of the Indian Army. The charismatic appeal of Subhas Chandra Bose,[17] after he took command of the 'second' INA in the summer of 1943, has also been widely cited.[18]

---

[13] Barkawi, 'Culture and Combat', p. 339, and Sundaram, 'Paper Tiger'.

[14] More than 50% of the total number of Indian Army POWs refused to join. The numbers of POWs who refused to join were even higher in the units captured in Hong Kong. See Gajendra Singh, 'Breaking the Chains', for more details.

[15] See Tuker, *Memory*, pp. 52–3. It is well known that the loyalty of many Indian soldiers was to the VCOs and officers in the battalion or regiment, not necessarily to the king-emperor. This was confirmed in numerous interviews with Indian and British officers, 1999–2009. See also comment by Gen. Auchinleck: 'the loyalty of our men was really to the officers of the regiment or unit, and ... although there may have been some abstract sentiments of loyalty and patriotism to the Government and to the King, the men's allegiance for all practical purposes was focused on the regiment, and particularly on the regimental officers, on whom they depended for their welfare, advancement and future prospects' (12 Feb. 1946, No. 1137, Auchinleck Papers, University of Manchester; also in Connell, *Auchinleck*, p. 947).

[16] Many historians and histories of the INA and INA interrogation results cited this reason.

[17] 'INA deeply affected by Subhas Bose's inspiring leadership and clever propaganda ... [T]he personal influence of Subhas Bose on all ranks of the INA is tremendous and undeniable.' See SEAC Weekly Security Intelligence Summary, no. 194, 20 Jul. 1945, L/WS/1/1506, OIOC, BL, for more details. Bose was a Bengali, educated at Calcutta University and Cambridge University. He passed the very difficult ICS exam, ranking fourth in the list. He later resigned to take up the nationalist cause. See Gordon, *Brothers Against the Raj*, and Toye, *The Springing Tiger*, for detailed discussions of Bose. For more recent analysis, see Bose, *His Majesty's Opponent*.

[18] See the extensive discussion by Gajendra Singh, 'Breaking the Chains', for more information. British intelligence and officials appeared to go back and forth during the war period regarding this reasoning. One common issue was the role of the VCOs or ICOs within a given regiment or battalion that had been captured. Many times the Indian POWs resisted the efforts of the INA, while others followed their ICOs or VCOs who decided to join. In the end, the Indian soldier was loyal to his NCOs, VCOs, ICOs, and British officers and to the regiment as a whole, not to the British Raj. This distinction was well known to many within the Indian Army. This, among many similar themes, was discussed in more than 100 interviews with British and Indian officers, 1999–2009. See also Barkawi, 'Culture and Combat', pp. 339–40.

The embarrassing defeat of the III Indian Corps in Malaya destroyed the myth of British capability and leadership in war for many of the Indian POWs. The over-expansion of the army and officer corps also played a role.[19] Another issue that has been cited for some of the ICOs who joined was the pre-war Indianisation process, which many considered 'prejudiced' and humiliating;[20] many officers who joined the INA had come from the 1/14th Punjab Regiment, one of the pre-war Indianised battalions.[21] Even Gen. Sir Claude Auchinleck believed that the tensions of the pre-war Indianisation process were one of the driving forces behind the motivations of some of the INA.[22] The rank and file pulled from all the various classes of the pre-war Indian Army; however, the INA recruited many more Sikhs, Jats, and Dogras than Punjabi Musalmans, Pathans, and Gurkhas.[23]

Captain Mohan Singh was made a major general by the IJA and tasked with raising and preparing the INA for operations in Burma and Assam. Fujiwara was replaced as the liaison officer with the INA from IGHQ by Colonel Iwakuro Hideo, who held less favourable views of the INA. Mohan Singh set out to create two divisions of 15,000 men each, a goal which the Japanese viewed as too ambitious. Many within the Japanese IGHQ and the Burma Army came over time to view the INA as deeply

---

[19] See Chapter 2 as well as Marston, *Phoenix*, and Moreman, *Jungle*, which discuss the negative impact of lack of professionalism in the early years of the war. See also Barkawi, 'Culture and Combat', p. 343, and 'Indian National Army – Counter measures' 1/7 Gurkha Rifles, Loose Archives, G46, Gurkha Museum, Winchester, UK: 'once things are going well troops are less likely to be affected by Indian National Army propaganda'. This was confirmed as the Fourteenth Army became stronger and better trained. In 1944 and 1945, the INA did not receive any support in terms of desertions, and actually lost many INA soldiers who surrendered to the Fourteenth Army during the Ha-Go and U-Go offensives. See also Roy, 'Military Loyalty', pp. 509–10, 517.

[20] See Cohen, 'Subhas Chandra Bose', p. 414; confirmed with Indian Army officers in interviews with the author, 1999–2009. See also Sundaram, 'Seditious Letters', and the discussions of the pre-war Indianised battalion, the 4/19th Hyderabad Regiment issues in Singapore, and the power of an unenlightened CO and his negative impact on a battalion, on the verge of fighting the Japanese.

[21] See Tuker, *Memory*, p. 52, for more discussion. He as well as other officers called for the disbandment of this battalion in the post-war period.

[22] Quoted in Connell, *Auchinleck*, p. 947. An INA officer specifically stated similar comments '[throughout] our career in the Indian Army there had been distinctions between the British Officers and the [ICOs]. The [ICOs] had not been treated as well as our English comrades or brother officers' (Barkawi, 'Culture and Combat', p. 332).

[23] Shah Nawaz Khan, *My Memories*, p. 26. Bose recognised that the majority of the recruits were Hindus and the potential impact of this within the INA. He specifically urged Hindus to be generous with members from other religious groups. See Bose, *His Majesty's Opponent*, p. 252. Some Indian Army historians have claimed that no Gurkhas joined the INA, but this is false. See Shah Nawaz Khan, *My Memories*, p. 26, and Ronald Hyam, *Britain's Declining Empire: The Road to Decolonisation, 1918–1968* (Cambridge University Press, 2007), p. 96.

suspicious, since it was an army of 'surrendered' personnel, which was anathema to the Bushido code of the IJA. By September 1942, however, due mostly to the 'propaganda' value of the INA, the IGHQ allowed the formation of the 1st INA Division and ancillary units.[24]

Relations between Mohan Singh and the IGHQ began to deteriorate by the end of 1942. Supplies for division and ancillary units became an ongoing issue, as did the IGHQ moving elements of the INA to the battlefront without consulting Mohan Singh. INA soldiers were used as camp followers to the IJA, as well as construction troops to build camps and airfields.[25] The situation came to a head as the Independent League began to question Mohan Singh's reliability, after he requested that all INA soldiers swear allegiance to him and only him. At around the same time, a senior officer of the INA also defected to the British at the first opportunity. Mohan Singh must have been aware that the IGHQ and Independent League were conspiring against him, and he dissolved the INA. The League and the IGHQ moved to arrest Singh in late December 1942.

The IGHQ recognised that there was a need to reorganise the INA. They sought the services of Subhas Chandra Bose as the new leader of the INA (he would also lead the Indian Independence League).[26] Bose was a nationalist, and interested in the violent overthrow of the Raj, unlike many in the Indian National Congress or Muslim League at the time. He had also helped organise the Free India Legion[27] and had been working in Germany since 1940. Bose arrived in June 1943 to take command of the INA or, as some referred to it, the second incarnation. He was considered to be a more adept political leader and strategist than Mohan Singh, who was in many ways a soldier first and a politician second.[28] The Japanese allowed Bose to proclaim the Provisional

---

[24] The names of the three 'guerrilla regiments' were Gandhi, Nehru, and Azad, and they numbered close to 9,000 men. The ancillary units numbered close to 4,000–5,000 men each. The choice of the term 'guerrilla' is odd, as the regiments served as normal conventional light infantry. It most likely had to do with the political connotations of the term.

[25] Tuker provides an eyewitness account of a POW describing INA being used as prison guards and firing parties, dealing with escaped Commonwealth POWs in Singapore. See his *Memory*, pp. 565–7.

[26] See C. A. Bayly and Harper, *Forgotten Armies*, p. 279.

[27] Many of the POWs for this organisation came from one formation, the 3rd Indian Motor Brigade, which had been ravaged in North Africa.

[28] During the height of the Bengal famine, Bose offered supplies of rice from Burma to relieve the suffering: C. A. Bayly and Harper, *Forgotten Armies*, p. 291. Many POWs considered Bose a better leader than Singh; Bose also refused to take a military title (*ibid.*, p. 322).

Government of Free India, Azad Hind, on 21 October 1943;[29] he also named himself head of state, foreign minister, and C-in-C of the INA.[30]

Bose was also interested in trying to mobilise the Indian communities of South East Asia to join the INA. He was only partially successful in this initiative; after the first INA was dissolved, only 9,000 former soldiers offered their services for the second incarnation, along with 25,000 Indian civilians, mostly Tamils.[31]

The second incarnation of the INA comprised three divisions and the independent Nehru Brigade. The 1st INA Division was mostly POWs (although some were scattered throughout the 2nd Division).[32] The 3rd Division was made up solely of Indian civilians. An officer training school was established at Nee Soon, and some officers also went to the Japanese Imperial Military Academy.[33] (One significant reason for the INA's eventual failure was the fact that, of the thirty-five ICOs and one hundred-plus VCOs recruited, most were rapidly promoted to senior-level positions for which they were inadequately trained, educated, or experienced.)

In early 1944, Bose met with senior Japanese Army officials to discuss the INA's potential involvement in the Japanese offensives planned for the Arakan and Imphal regions.[34] As Mohan Singh had before him, Bose encountered reluctance from IJA senior staff to allow the INA a central role in any major offensives. The reasons were the same: distrust of soldiers who switched sides; lack of training; and differing doctrinal practices, due to some of the soldiers having previous experience in the Indian Army.[35] Eventually the IJA agreed to designate one INA regiment, the Bose Brigade,[36] as part of the Ha-Go offensive into the Arakan, on the condition that their performance would determine the fate of the rest of the INA.

Once the Bose Brigade was shipped to Rangoon to prepare for the offensive, the IJA officers had to negotiate further with Bose regarding

---

[29] Connell, *Auchinleck*, p. 796.

[30] Maj. Gen. Shahid Hamid, *Disastrous Twilight: A Personal Record of the Partition of India* (Barnsley, UK: Leo Cooper, 1986), p. 16.

[31] C. A. Bayly and Harper, *Forgotten Armies*, p. 323. Not all of the recruits were nationalists; many were unemployed labourers who preferred service in the INA to Japanese forced labour camps (*ibid.*, p. 326).

[32] See Sundaram, 'Paper Tiger', pp. 37–8, as well as India Command Weekly Intelligence Summaries, no. 178, Part III, Appendix B, L/WS/1/1433, OIOC, BL.

[33] C. A. Bayly and Harper, *Forgotten Armies*, p. 325.

[34] See Chapter 2 for a wider discussion of Operations Ha-Go and U-Go and the eventual defeat of the IJA.

[35] C. A. Bayly and Harper, *Forgotten Armies*, p. 371.

[36] Bose pulled the 'best' from other units and regiments to fill out this specific brigade, knowing its performance was going to be judged.

command and control, specifically whether INA officers would command the battalions, companies, and platoons. In the end, the brigade was split into two and served under the command of various Japanese divisions, acting mostly as a secondary force, rather than spearheading an invasion of India, as Bose had hoped.[37]

Another argument for INA troops taking part in the offensives was to interact with and induce other Indian soldiers to switch sides. During the first Arakan offensive of 1942/3, twenty-three Sikh *jawans* from the 1/15th Punjab Regiment had defected to the INA, and later fourteen Hindu Jats from the same battalion had followed suit. The INA hoped to provoke more of this.[38] During the Ha-Go offensive of 1944, the INA again played a secondary role, and there was only one instance of Indian troops (Indian State Forces, not Indian Army) switching sides.[39]

Initially, INA troops in the Arakan stayed loyal to the INA and their IJA masters. However, as starvation and defeat began to take their toll, loyalties began to waver, and two companies from the Bose Brigade surrendered en masse to British forces in July 1944. By October 1944, the INA and IJA in the Arakan were retreating back into southern and central Burma, as the British counteroffensive truly took hold.[40] The INA's efforts in the U-Go offensive in Assam (Imphal region) met with a similar fate. The 1st INA Division[41] was deployed as part of the

---

[37] See comments from an INA officer to Bose in C. A. Bayly and Harper, *Forgotten Armies*, p. 374.

[38] Note that these two cases occurred in the same battalion, during the unsuccessful offensive in the Arakan. The lack of ability of the Indian Army to contend with the IJA and the jungle at this point is well documented. See Chapter 2 and Marston, *Phoenix*, for more detail. As with the units in the Malayan campaign of 1941/2, the battalion had been heavily 'milked' and leadership may have been an issue. See C. A. Bayly and Harper, *Forgotten Armies*, p. 274, for some discussion of the 1943 Arakan campaign and discussions of the INA. Gajendra Singh noted that some of the men claimed to have been duped by their VCOs; see his 'Breaking the Chains' for more details on the specific interrogations of the soldiers involved. See also *TOP*, III, 7 May 1943, 690, pp. 951–2, for more discussion of the 1/15th Punjab Regiment.

[39] Various Indian Princely States, such as Hyderabad, Patiala, Mysore, Jaipur, and Kashmir to name a few, raised and commanded their own military forces during the period of the Raj. These forces were used for internal security operations within their states. On occasion, such as the First and Second World Wars, various Indian State Forces served overseas alongside the Indian Army. During the lead-up to partition, some of the Indian State Forces were complicit in attacking the civilian populations inside and outside the Punjab. Indian Army forces often engaged some of these forces in battle. For a wider discussion see Gaylor, *Sons of John Company*, pp. 50–8. An outpost from the Indian State Forces (not Indian Army), Gwalior Lancers, switched sides to the INA. See Sundaram, 'Paper Tiger', p. 43, and Mason, *A Matter of Honour*, p. 517.

[40] See Sundaram, 'Paper Tiger', for more detail.

[41] Many other INA units were used as lines of communication troops in both the Arakan and Assam to support the IJA main effort.

offensive, but did not reach the front until April 1944, just as the offensive started to grind to a halt. Some British commanders thought that the INA had fought well in the Imphal, but it made little difference to the eventual outcome. The IJA had underestimated the reform that had taken place in the Fourteenth Army and they, along with their INA allies, were slowly destroyed in and around the Imphal Plain.

One characteristic episode involved the 4/5th Mahratta Light Infantry in a battle with the INA Nehru Brigade in July 1944. The Mahrattas were able to patrol very close to the Nehru Brigade's defensive positions, and their fire discipline unnerved the INA troops. The INA had estimated that only a platoon was attacking their position, and set out to induce the Mahrattas to switch sides. They received no response. The Mahrattas, meanwhile, had fully enveloped the INA positions and attacked, forcing the INA to fall back and suffer a significant number of surrendered, killed, and wounded along the way.[42]

The IJA began the general retreat from the Imphal fighting in August 1944, taking the 1st INA Division with it. The INA's performance in the IJA offensives of 1944 was not notably successful. Some 1,500 INA troops deployed to the Arakan and another 7,500 to the U-Go offensive. More than 2,000 men were killed or wounded, or died of starvation during the campaigns.[43] The 1st INA Division reached Mandalay by September 1944, where Bose learned more details of both campaigns. Bose felt that the INA had been misused and mistreated; he was vocal in his opinions and his desire to improve conditions for the employment of the INA.[44] Despite his issues with the IJA, however, he persevered with delivering his propaganda message: 'neither the INA nor he was the least disheartened: he would immediately set about preparing for another attack on Imphal. If need be, he must attack Imphal ten times.'[45]

The IJA began to plan for the defence of Burma in October 1944, as elements of the Fourteenth Army followed up their success in the Arakan and Assam with an advance towards central Burma. As discussed in Chapter 2, the IJA decided to defend the eastern bank of the Irrawaddy

---

[42] See Tuker, *Memory*, Appendix II, pp. 555–7, for a fuller description. In the end, the Fourteenth Army of 1944 and 1945 was a seasoned and professional force that in terms of tactical abilities far overshadowed the INA.

[43] Tuker stated that only 150 were killed and 1,500 died of starvation. He does say that, by the end of 1945, more than 5,000 surrendered or deserted and 7,000 were captured (*Memory*, p. 562). Mason provides different numbers for the fighting on the Imphal Plain: he claims more than 400 were killed, but not the 4,000 claimed by some Indian journalists in the post-war period. See Mason, *A Matter of Honour*, p. 517.

[44] Sundaram, 'Paper Tiger', pp. 49–50; see also India Command Weekly Intelligence Summaries, 10 Nov. 1944, L/WS/1/1433, OIOC, BL.

[45] Quoted in C. A. Bayly and Harper, *Forgotten Armies*, p. 393.

River, with their positions centred on Mandalay in the north and the major railhead of Meiktila to the south. Bose sought an independent sector of defence for the remainder of the INA units and formations, along with better equipment and supplies, if not complete independence for the INA, under his sole command. The IJA did not react favourably to these requests, responding that, with regard to supplies, all that could be done would be, but not to expect much. IJA leadership remained suspicious of the INA's loyalty, following the desertions that took place in the Ha-Go and U-Go operations. In the event, the IJA allowed the INA to fall under Bose's direct command for the short term, and directed elements of the INA to take part in the defence of the Irrawaddy.[46]

With the 2nd INA Division moved into positions along the Irrawaddy, the Nehru Brigade, commanded by Col G. S. Dhillon, was detached to support the IJA forces further south. Over the course of February 1945, however, the autonomy that Bose thought he had won for the INA ceased to exist as the 2nd INA Division and its units and formations were placed under the command of the IJA 15th Division. On 14 February 1945, leading elements of the 7th Indian Division crossed the Irrawaddy River, smashing through the IJA and elements of the Nehru Brigade. Within hours of the first assault, more than 250 INA troops laid down their weapons.[47] The Nehru Brigade and elements of the IJA counter-attacked the 7th Indian Division's beachhead, but were repulsed after heavy fighting.

Caught alongside the IJA in Extended Capital, the Fourteenth Army's envelopment operation, the INA slowly disintegrated. By the end of March, more than 2,000 INA troops had surrendered to the Fourteenth Army.[48] Brig. R. C. B. Bristow, who served as CO of the Dogra Machine Gun Battalion during the fighting on the central plains of Burma and drive to Rangoon, received word of the INA's presence in the area and wondered how his men would react. He noted that the 'awkward situation was happily resolved by the INA surrendering without a

[46] Connell, *Auchinleck*, p. 797, and Sundaram, 'Paper Tiger', pp. 51–2; see also Bulletin 174 and ALFSEA Weekly Letter, 48, WO 203/1194, NA.

[47] Many of the Indian Army officers interviewed for this book as well as for my *Phoenix* openly expressed their disdain for the INA when they encountered them in battle. They also noted that their men expressed no sympathy at the time for the INA. Some officers recalled having to restrain some of their men from summarily executing INA POWs: author's interviews with British and Indian officers, 1999–2009. See a fuller description of some of this fighting and the apparent lack of will on the behalf of the INA in Tuker, *Memory*, pp. 558–9. He details the surrender of some 200 INA to the 4/2nd Gurkha Rifles from 20th Indian Division.

[48] Hamid, *Disastrous*, p. 17.

fight'.[49] IJA officers' doubts about the INA's loyalty and fighting spirit[50] continued to grow,[51] and Slim had to issue orders that Indian Army soldiers were to take INA troops prisoner, not kill them out of hand. He recalled that 'our Indian and Gurkha troops were at times not too ready to let them [INA] surrender and orders had to be issued to give them a kinder welcome'.[52] Bose flew to Tokyo from Saigon on 18 August, following the initial Japanese surrender; his plane crashed and he was assumed dead.[53]

INA troops captured in 1944 and 1945 were shipped back to India and segregated. British and Indian authorities attempted to discover the various reasons for their defections, and during the war the Indian Army dealt with INA prisoners via standard military methods – namely courts martial. By the end of the war, about thirty INA members had been tried; of those, nine were executed for having carried out espionage or sabotage missions.[54] The ending of the war and the occupations of Burma, Malaya, and Singapore significantly increased the flow of captured INA troops back to India.

INA trials

During the summer months of 1945, the Indian Army conducted interviews with INA prisoners in Malaya, Burma, and India, and tried to determine what should be done with them: how loyal were they to the

---

[49] He also stated that he talked with some of the INA members who were Dogras. He formed the impression that 'they had been confused and subverted by a small group of turncoat ICOs who, convinced the British would lose the war, had cast their lot with the Japanese' (Bristow, *Memories*, p. 134).

[50] Japanese and British intelligence indicated that many officers below the level of battalion command were not 'true INA', and that many sought to surrender as soon as possible. A number of senior officers were viewed as loyal to Bose and his ideals. Within the first month of fighting along the Irrawaddy, more than 1,000 INA members deserted to the Fourteenth Army. Many of the deserters were former POWs and not the Indian civilians who had been recruited.

[51] Sundaram, 'Paper Tiger', p. 53.

[52] Quoted in Mason, *A Matter of Honour*, p. 518. See also SEAC Weekly Security Intelligence Summary, no. 189, 15 Jun. 1945, L/WS/1/1506, OIOC, BL, which stated, 'one unit in Rangoon reports that IORs [Indian other ranks] regard the INA as traitors and would not hesitate to shoot them if so ordered'.

[53] Debates continue regarding the mystery of Bose's death. Even in 2006, there were many who claimed that Bose did not die on the plane. See Sundaram, 'Indian National Army', p. 142.

[54] H. V. Hodson, *Great Divide: Britain, India and Pakistan* (London: Oxford University Press, 1969), p. 249; Connell, *Auchinleck*, p. 797. See also *TOP*, III, 13 Oct. 1942, 91, p. 127; 14 Oct. 1942, 94, pp. 129–30; and 24 Oct. 1942, 117, pp. 154–5, for a wider discussion of the 'sabotage' and 'espionage' efforts and their lack of ability to cause damage.

INA? Would they be able to rejoin the Indian Army? The CO of one of the INA Guerrilla Regiments, in his interview, warned that many INA, if returned to their regimental depots, would appear to be compliant, but would continue to cause problems. He voiced what was many commanders' greatest fear: 'a rapid permeation of nationalism through the entire Indian Army'. The report went on to state that such views 'reflect the mentality not only of some of the commanders but also of some of the rank and file who have been so influenced'.[55] A later report, dated 20 July 1945, reiterated this point. The officer reporting had spent time with 4,000 INA POWs; his finding was that 'they have been thoroughly imbued with Bose's ideas and ... it is doubtful if they can be rehabilitated as soldiers again'.[56]

The Indian Army set out to separate and classify the prisoners for potential prosecution, rehabilitation, dismissal, or re-entry into the Indian Army. Senior staff decided fairly early on not to prosecute the majority of the rank and file, but to focus on the leadership, both in the INA and in the German-sponsored Free India Legion. Interrogation centres carried out procedures to assess INA members' loyalty and to determine reasons why some POWs switched allegiance.

By early August 1945, the Indian Army established criteria for courts martial. INA prisoners were to be assessed and designated as one of three colours: black, grey, or white. These corresponded to the following criteria: black meant that 'they should be brought to trial for a criminal offence, or [that] their release would be dangerous'. Grey meant that they had been members of an enemy organisation and subjected to enemy propaganda, and affected accordingly, but were not considered to be fundamentally and incurably disloyal. White meant that their loyalty was beyond question.[57] The report which laid out these criteria also specified that all INA officers would automatically be labelled as 'black' and court-martialled. The initial estimate for courts martial, based upon this assumption, was given as 600. The report indicated that, for another 1,400 listed as 'black', carrying out a trial would be difficult. More troubling was the figure of 5,600 given for other INA personnel listed as 'black', for whom not enough evidence was available to take a prosecution forward. These men were to be dismissed from the army and detained under Ordinance IV of 1944;

---

[55] SEAC Weekly Security Intelligence Summary, no. 189, 15 Jun. 1945, L/WS/1/1506, OIOC, BL.
[56] SEAC Weekly Security Intelligence Summary, no. 194, 20 Jul. 1945, L/WS/1/1506, OIOC, BL.
[57] *TOP*, VI, 17, 11 Aug. 1945, p. 49.

this recommendation sparked much debate within the GOI and the Indian Army, as well as with HMG.[58]

INA members who were to be tried faced the prospect of execution or deportation for life. Greys were to be dismissed from the army and designated 'services no longer required'. They would receive a pension (excluding their time as POWs) and forty-two days' pay. This was considered necessary to accommodate the feelings of those still serving in the army. Whites were to be treated as other recovered POWs, and continue to serve in the army.[59]

As cases began to come to trial, the Indian National Congress began to speak out in defence of INA prisoners, even though it had vocally opposed both the INA's narrative and methods during the war.[60] The Muslim League and the Punjab Unionists followed suit.[61] By mid September, Nehru was becoming increasingly vocal in his view that trials of INA defendants should not move forward.

Indian Army officers challenged Nehru on his reversal. During a visit to the 16th Cavalry in autumn 1945, one officer confronted Nehru, pointing out that 'when he was in Ahmednagar jail he had condemned the activities of the INA but was now championing their cause and using it for political purposes'.[62] Wavell advised HMG that 'Congress are making great play in support of the INA, demanding their unconditional release and sometimes lauding them as heroes.'[63] In October, British intelligence and GOI began to hear rumours (later confirmed in the violence of 1946 and 1947) that former INA troops were being sought by various political militias to serve as a military training force.[64]

---

[58] See *TOP*, VI, 32, 33, 47, 60, Aug. 1945, pp. 75, 76, 107, 142–3, for more on the debates that began to erupt regarding the ability to hold more than 6,000 men in detention without trial.

[59] *TOP*, VI, 11 Aug. 1945, 17, pp. 50–1. See also Wavell's entry in his diary, Moon, ed., *Wavell: The Viceroy's Journal*, for 6 Aug. 1945, pp. 161–2.

[60] See Gordon, *Brothers Against the Raj*, pp. 551–2; Nehru was quoted in 1943 as stating that he would go to the front to fight Bose and the Japanese if they invaded.

[61] Tuker, *Memory*, pp. 62–3, and Cohen, 'Subhas Chandra Bose', p. 421.

[62] Hamid, *Disastrous*, p. 19. The 16th Cavalry was a pre-war Indianised regiment that did well during the war and continued to perform well in French Indo-China as part of the 20th Indian Division. See Chapter 4 for more details.

[63] *TOP*, VI, 127, 1 Oct. 1945, p. 305.

[64] *TOP*, VI, 135, 9 Oct. 1945, pp. 319–20, which discusses Nehru's plan to make use of the INA – large quantities of arms are said to have been smuggled into India from the Burma front – both to train Congress volunteers and as a Congress striking force; and also possibly to tamper with the Indian Army. Nehru is said to have had conversations about the use of the INA for subversive purposes (*ibid.*, p. 319). See also Wavell to Pethick-Lawrence, 6 Nov. 1945, *TOP*, VI, 194, p. 452, as well as Hamid's discussion of the Congress Volunteer Corps and Sikhs seeking the support of released INA prisoners in *Disastrous*, p. 20.

Many Indian Army POWs were perplexed by Congress's sudden support for the INA. One returned officer reported to the viceroy how 'he and others had been shocked on their return to India to find that men of the INA were in some political quarters acclaimed as national heroes while the POWs who had stuck it out were completely disregarded'.[65]

Congress's political U-turn also presented Gen. Auchinleck and the Indian Army with a major dilemma. Negative feeling in the army and among returning POWs about the INA demanded quick and decisive action towards those members designated as 'black'. Doing so, however, against the wishes of Congress was likely to create a political firestorm – one that would be played out in India, where the majority of the population felt little connection to the army and the ideals for which they purported to stand. The new secretary of state for India and Burma, Lord Pethick-Lawrence, began to ask pointed questions about how many death sentences were likely to be carried out; under what circumstances; and when clemency might be considered.[66] Wavell and Auchinleck, sensitive to the political situation and being put under pressure, responded by restricting still further the number of courts martial planned, and narrowing the circumstances under which the death penalty could be applied,[67] although they knew this would be badly received by Indian Army personnel.[68]

Congress formed the Office of the INA Defence Committee on 22 September 1945 and formally announced the defence team for the first courts martial on 15 October 1945. At this time, they also petitioned the viceroy to postpone or abandon the trials.[69] Some of the defence team's members – Sir Tej Bahadur Sapru, Jawaharlal Nehru, Shri Bhulabhai Desai, Dr K. N. Katju,[70] and Rai Bahadur Badri Das – were considered among the best legal minds in India.[71]

---

[65] *TOP*, VI, 135, 9 Oct. 1945, p. 322; see also Jenkins to Turnbull, 23 Oct. 1945, *TOP*, VI, 160, pp. 386–7, for details of an Indian Army Indian officer (Capt. Badhwar, a former POW) meeting with a member of Congress to tell him about the 'truth' of the INA and their brutality.

[66] Pethick-Lawrence to Wavell, 29 Oct. 1945, L/WS/1/1577, OIOC, BL. With the change of government in the UK, under the leadership of the Labour Party, Lord Pethick-Lawrence took over from Leo Amery on 3 August 1945.

[67] Wavell to Pethick-Lawrence, 2 Nov. 1945, L/WS/1/1577, OIOC, BL.

[68] One officer, Col Malik, did report on 29 November 1945 that there was widespread sympathy for some of the INA, within the IORs and some within the ICO ranks. See Box 6/16, Gen. Sir Richard O'Connor Papers, Liddell Hart Centre, KCL.

[69] *TOP*, VI, 143, 15 Oct. 1945, pp. 341–4.

[70] His son had been killed fighting the Japanese in 1943: Connell, *Auchinleck*, p. 800.

[71] See *TOP*, VI, 143, 15 Oct. 1945, pp. 341–4, for a detailed submission of the position of the INA Defence Committee and their opening claims regarding the position of the INA and the specific defendants.

The first trials were set for early November, and the first officers tried were Capt. Shah Nawaz;[72] Capt. P. K. Saghal of the 2/10th Baluch Regiment, who commanded one of the battalions in Nawaz's division; as did the final defendant, Lt G. S. Dhillon, of the 1/14th Punjab Regiment. These three men represented the three major religions of India: Hindu (Shagal), Muslim (Shaz), and Sikh (Dhillon). They were all charged with murder; with abetment of murder; and with waging war against the king-emperor.[73] Gen. Auchinleck received word that the three defendants had entrusted their defence to the INA Defence Committee, and the trial was scheduled to begin at the Red Fort on 5 November.[74]

Gen. Auchinleck had decided to hold the INA courts martial at the Red Fort in Delhi. His primary motivation in doing so was to confront the problem in an open forum, instead of holding trials in various cantonments or less public arenas and opening the Indian Army to charges of trying to conclude the business in secrecy. The Red Fort was also chosen partly for practical reasons: the three defendants were being held there; GHQ India was not far away; and the fort itself was a symbol of India's greatness. The main drawback to this location was that it placed the trials in the full glare of public and media scrutiny; symbolically, the Red Fort also raised unhappy imperial associations as the home of the last Moghul emperors. As things turned out, it was a decision that backfired badly for the Indian Army.[75]

At the start of the trials, the effect of the INA situation on the army as a whole was quite minimal, especially in the 'frontline' or veteran units that had recently been involved in the campaigns in Burma and Italy. A morale report in October 1945 specifically reported on reactions from *jawan*s and others to discussions about the INA that were occurring outside the army. The report indicated that 'the sudden collapse of Japan came as a surprise for Indian troops. They were enthusiastic and greatly enjoyed the glory of being part of the victorious forces ... Politics are affecting the Army more closely than ever before, though so far there is no evidence to show that the Army as a whole is taking an interest in politics ... So far reports indicate that large numbers of

---

[72] He was from the 1/14th Punjab Regiment and was a pre-war ICO, winner of the Sword of Honour at IMA Dehra Dun. He was made a major general by the Japanese and commanded an INA Division in 1945.

[73] Hodson, *Great Divide*, p. 251; Connell, *Auchinleck*, p. 801; and Gordon, *Brothers Against the Raj*, p. 552.

[74] Auchinleck to Sir Evan Jenkins, 20 Oct. 1945, No. 1108, Auchinleck Papers, University of Manchester.

[75] Connell, *Auchinleck*, p. 800, and Hamid, *Disastrous*, p. 17.

Sepoys are indifferent to the fate of the INA.'[76] Later reports would indicate a more complex response.[77]

Within days of the trials starting, the Indian media and much of the population were following the trials closely and, it appeared, were increasingly vocally supportive of the INA defendants.[78] Even more troubling for the GOI and the Indian Army was the manner in which Congress began to link the INA trials with the Quit India movement of 1942, and discussions of trials for people who took part in the suppression of Quit India in a future independent India. Congress leaders were making claims that the 'British could be turned out of India within a short time ... threatening the officials who took part in the suppression of the 1942 disturbances with trial and punishment as "war criminals"'.[79]

Auchinleck sent one of his senior Indian officers, Col K. S. Himatsinhji, to meet with one of the defence counsels, Desai, to discuss the ongoing trials. The report to Auchinleck was extremely telling: Desai candidly confirmed that 'the INA trials have given them the best weapon they ever had for their propaganda and that, if any of these are executed, it will only make them the greatest martyrs India has ever had'.[80] When Himatsinhji asked Desai, 'how are you going to reconcile those prisoners of war and other Indian soldiers who had suffered and fought not only the Japs but the INA and who demand the guilty INA personnel must be tried?', Desai replied, dismissively, that anyone who expressed this sentiment had been 'tutored' to say so.[81]

This last response shows how little the Indian National Congress really understood the culture of the Indian Army. Desai also demonstrated his lack of awareness about the INA's battlefield performance, when he reported to the colonel that the INA had nearly succeeded in capturing Kohima in 1944.[82]

---

[76] 31 Oct. 1945, L/WS/1/1636, OIOC, BL.   [77] See below for later reports.

[78] Wavell to Pethick-Lawrence, 7 Nov., *TOP*, VI, 190: 'The General Court Martial of the three INA officers has been adjourned for a fortnight after a two-day hearing ... The proceedings seem to have been dignified and so far the defence counsel have been content to behave quietly. The trial is being given a great deal of attention in the Press and indeed the local Congress paper the Hindustan Times contains little else' (p. 447). Wavell would add in a letter on 13 November 1945, 'the adjournment of the first trial for a fortnight has not led to any slackening in the stream of propaganda poured forth by the Nationalist press in favour of the INA': Wavell to Pethick-Lawrence, 13 Nov. 1945, *TOP*, VI, 208, p. 476.

[79] Wavell to Pethick-Lawrence, 6 Nov. 1945, *TOP*, VI, 194, p. 451.

[80] Letter from Col K. S. Himatsinhji to Auchinleck, 19 Nov. 1945, No. 1113, Auchinleck Papers, University of Manchester.

[81] *Ibid.*

[82] *Ibid.* See also No. 1114, a letter from Maj. C. M. Cockin, stating that the problem of the INA should be ignored until a new national government had been formed in India, noting the growing tension between British and Indian views on the subject.

In late November, Auchinleck called for a meeting of his senior military commanders at GHQ India in New Delhi. He wanted to assess the impact of the ongoing trials on the morale of the Indian Army, as well as on popular opinion generally, and to determine what should be done about INA trials that were still to come. Opinion on all of these matters was deeply divided among those attending the meetings; after they were over, Auchinleck received several letters from officers who had attended, and who felt that it was necessary for the trials to continue. One letter, written by Gen. Sir Richard O'Connor to Gen. Auchinleck, highlighted this dilemma: 'if there is sympathy for them in the Army, which I still doubt, then it is because we have allowed these arguments to be used without any sort of reply ... How can we expect to keep loyalty if we don't condemn disloyalty.'[83] Lt Gen. Geoffrey Scoones also sent a note, reiterating many of the same points, including intelligence reports that the Indian Army, so far, appeared not to have been affected. He also highlighted that, while he understood that Auchinleck was in a most difficult position, 'any leniency (call it what you will) will *not* attain our immediate objective'.[84]

On 19 and 20 November, Auchinleck met with members of the provincial leadership regarding growing political tensions and agitation among the Indian population. Violent protests in support of the INA had erupted in Madras, Delhi, Lahore, and Bombay; Calcutta had a general strike from 21 to 26 November, and several hundred were killed or wounded.[85] Representatives from the Punjab expressed their fears that they were facing civil unrest worse than the incidents of 1942, and requested that there be no further trials, except in cases of murder and atrocities.[86] They also asked Auchinleck to commute any death sentences. Auchinleck eventually conceded and agreed to limit the number of trials, in an effort to calm the unrest spreading throughout the countryside. He also agreed that every effort should be made to speed up the trials.[87] Auchinleck reiterated this position to Wavell two days later in a follow-up letter, contending that the more lenient course of action was best, even though he knew that many army commanders would disagree, believing that this course would be detrimental to the

---

[83] O'Connor to Auchinleck, 24 Nov. 1945, No. 1118, Auchinleck Papers, University of Manchester.

[84] Lt Gen. Geoffrey Scoones to Auchinleck, 24 Nov. 1945, No. 1117, Auchinleck Papers, University of Manchester.

[85] Lebra, *Jungle Alliance*, p. 208.

[86] See Auchinleck to Wavell, 24 Nov. 1945, Enclosure 2, *TOP*, VI, 233, pp. 530–6, for more details of the Punjab's response.

[87] Auchinleck to Wavell, 24 Nov. 1945, *TOP*, VI, 233, p. 536.

army's morale.[88] A letter from Sir George Cunningham (governor of the North-West Frontier) to Wavell on 29 November further illustrates the divide between the senior political and military leadership that Auchinleck had to contend with. Cunningham stated: 'Some Army officers of great experience with whom I have discussed the matter ... have said that leniency at this stage would have a disastrous effect on the army. I do not believe this to be true. Some Indian officers and soldiers, whose relations or close friends have suffered under the INA leaders, are no doubt thirsting for their blood.[89] But I am certain that they are comparatively few ... [T]he thing is daily becoming more and more purely Indian versus British ... [T]he only way of stopping the rot is by a clean cut, at once.'[90] Another governor, Sir H. Twyman, of the Central Provinces and Berar, discussing Congress's efforts to drum up support for the INA in the countryside, wrote, 'I do feel some uneasiness as to the attitude which Indian troops may adopt if called upon to fire on mobs.'[91] He also notes, later in the report, that one of the Special Branch officers had reported that sympathy for the INA was not widespread among Indian Army *jawans*, NCOs, VCOs, and officers, and that the closer to the war the men served, the less sympathy was to be found.[92]

This last point, in particular, is one that would be made repeatedly in the coming two years: that the support and steadfastness of the Indian Army tended to come from the 'veteran' and frontline forces – those who had fought and died alongside one another in the Second World War.

Gen. Tuker, from Eastern Command, one of most outspoken critics of any possible leniency with the INA, stated that '*The Statesman*, India's influential English daily newspaper, said that the weak and inept handling of the INA by our Army Headquarters would do incalculable harm

[88] Auchinleck to Wavell, 26 Nov. 1945, No. 1119, Auchinleck Papers, University of Manchester. He also went on in detail, 'I do not think any senior British officer today knows what is the real feeling among the Indian ranks regarding the INA. I myself feel, from my own instinct largely, but also from various sources, that there is a growing feeling of sympathy for the INA ... In spite of the advice of these Army commanders and the Adjutant-General, three of whom are Indian officers of long standing and great experience of Indian troops, I am still convinced that the course I have recommended to you is the safest and best.'

[89] This point was raised by Wavell in a letter to Lord Pethick-Lawrence on 1 October 1945: 'two battalions of Gurkhas who have been returned from Prisoner of War camps in Malaya are far more bitter about the INA than about the Japs ... [T]heir one request to me was to see that stern justice was dealt out to the INA' (*TOP*, VI, 127, 1 Oct. 1945, pp. 305–6).

[90] Cunningham to Wavell, 27 Nov. 1945, *TOP*, VI, 243, p. 546.

[91] Sir H. Twyman to Wavell, 26 Nov. 1945, *TOP*, VI, 239, p. 542.

[92] *Ibid.*, pp. 542–3.

to the Indian Army ... I have said that all British officers, a large number
of nationalist Indians, even men of the Congress Party who were not
withered by hatred ... expected that the Army would vindicate itself by
laying on thick and fast the punishment of the officers of the INA.'[93]
Tuker reported that many within Eastern Command, from the *jawans* to
the officers, condemned the activities of the INA and hoped for a tough
prosecution. He even went so far as to point out what he saw as a growing
disconnect between senior leadership and officers at the regimental level
in the matter of leniency.[94]

On 27 November, Wavell reported some ominous observations to
Lord Pethick-Lawrence. The first one, reported a month earlier, was
that propaganda posters had been found, openly threatening that if INA
officers were executed, 'twenty English dogs' would die. The second
confirmed earlier reports of released INA being recruited as 'trainers'
for various political militias, preparing for the possibility of violent guerrilla campaigns in the near future. He went on to declare that, as a result
of misperceptions in the media regarding the INA's motives, actions, and
apparently widespread support, the trials had become 'a threat to the
morale of the Indian Army'.[95] This view prompted Auchinleck to go
even further with clemency, in an attempt to avoid more bad press and
defuse rising tensions.[96] Wavell concurred with this course of action in a
letter to Sir George Cunningham, confirming that no additional trials
would be held, unless the accused was charged with committing 'gross
brutality' against any member of the Indian or British Army.[97] But the
Red Fort trials, already under way, would continue.

At the end of November, Auchinleck presented an in-depth assessment of the internal situation in India for the Chiefs of Staff Committee.
In this report, he was quite candid about the impact of the INA, mentioning early on, for example, the number of weapons lying about in
India following the war and his fear that ex-INA members would be able

---

[93] Tuker, *Memory*, pp. 58–9. Tuker spends quite a bit of time presenting the argument that
the army command did not do enough to create a counter-narrative to the INA, to
criticise their inept battlefield performance, or to speak plainly about the brutalities that
INA troops meted out to fellow Indian Army POWs: ' ... our army did little to correct
impressions' (*ibid.*, p. 61).

[94] *Ibid.*, pp. 67–70.

[95] Wavell to Pethick-Lawrence, 27 Nov. 1945, *TOP*, VI, 246, p. 554. This sentiment was
reported by a journalist, Shiva Rao, in a letter to the Board of Trade, which was
submitted to the cabinet in the UK. It openly stated, 'Even men in the army are being
influenced by the trial.' He also added, 'I am more than ever convinced that this trial is a
first class blunder' (28 Nov. 1945, *TOP*, VI, 248, p. 564).

[96] See Wavell to Pethick-Lawrence, 29 Nov. 1945, *TOP*, VI, 251, p. 566.

[97] Wavell to Sir G. Cunningham, 30 Nov. 1945, *TOP*, VI, 253, p. 573.

and willing to use them. (In fairness, he also cited demobilised Indian Army soldiers as a potential concern, fearing that they might also be influenced by Congress to take up arms.) He compared and contrasted the situation in 1945 with that during the Quit India movement of 1942, and concluded that a co-ordinated campaign in the post-war era would be far more dangerous, mainly because of the presence of large numbers of demobbed soldiers who, trained to disrupt and cause havoc in war, could cause great damage used as a political militia.[98]

Auchinleck also considered the loyalty of the Indian Army in some depth, and in the context of the ongoing INA trials. He asserted that, at present (November 1945), the Indian Army 'was capable of dealing with either communal or anti-Government disturbances and failures on their part to perform their duty would probably be few and isolated'.[99] However, he expressed doubt about the future, and stated bluntly that it was impossible to know what might happen in the next six months. He cited Congress's pro-INA campaign and indicated his certainty that it must have an impact on the Indian Army. He feared that Congress would keep up the pressure, especially in light of the Indian Army's continuing deployment in French Indo-China and the Netherlands East Indies,[100] and classified the debates raised by Congress regarding these deployments as potentially more explosive than the INA trials.[101]

Looking to the future, Auchinleck raised another issue that he anticipated causing problems in the coming months. Many British officers who had served in the Indian Army, both before and during the war, were being released as the army was drawn down.[102] Many of these experienced officers were being replaced by newly created ICOs who were unknown to the men in the regiments and battalions. Many of the veteran officers had proved themselves in battle, but the new ICOs had not, and Auchinleck feared they would not be able to command the necessary respect and authority to rein in their men if difficult situations arose. Auchinleck made it very clear that the future stability of the country was reliant upon professional and stable Indian Armed Forces; if this could not be maintained, widespread and uncontained violence

---

[98] 'Internal Situation in India, Appreciation by the Commander in Chief', 24 Nov. 1945, L/WS/1/1008, OIOC, BL.

[99] Ibid.

[100] See Chapter 4 for more discussion of these deployments.

[101] This was a highly contentious issue and will be dealt with in more detail in Chapter 4.

[102] Many officers were leaving due to the drawdown and the fact that there appeared to be no future for British officers in the Indian Army. See Chapter 6 for a more detailed discussion of the drawdown.

might be the result. He bluntly suggested that one way this could be done would be a firm and explicit declaration by HMG to the effect that, while they maintain their intention to grant self-government to India by constitutional methods, (i) any armed insurrection would be put down, by force if necessary and the leaders punished; (ii) government servants would be supported to the full; and (iii) police and troops acting in the execution of their duty would be protected at the time and thereafter.[103]

Following submission of this assessment, Auchinleck released a press communiqué on 1 December 1945, outlining the GOI and Indian Army's plans for INA officers and soldiers. This indicated that many INA members designated as 'black' were going to be released because they had not carried out 'brutal attacks' against fellow POWs or Indian Army troops. The communiqué did not state any specific numbers, but it was clear that numbers awaiting trial had dropped dramatically.[104]

The release of this communiqué, in conjunction with a counter-propaganda campaign, started to quiet things down.[105] Wavell was able to report favourable results through the last weeks of December; on the 20th he wrote that: 'We are taking active measures regarding units [propaganda in villages to praise serving soldiers and exploits of the Indian Army]. If we can get the feeling right in the units the man going on leave will constitute the best propaganda instrument in the village ... INA agitation in the press is on the decrease and there are signs that Congress do not wish to intensify it.'[106] He was not entirely confident, however, as indicated by a letter that he wrote to King George VI around the same time: 'interest in the INA trials, which might well cause such an explosion, has for the time being died down ... [A]s soon as the first verdicts and sentences are given in the next few days, the whole weight of

---

[103] 'Internal Situation in India, Appreciation by the Commander in Chief', 24 Nov. 1945, L/WS/1/1008, OIOC, BL. Prime Minister Clement Attlee agreed with this assessment and stated that the loyalty of the army was key. He asserted that the Army would receive the full support of HMG, and emphasised the need to spread the word of the 'deeds' of the Indian Army during the war as a counter-narrative. See Attlee to Pethick-Lawrence, 6 Dec. 1945, *TOP*, VI, 271, p. 616.

[104] Governor-General to Sec. of State, 2 Dec. 1945, *TOP*, VI, 258, pp. 586–7. The GOI received intelligence regarding the numbers of people detained without trial within the INA and how much strain it was causing among many moderate Indians within India. The press communiqué helped deal with this constant issue and irritant. See letter from Mr G. D. Birla, *TOP*, VI, 270, pp. 612–14.

[105] There had been discussions in both New Delhi and London to counteract the Congress INA propaganda. The main theme was the use of POWs who stood firm against the IJA and INA: to have these men return to villages and allow them to tell their stories. This started to have an impact; see Wavell to Pethick-Lawrence, 15 Jan. 1945, *TOP*, VI, 357, p. 797.

[106] Wavell to Pethick-Lawrence, 20 Dec. 1945, *TOP*, VI, 300, p. 665.

the Nationalist Press will again be directed towards securing their release or at least the commutation of their sentences.'[107]

The first trial ended on 31 December 1945, and the verdict was released on 1 January 1946. All three officers were found guilty of waging war against the king; but only Shah Nawaz was found guilty of abetment of murder. All three were sentenced to transportation for life and cashiering and forfeiture of pay and allowances for time served with the INA. Auchinleck commuted the sentence of transportation for life, citing the following rationale: 'I believe that to confirm the sentence of transportation on these two officers would have the effect of making them into martyrs and of intensifying the political campaign of bitterness and racial antipathy now being waged by Congress.'[108] Auchinleck felt that if the sentences were carried out, violence would ensue and put the loyalty of the Indian Army to an excruciating test. Auchinleck's decision caused dissension among Indian Army officers, even as he was being commended by senior Indian civilians.[109] Philip Mason, a noted author as well as an Indian civil servant,[110] asserted that Auchinleck's decision demanded great courage, but noted that, in the end, 'the trial and its outcome [were] seen as a defeat for Britain'.[111]

Lt Gen. Tuker, GOC Eastern Command, was outraged by Gen. Auchinleck's actions. As he himself recalled: 'Very soon the Press came out with the announcement that the army had decided to deal leniently with the INA offenders. While accepting that many were but sheep, the British officers, now getting first hand tales of the brutal treatment of loyal officers and men at the hands of some of the blackguards of the INA, became more incensed than ever and more out of sympathy with the higher military authorities ... [T]he Army took it upon itself to commute, reduce or set aside the sentences and thus, to the scandal of its officers, condone the offences. The courts martial had done their duty

---

[107] Wavell to HM King George VI, 31 Dec. 1945, *TOP*, VI, 322, p. 714. See also letter from Sir Bertrand Glancy, Governor of the Punjab, to Auchinleck, 29 Dec. 1945, No. 1125, Auchinleck Papers, University of Manchester, stating that, while there was some sympathy for the INA, the counter-argument of returned POWs was starting to have a positive impact as well.

[108] Report by Auchinleck on the first INA trial, 1 Jan. 1945, No. 1127, Auchinleck Papers, University of Manchester.

[109] See letters from Dr M. C. Dawar to Auchinleck, 3 Jan. 1946, No. 1128, and Sir Shanti Swarupa Bhatnagar to Auchinleck, 4 Jan. 1946, No. 1129, Auchinleck Papers, University of Manchester.

[110] He served during the Second World War as the deputy secretary in the Defence and War Department, secretary to the Chiefs of Staff Committee, and finally as joint secretary to the War Department in the post-war period. See Mason's very interesting account of serving in the ICS, *A Shaft of Sunlight*.

[111] Mason, *A Matter of Honour*, p. 522.

and imposed heavy penalties; the Army had no business to meddle with what should have been a political compromise. The sentences should have been confirmed, thus upholding the standards of loyalty of the Indian Army. If the Viceroy had thought fit to intervene and to direct that leniency should be shown, that was another matter.'[112] The logic of Tuker's argument does carry weight, and his views on the matter were echoed by many officers during interviews with retired Indian Army officers, as well as in a number of contemporary morale and intelligence reports.[113]

Examining intelligence and morale reports for January 1946 provides some interesting insights into what was being said at the time from various perspectives. These contradict Auchinleck's views to a certain extent, without completely supporting Tuker's. One report provides a good example: it stated that morale was very high at the moment of writing, attributing this to the army's still-recent victories and stating that the troops were rightly proud of their efforts in defeating the Italians, Germans, and Japanese. Discipline was reported as being quite high, and in one place the report specifically stated that the *jawan*s had little interest in politics. It goes on to discuss the INA, indicating that while there was some sympathy generally speaking, there was none for INA members who had been accused and found guilty of crimes against fellow Indian soldiers. The report concludes with the finding that 'there is no indication that Congress propaganda is having any marked effects, and all commanders insist that the trials are having no adverse effect on morale'.[114]

Intelligence reports for the month of January supported the comments stated in the morale reports. The report for 4 January 1946 indicated little interest in the trials expressed by the Indian other ranks (IORs), and that they were carrying out their duties as always.[115] The report for 18 January says much the same: 'first impressions regarding the first trials are that they have had little effect on the opinion of the bulk of the rank and file and may have if anything encouraged a slight decline in interest'.[116] The report went on to describe a difference of opinion between British and Indian officers: indicating that the Indian officers had no quarrel with how INA personnel were being handled, while British officers were surprised by what they considered as condoning this lack of loyalty.

---

[112] Tuker, *Memory*, pp. 67–8.
[113] Author's interviews with Indian Army officers, 1999–2009.
[114] 31 Jan. 1946, L/WS/1/1636, OIOC, BL.
[115] 4 Jan. 1946, L/MIL/17/5/4276, OIOC, BL.
[116] 18 Jan. 1946, L/MIL/17/5/4276, OIOC, BL.

The interesting side-note in this report concerned the VCOs, stating that, while British and Indian commissioned officers were willing to express and debate their views on the INA question, VCOs were reluctant to discuss the matter.[117] Overall, the reports were mixed; but they did not conform to Auchinleck's point of view that the situation was dire.

Following receipt of the reports for January 1946, Auchinleck made another controversial announcement. With three INA trials in progress and more about to commence,[118] he proposed 'to drop the charge of waging war against the King-Emperor and to include only charges of murder and brutality'.[119] He felt that some of those accused of waging war against the king-emperor were likely to be found not guilty, and that this verdict would overshadow the more serious charges of murder and brutality.

Wavell concurred with Auchinleck's decision,[120] and both Auchinleck and Wavell had immediate concerns regarding the trials that had already begun. On 10 February 1946, as Capt. Abdul Rashid was called to the court, student demonstrations began in earnest in Calcutta.[121] The Indian Army was called out to suppress the demonstrations and some students were killed. Interestingly, Congress distanced themselves from these demonstrations, although they were supported by the Communist Party of India.[122]

Although the student demonstrations were dealt with swiftly, Auchinleck began to feel more and more pressured about the INA trials, their outcomes, his commutation of sentences, and their apparent impact on the Indian Army. As a result, he decided to send out questionnaires throughout the army to assess feeling about the INA. The findings were thought-provoking. Auchinleck asked formation commanders for their views of the INA trials, as well as potential issues within the army. He also sent questionnaires to KCIOs and ICOs, asking for their views of the

---

[117] *Ibid.*

[118] Capt. Mohammed Burhanuddin, 2/10th Baluch, was being tried for waging war against the king-emperor and murder: Connell, *Auchinleck*, p. 813.

[119] Auchinleck to Wavell, 22 Jan. 1946, No. 1133, Auchinleck Papers, University of Manchester.

[120] Wavell to Auchinleck, 23 Jan. 1946, No. 1134, Auchinleck Papers, University of Manchester.

[121] There had been earlier student demonstrations in November 1945, as the INA trials commenced. At the same time, Capt. Burhanuddin's trial began. He was also found guilty of brutality, and sentenced to seven years' imprisonment. See letter from Auchinleck to Wavell, 19 Feb. 1946, No. 1139, Auchinleck Papers, University of Manchester. Wavell agreed to the sentence, even if it potentially carried a risk of more civil unrest. See Wavell to Auchinleck, 20 Feb. 1946, No. 1140, Auchinleck Papers, University of Manchester.

[122] Gordon, *Brothers Against the Raj*, p. 555.

INA trials.[123] On 12 February, Auchinleck wrote a memorandum, based upon the findings of the questionnaires and the views of senior officers, discussing the effects of the first INA trials 'on the Indian Army as a whole'. He summed up the Indian officers' points of view as follows: 'most admit the gravity of the offence and do not condone it, but practically all are sure that any attempt to enforce the sentence would have led to chaos in the country at large and probably to mutiny and dissension in the Army, culminating in its dissolution, probably on communal lines'.[124]

Interestingly, not all ICOs agreed with these findings, including one of Gen. Auchinleck's own aides. Lt Col (later Maj. Gen.) S. S. Hamid responded to Auchinleck, in part, that 'the ICOs feel that the three INA officers have been let off very lightly and the authorities have been bowed down to the politicians. This has had an adverse effect on their morale and they do not see much future in the Army.'[125]

Auchinleck also discussed the effects on the VCOs and rank and file of the army; here too he concluded that it did not affect many, especially within the infantry and combat arms, but that it had caused some issues in the support branches. Overall, he indicated that the majority within the ranks agreed with the decision to be lenient and that the issue should now be over. His findings clearly indicated that most of the criticism of the handling of the INA trials originated with the British officers of the Indian Army. As he concluded: 'the effect on many British officers has been bad, and has led to public criticism which has not been in accordance with the traditional loyalty I am entitled to expect. To these officers, perhaps not always perceptive or imaginative, an officer is an officer, whether he be Indian or British, and they make no allowance for birth or political aspirations or upbringing, nor do they begin to realise the great political stresses and strains now affecting this country. They are unable to differentiate between the British and Indian points of view.'[126]

---

[123] See Hamid, *Disastrous*, p. 20.

[124] Letter addressed by Auchinleck to army commanders, 12 Feb. 1946, No. 1137, Auchinleck Papers, University of Manchester.

[125] Maj. Gen. Hamid added more detail in his answers to the questionnaire. He specifically stated: 'The general feeling among ICOs is that the trial has been given undue publicity and should not have been held in Delhi, and for that reason, not even in India. After the original mistake of holding the trial in Delhi had been committed and public opinion aroused against it, the authorities should not have yielded to press or party propaganda but should have punished the accused according to existing laws, which would have shown that discipline in the Army is not subject to public opinion.' He goes on into more detail regarding the pressure he saw upon Auchinleck to commute the sentences. See Hamid, *Disastrous*, pp. 21–2, for more details.

[126] Letter addressed by Auchinleck to army commanders, 12 Feb. 1946, No. 1137, Auchinleck Papers, University of Manchester.

Auchinleck followed this with a discussion of the state of the army in 1941, focusing on some of the pre-war problems resulting from Indianisation. As he stated in the memorandum: 'Moreover, they forgot, if they ever knew, the great bitterness bred in the minds of many Indian officers in the early days of Indianisation by the discrimination, often very real, exercised against them, and the discourteous, contemptuous treatment often meted out to them by many British officers who should have known better.'[127]

Auchinleck concluded by stating bluntly that he commuted the sentences to support a larger goal: a viable, functional, and professional Indian Army, 'for the future, whatever Government may be set up in India. This can only be done if the British and Indian officers of that Army trust and respect each other and continue to work wholeheartedly together for the common cause as they have done in war.'[128]

No sooner had Auchinleck sent this memo than an Indian officer, Col K. S. Himatsinhji, reported on 17 February that the mood in most of the country was anti-British, and that Congress and the Muslim League were in agreement on the INA issue – one of the few things that the two parties could agree on at the time, amid tensions surrounding upcoming elections for an interim government and the debates on the possibility of an independent Muslim state.[129]

Royal Indian Navy mutiny

While the Indian Army struggled with how best to handle the INA trials, other branches of the military were encountering their own problems. In January 1946, the Royal Air Force (RAF) airmen stationed at Royal Indian Air Force (RIAF) bases in India and the Middle East demanded early demobilisation and better pay, and followed this with wilful disobedience of orders. This mutiny was peaceful and dealt with swiftly. Some members of the RIAF decided to follow their British counterparts' example, but their efforts were quashed almost immediately.[130] Some senior British officers, notably Gen. Tuker[131] of Eastern Command,

---

[127] *Ibid.*   [128] *Ibid.*

[129] Col K. S. Himatsinhji to Auchinleck, 17 Feb. 1946, No. 1138, Auchinleck Papers, University of Manchester.

[130] Hamid, *Disastrous*, p. 23.

[131] Auchinleck's military secretary, Hamid, made an entry in his diary regarding Tuker. On 28 March 1945, he met Tuker and described him as follows: 'Tuker is the most outstanding officer I have ever met. He is a fighting soldier as well as a great strategist, and is completely relaxed in a difficult situation. He is a great friend of Wavell, with whom he shares a love for poetry. He even attends Urdu *Mushairas* [recitations of poetry]' (*Disastrous*, pp. 46–7).

contended that at least some of the disobedience was the result of the soft sentences handed down in the first INA trials, pointing out that 'it was certainly used by the mutineers as a precedent for their conduct'.[132] (He also claimed that the RIAF actually declared their sympathy with the INA.)[133] Both mutinies were put down by British and Indian Army units, without any bloodshed. The next problem to flare up came from an Indian Pioneer unit in early February, near the Royal Indian Navy (RIN) depot in Calcutta. This was also handled swiftly, as was a second disturbance at the Signal Training Centre at Jubbulpore.[134]

These mutinies were dealt with quickly, the ringleaders were caught and tried swiftly, and the press appeared to be unaware of the situation. There were claims that Congress was behind at least some of these actions.[135] Some army officers also believed that since the units involved were not veteran or frontline forces, they were more susceptible to such problems.

The next major issue to arise originated in the Royal Indian Navy (RIN), not for the first time; the RIN had already suffered nine mutinies between 1942 and 1945.[136] The unrest began at the signal school HMIS *Talwar* in Bombay where, on 8 February, several sailors were court-martialled for insubordination. More alarming was the slogans that began to appear around the school, including 'Quit India', 'Kill the British White Bastards', and 'Revolt Now'.[137] By 17 February, many ratings from HMIS *Talwar* were refusing to touch food or go on parade; by the 18th, ratings from HMIS *Sutlej* and *Jumna* as well as ratings from the Castle and Fort Barracks in Bombay were following suit. Flag marches were established and the agitators threatened to take their mutiny off the naval base. The leadership of the mutiny brought out a list of demands, including the release of all INA prisoners. Gen. Sir Rob Lockhart, commander of Southern Command, was put in charge of putting down the mutiny. At first, a battalion from the 5th Mahratta

---

[132] Tuker, *Memory*, pp. 80–1.   [133] *Ibid.*, p. 84.

[134] *Ibid.*, pp. 80–98, and author's correspondence with Maj. G. E. Mitchell, Royal Indian Army Service Corps.

[135] Hamid, *Disastrous*, p. 24.

[136] Hamid goes into greater detail highlighting the major issues that existed in the RIN during the war period and the immediate post-war period. One of the key issues that Hamid cites was the issue of leadership, especially in terms of mid-level officers and below. See Hamid, *Disastrous*, pp. 24–5, for more detail. See also Wavell to Attlee, *TOP*, VI, 466, p. 1055: 'RIN has not the same background as army, proportion of experienced officers and petty officers is very small owing to the rapid expansion during the war, and [a] number of young and excitable men have been worked on by agitators from inside and outside. There may be service grievances but I do not think they are serious.'

[137] Hamid, *Disastrous*, p. 25.

Light Infantry, supported by British forces, was sent into Bombay to eject any sailors who had entered the city and push them back into their barracks. At first the Indian and British infantry and Royal Marines were able to round up troublemakers without much difficulty, and the Indian Army performed its task with professionalism.[138]

At the same time as events in Bombay, RIN personnel in Karachi began their own mutiny. Ratings from HMIS *Hindustan* opened fire upon army troops on shore in Karachi, but were rapidly silenced by Indian Army artillery. Seven ratings were killed and the rest surrendered.[139]

On 21 February, the mutineers in Bombay opened fire on some of the Indian and British Army positions on land. Again, the army was able to put this down swiftly; they prevented the ratings from surging back into Bombay, although some made it into the city. On the morning of the 22nd, rioting broke out in sections of Bombay in support of the mutineers.[140] By early evening two battalions were deployed as Aid to the Civil Power, supporting the Armed Police to restore order. Any RIN mutineers who were caught in the city were rounded up and placed back in the barracks. By the 23rd, when the rioting ended, there were three battalions patrolling the city. More than 1,000 people were arrested, another 1,000 were injured, and some 200 were killed, along with nine ratings and one officer. The Indian National Congress, who at first had been passively supportive of the mutineers, became alarmed by the scale of the violence in Bombay, and called for them to surrender. On the 23rd they did so, hoisting white flags on the various ships.[141]

Overall, this incident's effect on the army's internal cohesion or discipline appeared to be negligible.[142] In fact, the Indian Army received high praise for its handling of both the mutiny and the civil disturbances in Bombay. One observer recorded that 'during the RIN mutiny in Bombay and subsequent civil disturbances in the city, the morale of the Indian troops employed in settling the mutiny and in assisting the civil

---

[138] Wavell to Pethick-Lawrence, 22 Feb. 1946, *TOP*, VI, 461, p. 1048: 'there is no sign of trouble spreading to the Indian Army'.

[139] Hamid, *Disastrous*, pp. 25–6, and Tuker, *Memory*, pp. 86–91. For more detail, see Sir F. Mudie to Wavell, 27 Feb. 1946, *TOP*, VI, 474, pp. 1071–4. Mudie reports on the Karachi episode in very interesting detail.

[140] See Chapter 5 for a discussion of the communal violence that erupted in Calcutta in February 1946.

[141] Sir John Colville (Bombay) to Wavell, 27 Feb. 1946, *TOP*, VI, 478, pp. 1079–85.

[142] A minor disturbance occurred when twenty-five soldiers from the 17th Mahratta Light Infantry refused to follow orders after they arrived in Bombay from service in Malaya; this has been linked to issues surrounding customs examination and bad food on ship. See Intelligence Reports, No. 5, 1946, L/MIL/17/5/4276, OIOC, BL.

power was reported to have been high. Men carried out their duties efficiently and impartially.'[143] Another report commented: 'in spite of the political capital being made out of the army's conflicting loyalties, Indian troops of all classes carried out their duties in the RIN mutiny and civil riots to the complete satisfaction of their officers'.[144] A follow-up report stated flatly that there was little sympathy for the RIN ratings, especially from veteran and frontline army units, who looked down on the RIN and openly speculated that they must have had weak officers.[145] Auchinleck wrote personally to Lockhart: 'I will be most grateful if you will convey to all the troops concerned my appreciation of the restraint and discipline which they showed in most difficult circumstances and my deep gratitude for their help in relieving a most difficult situation.'[146] Interestingly, the Indian press attempted to subvert the efforts of the Indian Army by claiming that soldiers refused to carry out the orders of higher command to put down the mutinies.[147]

The continuation of the INA trials

In an attempt to celebrate the recent successes of the Indian Army in the Second World War and also shift some public attention away from the INA trials, the GOI and Indian Army organised a series of events during the week of 7 March. The highlight was the Victory Parade on the 7th itself in Delhi. Viceroy Wavell described it, both in his diary and in a letter to King George VI, as 'I think the most impressive parade and finest body of men I have seen in 45 years' service; I came away full of pride in the Indian Army.'[148]

The Indian National Congress boycotted both the parade and the celebration, and this increased the tension between Auchinleck and

---

[143] *Ibid.* As Tuker stated: 'the soldiers had done their job and done it properly' (*Memory*, p. 88).

[144] 30 Apr. 1946, L/WS/1/1636, OIOC, BL. It was also reported in the intelligence briefs; see India Command Fortnightly Intelligence Reports, 1 Mar. 1946, L/MIL/17/5/4276, OIOC, BL.

[145] India Command Fortnightly Intelligence Reports, 15 Mar. 1946, L/MIL/17/5/4276, OIOC, BL.

[146] 2 Mar. 1946, 8310/154-73 Lessons of the Royal Indian Navy Mutiny, Gen. Sir Robert Lockhart Papers, NAM.

[147] Tuker, *Memory*, pp. 93–8. Also, the governor of the Sind, Sir Mudie, stated: 'In today's Sind Observer there is a news item that a number of Indian Army men are in detention for refusing to take action against RIN mutineers. This is absolutely false and I have reason to believe that the Editor knows it to be false'. (Mudie to Wavell, 27 Feb. 1946, *TOP*, VI, 474, pp. 1073–4).

[148] Wavell to HM King George VI, 22 Mar. 1946, *TOP*, VI, 545, p. 1235; see also Moon, ed., *Wavell: The Viceroy's Journal*, p. 220.

Wavell on one side and the Congress leadership on the other. As the soldiers marched off the parade ground, various nationalist demonstrators jeered and derided the soldiers and their efforts. The mob of demonstrators then turned their attention to the city of Delhi, resulting in widespread burning and looting. The next day, Wavell met with Congress leadership, and berated them for these actions. As he reported to the king in his letter: 'I have never been more disgusted with Indian politics; and have taken the occasion, while seeing political leaders shortly afterwards [after the parade] to express myself plainly indeed to them about their insult to the Indian armed forces, who have saved India and so greatly raised their prestige. I told them that their folly in exalting the few thousand traitors of the INA, who were chiefly cowards and softlings of the Indian Army, and in belittling the great mass who had been loyal and saved India, would recoil on their own heads. They listened in silence and professed to agree, but I doubt whether there will be any change of heart, though I think some are beginning to realise their blunders.'[149]

Auchinleck, while expressing himself pleased with both the conduct of the army during the victory celebrations and the viceroy's dressing down of Indian politicians, nevertheless felt compelled by nationalist attempts to subvert his authority to set out clearly his views on the role of the army. He did so in a letter that was read out to Indian Army officers on 28 March 1946 by the adjutant general, Savory, in a radio broadcast. The letter, addressed to 'Every Officer of the Indian Army', asserted that

The magnificent divisions of the Indian Army are world renowned. The Indian soldier will go down in posterity as among the finest fighting soldiers of the world ... [I]f however, the army, through inefficiency or unreliability in the performance of its duties in the maintenance of law and order, fails to carry out the orders of the government in power at the time, then the internal situation may well develop into chaos ... The Army [is] the anchor of the country and ... its 'Great Duty' [is] to remain disciplined: efficient: and loyal to whatever government may be in power ... Thus may the Indian Army lead the way ... British officers, it is your duty to your country and to the army to which you belong to pass on to your Indian comrades, who are to follow you, in a spirit of unselfishness and service, all the experience and knowledge that you have gained in the past, so that they may, in their turn, serve the Indian Army as faithfully and truly as you have done.[150]

---

[149] Wavell to HM King George VI, 22 Mar. 1946, *TOP*, VI, 545, p. 1235; see also Moon, ed., *Wavell: The Viceroy's Journal*, p. 220.

[150] Morale Reports, 28 Mar. 1946, L/WS/1/1636, OIOC, BL; see also 28 Mar. 1946, No. 1144, Auchinleck Papers, University of Manchester. The adjutant general of the army, Savory had sent a note to Auchinleck on 20 March stating very similar views: 'The aim of the British and Indian officers should be to ensure that the Indian Army as handed over to the future Government of India should be loyal, efficient and a reliable army in

On the same day, Lt Gen. Tuker submitted a paper to Auchinleck, predicting that sooner or later communalism was certain to infiltrate the Indian Army. He reportedly wrote that 'the men are being subjected to nationalist propaganda, attending political meetings and coming in contact with political agitators ... Communal disturbances in their home areas and the tales of atrocities are a source of constant worry for them ... [A]nyone who disagrees with the above assessment is out of touch and living in a world of make-believe.'[151]

Wavell noted in his journal on 19 February, as the RIN mutiny began, that Gen. Auchinleck was very gloomy, and that he felt that Auchinleck was considering abandoning the INA trials completely.[152] One morale report for late March/early April highlighted the complexity of the situation within the army, pointing out that even the *jawans* were being forced to consider the INA question, as a result of pervasive political rhetoric and instability in the country generally and in the other armed forces specifically. The report also indicated that *jawans* and VCOs were beginning to feel some sympathy for the INA, believing that they had been misled by their officers and the Japanese. One key difference that this report focused on was the feelings of both Indian and British officers; it stated: 'many British and Indian officers [are] afraid that leniency shown in the trials might be widely accepted as a sign of government weakness'.[153]

One follow-up intelligence report from 12 April indicated a dangerous precedent: a commanding officer, discussing the political situation in the country, cited a situation that had arisen with some of the new ICOs in his unit. He stated: 'The ICO knows about his men but either does not

---

accordance with its past. Anything less would lead to chaos and anyone who thought otherwise was biting off his nose to spite his own face' (Morale Issues, 20 Mar. 1946, L/WS/1/1636, OIOC, BL). The nationalist *Hindustan Times* bluntly responded to Auchinleck's letter on 30 March: 'There is no doubt whatever that if the transfer of power is not quickly brought about, the foreign rulers of India cannot count upon the loyalty of the Indian Army. Nor can the Nationalist attach much importance.' It went on to accuse the British officers of the army of creating trouble. Lt Col Hamid retorted that 'to blame them and to doubt their loyalty at this stage is to dishearten them'. See Hamid, *Disastrous*, p. 47.

[151] Hamid, *Disastrous*, p. 46.
[152] Moon, ed., *Wavell: The Viceroy's Journal*, p. 215.
[153] Morale Reports, Mar.–Apr. 1946, L/WS/1/1636, OIOC, BL. An intelligence report from April also stated that the *jawans* were potentially becoming more politically conscious due to Congress and the Indian press. See India Command Fortnightly Intelligence Reports, 12 Apr. 1946, L/MIL/17/5/4276, OIOC, BL. One earlier intelligence report from 1 February 1946 did touch upon the officers' different points of view, noting that 'more senior ICOs showed surprise at the leniency shown and some fear that it may herald the entry of political influence in the service' (India Command Fortnightly Intelligence Reports, 1 Feb. 1946, L/MIL/17/5/4276, OIOC, BL).

wish to counter any unhealthy political thoughts or is afraid to do so [due to the political climate]. ICOs have been called upon to lecture to their men on the importance of the fighting services remaining unbiased on political issues, have shown reluctance to do so, not because they disagree with such a policy but because they feared to do anything that might appear to make them be seen as unnationalistic in the eyes of the men. One ICO complained of the difficulty he would experience in carrying out his duties in the Aid to the Civil Power. The fear of reprisals that might be instigated against his family worried him.'[154] The ideological gap – between veteran officers with battlefield experience and respect from their men on one side and newly arrived ICOs with minimal frontline experience and ability to impose their will on their men on the other – appeared to be widening.

The issue of the INA trials remained unresolved into April and May,[155] with pressure to discontinue them steadily increasing both from within India and from the United Kingdom.[156] After a long series of debates, Wavell and Auchinleck agreed in late April to cancel any further trials of INA personnel. They met with Nehru on 2 May to discuss the outstanding issues in person.[157]

Nehru had sent many messages regarding the INA situation, and met with Auchinleck and Wavell more than once, as had Muhammad Ali Jinnah, the head of the Muslim League. Wavell and Auchinleck had decided that those INA personnel who had already been found guilty would serve out their sentences;[158] this created another ongoing issue, as both Congress and the Muslim League responded to this decision by continuing to request that Wavell and Auchinleck release other INA prisoners. Wavell asked Nehru not to tell the Indian press that he had written to Auchinleck to try to influence his position, and Nehru agreed.

---

[154] India Command Fortnightly Intelligence Reports, 12 Apr. 1946, L/MIL/17/5/4276, OIOC, BL.

[155] Hamid specifically recalls a meeting on 4 April where the INA was discussed extensively: *Disastrous*, p. 49.

[156] See Moon, ed., *Wavell: The Viceroy's Journal*, entries for month of March and April; see also Record of Interview between Lt Gen. Sir A. Smith and Muhammad Ali Jinnah, 28 Mar. 1946, *TOP*, VII, 12, pp. 20–2, for some of the debates and discussions that continued in March and April regarding the INA. See also Meeting between Wavell and the Governors, 29 Mar. 1946, *TOP*, VII, 20, pp. 48–51.

[157] See Meeting with Nehru, 2 May 1946, *TOP*, VII, 177, p. 394. Hamid (*Disastrous*, p. 59) specifically stated that during the meeting, when Nehru pushed for the release of the convicted members of the INA, Wavell did not mince his words; he characterised the INA as weaklings and deserters, and declared that their release would affect the morale of the army.

[158] Fourteen men were tried and sentenced before Auchinleck discontinued the trials: Connell, *Auchinleck*, p. 817.

During the meeting, Wavell bluntly reiterated once again his contempt for the INA to Nehru. Interestingly, Nehru responded with the following: 'any body of men were a mixture; but that while he realised that some of the INA men had not joined from the best of motives and were not the best type of men, he had met many of them who were of the good type. He said that the attitude taken by the Congress Party towards the INA trials was not simply for political motives but in response to the real feeling in the country ... He said there was no intention to withhold admiration from the regular Indian Army, though they had hitherto felt this was a foreign instrument of repression.'[159] Wavell wrote after he entered this: 'I think, from what he said, that Congress has begun to realise that the INA is not entirely a creditable asset.'[160]

Nehru sent a note to Auchinleck on 4 May, thanking him for discontinuing the trials. In this note, Nehru went into considerable detail explaining why he had chosen to defend the INA; he also stressed that he understood and appreciated the Indian Army's sacrifices. He closed his letter with the following statement: 'I suppose that everyone who has given thought to the matter realizes fully that it is a dangerous and risky business to break the discipline of an army. It would obviously be harmful to do any injury to a fine instrument like the Indian Army, and yet, at every step, till major changes take place converting it into a real national army, we have to face the political issue which governs every aspect of Indian life today.'[161] Auchinleck's aide Hamid described in some detail the follow-on meeting between Auchinleck and Nehru, which took place the next day in Simla:[162] 'Nehru seems rather apologetic as a result of his advocating the cancellation of the INA trials. He probably realizes for the first time what effect the cancellation of the trials will have on the regular army. This is the same army that stood firm and fought well during the war while the INA indulged in atrocities against their comrades. During the conversation he seemed to make peace with the Auk [Auchinleck].'[163]

In spite of Nehru's political manoeuvring in the matter of the INA trials, his behaviour at this point indicated that he was beginning to realise that the Indian Army as an institution needed to be non-communal as well as apolitical, especially with independence coming soon. Perhaps he was also beginning to realise that he might have pushed

---

[159] Meeting with Nehru, 2 May 1946, *TOP*, VII, 177, p. 394.   [160] *Ibid.*
[161] Nehru to Auchinleck, 4 May 1946, No. 1149, Auchinleck Papers, University of Manchester.
[162] The Cabinet Mission had just started their rounds of talks with all the various political parties.
[163] Hamid, *Disastrous*, p. 60.

things too far. It also highlighted once again, unfortunately, his complete lack of understanding of the Indian Army as an organisation.

Conclusion

There can be no doubt that the INA trials placed significant strain on the Indian Army. Gen. Auchinleck, in his attempts to reinforce the success of the Indian Army during the Second World War and offset the INA's impact, was upstaged and outmanoeuvred by Nehru and the Indian National Congress. This was possible partly because of Auchinleck's decision to make the trials public in order to send a message. Nehru and many in the Indian National Congress may not have agreed with the INA's inception or purpose but, in the public presentation of the trials, they recognised a major political opportunity, and seized it. In the end, the INA would not disappear from the political upheaval in the coming months. The issue ended only with the granting of independence in August 1947.[164]

Auchinleck, pressured and buffeted by conflicting opinions about how best to handle INA personnel designated as 'black', had to steer as centrist a course as he could manage. Morale and intelligence reports, as well as opinions from his military commanders, varied greatly and there was little consensus to be found about the impact the trials were likely to have on Indian Army personnel. There were hints of potential issues for the future, demobbed soldiers being influenced and used by various political parties, former INA soldiers entering the 'militias' of various political parties, and the replacement of veteran officers with recently commissioned and non-veteran ICOs.

The irony in all of this is that, in the midst of political upheaval and civic disruption, the Indian Army coolly and professionally carried out its responsibilities in India Command, dealing with the civil disturbances and acting in Aid to the Civil Power. Indian Army troops in Burma, Malaya, French Indo-China, and the Netherlands East Indies also carried on with their duties, which were trying to say the least, without fuss or fanfare.[165] The Indian Army, severely provoked as it was, maintained its professional discipline and loyalty in a national maelstrom.

---

[164] See Chapter 7 for more details.   [165] See Chapter 4 for more information.

4 The Indian Army in French Indo-China and the Netherlands East Indies 1945–1946

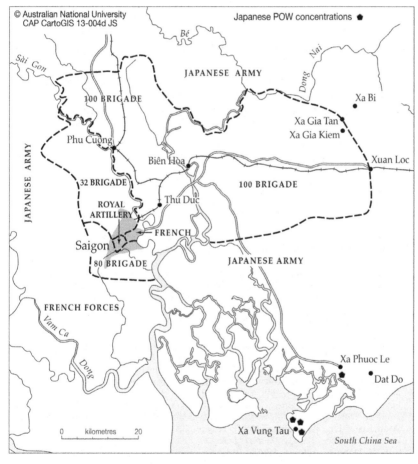

Map 4.1 20th Indian Division in and around Saigon

Indian troops should not be used for doing Britain's work against our friends who are fighting that same fight we are.[1]

Wars do not come to a clean end.[2]

This chapter focuses on a difficult and controversial aspect of the Second World War and its immediate aftermath: occupation responsibilities throughout the Japanese Empire. When His Majesty's Government in London agreed to expand the area of responsibility for South East Asia Command (SEAC) with regard to occupation duties in July 1945 at Potsdam, Germany, this put SEAC in the position of relying upon the largely volunteer Indian Army to carry out the mission.[3] The conscript British Army could not meet this need, as it was having great difficulties keeping numbers high enough amid demobilisation pressures at the end of the war in the east. In the immediate aftermath of the Second World War, the Indian Army found itself carrying out occupation duties not just in British colonies such as Burma and Malaya, but also in the colonies of French Indo-China and the Netherlands East Indies (later Indonesia).

The Indian Army's involvement in French Indo-China (FIC) and the Netherlands East Indies (NEI) was to prove one of its most controversial assignments.[4] In both places, Indian Army divisions

---

[1] Quoted in Geraint Hughes, 'A "Post-War" War: The British Occupation of French Indochina, September 1945–March 1946', *Small Wars & Insurgencies*, 17, 3 (2006), p. 276.

[2] Louis Allen, *The End of the War in Asia* (London: Hart-Davis MacGibbon, 1976), p. 267.

[3] All the senior officers mentioned in this chapter were Indian Army, except for Gens. Christison, Jack Dempsey, and Mountbatten.

[4] There has been considerable research into this period in the past twenty years, mostly within the context of the post-Second World War political environment; there has not been much specific emphasis on the Indian Army's role as distinct from the larger strategic context of British decolonisation and the impending conflict in French Indo-China that would engulf the French (and later the Americans) in two costly wars, as well as the Indonesian war of independence. For further details on the larger issues surrounding this chapter, see the following: John Springhall, 'Kicking Out the Vietminh: How Britain Allowed France to Reoccupy South Indo-China, 1945–1946', *Journal of Contemporary History*, 40, 1 (Jan. 2005), pp. 115–30; Ronald Spector, 'After Hiroshima: Allied Military Occupations and the Fate of Japan's Empire, 1945–1947', *Journal of Military History*, 69, 4 (Oct. 2005), pp. 1121–36; Peter Neville, *Britain in Vietnam: Prelude to Disaster, 1945–1946* (London: Routledge, 2007); Peter Dennis, *Troubled Days of Peace: Mountbatten and South East Asia Command, 1945–1946* (Manchester University Press, 1987); Hughes, 'A "Post-War" War'; Allen, *End of the War in Asia*; Peter Dunn, *The First Indo-China War* (London: C. Hurst & Co., 1985); F. S. V. Donnison, *British Military Administration in the Far East, 1943–1946* (London: HMSO, 1956); Kirby, *War Against Japan*, V; Mountbatten, *Report*; Vice-Admiral Lord Louis Mountbatten, *Post Surrender Tasks: Section E of the Report to the Combined Chiefs of Staff by the Supreme Allied Commander South-East Asia, 1943–1946* (London: HMSO, 1969); and *TOP*, V, VI, and VII; as well as papers of Gen. Sir Douglas Gracey, Liddell Hart Centre, KCL. For more details on the Netherlands East Indies, see John Springhall,

found themselves, as one officer would later state, in the position of 'piggy in the middle'.[5] The divisional and corps commanders had to navigate a minefield of political issues, involving emancipation of Allied prisoners of war[6] and civilians, disarming more than 300,000 Imperial Japanese soldiers, and eventually fighting counter-insurgency campaigns against nationalist guerrillas who perceived them as instruments of the returning French and Dutch colonial administrations. For some battalions, the campaigns during this period involved fighting almost as bitter as anything they had encountered against the Japanese in Burma.[7]

The occupation was further hampered by a poorly defined strategy: mission statements appeared to change over the course of the occupation, and indicate considerable gaps in understanding between SEAC, HMG, and India Command on what the Indian Army's remit and goals should be. Attempting to define, and articulate, why the Indian Army should be involved in occupation duties in non-British colonies and as a result find itself fighting a counter-insurgency campaign against nationalists that had nothing to do with India or the British Empire presented a number of problems for both the viceroy, Lord Wavell, and Gen. Sir Claude Auchinleck. Along with the post-war trials of Indian Army personnel who had joined the Indian National Army as Japanese prisoners of war, the Indian National Congress Party made significant political use of the Indian Army's involvement in FIC and the NEI, part of an ongoing debate on India's independence and the role of the army in that context.

While the Indian Army's involvement was being discussed and debated in New Delhi, the Indian Army itself quietly got on with carrying

---

'Disaster in Surabaya: The Death of Brigadier Mallaby During the British Occupation of Java, 1945–1946', *Journal of Imperial and Commonwealth History*, 24, 3 (Sep. 1996), pp. 422–43; Richard McMillan, *The British Occupation of Indonesia, 1945–1946* (London: Routledge, 2005); papers of Lt Gen. Sir Philip Christison, IWM; and papers of Lt Col A. J. F. Doulton, NAM.

[5] Author's interview with Maj. G. C. Coppen, 1 Nov. 1999.

[6] See Kirby, *War Against Japan*, V, Appendix 30, for a detailed discussion regarding the numbers of POWs in SEAC AO.

[7] A sad commentary regarding this point was the death of Lt Col Sarbjit Singh Kalha of the 2/1st Punjab Regiment at Sourabaya in Java, NEI. As noted in Chapter 2, he had risen to command the battalion during the Burma campaign and was highly respected. According to the 5th Indian divisional history, he was 'calm and unruffled in battle, fearless, and with delightful manners, he had won the DSO and Bar. His remarkable ability included that of commanding both British and Indian officers, and there was no one in his battalion or in the Division who did not hold him in the highest regard. He was one of those senior Indian Army officers whom India could least to afford to lose' (Brett-James, *Ball of Fire*, p. 463).

out their difficult duties with competence and dispatch. They were commended on all sides for their professionalism, providing a vivid example of how Jawaharlal Nehru[8] failed to comprehend the essential motivation of most Indian soldiers, VCOs, and officers, regardless of the circumstances or the problems therein: to perform to the best of their abilities.[9] To supply but one example from this period, consider the performance of the 23rd Indian Division in the NEI by assessing awards listings for gallantry and leadership: the Distinguished Service Order, the Military Cross, and the Military Medal. Nine DSOs were given to commanders during the Burma campaign, three in the NEI. Seventy MCs were given out in Burma; twenty-three were given out in the NEI. Last but not least, one hundred Military Medals were awarded in Burma, and another thirty-eight in the NEI. Then consider that the 23rd served just over one year in the NEI, compared to just under three years in Burma against the Japanese.[10]

One need only refer to the various war diaries and divisional and regimental histories to see that, for the men, VCOs, and officers, these campaigns were a strange continuation of the Second World War – and one which some authors felt should not have occurred.[11] Some units added battle honours to their credentials during this period; more than one indicated that they accomplished this without any obvious support from the British Army. The pre-war model of one British battalion in each Indian Brigade, to toughen it up, was a thing of the past by 1945 and 1946, and the Indian Army took responsibility for being both the spine and the body within all of the divisions: bearing the brunt of higher-level decision-making, expanding the area of responsibility for SEAC, and carrying out occupation duties in non-British colonies.

---

[8] Nehru attempted to use both the INA trials and the operations in FIC and the NEI as political levers against the viceroy and the CinC. His objections reached the United States, and the *New York Times* reported on a speech he gave late in 1945, in which he stated that Indian troops were 'doing Britain's dirty work against our friends [Viet Minh and Indonesian nationalists]' (*New York Times*, 1 Jan. 1945). The irony about the complexity of relationships among nationalist populations at the end of the war is exemplified by Ho Chi Minh, then operating in the northern section of Vietnam who, despite his nationalist credentials, was instrumental in the capture and handing over of the deputy commander of the Indian National Army, Maj. Gen. A. J. Chatterjee, to the British military.

[9] See Hughes, 'A "Post-War" War', p. 276: 'Indian and Gurkha troops who provided 20th Division with nearly all of its frontline soldiers, and who showed no qualms about treating local nationalists as the new enemy.' See also 80th Brigade security intelligence report, 23 Oct. 1945, WO 172/7218, NA.

[10] Doulton, *Fighting Cock*, p. 311.

[11] See McMillan, *British Occupation of Indonesia*.

Strategic context

As noted above, Lord Louis Mountbatten, commander of SEAC, arrived in Potsdam, Germany, on 24 July 1945, to meet with the Combined Chiefs of Staff. There he was informed that SEAC would be taking over responsibility for more of South East Asia – chiefly Borneo, Java, and Indo-China, all of which had previously been under the control of South West Pacific Area, or Gen. Douglas MacArthur's command. At first, Mountbatten did not feel that this would be too large a task for SEAC to take on. SEAC had already been planning Operation Zipper, the amphibious attack and campaign for Malaya and Singapore.

It was during the meetings in Potsdam that Mountbatten was advised of the impending atomic bomb drop on Japan. He was sworn to secrecy, but told to prepare for the possibility of an early Japanese capitulation. Mountbatten duly informed SEAC HQ in Kandy, Ceylon, without revealing information about the atomic bomb, to prepare for potentially imminent capitulation, and to begin planning to manage the enlarged area of responsibility that SEAC had inherited. SEAC HQ responded to this information with concern, fearing that Operation Zipper would not go forward if an early capitulation occurred. Military and political leaders in SEAC and London considered the invasion and reoccupation of Malaya and Singapore of particular psychological importance, necessary to wipe clean the humiliation of the 1942 Malayan and Singapore capitulations.[12]

Mountbatten immediately set out to prepare SEAC, chiefly formations from the Twelfth and Fourteenth Armies, to make ready to seize strategic areas from the Japanese in Burma and then prioritise specific areas expected to be handed over to SEAC control. On 13 August SEAC established priority areas as follows: Malaya, Saigon (Ho Chi Minh City), Bangkok, Batavia (Jakarta, NEI), Sourabaya (NEI), and Hong Kong. With this plan in place, SEAC was able to move quickly, and naval forces were able to begin carrying out Operation Zipper in short order.[13]

The increased level of responsibility caused consternation for some senior British officers, including Gen. Sir William Slim, commander of Allied Land Forces South East Asia (ALFSEA). As he wrote: 'The area of South East Asia Land Forces had suddenly expanded to include

---

[12] See letter to Foreign Office, 31 Jul. 1945, *Documents on British Policy Overseas*, Series 1, Vol. I, *1945* (London: HMSO, 1984), Calendar I to no. 599; also quoted in Dennis, *Troubled*, pp. 11–12.

[13] Saigon was placed high on the list because the Japanese HQ for their Southern Army was housed there: Dunn, *First Indo-China War*, p. 119.

Malaya, Singapore, Siam [Thailand], [the NEI], Hong Kong, Borneo
and the Andaman Islands ... [I]n two of them, Indo-China [FIC] and
[the NEI], nationalist movements armed from Japanese forces had
already seized power in the vacuum left by the sudden surrender.'[14]

Another major issue for Gens. Slim and Auchinleck, back at India
Command, was that Operation Python, the repatriation scheme for
British personnel, was also in full force.[15] Many conscripted British
officers, NCOs, and soldiers were being released from service due to
pressure on the British government with the war's end. With the
expanded area of operations for SEAC and the need to reoccupy many
areas, SEAC needed formations that were going to provide the capacity
required for occupation duties. The political reality of Operation Python
meant that this duty fell to the professional Indian Army,[16] and this was
unlikely to be welcomed by nationalist politicians in India.[17] Auchinleck
stressed to Mountbatten that it was not a foregone conclusion that all the
Indian Army troops that were needed could come from India Command.[18] SEAC had asked for the 7th Indian Division to deploy to Siam,
the 20th Indian Division to deploy to Indo-China, and the 23rd and 26th
Indian divisions to deploy to Malaya and then the NEI, with the 5th
Indian Division following on.[19] Auchinleck specifically cited the need for
troops for internal security duties in India, which would be necessary
later in the year and into 1946 as the INA trials moved forward. It was
clear that the political situation in India was extremely delicate; Mountbatten understood this and was quick to respond to Auchinleck that he

[14] Slim, *Defeat into Victory*, pp. 529–30.
[15] HMG made an announcement in February 1945 that all British soldiers, NCOs, and
     officers who had served in the Far East for three years and eight months would be
     repatriated to the UK and released from service. In June 1945 this was amended to three
     years and four months. This policy decision created significant difficulties for SEAC and
     GHQ India in manning British battalions in the Indian Army, as well as British divisions,
     during the final phases of the Burma campaign. Decisions made about expanding
     SEAC's area of responsibility extended its impact into the post-war period. See Kirby,
     War Against Japan, V, pp. 83–91, for a full description of its effects.
[16] As Ronald Spector noted: 'Mountbatten suffered from the most critical shortage of
     troops as well as the worst timing ... [A] large proportion of Mountbatten's non-
     British forces were divisions of the Indian Army ... [A] good number of the Indians
     were career soldiers and many of the rest were in no hurry to be discharged' (Spector,
     'After Hiroshima', pp. 1128–9).
[17] See below for more discussion.
[18] It is interesting to note that, in Mountbatten's private diary, he never alludes to any
     tension regarding the use of Indian Army troops or to Auchinleck's and Slim's concerns,
     despite mentioning both men numerous times. See Mountbatten, *Personal Diary of
     Admiral The Lord Louis Mountbatten: Supreme Allied Commander, South-East Asia,
     1943–1946*, ed. Philip Ziegler (London: Collins, 1988).
[19] Slim, *Defeat into Victory*, pp. 530–1, and Dunn, *First Indo-China War*, p. 124.

saw the need to be cautious. Even so, neither they nor HMG were prepared for what would be required of the Indian Army in the NEI and FIC or for the political fallout that would ensue.[20]

Even as planning went ahead, formations were earmarked and assigned; as shipping began to move, inter-Allied relations deteriorated. The American general Douglas MacArthur announced that he wished for all commanders to stop movement and for no landings to take place in the Japanese Empire until the formal surrender in Tokyo Bay had taken place. At this point, this ceremony was planned for 28 August. MacArthur's reasoning was that Japan had not yet signed any surrender treaty, and that unilateral action by theatre commanders could prejudice the surrender process, and ultimately lead to the Japanese commander of forces in South East Asia, Field Marshal Terauchi Hisaichi, refusing to obey surrender orders from SEAC.[21] It was well known that communications between Tokyo and field commanders were erratic at best during this time[22] and, while some of MacArthur's points may have been valid,[23] Mountbatten and SEAC were outraged. They complained bitterly to the Joint Chiefs, pointing out that some of their forces were already six days out from Rangoon and preparing to land in Malaya. The British Chiefs of Staff agreed with Mountbatten, but HMG in London disregarded these concerns and told Mountbatten and SEAC to halt the invasion of Malaya and follow MacArthur's instructions. To add insult to injury, not all Allied forces did the same. The Soviets ignored MacArthur and continued to destroy the Japanese Army in Manchuria; even worse, the American general Albert Wedemeyer,[24] serving with the Chinese Nationalist forces, did the same.[25] This delay contributed significantly to the subsequent issues that arose in the occupations of both the NEI and FIC; British/Indian forces lost time and traction in dealing with both Japanese and nationalist groups, the latter having successfully filled the political vacuum that had been created with the Japanese surrender.[26]

---

[20] Dennis, *Troubled*, p. 7.   [21] Dunn, *First Indo-China War*, p. 123.

[22] Dennis, *Troubled*, p. 13.

[23] It was feared that many Japanese soldiers would still fight on until they heard that the emperor had actually surrendered. It was estimated that there were close to 5 million Japanese soldiers in the empire, and their impression was that they had not been defeated.

[24] Gen. Wedemeyer had been the Chief of Staff to Mountbatten in SEAC, but in October 1944 he replaced Gen. Joseph Stillwell, to assume command of all US forces in China and to serve as Chiang Kai-shek's Chief of Staff.

[25] See letter to Mountbatten, 21 Aug. 1945, WO 172/1778, NA, and Dunn, *First Indo-China War*, p. 123.

[26] Dennis, *Troubled*, pp. 14–15. See also Slim's critical comments regarding this issue in *Defeat into Victory*, pp. 530–1.

The British/Indian Army mission for both the NEI and FIC continued to evolve over the next several months. Issues remain unresolved to this day regarding the intent of senior commanders and what actually occurred. Overall, the commanders had three specific aims in entering into each area: rescue Allied POWs, disarm the Japanese military, and maintain law and order to ensure internal security.[27] The ability of commanders to carry out these orders was compromised by the delay imposed by MacArthur, and the ensuing internal political maelstrom. The plight of the POWs was an excellent example of this; as Slim noted: 'Our men and those of our Allies were daily dying in their foul camps; thousands were at the limit of weakness and exhaustion.'[28]

SEAC's campaigns in the NEI and FIC began simultaneously; however, while the NEI campaign lasted through most of 1946, the FIC campaign was over for all intents and purposes by the end of February 1946. This chapter will first focus on the FIC campaign, named Operation Masterdom,[29] and then deal with operations in the NEI.

French Indo-China

The British were placed in charge of only part of French Indo-China; specifically, they were assigned to control the area south of the 16th parallel,[30] while the Chinese Nationalists controlled the area to the north. The British area of responsibility included not only southern Vietnam, but also Cambodia and parts of Laos. The Chinese troops, having disregarded MacArthur's orders, arrived in the area first, in early September. Their efforts were focused on pillage, rape, and loot in the northern areas of Indo-China.[31] The British mission was organised into two groups, the Control Commission[32] and the Allied Land Forces French Indo-China

---

[27] See ALFSEA Operational Directive No. 12, 28 Aug. 1945, 'Masterdom', WO 203/5444, NA, and Springhall, 'Kicking Out the Vietminh', p. 119.

[28] Slim, *Defeat into Victory*, pp. 530–1.

[29] See Operational Directive No. 12, 28 Aug. 1945, WO 203/5444, NA, and Springhall, 'Kicking Out the Vietminh', p. 119.

[30] In the end, the 20th Indian Division expended most of its time and effort in and around Saigon.

[31] See Springhall, 'Kicking out the Vietminh', p. 119, and Dunn, *First Indo-China War*, p. 139.

[32] This organisation was made up of resources from SEAC and reported directly back to SEAC HQ in Kandy, Ceylon. Gen. Gracey had an extensive list of tasks to fulfil for SEAC: assume control of HQ Japanese Southern Army; supervise the surrender; transmit SEAC orders to the Japanese; obtain information regarding Japanese dispositions and supplies; control Japanese communications; study the 'recovery of Allied prisoners of war and internees' (RAPWI) problem and render all possible aid;

Figure 4.1 Indian troops arrive in Saigon in 1945 © Imperial War Museums (Image No. SE 1772)

(ALFFIC),[33] and headed by the seasoned and well-respected 20th Indian Division commander, Maj. Gen. Douglas Gracey.[34]

As commander of Allied Land Forces South East Asia, Gen. Slim issued Operational Directive No. 8 to his senior commanders for the

report on Indo-China's lines of communication, airfields, and the port of Saigon; open river and sea approaches to Saigon; using Japanese resources, reduce size of Japanese HQs as soon as possible; and maintain liaison with the French local government, keeping Mountbatten informed. See 30 Aug. 1945, Box 4/2, Gracey Papers, Liddell Hart Centre, KCL.

[33] This was a larger organisation than the commission; it included French military forces and directly reported back to Gen. Sir William Slim and ALFSEA.

[34] Springhall, 'Kicking Out the Vietminh', p. 119.

military occupation of Malaya, Burma, the NEI, and FIC. Commanders were instructed to disarm and concentrate all Japanese forces; protect, succour, and ultimately evacuate Allied POWs and civilian internees; establish and maintain law and order; introduce food and other civil affairs supplies; and set up appropriate civil administration.[35] Gracey received further detailed orders; in addition to the points raised in Operational Directive No. 8, he was instructed to pay special attention to law and order and, more importantly, 'liberate Allied territory in so far as your resources permit', which to some on his staff implied possible future operations against the Vietnamese nationalists, the Viet Minh.[36] The terms of this last directive, compared to Gracey's actual actions, have led historians to see Gracey as potentially going beyond his remit.[37] Slim sent a message to Gracey that the French were to be in charge of civil administration; however, in designated key areas, he would be responsible for full authority over both the military and civilian but working through the French administration.

By the time the British were able to send troops into Indo-China, planning was beset with difficulties. The British had minimal intelligence about the Japanese Army in the area, as well as the state of the administration and relations with the Viet Minh.[38] The French had administered the area under five different colonies: Cochin-China, Tonkin, Annam, Cambodia, and Laos. Until March 1945, the Vichy French had worked alongside the Imperial Japanese Army, at which point they had been ousted by Japanese occupation forces. Before the British arrived, Ho Chi Minh had declared independence from the French authorities for the new nation of Vietnam, with the tacit support of the Japanese. The resistance movement was named the League for the Independence of Vietnam, or Viet Minh. The Viet Minh provisional executive committee in the south set out to fill the political vacuum there, acting at the behest of Ho Chi Minh.[39] The Viet Minh slowly started to take over governmental control in Saigon and the surrounding areas. On the same day as the Japanese surrender occurred, there were mass demonstrations in Saigon in support of the Viet Minh and of the declaration of independence. Violence erupted between French civilians, the Viet Minh, and

[35] ALFSEA Op. Directive No. 8, 23 Aug. 1945, Box 4/2, Gen. Gracey Papers, Liddell Hart Centre, KCL.

[36] Operational Directive No. 12, 28 Aug. 1945, Box 4/2, Gen. Gracey Papers, Liddell Hart Centre, KCL.

[37] See debate in Dunn, First Indo-China War, pp. 140–7.

[38] Ibid., p. 132,/2, Gracey Papers, Liddell Hart Centre, KCL. More information started to trickle out to the British, but it was not of a high quality.

[39] Kirby, War Against Japan, V, p. 290.

other political factions wishing to take advantage of the power vacuum. There were rumours of many people being killed, and escalating violence.[40]

The British needed to get troops to Saigon quickly, but were hampered by acute transport shortages by air and sea. This was the start of an ongoing problem for the British and, later, the French forces. The first elements of the 20th Indian Division, 80th Indian Brigade, arrived at Saigon's Tan Son Nhut airport on 8 September and immediately began to assess the situation.[41] More troops arrived on 11 September and Gracey arrived from Rangoon (Yangun) with his staff on 13 September.[42] Gracey immediately recognised the need for more troops, with the city and surrounding areas apparently in chaos. Ironically, Japanese troops were being used to provide security at the airfield. They would play both defensive and offensive roles under British command in the following days, weeks, and months, not just in FIC but also in the NEI.[43] This would lead to controversy, especially with the American and British press.

While one of the chief missions for Gracey and the Indian troops was disarming the Japanese, they recognised that they would need to keep a significant number in place as defensive and static forces.[44] Indian troops were slowly starting to arrive, and the rising violence between the French and the Vietnamese communities was causing problems.[45] As the days progressed, tensions between the British/Indians and the Viet Minh

---

[40] Springhall, 'Kicking Out the Vietminh', pp. 117–18.

[41] There is some discrepancy on the date: some authors such as Springhall state the first troops arrived on the 8th. The first detachment was more than one hundred soldiers from the 1/19th Hyderabad Regiment. Kirby, *War Against Japan*, V, p. 298, states that the first troops arrived on the 8th. The brigade would not be in fully in country until the 26th, due to the many transport issues.

[42] Upon arriving, Gracey and his staff walked past the small Viet Minh delegation and met with the Japanese contingent. This action specifically stated that the Allies did not recognise the Viet Minh as a legitimate government.

[43] Interestingly, many Indian Army veterans recalled, from their command of Japanese POWs, the professionalism and discipline that the Japanese displayed. Some even indicated their preference for commanding Japanese over their own Indian *jawans*: author's interviews with Indian Army officers, 1999–2009. 8th G/8th Gurkha Riles, Lt Col E. H. Russell, noted in a letter to his wife, upon arrival in Saigon, that 'the most incredible thing – really incredible thing – is to see the Japs. As we came down the gangplank, a Jap fatigue party took the men's kit from them, and loaded it onto lorries. They did it at the double. My right arm will fall off soon, as every Jap, even if he is 500 yards away, salutes, and one has to the return the salutes' (cited in 8th Gurkha Rifles Association, *Red Flash*, No. 15, Feb. 1992, p. 6).

[44] The process of disarming and rounding up soldiers and weapons was complicated. The British and Indian soldiers would do it first and then hand over the weapon stores to the French authorities and military, as the Japanese refused to deal with them.

[45] Kirby, *War Against Japan*, V, pp. 298–9.

increased apace. The Viet Minh were inciting Japanese soldiers not to surrender, but to desert with their weapons and join the Viet Minh.[46] They also set out to spread anti-British propaganda among the Indian soldiers in the division, but it fell on deaf ears.[47]

Gracey and his staff viewed the Viet Minh as a direct threat to law and order. On 19 September, SEAC issued contradictory directives, simultaneously ordering Gracey and the 20th Division to seize Saigon Radio and censor other broadcasts of the Viet Minh, and issuing a general statement about not interfering in local affairs.[48] Gracey and his staff decided on more far-reaching moves to contend with rising violence. Brig. Maunsell, Chief of Staff on the Control Commission, met with the Viet Minh provisional government on the 19th, and issued a proclamation closing all newspapers, banning Provisional Government seizure of buildings or other property, banning all public meetings, demonstrations, and processions, and the carrying of weapons, and enforcing a night curfew. He also asked for a list of all Vietnamese police and armed units. This amounted to declaring martial law, which Gracey then had to enforce, relying on the equivalent of two battalions of troops.[49] Gracey advised SEAC of his proclamation, asserting that: 'I would stress that though it may appear that I have interfered in the politics of the country, I have done so only in the interest of the maintenance of law and order and after close collaboration with some senior French representatives.'[50] Mountbatten backed Gracey at the time, although later in life he questioned Gracey's decisions at this point in the campaign.[51]

Gracey's proclamation was read out and in theory took effect on 21 September. In reality, however, without sufficient troops the British were limited in their ability to enforce its tenets, particularly the

---

[46] It was estimated that more than 2,000 Japanese soldiers did desert before and after the arrival of the British and Indian troops: Springhall, 'Kicking Out the Vietminh', p. 119.

[47] 'Report on Ops 80 Ind Inf BDE', Box 5/4, Gracey Papers, Liddell Hart Cenre, KCL; see page 6, 'propaganda to suborn Indian soldiers were freely posted up by Annamites [Viet Minh]. These had no effect at all.'

[48] It was stressed by Mountbatten in a communiqué: HMG's goals in sending British troops into FIC were fourfold – to control Field Marshal Terauchi's headquarters, which commanded the Japanese Armies in the Southern Regions; to disarm the Japanese; to release and repatriate Allied POWs and internees; and to maintain law and order until the arrival of French forces. He stressed that HMG had no intention of using British forces in FIC to crush resistance movements. See Dunn, *First Indo-China War*, p. 167.

[49] Gracey to Mountbatten, 19 Sep. 1945, WO 172/1784, NA.

[50] Gracey to Mountbatten, 21 Sep. 1945, WO 203/5562, NA; Dennis, *Troubled*, p. 39; and Springhall, 'Kicking Out the Vietminh', p. 120.

[51] See Mountbatten, *Post Surrender Tasks: Section E*, as well as Dunn, *First Indo-China War*, p. 173, and Dennis, *Troubled*, p. 41.

curfew. On the 22nd, former French POWs were released and rearmed to support the effort.[52] While at first this idea seemed like a good solution to the manpower problems in Saigon, it was to have wider repercussions within twenty-four hours. British and Indian troops had been moving through the city, trying to round up and disarm the Viet Minh police and armed groups. Units of the 80th Indian Brigade also moved against the Viet Minh-controlled administrative buildings, handing them over to the meagre French forces after they had taken possession. The French were able to seize control of the administrative elements of Saigon without too much bloodshed, pushing out the Viet Minh provisional government and raising the tricolour above the Hotel de Ville.[53] A *coup d'état* had occurred, however, and more blood was to be spilled.[54]

The released French POWs had been guarded by the Viet Minh, and had suffered at their hands. Unfortunately for Gracey and the British/ Indian forces, within twenty-four hours of the coup, French discipline began to break down, and French troops began to kill Viet Minh and suspected Viet Minh in retaliation. The French civilian population also became involved with the ensuing mob violence. This had repercussions for the British and Indian troops, and Gracey attempted to make the French commanders aware of the issues and get their men back in control. These men still fell under the command of Gracey, and he and his men would be accountable for the situation's deterioration.[55]

As a result of these developments, the Viet Minh began to consider the British as part of the attempt to reimpose French colonial government in

---

[52] The French 9th DIC (Colonial Infantry Division) was still not in Vietnam, but was to be released soon, to relieve the 20th Indian Division.

[53] See 'Saigon Control Commission, Political Report, 13 September to 9 October 1945', Gracey Papers, Liddell Hart Centre, KCL, for a more detailed account, as well as Dunn, *First Indo-China War*, pp. 183–9.

[54] Throughout this period, a series of debates was ongoing both in SEAC and in London, where the British mission began and ended. Mission creep had been occurring since mid August and there was at times a lack of clear strategy and end goal. Gen. Gracey felt that he had to carry out the coup to allow for law and order to be restored, and that the French forces and administration were best placed to implement this, since the Viet Minh was not a recognised organisation. See Dennis, *Troubled*, Springhall, 'Kicking Out the Vietminh', and especially Dunn, *First Indo-China War*, for a much more detailed account of the higher-level issues regarding strategy and joint British and French planning and thinking on Indo-China. An interesting document is the 'Report on Ops 80 Ind Inf BDE', found in Gen. Gracey's papers. It clearly outlines the need and planning for the seizure of key administrative buildings and centres in Saigon, stating: 'the stage was now set for the coup d'etat by the French to take over the civil administration in Saigon' (p. 4; 'Report on Ops 80 Ind Inf BDE', Gracey Papers, 23 Sep. 1945, Liddell Hart Centre, KCL).

[55] See Dunn, *First Indo-China War*, pp. 195–7, and Dennis, *Troubled*, pp. 43–8.

Indo-China.[56] Some authors cite this episode as the beginning of the first Indo-China war. The Viet Minh launched a general strike on 24 September, paralysing sections of the city by cutting off water or electricity. Violence also began to increase: on 25 September, more than 300 French and Eurasian families were butchered in a northern section of Saigon by Viet Minh and other paramilitary gangs. Violence escalated as the Viet Minh set up road blocks and British and Indian troops engaged them during their expanded patrols.[57] The sounds of gunfire, mortars, and other weapons were heard each night, as British/Indian, French, and Viet Minh forces skirmished through the city. Many Burma veterans noted the difficulty of fighting guerrillas in an urban environment.[58]

Mountbatten praised Gracey for his actions in communicating with the Chiefs of Staff,[59] but on the 24th he cabled Gracey and asserted that British and Indian troops should be used only in designated 'key areas'; the French and Japanese needed to handle sections outside Saigon.[60] Mountbatten appeared to be growing concerned that Gracey had exceeded his orders, and began to question his ability to command. Gen. Slim, by contrast, supported Gracey, and pushed Mountbatten to release all of the 20th Indian Division to provide support.[61] The course of action being contemplated was for British/Indian forces to take complete control of Saigon; this would require a whole division, to restore law and order and to repatriate POWs as well. Gen. Gracey was also expected to start working to find a political solution to the problems between the Viet Minh and the French, so as to allow the withdrawal of British and Indian forces.[62] It was also at this juncture that a politically fraught decision was made: to expand the use of Japanese troops.

[56] 'On September 23, armed and protected by the British forces, the French colonialists launched their attack and occupied Saigon. Our people replied by force of arms, and from that moment, our heroic resistance began' (Truong Chinh, *Primer for Revolt* (New York: Praeger, 1963), p. 17); see also Dunn, *First Indo-China War*, pp. 202–3.

[57] The first American casualty in the history of US intervention in Vietnam occurred during this period. Lt Col Thomas Dewey of the Office of Strategic Services (OSS) was killed in a Viet Minh ambush. The role and position of the US OSS during this period are controversial; see Dunn, *First Indo-China War*, and Dennis, *Troubled*, for a more detailed discussion of their stance in relation to the British and French activities.

[58] See war diaries from the 20th Indian Division for more information, WO 172, NA; see also Dunn, *First Indo-China War*, pp. 200–1.

[59] Dennis, *Troubled*, p. 50.

[60] See Dunn, *First Indo-China War*, pp. 200–10, and Dennis, *Troubled*, pp. 50–4.

[61] Springhall, 'Kicking Out the Vietminh', p. 124, as well as Hughes, 'A "Post-War" War', p. 271, and Dunn, *First Indo-China War*, pp. 229–30. At a meeting in Singapore on 28 September, Slim backed Gracey against Mountbatten that the whole division was needed to restore law and order in and around Saigon. See Hughes, 'A "Post-War" War', p. 270.

[62] Dennis, *Troubled*, pp. 59–61.

Not only would they be protecting airfields; they were also allocated to more offensive roles alongside British troops and sometimes under the command of British officers[63] to support Gracey's efforts to impose law and order in and around Saigon, until the rest of the 20th Indian Division and the follow-on French military forces arrived.[64] The Japanese refused to work for the French, and requested that all orders and actions be directed through the British command structure.[65] In the end, however, the main French build-up of forces took longer than expected.[66]

It was at this juncture that both Gen. Auchinleck and Viceroy Wavell began to note the political fallout that operations in FIC and the NEI were causing in India. Cognisant of the pressure on the Indian Army arising from the INA trials that were about to begin in New Delhi, Wavell stated to the secretary of state for India, Lord Pethick-Lawrence, on 1 October 1945:

The situation in French Indo-China and the Netherlands East Indies will give us some trouble. Indian troops are involved in both places, and we shall be attacked for allowing HMG to use them to suppress national movements. It was of course most necessary to disarm the Japanese, and to maintain law and order while this was being done. But I hope that HMG will be able to disengage the troops, both British and Indian, as soon as possible and leave the business to the French and the Dutch.[67]

---

[63] Author's interviews with Indian Army veterans, 1999–2009, and 1/1st Gurkha Rifles, War Diary, Oct. 1945, WO 172/7769, NA, as well as Dunn, *First Indo-China War*, p. 204.

[64] The Japanese forces followed a multi-pronged approach to the campaign. Some units clearly did not want to support the British and French, and actively aided the Viet Minh with weapons and lack of support to the British and Indian troops. Other units actively worked with British and Indian troops, and fought and died alongside them in battle with the Viet Minh. See Dunn, *First Indo-China War*, pp. 119–39, 149–55, 269–75, and 308–14, for a more in-depth discussion.

[65] Gracey reiterated this in a letter to Slim on 5 November: 'It is most necessary that I should continue to run the whole Japanese side of things as long as we are here. The Japanese will take anything from us, but will do nothing for the French.' Later in the letter, he noted a request from the Japanese command: 'We respectfully submit a request that all orders to our forces should be passed by a British officer and not a French officer, as we find it increasingly difficult to carry out the orders resulting from their shameless plans' (Gracey to Slim, 5 Nov. 1945, Box 5/4, Gracey Papers, Liddell Hart Centre, KCL).

[66] The 9th DIC was not formally in place until the end of November 1945, although other forces started to arrive in October and early November. Gen. Philippe Leclerc, commander of the French forces, arrived on 5 October. See SACSEA Joint Planning Staff, 'Turnover of Command', 19 Nov. 1945, WO 203/5608, NA, and Dennis, *Troubled*, pp. 59–61.

[67] Wavell to Pethick-Lawrence, 1 Oct. 1945, *TOP*, VI, 127, p. 306. Wavell would reiterate this point in a follow-on letter to Pethick-Lawrence on 9 October 1945. See *TOP*, VI, 135, p. 323.

Slim was aware of and in agreement with both Wavell and Auchinleck. He advised the chief of the Imperial General Staff, Alanbrooke, that 'directions we have been receiving from various sources seem to me to have been somewhat involved and at times contradictory'. In the same letter, he also recounted a conversation with the British secretary of state for war, Jack Lawson. He noted that, while Lawson intended that the British not become involved in nationalist struggles, French forces still operated under Slim's command, and that 'as long as we retain this command ... we cannot divorce ourselves from the responsibility for their actions'.[68]

Meanwhile, back in Saigon, the fighting continued. On 1 October, the same day that Wavell was asking for an end to the army's commitment, the British Chiefs of Staff reversed an earlier decision, and expanded Gracey's and the British and Indian troops' remit to work outside the Saigon area in support of the French. It was also on 1 October that talks were held between the British and the Viet Minh. Gracey's stated position was to curb violence and restore order in Indo-China. The Viet Minh expected the British to act as arbitrators, but Gracey was under strict orders not to do so, since such a role was political and outside his remit. A ceasefire was agreed, to take effect on the evening of the 2nd, and meetings between the French and Viet Minh were scheduled for the 3rd. Despite these efforts, sporadic fighting continued.[69] The truce ended definitively on 10 October, when the Viet Minh attacked a British/Indian engineer reconnaissance party. Gracey had warned the Viet Minh that they would reap the consequences of violence against his troops; he ordered his 20th Indian Division, veterans of the Burma campaign, and the newly arrived 32nd Indian Brigade, to clear the areas to the north of the city.[70] Brig. D. E. Taunton of the 80th Indian Brigade recalled that 'the moment rebel Annamites [the term used for the Viet Minh by British and Indian troops] attacked British troops I issued orders that we would cease to use minimum force and persuasion, but would use maximum brutal force in order to effect counter-measures in the quickest way and avoid unnecessary casualties to own troops'.[71]

---

[68] Slim to Alanbrooke, 6 Oct. 1945, annex to COS 9450 607 (0), CAB, 80/97, cited in Dennis, *Troubled*, p. 165.

[69] Gracey to Mountbatten, 1 Oct. 1945, WO 172/1786, NA, and Dennis, *Troubled*, pp. 66–7. See also Dunn, *First Indo-China War*, 'Truce', pp. 236–56, for a very detailed discussion of the truce talks and the higher-level political issues that occurred.

[70] Gracey was quick to point out that it was not going to be wanton killing; there would be no provocative use of force, and troops would cause minimal disturbance to law-abiding citizens. However, this did not mean he would not use all of his weapons against the violent elements of the Viet Minh. See Dunn, *First Indo-China War*, pp. 259–60.

[71] 'Report on Ops 80 Ind Inf BDE', Box 5/4, Gracey Papers, Liddle Hart Centre, KCL.

Mountbatten had agreed to this, asserting that 'I ordered strong action should be taken by the British/Indian forces to secure further key-points and so to widen and consolidate the perimeter of these areas. At the same time I insisted that further attempts to negotiate must continue.'[72]

The escalating violence in both FIC and the NEI increased political pressure on Auchinleck and Wavell in India. Auchinleck telegraphed the British Chiefs of Staff on 7 October, arguing that Indian troops must be withdrawn to alleviate political pressure.[73] Pethick-Lawrence responded to both Wavell and Auchinleck, confirming that it was HMG's intent to withdraw as soon as possible, but that, in the meantime, 'our endeavour [is] to keep out of political trouble in these areas as much as possible ... we can be entirely withdrawn not until French and Dutch troops arrive ... [W]e cannot totally disregard the interests of our French and Dutch Allies ... [I]n any case it is clearly our duty so long as we are the only people on the spot with effective forces to prevent ... conditions deteriorating into civil chaos with great loss of life.'[74]

Throughout October and November, the remaining units and forma-tions of the 20th Indian Division arrived; they set out to establish control in and around Saigon and to provide support for the French.[75] The French also began to arrive in early October; their commander, Gen. Philippe Leclerc, arrived on the 5th, along with the 5th Colonial Infan-try.[76] Fighting continued during this period between the British/Indians and the Viet Minh, and between the Viet Minh and the French.[77] Japanese troops were also utilised. The British also brought in more

---

[72] Mountbatten, *Post Surrender Tasks: Section E*, p. 282, and Dunn, *First Indo-China War*, p. 257.

[73] Auchinleck to the Chiefs of Staff, 7 Oct. 1945, L/WS/1/716, OIOC.

[74] Pethick-Lawrence to Wavell, 12 Oct. 1945, *TOP*, VI, 140, p. 337.

[75] Lt Col Russell, 3/8th Gurkhas, noted some of his frustration with the mission in a letter to his wife. On 23 October, after his battalion had lost more men killed and wounded, he wrote: 'what a bloody show this is. We had another man killed and two wounded, one rather badly ... I wouldn't mind so much if this was a pukka war, but our men are getting hit because a lot of bloody Annamites [Viet Minh] want to chuck the French out. I hope these French get a move on and take over the running of their own affairs' (*Red Flash*, No. 15, Feb. 1992, p. 6).

[76] Kirby, *War Against Japan*, V, pp. 302–3.

[77] For some battalions, serious fighting ensued. See the newsletters and histories of 9/14th Punjab and the 2/8th Punjab regiments in Boxes 5/5 and 5/12, Gen. Gracey Papers, Liddell Hart Centre, KCL, for more details of the actions, as well as Dunn, *First Indo-China War*, pp. 257–9. As one battalion stated: 'As far as the [battalion] was concerned the shooting season for the Annamites [Viet Minh] had opened.' See also battalion history of the 9/14th Punjab, which stated: 'it was an unsatisfactory sort of fighting. The enemy wore no uniform and usually did not carry arms visibly' (John Booth, *Ninth Battalion Fourteenth Punjab Regiment* (Cardiff: Western Mail and Echo Limited, 1948), p. 97).

Royal Air Force support, in the form of Spitfire fighter squadrons. These were to be used sparingly and under strict controls, but to be called upon if necessary.[78]

By 17 October, the last units and formations of the 20th Indian Division had arrived and were ready to move against the Viet Minh. It was decided to send the 100th Indian Infantry Brigade, commanded by Brig. C. H. B. Rodham, and supporting arms to the north and north-east of Saigon into the Thu Duc/Thu Dau Mot/Biên Hòa areas. Intelligence reports stated that the Viet Minh strength lay in these areas, and there was a clear need to break the Viet Minh ring of control surrounding Saigon. Rodham informed the Japanese command in the region that the 100th Brigade was coming to occupy the area and assume responsibility for the maintenance of law and order over the course of 23–25 October.[79] The Japanese were asked to continue disarming the Viet Minh, searching for weapons, and clearing areas around the main towns. The Japanese troops now fell under the command of Brig. Rodham and his brigade. The various units of the 100th Indian Brigade – the 1/1st Gurkha Rifles, 4/10th Gurkha Rifles, 14/13th Frontier Force Rifles,[80] and the 16th Light Cavalry[81] – carried out a well-planned and -executed operation to clear the areas to the north of Saigon. The Japanese carried out the static duties of defence, while the 100th operated mobile columns to destroy any opposition and deal with any road blocks.[82]

The units of the 100th Brigade defaulted to their war-time experience, and created combined arms mobile units. An example of this, an operation known as Gateforce, was established by the 14/13th FFRifles, who were based to the north-east of Saigon at Biên Hòa. Maj. L. D. Gates took his company, plus a squadron of armoured cars from the 16th Cavalry, a section of mortars from the 14/13th FFRifles, a detachment of Royal Engineers, and an attachment of Japanese troops, and pushed east towards Xuan Loc. They were ordered to create a patrol base in Xuan Loc on 29 October and patrol for three days, to try to destroy and capture 2,000 Viet Minh and members of the HQ staff who had been reported to have fled to the area. Gates was ordered to use maximum

[78] See Dunn, *First Indo-China War*, pp. 236–7, and Dennis, *Troubled*, p. 64.
[79] 100th Indian Infantry Brigade, War Diary, Nov. 1945, WO 172/7135, NA.
[80] This battalion was considered one of the best in the Burma campaign; at this point in the Indo-China campaign, it still had many of the veterans from Burma. See Marston, *Phoenix*, for much more detail on the battlefield performance of this battalion.
[81] This was a pre-war Indianised regiment and performed well during the war. It was commanded at this point by an Indian officer, Lt Col Joyanto Nath Chaudhuri.
[82] Dunn, *First Indo-China War*, pp. 270–7, and 100th Indian Infantry Brigade, War Diary, Nov. 1945, WO 172/7135, NA.

force to clear the area and track down and destroy the Viet Minh.[83] One of the most controversial aspects of this operation was the instruction to destroy any village that resisted their efforts.[84] Over the course of several days, Gateforce engaged elements of the Viet Minh and succeeded in destroying various roadblocks and fortified positions. After two days of fighting, it was estimated that close to 200 Viet Minh had been killed in the Xuan Loc region, thus, in theory, breaking the back of the overt Viet Minh military presence.[85] It was reported that Gateforce was also able to rescue some twenty French civilian hostages.[86]

The month of November brought about a partial shift in the campaign. As the 20th Indian Division was able to consolidate its gains, it decided to refocus on its primary operational task, disarming the Japanese Army.[87] More and more French troops were arriving in FIC and were able to start taking over key security tasks from British/Indian troops, as well as from the Japanese outside Saigon. The various units and formations of the 20th Indian Division continued to send out mobile combined arms patrols to show the flag and disrupt any Viet Minh attempts to seize key areas within the Saigon area of operations, at the same time as disarming the Japanese soldiers.[88] At around this time, Gen. Gracey

---

[83] 14/13th FFRifles War Diary, Nov. 1945, WO 172/7743, NA.

[84] Dunn, *First Indo-China War*, p. 280. This was not the first time that buildings were burned in retaliation by British and Indian troops. Members of the Bombay Sappers and Miners Company had destroyed huts after the killing of one of their men. See *ibid.*, p. 277. The issue with this is that although the Indian Army was an army that understood 'minimum force', many within the 20th Indian Division were mistakenly viewing this campaign through the prism of conventional operations, due to the level of violence and the military organisation and activities of the Viet Minh. It must also be remembered that the burning of villages followed the doctrinal practice of 'punitive expeditions' in the North-West Frontier Province over the previous eighty years. The British attempted to drop leaflets to inform the population, as they had done in the NWFP. See letter from Gracey to Mountbatten, 9 Nov. 1945, WO 203/4271, NA, and Dennis, *Troubled*, pp. 174–5, for some of Gracey's explanations for the destruction of houses and, potentially, villages.

[85] 14/13th FFRifles, War Diary, Nov. 1945, WO 172/7743, NA, and 100th Indian Infantry Brigade, War Diary, Nov. 1945, WO 172/7135, NA.

[86] Dunn, *First Indo-China War*, p. 282. By the end of November, eighteen British and Indian soldiers had been killed and fifty-one wounded, along with nineteen Japanese killed and thirteen missing. It was estimated that close to 400 Viet Minh had been killed and more than 400 had been captured by the 20th Indian Division; estimates from the French and Japanese were lacking. See Dunn, *First Indo-China War*, p. 285.

[87] Lt Col Russell of 3/8th Gurkhas wrote, in a letter to his wife, 'disarming the Japs is to start in a few days ... Unfortunately the Japs I have had under my command are to be disarmed by the RAF. I wish we were doing it, as I can't help liking the Jap Major who commands them, and I am sure he would prefer to be disarmed by us' (*Red Flash*, no. 15, Feb. 1992, p. 7).

[88] See 100th Indian Infantry Brigade War Diary for the month of November 1945, as it lists 'Jap Surrender Instr No 1' as well as other key tasks and operations for the brigade: WO 172/7135, NA.

made some key observations of the French Army's performance in Saigon. In a report to Gen. Slim on 5 November, he wrote: 'The French troops are leaving a pretty good trail of destruction behind them, which will result in such resentment that it will become progressively more difficult for them to implement their new policy, and, I am convinced, will result in guerrilla warfare, increased sabotage and arson as soon as we leave the country.'[89]

At the same time, Gen. Auchinleck, still pressing for the withdrawal of the Indian forces in the region, sought to make clear to the British Chiefs of Staff that the Indian Army was not an open-ended resource which they could use throughout Asia: 'If we continue to [send] Indian troops in[to] Java [and FIC], as HMG apparently propose to do, for the purpose of reinstating Dutch rule in the Netherlands East Indies [and French rule in FIC], we can have no defence whatever against the accusations that these troops are mercenary troops who are acting at the bidding of the British Government against the wishes of the Indian people.'[90] He followed up with a similar letter to the War Office on 15 November 1945.[91]

By the end of November, units of the 100th Indian Brigade had been used in mobile columns to engage pockets of the Viet Minh and had disarmed thousands of Japanese. The 14/13th FFRifles had disarmed more than a thousand Japanese on one day in November.[92] At the same time, some Japanese frontline units were still being employed in battle, doing a professional job and being commended for it.[93]

The complexity of the war and the 'strangeness' were staggering to many Burma campaign veterans.[94] The 9/12th Frontier Force

---

[89] Gracey to Slim, 5 Nov. 1945, Box 5/4, Gracey Papers, Liddell Hart Centre, KCL.

[90] Auchinleck to Wavell, 13 Nov. 1945, No. 1112, Auchinleck Papers, University of Manchester. He followed this with another letter on 20 November to G. E. B. Abell, private secretary to the Viceroy, No. 1116, stating that the Government of India should be consulted before Indian troops were used in other areas. Auchinleck and Wavell were under immense pressure due to the INA trials that were taking place and were aware of the potential additional pressure that would be applied to the Indian Army.

[91] Auchinleck to War Office, 15 Nov. 1945, L/WS/1/1488, OIOC.

[92] See both the battalion and the brigade war diaries, WO 172/7135 and WO 172/7743, NA, for more detail.

[93] Dunn, First Indo-China War, p. 311.

[94] Author's interview with Indian Army officers, 1999–2009. It is also noted in W. E. H. Condon, The Frontier Force Regiment (Aldershot: Gale & Polden, 1962), pp. 512–13: 'As the concentration of surrendered Japanese troops increased, the men of the battalion [9/12th FFR] had naturally to come into closer contact with their late enemies, and had the opportunity to observe them closely. It is recorded that their discipline was first class, and they co-operated and carried out orders 100 percent. Never was there a cause for complaint, and the men grew to respect them and showed a tendency to fraternize.' The 9/14th Punjab Regiment's battalion history, while respecting the Japanese soldiers' discipline, still could not see them as other than an enemy. As this history stated: 'Many

Regiment[95] was earmarked to set up a large Japanese internment area in Cap St Jacques (Vung Tau) to repatriate Japanese POWs.[96] On 28 November, the 32nd Indian Infantry Brigade handed over their area of responsibility north of Saigon. The drawdown was scheduled to begin in late November, in anticipation of Mountbatten's arrival to formally accept the surrender of Gen. Terauchi and his forces. While in Saigon, Mountbatten met with Gen. Gracey and the French army commander, Leclerc, to discuss the withdrawal of the 20th Indian Division, in response to both the needs of SEAC in other areas of operation (AOs) and the political pressure being applied by the Indian National Congress against the Government of India. The 32nd Brigade was earmarked to leave by the end of the year, and the 80th Brigade to leave with the divisional HQ and Gen. Gracey by the end of January 1946, as French forces geared up to take over.[97]

While the planning for withdrawal was in full swing, operations continued and took on a different tone during December. The 32nd Brigade carried out an operation to clear Han Phu Island of the Viet Minh, which it did with minimal casualties. By the 19th, it had relinquished command of the area to the French.[98] As 80th Indian Brigade was earmarked next, it slowly started to hand over various areas of responsibility to the French, at the same time as disarming the Japanese.[99] It became so quiet in their sector that the battalion was able to revert to peace-time training.[100] This was not true for the 100th Indian Brigade and its units, which continued to be engaged in various skirmishes with the Viet Minh at the same time they were disarming the Japanese and seizing arms stocks, during December 1945 and January 1946.[101]

---

of them [surrendering Japanese soldiers], handing over their swords which were family heirlooms, were in tears but after what we had seen of them [in Burma] our hearts were closed to any pity for the Jap' (Booth, *Ninth Battalion Fourteenth Punjab Regiment*, p. 99).

[95] The battalion arrived in FIC in early October 1945. It was initially commanded by an Indian commissioned officer (ICO), Lt Col Hayaud Din, who had commanded the battalion during the heavy fighting in Burma in 1945. The battalion had served throughout the Burma campaigns of 1943–5 with the 80th Indian Infantry Brigade. Upon the ending of the Burma campaign, the unit became the recce battalion for the division. During the first weeks of deployment to FIC, it served in the Cholon area of Saigon and participated in many clearing patrols of the area. In mid October it was ordered to proceed to Cap St Jacques to set up a series of internment camps for the Japanese POWs. See Jan.–Dec. 1945, WO 172/7738, NA, as well as Box 4/26, Gracey Papers, Liddell Hart Centre, KCL.

[96] 9/12 Frontier Force Regiment, War Diary, Dec. 1945, WO 172/7738, NA.

[97] See Dunn, *First Indo-China War*, pp. 314–16, for more details.

[98] 32nd Indian Infantry Brigade, Dec. 1945, WO 172/7098, NA.

[99] 80th Indian Infantry Brigade, Dec. 1945, WO 172/7128, NA.

[100] 9/12th FFR, Dec. 1945, WO 172/7738, NA, and see also Condon, *Frontier Force Regiment*, pp. 509–13.

[101] 100th Indian Infantry Brigade, Dec. 1945, WO 172/7135, NA.

While the British were beginning their process of withdrawal and handover, French 'arrogance' and lack of discipline, which had already caused problems in September, began to get out of hand again. Gen. Gracey sent a letter to Gen. Leclerc, bluntly stating his anger at the French units' arrogant and racist behaviour towards both the Japanese forces and his own Indian troops. He wrote, in part:

It might be of value for them [French troops] to realize that, had not the Japanese in most cases carried out my orders faithfully, there would have been a disaster of the first magnitude in Southern French Indo-China with a massacre of thousands of French people, and the destruction of a vast amount of French property ... [With regard to instances of disrespect towards Indian troops] the camaraderie which exists between officers of the Indian Army and their Gurkha and Indian soldiers must be explained to them. Our men, of whatever colour, are our friends and not considered 'black' men. They expect and deserve to be treated in every way as first-class soldiers and their treatment should be, and is, exactly the same as that of white troops.[102]

Gracey was similarly disturbed: 'There is no more fruitful source of friction between Indian Army officers and their men on one side, and French troops on the other, than when our Indian and Gurkha troops are regarded and treated as "black" by French officers and men. I mention this point particularly as cases have occurred in which it is obvious that our Indian Army traditions have not been understood.'[103] As noted previously, the 32nd and 80th Brigades began to hand over control to the French and organise withdrawal, in preparation for service in British Borneo and other AOs of SEAC in December. Meanwhile, the fighting continued, to the north and north-east of Saigon, in the 100th Brigade's AO, throughout December and early January. The brigade was stretched, due to the lack of supporting forces to the south and west. The 14/13th FFRifles carried out countless patrols in and around Biên Hòa, reverting to the term 'Sher Forces', which had originally referred to their patrolling activities in the Burma campaign. This exemplifies how many within the battalion saw this as a continuation of the Burma war, albeit against a different enemy.[104] While the battalion sent out Sher Forces to engage the Viet Minh, they slowly started to see a Viet Minh build-up of forces and became aware that the Viet Minh controlled the

---

[102] See 12 Dec. 1945, Box 4/16, Gracey Papers, Liddell Hart Centre, KCL; also quoted in Dunn, First Indo-China War, pp. 325–6, and Dennis, Troubled, p. 177.

[103] 12 Dec. 1945, Box 4/16, Gracey Papers, Liddell Hart Centre, KCL.

[104] Author's interviews with officers from the 14/13th FFRifles. See my Phoenix for more details on the 14/13th FFRifles and the Sher Forces, as well as Dec. 1945, WO 172/7743, NA.

night once again. Many patrols were able to surprise the Viet Minh, partially due to the jungle warfare experience they had earned in Burma.

A marked similarity between the campaigns in Burma and in FIC was evident in the Viet Minh attack on the patrol base at Biên Hòa. Overnight on 2/3 January 1946, a Viet Minh battalion attacked the main patrol base for the 14/13th FFRifles there, with attached troops from the Jats. The Viet Minh launched five well-coordinated, simultaneous attacks supported by heavy fire. The Indian troops were able to beat off the attacks, with heavy fire from machine guns and supporting mortars. The attack lasted for four hours and resulted in an estimated 100 Viet Minh killed, with no losses for the troops at Biên Hòa, including the Japanese, who were still defending.[105] While the Viet Minh lost the battle, many of their opponents noted their bravery afterwards.[106]

Units of the 100th Indian Brigade continued to send out patrols to keep up the pressure, before the brigade handed over responsibility to French forces.[107] The Viet Minh in return kept pressure on the brigade and the various patrol bases, including Biên Hòa. The 'mobile' ability provided by the 16th Light Cavalry's armoured cars ended with the 16th's departure on 12 January.[108] The 80th Indian Brigade had stood down the day before, and the 20th Division HQ and Gen. Gracey were scheduled to leave FIC at the end of the month for Malaya. The date set for the transfer of all forces, including some Indian battalions in FIC to French command, was 28 January, the day that Gracey was scheduled to leave.[109] More than 54,000 Japanese soldiers had been disarmed and concentrated at Cap St Jacques; 40 soldiers from the 20th Indian Division had died and more than 100 had been wounded between October and late January.[110] It is estimated that more than 2,000 Viet Minh were killed during the same period.[111] Initially the 100th Indian Brigade was assigned to support the French, but this was stopped in response to political pressures in India and objections from Auchinleck and the viceroy. The brigade left on two days, 8 and 9 February;[112] over the

---

[105] 14/13th FFRifles War Diary, Feb. 1946, WO 172/10272, NA.
[106] Dunn, *First Indo-China War*, p. 334.   [107] Dec. 1945, WO 172/7135, NA.
[108] See WO 172/7353 and WO 172/10060, NA, for more details of the 16th Light Calvary.
[109] 20th Indian Division HQ War Diary, Feb. 1946, WO 203/5995, NA.
[110] The Indian Army continued to assess the morale of the troops overseas, due to the INA trials and other potential threats. The intelligence reports generally indicated that 'Indian troops in Indo-China [were] not showing much interest in political events in India ... [and] carrying out their duty as loyally as ever': India Command Fortnightly Intelligence Reports, 1946, No. 2. 20 Jan. 1946, L/MIL/17/5/4276, OIOC, BL.
[111] Dunn, *First Indo-China War*, p. 341.
[112] Dec. 1945, WO 172/7135, NA.

course of January and February close to 12,000 troops from the 20th Indian Division withdrew from FIC.

The 9/12th FFR[113] and 2/8th Punjab remained in FIC, the latter to guard the mission in Saigon and the former to guard Cap St Jacques and continue the repatriation of Japanese POWs. Both battalions served until the end of March under the authority of Allied Commander's Inter-Service Liaison Mission to French Indo-China, under the command of a British brigadier, F. K. S. Maunsell. Only small miscellaneous subunits remained, including one company from 2/8th Punjab, until May 1946.[114]

Field Marshal Slim summed up the efforts of Gracey and the 20th Indian Division as follows: 'Gracey was faced with the most difficult politico-military situation in Allied territory, which he handled in a firm, cool, and altogether admirable manner.'[115] This assessment could serve for the whole of the Indian Army's performance in this campaign.

The Netherlands East Indies

As stated earlier, the operations in the Netherlands East Indies (NEI) lasted longer than those in FIC. The deployment of Indian Army forces also entailed close to three times the numbers,[116] and the fighting in the NEI was far more costly.[117] This was partially due to the quality of the Indonesian nationalist forces and to the burden of carrying out duties longer, because of the slow progress of arriving Dutch troops. The British official historian, Maj. Gen. S. Woodburn Kirby, recalled that 'They [the Indonesian nationalists] proved to be fanatical opponents and capable of fearful atrocities, as often as not against women and children.'[118]

As had already occurred in FIC, the Dutch colonial troops were not as disciplined as their Indian Army counterparts; this created problems for British commanders throughout the campaign.[119] Another similarity

---

[113] Condon notes an interesting aspect of the withdrawal of the 9/12th FFR in his book: 'on 29th of March the battalion embarked at Cap St Jacques ... Many Japanese senior officers and men lined the route to say goodbye to the Battalion, and it was a curious, if not pathetic, scene to find the very men who had fought against us so bitterly, now so manifestly sorry to bid the Battalion farewell' (*Frontier Force Regiment*, p. 513).

[114] Dunn, *First Indo-China War*, pp. 355–6.   [115] Slim, *Defeat into Victory*, p. 532.

[116] In the end, the 23rd, 26th, and 5th Indian Divisions and supporting elements were deployed to the NEI.

[117] More than 600 soldiers and officers were killed in Java and Sumatra, compared to just over 40 in FIC: Kirby, *War Against Japan*, V, Appendix 31, p. 544.

[118] *Ibid.*, p. 307.

[119] There are numerous references to issues with Dutch colonial troops, especially the Ambonese. See Kirby, *War Against Japan*, V, p. 339, and McMillan, *British Occupation of Indonesia*, p. 86, as quick references to the issues.

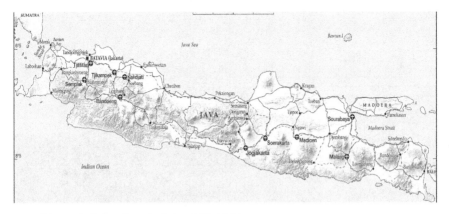

Map 4.2 Operations in Java 1945–1946

between the two operations was the loss of focus between developing the grand strategic vision and carrying out actual operations on the ground, due to a lack of clear direction from SEAC and London. Last but not least, the duration of operations in the NEI enabled nationalists in India to apply pressure to withdraw troops on both the viceroy, Lord Wavell, and the CinCI, Gen. Auchinleck.[120] Meanwhile, units and formations in the NEI attempted to focus on their mission, in the midst of a large-scale political debate that intensified with the ending of the INA trials in late spring 1946.[121]

The Imperial Japanese Army and Navy did not openly support nationalist organisations during their occupation of the NEI during the Second World War, but they gradually began to allow Indonesians access to positions in government administration. The Indonesian nationalist leader, Dr A. Soekarno or Sukarno, was allowed to create a movement that opposed western influence and co-operated with the occupying Japanese military authorities. From 1943, Indonesians were allowed

---

[120] Just as the 23rd Indian Division was landing in Batavia in western Java, Wavell was reporting to the secretary for India, Pethick-Lawrence, 'The Nationalist papers are taking much interest in the events in French Indo-China and Java. Some days ago I telegraphed to Mountbatten pointing out to him the undesirability of using Indian troops to deal with disturbances in eastern countries, and expressing the hope that they might be disengaged as soon as possible' (Wavell to Pethick-Lawrence, 9 Oct. 1945, *TOP*, VI, 135, p. 323).

[121] See Dennis, *Troubled*, for an in-depth discussion of the higher-level decision-making throughout the whole campaign, and the many back-and-forth debates and planning that occurred throughout this most difficult campaign.

Figure 4.2 Indian troops take cover from Indonesian nationalists, 1945
© Imperial War Museums (Image No. SE 6799)

more of a voice in running their occupied territory, although there was no question of outright independence. With the tide of war turning against the Japanese in summer 1945, a meeting was held in Singapore to discuss granting independence to the Indonesians, especially on the island of Java. Events overtook the debate, and on 17 August Sukarno declared independence for the NEI. The Japanese began to hand over adminis-tration and dispense arms to the nationalists.[122] By the end of August, the Japanese had given up control of law and order, and had withdrawn to camps to await the arrival of the Allies. They had also armed and trained many nationalists, who took over the governance of much of Java,

[122] Kirby, *War Against Japan*, V, pp. 309–10, and Dennis, *Troubled*, p. 81.

Figure 4.3 Indian troops identify mass graves in Java © Imperial War Museums (Image No. CF 1279)

and who were openly opposed to the return of the Dutch colonial authorities and prepared to fight any landing of Dutch soldiers.

The first intelligence reports on the Indonesian forces listed their strength at seven divisions. Some of the divisions were of limited value, but could operate as guerrilla bands. One division, stationed in eastern Java, had been well trained by the Japanese and, equipped with tanks and artillery, was prepared to oppose British operations in the area.[123]

---

[123] Kirby, *War Against Japan*, V, p. 312, and see Christison's comments, 'the one in East Java is tough and well led', in 'Life and Times of General Sir Philip Christison', p. 178, IWM.

The intelligence picture of what was going on in Java was not clear to SEAC. As Mountbatten noted: 'I had been given no hint of the political situation which had arisen in Java ... Dr H. J. Van Mook [of the Netherlands East Indies Provisional Government in Australia] had given me no reason [to suppose] that reoccupation of Java would present any operational problem, beyond that of rounding up the Japanese.'[124] Lt Gen. Sir Philip Christison stated, 'there was practically no Intelligence about the state of affairs'.[125] Reports came in throughout the month of September about rising levels of violence against Dutch settlers and potential colonial collaborators who were considered likely to support a Dutch return. Elements of Force 136[126] parachuted into Batavia on Java, and the Royal Navy (RN) deployed a cruiser force to the area in early September. The RN commander, Rear-Admiral W. R. Patterson, specifically warned on 18 September that Allied land forces were needed in Batavia to avoid further violence and lawlessness. Gen. Slim, Commander AFLSEA, ordered Fourteenth Army to release two brigades from the 23rd Indian Division, then serving in Malaya, to deploy to Batavia in the western part of Java and Sourabaya in the eastern section of Java. The first brigade group sailed on 1 October.[127]

Intelligence was still sketchy in early October 1945, when Lt Gen. Christison, commander of the XV Indian Corps, was appointed the Commander Allied Forces Netherlands East Indies. When asked during a press conference what sort of reception the Indian Army was likely to receive, he indicated that he did not expect hostility, since the Indonesians liked the Dutch.[128] This underestimation and lack of intelligence were to pose a major hurdle throughout the campaign.

Campaign aims and strategy became muddled very early on: as had already happened in Saigon, the intent of the mission did not align with the expectations of Indonesian nationalists. Christison, ordered to proceed to Batavia immediately, was told initially to disarm the Japanese, rescue Allied POWs and internees, and fill the vacuum between the Japanese capitulation and the returning Dutch administration. This last point proved, as it had in FIC, to be the most tricky and contentious.

---

[124] Quoted in Kirby, *War Against Japan*, V, p. 311.

[125] 'Life and Times of General Sir Philip Christison', p. 175, IWM.

[126] This was part of the British Special Operations Executive that had been working in South East Asia throughout the war and had carried out sabotage and the raising of local guerrilla forces to oppose the Japanese occupations.

[127] A battalion of British troops and supporting Royal Marine troops arrived in Batavia on 28 September to prepare for reinforcements coming behind.

[128] See 'Life and Times of General Sir Philip Christison', p. 176, IWM; and McMillan, *British Occupation of Indonesia*, p. 16, for more details.

Figure 4.4 Indian troops in Sourabaya counter-attack © Imperial War Museums (Image No. SE 5663)

Mountbatten attempted to limit this aspect of the mission to 'key areas', intending that Indian divisions would occupy and administer key urban areas only, maintaining law and order in the principal cities of Batavia and Sourabaya on Java and Padang, Medan and Palembang on Sumatra. The hinterland was to be the responsibility of the Dutch colonial administration and military. There would be some overlap, however, when Dutch administrators and military moved through the secured 'key areas' of British control into the countryside.[129]

---

[129] Kirby, *War Against Japan*, V, p. 314, and McMillan, *British Occupation of Indonesia*, pp. 19–20. The British secretary of state for war, Jack Lawson, specifically stated to Lt Gen. Christison, when they saw one another in Singapore, 'that nothing should be done to suggest your troops are going to re-impose Dutch Colonial rule. You must not take sides.' See 'Life and Times of General Sir Philip Christison', p. 176, IWM.

The operation's lack of strategic focus was demonstrated in one incident that took place around this time, and had long-term implications. Christison was ordered by the British secretary of war, Lawson, to endeavour to bring the Indonesian nationalist leadership and the Dutch together to find a political solution.[130] Dr C. O. Van der Plas, deputy governor of the NEI, who arrived in mid September with the RN, had rebroadcast a message from the queen of the Netherlands from earlier in the war,[131] outlining advances in self-government. In response, Sukarno sent a message to Christison, saying that he would support the Allied mission, since it was not there to re-impose pre-war Dutch colonial authority. Many moderates echoed this sentiment in indicating their co-operation to Allied staff. This turn of events greatly angered the Dutch authorities; they sent irate messages to Mountbatten and his staff, accusing Christison of mediating on their behalf and of recognising the Indonesian Republic as a legitimate entity. They also repudiated the broadcast from Van der Plas. Within days, Sukarno contacted Christison to advise that all co-operation would cease; that he would no longer try to restrain the extremists in his organisation; that he would oppose any Dutch landings; and that he and his supporters would fire on the British if they were found to be covering the Dutch landings.[132]

Due to the large scale of this campaign and space considerations, this chapter will focus primarily on the performance of Indian troops in Java, on account of its critical role in the campaign's progress and outcome. (This is in no way intended to minimise either the difficulty of the mission or the professional performance of the 26th Indian Division in Sumatra.)[133]

---

[130] See Dennis, *Troubled*, pp. 89–92, for details.

[131] See Kirby, *War Against Japan*, V, Appendix 24, for a full transcript of the radio message.

[132] *Ibid.*, pp. 315–16. Dennis, *Troubled*, deals with this issue in more detail. Mountbatten was asking the Chiefs of Staff to support his push that the Dutch government needed to be clear in their aims in the NEI, that negotiations should begin between the Dutch and the Indonesian Republic. In the end, the Dutch responded and became more set in their ways, presuming that they would dictate what was needed in the NEI and that the British troops were there to maintain law and order until the Dutch forces arrived. There was much tension and the issue would not be resolved until British and Indian troops left later in the year. See Dennis, *Troubled*, pp. 92–6.

[133] The occupation of the island of Sumatra followed a similar pattern to the occupation of Java, focusing on the taking of key towns (Medan, Padang, and Palembang) in an attempt to find Allied POWs. The 26th Indian Division arrived in late October 1945. As with Java, there was a rising tide of tensions with the local Indonesian forces. By early 1946, the 15,000 men from the 26th Division were engaged with Indonesian forces. As a former veteran stated, 'The treacherous manner of their deaths [an Indian officer and three *jawan*s were ambushed] and the gruesome mutilations inflicted on their bodies set the pattern of our dealing with them [the Indonesian fighters]. They simply became the

Western Java

The remainder of the 1st Indian Brigade, 23rd Indian Division, arrived in Batavia by 5 October. The tactical HQ of the XV Corps (later Allied Forces Netherlands East Indies) and 23rd Indian Division arrived on 6 October; the rest of the formation followed and were in place by the 10th.[134] For the first few days, the units of the brigade were made responsible for law and order and for guarding the internment camps. The Indonesian police force was brought under British control. Indonesian nationalists did not harass Indian and British forces at first, although they did begin to establish roadblocks. It was noted that, initially, British and Indian troops were able to visit cafes without arms.[135] On 10 October, the first violent engagements began between Indonesians and British/Indian forces; from that day forward, daily clashes were the norm.[136]

Similar issues arose in Batavia that 20th Indian Division troops had already encountered in Saigon. First, Dutch nationals living in the area began to make false reports of looting or armed Indonesian nationalists, in order to force British/Indian forces to patrol constantly. Indian battalions noted their frustration with this practice in their war diaries.[137] Second, Dutch 'Colonial Forces' in the area, the Koninklijk Nederlands-Indisch Leger (KNIL), were re-raised following the arrival of British forces[138] and quickly gained a reputation for lack of discipline and for over-reaction. The British commanders recognised that the KNIL were potentially a rallying point for the Indonesian nationalists. It was decided to redeploy them to the southern sector of the city and put them under Dutch command.[139]

---

enemy and we had a guerrilla war on our hands' (McMillan, *British Occupation of Indonesia*, p. 120). For a much wider discussion regarding the operations in Sumatra, see the following: McMillan, *British Occupation of Indonesia*, pp. 113–37; Kirby, *War Against Japan*, V, pp. 253–63; War Diaries of the 26th Indian Division, WO 172/7045 and WO 172/9893, NA; also '26th Indian Division in Sumatra', WO 203/6160, NA; various brigade and battalion war diaries from the division; and 'Life and Times of General Sir Philip Christison', p. 176, IWM.

[134] Kirby, *War Against Japan*, V, p. 319.

[135] 'At first I ordered all troops not on duty to walk about and enter shops and pubs unarmed and there was much camaraderie' ('Life and Times of General Sir Philip Christison', p. 180, IWM); McMillan, *British Occupation of Indonesia*, pp. 20–1.

[136] Kirby, *War Against Japan*, V, p. 321.

[137] See War Diary of the Indian State Forces, 1st Patialas, Oct. 1945, WO 172/7827, NA, and McMillan, *British Occupation of Indonesia*, p. 22.

[138] The KNIL recruited from two specific ethnic groups that were loyal and interested in seeing the return of the Netherlands to the islands. In the end, they had much to lose and wished to restore Indonesia to pre-war policies.

[139] McMillan, *British Occupation of Indonesia*, pp. 22–3.

British command soon discerned a need to extend its reach further into the interior in order to safeguard the internment camps.[140] In haste, a company from the 1/16th Punjab Regiment deployed to the town of Buitenzorg, a railway centre 100 miles to the south of Batavia. The decision to extend the British area of administration necessitated additional troops,[141] whose arrival exacerbated growing tensions.[142] Tactical intelligence concerning numbers of internees and armed nationalists was lacking.

The company was to be relieved as quickly as possible by the arrival of the 37th Indian Infantry Brigade. The 3/3rd Gurkhas arrived on 15 and 16 October, and were sent to Buitenzorg immediately as replacement troops. Once established, the Gurkhas quickly identified an impending humanitarian crisis, due to the larger than expected number of Allied POWs and civilian internees in the area. Co-ordinating with Japanese forces already stationed in the area, the Gurkhas undertook to maintain law and order and evacuate the internees. Tensions continued to rise as Indonesian extremists massacred hundreds of Eurasians. Gurkha forces had to rely upon the moderate nationalist authorities for electricity and water supplies, and continued, whatever else was happening, to carry out patrols in order to rescue as many internees as possible and ship them back to Batavia. Their mission continued through the end of 1945 and into 1946, when the 1/16th Punjab returned to the area.[143]

While it appeared that most Japanese soldiers and officers were supportive of imposing law and order under the authority of British and Indian forces,[144] this was not always the case. As noted previously,

---

[140] Lt Gen. Christison reported seeing paperback books showing white people and Eurasians being tortured, dismembered, and killed; these were confirmed by reports that came in each day: 'Life and Times of General Sir Philip Christison', p. 180, IWM.

[141] Lord Pethick-Lawrence noted in a letter to Lord Wavell on 16 October 1945 that a second Indian division was needed for Java and took priority over other areas, due to the attitude of the Indonesian nationalists. See Pethick-Lawrence to Wavell, 16 Oct. 1945, TOP, VI, 145, p. 346. Wavell, in responding to this request, highlighted significant concerns about the level of strain under which the Indian Army was operating due to the INA trials. He wrote: 'I think it right to let you know privately that in my opinion loyalty and discipline of the Indian Army may be subjected to severe strain owing to the agitation about the INA demobilization. I think it is most important that we should not add further strain of commitments in the Netherlands East Indies or French Indo-China. I am sure you will appreciate this and do your best to resist employment of additional Indian Divisions in Java' (Wavell to Pethick-Lawrence, 17 Oct. 1945, L/WS/1/726, OIOC, BL, and TOP, VI, 148, p. 360).

[142] See War Diary of 1/16th Punjab Regiment, Oct. 1945, WO 172/7753, NA.

[143] See War Diary of 3/3rd Gurkha Rifles, Oct.–Nov. 1945, WO 172/7775, NA, and McMillan, British Occupation of Indonesia, pp. 23–4.

[144] One Japanese officer, Maj. Kido, who worked heavily with the Gurkhas in central Java, was actually recommended for a British decoration, the Distinguished Service Order, by Gen. Christison: McMillan, British Occupation of Indonesia, p. 30.

some within the IJA had provided weapons and training to the Indonesian Republican forces before the British/Indian forces arrived. This did not go unnoticed, and resulted in the arrest of Maj. Gen. Nakamura Aketo, Japanese commander of all forces in central Java, along with some of his HQ. They were shipped to Singapore for trial, accused of disobeying their orders to surrender.[145]

The 3/5th Royal Gurkhas were sent to Bandoeng in October 1945, and almost immediately began active patrolling against insurgents in and around the area to liberate as many internees and POWs as possible. The 3/5th Gurkhas had less difficulty re-establishing law and order, due to the fact that Japanese forces, obeying orders, took back the town from the extremists.[146] Japanese forces in the area supported the Gurkhas in their efforts to create a bubble of security in and around the town, and Japanese tanks were used to destroy roadblocks and extremist positions that threatened the mission.[147]

Central Java

The lack of accurate intelligence within SEAC about numbers of camps and internees in the areas targeted for occupation was conclusively demonstrated by the campaign to land troops in Semarang. Originally, operations in central Java were not a priority: Sourabaya in the east was supposed to be the second major operational area for XV Corps. As with the rest of the operation, there were minimal forces available for the mission. The 3/10th Gurkhas from the 37th Brigade were re-embarked on transports and shipped to Semarang, 250 miles east of Batavia, in response to reports of fighting between nationalists and Japanese, with many internees still in camps, needing to be rescued.[148] On 19 October, the battalion landed in an almost deserted harbour; as they moved into the city they could hear sporadic gunfire, and were shortly fired upon themselves. In the aftermath, Indonesian nationalist officials came to claim that the firing had come from Japanese soldiers, while the apologetic Japanese commander characterised the incident as fighting that had erupted between insurgents and Japanese troops, resulting in a mistaken attack on the Gurkhas.[149]

---

[145] Kirby, *War Against Japan*, V, p. 321.   [146] Doulton, *Fighting Cock*, p. 246.
[147] See War Diary of 3/5th Gurkha Rifles, Oct.–Nov. 1945, WO 172/7779, NA, and McMillan, *British Occupation of Indonesia*, pp. 25–6.
[148] The battalion was specifically ordered to maintain law and order and not to take sides in any political matters. See War Diary of 3/10th Gurkha Rifles, Nov. 1945, WO 172/7792, NA, and McMillan, *British Occupation of Indonesia*, p. 27.
[149] Kirby, *War Against Japan*, V, p. 320.

Japanese troops in the area had been stationed to the south near some of the large internment camps in Ambarawa and Magelang. The Japanese commander had decided to move towards Semarang in an attempt to re-impose order, but had found his unit repeatedly engaging with insurgents. The Japanese helped the Gurkhas to re-establish control inside Semarang and to escort small detachments to Ambarawa and Magelang to support the feeding and repatriation of the Allied POWs and civilian internees.[150]

It was clear that the 3/10th Gurkhas could not hold the areas for which they had been given responsibility, and the decision was made to send the Third Brigade, the Royal Artillery Brigade, which had close to two battalions of infantry, to support the Gurkhas. Troops began arriving on 22 October. Upon arriving in Semarang, the 3/10th Gurkhas were ordered to move the whole battalion to Magelang. The battalion lacked transport and had to fight their way through numerous roadblocks. As the Gurkhas arrived, close to 5,000 extremists attacked their positions, bolstered by artillery and mortars. Japanese forces in the area came once again to support the Gurkhas; after a few days of heavy fighting, members of the Indonesian Republican government sought to negotiate a truce. After a series of talks, it was agreed that as soon as the British had gathered up all the internees and POWs in the area, they would withdraw back to Semarang. In the end, more than 2,500 internees were evacuated and the British withdrew from Magelang on 21 November.[151]

The extremists were slowly gathering strength as British and Indian forces began to withdraw from parts of central Java. Gurkhas, Japanese, and internees arriving from Magelang into Ambarawa witnessed chaos. While there had been a ceasefire in effect in Magelang, it was constantly being violated. As the Gurkhas and the internees moved towards and into Ambarawa, they had to fight their way through a series of roadblocks and ambushes.[152] The RAF was being used to destroy Indonesian positions, including artillery positions, which were bombarding the British lines. One internee camp was attacked and many British troops and women and children were killed. Allied Forces Netherlands East Indies (AFNEI) began to pull the 23rd Indian Division back towards Batavia and central Java, after the heavy fighting in Sourabaya and the arrival of more Indian Army reinforcements.[153]

[150] McMillan, *British Occupation of Indonesia*, p. 26.
[151] War Diary of 3/10th Gurkhas, Nov.–Dec. 1945, WO 172/7792, NA; McMillan, *British Occupation of Indonesia*, pp. 27–8; and Kirby, *War Against Japan*, V, p. 336.
[152] War Diary of 3/10th Gurkhas, Dec. 1945, WO 172/7792, NA, and Kirby, *War Against Japan*, V, p. 337.
[153] See pp. 185–92 for more discussion of the fighting in eastern Java, at Sourabaya.

On 27 November, elements of the 49th Brigade arrived and pushed out towards Ambarawa, to support the withdrawal of Gurkhas and internees to Semarang. British and Indian troops began to evacuate POWs and internees to Semarang; they completed this task on 8 December, and pulled out of Ambarawa a week later.[154] As reinforcements began to arrive in Semarang and the withdrawal from Ambarawa began, Indonesian insurgents closed in on Semarang. Violence in and around the town began to increase during mid November. Some of the fighting became so intense that naval gunfire support was called in. As at Semarang, the brigade was reinforced with troops from Ambarawa, and elements of 49th Brigade began to sweep the areas around the town, clearing out large numbers of insurgents.[155] On 11 January 1946, the 5th Parachute Brigade arrived to relieve the 49th Brigade, who then proceeded to move to Batavia to the west, where the 23rd Indian Division was concentrating its brigades. The 5th Parachute Brigade remained in Semarang for just over a month, until additional Dutch forces arrived and were able to take over responsibility.[156]

Eastern Java

Before considering the difficult campaign in eastern Java, in and around Sourabaya, it is necessary to provide a general picture of the 23rd Indian Division as of October 1945. The AFNEI and 23rd Indian Divisional HQ, along with the 1st Indian Brigade and the 37th Indian Infantry Brigade, were in the west, in the Batavia-Buitenzorg-Bandoeng area; the divisional troops or the Royal Artillery Brigade were in and around the Semarang-Ambarawa-Magelang area in central Java. There was continuous fighting in and around the British/Indian formations. Over the course of October and November, fighting increased in severity in some locations. Royal Navy ships were brought in to provide naval gunfire support. British and Indian forces did their best to track down and evacuate all Allied POWs and civilian internees, rounding up thousands and pulling them back to various harbours for repatriation.[157]

The last remaining brigade from the 23rd Indian Division, the 49th Indian Infantry Brigade, under the command of Brig. A. W. S. Mallaby, were ordered to land at Sourabaya, in eastern Java. They arrived on

---

[154] War Diary of 49th Indian Infantry Brigade, Dec. 1945, WO 172/7108, NA, and McMillan, *British Occupation of Indonesia*, pp. 28–9.
[155] War Diary of 49th Indian Infantry Brigade, Dec. 1945, WO 172/7108, NA, and Kirby, *War Against Japan*, V, pp. 338–9.
[156] Kirby, *War Against Japan*, V, p. 339, and Dennis, *Troubled*, p. 189.
[157] Kirby, *War Against Japan*, V, pp. 321–2.

25 October, encountering some of the best armed and trained Indonesian nationalist forces operating in the NEI. Lt Gen. Nagano Yuichiro, commander of the IJA 16th Army, reported to Gen. Christison that 'We have been training 7 divisions of Indonesian soldiers who never saw the Dutch. Most of these divisions are not formidable but the one in East Java is tough and well led. They will give you much trouble.'[158] The practice of deploying a brigade into a volatile area of operations was not new either to the 23rd Indian Division or to Christison, but eastern Java was a different matter. It rapidly became clear to SEAC that more troops would be necessary. On 17 October, even before the 49th Brigade had arrived in Sourabaya, more units, including Indian cavalry regiments, had been requested from Malaya and other regions to support the overstretched 23rd Indian Division. By the end of October, two brigades from the 5th Indian Division[159] were also en route to Java to provide additional support.[160]

Brig. Mallaby and his 49th Indian Brigade were ordered to carry out the same mission as other brigades and units: evacuate internees and disarmed Japanese military personnel, and maintain law and order.[161] The possibility of re-establishment of Dutch control was not specifically discussed with Indonesian Republicans at any point in the campaign. Upon their arrival into the harbour of Sourabaya, brigade staff noted the number of 'hostiles' in and around the area, and the British sent two officers to arrange to meet with Dr Moestopo (commander of the Indonesian (Japanese-trained and -equipped) Republican Army), the

---

[158] For more details regarding the conversation with Christison, see 'Life and Times of General Sir Philip Christison', p. 178, IWM.

[159] The dispatch of the 5th Indian Division caused much anger in New Delhi, as Auchinleck was under more and more pressure not to use 'Indian troops' in the NEI and FIC. He asked for the British 2nd Division to be sent, but Mountbatten over-ruled him, saying that the division was not ready and that he needed troops right away. See Dennis, *Troubled*, pp. 121–3.

[160] Brett-James, *Ball of Fire*, p. 451, and Kirby, *War Against Japan*, V, p. 322.

[161] McMillan goes into some detail regarding Mallaby's background and friction with his second-in-command, Col L. H. O. Pugh. Brig. Mallaby had spent most of the Second World War as a staff officer, serving as a major general as the director of Military Operations at GHQ India. He dropped a rank to brigadier to command the 49th Brigade as it prepared for the final push against the Japanese. Col Pugh had a distinguished career as a commander during the Burma campaign, winning the DSO and Bar. He commanded the 33rd Indian Infantry Brigade in 1944 and 1945. It appears that, with the reshuffling of the commands at the end of the war, Pugh became a second-in-command and a colonel once again, with Mallaby as his commander. According to many sources, the two men were completely different, Mallaby 'more relaxed' and Pugh 'a bit of a fire eater'. This apparently created significant friction, and the two men were barely speaking to one another by the time the brigade landed. See McMillan, *British Occupation of Indonesia*, pp. 33–4, for more details.

Tentara Keamanan Rakyat (TKR), and Dr Soerio (Indonesian governor of East Java). Tensions were high; Moestopo wanted to kill the small British delegation and throw their bodies into the harbour, while the British officers insisted that they had come in peace, and Soerio tried to act as mediator. Mallaby's staff received a signal not to land troops without Moestopo's permission, but Brig. Mallaby and his staff made it clear that they were not going to wait for permission to land troops. The British and Indian forces landed with fixed bayonets and loaded weapons, and began to seize key areas of the harbour and town. This bold action initially appeared to pay off as the Indonesians sent a small delegation to meet with Mallaby and his staff regarding arrangements for the future.[162] By this point, the British were in control of the port and most of the facilities, but not the power station and one of the key bridges.[163]

In the first round of talks, the British stressed that they had come to evacuate internees and maintain law and order, not to interfere in the internal politics of Indonesia. They also confirmed that there were no Dutch officials serving on brigade staff. A meeting between Moestopo and Mallaby on 26 October focused on the issues of arming and disarming the civilian population. Mallaby and Moestopo agreed that Indonesian uniformed soldiers and police were to remain armed, and carry out law-and-order operations alongside British and Indian forces. Armed civilians, meanwhile, were to be disarmed.[164] The Indonesians remained suspicious and continued to insist on British confirmation that no Dutch were to be landed. The British and the Indonesians moved quickly to set up boundaries of areas of responsibility and arrangements for internees to be processed.[165]

What happened next highlighted the disconnect between orders emanating from SEAC and 23rd Divisional HQ and the situation on the ground. On the morning of the 27th, an RAF Dakota transport flew over the town and dropped leaflets; this was part of an RAF operation that had been going on for several weeks, moving from the western part of Java to the east. The problem was that the leaflets did not account for any changes to the environment on the ground: they stated that the British Military Administration would supersede the Indonesian Republican government in the area and, more crucially, that all arms were to be

---

[162] See War Diary of 49th Indian Infantry Brigade, WO 172/7108, NA, and McMillan, *British Occupation of Indonesia*, p. 37.

[163] Dennis, *Troubled*, p. 123.

[164] McMillan, *British Occupation of Indonesia*, pp. 38–9.

[165] Kirby, *War Against Japan*, V, p. 323.

surrendered and that anyone bearing arms illegally would be shot by British and Indian troops. Many Indonesian nationalists considered this high-handed, and that they had been 'duped' by the British. This failure to communicate essentially negated all the hard work that had been done on the 26th. Moestopo met with Mallaby, but there was no consensus on what the future held. Mallaby did assert that he had not been made aware that the leaflets were going to be dropped, but also confirmed that he was obligated to follow the orders of his superior officer, Maj. Gen. D. C. Hawthorn from the 23rd Indian Division.[166] As a result, negotiations broke down.

On 29 October Indonesian forces, supported by artillery and tanks, attacked all the British and Indian positions in and around Soura-baya,[167] as well as internees' camps and convoys. Hundreds were killed, and several British officers and Indian VCOs were caught, tortured, and killed, and their bodies mutilated. Some British and Indian positions ran out of ammunition and were over-run and massacred by Indonesian forces. It is estimated that the 4,000 British and Indian forces stationed in the area were attacked by 20,000 armed soldiers of the TKR and supported by another 14,000 armed civilians.[168] The intensity of the fighting is best conveyed by an officer from the division: '49 Bde were fighting for their lives and for the lives of the internees they had come to protect, with the odds weighed heavily against them ... [T]here had been no time to move up reserves of ammunition and food which lay useless in the docks ... [F]ight they did with magnificent gallantry – in some cases until their ammunition was gone ... [T]here were desperate battles all over town.'[169] The Brigade HQ sustained more than 25 per cent casualties, and two platoons of the Rajputana Rifles were wiped out to the last man.[170] It was estimated that the Indonesians lost close to 6,000 men.[171]

---

[166] See *ibid.*, pp. 323–4, Dennis, *Troubled*, pp. 123–4, and McMillan, *British Occupation of Indonesia*, pp. 39–41, for more details. McMillan goes into detail about the disconnect between Brig. Mallaby and Maj. Gen. D. C. Hawthorn and the 'glossing over' of the leaflets by the divisional historian, Lt Col Doulton, in *Fighting Cock*.

[167] McMillan goes into some detail, stating that Mallaby did not reposition his forces to deal with a potential outbreak of violence and many officers did not understand why he did nothing to deal with a potential attack. See the comments in McMillan, *British Occupation of Indonesia*, pp. 41–4, especially the comments from the CO of 4/5th Mahratta Light Infantry.

[168] McMillan gives quite a bit of detail of the fighting and the loss of life: *British Occupation of Indonesia*, pp. 43–5. See also the war diaries of 49th Indian Infantry Brigade for more details.

[169] Doulton, *Fighting Cock*, p. 255.

[170] War Diary of 5/6 Rajputana Rifles, Nov. 1945, WO 172/7709, NA.

[171] Brett-James, *Ball of Fire*, p. 450.

Mountbatten sent Sukarno to Sourabaya to broker a ceasefire. Sukarno met with Mallaby and members of the Indonesian Republican government, and succeeded in doing so. On 30 October, Gen. Hawthorn arrived to meet with Sukarno and Mallaby; he ordered the brigade to pull back to positions in the harbour, take the airfield, and maintain some positions in the south, where there were internees, while the Indonesians held the city. Sukarno agreed to this plan, and he and Hawthorn flew back to Batavia. However, fighting broke out afresh within twenty-four hours; moderate voices in the Indonesian government were sidelined by extremists, who called for attacking British and Indian troops in and around Sourabaya, disregarding the orders of Sukarno.[172]

The almost immediate return to open warfare was partially due to the fact that many Indonesians believed that the British had caved in and surrendered. As a result, several units and subunits were caught inside the city; one company from the 6/5th Mahrattas, tasked with defending the International Bank Building, were ordered by the Indonesians to surrender their weapons. They refused and fighting erupted.

Not only was Mallaby unsuccessful in his attempts to negotiate an end to the fighting, two of his officers who had been working with Sukarno and attempting to negotiate a ceasefire were captured; they were killed and their bodies were mutilated. Mallaby and some of his staff returned to Bank Square in another attempt to end the fighting; they were ambushed and the brigadier was killed on 30 October.[173]

The actions of the Indonesian forces in Sourabaya further exacerbated problems in other parts of Java. The 3/10th Gurkhas encountered diffi-culties at Magelang, and withdrew to Semarang at the end of November. Tensions continued to rise in Batavia, and in eastern Java the Indonesian extremists demanded that the 49th Brigade in Sourabaya lay down their arms. The brigade had pulled back to a smaller perimeter that had been agreed before Mallaby's death; internees were evacuated, and a limited ceasefire prevailed for the first few days of November.[174] Gen. Christison issued a warning to all Indonesian extremists that 'unless those responsible for Mallaby's murder were handed over, [he] would bring the whole weight of [his] land, sea and air forces to bear on Surabaya'.[175] Royal Navy ships arrived into the Sourabaya harbour to

---

[172] See Kirby, *War Against Japan*, V, pp. 324–5, Dennis, *Troubled*, p. 124, and McMillan, *British Occupation of Indonesia*, pp. 46–8.
[173] See McMillan's very detailed and important analysis of this episode in *British Occupation of Indonesia*, pp. 48–50.
[174] *Ibid.*, pp. 51–2.
[175] 'Life and Times of General Sir Philip Christison', p. 185, IWM.

add support to the besieged 49th Brigade. During this period, some captured British and Indian troops were returned to the Brigade HQ.[176]

On 2 and 3 November, the 9th and 123rd Indian Infantry Brigades, from the 5th Indian Division, began disembarking in Sourabaya as reinforcements for the 49th Brigade. The concentration of the two brigades was kept secret, and the 49th Brigade continued to hold the new perimeter.[177] Maj. Gen. E. C. Mansergh, a highly respected divisional commander from the Burma campaign, assumed command of the three brigades in Sourabaya. Mansergh attempted to meet with moderates in Sourabaya on 7 November, in order to find a political solution. However, it rapidly became clear to divisional staff that the extremists were in charge and thought they were winning.[178] An ultimatum was delivered that the criminals involved in the killing of Mallaby and other British and Indian officers and men were to be handed over to British authorities. By 9 November, the two brigades had completed their disembarkation and were ready for offensive operations. On the same day, leaflets were dropped stating that the British were going to take action against the extremists in the town, and that no political settlement would be forthcoming.[179]

Meanwhile, opposition and tension in New Delhi were steadily increasing. On 7 November, Wavell telegraphed Pethick-Lawrence, warning that 'serious repercussions likely to arise here [in India] if Indian troops are used to suppress Indonesian movement and reinstate the Dutch'.[180] Pethick-Lawrence responded on 11 November that 'the position we have to deal with is one of extreme difficulty . . . [O]ur object has throughout been to avoid being involved in any hostilities with the Indonesians . . . [T]o abandon Java might lead to much wider withdrawals, facing us with serious loss of prestige in Malaya and Burma and leading to similar troubles there.'[181]

---

[176] Kirby, *War Against Japan*, V, p. 328.   [177] Brett-James, *Ball of Fire*, p. 452.

[178] The CO of the Dogra Machine Gun Battalion, Lt Col Bristow, noted this in his recollection of the arrival of 5th Indian Division. See his *Memories*, p. 139. Bristow would later witness the carnage of the Punjab in 1947 as one of the Punjab Boundary Force brigadiers.

[179] McMillan, *British Occupation of Indonesia*, p. 55; Brett-James, *Ball of Fire*, pp. 452–3; War Diaries of 9th Indian Infantry Brigade, WO 172/7085, and 123rd Indian Infantry Brigade, WO 172/7138, both NA.

[180] Wavell to Pethick-Lawrence, 7 Nov. 1945, L/WS/1/727, OIOC, BL, and *TOP*, VI, 198, p. 460.

[181] Pethick-Lawrence to Wavell, 11 Nov. 1945, L/WS/1/727, OIOC, BL, and *TOP*, VI, 206, pp. 474–5. Wavell responded on 27 November to Pethick-Lawrence, stating 'The INA trials have been embarrassing, but I think the use of Indian troops in Java and French Indo-China is more damaging in the long run because the case against it is, from the Indian point of view, almost a cast-iron one' (Wavell to Pethick-Lawrence, 27 Nov. 1945, *TOP*, VI, 246, p. 555).

At the same time, the 5th Indian Division was poised to mount a major offensive in Sourabaya, with Gen. Mansergh and his staff making plans to seize back the town and gain access to the nearby internee camps. When the ultimatum regarding the handover of those who had killed Mallaby and other British and Indian personnel went unanswered, the order was given to move into the city. The offensive to take back the town began early on the morning of 10 November;[182] British and Indian troops were attacked almost immediately by a considerable Indonesian force, supported by artillery and surrendered Japanese tanks. Within a few hours it was clear that the troops would need more support,[183] and both naval gunfire and RAF air cover were provided as British and Indian troops fought their way back into the town against stiff and heavy opposition. Both artillery and naval gunfire support were to be used only when needed, in an attempt to avoid too much damage, and tank support could be used only with the permission of the divisional commander.[184]

Taking back Sourabaya was a slow and bloody process;[185] the town was not cleared until 29 November, and even then sporadic fighting and house searches continued and the town was not declared fully secure until late December.[186] By the end of November, British and Indian troops had suffered more than 800 casualties, including just under 100 killed, but had also recorded nearly 200 personnel missing.[187]

While the 5th Indian Division was occupied in Sourabaya, tensions in New Delhi were increasing. A report submitted on 1 December by the Chiefs of Staff Committee described the internal situation in India. While the report discussed communal violence, anti-government activities, INA trials, and caches of unlicensed arms, it also focused on the 'effect of the political situation on the Armed Forces', indicating that the INA trials had affected morale among army personnel. It went on to express even greater concern over the continuing involvement of the Indian Army in FIC and the NEI, noting that 'Congress may intensify the present campaign against the use of the Indian troops in NEI and

---

[182] Indonesians would refer to this as 'Heroes' Day' from 1945 onwards.

[183] Doulton, *Fighting Cock*, p. 265.

[184] McMillan (*British Occupation of Indonesia*) makes the point that the British did not bombard the city at will, as is claimed by some; this is confirmed in both the 5th Indian Division and 13th Lancers war diaries, WO 172, NA. See also Brett-James, *Ball of Fire*, pp. 456–7, and 'Life and Times of General Sir Philip Christison', p. 186, IWM.

[185] Lt Col Bristow of the Dogra Machine Gun Battalion recalled that 'clearing the town street by street was a slow and costly operation which last[ed] 19 days': *Memories*, p. 139.

[186] Dennis, *Troubled*, p. 126; McMillan, *British Occupation of Indonesia*, pp. 54–7; Kirby, *War Against Japan*, V, pp. 333–6.

[187] Kirby, *War Against Japan*, V, p. 336.

FIC and thus attempt to suborn the army. This campaign in [the] long run [could] have even more dangerous effects than the INA campaign as it will be based on the accusation that the troops are mercenaries.'[188]

The units and formations of the 5th Indian Division (the 49th Indian Brigade having moved back to Semarang and then on to Batavia in late November to consolidate all of the 23rd Indian Division in one area) set out to continue in their mission of repatriation of internees and surrendered Japanese soldiers throughout the last months of 1945 and into early 1946. The British and Indians commanded the town and continued forays into the countryside to disrupt any build-up of Indonesian forces; the resulting actions employed more guerrilla tactics than before. British and Indian troops successfully foiled all Indonesian attempts at seizing key locations in and around the town.

Gen. Mansergh and his divisional staff set up a military government and began to lay the foundations of a civil administration, including police, law, education, and broadcasting. Dutch troops began to arrive in early February 1946, and the divisional staff began the handover process. On 23 April 1946, Mansergh left the division to take up the command position of GOC Allied Land Forces Netherlands East Indies. The various brigades began to withdraw by sea from Sourabaya in April, and the handover of control to the Dutch was completed on 8 May.[189]

End of British/Indian involvement and re-institution of Dutch authority

Fighting intensified in western Java in late November and December 1945 as the British/Indian offensive in Sourabaya continued. The extremists made a concerted effort to sever communications between Batavia and Bandoeng during this period; however, as more and more British/Indian units from central and eastern Java made their way back to

[188] The report went on to say, 'our action in Java and French Indo-China is already being represented as European repression of national risings of Eastern peoples. If this is made a major political issue as is likely, it may have a serious effect upon the loyalty of the Indian Armed Forces': 'Internal Situation in India', 1 Dec. 1945, L/WS/1/1008, OIOC, BL, and *TOP*, VI, 256, pp. 576–83. This report appeared to have some impact on the decision-makers in London. As Pethick-Lawrence stated to Wavell on 16 December 1945, 'in the meantime both I and [Gen. Sir Ashton Gerard Oswald Mosley] Mayne [military secretary to the India Office], who was at the meeting [meeting with the Chiefs of Staff in London] gave very strong expression to your views and to those of the Commander-in-Chief. I think that partly as a result of our representations it is now unlikely that a third Indian division will be sent to Java. This though it by no means meets Indian views entirely will at least not add seriously to the already grave position' (Pethick-Lawrence to Wavell, 16 Dec. 1945, *TOP*, VI, 273, p. 618).

[189] Brett-James, *Ball of Fire*, pp. 463–5.

Batavia (during consolidation of the 23rd Indian Division), pressure on the British began to decrease. As 1946 began, it was clear that the situation in Java had changed. British and Indian troops had secured Sourabaya and its environs; they had been successful in extricating numerous internees and Japanese POWs from central Java; and they were consolidating forces in Batavia and in the western interior.[190]

At the end of 1945, a meeting was held in Singapore to discuss the current and future situation in the area. Lt Gen. Christison sent a staff officer, a lieutenant colonel, to present on the final plans to deal with extremists in western Java to Lord Mountbatten and Lord Alanbrooke, chief of the Imperial General Staff. In discussing the possibility of casualties, Mountbatten made a specific request that Indian troops be used, saying that he did not want to see British wives widowed so long after the war's official end. The lieutenant colonel, greatly angered and offended by this, responded, 'Sir, do you really think it is different if Mrs Poop Singh is made a widow?'[191]

Just as the fighting in most of Java, where the British and Indians were stationed, began to die down, political pressure in New Delhi heightened once again. Wavell and Auchinleck let it be known that they were under intense pressure from the Indian National Congress and other nationalists to withdraw Indian troops from both FIC and the NEI. Pethick-Lawrence wrote to Prime Minister Attlee, emphasising the need for an early withdrawal from both places and noting that 'motions of protest' had been tabled in the Indian Assembly to oppose the employment of Indian troops in both locations, especially Java. Wavell, seconded by Pethick-Lawrence, asked for a specific withdrawal date to offset the motions that were to be debated on 21 January.[192] The discussion was picked up by the Chiefs of Staff in London and the prime minister; they expressed resistance to Lord Wavell making such a definitive announcement, and indicated that they were concerned about the impact of such a declaration on the talks that were continuing between the Dutch and the

---

[190] See Kirby, *War Against Japan*, V, p. 341, Dennis, *Troubled*, pp. 190–1, and McMillan, *British Occupation of Indonesia*, p. 61.

[191] 'Life and Times of General Sir Philip Christison', p. 188, IWM.

[192] See *TOP*, VI, 341 and 342, pp. 750–1, for more information. Also refer to Mss Eur D714/72, OIOC, BL. The terms of the motion were as follows: 'to discuss a specific and urgent matter of public importance, namely the using of Indian troops in the bombardment on the 10th of November and succeeding days of 1945 of Surabaya ... the sending of Indian troops to Indonesia to aid the British in their operations against the Indonesian struggle for independence ... to censure the GOI for permitting the use of Indian troops in Indonesia and Indo-China to suppress National Government there and to re-establish the Imperialist hold of the European powers' (*TOP*, VI, 364, pp. 811–12).

Indonesians. They agreed to meet again on 18 January, to see if there was a way for the viceroy to 'make a less categorical statement'.[193]

Wavell and his staff drafted a potential response to the motion that they anticipated in the Indian assembly: it emphasised 'the task [of the Indian divisions] of disarming, concentrating and evacuating the Japanese in the Netherlands East Indies and of rescuing Allied prisoners of war and internees. Political tranquility is essential to the successful accomplishment of this task ... [I]t is the intention of the British government to withdraw British and Indian troops as soon as their tasks have been fulfilled.'[194]

The fighting in FIC generated considerably less outcry in New Delhi. This was partially due to the smaller number of troops involved and the quicker withdrawal of the 20th Indian Division; the fighting in Java involved more troops and a longer handover. In addition to these logistical differences, the Indian nationalists perceived the Indian divisions in Java as more aggressive and inflicting more damage; they cited the attack on Sourabaya in particular as motivating 'motions' that they were planning to bring forward.[195] The response from HMG in London – over-ruling the objections of the viceroy, the commander-in-chief, India, and Pethick-Lawrence – indicated to many that the balance of power had not shifted from London, and that the voice of moderation in New Delhi had no real authority to stop the deployment or use of Indian troops in the NEI and FIC.

As of February 1946, large-scale violence had lessened significantly, but sniping, looting, and murder continued. AFNEI had been forced to redeploy forces in and around Java as the Dutch began to arrive to take over;[196] the 23rd Indian Division had consolidated outside Batavia and was attempting to control lines of communications into the interior and the key towns of Bandoeng and Buitenzorg.[197] There was some serious fighting in mid March, but units of the 23rd Indian Division, notably the 1st Patialas (Indian State Forces), were able to control the

---

[193] *TOP*, VI, 348, minute four, p. 764.   [194] *TOP*, VI, 368, Annex 1, 18 Jan., p. 819.

[195] See n. 192 for details of the specific parts of the motion.

[196] See Dennis, *Troubled*, and McMillan, *British Occupation of Indonesia*, for an in-depth discussion of the many layers of negotiations, relations, and planning for Dutch Army troops to return to the NEI and their takeover of the British and Indian positions in Java and NEI as a whole.

[197] The 1/16th Punjabis described the mission thus: 'the main tasks at Buitenzorg were the maintenance of road communications up to the Poentjak Pass on the Bandoeng road, and the preservation of law and order in the surrounding country. During the following three months [February–May] frequent clashes with bands of extremists took place.' See Lt Col J. P. Lawford, *Solah Punjab: The History of the 16th Punjab Regiment* (Aldershot: Gale & Polden, 1967), p. 235; see also WO 172/10280, NA.

situation.[198] Over the next months, British and Indian troops pulled back to Batavia as more and more Dutch troops came in to take over their positions. The 50th Indian Tank Brigade and 161st Indian Infantry Brigade (5th Indian Division) remained in Batavia, and the 5th Parachute Brigade held Semarang in central Java until the Dutch relieved them in the second half of February. Two brigades from the 5th Indian Division stayed in Sourabaya until April. British and Indian forces did not control much outside the coastal enclaves in central and eastern Java, but in western Java they did control portions of the interior. Throughout this period, and until the last British and Indian troops withdrew, they continued to undertake the withdrawal of Japanese soldiers, sailors, and airmen, as well as the rescue of Allied civilian and military internees.[199]

The year 1946 also brought major changes in the command structure. On 1 February, Christison was sent home to the UK to take up Northern Command; he was replaced first by Lt Gen. Sir Montagu Stopford as GOC ALFNEI and later, in April, by the recently promoted Mansergh, from the 5th Indian Division. Mountbatten was replaced on 1 June as commander SEAC by Stopford, who was made acting commander of ALFSEA.[200] By summer 1946, the 23rd Indian Division was the last formation left in Java. The division was withdrawn in four stages, throughout October and November, coinciding with the departure of the 26th Indian Division from Sumatra. With the final Indian divisions evacuated from the NEI, both SEAC and ALFSEA ceased to exist as of midnight on 30 November 1946.[201]

Final counts for British and Indian units show approximately 600 killed, 1,400 wounded, and 320 missing during the thirteen months of operations in Java.[202] The number of missing is the total from both the 23rd and the 5th Indian Divisions, and records indicate that some of these soldiers were deserters. Attempts by Indonesian nationalists to subvert the authority of the Indian and British commanders, and to entice Muslim soldiers to desert to their cause, have been documented. Col W. E. H. Condon, writing the 13th Frontier Force Rifles' regimental history, refers to this: discussing the role of the 8/13th FFRifles, working in and around Buitenzorg, in Java, under the command of the 36th Indian Infantry Brigade (Separate), he writes that

[198] See war diary of the 1st Patialas, Apr. 1946, WO 172/10343, NA, as well as Doulton, *Fighting Cock*, pp. 294–9.

[199] Kirby, *War Against Japan*, V, p. 342; McMillan, *British Occupation of Indonesia*, pp. 90–9.

[200] Kirby, *War Against Japan*, V, p. 348.   [201] *Ibid.*, p. 374.

[202] *Ibid.*, p. 351.

service in Java, coming as it did after a World War when all were hoping for release, put a very great strain on discipline and *esprit de corps*. Indeed, it would be difficult to find a situation containing more temptations to a soldier or a role calling for the use of more tact, patience and self-control. It is only fair to record that the conduct of the 8th Battalion was such that it was held up as an example to other troops in Java. General Stopford, in a letter ... circulated to all units on 6th March [1946] ... that the checking of the increase in desertion and preventable disease was a matter of unit discipline and *esprit de corps*.[203]

The senior staff at both India Command and SEAC continued the practice of assessing the morale of the Indian Army troops throughout the FIC and NEI campaigns, as they had during the Second World War and INA trials. War diaries and intelligence assessments make frequent reference to the impact of the mission and the INA trials on the Indian *jawan*s. The reporting diverged in many ways: some accounts indicate that Indian troops watched the INA trials with much interest,[204] while others note a complete lack of interest,[205] citing instead requests from the troops for information about rainfall and crops at home as well as their future prospects in the army.[206] Of the 45,000 fighting men who served in the NEI, some 700 soldiers did desert, representing about 1.6 per cent of the total force. As Richard McMillan has noted, 'the rate of desertion on both Java and Sumatra was small and can in no way have affected the operational effectiveness of the Army of occupation'.[207]

[203] W. E. H. Condon, *The Frontier Force Rifles* (Aldershot: Gale & Polden, 1953), p. 352. It must be noted that the battalion served with the 26th Indian Division in Burma, and had been on home leave since May when it was called up again and shipped to Java in November 1945. Interestingly, the battalion was commended for its morale; this could easily have been otherwise, given that the men had been on home leave already.

[204] See war diaries of 1st Indian Infantry Brigade, Feb. 1946, WO 172/9909, NA, discussing the 1/16th Punjabis; see also McMillan, *British Occupation of Indonesia*, p. 155.

[205] See War Diaries of 37th Indian Infantry Brigade, Jun. 1946, WO 172/9932, NA; see also McMillan, *British Occupation of Indonesia*, p. 155.

[206] See intelligence reports dealing with morale in L/WS/1/1636, OIOC, BL, as well as Intelligence Reports, L/MIL/17/5/4276, OIOC, BL, for the end of 1945 and first half of 1946, which highlight the issues of family, crops, and the future, more than duties in FIC, NEI, or the impact of the INA trials. Examples of such reporting include a report from January 1946, stated that 'morale of the Indian Army is at a high level ... Indian troops are rightly proud of the part played in the campaigns in this theatre [SEAC] and it is often felt that not enough publicity has been given to their achievements' (L/MIL/17/5/4276, OIOC, BL).

[207] McMillan, *British Occupation of Indonesia*, pp. 159–60. See his whole chapter, pp. 138–64, for more in-depth discussion of issues, especially within the Mahratta Light Infantry. The two Mahratta Light Infantry battalions, 49th Brigade, recorded quite a few desertions; but it must be remembered that these two battalions, outnumbered and lacking ammunition to hold their positions, suffered heavily during the early stages of the fighting in Sourabaya. One significant cause that McMillan did not discuss, but which came up at times in the Second World War, was weak

In both FIC and the NEI, British and Indian Army units were dropped into a difficult political situation, and left to contend with a muddled and shifting strategy. Despite this, as the 23rd Indian divisional history stated: 'We came to Java as soldiers, as soldiers we went away, and we cherished the thought that in performing our duty with steadfast courage and disciplined restraint we had played our part in averting what was so nearly a great human tragedy and had, perhaps, helped bring peace to a troubled land.'[208] Units and individual officers provided various perspectives in their assessments, including statements such as 'it was a relief when it became known that the sojourn was nearing an end. The role of the British forces had been a distasteful one.'[209] One veteran of the campaign later recalled: 'I believe that in 1945 and 1946 through much of South-East Asia the old Indian Army did a difficult job with humanity and success.'[210] Lt Col Bristow wrote that 'the loss of life in Java seemed unnecessary, and was deeply deplored. Veterans and heroes of Eritrea, the Western Desert, Imphal and Burma were killed in a futile conflict which was forced on us.'[211]

Conclusion

The 5th, 23rd, 20th, and 26th Indian Divisions' experiences in FIC and the NEI highlighted the complexity that underlies even the apparently simplest military engagement. These post-war deployments resoundingly contradict the common assertion that the Second World War was not politically complex. HMG was never quite clear about what role the British and the Indian Armies should play in supporting their European allies in the restoration of their former colonies. Furthermore, one cannot help but wonder whether HMG would have been as quick to allow the expansion of SEAC AO, if British soldiers, NCOs, and officers had been the ones to do the fighting. The political pressure brought to

officership. See also 'Intelligence Review Period Oct. 1945–Nov. 1946, Appendix A: Deserters Indian Troops', WO 203/2645, NA.

[208] Doulton, *Fighting Cock*, p. 302.

[209] This comes from the 1/16th Punjabis, the longest-serving battalion in Java: Lawford, *Solah Punjab*, p. 236.

[210] Patrick Davis, *Red Flash*, No. 16, Mar. 1993, p. 10. He served in the 4/8th Gurkhas and commanded A Company, which arrived later in the campaign, during the summer of 1946. In one of his letters to his mother, which was published in the same *Red Flash* edition (p. 8), he discussed his concerns about the deployment. He stated: 'We're still in Java ... We're all a little browned off to tell you the truth ... But I suppose someone has to be here ... We've only had five killed in a month, which is very light, but not at all pleasant. One doesn't enjoy losing lives in such a dim and doubtful cause.'

[211] Bristow, *Memories*, p. 140.

bear by Operation Python indicates that the likely answer is no. An additional irony is that the new Labour government, in haste to end the British presence in India, nevertheless saw the Indian Army as an Imperial Reserve with unlimited abilities to project British power and support for allies, with the added benefit of few casualties to trouble the British electorate.

The uneven and continually evolving strategy within SEAC also highlights some of the issues that had arisen between India Command and SEAC. While both the Fourteenth and Twelfth Armies fell under the command of SEAC, their formations were predominantly Indian. It was one thing to have forces working in former British colonies, such as Burma and Malaya – which Indian Army units did. Their roles in FIC and the NEI, on the other hand, created a major political issue in India, at the same time as the INA trials were getting under way. To Gen. Auchinleck, the long-term stability of the Indian Army was the most important factor for India during the period leading to independence, and he felt very strongly that involvement in these operations caused far too much unnecessary pressure.

The lack of clear strategy, and contradictory advice from both SEAC and London, left Indian Army and SEAC commanders to develop planning and strategy on their own, from the perspective of the unit on the ground. While this resulted in some mistakes, particularly in the early days, Indian Army commanders and troops were able to recover, regain the initiative to secure key areas, and repatriate thousands of Allied POWs and civilians. The divisional and corps staffs set out to carry out their mission, at first with minimal support; along strict military lines, they did a professional job. The officers, VCOs, NCOs, and soldiers of the 5th, 20th, 23rd, and 26th Indian Divisions carried out this difficult mission with the same level of professionalism and ability as they had shown in Burma from 1943 to the end of the war. Many veterans had remained with the divisions, and applied their experiences and knowledge to the campaigns in FIC and the NEI. Many of the officers, VCOs, NCOs, and *jawans* considered themselves professional soldiers and recent victorious veterans of Burma, and their job to carry out the orders of their commanders professionally – even when lack of strategy and political awareness at the highest levels left them in the middle of a series of difficult political and combat situations.

Ultimately, the Indian nationalists' rhetoric, though troublesome, had minimal impact on Indian forces.[212] This was partially due to the

---

[212] Brett-James, *Ball of Fire*, p. 465.

duration of the campaign, but more because they were veteran frontline troops, and as such tended to view their circumstances from the perspective of military professionals. This self-perception was reinforced by their interaction with Japanese forces; British and Indian troops, at first bemused by their role, came to respect and develop a feeling of camaraderie with their former enemy. Those who had been fighting and killing one another a few months previously discovered common ground as fellow professional soldiers, serving and dying alongside one another. In such paradoxes are embodied the fog and complexity of war.

The concluding remarks in the 5th Indian divisional history on the fighting in the NEI state run: 'To the individual Indian soldier this task must have presented serious problems. Their propagandists at home missed no opportunity of comparing the duties that had to be carried out in Indonesia with what they, in India, were fighting against in their efforts to rid India of British occupation ... [T]he soldiers had been away for years and were longing to return home. Yet, despite these important facts, they carried out their duty to their regiments, their officers and their Commander in the loyal, patient and self-sacrificing way so characteristic of the Indian soldier.'[213]

---

[213] *Ibid.*

5   1946, the year of difficulty: internal security and the rise of communal violence

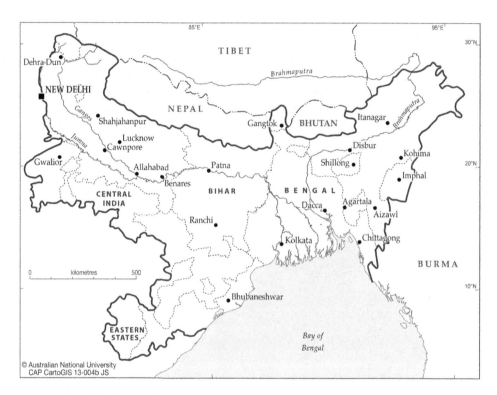

Map 5.1 Eastern Command 1946–1947

We are going to hand over to you a magnificent weapon – a weapon of the finest tempered steel, a blade that will never turn in your hand ... I have often wondered whether the people of India as a whole realise what the Indian Army has meant to them ... The Indian Army, the Indian soldiers, are the best ambassadors India has ever sent. They are a magnificent example of the Indian nation. If India is worthy of that Army then she is worthy of everything ... [This great army] was not solely due to intensive training but to the quality of the men – the virtue of courage, the virtue of loyalty and the virtue of endurance.[1]

This tribute to the Indian Army was made by Lt Gen. Sir Francis Tuker of Eastern Command in early 1946, speaking to a group of journalists in Calcutta. One of the journalists listening, in reporting the event added some of his own thoughts:

We earnestly hope that the Indian Army will maintain that high standard of efficiency and reliability of which General Tuker has been so proud ... One thing must be clear: the Army should not allow politics to interfere with its work. It is an excellent principle that it should have no politics. [Its job is to be] always ready to defend the country against aggressors, and not to side with one party or the other.[2]

The principle articulated here had already been strained by events such as the INA trials and the resulting violence which erupted within India. The summer of 1946 would prove a greater test than any the Indian Army had yet encountered in dealing with internal affairs.

Previous chapters have focused on the role of the Indian Army in the Second World War, and in internal security operations in French Indo-China and the Dutch East Indies. In all of these situations the army demonstrated a consistent standard of professionalism and discipline. The post-war era back in India opened a new phase, one of rising political and communal violence. This trend involved the Indian Army in a less obvious role – that of demobilised soldiers taking part in, and sometimes orchestrating, the violence. The events of 1946, especially in Eastern Command and the United Provinces, clearly indicated a new level of deterioration in community standards – one that would continue to increase in brutality and spread to the Indian Army's main recruiting area, the Punjab, by March 1947. The INA trials and the subsequent unrest that they provoked had demonstrated the Indian Army's capability in managing communal disturbances. Despite this, the senior command of both the army and the British Indian administration watched the unfolding of events in 1946 with some trepidation.

---

[1] Tuker, *Memory*, p. 573.   [2] *Ibid.*, pp. 573–4.

The historians Ian Talbot and Gurharpal Singh have highlighted the differences between the 1946 violence and what had come before:

five features differentiated the end of empire violence from 'traditional' communal riots. First, it contained a desire to squeeze out, or in modern parlance, to ethnically cleanse minority populations. This was evidenced both in the high casualty figures and the destruction of dwellings and businesses. Community life was so shattered that it could not be reconstituted in the affected locality. Second, violence was not about religious differences in the traditional riot, but occurred within the end of empire political context of the contest for power and territory. Local struggles responded to the wider issue of Pakistan ... Third, the Partition violence was more intense and sadistic than anything that had preceded it ... Fourth, linked with the previous characteristic, the violence spread from its traditional public arena of conflict to invade the private sphere. Women and children were caught up in the outbreaks and shown no mercy. Fifth, the violence evinced a high degree of planning and organization by para-military groups.[3]

This chapter will consider the role and functions, as well as the controversy, of the Indian Army acting as Aid to the Civil Power in India, and examine its performance in this capacity in 1946, as it attempted to quell the rising political and communal violence that would far surpass anything in its past experience. The events of 1946 provided, among other things, a clear indication that there were numerous issues requiring high-level attention within other government services, notably the Indian civil service and the Indian Police, which would only be exacerbated as independence drew near.[4] It also highlighted the difficult position in which this role placed the army, leading to speculation about what would happen if the violence spread to the Punjab, still the major recruiting area for the army.

---

[3] Ian Talbot and Gurharpal Singh, *The Partition of India* (Cambridge University Press, 2009), p. 66. The book provides an excellent overview of the very complicated process of partition of the subcontinent.

[4] The Indian civil service (ICS) in 1946 was close to crisis point, due to personnel shortfalls, post-war weariness, and the aftermath of numerous crises. Recruitment of British personnel to the ICS had in essence ended unofficially by 1943, causing a major personnel shortfall by 1946 – so much so that Sir Stafford Cripps, speaking in Parliament in March 1947, intimated that Britain no longer had the power to rule. Hyam specifically stated that 'recruitment dried up totally in 1943, and by December 1946 there were only 6008 European ICS [officers] left. Even if replacements could be recruited, it would take three to four years' training' (Hyam, *Britain's Declining Empire*, p. 114). See also comments by Pethick-Lawrence in *TOP*, VIII, 302, p. 551. For a much more detailed discussion of the issues within the ICS and Indian police in the run-up to independence, see David Potter, 'Manpower Shortage and the End of Colonialism: The Case of the Indian Civil Service', *Modern Asian Studies*, 7, 1 (1973), pp. 47–73. Potter also makes the contentious point that 'a fundamental shift in allegiance [occurred] on the part of the Indian ICS officers from the British Government to the nationalist forces in India' (*ibid.*, p. 71).

Lord Pethick-Lawrence, the secretary of state for India, in a telegram to the British prime minister, Clement Attlee, pinpointed the central importance of the Indian Army in a delicate political situation: 'it is clear that nearly everything depends upon the reliability and spirit of the Indian Army, provided that they do their duty, armed insurrection in India would not be an insoluble problem. If, however, the Indian Army were to go the other way, the picture would be very different.'[5] Gen. Claude Auchinleck,[6] the commander-in-chief, India (CinCI), responding to the telegram, wrote that:

the reliability and spirit of the Indian forces including the Police will be secured by a firm and explicit declaration by His Majesty's Government to the effect that while they maintain their intention to grant self-government to India by constitutional means: A. armed insurrection will be put down by force if necessary and leaders punished. B. government servants will be supported to the full. C. the police and the troops acting in the execution of their duty will be protected at the time and thereafter.[7]

Auchinleck's assertions would shortly be put to the test, as communal violence spread from Bengal to the Punjab.

The political landscape in 1946

The political developments of 1946, specifically the Cabinet Mission and the formation of the Interim Government, had a direct impact on events in India in the second half of the year, and consequently on the army's role in performing internal security duties.[8] Many historians feel that the Cabinet

---

[5] 'Prime Minister's Minute on the Indian Army Morale', 6 Dec. 1945, L/WS/1/943, OIOC, BL.

[6] Gen. Auchinleck became a field marshal on 31 May 1946. He received many letters of congratulations. See Auchinleck Papers, University of Manchester. See also his letter to the Indian Army thanking them for their many kind letters of congratulations. He specifically stated: 'I am deeply moved and greatly honoured by your kind messages coming to me from the Army' (Publicity, 1 Jun. 1946, L/WS/1/742, OIOC, BL). When mentioned in this chapter, his rank will relate to the time period under discussion.

[7] 'Auchinleck's response to the Prime Minister's Minute', 8 Dec. 1945, L/WS/1/943, OIOC, BL. Viceroy Wavell followed up Auchinleck's points and added: 'full publicity should be given to the arrival of all formations from overseas and the welcome arranged on a lavish scale'.

[8] Some of the most easily accessible primary sources dealing with the Cabinet Mission of 1946 and the formation and function of the Interim Government can be found in the *TOP*, VII–VIII. For some of the best sources to be found in secondary works, see Yasmin Khan, *The Great Partition: The Making of India and Pakistan* (New Haven: Yale University Press, 2007), esp. chapter 3; Brown, *Modern India*, and Brown, *Nehru: A Political Life* (New Haven: Yale University Press, 2004); Stanley Wolpert, *Shameful Flight: The Last Years of British Empire in India* (Oxford University Press, 2006), especially chapter 6; and the bibliography of Talbot and Singh, eds., *Partition*.

Mission of 1946 was the last hope for Congress and the League to make common cause and establish a coalition government that would lead India to independence. As Prime Minister Attlee stated, 'My colleagues are going to India with the intention of using their utmost endeavours to help her attain her freedom as speedily and fully as possible. What form of Government is to replace the present regime is for India to decide.'[9]

As has been discussed previously, the Indian National Congress party had decided not to support India's involvement in the Second World War, while the Muslim League and Punjab National Unionist Party did. As a result of their decision, and of the ongoing Quit India movement, Congress leaders were put in jail. The governance of many of the Congress-led provinces was disrupted;[10] British governors took over these provinces and carried out direct rule. Muhammad Ali Jinnah and the Muslim League filled much of the political vacuum left by Congress members' imprisonment; over time Jinnah and the League came to represent 'Muslims' as a whole and were focused in their efforts not to become a subjugated group under a Hindu-dominated independent India.[11] British authorities, recognising the growing rift between Hindu and Muslim political leaders, attempted to bring the two sides together during the war to discuss the potential for a multi-religious independent India. These efforts were entirely unsuccessful, and indeed it was during this period that calls for a Muslim Pakistan, separate from India, grew increasingly forceful.[12]

The talks took place in New Delhi and Simla over the course of three months and at first appeared to be successful in bringing the two main political parties to a partial solution.[13] The Cabinet Mission Plan was to create an All-India Government whose powers would encompass only foreign affairs and defence. All other powers would be devolved to the provinces.[14] Congress and the Muslim League agreed to the Cabinet

[9] 'India Statement by the Cabinet Mission and his Excellency, the Viceroy, 16 May, 1946', in Philips, ed., *Selected Documents, IV*, p. 378; see also Moon, ed., *Wavell: The Viceroy's Journal*, Appendix II, for more details.

[10] See Government of India Act, pp. 164–6; also in Philips, ed., *Selected Documents, IV*, pp. 320–35.

[11] Jinnah had made statements before the Second World War highlighting his fears: 'the majority community have shown their hand that Hindustan [India] is for the Hindus' (M. A. Jinnah on the Alienation of the Muslims from Congress, Oct. 1937, cited in Philips, ed., *Selected Documents, IV*, p. 347). See letters and speeches from Nehru as well as Jinnah describing and debating the issue in more detail: *ibid.*, pp. 336–60.

[12] *Ibid.*, pp. 336–7.

[13] This subject is too large to discuss in any great detail in this book. As stated earlier, see *TOP*, VII–VIII; Moon, ed., *Wavell: The Viceroy's Journal*; and Philips, ed., *Selected Documents, IV*, for much more detail and specific primary source materials.

[14] Talbot and Singh, eds., *Partition*, p. 40.

Mission 'Statement' of 16 May, even though it was characterised as having a weak central government.[15] This statement also specified that the Indian armed forces should not be divided,[16] as to do so 'would inflict a deadly blow on the long traditions and high degree of efficiency of the Indian Army and would entail the greatest dangers'.[17] Wavell met with Gen. Auchinleck to discuss the release of the statement and specifically asked about its potential impact on the army; Auchinleck replied that he anticipated none.[18]

Wavell ceased talks in early June and sought to create an Interim Government to focus on writing a new constitution and preparing for independence. On 16 June, Wavell and the Cabinet Mission issued a statement on the need for a strong and representative Interim Government, 'to conduct the very heavy and important business that has to be carried through'.[19] Invitations were sent out to leaders from both major parties, including Jinnah and Nehru, along with the senior leadership of various minority groups.[20] Wavell sent a report to the British cabinet on 29 June 1946, outlining a number of points that would be challenged and then confirmed in the final months of 1946. In discussing the Indian Army, he indicated that '[while] the loyalty and discipline of the Indian Army are at present to all appearances satisfactory, there are doubts whether the Indian Army would respond if asked to suppress a Congress mass movement, or deal with

[15] Wavell accused the Indian National Congress of wanting a strong centre and not backing down from that aim. See Moon, ed., *Wavell: The Viceroy's Journal*, 'Lord Wavell's Appreciation of Possibilities in India, May 1946', p. 483, and 'Resolution of the Congress Working Committee, 25th of June 1946', in Philips, ed., *Selected Documents, IV*, pp. 386–7, for more detail.

[16] Auchinleck's aide, Hamid, mentioned that many of the smaller minority groups, such as the Sikhs, felt frustrated with the findings and feared for their loss of position. The Sikh leadership appointed a Committee of Action, with former INA officers and soldiers filling the ranks, to fight the plan that was being developed. See Hamid, *Disastrous*, p. 73. Intelligence was also gained that Sikhs were arming themselves with weapons from American weapons dumps left behind from the Second World War. See Chapter 7. See also Hamid, *Disastrous*, p. 82.

[17] 'India Statement by the Cabinet Mission and His Excellency, the Viceroy, 16 May 1946', in Philips, ed., *Selected Documents, IV*, p. 380.

[18] 'Record of Meeting of Cabinet Delegation, Wavell and Auchinleck, 6 May 1946', *TOP*, VII, 202. The record stated that 'generally speaking the Intelligence reports about the state of the Army showed little sign that it had been permeated by any disruptive political forces'. However, it also reported that 'there was, however, more communal feeling in the Army now than there was two years ago and this was specially so in regard to the Indian officers' (p. 438).

[19] Moon, ed., *Wavell: The Viceroy's Journal*, p. 489, and Philips, ed., *Selected Documents, IV*, p. 385.

[20] See Moon, ed., *Wavell: The Viceroy's Journal*, p. 489, and Philips, ed., *Selected Documents, IV*, p. 385, for full list of the men invited.

widespread communal trouble, and in some areas the Police also would prove unreliable'.[21]

While His Majesty's Government and Wavell proceeded with plans for an interim government, the political wrangling that had begun during the earlier phases of the Cabinet Mission Plan became increasingly heated. The Congress party, which had initially been supportive of the plan, began to withdraw in early July;[22] the Muslim League followed suit later in the month.[23] As July went on and the political parties squabbled, lines were drawn across India along communal groupings, entrenching divisions that had previously been more malleable, and laying the ground for an outbreak of communal violence that would be more violent, organised, and deadly than any that had come before.

The effect on the Indian Army during this period appeared to be minimal. While interest in the news of the Cabinet Mission and the statement in May was in evidence in the various intelligence and morale reports, the findings generally indicated that many soldiers were 'feeling uncertain regarding the future of the Army as a whole and the individual as well'.[24] Some other reports noted that many VCOs and ICOs were taking an interest in the political developments that were taking place.[25] One report from July observed: 'the majority of the ICOs and VCOs appeared to follow the [political] developments closely and expressed their disgust at the discussions and the inability of the parties to come to an agreement'.[26]

On 24 August, Congress withdrew its objections to the Cabinet Mission Plan and agreed to help form an interim government; the

---

[21] 'Note for Cabinet on Present Position in India', 29 Jun. 1946, *TOP*, VII, 641. The report deals in detail with the potential issues within the ICS and the Indian police, due to the lack of numbers and the inevitable retirement of many of the British officials in the coming months. He was quite clear that the British at present 'no longer have the resources, nor I think the necessary prestige and confidence in ourselves' (p. 1086).

[22] There is some debate regarding the wording of Congress' acceptance of the plan. See Moon, ed., *Wavell: The Viceroy's Journal*, pp. 325 and 493, for more discussion. When Nehru took over presidency of Congress on 10 July, he began to pull away from Congress' support for the Cabinet Plan.

[23] Initially, the Muslim League appeared to accept the Cabinet Mission Plan, only to retract their position on 29 July. See Hamid, *Disastrous*, p. 84.

[24] Morale Reports, 30 Jul. 1946, L/WS/1/1636, OIOC, BL. Intelligence Report No. 12, 7 Jun. 1946 (L/MIL/17/5/4276, OIOC, BL), specifically states that 'Indian soldiers' minds appear to be more exercised by economic conditions in the homes and the chances of early release rather than by the imminent political changes and their implications.' This was reconfirmed a few weeks later in the 13th report.

[25] One report specifically stated that some ICOs were offering support to nationalist politicians. The report went on to state, 'the situation requires constant watching and any signs of communal feelings should be reported at once'. See Intelligence Reports, No. 12, 7 Jun. 1946, L/MIL/17/5/4276, OIOC, BL.

[26] Intelligence Reports, No. 14, 5 Jul. 1946, L/MIL/17/5/4276, OIOC, BL.

Muslim League refused to participate at this time. The Interim Government was sworn in on 2 September in New Delhi, acting as the viceroy's cabinet. Nehru was installed as the vice president, effectively the prime minister as well as member for external affairs and Commonwealth relations; in taking up this position, he promised to reshuffle the cabinet in the event that the Muslim League decided to participate.

The Muslim League finally agreed to join the Interim Government on 15 October and was assigned five of the thirteen cabinet positions.[27] However, this created additional tensions, as the Muslim League accepted the cabinet positions, but refused to participate in the Constituent Assembly. In early December, both Congress and other non-Muslim League members of the Interim Government asked the Muslim League members to step down from their cabinet positions, citing their refusal to participate fully in the assembly.[28]

The Interim Government post that directly affected the Indian Army was the member for defence, held by the former Punjab minister for development (1942–6), Sardar Baldev Singh, who also represented the Sikh minority. This was the first time that this key position was held by an Indian. Auchinleck was no longer a member of the viceroy's cabinet; he still had full authority over the military, but he now served as an adviser to Sardar Baldev Singh. Auchinleck was part of the newly formed Defence Members Committee, of which Singh was the chair.[29] Wavell agreed to the nominations put forward by Nehru,[30] including that of Singh, whom both considered the best choice available.[31] Initially, Auchinleck also supported the choice of Singh;[32] unfortunately, this cordiality did not last and relations became strained before the year was out.[33]

The army's role in internal security duties

The Indian Army had served as Aid to the Civil Power[34] (also known as internal security or IS) since the first years of the British Raj, and had consistently demonstrated a marked level of professionalism in

---

[27] India Press Release, *TOP*, VIII, 467, p. 736.

[28] See Sir Stafford Cripps, 'Reasons for the Transfer of Power', 5 Mar. 1947, in Philips, ed, *Selected Documents*, IV, pp. 393–7.

[29] Hamid, *Disastrous*, p. 100.

[30] Nehru to Lord Wavell, *TOP*, VIII, 1 Sep. 1946, 153, pp. 237 and 238.

[31] Moon, ed., *Wavell: The Viceroy's Journal*, p. 338: 'Singh was in the circumstances the best bet as War Minister.'

[32] *Ibid.*, pp. 350 and 357.   [33] See Chapter 6 for more detail.

[34] Aid to the Civil Power tended to focus on three main areas: minimum use of force, civil-military co-operation, and deterrence of unrest. British troops stationed in India also carried out this role, and there were many who felt that it was best to use British and

performing this most difficult and unpopular task.[35] The Government of India recognised that the Indian Army was the last line of defence in dealing with any popular uprising, and hence was very aware of the importance of maintaining its loyalty. It was often referred to as the 'Sword of the Raj' in the post-Mutiny (1857) period.[36]

In the pre-Amritsar (1919)[37] period, the Indian Army often resorted to martial law when faced with difficult situations. Imposing martial law meant that the military was effectively in charge of whatever area was in turmoil, and co-ordinated the effort to restore order. The definition of minimum force was less clear during martial law as well. After Amritsar, the military was pressured not to impose martial law, and to keep the civil authority in charge if at all possible. However, many soldiers, NCOs, VCOs, and officers remained unclear on both the definition and practical application of minimum force.[38]

A plethora of official and unofficial manuals and books describing the role of the army and the guiding principles of IS doctrine were written during the inter-war period (1919–39). The two most important of these proved to be Maj. Gen. Charles Gwynn's *Imperial Policing*, published in 1934, and the Indian Army manual, *Internal Security Instructions* (1937).[39] The latter followed on from the British Army manual, *Duties in the Aid of the Civil Power*, which was published the same year.

Gwynn's work was intended as an instruction manual to be read and discussed at the various British and imperial training centres and professional military education establishments, as well as read by the lay person.[40] His book presented a series of case studies in the

---

Gurkha troops, since they were 'foreign'; however, there were never enough to make this practical.

[35] There are many accounts by British and Indian Army officers of difficult experiences with internal security. One of the best and most accessible is by Field Marshal Slim, *Unofficial History*, pp. 75–98.

[36] See Omissi, *The Sepoy and the Raj*, for more discussion of this concept.

[37] For more details on the Amritsar incident, see the recent chapters by Nick Lloyd, 'The Indian Army and Civil Disorder: 1919–1922', in Roy, *The Indian Army in the Two World Wars*, pp. 335–58, and Johnson, 'The Indian Army and Internal Security', as well as Collett, *Butcher of Amritsar*.

[38] 'The Manual of Military Law contained over 900 pages, but only one page is allotted to Martial Law ... The soldier has very little to go upon' (quoted in Lloyd, 'The Indian Army and Civil Disorder', p. 337); see *ibid.*, pp. 348–52, for additional discussion of this issue. The debate regarding martial law and the use of minimum force would come to a head once again in the Punjab in 1947.

[39] Gwynn, *Imperial Policing*; L/MIL/17/5/4252, OIOC, BL.

[40] Gwynn explicitly articulated one of the most critical reasons for a better understanding of IS duties: 'In less serious cases, where armed rebellion is not encountered but disorder is of the nature of riots, communal or anti-government, which have passed out of civil control, there is the same necessity for firmness but an even greater necessity for

post-1918 period;[41] he attempted to draw relevant conclusions from each,[42] establishing four governing principles: primacy of the civil power; use of minimum force; firm and timely action; and co-operation between civil and military authorities. He emphasised the need to restore order as quickly as possible, and that the use of coercion was inherently necessary. He also discussed intelligence gathering, stressing its importance and the role of the police in obtaining it, declaring that 'in all internal trouble the basis of the intelligence system must depend on police information ... It is, however, essential that Army should maintain close touch with the police organisation.'[43]

Imperial Policing became a resource not only for operational training, but also for official military doctrine developed during the 1930s and 1940s. The War Office manual, *Duties in the Aid of the Civil Power*, clearly shows Gwynn's influence when it lists six principles for the army in IS duties: provision of adequate forces; necessity for offensive action; co-ordinated intelligence under military control; efficient inter-communication; mobility; and security measures to conceal preparations and movement of troops. In addition, it emphasises that the army should work under civilian leadership and support their efforts and use minimum force, with the ultimate end of restoration of law and order.[44]

Supported by these principles, the manual outlined the army's involvement in three phases. In the first, precautionary phase, the military should be standing by; in the second, while the police attempt to address the problem, the military should be staged forward, closer to the site of trouble, but still standing by. Only in the third phase is the military actually used to quell the disturbance.[45]

Two of Gwynn's governing principles, minimum force and civil–military co-operation, became the two central themes of Indian Army IS doctrine in the inter-war period and the violence in 1946 and 1947;

estimating correctly the degree of force required. Responsibility is often thrown on quite junior officers for the action necessary. Mistakes of judgment may have far-reaching results. Military failure can be retrieved, but where a population is antagonized or the authority of a Government seriously upset, a long period may elapse before confidence is restored and normal stable conditions are re-established' (Gwynn, *Imperial Policing*, p. 5).

[41] Interestingly, as an Irish-born officer, he omitted the difficult Irish war of independence.

[42] He was quite clear that situations faced by troops would vary greatly in their nature and intensity, that 'no hard and fast regulations would cover every case' (Gwynn, *Imperial Policing*, p. 10). Perhaps not surprisingly, his governing principles have continued to influence British counter-insurgency campaigns long after the 1930s.

[43] *Ibid.*, pp. 21–2.

[44] Johnson, 'The Indian Army and Internal Security', pp. 372–3.

[45] In practice, however, it is clear that the army was used as a deterrent as well, often deploying before the Indian police arrived: Raghavan, 'Protecting the Raj', pp. 260–1.

they were also the most contentious. Following the Amritsar incident of 1919, the British[46] and Indian Armies set out to further reinforce and maintain an understanding of minimum force in undertaking IS duties.[47]

The most basic definition of minimum force can be found in the *Manual of Military Law* (1929): 'the types of disturbance in which troops may be called upon to intervene matter little and the principles ... apply to each and every type ... [Force applied by an officer] must only be the amount which is necessary to effect the immediate object before him and must on no account use force with a view to its deterrent effects elsewhere or in the future.'[48] Practical application of this principle was as follows:[49] a section, platoon, or company would arrive at the scene of trouble, usually accompanied by the district magistrate or someone from the civil administration. The unit tended to make a square formation, with the commanding officer and the magistrate in the middle. The troops would be trying to cover all angles of attack. If the crowd did not disperse, the magistrate would sign a writ, IAFD-908, a bugle would sound, and the unit would issue a warning for the crowd to disperse. If the crowd still did not disperse, a second warning would sound and the police would be ordered to fall back. The commander would identify targets and allocate the number of rounds to be fired. The troops were ordered to fire to wound, rather than to kill. If the crowd dispersed, firing would cease and first aid would be given to the wounded. This was a model system, and did not always proceed as planned; however, army officers were both trained and educated to a high level always to work alongside the civil administration and wait for a writ to be issued before firing.[50]

Civil–military co-operation was the other defining principle that would be called into question in the post-war period. As the 1937 *Internal Security Instructions* stated: 'the success of internal security operations depends principally upon the cooperation between civil and military

---

[46] The British Army had to contend with difficult duties in Ireland in 1919–21 and in Iraq in the 1920s, and thus sought to solidify and codify doctrine for their troops as well.

[47] Minimum force in the pre-1919 period was a guiding principle. The issue then, as now, was practical interpretation and application. Army Regulations India, War Office, London, in vol. II, specifically states: 'apply as little force, and do as little injury, as may be consistent with dispersing the assembly' (p. 76); see also Johnson, 'The Indian Army and Internal Security', p. 372.

[48] *Manual of Military Law*, 1929, quoted in Raghavan, 'Protecting the Raj', p. 260.

[49] See Slim's account in his *Unofficial History*, as well as Bristow, *Memories*, p. 28, for more details. Bristow's account will be discussed in Chapter 7 as well, since he was a brigade commander in the Punjab Boundary Force.

[50] See the various Indian Army IS manuals and Raghavan, 'Protecting the Raj', pp. 264–6.

authorities'.[51] However, as the previous paragraph describes, the tactics involved meant that the local magistrate and police had to be present and accountable. During the inter-war period, this relationship worked well; the ICS district magistrate acted as the civilian representative, assisted by the commissioner of police. The commanding officer of the local military station in the given district provided the military component. The military also attached a liaison officer to the civilian administration; he read the intelligence reports and other information that came in to both the district magistrate and the police, meeting as necessary to co-ordinate intelligence. He worked with the civilians on future planning and assessing potential areas of unrest. Action plans were signed off by both the military and civilian officers. The military command would also forward relevant intelligence to the local magistrate. It was understood that the district magistrate and the police took the lead, since they interacted with the people on more occasions. As with any administrative situation, the functionality of a given district hinged to a great extent on the personalities involved and how they viewed their mutually supporting roles. IS situations naturally created occasional tensions during the inter-war period; however, the breakdown of security and questions of loyalty in the post-war period were to put an unprecedented level of strain on all those tasked with IS responsibilities.[52]

The next important doctrinal manual published was *Military Training Pamphlet (MTP)* No. 11, 'Notes on Training for Duties in the Aid to the Civil Power, 1941'. This manual highlighted the importance of civil–military co-operation: 'the success of all military measures in aid to the civil power depends very largely upon the co-operation between the civil and military authorities. Successful co-operation is only achieved when there is mutual confidence and understanding.'[53] *MTP 11* also noted that the military had been granted no new powers since the 1937 edition had been published, reiterated that 'civil authorities are in control', and further emphasised the use of minimum force: 'troops are not operating in an enemy country: there is no enemy to be annihilated'.[54]

As stated in Chapter 2, the Quit India movement of 1942 was a major challenge for both the GOI and the Indian Army, particularly in the recent aftermath of military defeats in Burma and Malaya. Despite these stresses, the Indian Army stood firm and was able to perform its duties

---

[51] L/MIL/17/5/4252, OIOC, BL.
[52] See the various Indian Army manuals listed in the chapter for more specific details.
[53] *MTP 11*, 'Notes on Training for Duties in the Aid to the Civil Power', 1941, L/MIL/17/5/2252, OIOC, BL, pp. 2–3.
[54] *Ibid.*, pp. 4–8.

without any questions of loyalty. This was even more notable because this was at a time when the Indian Army had lost significant numbers of experienced personnel to expansion, in addition to the blows to morale sustained following the defeats in Malaya and Burma. This, on the surface, would appear to be the time that the army was most vulnerable; but, even with half-trained officers, VCOs, and soldiers, it stood firm in the performance of a difficult task.

The Indian Army undertook a major internal defence exercise in 1946. This exercise identified several areas of concern, among them the use of minimum firepower, coping with inadequate numbers of soldiers, and when to institute martial law. The most telling opening comment from the report, however, was the note that 'civil administration was unable to participate in the exercise'. The civil administration's lack of understanding was also made apparent by this exercise, as they had to be advised that in future they would be expected to participate. The military was particularly concerned that civil administrators understand that the imposition of martial law did not mean an end of civil authority or responsibility.[55] The military might be temporarily in charge, but the civilian administration needed to remain active, to continue work in the executive and judicial branches.

The issues surrounding the use of force came in for a fair amount of discussion. As the political and communal climate in 1945–6 began to deteriorate, some commanders acknowledged that there was a potential need for some limitations to be lifted. The report 'recorded therefore that some guidance should be given by GHQ India to subordinate commanders as to the relaxation of the role of minimum force'.[56]

Following this exercise, the Indian Army revised its training materials in 1946, taking the opportunity to state bluntly that IS duties entailed a focus different from that which many officers and men, with experience in the Second World War, were used to.[57] *MTP 11-A*, 'Platoon Commander's Guide to Duties in the Aid to the Civil Power', stated that: 'in war the object is to kill the maximum number of the enemy in the shortest possible time. Aid to the civil power is not war. The sole object is to restore law and order, first by maximum of persuasion and patience, second by action of

---

[55] Specifically see 'Report on India Command Internal Defence Exercise', 1946, L/MIL/17/5/1816, OIOC, BL, section dealing with martial law, and the various thoughts on when the military should and should not take charge.

[56] *Ibid.*

[57] Many officers I interviewed highlighted that they needed retraining in IS duties due to their Second World War experience. They also noted that they felt the training was realistic and that the doctrine was well written and clear: author's interviews with Indian Army officers, 1999–2009.

the police, last by the use of minimum force by the military . . . [Y]ou will do your duty as a soldier and at the same time fulfil one of your obligations as a citizen.'[58] Officers were advised that, before the troops left the barracks on IS duties, they should 'ensure [the] men know they are called upon to act for the good of the country by upholding the lawful authority of the government which is essential for the wellbeing of any civilised country'.[59]

The 1946 edition also reiterated time-honoured practices of civil–military co-operation, stressing the need for the local magistrate's presence. A platoon commander 'must comply with the magistrate's request to take and seek military action ... [A]ll will avail themselves of the magistrate's advice during the military action but not ... be dominated by it.'[60] If a magistrate was not immediately available, the doctrine emphasised the need to locate one before officers could resort to force with a crowd. The doctrine also focused on the role of police in IS, since they often provided valuable intelligence about both the area of operations and the 'troublemakers' within the community. The manual also specified key points to consider when preparing to use 'minimum force':

a. Your object is not to kill but to incapacitate. b. Use your weapons and equipment in the manner in which you have been trained as soldiers. c. Be impartial. d. Use minimum force. e. Never use blanks. f. Never fire over the heads of the crowd. g. Never load by single rounds. h. Slow fire will suffice. i. Never use Brens [light machine guns]; rifles will suffice. j. Always aim at the legs not the body or head. k. Shout for effect. l. Stop the instant the crowd shows signs of breaking up. m. Never allow the crowd to get close. n. Secure the casualties immediately. o. Keep diary accounts.[61]

The increasing level and organisation of violent action in 1946 and, especially, 1947 called into question some of the prescriptions outlined in the 1946 manual. The Indian Army began to face demobilised soldiers, who were familiar with, and understood the limitations of, the manual. Many veterans were quick to recognise the differences between conventional war in North Africa, Italy, the Middle East, and Burma, and IS duties. However, many officers noted that the rising communal violence and, later, the fighting in the Punjab in particular were in many ways reminiscent of conventional war. As a result, many agreed with suggestions to lift some of the restrictions on the use of force.[62]

By mid 1946, the Indian Army had already encountered difficult IS situations, mainly responding to the political violence surrounding the trials of the INA. Their involvement had raised no issues regarding

---

[58] *MTP 11-A*, L/MIL/17/5/2253, OIOC, BL, pp. 1–2.   [59] *Ibid.*, p. 8.
[60] *Ibid.*, p. 4.   [61] *Ibid.*, pp. 6–8.
[62] Author's interviews with Indian Army officers, 1999–2009.

loyalty or performance, although some strain was noted. However, the second half of 1946 presented a different level of challenge: the Indian Army faced serious communal violence[63] in Calcutta, Eastern Bengal, Bihar, and the United Provinces, episodes which tried both its discipline and its loyalty.[64] During these outbursts, thousands of people were brutally killed and wounded in situations that had been allowed to rage unchecked for several days before the army was called in to re-assert government authority.

As noted in Chapter 3, the Indian Army had had to contend with serious violence earlier in 1946, in connection with the INA trials and the RIN mutiny.[65] Southern Command, which was in charge of all military operations in Bombay, in its report on lessons learned from IS operations to put down the RIN mutiny, contended that some principles of IS were not being applied by its sister services, chiefly the Indian Police. Voicing sentiments that were echoed later after the Calcutta riots, the report asserts that 'timely intelligence before and during disturbances is vital. There must be arrangements for pooling all intelligence ... [D]uring disturbances a central report centre to receive, collate, and disseminate reports from all sources should be established ... [T]here must be a combined intelligence staff operating permanently, probably under the chairmanship of the senior army staff.'[66] Southern Command also highlighted potential issues with training and knowledge of junior officers, emphasising that they must be better trained and that senior officers needed to stop interfering with their decision-making. This report also touched on the unresolved debate on use of minimum force, noting that 'training in IS duties must include training in dealing with really violent and determined mobs'.[67]

---

[63] As noted earlier, many weapons used during this and later violence were discarded by American troops after the Second World War. There were arms dumps throughout eastern India that had essentially been abandoned, providing caches of weapons and ammunition for political paramilitary volunteer organisations all over India: Tuker, *Memory*, pp. 125 and 135.

[64] See *ibid.*, pp. 597–605, for personal accounts of operating in Calcutta in the Aid to the Civil Power, as well as Hamid, *Disastrous*, pp. 186–90 and 208–9, for a detailed discussion of why British troops were gradually withdrawn and not allowed to carry out the Aid to the Civil Power in the Punjab in June, July, and August 1947.

[65] While intelligence reports indicated that the army had carried out its duties with professionalism, one report from April 1946 noted that some soldiers had been observed attending political rallies. The report did go on to say 'as far as can be ascertained this feeling is not yet either widespread or deep rooted': Morale Reports, 30 Apr. 1946, L/WS/1/1636, OIOC, BL.

[66] Lessons of the Royal Indian Navy Mutiny, 8310/154–73, Gen. Sir Robert Lockhart Papers, NAM.

[67] *Ibid.* The report highlighted other points, such as that all ranks must be warned that 'magistrates and police officials cannot order troops to open fire. These officials can only call upon troops to disperse rioters ... officers must be drawn to the rules about firing with automatic weapons.'

The Great Calcutta Killing (16–20 August 1946)

The Calcutta riots were linked to the political climate of July 1946, particularly the impending installation of the Interim Government (September 1946) under the leadership of Nehru of the Indian National Congress party.[68] Various Muslim officials had been invited to serve as part of the government;[69] however, on 27 July, Jinnah announced the Muslim League's rejection of the Cabinet Mission Plan, and called upon 'the Muslim nation to stand to a man behind their sole representative organisation, the Muslim League, and be ready for sacrifice'.[70] Jinnah followed this on 29 July with the call for direct action (strikes, closing of shops, disruption of transport) to take place on 16 August 'to achieve Pakistan'.[71] The Muslim League's approach was to protest the perceived inequitable treatment at the hands of the Hindus, led by Congress.[72]

In the run-up to August, both parties and their supporting newspapers inflamed tensions between the Muslim and Hindu communities.[73] The commander of Eastern Command, Lt Gen. Tuker,[74] recognised the day of Day of Direct Action's potential to spark widespread communal violence. He ordered military reinforcements, one British and two Gurkha battalions, to be ready to move into the city. Congress called for a remembrance day on 9 August to commemorate the Quit India movement of 1942; this was carried out with no violence, but communal tensions continued to rise. Gen. Tuker reported that the military commanders in the city, Brigs. James Patrick MacKinlay and Eric Sixsmith, restricted movement of the military forces in the city up to and on the

---

[68] See Suranjan Das, *Communal Riots in Bengal 1905–1947* (Bombay: Oxford University Press, 1991). Das specifically stated: 'What, however, most clearly distinguishes the 1946 violence from earlier outbreaks was its highly organized nature and direct links with institutional politics' (p. 176). For a general overview of the riots and the later violence in 1946, see Yasmin Khan, *Great Partition*, ch. 4, pp. 63–80, for background.

[69] Moon, ed., *Wavell: The Viceroy's Journal*, p. 334.

[70] Quoted in Das, *Communal Riots in Bengal*, p. 165. The League was in charge of the Bengal Ministry at this point.

[71] Muslims were to suspend all business, and public meetings were to be held to explain the League's rejection of the Cabinet Mission Plan. It also highlighted an element of violence as the League stated that it was to fight the contemplated caste-Hindu domination, as well as Jinnah's statement, 'we bid goodbye to constitutional methods': Das, *Communal Riots in Bengal*, p. 165.

[72] Tuker, *Memory*, pp. 153–4.

[73] See Das, *Communal Riots in Bengal*, pp. 166–70, for more details.

[74] For a more complete description of the key role Tuker's *While Memory Serves* has played in our understanding of this period, see Mary Doreen Wainwright, 'Keeping the Peace in India, 1946–1947: The Role of Lt General Sir Francis Tuker in Eastern Command', in C. H. Philips and Wainwright, eds., *The Partition of India: Policies and Perspective, 1935–1947* (London: George Allen and Unwin, 1970), pp. 127–47.

Figure 5.1 Calcutta riots, 1946 © Imperial War Museums
(Image No. HU 87261)

16th, so as not to exacerbate any tensions.[75] Gen. Tuker had to leave command for a series of meetings in London and New Delhi, and so placed Maj. Gen. Roy Bucher in charge.[76]

Just before serious communal violence broke out in Calcutta (and then spread to East Bengal, Bihar, and the United Provinces), a meeting took place on 13 August in the Chiefs of Staff Committee in New Delhi, where they were requested to discuss the 'Internal Situation in India'. They were asked to discuss a report on the findings of the Joint Intelligence Staff, which reported that, due to the current political and communal climate, future disturbances could lead to civil

[75] Tuker, *Memory*, p. 155.   [76] Wainwright, 'Keeping the Peace in India', p. 133.

war; and that, if civil war were to break out, the Indian Army could not be relied upon. Auchinleck gave it as his opinion that the report was too gloomy, indicating his belief that the situation in India had improved over the past two months. (Little did he realise how dangerous it was about to become.) In response to comments relating to the Indian Army, he asserted that 'the Army had been little affected'.[77] He did warn, however, that in the event of serious communal trouble, it would be impossible to call upon Muslim troops to take action against Muslims or Hindu troops to do the same with their co-religionists. He ended by reiterating that 'at present no such widespread trouble had arisen, and there were no signs of unreliability in the army at all'.[78]

The first reports of violence in Calcutta came in on 16 August; the governor of Bengal reported that disturbances had begun around 7 a.m. in certain sections of the city.[79] Hindus set up barricades to prevent Muslims from entering certain parts of the city, and Muslims tried to force Hindu shopkeepers to shut their shops. The Muslims were preparing to hold a major political rally at the Ochterlony Monument. Within hours, Muslims and Hindus were attacking one another in different sections of the city.[80] The police were able to deal with some of the outbursts, and the army was put on alert to support the police if needed.[81] From the start it was quite clear that the violence was communal in nature, as the governor reported: 'disturbances so far have been markedly communal and not, repeat not, in any way anti-British or anti-government'.[82] The rioting and violence increased overnight;[83] the army was called

---

[77] Chiefs of Staff Committee, 'Internal Situation in India', 13 Aug. 1946, L/WS/1/1030, OIOC, BL. Interestingly, one report, written in July 1946, claimed that 'there is said to have been a slight increase in communal feeling among IORs but no more than what might be expected in the circumstances' (Morale Reports, Jul. 1946, L/WS/1/1636, OIOC, BL). Auchinleck would later express concern in September 1946: 'Already many Muslim officers, for example, consider themselves as Muslims first and Indians second, though they may be proud to belong to the present Indian Army' (Morale Reports, Sep. 1946, L/WS/1/1637, OIOC, BL).

[78] Chiefs of Staff Committee, 'Internal Situation in India', 13 Aug. 1946, L/WS/1/1030, OIOC, BL.

[79] Sir F. Burrows to Pethick-Lawrence, 16 Aug. 1946, *TOP*, VIII, 154, p. 240.

[80] See Tuker's assessment in *Memory*, pp. 156–7.

[81] The York and Lancaster Regiment was ordered to prepare for movement at 3 p.m. See *ibid.*, p. 157. Tuker had claimed that the police had had issues with IS in the previous riots earlier in the year and that they might not be strong enough. See Wainwright, 'Keeping the Peace in India', p. 132.

[82] Burrows to Pethick-Lawrence, 16 Aug. 1946, *TOP*, VIII, 154, p. 240.

[83] The violence was bestial, highly organised, and aimed at all aspects of civil life. Women and children were specifically targeted. Rape and physical attacks on specific body parts were prevalent, and after these attacks the victims were often butchered in front of their

out[84] to take over some areas for patrolling, and a curfew was imposed.[85] The rest of the garrison, two British battalions, was deployed to other affected areas, and the Gurkhas were put on call. On the 17th, the Gurkhas entered into the city, as more troops from Eastern Command were called in, including more Indian troops. The army units were carrying out both motor and foot patrols, and were regularly engaging in heavy fighting against gangs of killing squads.[86]

A report from the governor on 18 August emphasised that the military was able to maintain law and order in the areas only by control and patrol; it also indicated the likelihood of former soldiers and INA involved in the violence, noting that 'gangs are still adopting guerrilla tactics with some success to evade our mobile patrols' and stating that more military were needed.[87] This combination of factors – the presence of demobilised soldiers in the community and the growing need for more troops – was to increasingly hamper the army's ability to quell communal violence through 1946 and into 1947, as the Indian Army was rapidly demobilised regardless, transferring large numbers of soldiers from its ranks into a fractured community.

During the day and evening of the 18th, British, Indian, and Gurkha units moved into northern Calcutta to clear out gangs and attempt to take control of the area. Additional troops were also arriving to help relieve the tired troops. Tuker reported a disturbing aspect to the situation that was to worsen as violence increased and spread from Calcutta to the rest of Eastern Command and later the Punjab: 'Police and soldiers were getting tired, and the load of quelling the violence was falling more and more on the troops as the police wearied and lost heart.'[88]

Concerns regarding the police's efforts and intelligence gathering were echoed in a later report by acting army commander Maj. Gen. Bucher. He reported the crucial breakdown of trust: 'troops waiting to be called out and those who have taken up precautionary positions must not place full reliance on information provided by the police or by the civil

---

families. See Tuker, *Memory*, and Das, *Communal Riots in Bengal*, for more details if you wish.

[84] Tuker would later accuse Bucher of 'being too much of a political soldier [who] did not step in with his army reinforcements, which I had left ready for him, until the killing had started. Had I been there, I would have seen that the soldiers were ready in central positions prepared to act' ('Record of 1946/1947', p. 7, Box 71/21/1/7, Tuker Papers, IWM).

[85] Burrows to Wavell, 17 Aug. 1946, *TOP*, VIII, 159 and 161, pp. 244 and 245.

[86] Tuker, *Memory*, pp. 159–62.

[87] Burrows to Wavell, 18 Aug. 1946, *TOP*, VIII, 169, p. 255.

[88] Tuker, *Memory*, pp. 161–2.

authorities'. This report also recommended that the military gather its own information: 'officer patrols must be constantly moving about the area in which troops are likely to be required so that they have an up to date and personal knowledge of what is going on'. The report went on to cover some key issues that would plague the army until independence, particularly with regard to interpreting IS doctrine. One example was defining a crowd as hostile after they began to disperse. As discussed earlier, crowds historically were allowed to disperse; however, after events in Calcutta, Bucher raised the idea of continuing to consider crowds hostile after they dispersed, given that they continued to re-form after contact and frequently attacked more than once. Bucher also discussed the use of tanks for patrolling, which had previously been considered contradictory to the idea of minimum force, asserting that 'tanks employed in patrolling were found to be invaluable ... They have considerable morale effect.' Discussing the use of Indian versus British troops, Bucher was unequivocal: 'Indian Army units must be used to a far greater degree in the aid to the civil power.'[89]

Discussions of IS duties during this period indicate concerns about breakdown in the accepted order, both in working with the police and the civil administration, and in the scope of behaviour expected from the population. These first incidents of 1946 provided a glimpse of what could happen if the system broke down. The police were not as co-operative as they had been in the past; they did not provide valuable intelligence; and they were not as focused on their own duties. In one egregious example, a lieutenant colonel in the intelligence section reported to Lt Gen. Tuker that 'during the riots the police made profits for their personal gain; money was demanded for security'.[90]

On the 19th, violence appeared to subside and some shops began to open. Clean-up and tending to the dead and wounded began.[91] The viceroy reported initial findings to Pethick-Lawrence on 21 August: three days of violence in Calcutta had produced more than 3,000 dead and 17,000 wounded.[92] The political parties, Congress and the Muslim League, blamed one another for the violence. Wavell reported that

---

[89] 'Lessons of the Calcutta Riots', 3 Oct. 1946, to the Chief of the General Staff, New Delhi, Gen. Sir Roy Bucher Papers, NAM.

[90] Lt Col GSO1 Intelligence Report to Lt Gen. Tuker, Box 71/21/4/6, Tuker Papers, IWM.

[91] See Tuker, *Memory*, p. 163, for a graphic description of the brutality demonstrated in the city. See also Appendix V, pp. 597–605, in Tuker, *Memory*, for a detailed description of a company commander's version of the violence and the clean-up.

[92] The final tally would increase to 4,400 dead: Wavell to Pethick-Lawrence, 28 Aug. 1946, *TOP*, VIII, 208, p. 323.

when it [violence] started the Hindus and Sikhs were every bit as fierce as the Muslims. The present estimate is that appreciably more Muslims than Hindus were killed. I have been told that savagery and enthusiasm for murder was terrible ... All ordinary human feelings seem to have completely deserted a considerable proportion of the population of the city. The number of troops employed is now 5 battalions of British and 4 battalions Indians and Gurkhas.[93]

Reports began to come into army HQ that ex-INA soldiers had been involved in the organised killings. INA men had come to Calcutta to celebrate INA Day on 18 August, and many former INA were employed in different parts of Calcutta. It also became apparent that the vast majority of the INA were Hindus. While the INA had claimed to be non-communal during the Second World War, the events of August 1946 indicated the harsh reality of communalism in the communities.[94]

Lord Pethick-Lawrence received a letter on 22 August from Horace Alexander, who headed the Friends Ambulance Unit in India, which highlights some of the major issues developing in Indian IS:

with regard to the police: they came in for such severe criticism last winter for acting too soon and too violently that one hesitates to criticise them for coming in too late this time. But I must record that I have not heard of any instance of effective intervention from the police during the whole of Friday or Saturday. I have heard several stories of the police looking on or refusing to intervene ... I realise that a Government that calls in the military too soon is instantly criticised for acting too harshly; and there will no doubt be some rather bitter comments from the Government side that the very people who criticised the Government last winter for using the military to excess were now clamouring for its use.[95]

The first major assessment on the violence in Calcutta was written up by Sir Frederick John Burrows on 22 August and sent to Pethick-Lawrence. This report outlines the lead-up to the outbreak, as well as the various efforts to contain the violence. Throughout, Brig. MacKinlay worked alongside the civil administration, adapting to conditions on the ground and recognising that his forces could not be dispersed, due to the level and orchestration of violence. Sir Frederick concluded that

the scale of the rioting was unprecedented. It was a pogrom between two armies ... [T]he only thing which prevented a complete collapse of the

---

[93] Wavell to Pethick-Lawrence, 21 Aug. 1946, *TOP*, VIII, 187, p. 274. Some Indian politicians called for more British troops to be deployed, only after calling for British troops to be withdrawn from India as a whole, as quickly as possible. Tuker also commented about the violence, 'it was unbridled savagery with homicidal maniacs let loose to kill and kill and to maim and burn' (*Memory*, p. 160).

[94] See Das, *Communal Riots in Bengal*, pp. 181–2, and his sources on p. 273 for more detail. INA members would be implicated in violence on both sides of the communal divide.

[95] Mr Horace Alexander to Pethick-Lawrence, 22 Aug. 1946, *TOP*, VIII, 194, p. 288.

administration was the three battalions of British troops, who were readily available for this sort of emergency [more troops were brought in from other areas]. Though the occasion and nature of the emergency could not be foreseen, the Army Commander and I had long agreed on the necessity of such a disposition of troops. I could not possibly have held Calcutta with the police alone, and I am extremely doubtful if Indian troops would have inspired sufficient confidence.[96]

Writing his own assessment of this period, Lt Gen. Tuker recalled a meeting on 18 August with a Muslim League official, Huseyn Shaheed Suhrawardy, who was chief minister for Bengal, and Indian and British officers. According to Tuker, Suhrawardy clearly showed his communal bias; however, he was confronted by several officers present, who asked why civilians could not live in harmony as officers and soldiers of various religious backgrounds could live in peace in the army. The chief minister responded that the unity in the army would not exist much longer. Lt Gen. Tuker commented that 'he was right and we knew it'.[97] Senior ICS officials expressed concern as well; the governor of the Punjab, Sir Evan Jenkins, wrote in a letter to Wavell that 'how far the Muslim soldiers of the Indian Army would support the present regime in an emergency is at least doubtful ... [T]he danger with the soldiers as with the rest of the Muslim population is the religious appeal.'[98]

Not all commanders shared this pessimism regarding the performance of the Indian troops. Maj. Gen. Bucher, who was acting army commander for the first two days of the Calcutta violence, met with Wavell on 26 August; Wavell, recording the meeting in his diary, commented that 'the Indian troops, including the transport companies, behaved very well indeed'.[99] Gen. Sir Reginald Savory, the adjutant general at the time, wrote to his wife that 'I find it most intensely interesting as I am fairly closely involved in things so far as the Army alone stands between order and chaos just now.'[100]

The first internal intelligence report examining the impact of the riots on the army was written in September; it concluded that 'although the political and communal situation remained tense throughout [August] the Indian services generally were unaffected by the course of events'.

---

[96] Burrows to Pethick-Lawrence, 22 Aug. 1946, *TOP*, VIII, 197, pp. 302–3. See the full document for more details on the way the governor and the army commander were able to deal with the violence.

[97] See Tuker, *Memory*, p. 162. Suhrawardy's communal bias was noted many times during the violence; see Moon, ed., *Wavell: The Viceroy's Journal*, 26 Aug., pp. 338–9.

[98] Jenkins to Wavell, 31 Aug. 1946, Wavell Papers, OIOC, BL.

[99] Moon, ed., *Wavell: The Viceroy's Journal*, 26 Aug. 1946, p. 339.

[100] Gen. Sir Reginald Savory to his wife, 28 Aug. 1946, 7603-93-80, Gen. Sir Reginald Savory Papers, NAM.

The report made specific mention of 'comradeship of active service in the Second World War' as a key element of the army's *esprit de corps*.[101] Field Marshal Auchinleck sent a note to Maj. Gen. Bucher on 24 September, commenting that 'action by the Army in support of the police is an unwelcome task calling for tact, forbearance, steadiness, firmness and impartiality. These qualities were shown in the most difficult circumstances by formation HQ and all units ... for which our soldiers, British and Indian, are justly proud.'[102]

A later intelligence report from October evaluating the Indian Army's performance during the August riots stated that 'all ranks employed in Calcutta during and after the riots are reported to have behaved in an exemplary manner and have received praise for their hard work, fairness and impartiality. The Calcutta calamity seems, if anything, to have drawn Indian soldiers of different communities closer together.'[103] This assessment of the Indian Army's performance appears to reflect the general opinion,[104] and these themes were reiterated in an internal 'morale report' prepared the same month:

the morale of the Indian troops generally appears to have remained steady, in spite of the testing nature of recent events. At no time has there been any marked communal feeling within the units, and indeed many reports for the period make a point of fact that Muslims and Hindus successfully played host to one another ... [C]ommunal relations within units appear to have withstood satisfactorily ... [T]he conduct of troops engaged in dealing with riots appears to have been entirely satisfactory and in many cases has earned the respect and appreciation of locals.[105]

Violence in East Bengal (Noakhali), October 1946

The first reports of tension and violence in East Bengal began in early September. Although Wavell had reported to Pethick-Lawrence that communal tensions were rising across India,[106] 300 people had been

---

[101] Intelligence Reports, No. 16, 2 Sep. 1946, L/MIL/17/5/4276, OIOC, BL.

[102] Auchinleck to Bucher, 24 Sep. 1946, Bucher Papers, 7901–87–3, NAM.

[103] Intelligence Reports, No. 17, 1 Oct. 1946, L/MIL/17/5/4276, OIOC, BL.

[104] Many observers noted that the army was still operating as a non-political and communal force; however, some senior officers (including Lt Gen. Tuker) also noted that most of the trouble occurred outside the Punjab, where most of the army had been recruited, and wondered how the army would fare when deployed on IS duties in their home areas. See Tuker, *Memory*, p. 137.

[105] Indian Army Morale, Report Ending Oct. 1946, L/WS/1/1637, OIOC, BL.

[106] There was rising tension in Bombay throughout September; however, it subsided when the police were able to take control of the situation early on. For more details, see letters of Sir A. Clow, Governor of Bombay, to Wavell, 17 Sep. 1946, *TOP*, VIII, 328, pp. 531–3, and 3 Oct. 1946, *TOP*, VIII, 399, pp. 648–9.

killed in East Bengal before any official report was made. Lt Gen. Tuker, Eastern Command GOC, and his staff recognised that East Bengal and other areas under his command were teetering on the brink of violence sparked by events in Calcutta. Tuker's information came from intelligence gained by the military branches; he noted that civil intelligence 'was sadly lacking ... [N]o authentic report ... came out of East Bengal.'[107]

The primary consideration for Lt Gen. Tuker and his staff in Eastern Command was where best to place the troops so as to have the best chance of quelling any violence before it spread too fast. Troops that had been deployed to Calcutta in August were redeployed to Chittagong in East Bengal and into Bihar.[108] Tuker reported that both he and the Bengal Army commander, Gen. R. P. I. Ranking, as well as government officials, began to hear rumours of violence in the districts of Noakhali and Tippera on 14 October. Ranking began to move police and troops into the area,[109] even though the reports asserted that the police could handle the situation alone.[110] Tensions existed, but there appeared to be no signs of incipient violence. This is in marked contrast to two letters that Wavell[111] received from citizens of Noakhali, also on 14 October, asserting that violence was rampant and that 'no police help available. Unless immediate military help rendered, entire Hindu population will

---

[107] Tuker, *Memory*, p. 170. Das recorded that 'the Noakhali–Tippera riot was in some respects an extension of the Calcutta carnage which had affected inter-communal relations throughout eastern Bengal ... and a sizable section within both communities [Hindu and Muslim] became eager to avenge the deaths of their co-religionists' (*Communal Riots in Bengal*, p. 195).

[108] Tuker describes the back-and-forth deployment of various units from Calcutta across East Bengal in early October in an attempt to offset any violence. See *Memory*, pp. 170–1.

[109] Interestingly, Shahid Hamid, Auchinleck's aide, noted that violence had erupted on the 10th in Noakhali district. See Hamid's entry in his diary for 10 October 1946, *Disastrous*, p. 108. Das indicates that this was the first day of riots and killings. He cites the address by the chief minister for Bengal, Ghulam Sarwar, to 15,000 Muslims, who turned around and looted the various Hindu shops in the area and then attacked the residences of two of the wealthiest Hindus in the area: *Communal Riots in Bengal*, p. 196. See also Tuker, *Memory*, Appendix VI, pp. 616–19, a personal account of a company commander from 4/2nd Gurkha Rifles, who recalled receiving word from the police on the 14th and troops moving out within an hour. See the whole report for specific details on the complexity of a company operating in the IS role. Sir F. Burrows, Governor of Bengal, also indicated that violence erupted on the 10th in a letter to Lord Pethick-Lawrence; see his letter, dated 16 Oct. 1946, *TOP*, VIII, 472, p. 743. He also mentions troops being moved around at an early stage.

[110] Tuker, *Memory*, p. 171.

[111] Wavell noted in his journal entry for 15 October 1946: 'serious troubles seem to have broken out in Eastern Bengal with much killing of isolated Hindu communities by Muslim terrorists'. See Moon, ed., *Wavell: The Viceroy's Journal*, p. 360.

be extinct.'[112] Press reports from the 16th described mass murder, kidnapping, and ethnic cleansing by Muslim gangs against Hindus in and around Noakhali.[113] It shortly became clear that communications in the area with the outside world had been compromised, leaving authorities in the dark about what was happening.[114]

The military and civilian administration met on the 16th and decided to deploy another 2,500 police and troops to the affected areas. Companies from several Indian Army battalions were sent in to restore order as quickly as possible. It was estimated that more than 1,000 armed Muslim men had been carrying out a well-organised violent pogrom. Intelligence also came in that ex-soldiers were among those involved. Mass conversions of Hindu women took place, and violence against women and children was high on the agenda, as it had been in Calcutta.[115] The local police and the civil administration were widely considered to be biased in favour of the Muslim population,[116] and failed to protect many of the Hindus in the area. The League's Bengal administration also attempted several times to obstruct the army's operations to clear out the Muslim gangs.[117]

By the 19th, most of the violence had subsided as police and troops moved out and killed, wounded, or captured members of the gangs.[118] Lt Gen. Tuker moved the 161st Indian Infantry Brigade, commanded by a Hindu, Brig. Pran Nath Thapar,[119] and its units

---

[112] Mr Sarat Chandra Bose to Wavell, 14 Oct. 1946, *TOP*, VIII, 452, p. 726. See also Das, *Communal Riots in Bengal*, pp. 192–3, for some of the background regarding the dates of violence and the reporting.

[113] Tuker, *Memory*, pp. 171–2.   [114] Talbot and Singh, eds., *Partition*, pp. 70–1.

[115] Das, *Communal Riots in Bengal*, p. 198.

[116] See the 'Minutes of Conference with the Governors of Bengal, United Provinces, Punjab Sind, and North-West Frontier Province, 8 August 1946', *TOP*, VIII, 132, for comments regarding the police in Bengal from the governor. He stated: 'The East Bengal Police who were 30% Muslims used to be good but were not as reliable as in the past ... Many [British] officials would want to go from the 1st of January 1947 ... even now there were less than 100 British ICS officers in the Province, and about the same number of Indian Police officers. The steel frame was now more like lath and plaster and more plaster than lath' (p. 205).

[117] See Das, *Communal Riots in Bengal*, p. 200, where he specifically states that the superintendent of police in Noakhali made his partisan views clear to all, and the Bengal chief minister Suhrawardy wanted troops to stop attempting to restore order in the area.

[118] Tuker, *Memory*, p. 175. Wainwright says the violence subsided by the 20th: 'Keeping the Peace in India', p. 135.

[119] Lt Gen. Tuker specifically made mention of Brig. Thapar's ability. He stated: 'he discharged his duties in these peculiarly difficult conditions with absolute impartiality, a deep sense of responsibility and competence, setting an example to all other Indian officers who were later to be employed all over eastern and northern India in these days of insensate cruelty and violence' (*Memory*, p. 619).

into the area.[120] The troops carried out sweeping operations alongside the police throughout the rest of October and November. The troops were vilified by the Muslim League's Bengal administration for their involvement; the adjutant of the 1/3rd Gurkhas recorded that 'officers had the impression that from Mr Suhrawardy, the Chief Minister, downwards, the bias was in favour of the Muslims and against their victims, and the ministers showed resentment, rather than gratitude, to the soldiers for all they had done to stop the disturbances. Police too who had acted against Muslims were not appreciated.'[121]

The army, along with some police, were able to quell the violence in the area, although it took time, due to defective information and mis-judgement by the local commander.[122] The army also sought out former soldiers living in the area and called them in to gain their assistance in re-establishing equilibrium in the community.[123] Before it was over, some 350 villages in the two districts had been affected;[124] the authorities estimated that, while only 300 people were killed, more than 50,000 Hindus became refugees.[125] After a series of interviews with various leaders and officials, Wavell summed up his findings in a letter to Pethick-Lawrence on 5 November: 'the police are undoubtedly demoral-ised and ineffective ... [T]he people at large have little confidence in their impartiality ... [T]he troops ... did excellent work and have restored order and confidence where they have been.'[126]

At around this time Auchinleck also wrote to the army commanders:

At our recent conference I discussed with you the excellent work which has been done and is being done by the British officers of the Indian Army,

---

[120] See Tuker, *Memory*, Appendix VI, pp. 606–19, for accounts of these operations by officers of the 4/7th Rajputs and the 1/3rd Gurkhas.

[121] *Ibid.*, p. 618.

[122] See letter from Wavell to Pethick-Lawrence, 5 Nov. 1946, *TOP*, IX, 8 enclosure, specifically for more details on the conversation with Maj. Gen. Bucher. Bucher did admit that the troops being well dispersed had quelled much of the violence. He also noted that the people in the districts had no faith in the police and the minister, and that the morale of the inspector general of police in Bengal was low, and felt that the police were not at the same standard as they had been in the past (pp. 14–15).

[123] Tuker, *Memory*, pp. 176–8. Tuker also mentions that both the Muslim and Hindu communities made accusations that the Indian Army troops were acting with too much vigour, always accusing troops of the opposite religion of being too zealous.

[124] The British authorities, both civil and military, stated repeatedly that, while the violence was appalling, it was blown out of proportion in comparison with the situation in Calcutta. They felt that Congress and Nehru were primarily responsible. See entries in *TOP*, VIII, Moon, ed., *Wavell: The Viceroy's Journal*, and Tuker, *Memory*, for more discussion.

[125] Talbot and Singh, eds., *Partition*, pp. 70–1. They also mention the well-organised element of the violence due to the presence of demobilised soldiers.

[126] Wavell to Pethick-Lawrence, 5 Nov. 1946, *TOP*, IX, 8 enclosure, p. 18.

particularly the old Regular officers and amongst them especially Commanding Officers of units. I realize very well how very difficult their present task is and that it is not likely to get easier in the future. I will be most grateful if you will take every opportunity of letting Commanding Officers know how much I appreciate the splendid way they are carrying on. They are doing a great service to the Army and to their country.[127]

Violence in Bihar

The violence in Calcutta and East Bengal was initially blamed on Muslims and support from the local Muslim League officials by many within the Hindu and Sikh communities. The fact that local League officials in Bengal did not do much to squelch their own communal violence caused dissension at the highest levels of the Interim Government, as League and Congress members blamed one another for supporting the violence.[128] At the end of October, violence broke out in Bihar, where Hindus attacked Muslims. The Congress-led government in Bihar was criticised for not dealing with the violence, as League-led governments had been following incidents in Calcutta and East Bengal. The Congress-led Provincial Government called for a protest day to remember the dead of Noakhali, and within days violence had erupted.[129] The chief minister for Bihar, S. K. Sinha, and his Congress colleagues initially refused to call in troops, asserting that 'prayer' would restore calm. Over the ensuing two weeks, more than 7,000 people were killed in Bihar, and some 50,000 displaced.[130]

The governor of Bihar, Sir Hugh Dow, in a letter to Wavell in early September, foresaw the coming violence; he indicated that communal tensions were extremely high, and cited the numbers of Biharis who were returning from the Calcutta violence and spreading tales. He called into question the Congress government and their officials, who he accused of 'undermining the authority and prestige of district officers, and even

---

[127] Auchinleck Papers, 20 Oct. 1946, No. 1196, University of Manchester; also quoted in Connell, *Auchinleck*, p. 851, and Hamid, *Disastrous*, p. 109. See 'Minutes of Conference with the Governors of Bengal, United Provinces, Punjab Sind, and North-West Frontier Province, 8 August 1946', *TOP*, VIII, 132, and the reply from the deputy commander-in-chief, India, Gen. Sir Arthur Smith, when asked about the reliability of Muslim troops: 'the probable attitude of Muslim troops ... according to a report the average Sepoy was taking very little interest in political matters' (p. 209).

[128] See letter from Nehru to Wavell, 15 Oct. 1946, *TOP*, VIII, 462, p. 732, and letter from 23 Oct. 1946, 496, pp. 781–4, for more description of the 'political accusations'.

[129] Sir H. Dow, Governor of Bihar, to Pethick-Lawrence, 29 Oct. 1946, *TOP*, VIII, 524, p. 831.

[130] Talbot and Singh, eds., *Partition*, p. 72.

when exhorting officers to do their duty have done it in a hectoring manner, threatening them with punishment ... and perhaps worst of all, the way in which the police have been handled has caused considerable doubts as to their dependability in an emergency ... I am not without hopes that there will be an improvement in some directions as the result of a Congress Ministry at the Centre, and the sobering effect of Calcutta on some of the leaders of the extreme groups.'[131] The Eastern Command GOC, Lt Gen. Tuker, was equally damning of the situation as it stood. He stated: 'We knew by now [early October] that the Bihar police were of little use. They had been rotted out by the very party of the Ministers who held office ... The police were therefore dispirited and incompetent.'[132]

The Noakhali Day of Remembrance went forward in the Chapra Saran District, and violence broke out on 25 October.[133] As in Calcutta and East Bengal, the violence was highly organised and well planned. As in Calcutta and (to a certain extent) Noakhali, women and children were specifically targeted. Lt Gen Tuker recorded that 'women and their babies were cut up, butchered, with an obscene devilry that a civilized people cannot even conjure forth in their imagination'.[134] It is interesting to note that Tuker reports that when he asked a group of Hindu soldiers why they used their weapons against the gangs of killers (co-religionists) with such effect, they stated, 'they would have liked to wipe them out after what they had seen'.[135]

Maj. Gen. R. Ekin, GOC of the Bihar and Orissa area, called upon the governor, Sir Hugh Dow, and the civilian administration to use more troops; he was sending units out on repeated 'flag marches' in an attempt to quiet things down. The area command was short on numbers, since three battalions had been moved to Calcutta and East Bengal in response to incidents there, and the closest reinforcements were in Ranchi, nearly 300 miles away. A company of the 4/3rd Gurkha Rifles was despatched to Chapra in response to Ekin's request, but even as they were on the move,

[131] Dow to Wavell, 7 Sep. 1946, *TOP*, VIII, 276, pp. 442–3.
[132] Tuker, *Memory*, p. 183. Talbot and Singh in *Partition of India* also highlighted this issue, noting that 'police lacked impartiality' (p. 73).
[133] See Tuker and Dow in a letter to Pethick-Lawrence, 29 Oct. 1946, *TOP*, VIII, 524, p. 831, where they state it began on the 25th, as do Talbot and Singh in *Partition*, p. 71.
[134] Tuker, *Memory*, p. 182. See also Vinita Damododaran, 'Bihar in the 1940s: Communities, Riots and the State', in Low and Brasted, eds., *Freedom*, pp. 175–98, which records that some Muslim men killed their wives and daughters as Hindu gangs closed in, for fear of what might happen to them at the hands of the Hindu mobs (p. 189). The butchery of Muslims in some villages was so great that they functionally ceased to exist (*ibid.*).
[135] Tuker, *Memory*, p. 182.

violence was spreading across Bihar from Chapra to the Patna, Monghyr, Bhagalput, and Gaya districts.[136] By 2 November, violence had spread throughout northern and southern Bihar.[137]

The available troops were playing catch-up with those elements of the police who were willing to support the army. During the early days, troops tended to come upon villages that had been recently been attacked; they would drive off the enemy, then rescue people who had survived. As time went on, more and more troops were earmarked for these missions. The normal mission plan for an army battalion was to split into company-sized formations, create a company base, and deploy multiple mobile patrols to intercede against the various gangs. Sections of men were frequently dropped off in villages to offset attacks by gangs; while generally outnumbered, units were able to inflict enough damage on an attacking mob to drive them off.[138] The 5th Indian Divisional HQ was moved to Dinapur to help organise and plan IS deployment.[139] Commanders sought out former soldiers in the community and asked them to serve as 'special constables', and many joined, as they had in Noakhali.[140] With centralisation of the army's efforts and the full resources of the 5th Indian Division (minus the 161st Brigade) available, the army and the police[141] began to get control of the situation by 6 November.[142]

During this period, Wavell's journal entries about the violence in Bihar were damning of the actions of both the League and Congress. On 6 November, he wrote that 'the situation in Bihar seems quite out of hand. It is of course the result of the violent communal propaganda on both sides and the lowering of the authority and morale of the services and the Police by the Ministry ... [A]s I have warned HMG on many occasions we have now the responsibility without the power, whereas the Indian Provincial Ministries have the power but little or no sense of responsibility.'[143] On the 7th, Wavell visited Bihar in person. He visited various

---

[136] Damododaran, 'Bihar in the 1940s', p. 188.

[137] See the account from the CO of the 1st Madras Regiment in Tuker, *Memory*, pp. 186–8, and accounts in Appendix VII, pp. 620–3.

[138] For more detail, see *ibid.*, where an officer from the 4/10th Gurkha Rifles describes his company's role in Bihar.

[139] The 5th Indian Division had returned from service in the NEI; one of its brigades, the 161st, had been placed in East Bengal to deal with the violence there.

[140] Tuker, *Memory*, pp. 622–3.

[141] Tuker felt that the police, when supported by the army, tended to perform better than expected, but still not to a consistently high standard: *Memory*, pp. 188–9.

[142] Dow to Wavell, 6 Nov. 1946, *TOP*, IX, 19, p. 39.

[143] Moon, ed., *Wavell: The Viceroy's Journal*, pp. 372–3. See also his letter of 22 November to Pethick-Lawrence, *TOP*, IX, 77, pp. 139–40, for a more nuanced discussion of the violence and the role of Congress and the League.

Congress, police, army, and League officials, as well as Nehru. Wavell noted afterwards that Nehru was trying to 'check the troubles'.[144] His assessment of the local Congress leadership was scathing, actually referring to the chief minister, Sinha, as a 'gangster'. He told Sinha in person 'that his government has disgraced and discredited Bihar; that it was criminal folly to allow Noakhali Day to be celebrated ... lowering the morale of the Police and [that,] in failing to control the Press, [his government] had led directly to the present tragedy'.[145]

It appears that decisions about use of minimum force were largely being left to individual commanders at this time.[146] One platoon had to contend with a mob of a thousand men; they fired into the crowd, fixed bayonets, and cleared them out. Most of the army's efforts, however, were focused on escorting refugees. The violence inflicted upon the Muslim community by the Hindus was immense; within a month, more than 60,000 refugees had left the province.[147] The efforts of Lt Col Venning and the 1st Madras Regiment during this period were highly commended. The regiment, who were all Hindus, carried out their difficult tasks against co-religionists with unflagging professionalism, inflicting heavy casualties and evacuating some 12,000 Muslim refugees.[148]

Wavell summed up the efforts of the Indian Army troops in Bihar in a telegram to Lord Pethick-Lawrence on 9 November as follows: 'The morale of the Indian troops is high and all ranks, irrespective of community, are determined to put down the disturbances.'[149] Intelligence reports coming into GHQ India, assessing the morale of the units in the field, were generally optimistic; one from November stated: 'a refreshing feature of the intelligence reports received during the last month is that most COs are of the opinion that the Army, generally speaking, continues to be free from communal squabbles which rage amongst civilians outside ... [D]espite an increasing interest in politics, there are still no

---

[144] Moon, ed., *Wavell: The Viceroy's Journal*, p. 373. Dow also indicated that Nehru was helpful: 'Nehru has been here for some days ... denouncing the atrocities committed by Hindus in Bihar' (Dow to Wavell, 6 Nov. 1946, *TOP*, IX, 19, p. 39).

[145] Moon, ed., *Wavell: The Viceroy's Journal*, p. 374.

[146] See description of Lt Col Venning and the 1st Madras in the village of Nagar Nahusa and their constant fighting against the killing squads that numbered close to 4,000 men: Tuker, *Memory*, pp. 189–90.

[147] Talbot and Singh, eds., *Partition*, p. 73.

[148] Tuker, *Memory*, p. 190. Tuker added, 'the record of Colonel Venning's operations supports everything that I have to say about the complete impartiality and soldierly behaviour of the Indian Army under this violent test. His men were nearly all Hindus and they fought against great odds with great determination against their co-religionists' (*ibid.*).

[149] Wavell to Pethick-Lawrence, 9 Nov. 1946, *TOP*, IX, 20, p. 40.

indications that the ranks are prepared to let ... political convictions affect ... relations with ... comrades or ... loyalty for the Army.'[150]

As had happened in Calcutta, the well-organised violence began to affect what was considered 'minimum force'. Governor Sir Hugh Dow raised this issue in a letter to Wavell on 23 November, where he described how, confronted with huge numbers of violent protestors, army troops and police had to shoot to kill large numbers within the mobs – actions which he and his ministry supported. However, he went on to point out that various community members were now accusing the army and police of using excessive force. He asserted that he considered this accusation quite unjustified, and asked for the viceroy's support for military and police efforts. He ended by stating: 'I have nothing but praise and admiration for the spirit in which every one of the military officers I have met is carrying out an extremely distasteful task.'[151]

Internal Indian Army intelligence reporting on morale concurred with this sentiment, stating that the army was carrying out its duties with professionalism and no hint of communalism. The reports highlighted that, when politics were discussed by soldiers, VCOs, or officers, discussions tended to focus on political parties' complicity in incidents of violence, and expressions of contempt for the political officials involved.[152]

Violence in Garhmukteshwar, November 1946

As violence began to subside in Bihar, it erupted in the United Provinces, near Garhmukteshwar in the Meerut district. The annual Kartik Purnima Mela, a Hindu festival, was being held to the north of the town in early November, and close to 1 million Hindu pilgrims had arrived in the area. The first few days of the festival were quiet, although the authorities were aware of rising communal tension.[153] The initial violence broke out on 6 November, in response to a rumour that a Hindu woman had been insulted by a Muslim at the festival. In retaliation, Muslim-owned stalls and bystanders were attacked, and within hours many Muslims who were at the fair had been raped, killed, or both. Once again, violence aimed at women and children was well organised.[154] Also once again, police appeared to stand

---

[150] Intelligence Reports, No. 18, Nov. 1946, L/MIL/17/5/4276, OIOC, BL.

[151] Dow to Wavell, 22/23 Nov. 1946, *TOP*, IX, 79, p. 150.

[152] Morale Reports, 31 Oct. 1946, L/WS/1/1637, OIOC, BL. One key finding was that: 'communal relations appear to have withstood satisfactorily ... and they had earned the respect and appreciation of the local civilians'.

[153] Tuker, *Memory*, p. 195.

[154] See *ibid.*, p. 198, for more detail. See also Sir F. Wylie, Governor of the United Provinces, to Pethick-Lawrence, 8 Nov. 1946, *TOP*, IX, 15, p. 30. Yasmin Khan, in

by and watch, without intervening. All of the police in the area were Hindu, and Lt Gen. Tuker believed that they genuinely feared for their own lives, and were not just avoiding confrontation with their co-religionists.[155]

The violence initially appeared to be contained at the fair; however, on the 7th, well-organised bands moved out from the fairgrounds to attack the Muslim section of Garhmukteshwar. There were numerous reports of former soldiers among the attackers, as well as members of the political militia, the Rashtriya Swayam Sevak Sangh (RSS Sangh), which included former INA members.[156] The mob descended upon the Muslim quarter, guided by local Hindus; women were raped and killed, children were slaughtered in front of their parents.[157] Police were heavily outnumbered and their minimal interventions were overtaken by well-organised attacks. The mobs cleared the town, then proceeded further afield and began clearing Muslims from the adjoining villages. The attacks went on for days, spreading to Meerut and Rohtak in the Punjab.

The army responded by calling out the Royal Garhwal Rifles from Meerut on 8 November, which tipped the balance and slowly restored order.[158] An Indian police officer, discussing attempts to curb communal violence, emphasised the importance of the army's presence: 'in spite of the official efforts to minimize the extent of this tragedy the news spread like wild fire, as we tried to dampen the smouldering tensions by arranging flag marches throughout the district by Army units available ... [T]he sight of tanks [Poona Horse] often with local police had some temporary effect in that the government forces were in control.'[159]

Rumours began to circulate almost immediately that the attacks had been organised before the festival took place, and the Congress-run United Province government came in for heavy criticism. News of the initial attacks was kept quiet from the authorities outside the district for several days, and this reinforced opinions that the local police were biased. One issue reiterated throughout all correspondence was the lack of troops to cover all the disturbances. This was only going to get worse, as violence spread and more troops were demobilised.[160]

'Out of Control? Partition Violence and the State in Uttar Pradesh', in Ian Talbot, ed., *The Deadly Embrace: Religion, Politics and Violence in India and Pakistan, 1947–2002* (Oxford University Press, 2007), pp. 36–59, writes that 'what transpired from late 1946 in UP was vicious targeted attacks on minorities, including women and children' (p. 41).

[155] Tuker, *Memory*, p. 198.   [156] Talbot and Singh, eds., *Partition*, p. 74.

[157] Initial estimates reported that more than 2,500 were killed on the first day: Sir Francis Vernie Wylie to Pethick-Lawrence, 9 Nov. 1946, *TOP*, IX, 21, p. 40.

[158] Tuker, *Memory*, pp. 200–1.

[159] Mss Eur C290 Channing Pearce, Indian Police, United Province, OIOC, BL.

[160] See Yasmin Khan, 'Out of Control?', pp. 38–9, for more discussion.

Wavell reported his initial findings on the recent communal violence to Pethick-Lawrence on 22 November 1946, and raised several points of interest. In particular, he was uncertain as to whether to place blame on the two major political parties (the Muslim League and the Indian National Congress):

The Muslims are to blame for their policy of 'direct action', which led to the Calcutta killings in August ... and for the Noakhali and Tippera disturbances, which were probably instigated by supporters of the Muslim League, though I am certain that the leaders of the Muslim League had nothing to do with it. But the retaliations in Bihar and the United Provinces have been, on a scale of numbers and degree of brutality, far beyond anything that I think has yet happened in India since British rule began. And they were undoubtedly organised, and organised very thoroughly, by supporters of Congress; again I am sure that the leaders were not involved, although I think that some of the Bihar Ministers acted recklessly and irresponsibly.

He went on to say that 'neither the Police nor the Indian officials can now be relied on thoroughly to act impartially'.[161] In a different report, he asserted that the Indian Army was carrying out its duties and avoiding any accusations of communalism – but wondered for how long this would be the case.[162]

Breakdown Plan and the Indian Army

Lord Wavell had begun work on a 'Breakdown Plan' in early June, in response to the difficulties encountered with the Cabinet Mission negotiations.[163] From June until mid January, Wavell, various governors, and Field Marshal Auchinleck discussed and debated details of a phased withdrawal from India in the event that the situation became untenable, or if outright civil war broke out.[164] Under the Breakdown Plan, many of

---

[161] Wavell to Pethick-Lawrence, 22 Nov. 1946, *TOP*, IX, 77, pp. 139–40.

[162] Note by Wavell of interview with Muslim League members of cabinet on 21 Nov. 1946, *TOP*, IX, 70, pp. 128–30.

[163] Some feel that the viceroy's decision to create the Breakdown Plan was a sign of desperation. However, to be fair to Wavell, as a military commander who had been left with a lack of planning in the opening stages of the war against Japan in late 1941 and early 1942, he did not want to be left trying to create a plan of withdrawal in the midst of a communal war. The behaviour of the various nationalist political parties and the rising communal violence at the time did make it appear that the situation was unravelling, something that many in London failed to understand or comprehend. Where Wavell needed to tread lightly was in mapping out the Indian Army's role in the Breakdown Plan.

[164] See the many entries in *TOP*, VII–VIII, and Moon, ed., *Wavell: The Viceroy's Journal*, for a more detailed discussion of the planning and thought processes.

the southern provinces (Orissa, Madras, Bombay, and the Central Provinces) would be granted independence immediately, as communal violence was non-existent in those areas during this period. In response to the violence in northern India, HMG planned to retain control for a short time longer, while attempting to implement a final political solution. The worst-case scenario laid out a withdrawal through the territory that would be the future Pakistan.

The Indian Army was essential to the implementation and success of the Breakdown Plan, and Wavell and the others expected that they would continue in their IS role.[165] A meeting focused specifically on the Indian Army's role in the plan was held in New Delhi on 30 November 1946; the plan was discussed in detail, as Lord Wavell prepared to travel to London to brief the plan in person. The specifics of the plan were:

(a) withdraw with minimum of disorder;
(b) maintain cohesion of the armed forces;
(c) administer shock to induce political leaders to adopt saner outlook;
(d) progressively reduce British responsibility in India while at the same time, and at each stage, strengthening position in the remaining territory.[166]

Discussion in the meeting about the army's anticipated position and morale during this period was frank. One comment recorded in the minutes put the position bluntly: '[We] cannot expect to maintain indefinitely the integrity of the Army, since it is known that British officers, who alone hold the Army together, are leaving soon.'[167]

Auchinleck was not happy about either the plan or the discussions. He reiterated that the Indian Army had repeatedly demonstrated that it stood firm against communalism. He maintained that the current British officers must remain with their units during the withdrawal, to maintain cohesion at all costs. He also pointed out that thus far the Indian Army was the only disciplined force in which communal interests were subordinate to duty. He was most damning in his last point of the meeting,

---

[165] Wavell was very clear about the continuing need for the Indian Army, writing that 'the continued existence of any semblance of law and order in the country depends almost entirely on the reliability and cohesion of the Indian Army' (Wavell to Pethick-Lawrence, 8 Sep. 1946, *TOP*, VIII, 286, p. 457). Pethick-Lawrence was not as confident about the loyalty of the Indian Army and how it would function if the plan was put into force. See his letter to the prime minister, 20 Sep. 1946, *TOP*, VIII, 342, esp. p. 553.

[166] Hamid attended the meeting with Auchinleck. See Hamid, *Disastrous*, p. 117.

[167] 30 Nov. 1946, Breakdown Plan, L/WS/1/1058, OIOC, BL.

when he declared: 'the effective announcement by HMG's Government of a phased withdrawal is likely to be very serious. This will create uncertainty, resulting in the deterioration of morale, and may lead to desertions with or without arms ... Finally, it may be necessary to face the possibility of wholesale disintegration of the Army in India.'[168]

Wavell briefed the plan to the British cabinet in London on 5 December, and specifically raised the issue of the Indian Army. He did not appear to express Auchinleck's concerns from the meeting on 30 November, stating that 'there was reasonable prospect of the Indian Army remaining unaffected and continuing to do its work of Frontier defence and maintenance of internal security'.[169] In a follow-up note to Pethick-Lawrence on 16 December 1946, Wavell referred to the Breakdown Plan, and reiterated that 'the Indian Armed Forces will be maintained intact as at present, under the command of and control of the CinCI. British officers and other ranks serving with the Indian Armed Forces will not be withdrawn and will continue to serve with their units.'[170]

Despite these assertions, Wavell's Breakdown Plan and his pessimistic views were not well received. The British secretary of state for foreign affairs, Ernest Bevin, was critical after the December meetings: he wrote to Prime Minister Attlee that Wavell was defeatist and should be recalled at once, and replaced by a person with the courage to uphold the dignity of the empire and the Commonwealth.[171] HMG rejected the Breakdown Plan in January 1947, and Wavell's 'pessimism' was cited as one of the reasons for his recall in February 1947.

The position of the Indian Army at the end of 1946

The Indian Army's performance throughout the difficult days of late 1946 was universally considered professional and non-communal, especially in comparison to the police and Indian officials.[172] The mood

---

[168] *Ibid.*, and see Hamid, *Disastrous*, p. 118.

[169] 'Record of Meeting at 10 Downing Street on 5 December 1946', *TOP*, IX, 157, p. 278.

[170] 'Lord Wavell's Alternative Draft of Statement on Indian Policy', *TOP*, IX, 196, p. 355.

[171] Mr Bevin to Attlee, 1 Jan. 1947, *TOP*, IX, 236, pp. 431–3. Bevin specifically stated that he felt the Indian Army was capable of handling the situation, but that, if the leadership of the army deteriorated, then the army could fall apart.

[172] Maj. James Wilson (later Lt Gen. Sir James Wilson) noted, when he was the academy adjutant at the Indian Military Academy (IMA, Dehra Dun) during 1946 and 1947, that '... the attitude of the Indian officers of the Army was different [from that of the police and civil service who were seen as communally biased]. The British officers, very much in the minority by now, received complete loyalty, support and co-operation from their Indian brother officers during this difficult period' (Lt Gen. Sir James Wilson, *Unusual Undertakings: A Military Memoir* (Barnsley, UK: Leo Cooper, 2002), p. 147).

was positive at the end of 1946, with various reports claiming that the situation was more settled. Auchinleck, in a major intelligence report on 15 November, highlighted several issues that would need to be addressed if there were to be any hope of calming things down conclusively, noting that: 'we have been able to compete [so far] with the considerable disturbances and consequent dispersion of troops'. He went on to assert, however, that 'we have not yet demobilized to the extent planned for 1 April 1947 . . . .[I]f the disturbances continue or increase, and the Army continues to be reduced, we shall find it increasingly difficult for the Army to carry out the calls made on it to give assistance to the Civil Power.'[173] The steady rate of demobilisation had already added to the problems in 1946, as report after report stressed the 'organised' behaviour of the killing squads in much of the violence. The director of intelligence at GHQ India raised similar issues in his report for the CinCI, and pointedly requested a halt to demobilisation, not only citing the recent violence, but also pointing out that the reasons for outbreaks of violence since August had not been removed and that all indications were that the situation would only get worse.[174]

Wavell noted in November that 'only the army had so far escaped any taint of communalism and was carrying out its duties'.[175] In response to the changing political mood and rise of communal violence, the Indian Army's Intelligence Branch decided late in 1946 that all subsequent intelligence reports would carry the heading, 'Political and Communal'.[176] The first official report under this heading, published in December 1946, recorded that 'COs continue to emphasise the spirit of co-operation and mutual good will existing between members of different communities in all the services . . . [M]ore reports have been reviewed commenting on the fairness and impartiality of Indian troops engaged in internal security duties . . . [A]ll ranks have come to realise the great responsibility that lies in their hands.'[177]

---

[173] 'Indian Political Situation, 15 November 1946, CinCI Appreciation of Internal Defence Situation', L/WS/1/1009, OIOC, BL. He went on to say that, until the police in Bihar and Calcutta were rehabilitated, the Indian Army could not be thinned out.

[174] Director of Intelligence Assessment, 23 Nov. 1946, L/WS/1/1009, OIOC, BL.

[175] 21 Nov. 1946, Wavell Papers, OIOC, BL. See Chapter 6 for a more detailed discussion of the demobilisation, division, and nationalisation of the Indian Army during 1946 and 1947.

[176] Field Marshal Auchinleck, in July, had created a small team to assess morale within the army. It was headed by Brig. A. A. Rudra and included three other ICOs. They reported directly to Auchinleck: Hamid, *Disastrous*, p. 84.

[177] Intelligence Reports, No. 19, 2 Dec. 1946, L/MIL/17/5/4276, OIOC, BL. The month's findings included several appendices; one reported that 'communal harmony amongst the IORs in this unit is very obvious and though the troops are drawn from many

However, Lt Gen. Tuker's account may provide a more accurate assessment of the mood of the community as 1946 drew to a close. Large-scale violence in Eastern Command had been contained, but communal tensions remained high. The army was stretched in its ability to respond to incidents of violence, and many British members of the ICS and police officers were leaving India. Observers questioned who would fill the growing administrative and security vacuum. And over all of these loomed the spectre of potential communal violence in the Punjab. Tuker wrote:

1946 passed into 1947, with trouble everywhere in Eastern Command, the aftermath of the horrors of Calcutta, East Bengal, Bihar and Garhmukteswar, and with a lurid and lowering sky in the Punjab – the one province to which we in the Army turned all our eyes, almost regardless of what might happen on our own doorstep. If the Punjab burst, the chances were that the mixed units of the Indian Army would burst also and that all of India would collapse ... [T]he feeling of responsibility was great: the feeling of frustration at the impotence of our Government, acute.[178]

Senior Indian officials, such as Sardar Baldev Singh, were concerned as well: 'the army had been well disciplined up to now and there had been no difficulty with Indian troops in Calcutta, but if bigger communal riots occurred some parts of the army might be affected'.[179]

An intelligence report from early 1947 describes how 'a feeling of quiet satisfaction appears to prevail amongst the Indian soldiers in general ... [T]roops of all castes are employed to deal with civil disturbances ... without any traces of communal discrimination arising.' A February 1947 report added more detail, commenting that 'interest in communal affairs exists and can hardly be otherwise, as men going on leave to areas

---

different classes, religions, and parties of India, they mingle freely with each other and relations amongst themselves [are] excellent'. Another went into greater detail: 'More reports have been received commenting on the fairness and impartiality of Indian troops that engaged in IS duties ... [A]ll ranks have come to realize the great responsibility that lies in their hands. They have seen murder and arson committed before the arrival of the military ... [T]he men carry out their duty in the knowledge that as yet the Army is above politics and that any action which they are called upon to take in good faith will always be supported by higher authority.' The question for many was how long the army would feel this way about their political masters.

[178] Tuker, *Memory*, p. 203. Wainwright also stated that the troops in Eastern Command had nothing but contempt for the fighting abilities of the communal gangs in Bengal and Bihar, which contributed to Tuker's assessment that things in Eastern Command should remain relatively stable in the coming months ('Keeping the Peace in India', p. 137).

[179] Indian Conference in London, 4 Dec. 1946, L/P&J/10/111, OIOC, BL; also found in 'Record of Meeting in the Secretary of State's Room at the India Office, London', *TOP*, IX, 155, p. 266. Singh would state later in the month, 'the Army has done its duty wonderfully well in recent disturbances'. See *TOP*, IX, enclosure to 211, p. 389.

where communal disturbances have taken place naturally absorb a certain amount of local attitudes ... however, relations between the different communities in units continue to be harmonious.'[180]

While the army appeared to be functioning well in the trials of late 1946 and early 1947, the abilities of the ICS and police to do their part in providing Aid to the Civil Power were being called into question. Wavell submitted a report in early December 1946, for circulation to the India and Burma Committee in London. The most challenging part of the report was the findings highlighted in 'Note on Morale of the Services in Provinces', which had been gathered from interviews and reports from across the country:

1942 [the Quit India movement] left a legacy of bitterness. Men guilty then of crimes of violence have been released and made into public heroes. Officials who did their duty then have been publicly disgraced ... [T]here has also been a steady deterioration of the administration, which was perhaps inevitable. There has been much political interference, and worst of all, Indian officials have felt compelled by political pressure to identify themselves with the Congress or the Muslim League instead of standing out as impartial members of an impartial Service ... [T]here may be a suspicion that the Services, reporting on their own morale, are now exaggerating, and that they are thinking of compensation and of their future and nothing else. This is unfair and untrue ... [T]he catastrophic effect of recent events on the Police service as a whole in Bengal and in Bihar can be judged by the ineffectiveness of the early action by the police both in the Calcutta disturbances and in the Bihar disturbances ... [T]hey were uncertain of support, and their experience had taught them that the best thing for the individual's future is to get out of a critical situation without having taken any definite action at all. The evidence of demoralization of the police in these two provinces is very convincing. Other services elsewhere might fail similarly under a similar test.[181]

A meeting of the British cabinet was convened on 10 December 1946 to discuss the recent troubles and political impasse in India in detail, as well as assess the morale of the police, ICS, and army. The prime minister raised the spectre of civil war and government collapse, and perhaps summed up the army's difficult position best when he advised the cabinet that 'the Indian Army, though the Commander in Chief had great personal

---

[180] Intelligence Reports, Nos. 20 and 21, L/17/5/4276, OIOC, BL.

[181] India and Burma Committee Paper IB (46) 41 'Morale of the Services in the Provinces of India', note by the Secretary of State for India, 5 Dec. 1946, *TOP*, IX, 156, pp. 269–70. See also Wavell's comments to the cabinet on 11 December 1946, where he reiterated the issues of morale within the Indian services and police. He did add a comment regarding the Indian Army: 'at present the Indian Army remained loyal, but a very severe and increasing strain was being put upon its discipline' (Cabinet, 11 Dec. 1946, *TOP*, IX, 186, p. 334).

influence with it, could not fairly be expected to prove a reliable instrument for maintaining public order in conditions tantamount to civil war'.[182]

As difficult as 1946 had been, there was no expectation of improvement in 1947. Issues of demobilisation and division of the army, as the date for independence and partition drew closer, would increasingly test the resolve of the Indian Army. The professionalism born out of the crucible of the Second World War, and honed and tested again in operations in South East Asia and in Aid to the Civil Power operations at home, were consistently commended by both the political and military leadership throughout 1946. How long it could continue in the face of mounting challenges was the question looming on the horizon as 1947 dawned.

[182] Cabinet Conclusions, 10 Dec. 1946, *TOP*, IX, 181, p. 319.

6   Demobilisation, nationalisation, and division of the army in the midst of chaos

> The armed forces as a whole have been built upon a non-communal basis. They have, fortunately for India, remained free from communal complications up until now ... [I]f even the mere indication of splitting the armed forces is allowed to gain ground at this stage, it will result in creating chaotic conditions in the ranks and disintegration will set in almost immediately ... [I]n the communally surcharged atmosphere ... such a contingency would be too disastrous to contemplate.[1]
>
> Sardar Baldev Singh, 25 April 1947

In the midst of growing communal violence in 1946 and 1947, major decisions were being made about the future organisation of the Indian Army. Following the army's expansion during the Second World War, it was of course necessary to decrease the army's size to a more economically sustainable level in the post-war period. However, it was necessary to balance economic considerations against the reality of increasing communal violence in India, as well as the mission of the Indian Army for 'imperial policing duties' in South East Asia, and the need for troops to fill both roles. The community situation created an additional consequence of demobilisation, which was to remove trained soldiers from one side of the equation and add them, demobilised and possibly dissatisfied, to the other, more volatile side.

Another concern during this period was the need to nationalise or Indianise the Indian Army's officer corps. There was no debate on whether this was the correct course of action, in recognition of the performance of Indian officers during the Second World War, as well as impending political changes; the critical question that remained was how fast it could be implemented without diminishing the professionalism of the army. And, as if these challenges were not sufficient, as 1947 dawned and the likelihood of partition became more and more apparent, the question began to emerge of how best to manage the division of the

---

[1] Mountbatten Papers, Official Correspondence Files: Armed Forces, 25 Apr. 1947, OIOC, BL.

Figure 6.1 Lord Wavell (middle) and General Claude Auchinleck (right) meet with Field Marshal Bernard Montgomery (left) in New Delhi © Imperial War Museums (Image No. IND 5205)

Indian Army into two separate forces, along communal lines. In this particular discussion, decisions about the Brigade of Gurkhas provided an additional challenge.

All of these issues, each complex in its own right, had to be resolved on an ever-changing time schedule and in the midst of dealing with unprecedented internal violence. Any army in history would have struggled to cope with fundamental changes in organisation, size, composition, officer ranks, and division. The performance of the Indian Army during these upheavals is a testament to the *esprit de corps* that still existed within its ranks.

Demobilisation

At the end of the war, the Indian Army stood at some 2.5 million men. As soon as peace was declared, the Indian and British governments moved quickly to demobilise most of the army, primarily as a cost-saving measure and with minimal reference to the societal, political, and economic

ramifications of such an undertaking. Various proposals were put
forward to slow plans for demobilisation; Gen. Auchinleck and the senior
command expressed both fear that too many issues remained unresolved
on the political side, and their belief that the Indian Army would be
required to serve as the backbone of a secure society. Matters, however,
had been taken out of their hands.

The issue of demobilisation had been discussed and debated early in
the war. In the pre-war Indian Army of 1914 and 1939, many soldiers,
NCOs, and VCOs had been given land grants for their service in the
army. Officials realised quite early on that this would be out of the
question for demobbed soldiers after the Second World War.[2] Instead,
as with the demobilisation following the First World War, the decision
was made to offer cash grants to soldiers who left the service at the end
of the war. By July 1942, a Directorate of Demobilization and Reconstruction had been created in preparation for the war's end.[3] These
preparations, however, proved to be inadequate in confronting many of
the realities of demobilisation. For example, an internal secret report
reported that 'the younger of these men know little of the land and
will, unless inducements are given, tend to crowd to the cities to seek
the opportunity to make use of their technical skill. Many will inevitably swell the ranks of the unemployed. Disgruntled many would turn
to the only other trade they know, fighting, and become dacoits
[criminals].'[4]

Other discussions during the war focused on the future size and
outlook of the Indian Army, at a time when the Indian Army had just
been defeated in the Far East. Field Marshal Wavell, then CinCI,
responded to a letter written by Secretary of State for India Leo Amery
on 16 January 1943, enquiring about the future composition and size of
the army. Wavell responded that any future committee to determine this
should be convened with little fanfare, pointing out that, 'We want
the officer and the soldier to be thinking entirely now of how to win the
present war and not of their future after it; and I am sure it would have an
unsettling effect if it became known that we were considering the futures

---

[2] There was one major exception. Men – NCOs, VCOs, and ICOs who received military
honours for gallantry – were given small land grants. See Anirudh Deshpande, 'Hopes
and Disillusionment: Recruitment, Demobilization and the Emergence of Discontent in
the Indian Armed Forces After the Second World War', *Indian Economic and Social
History Review*, Jun. 1996, p. 195.

[3] A specific section had been created in 1941, to lay out the future planning of
demobilisation. As the war progressed, its name would change and it would take on
other issues, such as welfare and amenities. See *Demobilization of the Indian Army*,
Adjutant General (Simla: Government of India Press, 1947), p. 1.

[4] Quoted in Deshpande, 'Hopes', p. 198.

of officers and men.'[5] Amery passed along Wavell's points to the then viceroy, the Marquess of Linlithgow, agreeing that any committee formed should be kept confidential and that some sort of assessment of the future position of India in twenty to thirty years' time was essential. He added that there must also be some sort of assessment of 'progressive Indianization in the higher ranks of the services and what role future British officers would play'.[6]

The Army Commanders Conferences at the end of the Second World War began to consider potential layout, size, and demobilisation scenarios for the post-war army. The first conference, which took place in August 1945, focused on the army's future mission, as well as the contentious issues of the size and composition of the officer corps. It also raised the possibility that, 'as regards to training, it may well be that troops will be required for police duties'.[7] The report for this conference focused on relationships between Indian and British officers, calling on all commanders to ensure complete integration and to remove anyone who did not support the effort.[8]

The General Staff Branch, New Delhi, proposed the first major planning of the size of the army for 1946 and 1947 in October 1945. They expected the army to have dropped from 2.5 million men to 700,000 men, NCOs, VCOs, and officers by the end of 1946. The tally was broken into two key areas: India and overseas. Internal numbers were broken down to 42 Indian battalions for frontier defence; 20 Indian battalions for internal defence; and 6 Indian divisions for general reserve (initially with 200,000 men overseas, although this number would change in response to demands for more troops in the NEI).[9] Another Army Commanders Conference took place in November 1945, to discuss some of the proposals for demobilisation, including scenarios for drawdown of various corps and divisions.[10] The CinCI declared that the future role of the Indian Army was to be trained for overseas duties and defence of India, with internal security listed as the third priority. He stressed that the army should not be used as a heavily armed police force.[11]

---

[5] Wavell to Marquess of Linlithgow, Viceroy of India, 25 Jan. 1943, *TOP*, III, 360, p. 539.
[6] Amery to Linlithgow, *TOP*, III, 8 Feb. 1943, 437, pp. 631–7.
[7] Army Commanders Conference, Aug. 1945, L/WS/1/1524, OIOC, BL.
[8] *Ibid.*
[9] Reorganisation of Post War Army in India, 30 Oct. 1945, L/WS/1/999, OIOC, BL.
[10] The CinCI asked for two corps, one armoured division, one airborne division, five infantry divisions, and two independent armoured brigades.
[11] Army Commanders Conference, Nov. 1945, L/WS/1/1524, OIOC, BL. Gen. Auchinleck sent a note to the War Office earlier in October, specifically stating that the roles of the army were (1) overseas; (2) frontier defence; and (3) Aid to the Civil Power. He was clear that he expected the Indian police to attempt to deal with this mission and that it would always be secondary for the army. See 24 Oct. 1945, L/WS/1/999, OIOC, BL.

The Army Conference in November 1945 also discussed the future of the officer corps, as well as the 'class composition' of the army. The CinCI understood that there were many officers, including senior officers, who had biases (for or against) various 'martial races'. He addressed this directly, noting that 'before the war, class composition was too haphazard and too much governed by personal likes and dislikes. A special committee has to be set up to examine the problem on a scientific basis. When the decisions of the committee are published and changes become necessary, army commanders are asked to accept these changes loyally and cheerfully ... for the good of the Army as a whole.'[12]

While discussions about plans for demobilisation were continued, events such as deployments to FIC and NEI and growing internal strife slowed the practical process down.[13] Reports indicated that nearly 1 million Indian soldiers, NCOs, and VCOs, as well as Indian and British officers, were to have been demobilised by early 1946. GHQ India asserted, however, that this goal could not be accomplished and still meet internal and external commitments.

The specific procedures for release were worked out in early February 1946, and involved three levels. The first level called for the release of any soldier, NCO, VCO, or officer categorised as medical level B or C; the CO had a vote in keeping any member of his regiment or battalion if they fell into either category. The second level encompassed all men who wished to leave and had served their contract. The third level comprised individuals who failed various intelligence tests. All COs were asked to use discretion in relation to deficiencies identified at all levels.[14]

---

[12] Army Commanders Conference, Nov. 1945, L/WS/1/1524, OIOC, BL. The first attempt to reform some of the pre-war practices came up in April 1946. The 16th Light Cavalry, a famous old Madras regiment, was to be reformed and reconstituted with recruits from Madras. It had formerly recruited from northern Indians, including Jats and Rajputs. Some soldiers who had been earmarked for demobilisation from the Madras region were offered a posting in the 16th Light Cavalry. The conversion was to occur in three phases: (a) formation of cadres, Madrassi instructors, calling for volunteers; (b) individual training; (c) collective training (Post War Organization of the Indian Army, GHQ India, 23 Apr. 1946, L/WS/1/1488, OIOC, BL).

[13] CinCI to War Office, 29 Nov. 1945, L/WS/1/1002, OIOC, BL. Auchinleck specifically states that initial planning (Plan 287) for demobilisation was not realistic in light of demands from SEAC for occupation duties and civil strife already present domestically. He had also expressed this opinion in a letter dated 27 November. The reasons stating why demobilisation had to slow down were (a) an increase rather than decrease in SEAC; (b) non-return from SEAC of certain formations; (c) no disbandment of units in India as they were needed for Aid to the Civil Power duties. See Demob and Release Scheme, 27 Nov. 1945, L/WS/1/930, OIOC, BL.

[14] 'Adjutant General Release Scheme – Indian Army', Demob and Release Scheme, 14 Feb. 1946, L/WS/1/931, OIOC, BL.

The list of overseas deployments in April 1946 underscores the demands being placed on the army at the same time as plans for demobilisation were being discussed. There were two Indian brigades still in the Middle East, and close to four divisions still in Burma. Malaya had nearly three divisions; Hong Kong had a brigade; the NEI had close to four divisions; Borneo and Siam had one division; and two brigades remained in Japan.[15] These were in addition to the units and formations in India fully engaged in dealing with internal security issues. There were forty-three battalions assigned to frontier defence, sixty British and Indian battalions on IS duties, and close to four divisions as the general reserve.[16]

During the period from VJ Day until the end of April 1946, close to 600,000 men, NCOs, VCOs, and officers were demobilised,[17] and more than 2,000 units were disbanded.[18] Internal reports from this period expressed concern about employment opportunities for these men. One early report indicated that, of the first 500,000 men demobilised, only 9,000 had found employment. It attempted to offset this number by recording that 35% of the released men had stated that they did not require employment, as they had individual means of livelihood, but still confirmed that some 50% of the 500,000 men demobilised were seeking employment.[19]

The Indian Army did not just release the men into the civil arena with no skills. One example: the Rajputana Rifles Regimental Centre, during the period from VJ Day to summer 1946, demobbed 6,000 men and 50 officers. Each regimental centre created a demobbed centre. The men went through a nine-week course, where they learned poultry farming and animal husbandry, as well as basic accounting. It was a requirement that men were to leave with two qualifications.[20] However, many issues

---

[15] Lt Gen. Cowan commanded the Indian troops in Japan. He wrote in 1946 to Gen. Auchinleck that there was a club there for the Indian troops, named the Auchinleck Club, because the CinCI 'is always thinking of his troops' (Publicity and Press Release, 29 Apr. 1946, L/WS/1/742, OIOC, BL).

[16] Plan for Demobilization of the Indian Army, Plan 287, Jan.–Apr. 1946, L/WS/1/1001, OIOC, BL.

[17] The average rate was 70,000 to 80,000 men per month. By the end of 1946, more than 1.3 million men had been demobilised. See *Demobilization of the Indian Army*, 'Releases – All Army Forces', p. 19.

[18] Publicity and Press Release, 'Reductions in GHQ Staff', 30 Apr. 1946, L/WS/1/742, OIOC, BL. An interesting reference was made on 8 May 1946 (*ibid.*) regarding the reduction of officer strength in GHQ India due to previous war-time pressures. It stated that more than 28 per cent of the officer positions had been lost since VJ Day.

[19] Publicity, 10 May 1946, L/WS/1/742, OIOC, BL.

[20] Publicity, 13 Jul. 1946, L/WS/1/742, OIOC, BL. The 14th Punjab Regimental Centre also offered courses in agricultural and other skills for the demobbed soldiers. In the event, however, only 30 per cent of demobbed soldiers took the courses over the two-year period. See Lt Col J. L. Cotton, 8002–68, NAM.

remained for some as they sought work upon demobilisation. Many of these individuals would come to haunt the Indian Army, since they took their dangerous skills and served as instructors for or leaders of the various political militias,[21] or served as bodyguards for politicians.[22]

Fears of a demobilised and militarised society began to surface in March 1946.[23] One intelligence report highlighted disaffection within the Jat Sikh ranks, who wondered why they were being demobbed and expressed anger at such a move.[24] An outside observer noted in East Bengal that 'the great majority of the depot staff and demobbed men were war-time recruits whose standard of discipline had suffered from hurried initial training [this was not entirely accurate after 1943] and then by the boredom of waiting for demobilization ... [T]hese men soon started to join in the INA and the political receptions.'[25] Demobilisation accelerated during the summer of 1946, as more units and formations were brought back to India from the Middle East and South East Asia.[26]

In early September, Jawaharlal Nehru, member for external affairs and Commonwealth relations within the Interim Government and head of the Indian National Congress, wrote a lengthy letter to Field Marshal Auchinleck outlining his views on the Indian Army. He emphasised the importance of the Indian Army feeling like a national army; removing communal feelings;[27] ending martial-race recruitment policies; and staffing with Indians from the top to the bottom. He also expressed his opinion that it should not be used to quell internal disturbances, or to carry out security duties in the former British colonies of South East Asia; and that all British troops should be removed. He did state that India should be proud of the army's efforts in the last war.[28]

---

[21] Ayesha Jalal describes both ex-INA and demobilised soldiers seeking employment in armed political militias. See Jalal, *Self and Sovereignty*, pp. 525–7. See also Chapter 7, dealing with 1947, for more details on the various militias.

[22] See Jalal, *Self and Sovereignty*, p. 524.

[23] See Deshpande, 'Hopes', pp. 193–205, for an in-depth discussion of key issues such as land allocation for veterans, retraining programmes instituted to help veterans back into civilian society, and reasons for the discontent among Indian other ranks.

[24] Intelligence Reports, Mar. 1946, L/MIL/17/5/4276, OIOC, BL.

[25] Mss Eur C290 Channing Pearce, Indian Police, OIOC, BL.

[26] Plan for Demobilization of the Indian Army, Plan 287, Oct. 1946, L/WS/1/1001, OIOC, BL.

[27] Lt Col Hamid was scathing in response to this point. He stated: 'Nehru did not care to remember that he was the one who inflamed communal feelings and bitter resentment in the Army by pleading the cause of the INA. He forgot that the Army carries out the orders of the duly constituted Government and had therefore nothing to fear from it' (Hamid, *Disastrous*, p. 104).

[28] Nehru to Auchinleck, 12 Sep. 1946, No. 1193, Auchinleck Papers, University of Manchester. See also Hamid's entry for 14 September 1946 in *Disastrous*, p. 102.

Auchinleck responded a few days later. He addressed many of Nehru's concerns, but his letter also indicates that Nehru was not fully aware of many of the institutional reforms that had taken place in the army during the war, or of feeling among army personnel regarding the future. Auchinleck's overarching theme was that there should be no slackening of discipline or obedience to a properly constituted authority. He asserted that his intent was to make the Indian Army a national one, and that he had always insisted on it being non-communal and non-political. He pointed out his own long record of pushing for a wider distribution of all races of India into the army, and the fact that the term 'martial races' was already forbidden usage.[29] He reiterated that the quelling of internal disturbances was chiefly the job of the police and not the army, but that the army's involvement had been required when the police had proved unequal to the task for various reasons. He noted that the army had urged the GOI repeatedly to strengthen the police, so that the army would not be required to act in the Aid to the Civil Power. He confirmed that nationalisation of the army was progressing, although hampered by a shortage of officers of sufficient quality, and stressed that complete nationalisation must be undertaken cautiously, so as not to undermine the stability and efficiency of the army. He was able to assure Nehru that all his issues had been addressed, including the issue of troops overseas.[30] Unfortunately, these exchanges mainly served to highlight the lack of communication and understanding between the future political leadership and the military high command.

By October 1946, there were 800,000 men, NCOs, VCOs, and officers in the Indian Army.[31] This number was due to be decreased to 387,000 by April 1947; one report stated that the bulk of the infantry would be demobilised during the months of November, December, and January as troops arrived back from service in Malaya, Japan, the Middle East, and the NEI.[32] With internal security problems on the rise at the end of 1946, GHQ India asserted that if 387,000 men were too few to deal with specific problems, the army needed to provide an alternative figure.[33]

---

[29] During the Second World War, the term had officially been dropped due to its political connotations and the need for many races to join the army.

[30] Auchinleck to Nehru, 17 Sep. 1946, No. 1194, Auchinleck Papers, University of Manchester, and Hamid, *Disastrous*, pp. 104–5.

[31] The 14th Punjab Regimental Centre demobbed 750 soldiers a month. It was ordered to handle 1,000 a month if need be: Cotton, 8002–68, NAM.

[32] More than six divisions of troops were serving overseas at this time. See Army Commanders Conference, Oct. 1946, L/WS/1/1523, OIOC, BL.

[33] Pethick-Lawrence in September had also called for the British troops that were in India to remain at full strength to support the Indian Army in IS duties as more were demobilised. This last issue would cause much debate within the Interim

In response, Field Marshal Auchinleck called for 500,000 to remain,[34] stating that 387,000 were not enough to carry out all the various duties of an army, particularly internal security.[35]

At the end of 1946, the Interim Government's minister for defence, Sardar Baldev Singh, wrote an assessment of the demobilisation process and Field Marshal Auchinleck's key role in it. He sent a letter to Prime Minister Attlee, requesting an extension of tenure for Auchinleck to serve as CinCI:

[he] has rendered very good service to the Armed Forces of this country and is popular with all Ranks. He has invaluable experience of many years to his credit and knows the country and its problems well. In the present uncertain political atmosphere of this country, I felt that I should have a man as Commander-In-Chief in whom I have full faith … Another important consideration … is the problem of reorganization of our Armed Force … We are in the process of demobilization and the task is heavy. From this point of view too, it is imperative that the Field Marshal should remain with us for some time.[36]

During the spring and summer of 1947, numbers of army personnel were drastically reduced; this process also involved the fracturing of units that had served together, in some cases since the 1840s.[37] In February 1947, the army stood at 736,000 officers and men; the demobilisation framework stated that, by April, there would be 434,000 troops left in the army.[38] Senior commanders fretted that 'the army cannot be looked upon by the civil power as an enormous reservoir … [O]fficers are noting that their numbers are too low to carry out all their duties and General Messervy [GOC Northern Command] stated that many units are below strength.'[39] It was also reported at this time that continued demobilisation and nationalisation would only increase the strain on the army.[40]

Alongside this internal upheaval, the communal violence in the Punjab was steadily worsening, reaching a crescendo in August 1947. Gen. Lockhart was put in command on the North-West Frontier in July

---

Government, as they wished to see more British troops withdrawn, mostly due to their costs: Pethick-Lawrence to Lawson, 19 Sep. 1946, L/WS/1/1091, OIOC, BL. See Nehru's letter to Wavell, 18 Sep. 1946, *TOP*, VIII, 331, p. 538, for more details.

[34] Indian Political Situation, Oct. 1946, L/WS/1/1009, OIOC, BL.

[35] Political Intelligence, Oct. 1946, L/WS/1/1009, OIOC, BL.

[36] Sardar Baldev Singh to Attlee, 12 Dec. 1946, *TOP*, IX, enclosure to 211, p. 389.

[37] See pp. 254–73, which focuses on the division and reconstitution of the army.

[38] Army Commanders Conference, Mar. 1947, L/WS/1/1524, OIOC, BL. See also the earlier report from 11 January 1947, called Plan 113, in L/WS/1/1000, and Plan for the Demobilization of the Indian Army, Plan 287, L/WS/1/1001, both OIOC, BL, for more detail. The initial plan in 1945 had estimated that only 321,000 men would be in the army by April 1947.

[39] Army Commanders Conference, Mar. 1947, L/WS/1/1524, OIOC, BL.

[40] *Ibid.*

1947; in an ominous letter to Messervy, whose Northern Command covered the Punjab, he wrote that there were not enough troops in the province to carry out internal security duties effectively.[41] Messervy was appointed the new CinC of the Pakistan Army in late July; he approached Mountbatten in early August to advise that the newly formed Pakistan Army was going to be just thirty-five battalions, rather than sixty-seven as originally anticipated, and that those thirty-five battalions were not going to be complete. As a result, he and his staff began the work of re-enlisting 10,000 former Punjabi Musalman and Pathan infantrymen back into the regular Pakistan Army.[42]

Nationalisation and division of the Indian Army

The state of the Indian Army's officer corps was far from ideal during the post-war period. Auchinleck, in an attempt to keep top-performing Indian officers in the army after the war's end, asked GHQ India to offer 'regular' commissions to 400 EICOs as early as February 1945.[43] In July 1945, Auchinleck advised the Indian Army that 'the process of Indian-isation should proceed as rapidly as is consistent with the maintenance of the military efficiency of the Indian Army'.[44] Despite these incentives, numbers were below optimum strength, and as violence erupted, the officer corps was not only stretched thin, but also lacking experience. In September 1945, the number of officers stood at 34,590 British and 8,340 Indians. By 1 April 1947, the numbers stood at 11,500 British officers and 8,400 Indian officers.[45]

The Indian Army had lost war-experienced British and Indian officers as a result of various decisions. Primary among these was the decision, in 1945, to award all future regular commissions to Indians.[46] This meant that British emergency commissioned officers (ECOs), as well as regulars, would gradually be replaced through the nationalisation process. However, the army's lower officer ranks were also being demobilised during this period; many experienced Indian commissioned officers (ICOs), not attracted by the prospect of 'peace-time' conditions, decided

---

[41] 8310–154/47, 25 Jul. 1947, Lockhart Papers, NAM. See also the planning for the future deployment of troops for Aid to the Civil Power duties in L/WS/1/1001, OIOC, BL, forecast in summer of 1946. They originally earmarked only twelve battalions; this was all well before the beginning of the communal civil war that would erupt in August 1946.

[42] Viceroy's Personal Report, No. 16, 8 Aug. 1947, *TOP*, XII, 385, pp. 590–606.

[43] Auchinleck to Gen. Mayne, Feb. 1945, L/WS/1/924, OIOC, BL.

[44] Auchinleck to Indian Army, Jul. 1945, L/WS/1/924, OIOC, BL.

[45] Barua, *Gentlemen of the Raj*, p. 130.

[46] Government of India to Sec. of State for India, 7 Oct. 1945, L/WS/1/924, OIOC, BL.

to leave the army instead. A large number of British officers also requested speedy demobilisation, so that they could seek employment, either as civilians in the UK or with the British Army.[47] An internal report from August 1945 stated that:

as regards actual numbers, there are now sufficient Indian officers to fill the junior officer cadre of the Indian Army of 1939 model ... [A]s regards seniority, practical experience, education and military qualifications, this position is very different. There are at present only 40 ICOs holding Lt Col commands and 20 Indian officers holding other Lt Col appointments. Even if these figures were doubled within the next few years, it would not suffice to fill even the number of post-war commands and first grade staff appointments, while the number qualified to hold more senior commands and staff appointments would be quite insufficient to merit the requirements of a post-war army of reasonable strength.[48]

As described earlier, the Army Commanders Conference of November 1945 began the process of restructuring the officer corps of the Indian Army. British ECOs would not be accepted for permanent or regular commissions, and British regular officers would gradually be phased out of the army. Serving British regular officers would still be able to request secondments, but they would no longer be made permanent.

The first formal announcement by the GOI regarding the nationalisation of the army came in early April 1946, when Gen. Auchinleck presented the 'Future of the Indian Army' to the Indian Assembly. At that moment the army had 39,100 officers, of which 27,640 were British officers and 9,240 were ICOs;[49] Auchinleck articulated the army's intention to

create a completely national army that is an army officered and manned throughout by Indians in the shortest possible space of time without lowering the very high standard of efficiency which maintains the Army today ... [I]t is the declared policy of the Government of India that the British officer element of the Indian Army shall be replaced by ICOs as soon as possible, compatible with the maintenance of the efficiency of the Army as a whole.[50]

---

[47] See L/WS/1/924 and L/WS/1/799, OIOC, BL.

[48] Principal Staff Officer to the Secretary of State for India, Aug. 1945, L/WS/1/924, OIOC, BL. The report discussed in detail the requirements for full nationalisation. However, the final findings were doomed to rejection by both the Indian Interim Government and HMG, as they stated that, at present levels, it would take twenty to twenty-five years for full nationalisation to be complete – an assessment that many senior officers agreed with. See letters from August to October in L/WS/1/924, OIOC, BL.

[49] Army Commanders Conference, May 1946, L/WS/1/942, OIOC, BL. It was estimated that the numbers would be 11,450 officers for the army in 1946, of which 4,230 would be BOs and 7,200 would be ICOs.

[50] Publicity and Press Release, 8 Apr. 1946, L/WS/1/742, OIOC, BL. Auchinleck estimated that the army would need 9,000 officers for the permanent peace-time

Lt Gen. Sir Richard O'Connor, commander of the North Western Army in India, wrote, in a letter to Sir George Cunningham, the former governor of the North-West Frontier Province: 'As you know we are doing all we can to induce young Indians of the right stamp to join the Army as regular officers so that the business of nationalisation ... proceeds as rapidly as possible without a loss of efficiency. It is nothing to do with the officers being Indian simply with gaining experience ... [T]he need for the closest possible co-operation between Indian and British officers of the Indian Army is very great.'[51]

While Auchinleck shared this opinion, he rapidly became very concerned about the numbers of both British officers and ICOs with valuable battlefield experience who were leaving the force. Auchinleck wanted BOs to serve on secondment with the newly formed Indian Army to help fill some of the gaps. A questionnaire was sent to 134 British officers with less than twenty years' service at the end of 1946 to assess their potential future. Seventy-five officers wished to be transferred to the British Army; thirty wanted to retire; and thirty-eight were willing to serve as seconded officers. Close to 150 officers with more than twenty years' service were asked as well: 60 wished to retire, and 46 were willing to serve on secondment. Another 33 stated they would serve on secondment, even if India left the Commonwealth.[52]

In October 1946, Auchinleck also grew worried about the standard of the Indian men attempting to gain admittance into the Indian Military Academy, Dehra Dun. He was under pressure from members of the Interim Government to accept potential cadets of a lower standard. He refused, asserting that

I am told by the Presidents of the Selection Board, including Indian officers of high calibre and by others competent to judge, that the general standard of the candidates coming before selection boards is very poor indeed, though I believe there is a slight improvement lately ... [T]he fact remains, however, that the percentage of rejections by the boards is very high and we have only been able to get enough suitable candidates to fill about half the vacancies at IMA ... [W]e must get enough Indian officers for the future Army and they

army. However, only 5,100 would be present by 1947. With many EICOs opting out, there were already 300 vacancies at IMA Dehra Dun (1,200 applied, but only 126 were suitable). He discussed the possible need for short-service commissions for British officers to help fill the void. He resisted calls to speed up promotion of various Indian officers to make up numbers. This issue was also highlighted in a statement by Aunchinleck to the War Office, Nov. 1945, L/WS/1/924, OIOC, BL. See later draft copy of letter to 'British officers' in Box 4/32, Gracey Papers, Liddell Hart Centre , KCL.

[51] Box 6/27, O'Connor Papers, Liddell Hart Centre, KCL.

[52] See letters from Sep. to Dec. 1946 as well as 'Results of Questionnaire', 1 Jan. 1947, L/WS/1/924, OIOC, BL.

must be good officers. So long as I am here, I will not agree with any lowering of the present standards.[53]

In early November 1946, senior commanders discussed the need for a nationalisation advisory committee. Some worried that such a committee, if formed from the Interim Government, would see itself as setting the timeline for full nationalisation. However, Auchinleck played down these concerns and confirmed that the committee would only offer advice.[54] On 19 November, it was announced that a 'Committee on Nationalisation of the Indian Armed Forces'[55] was to be set up to decide on the best ways to implement the policy of nationalisation and possible retention of British officers in the Indian Armed Forces as part of a transition process. The committee was to report back within six months on the findings.[56] On 22 November, Auchinleck sent a letter to all senior British officers, saying that, 'we are to go' and that, 'before we go, it is our bounden duty to do all we can to ensure the continued wellbeing and efficiency of our men and of the [a]rmy ... [W]e can only do this if we give freely and fully of our knowledge and experience to those who are to replace us in the higher commands and appointments ... [T]hey must be given actual experience in the art of command leadership ... I will appoint no officer, British or Indian, to any post unless I am sure in my own mind that he is properly fitted for it.'[57]

At the same time, recruitment of Indian officers was proving problematic. The defence member for the Indian cabinet within the Interim Government, Sardar Baldev Singh, advised the Central Assembly of the situation: 'present recruitment of officers for the Indian Army was unsatisfactory. The right material was not forthcoming ... The Indian Government will have to recruit officers from Britain.'[58] Col B. D. Bhanot of the Rajputana Rifles, a former Indian ECO, noted that 'regular British officers', with both pre-war and war-time experience, 'were of immense help and were worth their weight in gold'.[59] Auchinleck

---

[53] Army Commanders Conference, Oct. 1946, L/WS/1/1523, OIOC, BL. Auchinleck also discussed at this conference the constant need to assess their training. He stated: 'we must not lose the vigour and imagination with which our training was conducted in the war. We must have a constant change in outlook.'

[54] Chiefs of Staff Conferences, 2 Nov. 1946, L/WS/1/1096, OIOC, BL.

[55] The committee was headed by Sir N. Gopalaswami Ayyangar and the military lead was Maj. Gen. D. A. L. Wade; it included four Indian Armed Forces officers, including Brig. K. S. Thimayya.

[56] 19 Nov. 1946, L/MIL/7/19590, OIOC, BL.

[57] 22 Nov. 1946, No. 1199, Auchinleck Papers, University of Manchester, and Connell, *Auchinleck*, pp. 854–5.

[58] Post War Officering of the Indian Army, 7 Nov. 1946, L/WS/1/924, OIOC, BL.

[59] Author's correspondence with Col B. D. Bhanot.

expressed concerns about the larger ramifications of this situation in a meeting with Wavell, the viceroy at the time: 'the release of a large number of junior British officers from the Indian Army and their replacement by Indian officers . . . seems inevitable but will obviously weaken the army and tend to make it more susceptible to communal influence'.[60]

Recollecting on this period, Col. John Perkin, commander of 4/10th Baluch, 114th Indian Brigade, stated that 'only his company commanders and Viceroy Commissioned Officers had war experience'. Most of the platoon commanders were recent graduates of the Indian Military Academy. Although he expressed concerns about their capabilities, he felt they performed well,[61] contradicting to some extent Singh's earlier assessment of the quality of the Indian officers at IMA. The adjutant at the Indian Military Academy (the future Lt Gen. Sir James Wilson) confirmed that the quality of the first post-war intake of 126 officers that graduated in December 1946 was high;[62] it was the quantity that was the problem.[63] By the middle of 1947, it was estimated that close to 18,000 officers would be demobilised, including ICOs.[64]

Concerns about the potential performance of Indian officers in the face of rising communalism were discussed extensively in early 1947.[65] However, nationalisation was already in full flow. As of January 1947, there were 12,000 British officers in the army; it was anticipated that, by April 1947, this number would fall to 6,000 and by April 1948 to 4,000.[66] The first meeting of the Nationalisation Committee took place on 6 January. Brig. Kodendera Subayya Thimayya opened the meeting with a blistering statement on the nationalisation process, asserting that 'all Indians in the armed forces [have] the fullest confidence in the CinCI and know his

---

[60] Moon, ed., *Wavell: The Viceroy's Journal*, 6 Jan. 1947, p. 406. Gen. Hamid echoed this in his journal in June: 'Mountbatten is making things very difficult for the British officers. They are losing control and want to quit. There is already tension between Muslim, Hindu and Sikh officers' (*Disastrous*, p. 179).

[61] Author's interview with Col. John Perkin, 8 Jun. 2005.

[62] Wilson, *Unusual Undertakings*, p. 135.

[63] As one commander noted, 'there had to be a British rearguard, and the right choice was made; the British officers of the Indian Army. They knew the people and were trusted on both sides, which made them invaluable as organizers and mediators . . . Unfortunately that rearguard was not as strong as it could have been' (Bristow, *Memories*, p. 148).

[64] Army Commanders Conference, Nov. 1945, L/WS/1/1524, OIOC, BL.

[65] See letter from the governor of the Punjab, Sir E. Jenkins to Wavell, 14 Jan. 1947, *TOP*, IX, 274, pp. 499–500.

[66] India and Burma Committee, 21 Jan. 1947, *TOP*, IX, 288, p. 522. The *Daily Telegraph* was also reporting similar comments. 'It is . . . evident that the primary object is to further the policy of nationalization. It is well known that the proportion of Indian officers in the Indian Army is still small and supply of candidates of satisfactory standard has been extremely disappointing' (Demobilization and Release Scheme, 16 Jan. 1947, L/WS/1/931, OIOC, BL).

sympathetic views on nationalization. However, in spite of all the letters he had issued on the subject to all concerned, the average ICO was not convinced that the spirit of the letters was being carried out in practice.'[67] Another Indian, Brig. Kodandera Madappa Cariappa, stated in meetings in London that Congress expected to see the end of British officers in the army within five to eight years.[68]

In its February 1947 meeting, the Nationalisation Committee expressed its aim to complete nationalisation by July 1949. All British officers would be removed, and officers still required would form into the India Staff corps, which would serve at the senior levels in an advisory role as well as in command positions in some places.[69] The members of the meeting raised a number of contentious points. One British member pointed out that 'you will not have all the numbers you want of experienced officers ... [S]ome of them did extremely well in the war, but they left and it will be hard to get them back.'[70] Brig. Thimayya responded with the assertion that 'I know I am voicing the sentiments of many ICOs when I say that we feel dissatisfied with the progress of nationalization. For years we have seen that Indians have not been given a chance of filling important appointments. During the whole war we never had a single Indian who was allowed to do the job of the GSO 1 of a division.'[71]

The Commanders-in-Chief Committee, in responding to this meeting's findings, focused particularly on plans for senior Indian officer positions. They predicted a serious decline in professionalism if senior British officers were not kept in place, and anticipated that it would take ten years for enough Indian officers to be educated, trained, and ready for senior command.[72] Auchinleck supported these findings and

---

[67] 'Nationalization of the Indian Army', 6 Jan. 1947, 8204–797–1, Maj. Gen. D. A. L. Wade Papers, NAM.

[68] Wavell to Pethick-Lawrence, 26 Feb. 1947, *TOP*, IX, 469, pp. 819–22. Mountbatten later noted that it was brave of Brig. Cariappa to admit the need for British officers to remain for another five to eight years. See 'Record of interview between Lord Mountbatten and Mr Rajagopalachari', 11 Apr. 1947, *TOP*, X, 121, pp. 194–5. However, in later meetings within the Nationalisation Committee, Cariappa would claim that 'we have got to have an armed force officered by ourselves ... [W]e should have no non-Indians holding positions of command after June 1948' ('Nationalization of the Indian Army', 10 Apr. 1947, 8204–797–1, Wade Papers, NAM).

[69] Armed Forces Nationalization Committee, 2 Feb. 1947, L/WS/1/1096, OIOC, BL.

[70] 'Nationalization of the Indian Army', 2 Feb. 1947, 8204–797–1, Wade Papers, NAM. This sentiment was supported by a member of the committee, Lt Gen. Sir Arthur Smith: 'it is our considered opinion that, by 1 January 1949, there will NOT be enough Indian officers fit by experience to be given all the higher command and senior staff appointments without accepting a very big drop in the present high standard' (quoted in Barua, *Gentlemen of the Raj*, p. 129).

[71] 'Nationalization of the Indian Army', 6 Jan. 1947, 8204–797–1, Wade Papers, NAM.

[72] CinC Committee, 14 Feb. 1947, L/WS/1/1096, OIOC, BL.

reiterated them to Singh in a subsequent meeting. He made the additional point that fewer than 500 officers, of the 8,500 required, had more than eight years' service. He added that any attempt to attain full nationalisation by June 1948 'is to run a very grave risk of ... disintegration and disruption'.[73] Lt Gen. Sir Reginald Savory, adjutant general, supporting Auchinleck's position, expressed his own reservations about the nationalisation process, specifically his concerns that 'ICOs were becoming communally minded, drunk with prospects of early promotion and getting into cliques', and his fear that the 'Indian Army is due for imminent disintegration if India is divided'.[74]

Auchinleck followed up the theme of nationalisation at the Army Commanders Conference in New Delhi on 26 March, stressing that the issue was a complicated one, and that time for complete nationalisation was likely to be limited. He asked army commanders for their support of forthcoming nationalisation plans and emphasised that 'a smooth handover depends largely on British officers'.[75]

The potential division of the armed forces was an equally contentious issue, and there had been calls, as early as 1946, to restructure the Indian Army into communal units, in preparation for partition.[76] Gen. Tuker was one of the principal proponents of this strategy; Field Marshal Auchinleck opposed it completely. However, HMG's announcement in February 1947, proposing the handover of power by 1948, combined with rising communal violence and political deadlock between the Muslim League and Congress, brought it to the table once again. The first formal discussions about dividing the Indian Army took place in London in March 1947.

Gen. Geoffrey Scoones represented Auchinleck in meetings with the British CinC committee and the India and Burma Committee. Presenting to the India and Burma Committee of the British cabinet in London on the anticipated effects of partition of the country upon the Indian Army, Scoones stated: 'if the Army is to be handed over to more than one authority it cannot be handed over as an Army but only as communal forces to the respective sides; that once the process starts India will be deprived of any efficient defence and the internal situation will become dangerous. A partition of the armed forces will have to be planned in advance and on some definite assumption as regards to the political

---

[73] Auchinleck to Sardar Baldev Singh, 8 Mar. 1947, No. 1217, Auchinleck Papers, University of Manchester. See also Hamid's recollection of the meeting in *Disastrous*, p. 141.
[74] 20 Feb. 1947, 7603-93-83, Savory Papers, NAM.
[75] Hamid, *Disastrous*, p. 151.
[76] See Tuker, *Memory*, pp. 23 and 278.

future ... Therefore the longer the Indian Army remains in being the better.'[77]

Those present decided to create a secret plan to divide the army along communal lines, fearing that morale would suffer if the army found out too soon.[78] In a meeting on 13 March, Gen. Scoones reiterated his concerns: 'if it became known that the division of the Indian army on communal lines was being discussed, the effect on the morale of the Indian Army would be serious'.[79] The British Chiefs of Staff went into greater detail about the potential division of the forces, but asserted that 'in any event, there must be no splitting of the Indian armed forces while we [British] are responsible for the defence of India ... The Indian armed forces must therefore remain efficient [to deal with civil strife] and under unified control until the time of handing over power.'[80]

Auchinleck reiterated this last point in late March in a Viceroy Staff meeting, stressing that 'it would take five to ten years satisfactorily to divide the Indian Army'.[81] However, the Muslim League responded flatly that they did not want a unified army.[82] The Muslim League's focus was the fact that the army included few all-Muslim units,[83] and partition would necessitate ripping apart regiments along communal lines.[84] Doing so would inevitably lead to questions about levels of

[77] Gen. Scoones' remarks, Cabinet, India and Burma Committee, 4 Mar. 1947, *TOP*, IX, 480, p. 843. Mountbatten supported Scoones' sentiments. He asserted on 13 March, in another cabinet meeting, that it was 'essential that the unity of the Indian Army should be maintained': *TOP*, IX, 529, p. 940.

[78] Meeting of Ministers on Indian Questions, 13 Mar. 1947, L/P&J/10/78, OIOC, BL.

[79] *Ibid.*; also in *TOP*, IX, 530, pp. 940–5.

[80] Chiefs of Staff Committee, 18 Mar. 1947, L/WS/1/1045, OIOC, BL; also in *TOP*, IX, 544, pp. 974–81.

[81] 'Minutes of Viceroy's Fourth Staff Meeting', 28 Mar. 1947, *TOP*, X, 29, p. 35. Tuker agreed that it would take at least fifteen years to divide the army. According to Tuker, when he brought up the issue of 'classing' the army, the latter got angry and stated: 'the day the Indian Army is classed, I resign.' See 'A Record of 1945/47, India', p. 6, Tuker Papers, IWM.

[82] 'Minutes of Viceroy's Fourth Staff Meeting', 28 Mar. 1947, *TOP*, X, 29, pp. 35–8.

[83] See Tuker, *Memory*, Appendix XII, p. 653, which clearly lays out the structure of the Indian infantry regiments. Only four regiments – 5th Mahratta Light Infantry, 17th Dogra, 18th Royal Garhwal Rifles, and 19th Kumaon – were of one class (Hindu). The rest of the regiments had some combination. The final compilation showed that the Hindus represented the equivalent of 9⅓ of the regiments, the Muslims 6¾ of the regiments, the Sikhs 3⅔ of the regiments, and other sects 3¼ of the regiments. The nascent Pakistan Army was clearly at a disadvantage. These numbers did not include the Gurkha Brigade, which numbered close to forty battalions.

[84] See Jeffrey, *Punjab Boundary Force*, p. 492, for a description of the characteristic situation within one regiment. The 15th Punjab, with six battalions, had twelve Muslim, six Hindu, and six Sikh companies to divide within seventy-two days.

professionalism after the fact as officers, VCOs, and *jawan*s were taken out and dropped into other, newly made formations. Hindu and Sikh personnel were likely to fare better in this process than their Muslim counterparts, due to the organisational structure of the army of 1947.[85]

As discussions about the partition of India into Pakistan and Hindustan (India) became increasingly heated, political leaders from both sides began to suggest splitting up the armed forces before independence. In a meeting between Mountbatten and Muhammad Ali Jinnah on 7 April, Jinnah once again reiterated his position that the Indian armed forces needed to be divided, and that the future states of Pakistan and Hindustan must each be responsible for their own defence. Mountbatten responded by pointing out that a number of senior Indian officers had acknowledged that it would take at least five years before two independent armies could stand on their own without the support of British officers.[86] Mountbatten also asked how the army could be divided into two by June 1948 without serious communal repercussions.[87]

Meanwhile, other members of the Interim Government suggested that the army be divided along communal lines at some point in the future.[88] Liaquat Ali Khan, the deputy leader of the Muslim League, became the main proponent for discussing the partitioning of the army.[89]

Mountbatten met with Jinnah again on 8 April to discuss various issues, including the army. Mountbatten stated that as long as he was in charge of law and order in the country, division of the army would not occur. However, he did concede that, if HMG and the Interim

---

[85] As of March 1947, there were no all-Muslim armoured regiments, twelve Muslim artillery regiments, twelve Muslim engineer companies, one Muslim infantry battalion, and some miscellaneous service corps units; the remainder of the support services were mixed. In contrast, the Hindus and Sikhs could claim one armoured regiment, twenty-four artillery regiments, twenty-eight engineer companies, thirty-one infantry battalions, thirty Gurkha battalions (to be cut down to twenty), and forty-one transport companies, with the rest of the support services mixed units. Clearly, an army divided along communal lines would place the Muslims at a distinct disadvantage. See 'Note by Field Marshal Auchinleck on communal affiliation of the Indian Army', *TOP*, X, 43, pp. 62–3.

[86] Another issue was that many Muslim officers did not reside in the territory that would become Pakistan. Would Hindu, Sikh, or Muslim officers be forced to leave their homes and their regiments to appease the politicians?

[87] 'Record of interview between Rear-Admiral Lord Mountbatten and Mr Jinnah', 7 Apr. 1947, *TOP*, X, 92, p. 149.

[88] See Liaquat Ali Khan to Mountbatten, 7 Apr. 1947, L/P&J/10/79, OIOC, BL; also in *TOP*, X, 94, pp. 151–3. Khan would follow up with another letter stating that he did not expect the army to divide at the moment, but that some planning was needed for the future eventuality. See *TOP*, X, 135, pp. 220–1.

[89] Khan met with Mountbatten multiple times and communicated with him throughout April and May; see *TOP*, X and XI.

Government decided on partition as the way forward, he would set up committees to discuss the needs of a divided army, on the proviso that it would still serve under a central authority.[90] He reiterated these positions a few days later and added that nationalisation would weaken the army and that to add division of the armed forces on top of that would create too much pressure.[91] The need to maintain law and order was reiterated in the Viceroy Staff Meeting on 10 April 1947: 'there would be no question of division [of armed forces] until after June, 1948, because it would compromise his [Mountbatten's] mandate to ensure maintenance of law and order'.[92]

Meetings of the Nationalisation Committee during early April were equally heated, as various members questioned the validity of the claims that the British were intent on nationalisation. The members were split on whether the Indian Army could truly nationalise by June 1948.[93] Mountbatten met with Auchinleck on 14 April to discuss the matter in more detail. Auchinleck confirmed that, at that moment, the officer corps was dominated by Hindus and Sikhs, and reiterated that division would cause too much stress and would take more than five years to achieve. He agreed that nothing should be done until June 1948. He also predicted that a partition of the Punjab might spark a civil war. Such a schism would reverberate throughout the army, and there was no guarantee that the army could hold together. However, he assessed the army as 'loyal at [that] moment'.[94]

Tensions increased as the various Indian parties openly discussed the need for divisions in Bengal, the Punjab, and a future separate Pakistan. In mid April Mountbatten was still expressing strong opposition, going so far as to say that he would stop partitioning of the army: 'I considered

[90] 'Record of interview between Mountbatten and Jinnah', 8 Apr. 1947, *TOP*, X, 101, pp. 158–61.

[91] 'Record of interview between Mountbatten and Jinnah', 9 Apr. 1947, *TOP*, X, 105, pp. 163–4. Mountbatten was holding firm on the issue of a central authority controlling the armed forces as well (*ibid.*, p. 163). He also responded to Khan, stating that: 'I could not agree to splitting up the Army while Parliament is responsible for India ... [I]f any form of partition were decided on I should, of course, be prepared to agree to an investigation as to the need for, and if proved, the method of, implementing a partition of the Armed Forces' (Mountbatten to Liaquat Ali Khan, 9 Apr. 1947, *TOP*, X, 106, p. 165).

[92] 'Viceroy's Staff Meetings', 10 Apr. 1947, *TOP*, X, 110, p. 178.

[93] Brigs. Cariappa and Thimayya both questioned whether the British were serious about nationalisation, given the proposed timetable. Brig. Akbar Khan specifically stated: 'I do not think this can be done. We do not have enough sufficient[ly qualified] Indian Officers to take all appointments by next year' ('Nationalization of the Indian Army', meetings in Apr. 1947, 8204–797–1, Wade Papers, NAM).

[94] Viceroy Interview No. 64, 14 Apr. 1947, Mountbatten Papers, OIOC, BL; also in *TOP*, X, 138, p, 226. See also Hamid's entry for 14 April, *Disastrous*, p. 161.

it my duty to ensure that no steps were taken which would weaken the Indian Army as the ultimate resource on which the country depended for maintaining internal security.'[95]

Mountbatten met with Jinnah on 23 April to discuss the political impasse of potential partition, and the issue of the army came up once again. Jinnah did state that he hoped at least for a 'plan' to be developed for division, even if it did not occur until after independence.[96] Auchinleck responded to the questions and proposals of Liaquat Ali Khan and stated his thoughts to Sardar Baldev Singh, and once again stressed his view that division of the army was the wrong course. The process was immensely complicated and would be a lengthy business. It would affect all aspects of the army, and the armed forces in general. With the nationalisation process already under way, this was simply 'a bridge too far'. He added that any discussion of division of the army should be done only at the highest levels, so as not to hurt morale in any way.[97] Singh, the defence minister, supported Auchinleck's findings. However, support from Singh was, as it turned out, a double-edged sword: evidence was coming to light that he was treasurer of a fund to buy weapons for Sikhs in the Punjab in preparation for an anticipated civil war.

Both men's thoughts on the subject were submitted alongside Liaquat Ali Khan's proposals to the Defence Committee, and a meeting was held on 25 April.[98] Khan reiterated that, if a political decision was made regarding a future independent Pakistan, a plan was needed for the army. It was during this meeting that Mountbatten began to shift his opinion in favour of starting to plan the division of the army. He called for an 'Expert Committee' to be formed to provide evidence and ideas on potential plans. However, no actions were to be taken until a political decision had been made.[99] Auchinleck was asked for specific names to sit on the committee, and people to be brought in to discuss the issues in more detail. The one concession to both Auchinleck and Sardar Baldev Singh was the final comment by Mountbatten that, while either

---

[95]   Mountbatten to Pethick-Lawrence, 17 Apr. 1947, *TOP*, X, 164, p. 295.

[96]   Minutes of Meeting of 23 Apr., *TOP*, X, 203, pp. 378–82.

[97]   Memo from Field Marshal Auchinleck on the implications of proposals by Liaquat Ali Khan, 20 Apr. 1947, No. 1223, Auchinleck Papers, University of Manchester. See also Hamid, *Disastrous*, Appendix VIII, p. 330, for full text of the memo. See Connell, *Auchinleck*, pp. 877–80, for more details of the meeting as well.

[98]   At the time, Mountbatten was still supporting their views over Khan's demands; see 'Viceroy's Personal Report, No. 4', 24 Apr. 1947, *TOP*, X, 211, pp. 403–11.

[99]   See Hamid's entries for the 25th of April, in *Disastrous*, p. 164, and Connell, *Auchinleck*, pp. 879–81. See also Nos. 1225 and 1226, Auchinleck Papers, University of Manchester, which discuss the meetings in detail as well as *TOP*, X, 215, pp. 419–23, and 221, pp. 433–7.

nationalisation or, possibly, division of the army could be achieved by June 1948, they could not be carried out together without seriously affecting the professionalism and morale of the army. A decision had to be made about which one took priority.[100]

By late April, Lord Mountbatten was openly admitting that partition[101] of the country was inevitable; even Field Marshal Auchinleck had come to the same conclusion.[102] Mountbatten was still philosophically against partition, but he admitted in a meeting with the chief minister of Bengal, Huseyn Shaheed Suhrawardy, on 26 April, that he was being asked to partition the Punjab, Bengal, and Assam. In light of this the question of dividing the army, already tricky, became even more complicated, especially when Suhrawardy asked if Bengal could form its own army.[103]

The issue of a Bengal army was raised again in a meeting of Mountbatten's advisers on 1 May. Mountbatten responded that any discussion of Bengal having its own army would have to be dealt with whenever Hindustan and Pakistan discussed the future of their own armies.[104] This issue continued to be discussed, along with the earlier assertion that nationalisation and division could not be carried out simultaneously, in a series of meetings in early May. In one of these, Lord Mountbatten stated:

the present Armed Forces may have to be divided into [two] or even more separate entities. This is under investigation by the Defence Committee and the difficulties of replacing the 8,000 British officers by Indian Officers by the end of June 1948 are such that I do not believe that on top of this, it will be possible to get very far with any partition of the forces before this date. All parties are

---

[100] 'Minutes of Defence Committee Meeting, 26 Apr. 1947', No. 1226, Auchinleck Papers, University of Manchester, and see 'Defence Committee India, minutes of Third meeting, 25 Apr. 1947', *TOP*, X, 221, pp. 433–7, as well as Lionel Carter, ed., *Mountbatten's Report on the Last Viceroyalty: 22 March–15 August 1947* (New Delhi: Manohar, 2003), p. 128.

[101] As stated in Chapter 5, the political background to partition is quite large and falls outside the remit of this book. However, the following books and articles can provide a much needed background to the wider issue if required. Some of the key texts for this period include: Low and Brasted, eds., *Freedom*; *TOP*; Urvashi Butalia, *The Other Side of Silence: Voices from Partition* (London: C. Hurst, 2000); Yasmin Khan, *Great Partition*; Ian Talbot, *Divided Cities: Partition and Its Aftermath in Lahore and Amritsar, 1947–1957* (Oxford University Press, 2006); Ian Talbot and Gurharpal Singh, eds., *Region and Partition: Bengal, Punjab and the Partition of the Subcontinent* (Oxford University Press, 1999); Talbot, *Khizr Tiwana*; and Penderel Moon, *Divide and Quit: An Eye-witness Account of the Partition of India* (London: Chatto & Windus, 1962).

[102] Connell, *Auchinleck*, p. 882.

[103] 'Record of interview between Mountbatten and Mr Suhrawardy', 26 Apr. 1947, *TOP*, X, 227, pp. 448–60.

[104] 'Minutes of Viceroy's Ninth Misc. Meeting', 1 May 1947, *TOP*, X, 264, pp. 507–13.

therefore agreed on the need to keep the present Armed Forces as a single force until plans for their orderly separation can be put into operation.[105]

This point was raised in a meeting with Nehru on 10 May; he concurred that it would be impossible to both nationalise and divide the army by June 1948, and that any attempt to do both would probably result in collapse. However, if nationalisation was slowed down and some planning on partition was done – and done gradually – it might be feasible. Nehru agreed that division of the army should not be discussed until a definite decision had been made on which parts of India were going to separate; in fact, he felt that, even once this had been decided, the army should continue to 'function as whole'.[106] The Muslim League, unsatisfied, continued to fear that Congress and India or Hindustan would truly be in charge of a 'unified Army'. In a speech in New Delhi on 11 May, Jinnah asserted that partition was coming and that the division of the armed forces needed to be dealt with immediately: 'if the British decide that India must be divided and it follows that the armed forces must be divided and power transferred to the divided parts, then the Central government must be dissolved and all power should be transferred to the two Constituent Assemblies formed and representing Pakistan and Hindustan'.[107]

In a meeting in London with the Chiefs of Staff, Lord Ismay (military adviser to Mountbatten and a good friend of Auchinleck) was asked about the position of the Indian Army following Jinnah's speech and the trend of discussion towards partition of the subcontinent. Ismay responded that Jinnah was opposed to any unified army of all races or religions, and wanted a Muslim army.

The political situation continued to deteriorate and communal violence continued to increase.[108] In an attempt to stabilise the political situation, Mountbatten determined to press HMG for an early transfer of power. In the event he made his case successfully; he recommended that the armed forces should be divided by territorial basis of recruitment and that mixed units be entrusted to a committee headed by Auchinleck and the Chiefs of Staff of the two states, and divided accordingly.[109] It was

---

[105] 'Viceroy's Personal Report', no. 5, *TOP*, X, 276, Annex II, p. 547.
[106] 'Minutes of Viceroy's 11th misc. meeting', 10 May 1947, *TOP*, X, 382, pp. 731–8. These findings were sent to London on 11 May, reiterating that nationalisation would slow down and that if partition of the army was to take place, it would be done in an orderly manner. This telegram also discussed the possibility of a transfer of power earlier than June 1948. See Mountbatten to Ismay, 11 May 1947, *TOP*, X, 409, p. 774.
[107] 'Statement by Mr Jinnah at New Delhi', 11 May 1947, *TOP*, X, 411, p. 778.
[108] See Chapter 7 for more information.
[109] 'Minutes of Viceroy's 33rd Staff Meeting', 16 May 1947, *TOP*, X, 454, pp. 841–3. The last points were reinforced throughout the rest of the month in correspondence; see specifically nos. 466, pp. 861–2, and 477, pp. 888–9. See also the series of

immediately apparent that the issue of division would dominate the army as soon as it became known, so it was decided to slow down nationalisation in an attempt to retain as many British officers as possible for the anticipated upheaval.[110] By late May, tensions were increasing steadily as the Indian political parties failed to reach consensus on most issues. Mountbatten planned to have one last meeting on 2 June to see if any impasse could be broken; if not, HMG planned to announce that attempts at a Union of India had broken down irrevocably, and that partition was now the only viable way forward.[111]

On 27 May, Auchinleck weighed in with his views on division of the army, emphasising the number and complexity of issues requiring resolution. Considering communally based forces, he pointed out that

it is not merely a matter of saying Muslims to the left, Hindus to the right. In all three forces there are many officers and men whose homes are in parts of India which must inevitably come under the rule of the opposite community or party. In dividing these forces, each such case will have to be decided individually as no officer or man could be compelled to serve a government of which he does not approve … [I]n the Army there are certain fighting units which consist, so far as the rank and file are concerned, wholly of Hindus or Muslims, but this does not apply to their officers. British, Muslim, and all other classes of Indian Officers are completely mixed throughout the Army without any regard to their race or religion.[112]

This last issue, in particular, caused many heartaches in the following months, as Sikhs, Muslim, and Hindu officers asked to remain with their regiments irrespective of whether the unit went to Pakistan or India.[113] The British cabinet met on 28 May to discuss a variety of issues, including Auchinleck's note. They agreed in principle to his points, with the Treasury asking to be consulted about the financial implications of British officers serving on for a longer period than had originally been intended.[114]

Auchinleck's note discussed a number of things in detail; one gets the sense that he was not convinced that key people in the Indian political

correspondence in the same volume (nos. 455–77, pp. 843–88) for a more detailed discussion on the various debates surrounding the issue of partition as a whole.

[110] India and Burma Committee, 25th Meeting, 19 May 1947, *TOP*, X, 485. They specifically stated: 'the new plan [division] would necessitate a reversal of the existing policy of progressive nationalization: and the difficulties of division would be greatly eased if the greater part of the 6,000 British officers, with whom we should have dispensed by June, 1948, could be retained during the process of division' (p. 901).

[111] Cabinet Conclusions, 23 May 1947, *TOP*, X, 521, pp. 963–8.

[112] 'Division of the Armed Forces of India between Pakistan and Hindustan', note by Field Marshal Auchlinleck, 27 May 1947, *TOP*, X, 547, pp. 1004–8.

[113] Author's interviews with Indian Army officers, 1999–2009.

[114] India and Burma Committee, 28th Meeting, 28 May 1947, *TOP*, X, 553, pp. 1013–23.

parties, nor those in the viceroy's and HMG's inner circles, fully comprehended the difficulties that lay ahead. He stressed the need for a central control mechanism of the army's administration during the process of dismemberment, as well as the rationale for retaining British officers and the clear guidelines needed in order to ensure this. He insisted that they be volunteers and that they retain their privileges and position as officers serving under the Crown. In particular, he insisted that they serve under the central control of the CinCI[115] so that, until the division process was complete, the CinCI would be free to post and employ all British officers serving in the Indian Armed Forces as he saw fit. British officers could not be forced or ordered by the Indian Dominion governments to take actions that would be repugnant to their code of behaviour as officers or to their allegiance to the king. He also emphasised the necessity of suspending the proposed programme of nationalisation of the officer corps, asserting that, if it were not suspended, there would be collapse; and that this fact needed to be communicated to and accepted by Indian leaders, and explained by them to the public and to the ICOs of the armed forces. During the division phase, central control of the forces would be placed under the Joint Defence Council, which would include the CinCI, the governor general, and ministers from Pakistan and Hindustan. The HQs for the various services would be kept in New Delhi until the job was done.[116]

Mountbatten met with Indian leaders on 2 June to discuss the newly named Partition Plan, and possible changes in the handover date of Dominion status.[117] The issue of defence was touched upon, mostly covering the retention of British officers for the Indian Armed Forces. However, Mountbatten stated bluntly that 'it was far more difficult to persuade British officers to serve on at the present time than it had been a year previously. The principal reason for this was the increase in communal warfare and strife.'[118]

---

[115] This position would be elevated to supreme commander-in-chief, to serve over the two new CinCs set up for India and Pakistan. Auchinleck would serve as the supreme commander.

[116] 'Division of the Armed Forces of India between Pakistan and Hindustan', Note by Field Marshal Auchlinleck, 27 May 1947, *TOP*, X, 547, pp. 1004–8. See the full text for much more detail.

[117] Congress agreed to the plan in writing; Jinnah also agreed, first verbally and later in writing. See Yasmin Khan, *Great Partition*, ch. 5, pp. 81–103, for more details and Hamid, *Disastrous*, pp. 175–6.

[118] Minutes of the Meeting of the Viceroy with the Indian Leaders, 2 Jun. 1947, *TOP*, XI, 23, pp. 39–48. See comments from Gen. Messervy in the Sir Evan Jenkins note, *TOP*, XI, 98, pp. 177–82, where he expected that only 400 British officers would stay on after independence, which of course would create a major shortfall for the two armies, during

Mountbatten continued to present the implications of partition to the leadership with a series of memos. An expert committee was to be set up to oversee demarcations of land boundaries and government offices, including defence. The CinCI was to set up a committee to report their findings and work to a Partition Committee.[119] On 3 June, Mountbatten met with Indian leaders to discuss issues pertaining to partition in greater detail; prominent among them was the division of the armed forces. Mountbatten advised the meeting that he had met with Auchinleck and other army commanders on 2 June and they wanted him to convey their strong feelings that the process of division must not compromise the army in dealing with ongoing communal violence. They also stressed that morale must be maintained, or else chaos could ensue. The 3 June meeting considered, among others, the question of how to divide the army: whether along territorial or communal lines, and what to do with officers who wished to serve in India, but were not Sikh or Hindu, or in Pakistan, but were not Muslim.[120]

On 3 June, Mountbatten informed Auchinleck unequivocally[121] that it would be necessary to divide the armed forces[122] before independence, a development which outraged many senior British officers.[123] The adjutant general of the Indian Army, Gen. Sir Reginald Savory, believed that the politicians wanted to divide the army as quickly as possible, no matter what it cost.[124] On 4 June, Mountbatten announced a further complicating factor: independence was to be granted on 15 August 1947, instead of June 1948 as originally planned. According to people close to Auchinleck, this caused nothing but dismay in the headquarters. Many felt that things would now only get worse, and several army commanders

---

the division phase and the 'communal civil war' that would clearly erupt by the middle of August.

[119] Viceroy's Conference Paper, 2 Jun. 1947, *TOP*, XI, 28, pp. 53–6.

[120] Minutes of the Meeting of the Viceroy with the Indian Leaders, 3 Jun. 1947, *TOP*, XI, 39, pp. 72–8. See also no. 53, section 10, pp. 104–5, for more on this discussion.

[121] Maj. Gen. Hamid claimed in his memoirs that Auchinleck was not informed about the division of the armed forces, and that the British cabinet and Mountbatten felt that Auchinleck was old-fashioned and wished to see him go. However, there is clear evidence that there had been multiple conversations on this topic between Mountbatten and Auchinleck since late April. Mountbatten may have wished to see the back of Auchinleck, but he recognised Auchinleck's great popularity in the army and the further uproar that the latter's departure would cause. The salient point that Hamid makes is that Auchinleck made it clear, as did many other senior officers, that the division of the armed forces must be done slowly and carefully to avoid exacerbating problems that were already evident. See Hamid, *Disastrous*, p. 178.

[122] Ayesha Jalal, *The State of Martial Rule: The Origins of Pakistan's Political Economy of Defence* (Cambridge University Press, 1990), pp. 37–44.

[123] Yasmin Khan, *Great Partition*, pp. 96–7, and Hamid, *Disastrous*, p. 177.

[124] Letter, 28 Jun. 1947, 7603-93-80, Savory Papers, NAM.

demanded at least a year to prepare the division of the army.[125] Mountbatten refused, and ordered Auchinleck and his planners to start the planning with the new date of independence in mind.[126]

The plan for the division of the armed forces became official and public on 11 June when Auchinleck announced the establishment of a committee focusing on the 'Reconstitution of the Armed Forces of India'. (It had been decided to refer to the division of the armed forces as 'reconstitution' in an attempt to avoid the negative ramifications of the word 'division'.)[127] Auchinleck had officially stated only four days previously that it would take three years to undertake the division properly; in response, he had been given less than three months.[128]

Following his announcement, Auchinleck began to campaign for British officers to remain during the run-up to independence, stressing the necessity of their presence during reconstitution of the armed forces. On 11 June he wrote to Lord Ismay that 'I cannot stress too strongly my conviction that the success of any plan for the division of the Indian Armed Forces depends upon the willing co-operation of the British officers now serving with them, the great majority of whom it will be essential to retain during the process of reconstitution.'[129] Lt Gen. Tuker agreed wholeheartedly with Auchinleck on this issue. He stated: 'we learnt that the prestige of the British officers of the Army was very high and that Hindustan would ask for the services of many of them'.[130] Lt Gen Tuker also claimed that many ICOs wished for nationalisation to progress at a reasonable rate and did not support Indian political leaders who were pushing for accelerated promotions.[131]

On 16 June, Mountbatten indicated in a meeting that he had spoken with Auchinleck over the previous few days. He characterised Auchinleck

---

[125] Tuker refers to this in *Memory*, p. 351. The specific legal and official announcement was read through the Indian Independence Act, 18 Jul. 1947. See Philips, ed., *Select Documents, IV*, pp. 407–11, for more specific details.

[126] See Hamid's entry for 4 June and the many opinions and debates that erupted around Field Marshal Auchinleck, in *Disastrous*, pp. 178–81.

[127] See Carter, ed., *Mountbatten's Report*, p. 188. While they believed that the terminology might help, many of the officers, VCOs, and soldiers knew exactly what was going on. See also Yasmin Khan, *Great Partition*, p. 96.

[128] See 'Reconstitution of the Armed Forces of India, CinCI, Paper No. 1/47', 11 Jun. 1947, *TOP*, XI, 210, enclosure 2, pp. 406–14, for more detail on the organisation of the committee. See also Hamid, *Disastrous*, p. 182.

[129] Auchinleck to Ismay, 11 Jun. 1947, No. 1229, Auchinleck Papers, University of Manchester; also quoted in Connell, *Auchinleck*, p. 889. He also added: 'The goodwill of the British officers is more likely to be secured if the Partition Committee – on behalf of the future governments of Hindustan and Pakistan – openly state that services of the British are essential to the success of reconstitution, notwithstanding the "Quit India" cry of the past.'

[130] Tuker, *Memory*, p. 351.   [131] *Ibid.*

as 'now satisfied that the division of the Indian Armed Forces could be carried out without vitally impairing their efficiency, provided that there was goodwill and trust, and provided that political pressure was not applied to hurry the process unduly'.[132] Adherence to these last critical points – or the lack thereof – would facilitate or hinder the daunting task that Auchinleck and his staff faced in the coming months.

In hindsight, it is apparent that Auchinleck was so closely involved with the army that he failed to recognise the political inevitability of partition, and the necessary division of the ICS, police, and army. Auchinleck deserves credit for his efforts to maintain a unified force that would provide security during the period before and immediately following independence but, assessed after the fact, it is clear that this option was never going to be acceptable to the rival political factions within the Interim Government, who wanted to control all the security assets as soon as possible. This proved to be a difficult and costly mistake for Auchinleck; it also highlights his attempts to keep the army out of politics, not grasping how important control of the army would be in a partition scenario.[133]

The first major discussions concerning the division of the armed forces revealed the scope and difficulty of the decisions to be made.[134] Auchinleck stressed that planning for division should be carried out impartially, logically, and without rancour, and that the integrity and reliability of the armed forces should in no sense be prejudiced. He also reiterated his opinion that it would be impossible to carry on with nationalisation at the same time.[135] Despite his words, however, political wrangling remained the order of the day. Liaquat Ali Khan met with Ismay on 20 June 1947 and demanded that Pakistan have its army, under its own CinC, in place by 15 August. Ismay responded emphatically 'that unless there was to be chaos, the whole Army must be under a single central administration'.[136]

Jinnah also raised the issue of the Pakistan Army in a meeting with Mountbatten on 23 June, reiterating the demand that Pakistan have its army and CinC in place by 15 August. Mountbatten agreed but responded that, for administrative matters, Auchinleck should oversee

---

[132] Minutes of Viceroy's 43rd Staff Meeting, 16 Jun. 1947, *TOP*, XI, 216, pp. 419–20.

[133] There is some validity to Tuker's statement: 'But at the head of the Army was unfortunately Auchinleck who wished to be regarded rather like the patriarch Moses as the father figure of the Indian Army. This was all a matter of emotion. It seemed that whatever "the Auk" [Auchinleck] said must of course be perfectly right for the Indian Army' ('A Record of 1945/47, India', p. 5, Tuker Papers, IWM).

[134] For much detail see the Meeting of the Special Committee of the Indian Cabinet, 16 Jun. 1947, *TOP*, XI, 217, pp. 421–6.

[135] CinCI Weekly Conference, 19 Jun. 1947, L/WS/1/1125, OIOC, BL.

[136] Ismay to Mountbatten, 20 Jun. 1947, *TOP*, XI, 275, p. 534.

both armies. Jinnah then stated that Muslims no longer had faith in Auchinleck. Mountbatten claimed to have asserted in response that 'there was no more reliable or respected officer in India than Auchinleck'.[137] Ironically, Auchinleck was accused of being pro-Muslim by Congress with equal vehemence. The fact that he was being accused by both sides as favouring the other is perhaps an indicator of his impartiality.[138]

With plans now moving inexorably forward towards partition and division of the armed forces, Auchinleck reiterated to the viceroy and the Partition Committee that nationalisation of the officer corps must be suspended. He referred to discussions in the 25 April meeting, emphasising that, with the timeline shortened from June 1948 to August 1947, there was no hope of nationalising so quickly. The 8,200 British officers in the army as of June 1947 must be retained to deal with reconstitution and rising communal violence. In concluding his arguments, Auchinleck presented his most political comments yet:

there is every reason to believe that, in the present circumstances, many serving British officers are not really desirous of continuing their service in India. This attitude is the result of the frequent and emphatically expressed desire of Indians of various shades of opinion to be rid of the British officer element in the Armed Forces; and the markedly unfriendly and mistrustful attitude frequently adopted towards them by some Indians; and their disappointment that, for political reasons, the forces – of which they are so justly proud – are to be remoulded into separate entities.[139]

Tuker supported Auchinleck's position, adding that division of the once-proud army was too much for many officers to bear. Many officers were also unwilling to serve under the command of Jawaharlal Nehru, the man who had defended the INA during the trials in 1945 and 1946, accused the army of being the oppressor of the Indian people, and, most recently (in June 1947), blamed British officers for

---

[137] Record of interview between Mountbatten and Jinnah, 23 Jun. 1947, *TOP*, XI, 311, p. 382.

[138] See also Auchinleck's letter to Ismay, on 11 June 1947, where he lays out similar comments. A memorial to Auchinleck, put up by the Pakistan Army thanking him for his leadership, still stands in the cantonment at Peshawar.

[139] Auchinleck continued, 'it must be appreciated, therefore, that it is asking a great deal of the British Officer, after hearing the cry "Quit India" reiterated so loudly and so often in the past, to acquiesce readily to a request to stay. For this reason, I think Indian leaders must say publicly that they need the help of the British officers. Such a statement should encourage the officer to hope that he will be respected and trusted and treated as a friend which is what he desires.' See Note by Auchinleck, 23 Jun. 1947, *TOP*, XI, 312, p. 385.

not having done enough to stop the communal violence that was sweeping across northern India.[140]

In an effort to address demands made by both Khan and Jinnah, Auchinleck briefed members of the Special Committee of the Indian cabinet on 26 June. He and Mountbatten had agreed that each Dominion should have its own CinC who would be responsible for its army, but that administrative control of both armies would still rest with Joint Headquarters under Field Marshal Auchinleck's command. They hoped to ensure that most of the forces would be relocated to their appropriate places by 15 August.

The Partition Council met next on 30 June 1947, and the reconstitution of the armed forces was discussed in great detail. Six guiding principles were worked out. The first was that India and Pakistan would have operational control of their forces from 15 August. Second, heads of the various services would be appointed and would be responsible to the new heads of state. Third, all existing armed forces of India would remain under single administrative control until the respective Dominions were capable of taking over. Fourth, the forces would fall under the Joint Defence Council, headed by Field Marshal Auchinleck (to be named supreme commander) and include the governors general, defence ministers, and CinCs. Fifth, Auchinleck's title would change effective 15 August, and remain so until his work was complete. He would have no operational control of the armies, nor would he be responsible for law and order.[141]

Sixth, and perhaps most important, the actual division of the army was scheduled to happen in two phases. In the first phase, units would be divided down to company and squadron levels by 15 August 1947. The second phase was intended to focus on individuals, ascertaining their intentions with regard to partition. To avoid a breakdown in discipline and morale, the process would be done in stages, but would proceed as rapidly as possible. Mountbatten asked Auchinleck to come up with candidates for the new CinC positions for Pakistan and India.[142] There was also one additional change: when the Punjab

---

[140] Author's interviews with the Indian Army officers, 1999–2009; and Tuker, *Memory*, pp. 352–3.

[141] Hamid, *Disastrous*, p. 195.

[142] See Meeting of the Special Committee of the Indian Cabinet, 26 Jun. 1947, *TOP*, XI, 354, pp. 679–91; Notes by Mr Patel, 27 Jun. 1947, *TOP*, XI, 372, pp. 693–700; and Meeting of Partition Council, Note by HE the Viceroy regarding the Partition of the Armed Forces, 30 Jun. 1947, *TOP*, XI, 416, pp. 756–60, for much more detail on the particulars. See plans for the Armed Forces Reconstitution, 5 Jul. 1947, No. 1239, Auchinleck Papers, University of Manchester, for more detail.

Boundary Force[143] was formed in July 1947, it fell under the command of the supreme commander.[144]

One other decision made during this meeting was to have a significant impact on the army. The second phase of division (the 'intentions' phase) concluded with a decision that 'any Muslim domiciled in Pakistan would not have the option to serve in India, and any non-Muslim domiciled in India would not have the option to join the armed forces of Pakistan'.[145] In the event, many officers with Muslim backgrounds were denied commissions in the new Indian Army, while Hindus were similarly rejected from the independent Pakistan Army, even though these officers had gladly commanded men and VCOs from other religious backgrounds, and viewed their regiments as their home. Col B. D. Bhanot described to me how one of his fellow regimental officers, a Muslim, expressed his wish to remain with the Rajputana Rifles. He was told in no uncertain terms to either leave the army or transfer to Pakistan.[146] Many officers in both India and Pakistan found this choice a heart-wrenching one; while many ultimately may have chosen to move over to the opposite sides of the demarcation lines, they were aggrieved at being forced to do so.[147]

Tensions escalated rapidly in areas of the country that were going to be demarcated, particularly the Punjab. The disruption and division were evident by late June, and feelings ran high in the Indian Army. Savory, the adjutant general, noted his feelings in two different letters to his wife. In the first, written in late June, he stated, 'the political leaders of India are intent on splitting the Indian Army as rapidly as they possibly can, irrespective of the cost'.[148] In the second, dated 4 July 1947, he noted that 'the splitting of the Indian Army is now actually beginning and I cannot say I find it particularly pleasant. The whole thing is foolish.'[149] Gen. Lockhart, GOC, Southern Command (later CinCI), wrote in June 1947 that 'the army is anxiously awaiting information about the splitting of the army. There have been no signs whatsoever of any communal feeling amongst the troops employed in the Punjab.'[150]

In early July, Nehru raised the issue of nationalisation once again, even though all sides had agreed to stop the process due to reconstitution of the armed forces. He confirmed that he understood why it had to slow down, but that he wished for it to start once again. He asked why various

---

[143] See Chapter 7 for much more detail.
[144] Hamid, *Disastrous*, p. 218.   [145] Carter, ed., *Mountbatten's Report*, p. 190.
[146] Author's correspondence with Col Bhanot, 6th Rajputana Rifles.
[147] Author's interviews and correspondence with Indian and Pakistani officers, 1999–2009.
[148] Letter, 28 Jun. 1947, 7603-93-80, Savory Papers, NAM.
[149] Letter, 4 Jul. 1947, 7603-93-80, Savory Papers, NAM.
[150] 16 Jun. 1947, 8310–154/47, Lockhart Papers, NAM.

promotions of senior Indian officers had not taken place over the last few months, and for senior Indian officers to be associated with the reconstitution committees.[151] He was subsequently taken to task a few days later by the chief of the General Staff, Lt Gen. Sir A. Smith, who pointed out in a meeting that 'he [Nehru] had forgotten that the Indian Cabinet, some weeks ago, agreed that rapid nationalization to effect completion by June 1948, should be stopped, and that we should revert to the normal rate of nationalization'.[152] Nehru's actions indicate that either he still failed to understand the army and the role of officer education and training to take senior command positions, or that he did not care about the potential impact on the efficiency and performance of the army. Either of these is disturbing, particularly at a time when tensions were already high and getting higher.[153]

Interestingly, Nehru had appeared to withdraw some of his objections regarding nationalisation only a day earlier. On 12 July 1947, Mountbatten issued a statement to all British officers and other service personnel in India stating that

all concerned [Indian political leaders agree] that British officers are needed for the period during which the Armed Forces are being divided and reconstituted. The CinC and Senior officers of all the three Defence Headquarters are staying on for this period. Auchinleck, who is assuming the title Supreme Commander, will be responsible under the general direction of the Joint Defence Council of the two new Dominions for reconstituting the Armed Forces ... The strain which will be thrown on Officers of the Indian Services in carrying out this reconstitution, in addition to ordinary administration and training, will be considerable and if a large number of highly trained and experienced British offices are suddenly removed the risk of a serious breakdown will be very real. Pandit Nehru and Mr Jinnah have expressed the desire and hope that the requisite number of British Officers and Other Ranks will stay on.[154]

The Partition Council echoed the need for British officers to remain during meetings in mid July. Mountbatten and the Indian political leadership openly admitted that if many of the senior British leadership

---

[151] Nehru to Mountbatten, 11 Jul. 1947, *TOP*, XII, 69, pp. 105–7.

[152] Record of interview between Nehru and Lt Gen. Sir A. Smith, 13 Jul. 1947, *TOP*, XII, 88, p. 129.

[153] Record of interview between Mountbatten and Auchinleck, 15 Jul. 1947, *TOP*, XII, 113, pp. 165–7. During this meeting Sardar Baldev Singh's accusations that various British officers, including Auchinleck, were pro-Pakistan in their feelings, were raised and discussed. Mountbatten agreed that it was unprofessional behaviour on the part of the defence minister. Auchinleck did subsequently agree that a few more Indian officers would be promoted to major general by 15 August.

[154] Statement by Mountbatten to the British personnel of the Indian Armed Forces, 12 Jul. 1947, *TOP*, XII, 80, pp. 116–17.

were to leave on 15 August, there was a serious risk that the army would break down completely. Auchinleck was clear that he did not expect that many mid-level officers would remain after 15 August, in light of the violence and repeated attacks to which they had been subjected by the Indian press and political leadership in the last few years. He insisted that an appeal to the officers from Mountbatten, Nehru, and Jinnah was necessary to boost morale and resolve. Mountbatten was able to convince both leaders to co-operate, and the appeal was made.[155]

At about this same time, announcements were made that Lt Gen. Messervy[156] was to be the CinC of the new Pakistan Army[157] and Lt Gen. Lockhart[158] the CinC of the new Indian Army. Both appointments would be effective as of 15 August.[159] Field Marshal Auchinleck wrote to both men, laying out his ideas regarding the role of the supreme commander and emphasising his hopes for mutual co-operation among the three of them to deal with the coming difficult months. He specifically stated: 'If reconstitution of the Armed Forces is to be carried out rapidly and efficiently and without friction, we shall all of us, in your HQs and mine, have to work together in the closest co-operation and with the firm intention of doing all we can to help each other in our common task. I have already impressed this necessity on the officers who are to serve on my staff when I become Supreme Commander, and I am sure you will do the same with yours.'[160]

In the end, 2,537 officers opted to stay and serve in the Indian and Pakistani armies and 2,568 decided to opt out of service on 15 August. Close to 1,000 other ranks (94 per cent of the total) also decided to stay

[155] Viceroy's Personal Report, 18 Jul. 1947, *TOP*, XII, 162, pp. 225–32.

[156] As noted earlier he joined the Indian Army (Hodson's Horse) in 1914 and served in both the First and Second World Wars with distinction.

[157] Minutes of Viceroy's 21st Misc. Meeting, 20 Jul. 1947, *TOP*, XII, 184, pp. 272–6. Many Pakistani officers noted that they had expected Tuker to be appointed CinC for Pakistan. See Hamid, *Disastrous*, p. 183.

[158] As noted previously he joined the Indian Army (51st Sikhs, or 1/12 FFR) in 1914 and served in both the First and Second World Wars with distinction.

[159] Mountbatten to Earl of Listowel, new sec. of state for India, 25 Jul. 1947, *TOP*, XII, 227, pp. 330–2. Gen. Sir William Slim had been approached to take the CinC position, but turned it down. Both Messervy and Lockhart were promoted to full general on 15 August. Two senior Royal Navy officers were appointed the respective heads of the Pakistan Navy and the Indian Navy. Two air marshals from the RAF were appointed to command the new Dominions' air forces. See Mountbatten to Listowel, 27 Jul. 1947, *TOP*, XII, 253, p. 371.

[160] Auchinleck to Lockhart and Messervy, No. 1240, Auchinleck Papers, University of Manchester. Auchinleck also sent letters to the naval and air force officers, reiterating similar sentiments; see Nos. 1242 and 1244, Auchinleck Papers, University of Manchester.

on in India and Pakistan.[161] By early July, the Reconstitution Committee had also decided on the division of the various infantry and cavalry units for each army.[162] It must be remembered in considering this task that, while many of the battalions were still split along various communal lines, up to two-thirds could be of one communal class and would have to shift over to the other state. Subsidiary items such as stores, factories, vehicles, and so forth, would ultimately be allocated 30% to Pakistan and 70% to India.[163] Pakistan was eventually assigned 140,000 men out of the 410,000 within the army, 40% of the navy, and 30% of the air force.[164]

Within a few days of these announcements being made, Nehru appeared to launch an attack against the integrity of Auchinleck.[165] Mountbatten responded that he had faith in Auchinleck's integrity and impartiality.[166] This did not put an end to the matter, as many within Congress, including Sardar Baldev Singh, continued to express their belief that Auchinleck, as well as many other senior British officers, were pro-Pakistan. Mountbatten was firm in their defence, asserting that the officers were trying to be fair in carrying out reconstitution of the armed forces.[167] According to Lt Gen. Savory, Singh's attack was an attempt to

---

[161] Viceroy's Personal Report No. 17, 16 Aug. 1947, *TOP*, XII, 489, pp. 757–83.

[162] In terms of the infantry regiments, the split was as follows: Pakistan, 1st Punjab, 8th Punjab, 10th Baluch, 12th Frontier Force Regiment, 13th Frontier Force Rifles, 14th Punjab, 15th Punjab, and 16th Punjab; India, 2nd Punjab, 3rd Madras, 4th Indian Grenadiers, 5th Mahratta Light Infantry, 6th Rajputana Rifles, 7th Rajput, 9th Jat, 11th Sikh, 17th Dogra, 18th Royal Garhwal Rifles, 19th Kumaon, Assam Regiment, Sikh Light Infantry, Mahar, and Bihar Regiments. The cavalry regiments were divided thus: Pakistan, 5th Probyn's Horse, 6th Duke of Connaught's Own Lancers, Guides Cavalry (Frontier Force), 11th Prince Albert Victor's Own Cavalry (Frontier Force), Sam Browne's Cavalry (12th Frontier Force), 13th Duke of Connaught's Own Lancers, 19th King George V's Own Lancers; India, Skinner's Horse, 2nd Royal Lancers, 3rd Cavalry, Hodson's Horse, 7th Light Cavalry, 8th King George V's Own Light Cavalry, Royal Deccan Horse (9th Horse), Scinde Horse (14th Prince of Wales's Own Cavalry), 15th Lancers, 16th Light Cavalry, Poona Horse (17th Queen Victoria's Own Cavalry), 18th King Edward VII's Own Cavalry, 20th Lancers, and Central India Horse.

[163] Pakistan claimed that it did not receive all the stores and equipment it had been allotted and there is validity to this statement. One key reason for this was due to the outbreak of war between the two states by the end of 1947.

[164] Jalal, *State of Martial Rule*, p. 42.

[165] See Nehru to Mountbatten, 26 Jul. 1947, *TOP*, XII, 247, pp. 365–6, for more details.

[166] Record of interview between Mountbatten and Nehru, 29 Jul. 1947, *TOP*, XII, 270, pp. 399–400.

[167] Viceroy's Personal Report, No. 15, 1 Aug. 1947, *TOP*, XII, 302, pp. 443–56. The tensions did not go away, as Singh continued the pressure and accusations that Auchinleck and his senior officers were pro-Pakistan. See Viceroy's Personal Record, No. 16, *TOP*, XII, 385, pp. 590–606, for more details and for Mountbatten's continued support of Auchinleck and the senior British officers. Hamid also refers to this issue on 29 July; see *Disastrous*, p. 212.

rid India of Auchinleck and stop him from taking the supreme commander's position. In response, Mountbatten asked Savory to meet with Auchinleck and ask him to stop dabbling in politics. Savory was outraged by this request, as was Auchinleck when it came to his attention. He threatened to resign if he did not receive the support he expected, and demanded an apology from Singh.[168] In early August, Mountbatten made it clear to Singh[169] that it was necessary to mend the relationship with Auchinleck, and Singh acceded to this political reality.[170] Thus ended this particular conflict, but not the political friction and growing pains of the partition process.[171]

On the evening of 6 August, a dinner and party were held at the Imperial Delhi Gymkhana. Many of the senior political and military leadership of the future independent India and Pakistan attended. The future CinCs of India and Pakistan as well as other officers mingled and discussed the future. Two speeches by two of the most senior Indian and Pakistani officers illuminate the ending of the Indian Army as many knew it at the time. Brig. Cariappa, of India, spoke first:

I associate the honest and sincere wishes of every one of us here, and all of those with the Services outside, that we shall meet each other frequently as the best of friends in the same spirit of good comradeship that we have had the good fortune to enjoy all these years. We have worked together so long on the same team. We hope we shall continue to work together in the same spirit for the defence of the two Dominions against external aggression. Comrades-in-arms, during all our life in the various Services we have lived together, worked together and fought together in the various battlefields on which our magnificent Armed Forces have fought with the highest degree of fellowship and comradeship. May this spirit continue even after we are separated.[172]

The senior Pakistan officer, Brig. A. M. Raza, responded that he was

deeply touched by the true spirit of comradeship and genuine feelings of brotherhood evinced and expressed by General Cariappa, I assure everyone of the innate desire of all who are in this distinguished gathering and particularly of my brothers in arms. The Armed Forces of Pakistan will always uphold their traditions under which they served shoulder to shoulder with the Indian Armed Forces and will continue to do so whenever required, not only in the interest of our own people ... but also for the universal security

---

[168] See Hamid's entry for 29 and 30 July, in *Disastrous*, p. 212.

[169] Carter, ed., *Mountbatten's Report*, p. 264.

[170] Viceroy's Personal Report, No. 17, 16 Aug. 1947, *TOP*, XII, 489, pp. 757–83. Hamid also makes reference to Sardar Baldev Singh and Auchinleck having normal relations once again by 1 August; see *Disastrous*, p. 218. Mountbatten confirms this in his *Report*; see Carter, ed., *Mountbatten's Report*, p. 264.

[171] See the Conclusion for more details.   [172] Hamid, *Disastrous*, pp. 221–2.

which is the aim and object of humanity that has suffered the unprecedented horrors of two devastating world wars within a few decades.[173]

Despite these declarations of solidarity, Lt Gen. Savory commented the next day that 'India is finished so far as the Army is concerned ... [T]hey have many problems facing them ... I am sick of the whole business here.'[174] His, although the more pessimistic view, proved to be the more prescient one; communal violence across India and Pakistan continued to increase up to and beyond 15 August and culminated, by year's end, with the two armies fighting one another in Kashmir.[175]

The last order of the Indian Army was issued on 14 August. Named the Special India Army Order, it was issued by Field Marshal Claude Auchinleck and signed by Lt Gen. Sir R. A. Savory as the adjutant general in India and stated 'Discontinuance of India Army Orders. This is the last India Army Order.'[176]

Division of the Gurkha Rifle Brigade

While the senior command of the Indian Army was contending with the demobilisation, nationalisation, and division of the Indian Army as a whole, there was also the special case to consider: the future role and mission of the ten Gurkha Rifle Regiments. As noted in previous chapters, the Gurkhas had been recruited since 1815 from the independent kingdom of Nepal,[177] first for service in the East India Company and then into the Indian Army. Their recruitment was expanded in the post-Mutiny phase, alongside the expansion of recruitment from the peoples of the Punjab and northern India. During the First World War, some 114,000 men were recruited to the Gurkhas; in the Second World War, the ten regiments were expanded to include more than 200,000 men.[178] The officers for the Gurkhas were entirely British; from the earliest stages of the Indian Army's Indianisation or nationalisation process, begun in the 1920s, the Gurkha regiments were exempted.[179]

---

[173] *Ibid.*, p. 221.   [174] 7 Aug. 1947, 7603–93–80, Savory Papers, NAM.

[175] See Conclusion for more information.

[176] 14 Aug. 1947, No. 1246, Auchinleck Papers, University of Manchester.

[177] Segauli Treaty of 1815, after the Nepal War.

[178] During the Second World War, fifty-one infantry battalions existed, of which thirty-one were raised during the war: 'Defence Committee Paper "The Future of the Gurkhas"', 7 Mar. 1947, *TOP*, IX, 503, p. 885.

[179] In March 1947, the British government admitted, 'nor has there been any written undertaking that Gurkha units would only be officered by British officers, though there has been an understanding to this effect, which has hitherto been observed' (*ibid.*).

The first major discussions on the future of the Gurkhas occurred as the Second World War was drawing to a close.[180] HMG recognised the need for a strategic reserve for the Far East, as the likelihood was slim of the Indian Army continuing to serve in its traditional capacity of 'Imperial Reserve' for much longer.[181]

The primary challenge for Field Marshal Auchinleck, Lord Wavell (and later Lord Mountbatten), and CIGS in London, Lord Alanbrooke, was not only what to do with the Gurkha Rifles, but also to determine the Indian political leadership's position on the issue. Auchinleck met with the Maharaja of Nepal at the end of October 1945 to discuss the matter; the Maharaja supported the proposal to transfer affiliation of the Gurkha regiments to the British Army, but was hesitant to make the same arrangement with India, given the Maharaja's reservations about Gurkhas serving under Indian officers.[182]

CIGS met with Auchinleck in December 1945, stressing the need for the Gurkhas to help fill the shortage of British troops for overseas garrisons. Auchinleck made it clear that Gurkhas would have to be completely separated from the Indian Army and any attachment to the Government of India to avoid political issues in the future.[183] Wavell reiterated Auchinleck's points, and reiterated the necessity of recruiting the Gurkhas for future defence planning for the Far East.[184] Two significant issues shortly arose that would shape discussions between the British government and the future independent Indian government: the first was that the British Treasury agreed to pay only for the future employment of eight permanent battalions, or four of the ten regiments.[185] The second was that the Indian Interim Government announced in late October 1946 that it wished to retain all Gurkha battalions in the future Indian Army, and expressed its opposition to HMG's plan to employ Gurkhas

---

[180] Discussions between Wavell, Auchinleck, and Lord Alanbrooke, CIGS; see *TOP*, V, 346, pp. 767–76, for more details as well as Auchinleck to Wavell, 28 Mar. 1945, No. 1085, Auchinleck Papers, University of Manchester. See also Wavell to Pethick-Lawrence, Aug. 1945, L/WS/1/1023, OIOC, BL.

[181] See Raffi Gregorian, *The British Army, the Gurkhas and Cold War Strategy in Far East, 1947–1954* (London: Palgrave, 2002), esp. pp. 32–8, for specific background and discussion on British thoughts for the future of the Gurkha Rifles as a strategic reserve; see also David Omissi, 'A Dismal Story? Britain, the Gurkhas and the Partition of India, 1945–1948', in Alan Jeffreys and Patrick Rose, eds., *The Indian Army, 1939–1947* (Farnham, UK: Ashgate, 2012), pp. 195–214.

[182] Wavell to Pethick-Lawrence, 5 Aug. 1945, *TOP*, VI, 4, pp. 27–33.

[183] Wavell to Pethick-Lawrence, L/WS/1/1023, OIOC, BL; also reproduced in *TOP*, VI, 325, pp. 720–1. See also Pethick-Lawrence to Wavell, 26 Sep. 1946, L/WS/1/1023, OIOC, BL, for specific statements.

[184] *TOP*, VI, 325, pp. 720–1.

[185] Lawson to Arthur Henderson, 31 May 1946, L/WS/1/1023, OIOC, BL.

on imperial duties, which it considered a continuation of the calculated use of Indian Army troops in FIC and the NEI.[186]

The British realised that a negotiated settlement would be necessary. At first, the Interim Government called for three-way talks involving HMG, India, and Nepal. The War Office was able to negotiate for meetings first between the British and the Indians, and then with Nepal. However, before the talks could begin, HMG needed to decide how many would be needed, as well as making assessments about the future size of the British Army, a likely date for independence, subsequent plans for the Indian Army, and what potential impact the last of these might have on already growing communal violence.[187]

By late February 1947, the British Chiefs of Staff in London had decided that they wished for close to 25,000 Gurkhas to be transferred to the British Army for service in the Far East.[188] One issue that remained to be resolved was how long the Gurkhas would be in service to the British Army. Pethick-Lawrence informed Wavell that 'the War Office have now agreed to continue with the negotiations but on the lines of a short-term bid for a few Gurkha units for a period of five years'.[189] The British Chiefs of Staff met on 5 March and laid out their plans on how to negotiate the transfer of some of the Gurkhas. The CIGS, now Field Marshal Viscount Montgomery of Alamein, expressed British interest in having at least four regiments, which would be enough to provide the infantry element of a division in Malaya. He qualified the offer by saying that it 'would not be made unless the Indian Government expressed their approval of it'.[190] On 17 March, the Defence Committee decided that HMG would open negotiations with the governments of

---

[186] The Interim Government specified that it wanted Gurkha battalions to be retained and to be officered by Indian officers, as well as its opposition to 'the employment of Gurkha troops by HMG for Imperial purposes' (Wavell to Pethick-Lawrence, 30 Oct. 1946, *TOP*, VIII, 534, pp. 841–6); GOI Defence Dept to Sec. of State for India, 8 Nov. 1946, *TOP*, IX, 16, pp. 30–2; also see paragraph 6 in 'Defence Committee Paper "The Future of the Gurkhas"', 7 Mar. 1947, *TOP*, IX, 503, p. 885, for more detail.

[187] Gregorian, *British Army*, p. 38, and see Pethick-Lawrence to Wavell, 27 Feb. 1947, *TOP*, IX, 473, pp. 825–7.

[188] Those Gurkhas who were eventually transferred to the British Army were sent to Malaya to form a Gurkha Division, later numbered the 17th in honour of the old 17th Indian Division from the Burma campaign. While in Malaya, the Gurkhas formed the largest infantry force involved in the Malayan Emergency, and did much of the fighting in that campaign. The Gurkhas next became heavily involved in Konfrontasi or the Borneo Confrontation, and went on to serve in Hong Kong from the late 1960s until the end of the British presence there in the late 1990s.

[189] Pethick-Lawrence to Wavell, 27 Feb. 1947, *TOP*, IX, 473, p. 826.

[190] Chiefs of Staff Committee Meeting, 5 Mar. 1947, L/WS/1/1045, OIOC, BL. See also 'Defence Committee Paper "The Future of the Gurkhas"', 7 Mar. 1947, *TOP*, IX, 503, p. 885, for a summary of the lead-up to March 1947.

India and Nepal to secure the transfer of 25,000 men into the British Army, with no time limits to be stipulated for their terms of employment.[191] On 18 March 1947, the British formally announced its proposal to transfer four regular Gurkha regiments to the British Army, supplemented by further direct recruitment to reach a target of 25,000 men.[192]

Formal negotiations began in April. The British team was headed by Maj. Gen. Lewis Lyne, who was sent out to India in mid April to open talks with the Interim Government and the Nepalese government.[193] He reported on progress to Lord Mountbatten in early May; Mountbatten conveyed to the new secretary of state for India, Earl Listowel, that talks were going well and that it appeared as if both the British and Indians would succeed in their aims of securing the future employment of Gurkhas. He added the caveat that nothing was set and that the greatest care would be needed to weave through the final stages.[194]

Issues arose with the negotiations as well; things did not go smoothly during May and important decisions were not made.[195] In early June, Mountbatten asked Prime Minister Attlee for Field Marshal Viscount Montgomery to meet with Sardar Baldev Singh and Jawaharlal Nehru, to try to clinch the deal when he visited India later in the month.[196] Attlee agreed, and Montgomery was sent to meet with Nehru on either 23 or 24 June.[197]

Montgomery and Nehru met on both days, and Montgomery reported to London that 'I have to report to you [Attlee] that Mr Nehru has agreed in principle that we can proceed in the matter [the transfer of the Gurkhas]. There are of course many details still to be settled and I am arranging for a Mission from the War Office to come to Delhi to work out these details and then proceed to Nepal.'[198] Montgomery also reported along different channels that he had promised Nehru that the Gurkhas 'would not be used locally and certainly not against people's movements for freedom'.[199] While Montgomery had moved the discussions along,

[191] Defence Committee Meeting, 17 Mar. 1947, L/WS/1/1023, OIOC, BL.
[192] See Gregorian, *British Army*, pp. 38–9.
[193] Carter, ed., *Mountbatten's Report*, p. 129.
[194] Mountbatten to Listowel, 8 May 1947, *TOP*, X, 353, pp. 679–81. This was also confirmed in a letter from 19 May 1947 between Mr Harris and Sir A. Lascelles, *TOP*, X, 484, p. 895.
[195] Carter, ed., *Mountbatten's Report*, p. 191.
[196] Mountbatten to Attlee, 12 Jun. 1947, *TOP*, XI, 173, p. 318.
[197] Attlee to Mountbatten, 18 Jun. 1947, L/WS/1/1024, OIOC, BL.
[198] Montgomery to Attlee, 24 Jun. 1947, *TOP*, XI, 330, p. 608.
[199] Quoted in Gregorian, *British Army*, p. 40. According to Montgomery, the meetings between the two men were very cordial. See the letters to and from the men in L/WS/1/1024, OIOC, BL, dated 24 June 1947, and also reproduced in *TOP*, XI, 331 and 332,

by mid July it was still not clear what the final arrangements would be in terms of assignments for specific division of the Gurkha Rifles Regiments. Auchinleck was concerned; he could not ask which Gurkhas would like to stay on versus which were interested in moving over to the British Army. Nor could he advise the British officers concerned which regiments were going to move.[200]

A final agreement was reached about the future of the Gurkha Rifles on 7 August. The units selected for service with the British Army were the 1st and 2nd Battalions of the 2nd King Edward VII's Own Gurkha Rifles, the 6th Gurkha Rifles, 7th Gurkha Rifles, and 10th Gurkha Rifles along with their regimental centres.[201] The remaining six regiments – 1st King George V's Own Gurkha Rifles, 3rd Queen Alexandra's Own Gurkha Rifles, 4th Prince of Wales's Own Gurkha Rifles, 5th Royal Gurkha Rifles (Frontier Force), 8th Gurkha Rifles, and 9th Gurkha Rifles – would remain with the army of the Dominion of India. No Gurkha would be forced to serve in either force, but would have the option of volunteering for his preferred service.

The agreement was specific about the role of the Gurkhas in the coming months: all Gurkhas serving within India would serve under the command of the CinC of India. Those in Pakistan as of 15 August would serve under the command of the Pakistan CinC until they could be moved into India. Gurkha battalions still overseas would serve under the supreme commander. As with the rest of the Indian Army, the administrative elements of the Gurkha regiments would fall under the supreme commander, until the Dominions were capable of taking over

---

pp. 609–10. For a much more detailed record of the conversations and the issues raised by Nehru, see enclosure to correspondence of 28 Jun. 1947, *TOP*, XI, 388, pp. 720–6.

[200] Record of interview between Mountbatten and Auchinleck, 15 Jul. 1947, *TOP*, XII, 113, pp. 165–7.

[201] These regiments recruited from both eastern and western Nepal. The 2nd Gurkha Rifles were also closely associated with various British regiments due to its performance at Delhi during the Indian Mutiny. The famous 5th Royal Gurkha Rifles (Frontier Force) went to India. Tuker also indicated that administrative issues were key in the selection of these regiments. Three of the regiments had one of their battalions in Burma, and HMG did not want to move them back to India and then back out to Malaya. He was clear that it was a major surprise that the specific regiments were selected, since only the 2nd King Edward's Own Gurkha Rifles was seen as one of the senior regiments. The 1st King George's Own and 3rd Queen Alexandra's Own were raised in 1815 alongside the 2nd Gurkha Rifles. The 6th, 7th, and 10th Gurkha Rifles were seen as 'new' regiments within the Gurkha Rifles family: Tuker, *Memory*, p. 638. See also the regimental histories of the various Gurkha Rifles. When the regimental histories deal with this period, there is often perplexity about the selection process. As stated in Lt Col G. R. Stevens, *History of the 2nd King Edward VII's Own Gurkha Rifles*, vol. *III* (Aldershot: Gale & Polden, 1952), p. 309: 'British choice fell upon regiments with battalions still serving abroad.'

the mission.[202] The Maharaja of Nepal met with the British High Commissioner from India, and expressed his satisfaction with the results of the division of the Gurkha Rifles between India and the UK.[203]

The decision had been taken so late that GHQ India had to create a referendum to assess the choices for the various soldiers and officers from within the regiments. The initial choices were three: continue in service with Indian Army regiments; transfer to service with British Army regiments; or discharge. However, the various conditions of service and implications for the future were not entirely clear, and GHQ India received many more questions than definitive answers from those who were targeted by the referendum.[204] The other impact of the late decision meant that all regiments, including those destined for the British Army, would remain in India and Pakistan up to and after independence and would be involved in dealing with continuing communal violence.

Conclusion

As has been discussed throughout, the Indian Army was the most stable organisation of the GOI and the Interim Government during the last days of the Raj. Any containment of the outbreak of widespread communal violence, which in the Punjab and parts of northern India was outright civil war, was largely due to the army's involvement, and from the start it had insufficient numbers to intervene on an appropriate scale. Why then try to nationalise, demobilise, *and* divide the army in the midst of an already volatile situation?

The Indian Army was an organisation that was not well understood outside its own ranks, partially due to more than a hundred years' worth of efforts to keep it clear of political and communal intrigue. The original intent of this effort was, of course, to safeguard the security of the British Raj against internal strife, but one of the unanticipated outcomes was that by 1945 it was one of the few institutions in British India that was both communally integrated and effective. Seen from the outside, the nuances of its internal functioning were easy to overlook or ignore by those who wanted to focus solely on its prospective role as the military force of an independent state. Many within the nationalist community neither understood nor were willing to try to understand the army's

---

[202] Mountbatten to Listowel, 7 Aug. 1947, *TOP*, XII, 370, p. 569.
[203] UK High Commissioner in India to Cabinet Office, 12 Aug. 1947, *TOP*, XII, 439, pp. 678–9.
[204] See the various regimental histories of the 2nd, 6th, 7th, and 10th Gurkha Rifles for more information. See also John Cross, *In Gurkha Company* (London: Leo Cooper, 1981), for more details.

particular idiosyncrasies, and how they strengthened it as an organisation. Their main focus was on how best to use the army as a political lever against rival factions and the viceroy to attain their ultimate goal of independence and a satisfactory division of the spoils of the British Raj.

There is no question that the Indian Army had to demobilise at the end of the Second World War. What is questionable is the way in which such an important undertaking was handled, especially the lack of attention paid to how the world, particularly India, had changed with the end of the war. HMG, in fulfilling its occupation duties in the Far East, used the Indian Army in its long-standing role of Imperial Reserve without giving any thought to what impact this might have on the political situation in India, or what would become of the formations and units when they returned home. In its other major role of 1946, fulfilling internal security duties, the Indian Army also confronted a situation significantly different from any in its past, in terms of levels of violence, organisation of killing, and political support. As 1946 came to a close, the Indian Army was widely praised for its actions and for its apparent impartiality. Meanwhile, demobilisation continued and even accelerated, despite the trend of spreading violence across India.

What could the GOI have done with all the demobbed Indian Army soldiers who still wished to serve in some capacity? In the end, many found their way into various political militias, due to their ability to train groups in military skills as the communal civil war escalated. Units in Northern and Eastern Command, as well as in the Punjab Boundary Force, met and fought these well-led, -trained, and -equipped killing squads through the spring and summer of 1947. While demobilisation could not have been avoided entirely, the GOI and Interim Government could have found ways to slow it, for two compelling reasons: one, to keep more soldiers in uniform to contend with the rising violence; and, two, to keep demobbed soldiers from becoming a political liability for the government by contributing their skills and knowledge to one of the political militias – skills that some within the Interim Government actually sought out for their own political factions.

Most people within the army accepted initiatives towards nationalisation of the officer corps, both before and after the Second World War.[205] The over-riding issue for many within the army, including some of the ICOs, was the feeling that nationalisation needed to occur at the proper speed and with the correct levers in place to promote the correct people up the chain of command. The idea of handing all the reins of command

---

[205] See Marston, *Phoenix*, as well as Chapter 2 of this book for more detail.

and power to officers with minimal experience, training, and education, was generally considered to be a recipe for disaster. Field Marshal Auchinleck and Lt Gen. Savory were early proponents of nationalisation and wanted it to continue after the war, but at a realistic speed. Both were against the findings of the Willcox Committee, which stated in 1945 that it would take twenty-five years for the army to completely nationalise; they understood that such a timeline was unrealistic, but that accomplishing nationalisation within a year was equally unfeasible. The political decisions made by Lord Mountbatten and Prime Minister Attlee regarding transfer of power also had a significant, if unintended, impact on plans for nationalisation.

The division and reconstitution of the Indian Army and the Gurkha Rifle Regiments formed one more demand placed upon an army already under severe strain. Once again the political leadership, in both New Delhi and London, did not consider the potential impact of their actions, because they either did not understand the army's organisation or did not care about it. Either way, they pushed the army almost to breaking point to achieve specific political ends for both nations. Their actions created confusion and raised questions of loyalty as officers, VCOs, NCOs, and soldiers were transferred to different units and new states, in the middle of an ongoing communal civil war.

Many armies undergo gradual change and reform to integrate organisation shifts; but what was asked of and done to the Indian Army during the final months of the Raj would have broken most of the world's armies, especially if they had to contend simultaneously with a communal civil war in their own country.

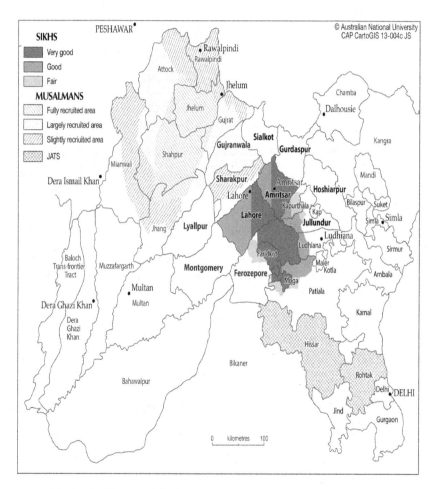

Map 7.1 Punjab 1947 and the communal breakdown

The mixed composition of the Punjab Boundary Force [Indian Army troops], as far as [Brigade] HQ was concerned, had through all this behaved reasonably. Muslim and neutral troops [Gurkhas and non-Punjabi] had taken forceful action against mobs. Hindu and Sikh troops had done their duty though they inflicted very few casualties, and to this degree they had failed. Mixed composition patrols under British officers had done extremely well. There had been no incidents between troops though tension was definitely growing ... Muslim officers worked flat out to protect their own community ... Hindu and Sikh officers had to be persuaded in most cases to do their duty ... [T]he civil administration and the police were completely and utterly useless.[1]

Brigadier from the Punjab Boundary Force

[W]hen we set forth upon our present duties I told you it was going to be a difficult task ... [O]fficers and men have worked loyally and without sparing themselves. I know the strain and fatigue that you have been subjected to and I know the strains and tugs of loyalties involved. We have been accused of partiality by both parties and that in itself is good evidence of the practical measures of overall impartiality which you have achieved in circumstances of unparalleled difficulty ... [I]t will be agreed that you in the PBF have ultimately upheld the honour of the old Indian Army, by your devotion to duty.[2]

Maj. Gen. Pete Rees, General Officer Commanding of
the Punjab Boundary Force

As these quotations indicate, 1947 was probably the most difficult year in the Indian Army's long history, as well as marking the end of the British Raj. Taken together, these quotes also illustrate the complexities involved in considering the army's ability to work together and remain professional, even in the midst of a communal war involving a level of ethnic cleansing not seen since the Second World War and rarely witnessed since.[3]

In 1947, the Indian Army faced the fallout from political issues that had not been resolved in 1946, as well as the looming partitioning of the subcontinent into Muslim Pakistan and Hindu-dominated India. As had been widely anticipated by many within the Indian Army, the force was taxed to high levels by growing communal violence, no longer just in Eastern Command, but throughout most of northern India, including the strategically important province of the Punjab. As violence accelerated, the various enablers of internal security duties, the Indian civil

---

[1] Tuker, *Memory*, p. 448.

[2] Special orders of the day, 31 Aug. 1947, File 59, Maj. Gen. Pete Rees Papers, OIOC, BL.

[3] There are hundreds of monographs and articles that deal with aspects of the partition of the subcontinent and the reasons for the 'communal outbreaks'.

service,[4] and Indian police[5] effectively ceased to function in many places, notably the Punjab. The army, meanwhile, in addition to carrying the heaviest IS load, continued to demobilise, nationalise the officer corps, and, most difficult, begin the process of dividing itself along class and communal lines, in accordance with political decisions driven by the need to establish independent armies for both Pakistan and India. An in-depth analysis of the political dynamics of the era falls outside the scope of this work; however, it is necessary to discuss some aspects of the political situation as they influenced the events of 1947.

The situation in the Punjab and northern India was particularly fraught because of the large number of retired and demobilised soldiers from the Sikh, Muslim, and Hindu communities who lived in the various districts. Many of these, at a loose end and in need of occupation, were ready and willing to put their military skills at the disposal of local political and religious leaders, by joining militias to carry out 'cleansing operations'.[6] Contemporary accusations that many of the Sikh *jatha*s were trained and led by former soldiers, INA members, and VCOs have since been substantiated. However, still more dangerous was the participation of the Punjab Princely States and their militaries and armouries.[7] When the situation in the Punjab began to deteriorate, the Maharaja of Patiala stated publicly that his army was ready to protect the Sikh community, and other Princely States followed suit. *Jatha*s began to form into units and receive professional-level training.[8] By May 1947, intelligence reports increasingly emphasised the collusion of the Sikh Princely States with the Sikh

---

[4] As noted in Chapter 5, for an in-depth discussion of the manpower shortages in the ICS, see Potter, 'Manpower Shortage'. Potter clearly shows that, before the end of the Raj, the ICS was in poor shape. It had been contracting since the 1930s; it was thin on the ground as of 1945, with close to 400 British officers, many of whom were nearing retirement. The other 500 officers were Indian, whose loyalty was widely questioned, both in London and by the Government of India (*ibid.*, pp. 68–9).

[5] The police would be accused in most districts of ceasing to function and then taking part in the violence; see below for more discussion. See Ian Talbot, 'The 1947 Violence in the Punjab', in Talbot, ed., *Deadly Embrace*, for more detail on the political background, esp. pp. 6–7.

[6] See Jalal, *Self and Sovereignty*, pp. 524–45, and Lucy Chester, *Borders and Conflict in South Asia: The Radcliffe Boundary Commission and the Partition of the Punjab* (Manchester University Press, 2009), p. 132.

[7] Aiyar, 'Anarchy', pp. 25–30; Talbot states, 'Sikh jathas were sometimes accompanied by soldiers from Jammu and Kashmir and the Sikh Princely States ... [T]roops from the princely states not only attacked the Muslim inhabitants ... but joined in the assaults on the neighbouring districts of the British administered Punjab' ('The 1947 Violence in the Punjab', p. 10). See also Copland, 'Master', p. 661: 'the Punjab states exercised considerable political and cultural clout in the larger provincial arena, especially in regard to the Sikh community'.

[8] Copland, 'Master', pp. 678 and 680.

jathas. The Princely States provided not only weapons, but also soldiers and officers from their state forces.[9] Ian Copland claims that Patiala and Nabha provided rifles, revolvers, and ammunition; Faridkot jeeps and trucks; Kapurthala money; and Kalsa training facilities for RSS cadres from Ambala.[10] All this activity was initially clandestine, but by mid July soldiers and officers from the State Forces were seen in British Punjab territory, leading and fighting alongside Sikh *jathas*.[11] In August, a report on the Sikh *jathas* described how 'in villages and cities the PBF were continually involved in very tough street fighting, coming up against accurate sniping, bombing, and rifle and machine gun fire'.[12] The Princely States not only provided support to military-style violence, but also the logistical support to continue the bloodshed.[13]

This chapter ends with the disbandment of the PBF on 1 September 1947. While the Indian Army was officially divided on 15 August, the PBF served intact until the end of the month. From that point forwards, remaining British officers served in the independent Indian and Pakistan Armies, which will be discussed in the conclusion. As 1947 progressed and northern India began to rip itself apart, unresolved political issues continued to complicate situations and hamper the army. One that loomed large was the ongoing saga of the Indian National Army.

The INA debate re-emerges

As 1946 drew to its end, the Indian Army and Field Marshal Auchinleck felt they had alleviated some of the tensions with the Interim Government, since their efforts in dealing with communal violence since August had been noted and appreciated.[14] However, this all changed at the end of the year when Sardar Baldev Singh, the defence member for the Interim Government, sent a letter to Auchinleck, calling for the release of all INA prisoners. He advised that discussion in the Central Legislative Assembly was moving towards calling for a resolution on the matter, and stated that the Indian people wished for the men to be released. He made it clear that the Interim Government would not push for the men to

---

[9] Sir John Colville to Secretary of State for India, 26 May 1947, L/WS/1/1010, OIOC, BL. See Hamid, *Disastrous*, p. 225, and Aiyar, 'Anarchy', p. 18.

[10] Copland, 'Master', pp. 680–1.

[11] *Ibid.*, p. 682.

[12] See Report on Communal Violence, File 48, Rees Papers, OIOC, BL.

[13] Copland, 'Master', p. 697.

[14] As Lt Gen. Tuker noted: 'The prestige of the Army was high and all men turned to it for protection' (*Memory*, p. 207). The British prime minister, Clement Attlee, stated the same, 'The Indian Army has so far stood up well and has not exhibited communal leanings': Attlee to Bevin, 2 Jan. 1947, *TOP*, IX, 243, p. 445.

be reinstated into the army, and included a letter from Nehru echoing the same points.[15]

Auchinleck responded to both letters on 6 January 1947, stating explicitly that he opposed the proposal to release the INA prisoners, on the grounds that it would strain the officer corps to breaking point. He cited senior British officers in particular, saying that 'The senior British officers of the Army, on whom, to a very large extent, the continuance of the present excellent demeanour of the Army depends, would, I feel, regard this action as a betrayal of the principles to which they have throughout their service been taught to adhere and would in consequence, be likely to lose faith in me as CinCI ... These British officers have helped to a very great extent to make the Indian Army what it is today and I cannot view with any equanimity any action which might seriously impair their morale in the troublesome months which appear to lie ahead of us.'[16]

Singh responded by circulating a copy of Auchinleck's letter within the Interim Government, and by paying a visit to Wavell on the morning of 9 January 1947. Singh expressed his opinion that the assembly would push not only for release, but also for back pay and reinstatement into the army.[17] Wavell recorded his response to Singh:

I warned him most forcibly indeed that any concession to the INA, even to the release of these prisoners, would be fatal for the Indian Army; that it would almost certainly make it impossible for the CinCI, or any senior officer of the British Army, to remain responsible for the Indian Army and I should find it impossible to accept responsibility for the security of India if the confidence of the Army was to be shaken in this way.[18]

Field Marshal Auchinleck met with the viceroy that evening; he advised that he had met with senior British officers, and that they were determined that no INA prisoners should be released. He also advised that he would resign if the proposed release occurred.[19] Lt Gen. Tuker

---

[15] Singh to Auchinleck, 30 Dec. 1946, No. 1204, Auchinleck Papers, University of Manchester; also reproduced in Connell, *Auchinleck*, pp. 855–7, and Hamid, *Disastrous*, pp. 121–2. Hamid specifically states that Auchinleck was furious.

[16] Auchinleck to Singh, 6 Jan. 1947, No. 1208, Auchinleck Papers, University of Manchester; also reproduced in Hamid, *Disastrous*, pp. 124–5, and Connell, *Auchinleck*, pp. 859–60.

[17] There is some confusion in the records about Singh's own position on these issues; some sources indicate that he opposed back pay and reinstatement, while Connell specifically states that Singh was in favour of back pay; see *Auchinleck*, p. 859.

[18] Wavell to Auchinleck, 9 Jan. 1947, Auchinleck Papers, University of Manchester; also in Connell, *Auchinleck*, pp. 859–60, and Hamid, *Disastrous*, pp. 125–6. He stated to Pethick-Lawrence the day before he that could not 'possibly give way': Wavell to Pethick-Lawrence, 8 Jan. 1947, *TOP*, IX, 263, p. 487.

[19] See Hamid, *Disastrous*, p. 126, and Connell, *Auchinleck*, p. 860.

recalled that it was clear that Auchinleck would not and could not back down, as to do so could result in a breakdown in army discipline.[20] Nehru met with Auchinleck on the 14th, and Singh with Wavell on the 20th, both stressing the need to release the INA prisoners. Wavell responded that he would have nothing to do with it and that, if it occurred, it would probably mean the disintegration of the Indian Army.[21]

Despite opposition, the issue did not disappear; in a letter to Lord Pethick-Lawrence dated 21 January 1947, Lord Wavell indicated that Singh was still pressing the INA issue, citing pressure on him from the left wing of the Congress Party, including Sarat Chandra Bose, Chandra Bose's brother. Wavell considered Singh nothing more than a mouthpiece for Nehru, and also believed that petitions for the release of prisoners and back pay would later shift to demands for reinstatement into the army. Wavell was unequivocal that he supported Auchinleck's objections;[22] he stated that he would refuse to have the issue discussed in cabinet, and would refer it to HMG for resolution. He advised Pethick-Lawrence of this, concluding that 'I trust I shall have full support of His Majesty's Government in resisting these demands, the acceptance of which would I am sure result in the beginning of the disintegration of the Indian Army, which is essential to avoid.'[23]

The India and Burma Committee met in London on 22 January to discuss Singh's proposals and Wavell's comments. The committee agreed with Wavell and Auchinleck's assessment, particularly the contention that any release of the INA would be detrimental to the morale of the Indian Army. They agreed that Wavell should meet with Singh and Nehru and emphasise the need to drop the proposal. If they refused to do so, Wavell had the right to over-rule the motion within the cabinet, as being prejudicial to the interests of British India.[24]

Following this decision, Wavell and Auchinleck met with Singh, Nehru, and Liaquat Ali Khan on the 24th to discuss the matter. They laid out their reasons why they considered proposals for INA release

---

[20] Tuker, *Memory*, p. 210.   [21] Hamid, *Disastrous*, p. 128.

[22] He specifically stated: '[Auchinleck] considers acceptance would be fatal to morale of the Indian Army and would make his position impossible' (Wavell to Pethick-Lawrence, 21 Jan. 1947, L/WS/1/1578, OIOC, BL); also in *TOP*, IX, 289, pp. 522–3, and Connell, *Auchinleck*, p. 680.

[23] Wavell to Pethick-Lawrence, 21 Jan. 1947, L/WS/1/1578, OIOC, BL; also in *TOP*, IX, 289, pp. 522–3, and Connell, *Auchinleck*, p. 680.

[24] See Minute of 6th Meeting of the India and Burma Committee, 22 Jan. 1947, L/WS/1/1578, OIOC, BL; also Telegram from Pethick-Lawrence to Wavell, 22 Jan. 1947, BL (also in *TOP*, IX, 295–6 and 301, pp. 528–9 and 537–40).

unacceptable. In reporting the meetings, Wavell characterised the tone as 'cordial', but indicated that he felt unsure about what the end result would be.[25]

In mid February, Singh and others within the Interim Government agreed to drop the issue of back pay for the INA, but continued to insist on release of the final prisoners; Auchinleck and Wavell continued to resist.[26] On 18 February, Nehru informed Wavell that the resolution would be brought up in the assembly,[27] and on 19 March, Wavell summoned the cabinet at night and informed them that he was over-ruling their efforts.[28] Interestingly, Nehru kept this veto silent within the Interim Government. He waited until the new viceroy, Lord Mount-batten, arrived later in the month.

Nehru informed Mountbatten that a resolution on the INA was going to go forward during the first week of April. Mountbatten met with Auchinleck, who reiterated his opposition, along with that of many senior officers of the Indian Army. Mountbatten, however, felt sure there had to be some compromise position acceptable to Nehru and the Interim Government as well as the army,[29] and a meeting was called for 2 April to attempt to find one.[30] Mountbatten reported afterwards that a com-promise was reached following a tense meeting: 'what we have in mind is that these advisers [who came from the army as well as from the Interim Government] should examine the proceedings of the various Courts Martial and give their opinion as to the desirability of reviewing the findings and sentences in each case, and make a report to the CinCI whether in their opinion the findings and sentences should be altered or

[25] Wavell to Pethick-Lawrence, 24 Jan. 1947, L/WS/1/1578, OIOC, BL. See also Moon, ed., *Wavell: The Viceroy's Journal*, p. 414.

[26] Wavell to Pethick-Lawrence, 12 Feb. 1947, *TOP*, IX, 383, pp. 681–6. See also Moon, ed., *Wavell: The Viceroy's Journal*, 11 Feb. 1947, pp. 418–19.

[27] Wavell to Pethick-Lawrence, 18 Feb. 1947, *TOP*, IX, 422, p. 753. See the end of the document on p. 770 for a complete breakdown of all the INA and the German-sponsored Legion Freies Indien that had been brought in and assessed as black, grey, and white. There were more than 100 black and grey officers, and 16,000 IORs and VCOs.

[28] There was a series of letters back and forth before 19 March, discussing whether Wavell should over-rule or if Mountbatten, the newly appointed viceroy, should take up the issue. Pethick-Lawrence directed Wavell to conclude the issue before Mountbatten arrived. See *TOP*, IX, 488, pp. 863–4; 507, p. 894; 526, pp. 926–8; 530, pp. 940–50; and 551, pp. 990–2, for more details. See also Moon, ed., *Wavell: The Viceroy's Journal*, 19 Mar. 1947, pp. 430–1.

[29] Record of interview between Lord Mountbatten and Field Marshal Auchinleck, 1 Apr. 1947, *TOP*, X, 50, p. 74.

[30] See *TOP*, X, 52, pp. 75–83, for a full description of the meeting in detail. See also 60–2, pp. 94–8, for details of the possible resolutions.

modified in any manner'.[31] In return, the Interim Government agreed to drop the motion.[32]

The INA debate was destined to end on 15 August, Independence Day, when Lord Mountbatten had agreed that a general amnesty for the remaining eleven INA prisoners would take effect, on the condition that publicity would be kept to a minimum.[33] The assessments of court proceedings resulted in the decision to reduce most of the sentences, allowing the INA to fall within the guidelines of the general amnesty. This was agreed to by Auchinleck and Nehru; Auchinleck also emphasised the need for the amnesty to occur only on 15 August – not before.[34] Mountbatten echoed this point: 'it does seem important that the scheme should be put into effect as inconspicuously as possible, and that great care should be exercised to prevent publicity, which might have a serious effect on the morale of the army'.[35]

The political landscape in early 1947

The first major political decision of 1947 was British prime minister Clement Attlee's statement on the transfer of power, made in the House of Commons on 20 February. The crux of his speech was the announcement that the British would transfer power no later than June 1948; he stated that 'it was for the Indian people themselves to choose their future status and constitution and that in the opinion of His Majesty's Government the time had come for responsibility for the Government of India to pass into Indian hands'.[36] He went on to present a number of related issues requiring resolution, such as the structure of future relationships with the Indian Princely States. He also stressed the importance of maintaining the effectiveness of the civil administration and the Indian Army during the transition.[37] Finally, he announced the end of Lord

---

[31] Mountbatten to Pethick-Lawrence (about the INA), 2 Apr. 1947, *TOP*, X, 63, p. 98. There was a follow-on letter from 3 April from Mountbatten discussing a small amendment to the formula. See Mountbatten to Auchinleck, 3 Apr. 1947, No. 1220, Auchinleck Papers, University of Manchester; also in Connell, *Auchinleck*, pp. 870–1.

[32] Viceroy's Personal Reports No. 2, 9 Apr. 1947, *TOP*, X, 108, pp. 167–72: 'motion was eventually withdrawn'.

[33] 'Record of interview between Lord Mountbatten, Mr Jinnah and Mr Liaquat Ali Khan', 29 Jul. 1947, *TOP*, X, 279, pp. 550–4.

[34] Viceroy's Personal Reports, 1 Aug. 1947, *TOP*, X, 302, pp. 603–4.

[35] Mountbatten Papers, Letters to and from the Secretary of State for India, 9 Aug. 1947, *TOP*, X, 402, p. 756.

[36] *TOP*, IX, 438, p. 773.

[37] Indian Policy, Statement of 20 Feb. 1947, *TOP*, IX, 438, pp. 773–5.

Wavell's tenure as viceroy, and the appointment of Lord Mountbatten to replace him as the final holder of that post.[38]

Reaction to this announcement was mixed in India; many within the Interim Government were pleased by what it indicated, but the language of the speech left considerable room for interpretation. Discussion of partition into two independent states, Pakistan and Hindustan, continued unabated and, if anything, appeared increasingly likely.[39] Mountbatten was specifically advised by the prime minister that he was to work with the Interim Government, and to treat it as the future Dominion government, emphasising that 'it is essential that there should be the fullest co-operation with the Indian leaders in all steps that are taken as to the withdrawal of British power so that the process may go forward as smoothly as possible'.[40]

Field Marshal Auchinleck was, as always, concerned about the announcement's impact on the Indian Army. Various reports coming in from the army's intelligence branch in the first two months of 1947 were very favourable, indicating that 'a feeling of quiet satisfaction appears to prevail amongst Indian soldiers in general ... [T]he unpleasant task [of IS duties] is carried out with firmness and determination without any traces of communal discrimination arising ... [T]he men feel proud of the fact that the Indian Army continues to set a fine example of unity to the country.' The report from February noted that 'interest in communal affairs exists and can hardly be otherwise, as men going on leave to areas where communal disturbances have taken place naturally absorb a certain amount of local flavour. However, relations amongst the regiments still remain harmonious.'[41]

Even before the statement was released, Auchinleck advised Wavell of his concern that the announcement was 'likely to be detrimental to the stability of the Indian Armed forces and may result in widespread indiscipline and communal trouble'.[42] Wavell, in turn, pointed out to the Chiefs of Staff in London that what might be good politically might be thoroughly bad militarily, noting the possibility of 'far reaching effects on the Indian Army ... The Indian Army is about the only stable element in

---

[38] Moon, ed., *Wavell: The Viceroy's Journal*, pp. 422–3.
[39] See letter from Gandhi to Nehru of 21 Feb. 1947 and Nehru to Gandhi on 24 Feb. 1947, in Michael Brecher, *Nehru: A Political Biography* (New York: Oxford University Press, 2005), p. 335; also in Connell, *Auchinleck*, p. 862.
[40] Attlee to Mountbatten, Mar. 1947, in Connell, *Auchinleck*, pp. 864–5.
[41] Intelligence Reports, No. 20, 8 Jan. 1947, and No. 21, 1 Feb. 1947, L/MIL/17/5/4276, OIOC, BL.
[42] Wavell to Pethick-Lawrence, 17 Feb. 1947, *TOP*, IX, 412, p. 734. Wavell also noted that Auchinleck felt that authority of the British officers within in the army would be weakened as well.

India and its disruption may lead to disaster.'[43] In a letter to Lt Gen. Scoones on 2 March 1947, Auchinleck referred to how the 'recent announcement by HMG has, as you will have realized, come as a considerable shock to very many people ... who thought it would be much more gradual ... I do not see how it can fail to have an unsettling effect on the Indian officers and men of the Armed Forces and I am feeling considerable anxiety about this.'[44] Within days, in confirmation of his fears, communal and politically motivated violence erupted across northern India, with the Punjab becoming centre stage.

Aid to the Civil Power in Eastern Command: March to September 1947

HMG's announcement of a date for independence and the potential for a partitioned country exacerbated tensions in Eastern Command considerably.[45] As communal violence broke out in the Punjab, it also began to affect the men of the various populations serving in Eastern Command.[46] Sikhs and Hindus returning to Calcutta and other districts spread news of Muslim-inspired violence, forgetting or omitting the fact that all three communities were involved. On the evening of 16 March, the first incidents of violence broke out in northern Calcutta between gangs of Muslims and Hindus.[47] The army and police, after countless engagements and patrols, were able to bring the situation under control by early April, but not before nearly 1,200 people had been killed.[48]

Throughout March and April, there were sporadic outbreaks of communal violence within Eastern Command,[49] along with riots and police mutinies. The police in Calcutta, both Muslim and Hindu (Gurkhas), were becoming increasingly partisan; in mid April the chief minister of Bengal, Suhrawardy, ordered the recruitment of some 600 Punjabi Musalmans, former soldiers, to offset the 1,000 Gurkha policemen in

---

[43] Wavell to Chiefs of Staff, 20 Feb. 1947, L/WS/1/1009, OIOC, BL.

[44] Auchinleck to Scoones, 2 Mar. 1947, No. 1215, Auchinleck Papers, University of Manchester; also in Connell, *Auchinleck*, p. 863.

[45] See Wainwright, 'Keeping the Peace in India', for an interesting view on the overall issues for the British administration and Indian Army. She states, 'the administration might have been quite capable of functioning effectively, the army quite capable of imposing order, but the British people and government at home were no longer willing to settle the Indian problem by force. All that could be done by the British authorities therefore was to contain the situation as far as practicable, and restore order as quickly as possible once disturbances had broken out' (p. 27).

[46] See Yasmin Khan, 'Out of Control?', for more background on the violence in the UP.

[47] Tuker, *Memory*, p. 228.   [48] *Ibid.*, pp. 229–30.

[49] As stated earlier, it included the provinces of Bengal, Assam, United Provinces, and Bihar.

Calcutta. Within days, there was an incident involving the two groups firing upon one another,[50] and the chief minister and his government were accused of exacerbating communal tension by recruiting PMs.[51] The army, once again, was commended for maintaining professionalism during this tense period.[52] The tensions remained; in mid July the governor of Bengal, Sir Frederick Burrows, reported his fear that the PM police would prove unreliable and partisan when the Boundary Commission announced its findings in mid August.[53]

The governor's fears were not unreasonable; Indian Army troops had been stationed in Bihar since the first outbreaks of communal violence in 1946. In late March 1947, communal tensions in Bihar began to escalate once again; the army carried out numerous flag marches in rural districts, to demonstrate its presence and preparedness to quell any violence. On 24 March, a police mutiny erupted at Patna; within minutes, the army was summoned to arrest the mutineers, who had overtaken the police in the barracks and the armoury. The inspector general of police and district magistrate were also called in; within hours, the mutineers were surrounded by both British and Indian troops, and gave up without a fight.

No sooner had this episode ended than another strike erupted at Gaya; once again the army was summoned to assist. Hard on the heels of this incident came reports of more strikes planned across the province over the course of 25 and 26 March. The causes for the initial mutiny were described as 'the culmination of a year's subversive activity amongst the police which, despite consistent warnings, ministers have failed to check. Military assistance at the moment is adequate.'[54] The next flash point was Monghyar, where again mutineers seized the armoury. These scattered mutinies were easily contained by the army.

Former INA soldiers also made their presence felt. The Bihar government had hired some and formed them into an 'Anti-Smuggling Corps' that was given the mission of stopping rice from being shipped out of Bihar to other provinces.[55] This corps was an ill-disciplined force which gained a reputation for being 'trigger happy', and the Bihar government agreed to disband them after Lt Gen. Tuker's command lodged

---

[50] Record of interview between Lord Mountbatten and Mr Tyson, 15 Apr. 1947, *TOP*, X, 154, p. 263.

[51] Viceroy's Personal Report, No. 4, 24 Apr. 1947, *TOP*, X, 211, pp. 403–11.

[52] See letter to the commanding officer of the 2nd Kumaon Regiment on 23 May 1947, in which the battalion was praised warmly for its abilities: Box 71/21/4/6, Tuker Papers, IWM.

[53] Burrows to Mountbatten, 18 Jul. 1947, *TOP*, XII, 161, p. 224.

[54] Governor Bihar to Secretary of State for India, 27 Mar. 1947, L/WS/1/1009, OIOC, BL.

[55] Tuker, *Memory*, pp. 222 and 230–1.

numerous protests. Lord Mountbatten also expressed his contempt for the Bihar government's practice of recruiting ex-INA personnel to district police organisations.[56]

On 3 June 1947, Mountbatten and HMG announced plans for the partition of the subcontinent into two Dominions, along with an earlier date for independence.[57] Tuker and his commanders braced for a violent public response, centring on the United Provinces and especially Calcutta.[58] On the day of the announcement, things were quiet. On 4 June, violence erupted between Hindu and Muslim gangs. The police and army, working co-operatively, were able to quell much of the violence.[59] As of late June, Tuker was still reporting that the army was carrying out its duties in a professional manner and was being commended by the police,[60] even as nationalist newspapers in Eastern Command published inflammatory stories and political and communal violence increased steadily. Tuker deployed a border cordon and 'mobile columns' to the border regions of UP and Punjab to block any Sikh or any other armed incursions into his command.[61]

Outbreaks of violence continued in large and small communities across the United Provinces, including Cawnpore and Assam in the east[62] as the month progressed, but the police and army continued to work together effectively.[63] Interestingly, Bihar and Orissa remained fairly quiet, even as the rest of Eastern Command became more and more tense. However, violence continued to increase in Calcutta, which had been the epicentre of politically and communally driven violence throughout 1946.[64] Tuker reported that violent communal attacks were on a steady increase throughout the month of June, recording that

---

[56] See Record of Interview between Lord Mountbatten and Mr Sri Krishna Sinha, 2 May 1947, *TOP*, X, 285, p. 564.

[57] See Philips, ed., *Select Documents, IV*, pp. 397–402, for more detail. The Indian Independence Act, 18 July 1947, announced the date of 15 August 1947. See *ibid.*, pp. 407–11, for more details.

[58] Wainwright, 'Keeping the Peace in India', p. 139.

[59] Tuker, *Memory*, pp. 295–7.   [60] See Tuker, *Memory*, p. 299 and Appendix IV.

[61] Wainwright, 'Keeping the Peace in India', p. 139.

[62] Violence had erupted between the various private armies of the political wings in Assam and the paramilitary organisation in May; the Assam Rifles had dealt swiftly with the situation. See Viceroy's Personal Report No. 6, 8 May 1947, *TOP*, X, 354, pp. 681–92.

[63] Even as independence arrived, the police in Cawnpore appeared to be capable of dealing with any flare-ups. The senior superintendent of police, George Boon, reported that 'we sent out orders to the armed motor patrols to find trouble and to put it down ruthlessly. They were to shoot to kill anyone attacking, looting or starting fires' (in 'Memories of August 1947', *Chowkidar*, vol. 8, no. 2 (Autumn 1997), compiled by Rosie Llewellyn-Jones, pp. 2–3).

[64] Tuker, *Memory*, pp. 341–6.

'Calcutta had passed beyond gangster methods, it was in the grip of anarchy.'[65]

With a month to go before independence and violence still on the rise, it was decided to heavily reinforce the police in Calcutta. By mid July three British battalions, seven Indian and Gurkha battalions, and one cavalry regiment were in place to provide support,[66] with the aim of supporting the police leading efforts to deal with the violence. This deployment was a temporary surge for the last month of the Raj;[67] the British battalions were scheduled to pull out by 15 August,[68] and all but four Indian and Gurkha battalions would be redeployed to other sectors of Eastern Command or shipped to Pakistan as part of the reconstitution process.[69]

Lt Gen. Tuker communicated five key themes to his command in anticipation of the difficult month ahead. First, anxiety and violence had created an environment of defeatist thoughts and views within all classes. Second, it was essential that confidence be restored within the army, and that the army set the example of soldierly discipline and efficiency. Third, refugees should be restored as soon as possible and treated with sympathy and kindness, and troops should act with vigour against all wrongdoers. Fourth, personnel should counter defeatist attitudes and rumours that might cause friction within the army; anyone

[65] *Ibid.*, p. 349. The viceroy made specific reference to the use of firearms in Calcutta in his Personal Report, No. 12, from 11 Jul. 1947, *TOP*, XII, 65, pp. 92–102.

[66] Garrison numbers in Calcutta, Box 71/21/4/6, Tuker Papers, IWM. See also Burrows to Mountbatten, 18 Jul. 1947, *TOP*, XII, 161, p. 224.

[67] Mountbatten specifically asked Nehru for more forces to come to Calcutta to avoid a major communal war on and after 15 August. See Mountbatten to Nehru, 21 Jul. 1947, *TOP*, XII, 193, pp. 282–3, and Nehru's response in 194, pp. 283–5.

[68] The British battalions stationed in India had done stellar work in IS duties since 1945. Decisions were being made to remove British battalions and units from IS duty gradually, going back to 1946. This process began with removing British battalions from Indian divisions and organising them into 'Independent Brigades'. By the summer of 1947, there were six brigade groups in the country. Nehru was keen for the British troops to leave as soon as possible after independence, and for them not to be used for IS duties in the lead-up to 15 August. Nehru and many within Congress viewed the British Army troops as 'foreign and [representing] foreign rule'. At a meeting in June 1947 with the CIGS, Field Marshal Montgomery, it was decided that it would take six months after independence for all British troops to leave India, due to shipping constraints. The first British troops left Bombay two days after independence. See Carter, ed., *Mountbatten's Report*, pp. 80 and 191, as well as Auchinleck to Lord Alanbrooke, 9 Feb. 1946, No. 1136, Auchinleck Papers, University of Manchester. A corollary to all of this was that all British troops had been removed from the 4th Indian Division, so no British battalions served in the Punjab. As the carnage and disruption spread, however, Nehru asked for British troops to be deployed in New Delhi. See Conclusion, pp. 338–51, for more details.

[69] Tuker, *Memory*, pp. 378–9.

putting self-interest before duty would be dismissed. Fifth, all points that he had raised should be brought to the notice of all within the command.[70]

Tuker and some of his senior staff met with the viceroy and the governor of Bengal on 30 July. The viceroy specifically asked if there was a need for a 'Joint Command' for Bengal, similar to what had been created for the Punjab – the PBF. Tuker asserted that there was no need for such an organisation,[71] and Maj. Gen. Ranking (the military commander in Bengal) and the governor of Bengal agreed. While they anticipated more trouble in Calcutta, the military command had drawn up specific plans to defend key locations within the city and then to take back the rest of the city by force, if need be. Tuker also confirmed that there were enough troops to deal with Calcutta, and that no further trouble was anticipated in East Bengal.[72]

Lord Mountbatten having indicated his confidence in the commanders and the military plan for Calcutta,[73] Lt Gen. Tuker sent a lengthy signal to his commanders in early August, outlining the keys for success in the coming weeks, reiterating the themes outlined above. Anticipating that his forces might become too stretched to deal with increasing violence as 15 August approached, he also advised his dwindling staff across Eastern Command that, if troubles erupted that were beyond the civil departments' capacity, area commanders should not hesitate to demand martial law. They should also be prepared to use more force than had been used in the past.[74]

There was some discussion of Tuker inheriting Delhi as part of his responsibilities after 1 August, as well as part of the eastern Punjab which bordered UP. Tuker made it clear that this would be difficult for his command, so Army HQ took command of Delhi and the PBF took over most of the Punjab.[75]

Overall, the Indian Army in Eastern Command was able to keep most of the violence that erupted to a manageable level during the period up to and immediately following independence. An officer from the 4/2nd King Edward VII's Own Gurkhas recalled that

---

[70] Signal, Jul. 1947, Box 71/21/4/4, Tuker Papers, IWM.

[71] He had done a battlefield circulation across the region over the previous weeks to assess the situation and felt that all was in hand. The 9th Brigade from the 5th Indian Division was on call to deal with any possible 'border issues': Wainwright, 'Keeping the Peace in India', p. 140. See below, pp. 311–37, for more discussion on the PBF.

[72] Record of interview between Mountbatten, Tuker, Ranking, and Burrows, 30 Jul. 1947, *TOP*, XII, 289, pp. 422–3.

[73] Viceroy's Personal Report, no. 15, 1 Aug. 1947, *TOP*, XII, 302, para. 9, pp. 443–56.

[74] Tuker, *Memory*, p. 406.   [75] Wainwright, 'Keeping the Peace in India', pp. 139–40.

on the eve of India's independence I was fully armed at the front of the officers' mess ... [T]wo other Companies were seated on their beds in barrack rooms ready to move at short notice ... Calcutta suffered a riot nearly every day in one part or another ... At independence it was expected that the balloon really would go up, hence our standing by ready to go where needed. Midnight came and went and nothing happened. No orders from Brigade, none of the unmistakable sounds of a communal riot ... I would like to finish by saying that the peace continued but Hindus and Muslims were at each other's throats again in a very short notice.[76]

Nehru commended the Indian Army units in the UP area in a letter to a British general. He stated: 'I shall be glad if you kindly convey to the troops under your command a message on my behalf thanking them for the cheerful and devoted manner in which they have in these difficult times invariably come out to help in the maintenance of law and order in this province.'[77] Tuker sent a signal to the troops in Calcutta and Bengal: 'please express to all of the officers and men ... [M]y thanks for their excellent work in the very trying circumstances in Calcutta during all these past weeks. Their complete impartiality and their good discipline have won the confidence of all in Calcutta and have raised the name of the troops of this command higher than ever before.'[78] This applied throughout Eastern Command;[79] however, the violence in the Punjab was of another order altogether.

Aid to the Civil Power and violence in the Punjab (Northern Command): March to September 1947

Prime Minister Attlee's speech on the plan for transfer of power naturally had an impact in the Punjab, the area where officials and officers most feared outbreaks of violence. The multi-sectarian Unionist Party of the Punjab had been soundly defeated by the Muslim League in the provincial elections of February 1946, winning seventy-five of the eighty-six seats reserved for Muslim candidates. According to Tan Tai Yong, 'at the end of the war, the Muslim elements within this larger

[76] 'Memories of August 1947', *Chowdikar*, account by Maj. John Thresh, pp. 10–11. See chapter 33, pp. 424–9, in Tuker's *While Memory Serves* for a narrative of the 'last Calcutta riot' of September 1947.

[77] Tuker, *Memory*, p. 465.

[78] Box 71/21/4/6, Tuker Papers, IWM. See also the letter from Tuker to Auchinleck from November 1947, where he states that 'the Army as a whole in Eastern Command has behaved quite wonderfully in all these troubles hitherto, we've had no friction at all in the units and I hope we won't'.

[79] See Wainwright, 'Keeping the Peace in India', p. 141.

rural–military elite, pressured by the increasingly popular appeal of Pakistan, made a tactical shift from the Unionist Party to the Muslim League'.[80]

As a result of this shift, Sir Khizr Hayat Tiwana remained in charge as the prime minister of the Punjab, but with less power.[81] Many observers felt that he miscalculated when he formed his Coalition Cabinet, appointing three Muslims (from his own party), two Hindus (from Congress), and one Sikh. Many Muslims considered his actions a betrayal. The Muslim League had no seat in the cabinet, even though they had most of the Muslim seats.[82]

By 1947, the Provincial Government of the Punjab was clearly becoming more sectarian. Members largely fell into two clear camps: the Muslim League, hoping for the establishment of a Pakistan; and Hindus and Sikhs, clamouring to avoid the possibility of a partitioned Punjab. The governor of the Punjab, Sir Evan Jenkins, reported to Lord Wavell in August 1946 on the communal position in the Punjab, emphasising the fracturing of society along communal lines: 'We have here the material for a vast communal upheaval ... [W]hat the Punjab needs at the present stage of its social and economic development is a Government representing all three communities ... with a marked rural bias ... [S]uch a Government could be formed by a Coalition based upon genuine common interest, or by a revived and strengthened Unionist Party.' He went on to conclude that the Coalition Ministry needed to confront the following: (a) the communal press, (b) violent speakers, (c) private armies, (d) lawlessness of all kinds, and (e) how to make clear by actions its support of district officers in the use of law-and-order powers. He warned that, if these points were not addressed, upheaval would ensue: 'it will begin with communal rioting in the towns on an unprecedented scale. The Sikh villagers of the Central Punjab and the Jats of the East will join in before long, and the Muslim villagers of the North and the West will follow suit.'[83]

The presence of private armies, and the inability of the Punjab Ministry to rein them in, were disquieting additional complications to an

[80] See Tan Tai Yong, 'Punjab and the Making of Pakistan: The Roots of a Civil–Military State', in Low and Brasted, eds., *Freedom*, p. 210. Yong elaborates: 'In 1947, the military-administrative superstructure held together Western Punjab amidst the unprecedented violence and upheaval brought about by independence and partition' (*ibid.*). See also Talbot, *Divided Cities*, pp. 37–8.

[81] See Talbot, *Khizr Tiwana*, for a more detailed account of Khizr Tiwana's tenure, specifically pp. 145–66 for issues in early 1947.

[82] See comments by Hamid, *Disastrous*, p. 130.

[83] Jenkins to Wavell, 31 Aug. 1946, 'Appreciation of Punjab Situation at the end of August 1946', *TOP*, VIII, 233, pp. 371–6.

already complex situation.[84] Sir Evan Jenkins reported in late 1946 that numbers recruited to private armies were rapidly expanding on both sides of the communal divide. He attributed this to the 'removal of restrictions by expiry of the Defence of India Rules of 1946 and the current communal tension'.[85] Sir Khizr Tiwana moved against fellow Muslim armed civilians in the Muslim League Volunteers, when the authorities arrested more than 100 of them.[86] In early 1947, Jenkins pressured Khizr Tiwana to take action against the large private armies that had been forming over the last months as communal violence spread from the east to the north.[87] The power and strength of the private armies were assessed in an intelligence report in February 1947. The men attended various training camps, where former INA soldiers as well as demobilised Indian Army soldiers were reportedly providing the training, and some were reportedly wearing 'military' uniforms. Many reports focusing on the rise of the 'volunteer para-military movements' hinted at the fact that the organisations were exceptionally well drilled in military skills, without apparently speculating on the reasons for this.

Senior officers assumed that former soldiers or even VCOs were behind some of the professional drill techniques (and later fighting quality) that these organisations demonstrated.[88] The authorities estimated that para-military organisations across India comprised more than 500,000 members,[89] and their impact on the violence in the Punjab during the spring and summer of 1947 is apparent from orders issued from the governor's office, specifically a 'ban on military drill, carrying of arms and processions'.[90] Many of the weapons in question came from Second

---

[84] The various organisations were listed in early 1947 as the following, including numbers: National Volunteer Corps or Rashtriya Swayam Sewak Sangh (RSS) (Hindu, 100,000); Muslim League Nationalist Guards (Muslim, 92,000); Khaksars (Muslim, 12,000); Ahars (Muslim, 3,000); Azad Hindu Volunteer Corps (Hindu, 58,000); Red Shirts (Congress Moslem, 12,500); Azad Hind, Congress left wing (Hindu, 8,500); and a variety of the smaller organisations. See 'Volunteer Organizations in India', 22 Jan. 1947, L/WS/1/745, OIOC, BL.

[85] Indian Political Intelligence, 22 Jan. 1947, L/WS/1/1009, OIOC, BL.

[86] Wavell to Pethick-Lawrence, 27 Nov. 1946, *TOP*, IX, 107, pp. 195–7.

[87] See Jenkins to Pethick-Lawrence, 26 Jan., in Rukhsana Zafar, ed., *Disturbances in the Punjab: 1947* (Islamabad: National Documentation Centre, 1995), pp. 33–4.

[88] Tuker had no doubt that this was what was happening: 'many ex-servicemen provided a trained nucleus, and acted as experienced leaders [for the *jathas*]' (*Memory*, p. 147). See also Copland, 'Master', pp. 687–9, and Talbot, *Divided Cities*, pp. 37–8.

[89] See Intelligence Correspondence with War Office, 22 Jan. 1947, L/WS/1/745, OIOC, BL. A senior Indian policeman also stated that 'these [demobbed soldiers] very soon started to join in the INA receptions and organisations': Mss Eur C290 Channing Pearce, IP, OIOC, BL.

[90] Political Situation, Governor of Punjab to Sec. of State for India, 22 Feb. 1947, L/WS/1/1009, OIOC, BL.

World War arsenals and dumps that had not been destroyed when US forces[91] left the area; military intelligence received information that many of the weapons had been seized and distributed to volunteer organisations.[92] Intelligence reports also stated bluntly that 'India's so-called volunteer organisations are in fact private and communal armies.'[93]

On 24 January 1947, the Coalition Ministry moved to outlaw and arrest many of the senior leadership of the various private armies, chiefly the Hindu RSS and the Muslim League Nationalist Guards. The Muslim League responded immediately, lodging formal complaints against the action, calling on the viceroy to reverse the actions of the Punjab ministry,[94] and launching a mass civil disobedience campaign. The Punjab Ministry, feeling the pressure, removed the ban on the Muslim League Guards.[95] On 2 March 1947, Khizr Tiwana resigned from his position and dissolved the Coalition Ministry.[96] Despite the coalition's efforts, the Punjab was becoming steadily more divided, and the call for partition of the Punjab more pronounced.[97] Governor Sir Evan Jenkins reported on 4 March 1947 that 'There has been much communal tension ... Congress and Sikhs are determined to resist Muslim rule ... [N]o progress in forming Coalition ... [S]ituation is grave and without Coalition communal trouble on a large scale seems inevitable.'[98] As Yasmin Khan wrote, 'the resignation of Khizr as premier of Punjab on 2 March and the collapse of his fated ministry was the final

---

[91] The United States had supported British efforts in the Burma campaign, as well as providing a regimental combat team, weapons, and advisers for the Nationalist Chinese forces fighting in northern Burma. There were supply dumps spread throughout eastern India. While the American forces carried out demobilisation procedures for some of these areas, not all dumps were closed to a consistent professional standard.

[92] Hamid, *Disastrous*, pp. 168–9. See also Tuker, *Memory*.

[93] Indian Political Intelligence, 22 Jan. 1947, L/WS/1/1009, OIOC, BL.

[94] See letters and correspondence from Jenkins, Pethick-Lawrence, and Wavell, *TOP*, IX, 310–14, pp. 556–63, for much more detail.

[95] Wavell to King George VI, 24 Feb. 1947, *TOP*, IX, 460, pp. 801–11.

[96] For full details of the reasons for his resignation, see letter from Jenkins to Wavell, 3 Mar. 1947, *TOP*, IX, 476, pp. 829–34. See also Talbot, 'The 1947 Violence in the Punjab', for more specific political background, esp. p. 3.

[97] See India and Burma Committee, Meeting 5 Feb. 1947, *TOP*, IX, 346, pp. 617–20; Jenkins to Pethick-Lawrence, 8 Feb. 1947, *TOP*, IX, 366, pp. 654–5. Wavell sent a note to Pethick-Lawrence on 12 February, laying out the opinion that no one group could hope to govern the Punjab without forming some type of coalition. If this did not succeed, then partition was inevitable: Wavell to Pethick-Lawrence, 12 Feb. 1947, *TOP*, IX, 383, pp. 681–6. See also the follow-up summary of Lord Wavell's meeting with Nehru on 22 Feb. 1947, *TOP*, IX, 448, pp. 785–6.

[98] Jenkins to Pethick-Lawrence, 4 Mar. 1947, *TOP*, IX, 481, p. 851. See the Punjab Police Special Branch report for the week ending 8 March in Zafar, ed., *Disturbances*, pp. 83–5, as well as NDC Accession No. S415. It gives a very detailed description of the outbreak and rapid expansion of the violence.

straw ... Master Tara Singh unsheathed his sword on the Punjab Assembly Building and other Sikh leaders called for Sikh rule once again in the Punjab. The communal civil war began.'[99] Ian Talbot stated that 'By the end of the first week of March ... quarters of most of the major cities in the Punjab were burning.'[100] The violence spread to many of the Muslim-dominated western Punjab districts, where large numbers of Sikhs were driven from their homes. It was clear from the outset that the violence was well organised, a trend that continued in the Punjab.[101]

On 5 March, Governor Jenkins requested drastic measures, in an attempt to deal with the inevitable civil war. He attempted to reform the Coalition Ministry, even as the government began to break down. He advised Lord Wavell that 'HMG must be quite clear as to the realities. During the next sixteen months [up to June 1948] order can be maintained in the Punjab whether under communal Ministry or Section 93 only by the use of force. Under communal ministry British officers and Indian Army will be used to conquer Punjab for the community in power.'[102]

The principal concern for many in the army command was the noticeable deterioration in performance of IS duties and procedures brought about by the drop in numbers and professionalism in the police and the ICS. They were not alone in this assessment, as evidenced by what passed in a meeting between Jenkins and Nehru on 14 March. Nehru had arrived in the Punjab to assess the situation; he had rapidly come to the conclusion that the 'solution to our problem in seriously disturbed areas ... was to hand over to the Military Commanders. Rightly or wrongly the communities had lost confidence in the services [police].'[103] Nehru went even further, raising the possibility of more draconian measures to be applied if violence continued to escalate.[104] His sentiments in this situation had changed notably from those expressed before the previous year's violence in other parts of northern India.

---

[99] Yasmin Khan, *Great Partition*, p. 83. See her ch. 5 for more background to the violence.
[100] Talbot, *Divided Cities*, p. 39.
[101] Talbot, 'The 1947 Violence in the Punjab', pp. 4–5.
[102] Jenkins to Pethick-Lawrence, 6 Mar. 1947, L/WS/1/1009, OIOC, BL.; see also similar correspondence between Jenkins and Wavell, 5 Mar. 1947, *TOP*, IX, 493, p. 869. See letter of 7 March 1947 from Jenkins to Wavell, which discusses in detail the communal make-up of the province, based upon the 1941 census: *TOP*, IX, 501, pp. 878–84.
[103] Note by Jenkins, 14 Mar. 1947, *TOP*, IX, 532, pp. 952–3. Jenkins specifically mentioned that Nehru stated 'In Bihar firm action by the Army had had an electric effect. I replied that troops were operating in large numbers in the disturbed areas and had been told to interpret the principle of "minimum force" in a sensible way' (p. 952).
[104] Hamid goes into some detail about the meeting as did Jenkins. See *Disastrous*, p. 143.

As violence escalated throughout the month of March, weaknesses in both the internal security doctrine and the civil administration became apparent. Lt Gen. Messervy (GOC Northern Command) advised that 'civil intelligence works too slowly to give quick enough results and timely warning. It also breaks down completely in the rural areas where the trouble starts. The military intelligence net is now being established ... [T]he details are not yet fully worked out but it is ideal to have one reliable agent on every patrol ... [T]roops must also gather intelligence.'[105]

The growing violence affected training of recruits as well as officers. The commandant of the 14th Punjab Regimental Centre noted: 'recent training was seriously handicapped ... due to the necessity of employing all ranks capable of handling a gun on civil defence. This entailed using recruits with only three months' service ... [I]t was in accordance with orders from higher authority and could not be avoided.'[106]

The manual *MTP 11-A* reiterated that 'minimum force is the least amount of force necessary to achieve the immediate object ... [Y]our object is not to kill but to incapacitate temporarily ... [S]hoot for effect ... [S]top the instant the crowd shows signs of breaking up ... [S]ecure the casualties immediately.'[107] However, the escalating level of violence in the Punjab and resulting breakdowns in civil–military communications began to undermine the principle.[108] Jenkins remained firm that Central Ordnance was to be used with discretion by military commanders.[109]

Messervy was forced to issue a new set of orders for Internal Defence in March 1947. He noted the change in circumstances, writing that 'It has been stressed that troops must act with speed and determination ... [T]he doctrine of minimum force is no longer the predominant factor ... [A]ll officers, VCOs, NCOs, must realise that although they have been granted these wide powers careless or reckless action on their part ... [in] exercising these powers will not be condoned.' Regarding civil–military relations, he advised that '[a]ll leaders ... remember ... a. intelligence! find out what is going [on;] b. dispel all false rumours and see that the truth is known[;] c. help all you have wounded, bring the terrorised to safety and [the] guilty to justice[;] d. enforce the strictest discipline to ensure that your unit or sub unit gives no cause for accusation

---

[105] 'Some remarks on the disturbances in the Punjab', Mar. 1947, File 50, Rees Papers, OIOC, BL.

[106] Cotton, 8002–68, NAM.

[107] *MTP 11-A*, p. 6. See Chapter 5 for more description of the manual.

[108] See Jenkins to Wavell, 17 Mar. 1947, *TOP*, IX, 540, pp. 965–71, where he reported that 'troops were able to inflict fairly heavy casualties on the attackers'.

[109] Note by Jenkins, 20 Mar. 1947, *TOP*, IX, 555, pp. 996–8.

by the civil population. If your discipline is really good the vast mass of people will welcome your presence and do all they can to help.'[110]

In another internal paper discussing the disturbances in the Punjab, Messervy highlighted other emerging issues. For example, he identified concerns regarding the professionalism of the Punjab Police.[111] While they did not collapse, there were many reports of their collusion or lack of drive to stop violence against one part of the community. He noted that, while 'the army has been steady and disciplined throughout ... there have been a few cases of Muslim troops not acting with [the] energy or alacrity with which they should have done'. He also documented two cases of ICOs who were accused of bias, and the ongoing investigation into these cases. Gen. Messervy's report also highlighted the need to make clear within the province that any 'pensioners engaged in the disturbances, or not co-operating with the Government to prevent them, [will] lose their pensions'. He specifically asserted that 'the districts affected are as heavily recruited as any in India. There is little doubt, I fear, that ex-soldiers and pensioners, some of the latter even including VCOs, have been heavily involved in many areas. In others they did very well and helped to save many of the minority community.'[112] This last statement confirmed, in many senior officers' minds, the potential threat of a large, demobilised, militarised society with no loyalty except to their communal leaders.[113]

Lt Gen. Messervy's report also discussed the issues regarding the use of martial law in the Punjab. He felt that if it were imposed, it would be

---

[110] 'Some remarks on the disturbances in the Punjab', Mar. 1947, File 50, Rees Papers, OIOC, BL.

[111] This concern was also noted in an intelligence report to Auchinleck in May 1947: 'it would appear that the police, particularly in those districts which have suffered in the previous disturbances, will tend to become partisan' (Auk GOC Personal Intelligence – Punjab, File 50, Rees Papers, OIOC, BL). Senior officers within the Punjab Police attempted to counter these claims. The senior superintendent of police in Lahore in February 1947, S. Supt. John Morton, stated: 'In these conditions [communal violence] it never ceased to amaze [me] ... the staunchness and loyalty of my police in doing their duty without fear or communal bias ... [W]hilst it would be naïve to deny that there [was] some truth in these assertions [police partiality] the fact that my men possessed a strong sense of public duty ... [S]o far as my police were concerned, they were remaining marvellously staunch' (Mss Eur D1003 Morton, 4 Feb. 1947, OIOC, BL). Morton's command ended later the same month. The loyalty of his men appeared to deteriorate later in the year.

[112] Official Correspondence, Political Situation in India, 22 Mar. 1947, Mountbatten Papers, OIOC, BL. See also earlier account from Jenkins to Wavell, on 17 Mar. 1947, *TOP*, IX, 540: 'the commander of 7th Division [Maj. Gen. Q. de T. Lovett] told me when I saw him yesterday that attacks on non-Muslims had been led in some cases by retired Army officers – some of them pensioners with honorary commissioned ranks' (p. 967).

[113] See Chapter 6 for an in-depth discussion of the demobilisation and division of the army.

used by the Muslim League as political propaganda, and to fuel accusations of the army being used as an anti-Pakistan instrument. He gave it as his opinion that, at that stage, the army had been given the correct extra powers to deal with the situation.[114]

Nehru and Auchinleck had both initially been in favour of imposing martial law[115] in the Punjab, but Auchinleck withdrew his support and backed Messervy's position instead, chiefly on the grounds of lack of troops to impose martial law effectively.[116] As a result, the Punjab Disturbed Areas Act[117] was imposed instead, giving officials wide powers to curb riots, and impose a death penalty on people who had committed or attempted murder or kidnapping.[118]

By the end of March, it appeared that most of the overt violence had subsided in the Punjab.[119] Lord Wavell had sent Field Marshal Auchinleck a letter, one of his last as viceroy, expressing his thanks for the excellent work the army had done in re-establishing control in the Punjab.[120] However, Sir Evan Jenkins was quite clear that there still existed a large undercurrent of unrest and that the Sikhs, in particular, were quite upset. Jenkins also emphasised that he and the GOI still

---

[114] Official Correspondence, Political Situation in India, 22 Mar. 1947, Mountbatten Papers, OIOC, BL. He listed the extra powers as the following: (a) pensioners actively engaged in the disturbances or not co-operating with the government to prevent them to lose their pensions; (b) land grants of participants or non-cooperators, similarly, to be forfeited. Another four powers which had not been promulgated initially, but were in place, included: (a) powers of arrest given to all military officers; (b) death penalty for arson, looting, and murderous attacks; (c) collective fines on towns and villages involved; (d) abrogation of the minimum force principle.

[115] Reports quoted Nehru as saying, 'troops should be empowered to be utterly ruthless and to shoot on sight'; Jinnah apparently held similar sentiments, declaring 'I don't care if you shoot Moslems or not, it has to be stopped' (quoted in Wolpert, *Shameful Flight*, p. 160).

[116] Hamid, *Disastrous*, p. 154.

[117] Jenkins specifically laid out what the act meant: 'have given authority to Magistrates and Police and to officers of the Armed Force respectively to use extreme force, with or without warning, against persons who in a disturbed area disobey orders prohibiting gatherings of five or more persons or the carrying of weapons or articles capable of being used as weapons ... [W]hen disturbances are widespread and as serious as these have been it is essential that Magistrates, Police and troops should have the power to deal summarily with persons who disregard lawful orders, even though this may use more than what appears at first sight to be "the minimum force".' See Jenkins to Mountbatten, MB 124, OIOC, BL, and reproduced in Kirpal Singh, ed., *Partition of the Punjab*, pp. 31–2.

[118] Talbot, 'The 1947 Violence in the Punjab', p. 7.

[119] Aiyar, 'Anarchy', p. 17. See the Sikh propaganda pamphlet in Zafar, ed., *Disturbances*, pp. 131–3, which highlights the inflammatory language and accusations from different communities that would play heavily into narratives of revenge by the Sikhs against the Muslims.

[120] Wavell to Auchinleck, 22 Mar. 1947, No. 1219, Auchinleck Papers, University of Manchester.

needed to govern the province under Section 93, as the Muslim League had failed in trying to form a government.[121]

It was reported at this time that the army had performed well in its duties, but was under great strain and, ironically, was being criticised once again by some within Congress for not doing enough to stop the violence. Auchinleck was quite concerned with the impact of the situation on the army as a whole, given the considerable percentage of personnel who had been recruited from the Punjab. However, as March came to an end, things appeared to be somewhat contained for the moment.[122] Most of the violence had been in the Muslim majority districts of the Western Punjab. It was estimated that close to 10,000 people were killed during this period, and that more than 40,000 Sikhs became refugees.[123]

The impact of events on the army was being closely monitored by the intelligence branch for obvious reasons. The first major report, compiled after the violence in March, indicated favourable outcomes, noting that most soldiers recognised that the efficiency of the army was key, and that this could be achieved only if politics and communalism were kept out of the army. The British and Indian units had acquitted themselves well during the recent violence, and the population had confidence in the army when it operated in their villages and districts. In the eyes of the civilian population, the army had maintained its ability to operate impartially and professionally. The report did indicate certain levels of upset within various units, arising from the desire of some soldiers to know the whereabouts and conditions of their families living in the Punjab.[124]

In a letter dated 7 April, Mountbatten advised Gandhi that the immediate disturbances in the Punjab had been dealt with, but that the root causes still existed.[125] He had written in his own reports that the country was still in an unsettled state, not just in the Punjab but also in Bihar, Calcutta, Bombay, Delhi, and the NWFP. He had also noted that 'In the Punjab all parties are seriously preparing for civil war, and of these the most businesslike and serious are the Sikhs.'[126] This last development was clear to all in the

---

[121] The viceroy would later state in April that the only hope for a unified Punjab rested with either a union or a coalition government and that, if this could not be achieved, partition was inevitable. See Viceroy's Personal Report, No. 2, 9 Apr. 1947, *TOP*, X, 108, pp. 167–72.

[122] India and Burma Committee, 28 Mar. 1947, Minute 1, *TOP*, X, 30, pp. 38–44. See also letter from Jenkins to Mountbatten, 31 Mar. 1947, *TOP*, X, 40, p. 59.

[123] Talbot and Singh, eds., *Partition*, pp. 75–6.

[124] Intelligence Reports, No. 23, 5 Apr. 1947, L/MIL/17/5/4276, OIOC, BL.

[125] Mountbatten to Gandhi, 7 Apr. 1947, *TOP*, X, 90, pp. 147–8.

[126] Viceroy's Personal Report, No. 1, 2 Apr. 1947, *TOP*, X, 59, p. 90.

Punjab[127] and in New Delhi, and accusations were aimed at the higher levels of the Interim Government to the effect that Baldev Singh was helping to raise funds for weapons for Sikh *jathas*; that there were clear links with some of the Sikh Princely States[128] in the Punjab to support *jathas*; and that the Sikhs had undertaken organised and financed incursions into the British-administered districts of the Punjab.[129] The Muslim League also accused the GOI and the governor of the Punjab of being pro-Sikh.[130]

Tensions remained high and sporadic violence erupted throughout the Punjab in April and May.[131] Conscious of the unrest seething under the surface, the clear political deadlock, and the visible arming of the Sikh *jathas*, Jenkins specifically requested at least two divisions to be deployed to the Punjab in May in preparation for the announcement of the partition of India and, more importantly, of the Punjab.[132] Lord Mountbatten agreed and asked the deputy CinCI, Lt Gen. Smith, to have a second division in the Punjab by early June, in anticipation of the upcoming announcement regarding not only the likelihood of partition, but also an earlier date for independence. According to Mountbatten, he had the unanimous support of the Indian cabinet to deploy an extra division, to stamp out communal violence with the 'utmost rigour'. He added, 'I particularly wished to have tanks, armoured cars, and aircraft used so that the poorly armed insurgent armies would feel that their resistance was futile since they were being mown down without a chance of killing any of the regular armed forces.'[133]

---

[127] Talbot, *Divided Cities*, quotes Jenkins: 'all communities were arming for a struggle which seemed inevitable' (p. 58).

[128] Many British officials from the Indian Political Service and British officers attached to the State Forces had begun to leave as part of the drawdown. Most State Forces were completely 'Indianised' by the summer of 1947.

[129] Jenkins to Mountbatten, 9 Apr. 1947, *TOP*, X, 109, pp. 172–6. See Minutes of Viceroy's 13th Misc Meeting, 11 May 1947, *TOP*, X, 404, pp. 759–62; Mr Abbott to Captain Brockman, 21 May 1947, *TOP*, X, 510, p. 942; Brockman to Sir John Colville, 22 May 1947, *TOP*, X, 511, p. 943; and Copland, 'Master', for more details and evidence. Hamid also notes this episode and included a specific pamphlet in his book: see *Disastrous*, pp. 158–9.

[130] Liaquat Ali Khan to Mountbatten, 15 Apr. 1947, *TOP*, X, 148, pp. 255–9. See Jenkins' response of 16 Apr. 1947, in *TOP*, X, 160, pp. 281–4. Jenkins had been accused as being pro-Muslim by many with the Congress Party; see Carter, ed., *Mountbatten's Report*, p. 110.

[131] See the various letters and reports back and forth between Jenkins and the viceroy in *TOP*, X and XI.

[132] Mountbatten to Gen. Sir Hastings Ismay, 11 May 1947, *TOP*, X, 410, p. 776. Mountbatten stated that a second division could not be deployed right away due to the potential unrest in other areas. He specifically told Ismay to alert Auchinleck to the potential division of the Punjab and the future impact on the need for more troops. According to Mountbatten, Jenkins actually asked for four divisions for the Punjab to stop a future civil war. See Carter, ed., *Mountbatten's Report*, p. 110.

[133] Lt Gen. Smith wanted a similar ordinance in place for Bengal as well. See Record of Interview between Mountbatten and Smith, 15 May 1947, *TOP*, X, 445, p. 828.

Mountbatten was initially vocal in expressing his desire that any communal civil war be ruthlessly crushed in the first instance,[134] although he would later temporise on this issue. In a letter to the governors written in May, he asserted that 'the long standing principle of using minimum force ... must be maintained'.[135] However, any course of action that the government wished to take was hampered by the lack of troops available; between demobilisation and the rising communal violence across northern and eastern India, the army was too short of troops to deploy an additional division to the Punjab.[136]

The Indian Army continued to receive commendation for their apparent impartiality during the violence up until the end of May. The various intelligence branches kept tabs on the 'pulse' of the army to identify any potential issues of communalism or political influence. An intelligence report focusing on this period notes that 'reports from units employed on IS duties continue to stress impartiality shown by the troops in carrying out their duties ... [U]nfortunately many VCOs who were on leave or pensioned took no action to prevent the disturbances in their villages or in a few cases went to the extent of participating.'[137] The army closely monitored the reactions of the men serving in the Punjab through the intelligence branch, especially those regiments that recruited heavily from the region. Infantry battalions were required to send in quarterly reports discussing various matters, including morale issues. Many commanding officers noted that morale remained high within the units. One report stated that 'during the period of review a high state of morale has been maintained. Recent disturbances in the Punjab caused concern and anxiety but fortunately the affected areas only had an indirect effect.' The same report, however, noted that 'releases [had] caused considerable upset in the battalion, the changeover in officers [had] been ... drastic and the hasty clearing of British ECOs [had] not been to the benefit to the battalion'.[138] Other battalions reported that morale was high and that 'the trouble in the Punjab has been strongly denounced by ... PMs and Jats and Rajputs'.[139]

---

[134] Mountbatten to Jenkins, 17 May 1947, *TOP*, X, 468, p. 863.

[135] See *TOP*, X, 468, note 2, p. 863, as well as Carter, ed., *Mountbatten's Report*, p. 115. He added, 'I asked HMG for their support if it was decided to use drastic measures against those starting a communal war, pointing out that, if even 10,000 fanatics were wiped out by the Armed Forces in the first round, this might stop the whole population of India from becoming involved.'

[136] *TOP*, X, 500, note 2, p. 927, and see Colville to Sardar Patel, 24 May 1947, *TOP*, X, 531, p. 979, where it is laid out that things are tight regarding troops being deployed for fear of their being thinly spread in other parts of the country. Colville does mention that the 4th Indian Division is on its way to Northern Command. The 4th Indian Division would form the future nucleus of the Punjab Boundary Force.

[137] Intelligence Reports, Nos. 23–5, Apr.–Jun. 1947, L/MIL/17/5/4276, OIOC, BL.

[138] 2nd Rajput Regiment, Mar. 1947, WO 268/458, NA.

[139] 4/6th Rajputana Rifles, Apr. 1947, WO 268/453, NA.

It was clear to all working and serving in the Punjab that communal tension was at a high pitch. Violence had continued throughout the previous weeks and months. Another major and contributing incident, often referred to as the Meo rising, occurred in March along the border of the Punjab and the United Provinces, west of Delhi in the Gurgaon district. This episode proved a microcosm of the episodes of violence flaring up across the Punjab: the police's inability to cope with the situation,[140] leading to the collapse of law and order generally;[141] a demobilised citizenry willing to use their previous military skills and training to devastating effect against their neighbours; the army lacking sufficient personnel to contend with a vast area and therefore being accused of not doing enough; and, most damaging, intervention from the Indian Princely States in the form of weapons, supplies, soldiers, and equipment to support a communal civil war.[142]

The Meo rising began when the Muslim population, called Meos, were attacked by well-organised bands of Hindu Jats, Ahirs, and Gujars in late March 1947. By early April, reports indicated villages being attacked and burned by all sides, and the police and army struggling to quell the violence.[143] By early June, more than fifty Muslim villages had been destroyed.[144] The Muslim League, outraged by the attacks, called upon the viceroy to deploy more troops to the area. Liaquat Ali Khan also questioned the class composition of the troops who had been deployed, and called for Muslim companies to deploy in support.[145]

Accusations and evidence emerged in June of intervention by Indian State Forces from Alwar and Bharatpur in the destruction of the Muslim villages, both inside their own states and in British India.[146] Jenkins re-asserted that armed groups from the Indian Princely States could

---

[140] Tuker is especially damning of the police efforts: see *Memory*, pp. 326–7.

[141] Zafar, ed., *Disturbances*, pp. 206–8.

[142] See 4th Report, Box 71/21/4/4, Tuker Papers, IWM, for discussions of the Indian State Forces getting involved in the fighting and killing.

[143] Jenkins to Viceroy, 3 Apr. 1947, L/WS/1/1010, OIOC, BL.

[144] By July this number increased, as did the number of Hindu villages attacked and burned by the Meos.

[145] Liaquat Ali Khan to Mountbatten, 31 May 1947, *TOP*, XI, 11, pp. 20–2. A company of Gurkhas and three companies from the Rajputana Rifles had been deployed to the area, later replaced by Sikh soldiers. See Khan's letter from 17 June 1947 to Mountbatten, as well as Ismay's response of the same day, detailing his argument and pushing hard for Muslim troops to be deployed to protect Muslim lives. He also called for the use of 'maximum force' if need be: *TOP*, XI, 232 and 234, pp. 451–4 and 456–7.

[146] Mss Eur C290 Channing Pearce, IP, OIOC, BL. This was not the only evidence, as armed parties from the Indian States of Faridkot and Nabha were caught in Lahore by the police and the Indian Army.

not enter British-administered areas without permission,[147] but this incident was a harbinger of things to come, and weapons, soldiers, and heavy equipment from the Indian States continued to make their way into the Punjab to support various sides in the coming civil war.[148]

In late May, Field Marshal Auchinleck and Lt Col Hamid returned to India from exercises and meetings in the UK. Hamid observed that 'On our return to Delhi the Army was in good shape ... At the moment there is little communal feeling among them. But once they come in touch with their kith and kin in the cities and villages it is bound to affect them. There has been no case of disobedience in the Armed Forces so far.'[149] Lt Gen. Tuker, from his position in Eastern Command, also commended the performance of the army during the difficult first months in the Punjab, noting that 'the army again earned for itself, at the very hearth of its own Punjab homes, a great name for impartiality and the gratitude of all and sundry'.[150] A letter from a senior officer to Sir Evan Jenkins highlighted the difficulty of the Indians' position:

many of the loyal supporters of law and order in the employ of either the ICS, [the] police, [or the] IA [Indian Army] are inevitably looking over their shoulders and wondering how their actions will be construed ... [A]lthough the loyalty of the army has remained outwardly unshaken by communal disturbances and political events ... it would not be unrealistic to question the loyalty in the event of an unpopular order by HMG.[151]

Another worrying development mentioned in many of the battalion war diaries from this period was the loss of veteran commissioned officers, both British and Indian, to demobilisation, nationalisation, and division.[152] In late March 1947, the 2nd Rajputs recorded that 'release has considerably upset the battalion, the changeover in officers has been

---

[147] Jenkins to Mountbatten, 31 May 1947, *TOP*, XI, 12, p. 24.

[148] See Tuker, *Memory*, p. 317, for a map of the district. The other issue within the States was the attacks on the minority populations within, causing a large refugee problem in the border areas. The Indian State Forces by the end of August were openly accused of attacking and killing Indian Army pensioners and families of serving Indian soldiers and officers in the Punjab. See Tuker's description of the attacks within the Princely States, around the Gurgaon district, *ibid.*, pp. 326–40, and 'Reports on Disturbances', Box 71/ 21/1/7, Tuker Papers, IWM.

[149] Hamid, *Disastrous*, p. 173. He added in his entry, 'a tribute must be paid to the British officers in the various Indian units. They are putting up a magnificent show and are trying their best to be completely impartial. I think it is correct to say that they are largely responsible for keeping the Indian Army sane. Of course, there are many Indian officers who are also non-political, dedicated to their profession and who are performing their duties impartially.'

[150] Tuker, *Memory*, p. 228.

[151] Auk GOC Personal Intelligence – Punjab, File 50, Rees Papers, OIOC, BL.

[152] See Chapter 6 for more detailed discussion.

particularly drastic and the haste of the release of British ECOs has not been to the benefit of the battalion.'[153] The 1st Indian Grenadiers reported that 'morale of the unit is high, but minor shocks have been caused by deteriorating officer situation, continual changeover of coy commanders, etc due to the release of ECOs and EICOs with veteran experience'.[154]

On 2 and 3 June, Lord Mountbatten met with members of the Indian political leadership; on the 3rd, he announced to the world that India was to be partitioned into two separate countries and establish its independence in August 1947.[155] Recognising the inevitability that both the Punjab and Bengal would need to be partitioned, a Punjab and Bengal Boundary Commission,[156] chaired by Sir Cyril Radcliffe, was established to demarcate the boundaries between a future India and Pakistan.[157]

Violence in Gurgaon continued unabated over the first week of June; the Meos had begun organising and attacking Hindu villages and razing them to the ground. It was being reported that the attacks were well organised, and that many of the insurgents were well armed. Another ominous development was reports of unprovoked attacks on the military.[158] The Indian Army troops already present were insufficient to cover the whole of the area affected, which was estimated to be more than 1,000 square miles.[159] Field Marshal Auchinleck decided to send a full brigade to the district in an attempt to quell the violence once and for all.

Things in Lahore and Amritsar appeared to be quieter than expected following the announcement, compared to the flare-up of violence in Calcutta. This caused the viceroy to report, perhaps over-optimistically, that 'Generally speaking His Majesty's Government's statement [of the 3rd of June] has eased the tension throughout the country and the real fear of communal war on a large scale has disappeared.'[160] Auchinleck

---

[153] 2nd Rajput, 31 Mar. 1947, WO 268/458, NA.

[154] 1st Indian Grenadiers, WO 268/446, NA.

[155] See Yasmin Khan, *Great Partition*, chapter 5, for a very good summary of the background of the decisions taken in early June.

[156] Radcliffe arrived in India only on 8 July, just over a month before independence. For a recent and exhaustive analysis of the process and findings, see Chester, *Borders and Conflict in South Asia*.

[157] Talbot and Singh, eds., *Partition*, p. 44.

[158] Viceroy's Personal Report, No. 8, 5 Jun. 1947, *TOP*, XI, 91, pp. 158–65.

[159] See description of an attack by the Meos on a Jat village in Tuker, *Memory*, p. 320: 'mortars were booming for miles around, cannons firing, and rifle attacks were made'.

[160] Viceroy's Personal Report, No. 9, 12 Jun. 1947, *TOP*, XI, 162, p. 301. He also reported that Auchinleck had carried out an assessment of the Indian Army's reaction to the coming division of the country and the army, writing that 'in general the solution is thought to be the best possible, though nearly all regret partition. Many of the troops have not yet realized the full implication of the plan, though they are obviously concerned at the inevitable splitting of the Services.' See also the multiple letters and

appeared to be more realistic in his assessment, stating that the 'situation seems to be under control at present from a military point of view though we quite realize trouble may increase and spread'.[161] Jenkins reported on 15 June that most of the violence in the district was being subdued, but also that he still needed more troops and that the army was stretched throughout the province.[162] Even though Gurgaon appeared to be settling down somewhat, violence was erupting in the surrounding Princely States,[163] and the potential for outbreaks in the large cities of Lahore and Amritsar was his greatest anxiety at that moment.

The Indian Army had redeployed the 4th Indian Division, under the command of Maj. Gen. Pete Rees, from Southern Command in late May.[164] Southern Command still had forces to deal with any violence, but was not taxed to the same levels as Eastern or Northern Command, except for the communal violence in Bombay. The GOC of Southern Command, Lt Gen. Sir Robert Lockhart, reporting on the IS situation, noted that 'I feel that the risk of serious trouble in Southern Command is much less than in either of the other two commands [Eastern and Northern] and we must accept reductions to help them.'[165]

By 31 May, there were sixteen battalions in and around Lahore.[166] The 4th Division made it clear to its men that they would be operating under the Punjab Disturbed Area Ordinance, which covered key issues including use of force when dealing with armed groups; disarming of citizens with weapons; powers of arrest without warrant of people who have either just committed a violent act or are about to do so; and recovery of stolen property or weapons. The ordinance specified that the army was still in support; that they should try to have police in the lead, and avoid appearing to take action without police in the area. Gen. Rees emphasised to his men that 'all officers, warrant officers, VCOs, NCOs must realize that although they have been granted these

---

telegrams for the months April to July in L/WS/1/1010, OIOC, BL, for evidence that tensions had not subsided.

[161] Auchinleck to Jenkins, 13 Jun. 1947, *TOP*, XI, 179, p. 333.

[162] Jenkins to Mountbatten, 15 Jun. 1947, *TOP*, XI, 209, p. 405.

[163] See Tuker, *Memory*, pp. 326–40, for a more detailed discussion of the violence in and around Gurgaon. Tuker reported that most of the violence finally subsided by mid July: *ibid.*, p. 391.

[164] Colville to Secretary of State for India, 26 May 1947, L/WS/1/1010, OIOC, BL.

[165] 'Internal Situation in Southern Command, 16 June 1947', 8310-154/47, Lockhart Papers, NAM. See also a report from John Griffiths, an ICS official, in Southern Command: 'the military were scarce in south India' ('Memories of August 1947', *Chowdikar*, p. 4).

[166] Minutes of Viceroy's Thirty Fourth Meeting, 31 May 1947, *TOP*, XI, 2, pp. 1–6.

wide powers, careless or reckless action on their part will not be condoned'.[167]

Lt Gen. Messervy moved his tactical HQ to Government House in Lahore before the 3 June announcement,[168] and prepared by advising his command that 'in the past the army has been loath to use force except as a last resort ... [S]tress has always been laid on the law of minimum force ... [I]t is now realized and rightly so that immediate strong action is far more effective ... [T]he law of minimum force still applies to every situation but this force can be applied immediately.'[169] The three major generals in charge of the three military areas were tied in closely with Messervy's HQ and with Sir Evan Jenkins, and in early June all felt that sufficient planning and organisation were in place for whatever might come next, other than the continuing problem of understrength battalions.[170]

Jenkins met with various political leaders on 23 June to discuss current conditions. He was aware that the police and the army could only react to whatever communal violence was coming; that they would be lacking in numbers; and that the populations themselves as well as the political leadership needed to change public opinion.[171] The viceroy met with senior Sikh leadership, including the Maharaja of Patiala, and impressed upon them that if the 'Sikhs showed any sign of fight they would have the Armed Forces of India against them and would be crushed. [The Maharajah] fully realized this and undertook to do everything in his power to try to steady them.'[172]

Jenkins' and Mountbatten's attempts to divert events away from communal violence ultimately failed, although political leaders expressed themselves as in agreement with their sentiments. Mountbatten reported to Jenkins on his conversations with Jinnah and Nehru about the GOI's plans, including Jinnah's statement that 'I don't care whether you shoot Muslims or not, it has got to be stopped', and Nehru's similarly stark declaration, 'Martial law should be declared forthwith in Lahore,

---

[167] 'Internal Security – Legal', File 50, Rees Papers, OIOC, BL.

[168] Jenkins stated that this command arrangement worked very well: 'Our liaison with Northern Command is excellent ... a very useful experiment which can be repeated if necessary' (Jenkins to Mountbatten, 15 Jun. 1947, *TOP*, XI, 209, p. 405).

[169] 'Northern Command Orders for Internal Defence, June 1947', File 50, Rees Papers, OIOC, BL. See also 'Firm Action to Suppress Lawlessness', *Civil Military Gazette*, Lahore, 3 Jun. 1947, which lays out in a press conference that if Northern Command 'have to take action to suppress lawlessness we will take firm action ... [T]he army is not an inferior organization, we do not take sides, we do not fight for one community against another' (reproduced in Kirpal Singh, ed., *Partition of the Punjab*, pp. 99–100).

[170] Jenkins to Mountbatten, 31 May 1947, *TOP*, XI, 12, p. 24. See Chapter 6 for a more in-depth discussion of the demobilisation issues.

[171] Note by Sir Evan Jenkins, 23 Jun. 1947, *TOP*, XI, 305.

[172] Viceroy's Personal Report, No. 12, *TOP*, XII, 65, p. 94.

Amritsar and any other area you think fit ... Whole operation should be handed over to the military ... [T]he troops should be empowered to be utterly ruthless and to shoot at sight.'[173] These sentiments were in stark contrast to Jinnah's and Nehru's previous constant criticism of the army's role as Aid to the Civil Power, and their belief that the army was operating illegally in this role. As events progressed and communal violence worsened, both abandoned their former positions; they wanted the situation dealt with as quickly as possible, even if it meant the death of many, and at the hands of the army.

As the Punjab and the Bengal provinces waited to hear the findings of the Boundary Commission, things became more and more tense. On 11 July, Jenkins recorded that communal tensions were high in most of the area, noting that 'communal feeling is now unbelievably bad'. More dangerous for the Indian Army, he reported that 'the Higher Services [the ICS and police] have virtually disintegrated ... In the ICS not one non-Muslim Indian is prepared to serve in West Punjab, and only one Muslim is prepared to serve in East Punjab. Hatred and suspicion are entirely undisguised.'[174] Even so, the Indian Army continued to report that 'the announcement of [partition] has no way tended to promote communalism in the army. Discussions which do occur between communities are reported to be free and sincere. There has been no report of Hindu-Sikh-Muslim friction from any unit.' The report did include the caveat that 'the average Indian Other Rank has yet to grasp the final implications of the announcement'.[175]

It was increasingly clear to both the civilian and military chains of command that the Punjab was facing significant disruption in the coming weeks, and possibly months, and all signs indicated that the ICS and police[176] were unequipped to deal with the coming crisis. Auchinleck proposed that areas adjoining the proposed independent states which experienced violence after 15 August be designated 'disturbed areas'. Auchinleck further recommended that areas deemed disturbed were subject to the jurisdiction of a 'Supreme Commander[177] [who], acting on the

---

[173] Mountbatten to Jenkins, 24 Jun. 1947, in Zafar, ed., *Disturbances*, pp. 260–1.

[174] Governor's Appreciation, enclosure to no. 81, Note by Sir George Abell, *TOP*, XII, 81, p. 120.

[175] Intelligence Reports, No. 26, Jul. 1947, L/MIL/17/5/4276, OIOC, BL.

[176] It was reported that the Punjab additional or auxiliary police by this time had several thousand demobbed soldiers within their ranks. As the regular police became less and less effective, the fact that auxiliary police had military skills ultimately contributed to the carnage. See Mss Eur Photo Eur 436 Gerald Robert Savage, Punjab Police, OIOC, BL.

[177] With the division of the Indian armed forces and independence, it was decided to appoint Auchinleck the supreme commander of the armed forces, directly in charge of the division of the forces and dealing with administrative aspects for the two new Dominions. Each Dominion would have a specific CinC who would be in charge of

request of the Joint Defence Council, will specially appoint a BRITISH Commander, with an adequate HQ, who will have MILITARY control over the area and of such troops and air forces that are considered by him to be necessary. These troops should be allotted, by the CinCs of the two Dominions, at the request of the Joint Defence Council.'[178]

The Punjab Boundary Force

On 17 July 1947, the Partition Council met and discussed the proposal from Field Marshal Auchinleck, who presented it personally.[179] After a series of questions and debates, the council decided to approve the proposal using the following framework:

(1) Action to deal with violence in the disturbed areas should be on the lines indicated by the CinC.
(2) Maj. Gen. Pete Rees,[180] commander of the 4th Indian Division, should be appointed as joint commander on the behalf of both Dominions.

Rees would be given a remit to control troops operating in specific areas of the Punjab, operating in a chain of command through the Joint Defence Council and the supreme commander. Senior Muslim and Sikh officers would serve as advisers on Rees' staff, and troops would be in defined zones no later than 8 August. No changes in the law governing the use of troops in Aid to the Civil Power would be allowed after 15 August.[181] With this decision, the Punjab Boundary Force was born.[182]

---

the operational responsibility of the new armies. See Chapter 6 for a much more detailed discussion of the division and the creation of the Joint Defence Council and the supreme commander position.

[178] Auchinleck to Mountbatten, Jul. 1947, *TOP*, XII, 102, p. 146.

[179] Jinnah and Khan as well as senior representatives of the future Dominion of India were present at the meeting. See Box 71/21/4/6, Tuker Papers, IWM, for many letters from soldiers, NCOs, VCOs, and officers detailing the violence in Punjab throughout the month of August. Some are reproduced in Tuker, *Memory*, ch. 34, pp. 430–52.

[180] According to Mountbatten's private secretary, Alan Campbell-Johnson, Mountbatten described Pete Rees as one of the ablest divisional commanders in the Burma campaign. According to Campbell-Johnson, Nehru was also very impressed with Rees. See Alan Campbell-Johnson, *Mission with Mountbatten* (London: Robert Hale Ltd, 1951), p. 175.

[181] Meeting of the Partition Council, 17 Jul. 1947, *TOP*, XII, 148, pp. 206–11; also in Zafar, ed., *Disturbances*, pp. 294–6. Robin Jeffrey in 'The Punjab Boundary Force and the Problem of Order, August 1947', *Modern Asian Studies*, 8, 4 (1974), p. 497, claims that senior army commanders had not been consulted. The plan came from Auchinleck and other senior army officers who were in the council meeting.

[182] For a complete breakdown of all the units and subunits within the PBF, see 'Strength and Composition of Boundary Force', *Constituent Assembly of India Debates (Legislature)*, vol. I, 201–4, reproduced in Kirpal Singh, ed., *Partition of the Punjab*, pp. 560–4.

Mountbatten, Auchinleck, Messervy, and Rees attended another meeting on 20 July to discuss planning specifics for the PBF. It was decided that selected districts (Amritsar, Ferozepore, Gujranwala, Gurdaspur, Hoshiarpur, Jullundur, Lahore, Lyallpur, Montgomery, Sheikhupura, and Sialkot) would have special military measures enacted in response to present and anticipated levels of communal violence.[183] The population of these districts amounted to 14.5 million and the communal breakdown was 55% Muslim, 25% Hindu, and 20% Sikh.[184] All of these communities ultimately became involved in communal violence.[185]

Imposition of martial law came up for discussion again at this meeting; Messervy reiterated that there were insufficient troops to carry it out, and recommended that the Punjab Disturbed Areas Act, Public Safety Act, and the Governor-General's Ordinance on Special Powers for the Armed Forces, already in place, should be continued for the time being.[186] Rees and the PBF would be responsible to the Dominion governments through the supreme commander and the Joint Defence Council; the troops were to take over in the named districts on 1 August.[187]

The PBF initially drew its units and formations from the 4th Indian Division which, as noted previously, had arrived in the Punjab at the end of May and early June, with violence in the area already escalating. Divisional staff immediately identified the need for a joint civil–military HQ, but the anticipated departure of British ICS and police proved an obstacle to establishing one. They did manage to organise weekly conferences to discuss the growing problems in the Punjab, at least until all British civilian staff were withdrawn from the area around 4 August. British staff had failed to hand

---

[183] This list of districts was later confirmed by Jenkins and ratified in a meeting of the Partition Council on 22 July. See *TOP*, XII, 205, pp. 301–2, for more details. Ludhiana was added on 24 July: see *TOP*, XII, 224, p. 326.

[184] File 48, Rees Papers, OIOC, BL.   [185] Aiyar, 'Anarchy', p. 17.

[186] 20 Jul. 1947, Mountbatten Papers, OIOC, BL. The basic points that were covered in these ordinances highlighted how dire things were getting: 'Government of India empowers any officer, warrant officer, VCO, or NCO to act as follows: a. fire upon or otherwise use force upon a person – contravening an order, prohibiting the assembly of 5 or more people, prohibiting the carrying of a weapon; b. to arrest without warrant any person who has committed an offence or reasonable suspicion exists that he has committed or about to – make an arrest, recover any person he believes is wrongly restrained, recover any property he suspects to be stolen, recover any arms' (Personal Intelligence Punjab, 1 Jun. 1947, File 50, Rees Papers, OIOC, BL). These laws were confirmed in a telegram from Jenkins to Mountbatten for all the districts of the Punjab on 31 July 1947 (*TOP*, XII, 299, p. 440).

[187] Minutes of Viceroy's Twenty-First Misc. Meeting, 20 Jul. 1947, *TOP*, XII, 184, pp. 272–6. Despite numerous discussions, the decision was ultimately made not to establish a similar organisation in Bengal. See minutes from relevant meetings, as well as the section above focusing on violence in Eastern Command.

over their intelligence contacts within the community to their Indian successors, which resulted in a communications and intelligence breakdown.[188]

It was already clear to the senior command that there had been efforts over the previous weeks to subvert the loyalty of the troops within the 4th Indian Division, as well as within all units and formations serving in the Punjab.[189] Lord Mountbatten felt that the presence of British officers with all units and subunits of the PBF[190] would help to safeguard against attempts at subversion, and restrain the troops from fighting one another as a separate entity.[191] The last intelligence report for the Indian Army, submitted on 2 August, seems to validate this theory: 'the integrity and impartiality of the Indian troops [have] remained unchanged. The way in which the civilian population has welcomed the Army wherever it has gone has come as a pleasant surprise to the troops.'[192] Reports from several other units designated to serve with the PBF reported similar sentiments as August 1947 dawned.[193]

Orders for the PBF directed Maj. Gen. Rees, along with two senior Indian military advisers, one a Sikh and the other a Muslim,[194] as follows:

a. [That troops would] deal with the disturbances on or after 15th of August in accordance with the guide lines as indicated by the C-in-C.
b. [That m]ilitary control would be exercised by Major General Rees.
c. That the zones of operations [would] be defined and approved by the Partition Council.
d. That troops would be in position by 8 August.

---

[188] See Tuker, *Memory*, pp. 441–2, as well as Bristow, *Memories*, p. 161.
[189] In the end the following brigades and units were part of the PBF: 114th Brigade (4/10th Baluch, 2/17th Dogras, 5/13th FFRifles), 14th (Para) Brigade (3/7th Rajputs, 1/2nd Punjab, 3/10th Baluch), 43rd (Lorried) Brigade (2/7th Rajput, 1/10th Baluch, 2/8th Gurkha Rifles, 3/3rd Queen Mary's Own Gurkha Rifles, 18th Cavalry, 4/12th FFR), 5th Brigade (1/4th Indian Grenadiers, 5th Rajputana Rifles, 1/9th Gurkha Rifles), 11th Brigade (4th Kumaon, 3/12th FFR, 1st Sikh Light Infantry, 3rd Mahar). Other extra battalions would serve on different detachments as well as the various regimental centres that fell within the twelve districts. See File 53, Rees Papers, OIOC, BL. No British troops were to be used, as stated earlier, which did cause some issues for some commanders. See Hamid, *Disastrous*, p. 209, as well as various letters in *TOP*, XII.
[190] See Kirpal Singh, ed., *Partition of the Punjab*, pp. 561–4.
[191] Meeting of the Provisional Joint Defence Committee, 29 Jul. 1947, *TOP*, XII, 276, pp. 403–4.
[192] Intelligence Reports, 2 Aug. 1947, L/MIL/17/5/4276, OIOC, BL.
[193] 1st Sikh Light Infantry, 2nd Quarterly Report, 31 Jul. 1947, WO 268/488, NA. This report also includes an account of two sepoys deserting with their weapons. See also 4/12th Frontier Force Regiment, WO 268/180, NA.
[194] Brig. Dhigambir Singh and Brig. Mohammad Ayub Khan.

e. That there should be no change in the law governing the use of troops
   in the aid of the civil power after 15th August, for such a period as
   these forces are employed.
f. That the troops would be drawn, as far as possible, equally from both
   Dominions and [would] be units of mixed composition. It was realised that the reconstruction may be delayed.
g. That the troops employed on these duties [would] be directly under
   the Supreme Commander, who [would] be directed by the Joint
   Defence Council.
h. [That] if any air support was required the AOC-in-C [would] decide
   in consultation with General Rees.[195]

On 1 August, Gen. Rees gathered his senior commanders and other
officers. He said, in part,

We are going to [be] the last representatives of the old Indian Army. The honour
and integrity of the Indian Army of which we are so proud [are] at stake and in
our hands and you and I, officers, VCOs, and men, have got to ensure that we
uphold and maintain our tradition ... We are a neutral force, operating in a
defined area, holding the scales of justice impartially under the direct orders of
the Supreme Commander, Field Marshal Auchinleck. We will continue to
operate after the 15th of August for as long as shall prove necessary to maintain
law and order and there is no question of units being ordered off to Pakistan or
India ... [There is an] absolute necessity for law and order, and in carrying out of
our duties, if we come in conflict with people who defy law and order and use
violence, we will use force ... I promise officers and men that provided they act in
all honesty of purpose I will back them up completely.[196]

The operational orders given to the troops on 1 August also highlighted
ongoing disputes with the Princely States, asserting that the PBF had the
right to pursue 'insurgents' who crossed into the Princely States.[197]
Maj. Peter Riches, Gen. Rees' aide-de-camp, commented that the general feeling at PBF HQ at the time was that, while they would do all they

[195] Hamid, *Disastrous*, p. 205.
[196] 'Special Order of the day, 1st August 1947', File 59, Rees Papers, OIOC, BL. The
acting commander of the 43rd Brigade, Lt Col Fergus Macartney, 2/8th Gurkha Rifles,
also noted an important aspect of the meeting and the potential pitfalls of the coming
month. He called for the restriction of Sikhs to be allowed only to carry ceremonial
kirpans (swords) and not the larger three-foot-long weapons. He was abruptly shouted
down by Brig. Dhigambir Singh in the meeting and asked to withdraw his ideas: Fergus
Macartney, Private Manuscript, Punjab Boundary Force; reproduced in *Red Flash*, No.
21, 1997, p. 6.
[197] Operational Order, 1st Aug. 1947, File 69, Rees Papers, OIOC, BL. There appears to
be some dispute about this: Copland writes that units were *not* allowed to chase *jatha*s
back into the States ('Master', p. 690), while Jeffrey states that they could enter the
Princely States, noting that 'where time permits the local political officer should be
previously informed' ('The Punjab Boundary Force', p. 505).

could, they expected no support from the British and Indian media, who were of the opinion that 'the PBF [couldn't] win'.[198] Auchinleck, however, had faith in Rees and the PBF; if he had any doubts about what the PBF would be able to accomplish, he kept them to himself. He wrote to Rees: 'I have just read your PBF operational instructions and this is to tell you I think it is excellent and I am sure that it will be of the greatest value to your troops ... I have ... complete confidence in you and your troops, and I am sure you will do the job as the [a]rmy has always done the job in the past!'[199]

As stated above, the violence in the Punjab escalated as 15 August approached.[200] Swarna Aiyar stated that its peak occurred between the 13th and the 19th, coinciding with the announcement of the boundary commission findings and independence.[201] Many authors state that much of this violence was well organised by Sikh leadership and former Sikh soldiers, to avenge the loss of the Punjab and to enact revenge attacks for the March attacks in the western Punjab.[202] The units from the PBF, spread throughout the province, began reporting problems with intelligence gathering almost immediately. They recorded that 'in late July and early August it was exceedingly difficult to get information as to the scale and type of trouble to expect ... [I]t is very necessary for the fighting services to be aware of the problems of the civil service.'[203]

Riches concurred that HQ believed that the Punjab Police were not viable, and hence intelligence was drying up all around the districts. As he put it, from 2 August, 'the PBF was a reaction force – it could not pre-empt many of the attacks'.[204] It was quickly apparent that the PBF was going to have a difficult time of it. One report described: 'situation in Amritsar, Jullundur and rural areas most unsatisfactory. Patrolling by the PBF is being intensified and special measures taken to protect trains.'[205]

---

[198] Author's interview with Maj. Peter Riches, 3 May 2005. Hamid reinforces this sentiment in his journal entry for 20 July: 'I feel that the positioning of the Boundary Force has come too late to exercise any effective control. General Rees is a very capable Commander but this task is beyond him. Political factors will come into play and he will be pressurized from all directions, and even maligned' (*Disastrous*, p. 207).

[199] Auchinleck to Rees, 14 Aug. 1947, File 73, Rees Papers, OIOC, BL.

[200] See Yasmin Khan, *Great Partition*, ch. 7, pp. 128–42, for more background on the violence in August.

[201] Aiyar, 'Anarchy', p. 17.

[202] Ian Talbot specifically stated 'whether or not there was an actual Sikh plan ... Sikh jathas led the attacks on Muslims that ethnically cleansed them from East Punjab. From May onwards, there had been a widespread collection of funds ... [and] import of weapons' ('The 1947 Violence in the Punjab', p. 9).

[203] Report on Communal Violence, File 48, Rees Papers, OIOC, BL.

[204] Author's interview with Maj. Riches, 3 May 2005.

[205] 2 Aug. 1947, L/WS/1/1010, OIOC, BL.

Nehru and other senior Indian political leaders, meanwhile, dismissed the Punjab government as callous and incompetent. They accused magistrates and police of being inept and partial, and further claimed that the police were actively involved with murder and arson. Governor Jenkins wrote a scathing letter to Mountbatten on 4 August, focusing on these accusations and the ongoing violence in the region. In response to the Indian political leaders' comments, he wrote 'this criticism does not come well from persons who have themselves shown gross partiality and encouraged it in others ... [T]hese critics themselves participate in the events which they profess to deplore.' His comment on the PBF was, 'I think the soldiers know their business and are doing it very well.'[206]

Col John Perkin, commander of 4/10th Baluch, confirmed that the PBF encountered problems with the police; at times, his men and officers had difficulty gathering intelligence in a given area, due to the complete collapse of the police.[207] The deputy inspector general of the Punjab Police in Jullundur district attempted to provide an explanation for this: 'Small police station staffs were swamped by events happening all around them. Isolated constables found themselves faced with situations impossible to meet unlike the army who lived and worked in units and were adequately officered [though not according to the General Staff]. The policemen all too often were inevitably out on [their] own.'[208]

Rees called in his commanders on 4 August for a conference. He advised his senior commanders to allow the junior commanders more flexibility to respond to situations as quickly as possible, without waiting for permission. He emphasised that officers must become familiar with the area, but not get too close to the people. Officers must get to know the leaders in the area, but keep the men away from such meetings. He ended the meeting with these words: 'the honour and reputation of the Indian Army of which we are so proud [are] at stake'.[209]

On the same day that this conference took place, the first major escalation in the level of violence occurred when a well-organised Sikh *jatha* surrounded two Muslim villages, burned them to the ground, and killed all the inhabitants. An officer who witnessed the violence described how: 'women and children had their limbs hacked off and their breasts amputated before being killed. Pregnant mothers were sliced open. Babies were left impaled on upright spears dug into the ground. Burnt corpses littered the

---

[206] 4 Aug. 1947, Mss Eur D807, Sir Evan Jenkins Papers, OIOC, BL.
[207] Author's interview with Col. Perkin, 8 Jun. 2005.
[208] Mss Eur F161/145, Indian Police, OIOC, BL, and see Bristow, *Memories*, pp. 15–153, for more discussion on the issues regarding the police in Jullundur later in the month.
[209] 'PBF Lahore Conference', 4 Aug. 1947, File 53, Rees Papers, OIOC, BL.

narrow streets ... [S]uch scenes were our daily sights combined with even worse horrors as we were directed by brigade to follow up incidents.'[210]

In a letter dated 8 August, Jenkins wrote to Mountbatten that intense communal violence had erupted at least once in nine of the twelve districts of the Punjab. The initial reports stated that casualties appeared to be at least 100 a day. Reporting by the police, however, had fallen off due to transfers. Jenkins wrote that the 'police in the East Punjab are unsteady and Moslem policemen in Amritsar intend to desert to West Punjab on the 15th August'.[211] He also cited problems with the PBF, chiefly insufficient numbers of soldiers. Jenkins urgently called for more reinforcements,[212] but the lack of available troops was one of the unintended consequences of the demobilisation process of the previous two years.[213]

At about this time, army officers in Lahore began to report that Muslim police were actively engaged in communal violence against Hindu- and Sikh-owned businesses and homes.[214] One Indian officer stated: 'I would like to stress that I am quite convinced that the police were deliberately organising the whole affair from start to finish and had no intention whatsoever of taking any action towards stopping it.'[215]

It was also at this time that various groups in the community accused the PBF of showing 'partiality'. The first questions were raised regarding the loyalty of Sikh soldiers in the PBF and the viceroy's bodyguard. Field Marshal Auchinleck was specifically asked to have the intelligence branch look into the issue.[216] Hindu leaders in Lahore also accused Muslim troops from the 5/13th Frontier Force Rifles of being biased, claiming

---

[210] Maj. P. H. James, 'Transfer of Sovereignty', *Royal Engineers Journal*, 111, 2 (Aug. 1997), p. 118.

[211] Official correspondence: Punjab, 8 Aug. 1947, Mountbatten Papers, OIOC, BL. See also the various Mss Eur in the OIOC, from the Punjab Police, which describe some of these issues in candid detail.

[212] Official correspondence: Punjab, 8 Aug. 1947, Mountbatten Papers, OIOC, BL. Auchinleck did not have any spare troops to send, and advised Jenkins of this on the 9th, although he told Maj. Gen. Rees that he would try his best to get some sort of reinforcements. See Minutes of Viceroy's Sixty-Ninth Staff Meeting, 9 Aug., 1947, *TOP*, XII, 389, pp. 610–12, and Hamid, *Disastrous*, p. 223.

[213] See Chapter 6 for more details.

[214] See Ian Talbot, 'A Tale of Two Cities: The Aftermath of Partition for Lahore and Amritsar, 1947–1957', *Modern Asian Studies*, 41, 1 (2007), pp. 151–85, for an in-depth discussion of the levels of destruction within two of the main urban centres of the Punjab.

[215] Intelligence Report – Civil Disturbances Lahore by Lt Col Alluf Qadir, 13 Aug. 1947, File 54, Rees Papers, OIOC, BL.

[216] Minutes of Viceroy's Sixty Ninth Staff Meeting, 9 Aug. 1947, *TOP*, XII, 389, pp. 610–12.

that 'the [military patrol] party returned uttering filthy abuses against Hindus with a threat of setting the Hindus right [by using violence] immediately'.[217] These were contradicted by other reports that Hindu and Sikh troops were performing extremely well against gangs of other Hindus and Sikhs.[218] In response to many allegations, Gen. Rees sent out a personal letter to his brigade commanders, saying that 'it is certain that we will have a lot of exaggerated and even false stories about our activities ... [I]t is suitable for me to go on now and remind you all to tell your junior leaders to make notes as notes are invaluable in any subsequent enquiries.'[219]

Reports of communal tensions developing within units were also beginning to come in.[220] Maj. Gen. D. C. Hawthorn contradicted some of the comments; when discussing information reported to him by Rees, he asserted that, 'the troops are unaffected by the communal tension and are carrying out all that is asked of them magnificently'.[221] Auchinleck, reading this assertion, presciently wrote in the margin, '[For] how long? C.J.A.'[222]

The note from Hawthorn also touched, once again, upon the ongoing problem of civil–military co-operation. It reiterated that 'sources of information [are] drying up', and discussed an incident in Amritsar when a Hindu superintendent of police disarmed the Muslim police.[223] Brig. Stewart, commander of one of the brigades, reported that 'attacks on villages are almost continuous ... [They] occur all over the district, which makes it difficult for anyone to anticipate their intentions in view of the size of the district ... [T]roops are very thin on the ground and in many cases no communications exist ... [A]ll battalions are going flat out with patrols, ambushes and sweeps, no effort is being spared to get at these gangs.'[224] Even Sir Percival Griffiths, in his book, *To Guard My*

[217] Letter from Hindu Leaders, Lahore, to Rees, 9 Aug. 1947, File 54, Rees Papers, OIOC, BL.

[218] See Rees Personal Logs, 10 Aug. 1947, File 68, Rees Papers, OIOC, BL.

[219] Rees to his brigade commanders, 9 Aug. 1947, File 58, Rees Papers, OIOC, BL.

[220] On 11 August, Muslim members of the 4/12th Frontier Force Regiment accused non-Muslim troops of firing indiscriminately and unjustifiably on Muslim civilians. See 30 Sep. 1947, WO 268/180, NA. The 2/2nd Punjab Regiment report listed that many men were concerned about the findings of the Boundary Commission. See Oct. 1947, WO 268/457, NA.

[221] 11 Aug. 1947, R/3/1/171, OIOC, BL; also in Zafar, ed., *Disturbances*, pp. 331–4, and Kirpal Singh, ed., *Partition of the Punjab*, pp. 466–7.

[222] 11 Aug. 1947, R/3/1/171, OIOC, BL; also in Zafar, ed., *Disturbances*, pp. 331–4, and Kirpal Singh, ed., *Partition of the Punjab*, pp. 466–7.

[223] See Rees Personal Logs, 10 Aug. 1947, File 68, Rees Papers, OIOC, BL. See also Jenkins to Mountbatten, 12 Aug. 1947, L/WS/1/1010, OIOC, BL.

[224] Misc. drafts and reports, 10 Aug. 1947, File 51, Rees Papers, OIOC, BL.

People: History of the Indian Police, hinted at this fundamental issue: 'Mountbatten rightly observed at a later date that there had been a general rundown of the administration and for a time the intelligence organisation of the police did fall below its previous well-known competence.'[225]

Governor Jenkins also emphasised concerns about the police in a report to the Government of India. He wrote that 'police in Lahore and Amritsar are now unreliable. There was serious indiscipline at the recruiting training centre ... I am still waiting for news of the state of the rural police stations ... some of which are said to have stopped functioning ... [W]e have no strength of troops and police required to restore order.'[226] Jenkins reported to Mountbatten on 12 August that the PBF and the commander had too great a task to deal with, pointing out that the PBF was required to cover some 17,000 villages and towns and reiterating that he would have needed two full divisions to carry out this mission effectively. The PBF was not at full strength and, with training centres added, numbered just over 9,000 effectives.[227]

Other reports from this period described gun battles between police and army troops on 12 and 13 August.[228] The district commissioner for Amritsar and Lahore commented that 'the public started to distrust the police and later the troops'.[229] The 5th Brigade reported a major clash between an armed group of 100 villagers and a patrol. It claimed that the patrol came under 'fire from a dozen [Muslim] police in company with a mob ... [T]he police were attempting to obtain [the] weapons with which we were armed and [the] ambush was expressly aimed as an attack on the army.'[230]

Issues with the police were not linked to any one area or communal group; units of the PBF reported 'partiality' within the police force throughout the month of August. Reports came from both Amritsar and Lahore of 'many complaints regarding the ineffectiveness and partiality of the police'.[231]

---

[225] Sir Percival Griffiths, *To Guard My People: History of the Indian Police* (London: Benn, 1971). Brig. Bristow concurred: 'The Indian Police had a fine record, but, after sudden reconstitution in the atmosphere of a communal war, they lost all sense of impartial duty' (*Memories*, p. 202).

[226] Punjab Government to Government of India, 12 Aug. 1947, L/WS/1/1010, OIOC, BL.

[227] Jenkins to Mountbatten, 12 Aug. 1947, R/3/1/171, OIOC, BL; also in Kirpal Singh, ed., *Partition of the Punjab*, pp. 472–3.

[228] Punjab Government to Government of India, 13 Aug. 1947, L/WS/1/1010, OIOC, BL.

[229] Mss Eur F409, George Brander, ICS, OIOC, BL.

[230] Communal Subjects, 12 Aug. 1947, File 54, Rees Papers, OIOC, BL. See also Hamid's entry for 13 August, in *Disastrous*, pp. 224–7.

[231] See Official Logs, 14–19 Aug. 1947, Files 54 and 62, Rees Papers, OIOC, BL.

It was also during the run-up to independence that attacks on trains between the two future states began to increase, with specific railway stations targeted as well. Attacks against both trains and stations increased throughout the month and only began to abate in late September.[232] As one British officer observed in the aftermath of an attack on a refugee train: 'I do not think I have ever witnessed such cold-bloodedness by any human beings as I witnessed last night ... In every carriage without exception the dead and dying were mixed up with the wounded – it was certainly a train of death.'[233]

The situation reached crisis point on the eve of independence. Jenkins, in one of his last letters, wrote to Rees on 14 August: 'before I leave I must thank you and the 4th Indian Division and PBF for all the help you have given us during this difficult time. Troops can seldom have had a more arduous and unpleasant task as the aid to the civil power ... [H]ow deeply we are in your debt, and what confidence we have had in your troops and in yourself.'[234] It was also on this day that Rees reported a drop in efficiency with some of his units and formations, due to the loss of British officers and shortage overall of veteran commanders.[235] As the new independent states of India and Pakistan were created on the 15th, Auchinleck submitted a report on the conditions in the Punjab for the Joint Defence Council. He described many of the problems presented here and added further comments regarding the PBF:

two more brigades ... are being sent to reinforce the PBF but no amount of troops can stop the indiscriminate butchery that appears to be going on on both sides ... General Rees and his brigade commanders are doing all they can and so the troops have been completely impartial and extremely well disciplined, in spite of baseless and mischievous stories to the contrary which are being printed, in some cases by people in responsible positions. Such stories do possible harm and may result in the troops ceasing to be impartial, in which event, the situation, bad as it is now, would become truly horrible.[236]

Mountbatten summarised his thoughts on the situation in the Punjab on 16 August in a long internal report. He discussed the issues with police becoming sectarian and refusing to protect peoples who were not of their

---

[232] See Aiyar, 'Anarchy', pp. 18–24, especially the vivid account of a train leaving Pakistan for India on pp. 20–1, as well as 'Report on the PBF', L/MIL/17/5/4319, OIOC, BL, for more details.

[233] Tuker, *Memory*, pp. 481 and 484. The officer specifically compared the attacks to the Nazis in the Second World War and actually stated they were worse than the Nazis.

[234] Misc. drafts and reports, 14 Aug. 1947, File 51, Rees Papers, OIOC, BL. Sir Evan Jenkins appeared to contradict himself later in October 1947, for reasons that are unclear.

[235] Lahore Conference meeting, 14 Aug. 1947, File 51, Rees Papers, OIOC, BL.

[236] Note by Auchinleck, 15 Aug. 1947, R/3/1/171, OIOC, BL.

religion. He claimed that, if it had not been for the PBF, the violence in Amritsar would have been a holocaust in the making. He specifically called for various senior political leaders of both Dominions to meet with Rees and create a working plan to deal with the rising violence. He asserted, 'It is quite clear and we all agreed, that the soldiers are doing everything that is humanly possible to try and hold the situation, and although it was decided, among other things to reinforce the Boundary Force by two more brigades ... the situation is long past mere military action and requires political leadership of the highest order.'[237]

After the 15th, things did indeed get worse.[238] By the end of the month, there were accusations of troops firing upon one another, although actual reports are limited to a few small incidents. As one officer responded: 'due to the atrocities committed here, and I don't think there can be any worse in history, it is quite natural that the troops in the PBF should get affected. To a very small extent they have been, but the incidents in this respect are negligible. Unfortunately they have been exaggerated and given big publicity, which tends to make matters worse.'[239] The Joint Defence Council met on 16 August to discuss the security situation; Auchinleck stressed the need to keep the PBF in place, and reiterated that 'troops have so far been impartial and well disciplined, despite stories to the contrary'.[240]

On 16 August, Mountbatten made the findings of the Punjab Boundary Commission public to the political leaders of Pakistan and India, and on 17 August to the populations of both countries.[241] Independence brought still more bloodletting as Sikhs, Hindus, and Muslims set out to destroy one another. In the months following independence, some 13 million people set out to cross the newly established borders in both directions – an undertaking that would tax the PBF to the breaking point.

Mountbatten also wrote a personal report on the 16th, documenting the previous fifteen days and setting out what he thought was needed in the coming months. He wrote:

rumours [about] the decision of the Boundary Commission in the Punjab had been sufficient to start large scale rioting which would undoubtedly have been a

---

[237] Viceroy's Personal Report, No. 17, 16 Aug. 1947, *TOP*, XII, 489, p. 763; also in Carter, ed., *Mountbatten's Report*, pp. 280–1.

[238] See Rees Papers (OIOC, BL) for specific situation reports (SITREPS) from the 15th until the end of the month. The SITREPS are also reproduced in Kirpal Singh, ed., *Partition of the Punjab*, pp. 514–17.

[239] Tuker, *Memory*, p. 435.

[240] 'Informal Minutes of the Joint Defence Council Meeting, 16 August 1947', reproduced in Kirpal Singh, ed., *Partition of the Punjab*, pp. 489–94.

[241] See Hamid, *Disastrous*, pp. 234–5.

communal war on a big scale if it had not been for the joint Punjab Boundary Force ... In Amritsar ... but for the presence of the PBF there would now be a complete holocaust in the city. Local Muslim leaders are trying to persuade the Muslim soldiers to follow the example of the police [to become communal] but so far without apparent success ... It is quite clear that the soldiers are doing everything that is humanly possible to try and hold the situation ... [T]he situation is long past mere military action and requires political leadership of a high order.[242]

Military commanders held politicians on both sides largely responsible for the communal violence.[243] Gen. Rees reinforced this view:

It is good, and encouraging to all PBF officers and men, and to me personally, to know that we have your confidence and your backing. I will do all that lies in my power to see that we carry out our task as you would wish us to ... The hard truth is that without the neutral Indian Army the slaughter and terror would have been desperate and completely out of control ... [W]e are having heavy communal propaganda levelled at our officers and men ... but I am combating it through the ICOs, Subedars and VCOs and they and the men realise and agree that unlimited bloodshed and terror would have been reigning in the central Punjab today ... if they were not standing firm and rock like as the IA always [is] when called upon.[244]

Field Marshal Auchinleck forwarded the above letter to Lord Mountbatten with the additional comment that 'I am sure that Rees is right and that any attempt to replace the PBF by dominion controlled forces forbidden to cross the common boundary would be likely to end in disaster and possibly an open clash. This is my opinion which is shared by Arthur Smith and [Lt Gen.] Lockhart.'[245]

Despite such confident reports, it was clear that some army personnel were beginning to falter. An interesting observation came from a British officer serving in a training battalion in Lahore. He noted that after 15 August the Muslim soldiers, who had been apolitical and non-communal before independence, became fanatically nationalistic about Pakistan. They viewed all non-Muslims as suspect. He saw that the Hindu and Sikh soldiers became very apprehensive about this, and the non-Muslim troops

---

[242] Viceroy's Personal Report No. 17, 16 Aug. 1947, L/PO/6/123, OIOC, BL; also in Carter, ed., *Mountbatten's Report.*

[243] Gen. Savory's comment on this situation was: 'Sad to see the approaching end of an Empire. Sad not so much because of our departure but because of what we are leaving behind us which looks like bloodshed and anarchy now raging in the Punjab and elsewhere ... The end of Nehru's Government which will be remembered for wrecking the law and order which the British had tried their level best to bring about in the subcontinent' (quoted in Hamid, *Disastrous*, p. 231).

[244] 17 Aug. 1947, File 73, Rees Papers, OIOC, BL; also in No. 1247, Auchinleck Papers, University of Manchester.

[245] Auchinleck to Mountbatten, 20 Aug. 1947, R/3/1/171, OIOC, BL; also in Kirpal Singh, ed., *Partition of the Punjab*, pp. 496–7.

transferred to India within days.[246] Another issue arose after the 15th: reports circulated inside the army of a company from the Sikh Light Infantry firing upon a company of Muslim troops from the 8th Punjab Regiment. As one senior officer noted: 'This was the real start of the breakdown of the army. It was hushed up as much as possible, but rumour magnified the event even more.'[247] Brig. Bristow described another incident in Jullundur, involving Jat soldiers from the Punjab who refused to stop Sikh *jatha*s from killing and burning Muslims and their homes. The VCO conveyed to the brigadier that 'the Raj had ended, and the conflict should be left to them to settle in their own way'.[248]

On 19 August, reports[249] came in describing the killing, in Amritsar, of two British officers[250] from the 33rd King George V's Own Bengal Sappers and Miners. The commanding officer described how the officers had been fired upon at a post where both military and policemen were present. The commanding officer went to retrieve the bodies and confront the commander, and described the situation and its effect upon the squadron:

I went with the standby troop directly to the area, ready to demolish the rogue post, but was met by a company commander, a British officer, who begged me to let him sort out the situation ... The troops in the post were probably from his battalion, of the Rajputana Rifles I believe. Any attack on the post would involve open warfare between a largely Hindu company and our Muslim squadron. Some soldiers in the city had become unreliable and unstable, a rare event even in those difficult days ... It was difficult to prevent NCOs and sappers breaking out that night, particularly our Pathans who could not forgive the unprovoked slaughter of their officers any more than our officers and VCOs would accept the situation.[251]

Rees went and spoke with the squadron the next morning, and stated that an investigation would commence as soon as possible. Members of the Rajputana Rifles reported that they had been fired upon first. It was never clear who was in charge of the police or troops at the post.[252] In the end,

[246] Mss Eur C416 Col Peter Green, Indian Army, OIOC, BL.
[247] There is another description of the 2/8th Gurkhas chasing down a jeep that was known for shooting into crowds at railway stations. The occupants were reputed to be Sikh soldiers. The jeep was captured with the Deputy Assistant Quarter Master General of the 14th Para Brigade and a couple of other Sikh soldiers: Macartney, CO 2/8th Gurkhas, PBF, in *Red Flash*, No. 21, 1997, p. 8.
[248] Bristow, *Memories*, pp. 152–3.
[249] Hamid notes this in his journal; see *Disastrous*, p. 237.
[250] Capt. Nick Powell and Lt Bill Image.
[251] James, 'Transfer of Sovereignty', pp. 118–19.
[252] PBF Rough Conference Notes, 20 Aug. 1947, File 56, Rees Papers, OIOC, BL. There is no evidence of any board of inquiry taking place. The only fallout appears to be a point raised on 3 September, by Gen. Rees, that the CO of the 5/6th Rajputana Rifles needed to be replaced as soon as possible. See 'Notes for 4th Indian Division', 3 Sep. 1947, File 74, Rees Papers, OIOC, BL.

the members of the 33rd Squadron retained their composure and their discipline. Brig. D. A. Barker-Wyatt noted that 'it was surprising after the squadron's experiences in Amritsar, where they had seen so many people of their own religion massacred, but their discipline and loyalty prevailed.'[253]

The pressures upon senior officers began to be unbearable. The brigadier in charge of the 11th Indian Brigade sent a note to Gen. Rees on the 20th. He wrote: 'I have to request that I be replaced by another officer in my present appointment ... [I]n the last four days there have been two massacres of defenceless Muslims which could have been prevented if I had the co-operation of the civil authorities. I now feel that I can not conscientiously continue to work under these circumstances.'[254]

Accusations continued on both sides. The magistrate of a sub-area in Sialkot accused the PBF: 'troops at present employed in Sialkot city are working against the interest of Muslims in that they are arresting Muslims from inside their homes and bringing them in as curfew breakers'. (Ironically, the battalion in question was commanded by a Muslim.) The commander defended his unit with these words: 'the Boundary force is impartially working to restore order. We are here to maintain law and order irrespective of communal spirits.'[255]

Nor was this the only issue between the army and civil authorities. Rees received word that the CO of the 1/12th Frontier Force Regiment had threatened to arrest and lock up the local magistrate for his apparent 'partiality'.[256] Concerns about the availability of weapons also continued. The 43rd Lorried Brigade reported that 80 per cent of the Muslim police

---

[253] Author's interview with Brig. D. A. Barker-Wyatt, 10 Sep. 2005. He privately published his experiences as a six-page article, 'Partition of India 1947: The Memoirs and Experiences of a Sapper Subaltern with the 2nd Indian Airborne Division'. He goes into some detail of the squadron carrying out difficult tasks as Sikhs, Hindus, and Muslims worked well together. He reported in the interview that the 4 (Bengal) Field Company was Pakistan-bound. The company was stopped on the Indian side of the border and ordered to give up their weapons and their equipment. A major fight almost ensued; it was ended only with the intervention of Lt Col M. C. A. Henniker and a meeting with the Indian Army officer involved. The men were allowed to proceed into Pakistan.

[254] 20 Aug. 1947, File 54, Rees Papers, OIOC, BL. Messervy made a telephone call on 22 August 1947 to the Deputy Chief of the General Staff, stating 'one Brigade commander and one Regimental Centre Commander [have] said that they were unwilling to continue to serve in the present conditions, because the orders they were receiving from the Civil [Service] appeared to be meant to increase the troubles and massacres rather than stop them. There must be something very wrong with the attitude of the Civil [Service] when British officers took this line' (Cat. No. R/3/1/171, OIOC, BL; also in Zafar, ed., *Disturbances*, pp. 358–9).

[255] 20 Aug. 1947, File 54, Rees Papers, OIOC, BL.

[256] See 20 Aug. 1947, File 71, Rees Papers, OIOC, BL.

in the Ferozepore district had gone, and that their weapons were not adequately guarded.[257]

Yet another issue arose on 21 August, this time with the 1/2nd Punjab Regiment.[258] The battalion, composed mostly of Dogras and Jat Sikhs, was stationed in Montgomery in Pakistan, and reports came in that both the Muslim police and civilians were attempting to antagonise the Hindu and Sikh troops. The commanding officer, Lt Col Gurbachan Singh, a Sikh, asked that his non-Muslim troops be moved as soon as possible.[259] The governor of the now-divided Punjab region (West Punjab), Sir Francis Mudie, wrote to Gen. Rees concerning Lt Col Singh. He called for Singh to be relieved of command, saying that 'Muslim League leaders say that they cannot go out to the villages to keep the Muslims in order for fear of being shot by Sikh soldiers. I cannot say that this fear is justified ... I do not know if Singh is normally communal, but there is no doubt about his being at present in an extreme state of communal excitement which makes his presence in Montgomery and other districts in command of Sikh troops extremely dangerous to the public.'[260]

At the same time that this report was generated, Savory received a letter highlighting a different point of view regarding Muslim–Sikh relations. The letter, from Lt Col Mahammed Siddeq, MC, 7/11th Sikhs, stated, in part: 'I belong to West Punjab and being a Muslim have no choice but to serve in Pakistan. I am a most disappointed person today. The Indian Army is systematically being destroyed ... to satisfy the politicians ... I love my Sikhs.'[261]

PBF units attempted to intercept the armed mobs before they caused damage to defenceless villages or sections of cities throughout the Punjab. As Maj. P. H. James noted: 'Occasionally we arrived in time to save a village and to disperse or destroy some of the attackers, but often we only knew of the event when we observed smoke from burning homes some miles away.'[262] Col Fergus Macartney noted that at times he was successful in quelling violence, such as when his battalion was sent into the Railway Station area of Lahore. He reported: 'Our really hard work then started – continuous patrolling day and night both on foot and in motor transport. I'm glad to say I got my area under control quickly, and

[257] Aug. 1947, File 23, Rees Papers, OIOC, BL.

[258] A number of sources have cited this battalion as a 'problem' unit. See Jeffrey, 'The Punjab Boundary Force', p. 510; Macartney, in Red Flash, No. 21, 1997, p. 9; and Rees Papers, OIOC, BL.

[259] 21 Aug. 1947, File 54, Rees Papers, OIOC, BL.

[260] 23 Aug. 1947, File 51, Rees Papers, OIOC, BL.

[261] 27 Aug. 1947, Savory Papers, NAM.

[262] James, 'Transfer of Sovereignty', p. 118.

in fact we opened fire twice, each time on gangs of Muslim hooligans killing a stray Hindu.'[263] Brig. R. C. B. Bristow, commander of the Dogra Regimental Centre in Jullundur and then the 11th Indian Brigade, noted a short but brisk engagement:

I was returning to the Cantonment ... when suddenly out of the left I spotted a large Jatha advancing on the City [Jullundur] ... [T]he Muslims were then concentrated in certain areas ... only lightly guarded through lack of troops ... I was being followed by a jeep of the Brigade Defence Platoon with three Gurkhas and a Bren gun ... ordering the Gurkhas into action ... [A]fter an ominous pause a few Sikhs with firearms emerged, and began to skirmish towards us with all the skill of trained soldiers ... [T]he Gurkhas responded to each rush with a determined burst of fire, and soon brought the attack to a halt ... [T]hat incident showed that large armed Jathas could be dispersed by a few resolute soldiers, who were prepared to fire.[264]

The commandant of the 14th Punjab Regimental Centre summed up his views succinctly:

no one was prepared for the wave of communal feeling that surged amongst the population ... [I]t must however be placed on record the steadfast loyalty of all ranks in the regiment ... [A]ll ranks carried out their duties often in the most trying circumstances to the best of their abilities and without any complaints ... [T]he centre provided a mobile column for the policing of Ferozorpore after the civil police ceased to exist.[265]

Near the end of August, commanders reported tensions among the different companies of one battalion of the 10th Baluch Regiment. One dispute came to a head, with the Dogra company and Punjabi Musalman company nearly coming to blows. The news reached Auchinleck, who called for the removal of the Dogra company to India.[266] Lt Gen. Tuker referred to this in his journal for 28 August, noting that 'the Punjab Boundary Force is now going communal. That is no wonder. At Delhi they want my 5th Division to come up and replace the now tired 4th Division. I have said that I do not recommend it as 5th should crack up sooner than the PBF since the 5th have been at this civil disturbance business for a year with hardly a pause.'[267]

---

[263] Macartney, in *Red Flash*, No. 21, 1997, p. 7.   [264] Bristow, *Memories*, p. 167.

[265] Cotton, 8002–68, NAM.

[266] See PBF Combined Log 25 and 27 Aug. 1947, File 62, Rees Papers, OIOC, BL. See also 'Secret Report on the Punjab Disturbances', p. 16, Box 71/21/10/4, Tuker Papers, IWM: 'the officer in charge [of Baluch troops] is under close arrest pending a court martial, troops have been confined to barracks and the CO has been suspended'.

[267] Tuker, *Memory*, pp. 399–400. Tuker went on to say, 'Punjab Police completely communal now. I replied that there was only one way of getting permanent peace in the Punjab and that was to concentrate all Gurkha battalions up there and Madrassis

The Punjab Police Special Branch was reporting that neither the police nor the army was up for the challenge. One report, on 30 August 1947, stated that 'the situation in Montgomery district deteriorated considerably, the Dogra and Sikh troops operating in the district having been responsible for it to some extent'.[268] While a secret report filed in September 1947 confirmed the Baluch accusation, it contradicted several points made by some observers in the Punjab, as well as Lt Gen. Tuker's comments. It explicitly stated that there were no incidents in East Punjab of any troops being involved in violence, and went on to state that some companies from the Baluch battalion in question in West Punjab appeared to have attacked non-Muslim refugees. It stated that the CO was under arrest and the troops were confined to barracks, and declared that 'this is the only case of the Army taking a communal turn'.[269]

Reports from this period describe a variety of situations involving the army. Lt Col R. N. P. Reynolds, from the 2/9th Gurkhas, reported on movement of 5,000 Muslim civilians from East Punjab to the border with Pakistan, under the protection of a company from the Mahar Regiment commanded by a Hindu major. Reynolds noted that Hindu police in the area were communal, and recounted how, as the column of civilians came to the border area: 'I asked at the police station if [five dead Muslim civilians] could be removed, I was informed it was not in their area, and they didn't seem to be interested. The police station was on other side of the road.'[270]

As noted previously, most members of the Punjab Police, Muslims and Sikhs included, could be communally focused. As a senior British officer, then still serving in the Punjab Police, noted, 'it would be quite wrong to say that the Punjab Police were free of communalism . . . [I]t could hardly be expected of them to maintain an entirely impartial attitude when members of their own religion were involved.'[271] The Royal Garhwal Rifles was also commended for its professionalism when dealing with escorting Muslim refugees to Pakistan, as well as for its impartiality in dealing harshly with Sikhs who wished to attack the refugees.[272]

When the Joint Defence Council (JDC) met on 25 August, members called for the end of the PBF and final division of the units to

---

and other reliable people and all guns and tanks and knock the Sikhs clean out of the ring. Put the area under martial law with a military governor and deal with it.'

[268] Zafar, ed., *Disturbances*, pp. 368–9; also NDC Accession No. S. 415.
[269] 'Secret Report on Punjab Disturbances', Box 71/21/10/4, Tuker Papers, IWM.
[270] Mss Eur D917 Lt Col R. N. P. Reynolds, OIOC, BL.
[271] Mss Eur F161/145 India Police, 'Punjab Police (Gamsford)', Aug. 1947, OIOC, BL.
[272] Box 71/21/10/4, Tuker Papers, IWM.

assignment in Pakistan and India.[273] At the same time that the JDC was calling for an end to the PBF, the 5th Indian Brigade accused Sardar Baldev Singh, the defence minister, of providing weapons to Sikhs in the fighting.[274] On the same day, a *Times* correspondent openly accused Hindu and Sikh soldiers of standing by while violence was perpetrated against Muslims.[275] The *Hindustan Times* took its cue from the London *Times* and printed an article on the 27th, claiming that British officers of the PBF and British ICS had not risen to the occasion, but had allowed the atrocities to go on.[276]

In spite of all this, many still believed that the PBF had carried out its duties to the best of its ability, and that it remained a viable force. Gen. Savory wrote to his wife that 'Things in the Punjab are very bad, with Sikhs going quite mad … [T]he troops have been quite remarkable, however, one does wonder how much longer will they be able to stand the communal strain … [T]he partitioning of the Indian Army is going with great speed. The poor old Indian Army. It is too sad … British officers can do nothing except to try to keep the two Dominion armies stable and stop them from becoming violently communal.'[277] Other officers felt that the situation was much more tenuous.[278] By the end of August 1947, the PBF had suffered twelve killed and thirty-two wounded.[279]

---

[273] Gen. Rees wrote rough notes stating that the force should be disbanded in light of tensions rising to a near-explosive point. See Jeffrey, 'The Punjab Boundary Force', p. 515. However, other historians claim that during the meeting he defended the PBF, which is consistent with his actions during this period. Rees may have agreed to disband the force, but he wanted the decision to be made by Auchinleck and himself, not by the politicians, whom he blamed for the communal violence.

[274] 25 Aug. 1947, File 61, Rees Papers, OIOC, BL.

[275] See article in *The Times*, 'Massacres in the Punjab – Muslims butchered by armed mobs of Sikhs', 25 Aug. 1947. As noted by Mountbatten's private secretary Campbell-Johnson on 27 August 1947: 'Pete Rees received very few thanks from either side for his efforts to carry out a task of unparalleled difficulty. Without the wholehearted backing of the Governments and the Press on both sides, the positions of the PBF and its commander became rapidly untenable, and otherwise steady and experienced troops began to feel the tug of communal loyalties deeper even than their military discipline' (*Mission*, p. 176).

[276] Hamid, *Disastrous*, p. 239. Campbell-Johnson, *Mission*, also stated that on the 27th Mountbatten was being persuaded that there was a need to disband the PBF; however, he was clear about its performance: 'the PBF was undoubtedly the best military answer to the problem, he was ready to concede that in this instance psychological reasons might outweigh purely military ones' (p. 174).

[277] 27 Aug. 1947, 7603-93-80, Savory Papers, NAM.

[278] 'Trouble started in the mixed regiments of the 43 Bde, 1/Baluch and 1/2 Punjab. They became close to being non-effective, particularly the 1/2 Punjab with its Sikh CO. They had to be removed from the Brigade and broken up.' This refers to the officer discussed previously who was causing problems on the 21st: Macartney, in *Red Flash*, No. 21, 1997, p. 9.

[279] Misc Correspondence, 'Casualties', Oct. 1947, Rees Papers, OIOC, BL.

Did the army lose cohesion and become communal?

The decision to disband the PBF was taken overnight on 1/2 September.[280] Gen. Rees issued a memo to his troops on 31 August, ordering units to release companies and squadrons to either Pakistan or India, based upon their communal background. Rees stated, 'there was a good measure of confidence that the PBF would be adequate to deal with any situation likely to arise. Its units had no trace of communal feeling and all over India expressions of goodwill were received ... [I]n the event the ingrained mutual trust of generations dissipated exceedingly rapidly.'[281] Others had a more nuanced response to what was happening. One British officer noted that 'Due to the atrocities committed here and I don't think there can be any worse in history, it is quite natural that the troops in the PBF should get affected to any small extent they have been but the incidents in this respect are negligible. Unfortunately they have been exaggerated.'[282]

The 'newer' regiments, the Mahar and Bihar, generally performed well during the disturbances. Their ranks had not been recruited from the Punjab, which meant they were less likely to be pulled by conflicting loyalties. As Brig. Bristow noted: 'those living at a distance from and unaffected by the new border [were] more prepared to do their duty, especially men of low caste like the Mahars, who were not fanatical about religion'. He also recorded that 'it [the Mahar regiment] did splendid work [with a Sikh as the commanding officer] ... [A]s a [single] class only unit recently recruited they were anxious to prove themselves good soldiers by doing their duty and succeeded, for Muslims acclaimed them as their saviours.'[283] Another British officer from the Gurkha Rifles

---

[280] The Joint Defence Council meeting held on 29 August 1947 decided to end the role of the PBF. For specifics, see Kirpal Singh, ed., *Partition of the Punjab*, pp. 503–8. On 1 September, after an outbreak of violence, witnesses at Ambala Cantonment Station accused soldiers, predominantly Sikh, of not doing enough for dying and wounded Muslims who arrived on a train. The soldiers plus one officer were put under arrest by the lieutenant colonel of the 2/1st Gurkha Rifles, who happened to be travelling through: Tuker, *Memory*, pp. 436–7. The one key issue that is not discussed in any great detail is that some reported examples of troops behaving inappropriately could possibly have been Indian State Forces, taken by the media and politicians as regular Indian Army forces. There is nothing but overwhelming evidence demonstrating that many of the Indian State Forces actively took part in the violence and at times specifically sought to kill Indian Army pensioners and families of active duty soldiers, NCOs, VCOs, and officers.

[281] 'Draft Report', File 62, Rees Papers, OIOC, BL.

[282] 'Notes from a British Officer in the PBF', 29 Aug. 1947, Box 71/21/10/4, Tuker Papers, IWM.

[283] Bristow, *Memories*, p. 176, and Tuker, *Memory*, pp. 446 and 449.

discussed the issue of Punjabi recruited regiments in more detail, recalling

... [m]ixed composition patrols when British officers had done very well. There had been no incidents between troops though tension was definitely growing but complaints were dealt with and disciplinary action taken if necessary. This I feel was entirely due to the few remaining British officers who moved freely amongst all troops. Muslim officers worked flat out to protect their own community and they were kept in hand by British officers. Hindu and Sikh officers had to be persuaded in most cases to do their duty ... as will be appreciated the most effective troops were non-Muslim or non-Punjabi Hindu. The Christian and Mahar troops stood very high in my estimation as they were impartial and worked extremely hard ... Hindu and Sikh performance was entirely down to the British officer.[284]

Such comments have prompted both contemporary and retrospective observers to ask: why did the army not deploy troops in the Punjab that had been recruited from elsewhere? There are several reasons, but the most important is that there were simply not enough troops available from other areas of the country to carry out the task of policing the Punjab. The Indian Army had traditionally targeted the Punjab for recruitment, and Second World War recruitment had followed this tradition.[285] Alternative solutions, such as requests to deploy British Army and Gurkha units along the new border, were often stymied by political considerations; for example, Nehru's objections prevented deployment of British troops. (The Gurkhas did deploy several battalions, and these performed well.) It should also be noted that Punjabi-recruited regiments generally functioned well as Aid to the Civil Power outside the Punjab.[286] The future president of Pakistan, Mohammad Ayub Khan, who served as a brigadier on Maj. Gen. Rees' staff, stated openly:

there was severe criticism of the Boundary Force and I also came in for a deal of blame ... [T]he Boundary Force was doomed to failure from the beginning ... [T]his was the unhappiest period of my life. I had never before seen anything so terrible and brutal. Women and children were mutilated and innocent people butchered mercilessly. All human qualities seemed to have been snuffed out and the whole edifice of culture and civilization crumbled during these terrible weeks ... I used to ask myself, 'what can be done to stop this madness?'[287]

---

[284] 'Letter from a Gurkha Rifles Officer', Box 71/21/4/6, Tuker Papers, IWM.
[285] See Talbot, *Punjab and the Raj*, for more background in the role of the Punjab within the British Indian Empire. See Omissi, *The Sepoy and the Raj*, Marston, *Phoenix*, and Peers, 'Martial Races', for more discussion of the recruitment practices in the Punjab region.
[286] See Chapter 5, dealing with the Indian Army in Eastern Command.
[287] Mohammad Ayub Khan, *Friends Not Masters: A Political Autobiography* (Oxford University Press, 1967), pp. 15–17.

Nehru, the newly created prime minister of India, sent Rees a letter on 3 September, discussing the ongoing situation but mentioning the military only in passing:[288]

I have visited the Punjab on three occasions during the last 16 days and I have visited many of the districts and had long chats with the district officials and military commanders there ... In the East Punjab the chief trouble has been due to the organised Sikh Jathas functioning often with the connivance of the police, the petty local authorities and sometimes even some soldiers. In the West Punjab there have been no such Jathas but Muslim gangs have functioned in the same way in many places aided by the police and local authority ... I think the intelligence system has been rather weak in the past and the PBF as it was too thinly spread out over all this area to keep full control over the situation.[289]

The *Civil and Military Gazette* wrote on 7 September that 'The Indian Army has always been regarded as a disciplined force by the bulk of the population. There have been no complaints of lack of discipline, nor has there been any instance of troops having been participating in looting. There have been several instances of partiality and communal bias. There have been reckless shootings and their co-operation with the civil authority has been lacking.'[290] Field Marshal Auchinleck wrote a positive assessment of the situation to Gen. Rees on 13 September; he congratulated him on his excellent work and stressed that, while the PBF would have been suitable for normal Aid to the Civil Power duties, the situation in August was on a completely different scale. No one had anticipated what had occurred, and Auchinleck pointedly commented on the collapse of civil administration and police, which had forced a burden upon the PBF beyond their capabilities.[291] Governor Jenkins offered a different opinion in a meeting back in the UK on 14 October 1947: 'He put the tragedy down to the failure of the Indian Army in the Border Force to take action against their own community.'[292] Why he made this statement at this juncture is not clear, particularly since he had explicitly stated the opposite to Rees in August 1947. He appears to be shifting blame from the ICS to the army, despite ample evidence, documented

---

[288] Only a few weeks previously, as noted by Campbell-Johnson, 'Nehru had indicated that he was very impressed with Rees' (*Mission*, p. 175).

[289] 3 Sep. 1947, File 73 Misc Correspondence, Rees Papers, OIOC, BL.

[290] 7 Sep. 1947, File 67 Press Cuttings, Rees Papers, OIOC, BL. It was reported on 4 September that three Sikh civilians had been killed by members of the 1/12th FFR; on 2 September, a magistrate was killed by Muslim soldiers. See File 68, 'Personal Logs', Rees Papers, OIOC, BL.

[291] Auchinleck to Rees, 13 Sep. 1947, No. 1256, Auchinleck Papers, University of Manchester; also in Connell, *Auchinleck*, p. 911. See also Auchinleck's comments in Hamid, *Disastrous*, pp. 248–9.

[292] Moon, ed., *Wavell: The Viceroy's Journal*, p. 436.

throughout the period, that while the ICS and police in the Punjab had ceased to function as institutions the army had not.[293]

The final report on the role of the PBF was published in November 1947. It included the following statements:

the civil administration ... virtually ceased to function ... [T]he police became completely partisan ... [T]he troops of the PBF were subjected to a strain which must be unprecedented ... [W]ell before [15 August] the intelligence sources were drying up. The British police and ICS officers were leaving and where their successors were concerned, the communal factor came very much into the consideration ... [T]he intelligence machinery itself virtually ceased to function – personnel were split and scattered, suspicion and hatred permeated the ranks of those who had worked together efficiently, the whole civil government machinery of collection, collation, timely dissemination to all intents and purposes went out of commission ... [T]he army, operating in the aid to the civil power, naturally relies mainly on the intelligence services of the civil government. Already in the Punjab, however, it had become clear that the army must supplement these by its own efforts ... [This] had become apparent in April/May and considerable efforts made to build up an efficient supplementary system of army intelligence. But of course the building up of an intelligence system takes time and continuity of key personnel.[294]

Maj. Gen. Rees was more direct: in a letter to Gen. Sir Richard O'Connor, the adjutant general of the British Army at the time, he stated bluntly: 'I am sure [Indian and Pakistani politicians] will realize that it was only the PBF that stood between them and complete chaos and anarchy.'[295]

The Indian Army was, essentially, set up to act as a police force, providing support to the civil police, who were expected to provide the intelligence required for effective operations. The district commissioner for Lahore and Amritsar, in documenting his experiences of this period, wrote: 'As regards the military and security aspects of partition operations. I think the outstanding lesson which we learned was [the] critical importance of first class intelligence.'[296] This was a system that had been proven effective in fifty years of operations.

The PBF, initially comprising only five brigades,[297] was asked to cover twelve districts[298] within the Punjab: an area comprising 37,500 square

---

[293] See letter of 14 Aug. 1947, File 51 Misc. Drafts and Reports, Rees Papers, OIOC, BL.

[294] Report of the PBF, Nov. 1947, L/WS/1/1134, OIOC, BL.

[295] Rees to O'Connor, 15 Nov. 1947, Box 6/29, O'Connor Papers, Liddell Hart Centre, KCL.

[296] Mss Eur F409 George Brander, ICS, OIOC, BL.

[297] The 5th Indian, 11th Indian, 14th Para, 114th Indian, and 43rd Lorried Brigades. Many of the battalions were under strength for both men and officers; see Jeffrey, 'The Punjab Boundary Force', p. 498, and Tuker, Memory, p. 447.

[298] 20 Jul. 1947, Mountbatten Papers, OIOC, BL.

miles and a population of 14.5 million, many of whom were demobilised soldiers.[299] Many of the units that made up the PBF came from regiments that recruited heavily in the Punjab.[300] These men were called upon to protect the lives of people who might be implicated in the killing of their own families.

No one could have predicted the level of violence that erupted and the fact that the police and the civil administration, already under incredible communal pressure, ceased, for all intents and purposes, to operate with any cohesion. Their breakdown left the PBF to handle the situation as best they could, operating under strength and in a situation of unprecedented social disruption. Lt Gen. Sir Francis Tuker commented that 'many people were encouraged to kill that summer by the almost total collapse, in the Punjab, of the legal sanctions which normally operate in civil society to inhibit such behaviour. "It appears as if there is not Government ruling over this area", wrote a Jemadar of the Indian Army, "everybody [at] present [is] at liberty to kill as many [people] as he likes".'[301]

Although there were instances of subunits not performing their duties, there were many more examples of professionalism maintained, at times in situations of extreme stress. As noted above, the Indian Army outside the Punjab performed well in IS duties; even formations that served in the Punjab, but did not serve with the PBF, carried out their duties. An internal report from GOC HQ Eastern Command specifically praised the 80th Indian Brigade, noting that 'the behaviour of the Indian soldier is almost beyond praise. He has shown to the whole district that the Indian soldier has no communal feeling in the execution of his duty.'[302]

An officer serving with the 25th Indian Brigade in northern Punjab vividly recalls the tensions at the time, as well as the process of splitting up the units within the brigade. He highlighted an issue that was raised in a variety of reports: the quality of available officers: 'the impartiality

---

[299] There are many misconceptions regarding the numbers of troops allocated to the PBF. Estimates have ranged as high as 55,000 soldiers; but documentary evidence indicates that total numbers, after reinforcements, never exceeded 25,000. See Campbell-Johnson, *Mission*, p. 139; Yasmin Khan, *Great Partition*, p. 129; Jeffrey, 'The Punjab Boundary Force', pp. 498–9; Bristow, *Memories*, p. 158; and Alex von Tunzelmann, *Indian Summer* (New York: Henry Holt, 2007), p. 196, for examples of this issue.

[300] Regiments such as the 12th Frontier Force Regiment, 13th Frontier Force Rifles, 1st Punjab, 2nd Punjab, 10th Baluch, and 17th Dogras recruited local Sikhs, Punjabi Musalmans, and Hindu Dogras into their ranks. Many of the regimental centres for the Indian Army were also based in the province.

[301] Tuker, *Memory*, p. 433; quote in Copland, 'Master', p. 697.

[302] 'Special Notes from GOC HQ Eastern Command dealing with the Riots', 7707–35, NAM.

of the British officers was the key stone to our discipline and efficiency'. He openly questioned the professionalism of one of the Pakistani senior officers in the brigade, and asserted that 'our units were very willing to do all they could to maintain law and order ... [S] ome of our units still comprised Hindus and Muslims. We had no fear that religious mania would affect the troops for they were loyal and well-disciplined under their officers ... [O]ur sepoys were magnificent in carrying out their awful and shocking duties and helping when they could irrespective of caste and religion, sometimes having to fire on their own co-religionists.'[303]

Brig. Bristow, who was engaged in Punjab operations during August 1947, however, summarised the gap in which the PBF found itself stranded, with doctrine and history on one side and the realities of the Punjab on the other: 'The normal internal security role of the army was to support the civil power in maintaining law and order, but we faced a crisis in which the civil power was ineffective, law and order had completely broken down, and the reliability of the troops varied.'[304]

While some subunits of the PBF did succumb to communal pressure, especially after 15 August, to make the blanket statement that the PBF failed in its role, whether due to the collapse of the Indian Army, to politics, or to communalism, is to radically oversimplify the complexities of the situation. It is possible that the PBF *did* fail in its mission to stop the violence. As this chapter has tried to demonstrate, the reasons why it may have failed had less to do with lack of discipline in the force during the violence, and more to do with factors that were outside its control. The fact that the PBF and the Indian Army, as institutions, did *not* collapse is a real and lasting testament to the professionalism of the force. As the events of 1947 clearly show, there were concerted efforts to undermine the integrity of the Indian Army from many of the same people who would later claim that the PBF was not viable and had possibly played a role in the violence in the Punjab. As Ian Copland noted, 'while recent work by Suranjan Das and Swarna Aiyer makes it clear that in many cases the aggressors operated in organized groups under "military style" leadership, apparently to a plan, researchers have yet to determine where and by whom these shadowy schemes were

[303] Maj. MacDwyer, 'Memoirs', pp. 135–49, 7809–3, NAM.
[304] Bristow, *Memories*, p. 164. The commander of the 14th Punjab Regimental Centre aired similar sentiments, declaring that 'No human was prepared for the wave of communal feeling that surged up in the civilian population ... It must be placed on the record the steadfast loyalty of all ranks in the regiment on account of the civil disturbances of the gravest kind' (Col J. C. Cotton, 8002–68, NAM).

devised or how they were implemented; nor has anyone succeeded in unravelling the links – that must surely have existed – between the actual perpetrators and the fire-brand Bengali, Bihari and Punjabi politicians'.[305]

The Indian Army went through a period of instability that could have destroyed any military organisation. Its experience in the events surrounding independence and partition is unique in the annals of military history and decolonisation. No other force has had to deal with such extreme and varied pressures. The communal violence that erupted in the Punjab in March 1947 and continued into November, with varying degrees of intensity,[306] tested the Indian Army at the same time that major changes were occurring in its structure.[307]

Many of the decisions taken over the previous two years – 'public' INA trials, demobilisation, division of the army – only increased the difficulties for a force asked to serve as police, government, and military in a region that was tearing itself apart. Looking at the whole picture, it seems beyond question that the PBF did what it could. That issues arose with some subunits exhibiting partisan behaviour is not in question; but to claim that the PBF did not succeed in any way is inaccurate. It is not an exaggeration to say that, without the intervention of the PBF, the number of people killed in the Punjab could easily have been double the number listed today. The Indian Army was essentially asked to prevent, or to attempt to contain, a civil war erupting among the various ethnic and religious groups from which its own soldiers, officers, and VCOs were drawn. The fact that a small proportion of troops demonstrated bias is surprising only because it was not more widespread. Any military force confronted with the carnage of the Punjab would have been hard pressed indeed trying not only to stop the killings, but also to prevent its own units from becoming emotionally involved in the situation, even if they had to become physically involved. It is hard to determine whether the Indian Army was close to disintegration, due to the fact that there are

[305] Copland states later in his article: 'I want to conclude by suggesting that the question of responsibility for the east Punjab massacres cannot begin and end with the Akalis [Princely States] and their princely allies, but must also comprehend the Congressmen at the Centre who sent wholly wrong and mischievous signals to the Sikh perpetrators. During the six months that the killings went on, the Union government did virtually nothing to stop them' ('Master', pp. 659 and 703).

[306] Swarna Aiyar divided the violence into three different phases: three weeks of March, confined to the West Punjab; April–July, sporadic outbreaks; and August, sustained incidents, which peaked during the week of 13th to the 19th: Aiyar, 'Anarchy', pp. 16–17.

[307] See Chapter 6 for a detailed discussion of the demobilisation, division, and nationalisation of the Indian Army.

minimal examples, but what was worrying for some was that some units did exhibit communal feelings, and that was damning and fearful enough for many since, if the army had collapsed in the Punjab, there would have been nothing left but anarchy.

In a letter written in 1970, Sir Francis Mudie stated the following key points regarding the PBF (which could not be substantiated from archival sources): 'the trouble with the PBF was that it was operating in a vacuum, an army responsible to no government ... [I]t weakened Rees's position ... and in fact there were instances of soldiers fighting amongst themselves and firing at their British officers or so it was reported to me ... General Rees did his best, but he had been given an impossible job and I was very sorry for him.'[308] It is clear that there were a few instances of this sort, but they appear from the documentary evidence to be very isolated events. As the GOC for Bihar and Orissa specifically commented, a common theme, 'It is interesting to note particularly amongst the fighting units when there are shared memories of past battles against a common enemy and proud knowledge of regimental achievement and tradition, that the strong ties of loyalty which bind the Indian soldier to his unit and his officer are not easily broken.'[309]

[308] Mss Eur F164, Sir Robert Francis Mudie Papers, 1970, OIOC, BL.
[309] Sep. 1947, Notes of GOC, Box 71/21/4/6, Tuker Papers, IWM.

Conclusion: The end of the British Indian Army

> The PBF may have been ineffective, but on a smaller scale, countless people were saved by the bravery of individuals who defied their co-religionists and sheltered, supplied or otherwise protected their neighbours.[1]

With the ending of the PBF's mission on 1 September, the British Indian Army's history, for all intents and purposes, also came to an end. Unfortunately, the violence did not, but continued on both sides

Figure C.1 End of the Raj © Imperial War Museums (Image No. HU 66178)

[1] Chester, *Borders and Conflict in South Asia*, p. 132.

338

of the border.[2] Unrest had spread to the streets of Delhi, and chaos reigned across the newly independent states of India and Pakistan. In September, two British battalions were brought into Delhi to help quell the violence, in direct contravention of decisions made before August 1947, which prohibited the use of British troops following partition.[3]

As the GOC of the PBF, Maj. Gen. Pete Rees was routinely vilified in the Indian press; following the PBF's dissolution, he was offered a senior position in the newly formed Military Evacuation Organization (MEO). This organisation, which was established on both sides of the border to facilitate evacuation of refugees, employed military personnel from both sides to provide transport and escort.[4] The organisation and its performance were generally commended throughout the remainder of 1947;[5] there were, however, some troubling reports regarding the poor performance of some units who were tasked with protecting refugees that were not of their caste.[6]

Col Mohammed Sher Khan was sent into East Punjab in September 1947 to report back to the supreme commander about the situation there. He advised that the violence appeared to be dropping in intensity, but suggested that one reason for this was lack of targets. He also addressed the fact that the number of attacks on the railways had begun to dissipate. He was scathing in his assessment of the state of the civil administration, bluntly declaring that it did not exist, and that the IP were not only still ineffective, but were actively involved in the violence and looting of Muslim communities that remained.

---

[2] Tuker, *Memory*, ch. 37, pp. 479–95, gives many accounts of military units attempting to deal with communal violence and evidence of units and commanders carrying out this difficult mission, even though the soldiers were beginning to falter in some units.

[3] Hamid, *Disastrous*, pp. 246–7. This was a major decision that was negotiated and debated throughout 1947, up to and including August. It was explicitly specified that British Army units would not be used in the Punjab, a decision that was agreed by both India and Pakistan. See many letters and correspondence regarding this issue in *TOP*, X–XII. There was also another request for British troops still in country to be used as a protection force for the various refugee camps; it stipulated that they would not be used in any 'military duties'. See both the 11th and 12th Meeting Emergency Committee Meetings, 8 and 16 Sep. 1947, DO 133/62, NA.

[4] Kirpal Singh, ed., *Partition of the Punjab*, item 183, 'Raising of the Evacuation Organization', pp. 544–6. See the various entries and correspondence covered *ibid.*, pp. 530–70, and 'Emergency Committee Papers and Minutes', DO 133/61–2, NA, for more details on the running of the MEO.

[5] The Prime Minister remarked that the MEO of the two Dominions 'seemed to be co-operating very satisfactorily': Minutes 23rd Meeting Emergency Committee Meeting, 17 Oct. 1947, DO 133/62, NA. Various authors have stated similar sentiments.

[6] See the various minutes from the Emergency Committee Reports for September–October; see DO 133/60–2, NA.

Khan was not alone in expressing feelings of exasperation towards the IP; other officials were much the same, including the governor, who reportedly stated, 'I would not be sorry if the Army shot them including their officers.'[7] Khan did report some issues with soldiers as well,[8] including that 'the non-Muslim soldiers do not provide adequate protection for the trains or columns ... [T]his does not apply to Gurkha or Garhwali troops or to a certain extent non-Punjabi troops, but if they are commanded by a non-Muslim officer other than a British officer then their action is also not as vigorous as it should be.'[9] Other reports, however, specifically stated that the same battalions did stellar work in protecting refugees. The 1/1st Punjab Regiment was commended for its services in Lahore, and the 1st Punjab Regimental Centre in Jhelum was commended for its efforts to protect more than 5,000 Sikh and Hindu refugees during the month of September.

The division of the army continued in the weeks leading up to and following independence, under the command of the supreme commander, Field Marshal Claude Auchinleck. Gen. Sir Reginald Savory reported in September,

The poor old Indian Army is in the process of being partitioned in spite of all that is happening we are succeeding to a great extent in unravelling the major units and transferring them to the right side ... [I]n spite of this momentum the traditions of the Indian Army are able to stand as the sole barrier between India and anarchy. The men are bewildered but still trying to do their duty. They are under great strain, with constant duties ... [plus the] still greater strain of communalism.[10]

The division process continued as various subunits moved out from different cantonments to either India or Pakistan, often escorted by

---

[7] 'Report on East Punjab Situation', 24 Sep. 1947, Mss Eur F164/14 Mudie, OIOC, BL.

[8] Tuker referred to the increased tensions as Muslim soldiers waited to be moved to Pakistan and to the fears of many from the Punjab for their families. He also reported Hindu troops killing and wounding fellow co-religionists who were attacking Muslim villages or refugees. It is hard to state that all the troops were communally biased, as many reports would contradict other rumours. See *Memory*, pp. 471–8.

[9] 'Report on East Punjab Situation', Mss Eur F164/14 Mudie, OIOC, BL; see subsection, 'Military', 24 Sep. 1947. Col Khan felt that the columns or trains with Muslim soldiers tended not to be attacked by Sikh *jatha*s or other militias. Interestingly, a lieutenant colonel from the Madras Regiment was accused of shooting at police in Delhi. He later apologised for losing his head, but relations between the police and army, already tense, became more so. See 'Minutes of Emergency Committee Meeting', 15th Meeting, 22 Sep. 1947, DO 133/62, NA.

[10] Letter to Gen. Scoones, Sep. 1947, 7603-93-81, Savory Papers, NAM. Gen. Bucher stated on 19 July 1948, in a letter to Gen. Savory, 'I have been doing a lot of touring [of regimental centres] and everyone from the Commanding Officer down is determined to maintain the old standards' (7603-93-82, Savory Papers, NAM).

troops from the same battalion or regiment. For example, the 1/16th Punjab Regiment was earmarked for Pakistan. The battalion left Eastern Command on 5 August and the Dogra and Sikh companies were left in Ramgarh, to join the Dogra Regiment and the 7th Battalion, Sikh Regiment.[11]

The transfer of the Sikh and Dogra companies from the 5/12th (Guides) Frontier Force Regiment illustrated the precariousness of the situation in both Dominions after partition. The Guides were stationed at Razmak on the frontier. The Dogra D Company was detached to the 3/4th Bombay Grenadiers at Thal on the frontier. When the battalion was ordered to move to India in September 1947, the train was attacked by Pashtun tribesmen. The Dogras and the Grenadiers were able to beat off the attack, but lost six men killed and twelve wounded. This episode shocked the officers, VCOs, NCOs, and soldiers in the Guides. The Sikh B Company still needed to be transported to India. The Sikhs were put on alert to move at an hour's notice, for over three weeks, as Supreme Command co-ordinated trains or trucks plus escorts for subunits moving to and fro. The Sikhs and the Muslims had a traditional farewell *bara-khana*. The battalion went out on 'road clearing' without the Sikh company. The Sikhs were put into trucks and moved towards India. The rest of the battalion did not know the move had occurred until they returned to barracks; only the lieutenant colonel and the subedar major were aware. Word reached the battalion that the Sikhs had arrived safely in Jubbulpore and joined the 7/11th Sikhs.[12]

The rest of the companies were filled with Punjabi Musalmans from the 7th Rajput Regiment[13] as well as soldiers from the regimental centre.[14] The 1/12th FFR served in the PBF; following the PBF's dissolution, it was shipped to Lyallpur in Pakistan with its Sikh and Dogra companies and spent the month of September escorting non-Muslim refugees to the India/Pakistan border. On 23 September, the battalion escorted its Sikhs and Dogras to the border, where they marched across the border to join the 1/2nd Punjab Regiment.[15] Lt Col J. C. Bell, 3/12th

---

[11] Lawford, *Solah Punjab*. Lt Col Lawford reported that the two companies 'said goodbye to the battalion for the last time, amid many manifestations of regret by all who were present' (*ibid.*, p. 280).

[12] Lt Gen. George MacMunn, *History of the Guides, 1922–1947* (Aldershot: Gale & Polden, 1950), p. 181.

[13] For a meticulously detailed history of the specifics of the very complicated division of the army (including where specific companies from specific battalions were assigned during the months of September, October, and November 1947), see Gaylor, *Sons of John Company*, as well as the many Indian Army regimental histories published in the past forty years in the UK, Pakistan, and India.

[14] Condon, *Frontier Force Regiment*, pp. 560–1.   [15] *Ibid.*, p. 564.

Frontier Force Regiment, summed up many sentiments when he sent a note to Gen. Savory and Field Marshal Auchinleck from Pakistan on 18 October 1947, stating that 'we are all Muslim now ... [I]t was a sad moment ... [T]he senior Sikh VCO wept in my office as he was about to go to India. In spite of this I think everyone felt that it was time to part.'[16]

As discussed earlier, the issue of the Brigade of Gurkhas was still being negotiated as independence dawned. Gurkha units had carried out IS duties throughout India, and been commended for their professionalism. Their conditions of future service, whether with the British Army, the Indian Army, or options for return to civil life, remained under discussion throughout September and October 1947. The delay, indecision, and impending division of troops caused considerable consternation for VCOs, NCOs, and soldiers. Reports from September indicated that more than half of the Gurkhas were willing to serve in the Indian Army, including Gurkhas from the regiments destined for the British Army.[17]

On 3 November 1947, the 1/2nd King Edward's Own Gurkhas came close to mutiny. Frustrated by concern and tension about their future, they refused to parade. The men had been incorrectly informed that they were to move to the Punjab, which to some meant movement to Malaya and British service. They resented having not been consulted about whether they wanted to opt for India, Britain, or Nepal.[18]

The tripartite agreement resolving the Gurkhas' future was concluded on 9 November 1947 among Britain, India, and Nepal. India received twelve of the twenty battalions. Four regiments (eight battalions) were selected for British service; these held a referendum for the men to decide their future: remain with the Indian Army, transfer to the British Army, or be discharged. By January 1948, 3,500 Gurkhas had opted to remain in British service,[19] and were immediately shipped to Malaya, just as the Malayan Emergency began.[20]

---

[16] Letter to Gen. Scoones, 18 Oct. 1947, 7603-93-83, Savory Papers, NAM; also 18 Oct. 1947, No. 1268, Auchinleck Papers, University of Manchester.

[17] Auchinleck to Scoones, 15 Sep. 1947, No. 1259, Auchinleck Papers, University of Manchester. This result surprised many British officers, who thought that more than half would want to serve with the British Army.

[18] In the end, just over 300 out of 700 troops from the battalion chose to remain in British service. See Auchinleck to Chiefs of Staff, UK, L/WS/1/1025, OIOC, BL; Gregorian, *British Army*, p. 41; Omissi, 'A Dismal Story?', p. 211; and Stevens, *History of the 2nd King Edward VII's Own Gurkha Rifles, vol. III*, pp. 312–13.

[19] Gregorian, *British Army*, p. 42, and Omissi, 'A Dismal Story?', p. 212.

[20] The British Gurkha regiments were under strength and, following partition, lacking in veteran VCOs, NCOs, and soldiers. Both of these factors would cause issues for Malaya Command as they attempted to get to grips with the violence of the Malayan Emergency. See Daniel Marston, 'Lost and Found in the Jungle', in Hew Strachan, ed., *Big Wars and Small Wars* (London: Routledge, 2004), pp. 96–114, for more details.

Auchinleck's end of tenure as supreme commander

The PBF's disbandment also signalled Field Marshal Auchinleck's final official operational mission. However, in practice, some 2,000 British officers remained after independence, serving in positions from the highest levels of the Pakistan and Indian Armies to battalion commands on both sides of the divided subcontinent. As the two fledgling armies attempted to contend with communal conflict in northern India, the two newly formed states prepared for war as the crisis in the Kashmir intensified.

For many people, the British Indian Army truly came to an end with the resignation of Auchinleck as the supreme commander. His position after the end of the PBF was in many ways the most difficult of his career. As the governments of India and Pakistan became increasingly hostile to one another, each sought more and more from the divided Indian Army, openly preparing for armed conflict. In addition to this pressure, Auchinleck also began to accuse the Indian government openly of failing to deal with the violence. His criticism was rooted in the expectation that it was only a matter of time before the press and the Indian government attempted to blame him and his staff for the deteriorating situation.[21]

Auchinleck was frank with Scoones about his fears for the future. In September 1947, he wrote:

our position as a neutral body trying to partition the Armed Forces to the equal advantage of both Dominions is not, as you will realize, exactly an easy one ... The Army has become infected with the communal virus ... [W]e expect not more than about 3,000 British officers out of a rough total of 9,000 to volunteer to remain on during Reconstitution ... [T]here are not enough officers ... to go around ... [T]he quality of such officers as there are is nothing like high enough to enable us to find sufficient officers of requisite experience and knowledge to fill the high command and staff appointments. This has been pointed out many times to both Governments and is still being pointed out by me ... I do not think, however, that facts such as this make much impression on people who are determined to nationalise the officer cadres as quickly as possible, which appears to be the case so far as the Indian Government is concerned. In Pakistan the authorities seem to be much more reasonable.[22]

While contending with these issues and the ongoing division of the armed forces, Auchinleck continued to plan for the drawdown of his HQ. The expected end date was 1 April 1948.[23]

---

[21] See Hamid's entries for 2 and 4 September 1947, in *Disastrous*, p. 245.
[22] Auchinleck to Scoones, 15 Sep. 1947, No. 1259, Auchinleck Papers, University of Manchester; also in Connell, *Auchinleck*, pp. 913–15.
[23] Hamid, *Disastrous*, p. 247.

Lt Col Hamid met with Auchinleck in Rawalpindi for one of the final times on 23 September, just after his family had been evacuated to Pakistan. According to Hamid, Auchinleck felt that HMG had let him down; he felt that Mountbatten was no longer impartial, and that his own position was becoming untenable. Hamid advised Auchinleck to stand down, and described him afterwards as 'a very sad man carrying within him a deep sense of failure'.[24]

Within days of this meeting, Mountbatten, now the governor-general of India, sent Auchinleck a letter stating that the supreme commander position was no longer considered workable by many members of the Indian cabinet. He advised Auchinleck frankly that criticisms of both the position and Auchinleck personally had begun back in August. Mountbatten went on to say that, while he had created the position especially to assist the two newly formed governments with the key administrative job of dividing up the armed forces in general and the army in particular, the Indian leadership remained suspicious of the position's true purpose. Mountbatten had asserted repeatedly to the Indian cabinet that operational control of the armed forces remained with them, through the current CinC, Gen. Lockhart, and it was clear that he could not argue any longer or, apparently, convince the Indian politicians. The only solution was for HQ, and Auchinleck's position, to go.[25]

On 28 September, Auchinleck delivered a report on the situation in India and Pakistan to the prime minister, chief of the Imperial General Staff, and the chiefs of the Air and Naval Staffs. His report, in two large parts, covered a wide range of issues, including tensions surrounding the division of the assets of the armed forces (describing India in this instance as difficult and Pakistan as co-operative), and the future of the Gurkha units.

Auchinleck's report also addressed some very contentious topics. One such involved the morale and retention of British officers who had chosen to 'stay on' after independence. Auchinleck described the officers' current state of mind: 'the conditions of massacre and bestiality of the worst kind in which many of these British officers have been working continuously for many weeks have sickened them. They have also lost faith in their cloth and in their men, of whom they were so proud

---

[24] Ibid., pp. 252–3.
[25] Mountbatten to Auchinleck, 26 Sep. 1947, No. 1260, Auchinleck Papers, University of Manchester; also in Connell, *Auchinleck*, pp. 915–19. Ismay sent Auchinleck a note stating that he had seen Mountbatten's note and felt it was the best solution, due to the tension with the Indian government. See Ismay to Auchinleck, 26 Sep. 1947, No. 1261, Auchinleck Papers, University of Manchester; partially reproduced in Connell, *Auchinleck*, pp. 919–20.

a short two months back.'[26] He went on to discuss an assessment of British officers serving on both sides of the recently divided Punjab, which stated bluntly that morale was lower than ever experienced in the past. The reasons for this low morale came down to '1. Disgust at the appalling scenes they were forced to see in the execution of their duty. 2. A sense of frustration owing to the almost total lack of aid and support from the civil authorities. 3. A conviction that the exercise of impartiality is no longer possible or indeed desired by those in authority. 4. A feeling that their efforts are entirely unrecognized by either Dominion Government.'[27] Many of the British officers were now calling to end their contracts within the following three months.

Auchinleck also reported that communal feelings were so heightened that it was only a matter of time before open hostilities occurred between the two states. He made it clear that British officers were to desist at once from any command positions if this was to occur. The Joint Defence Council made the Dominion governments aware of this fact, in the case of war.[28]

Auchinleck followed up this report with a damning letter to Gen. Sir Richard O'Connor, adjutant general of the British Army, on 3 October 1947, in which he declared 'in two short months unless conditions could have completely changed our fine army is gone, ruined ... British officers are disenchanted and have lost their magnificent morale and pride ... It is heartbreaking ... British officers have done splendidly and have been steady and loyal in the most terrible and distasteful circumstances ... [G]od help this country.'[29]

The pressure was mounting on Auchinleck to begin the process of winding down his HQ, moving up the original date of April 1948 to (at first) the end of 1947. He made it clear, in letters to Gen. Sir Geoffrey Scoones (then principal staff officer, Commonwealth Relations Office) and Mountbatten, that he was aware of the Indian government's desire to remove him and his staff,[30] but reminded Mountbatten that he also

---

[26] Auchinleck, 'Report on the Situation in India and Pakistan, 28 Sep. 1947, No. 1262, Auchinleck Papers, University of Manchester; partially reproduced in Connell, *Auchinleck*, pp. 920–4.

[27] *Ibid.* It stated that five British officers had been killed over a period of a week, trying to protect refugees on both sides of the border.

[28] *Ibid.*

[29] Auchinleck to O'Connor, 3 Oct. 1947, Box 7/13, O'Connor Papers, Liddell Hart Centre, KCL.

[30] He specifically stated to Scoones: 'as you know, there is a violent animosity towards my HQ, the JDC, and indeed any form of joint activity, which may help to secure anything for Pakistan at the expense of India, in the minds of the Indian Government, and they have put every possible pressure on Mountbatten to get rid of me and my HQ'

served the Pakistan government, and that they would have to be consulted as well.[31] A few days later, Auchinleck changed the proposed end
date for his position and command to 30 November, and recommended
that the Reconstitution Committee should also cease on that day.[32]

The JDC met on 16 October in Lahore, to discuss this and other
issues. Field Marshal Auchinleck reiterated his recommendation that
his HQ and position be terminated as of 30 November, and a heated
debate ensued. The Indian representatives agreed with the proposal, as
did Lord Mountbatten. The Pakistan representatives, including the
prime minister, Liaquat Ali Khan, were adamantly opposed to the
proposal, and determined that the Supreme HQ should remain open.
This allowed Auchinleck to more fully articulate his position:

My reasons for that recommendation are stated – as mildly as possible – in the
paper which is before the meeting. In the present atmosphere it has become
impossible for me and my officers to carry on with our task after November 30.
I am not prepared to keep my officers in this impossible situation. Continual
innuendos and accusations are being levelled against my HQ. I and my officers
cannot continue, in such circumstances, to perform a task for which co-operation
is necessary. I have not made this proposal in any desire to run away from the
completion of my responsibilities, but because of the situation I cannot for much
longer discharge those responsibilities.[33]

The debate continued, but the only resolution achieved in the meeting
was that the two states agreed to go away and discuss the ramifications
with their respective cabinets.[34]

Auchinleck had made up his mind and within two weeks HMG had
agreed with his proposal to close down the HQ and terminate his
command position.[35] The Indian Government had agreed as well, but
not the Pakistan Government.[36] As the wrangling continued, a larger
problem emerged: the Jammu and Kashmir crisis. On 24 October, 5,000

(Auchinleck to Scoones, 5 Oct. 1947, No. 1263, Auchinleck Papers, University of
    Manchester).
[31] Auchinleck to Mountbatten, 6 Oct. 1947, No. 1264, Auchinleck Papers, University of
    Manchester.
[32] Note for the Joint Defence Council Meeting to Be Held on the 16 of October in Lahore,
    13 Oct. 1947, No. 1266, Auchinleck Papers, University of Manchester.
[33] Minutes of the Joint Defence Council Meeting held on the 16 of October, No. 1267,
    Auchinleck Papers, University of Manchester; also in Connell, *Auchinleck*, pp. 925–9.
[34] The arguing continued between the senior leadership; see telegrams from Nehru to Ali
    Khan, 18 Oct. 1947, No. 1270, and Ali Khan to Nehru, 24 Oct. 1947, No. 1273,
    Auchinleck Papers, University of Manchester, for more details.
[35] It was formally announced on 13 November: Hamid, *Disastrous*, p. 282.
[36] See the various letters in Auchinleck Papers (University of Manchester), for the rest of
    October and early November, from No. 1271 onwards, for more specific debates and
    discussions.

tribesmen from the NWFP crossed the border to support the Muslims who had risen in opposition to any forced annexation by India. The Maharajah of Kashmir and Jammu announced on the 26th that the state would accede to India, and asked for Indian military support to deal with the resulting violence. The Indian government obliged, airlifting in a battalion of troops on 27 October. Gen. Sir Robert Lockhart, CinCI, could take no other course of action; Kashmir was now part of India, and providing military support did not violate any rules regarding the use of British officers in the field.

Auchinleck received word from Gen. Gracey (who was acting CinC Pakistan while Gen. Messervy was on leave) that Jinnah had ordered him on the evening of 27/8 October to send Pakistan army troops into Jammu and Kashmir. Gracey made it clear to Jinnah that such an order could not be obeyed; if it were, the 'stand down' order and withdrawal of all British officers would be in effect, since this action would constitute an invasion of Indian territory. Auchinleck flew to Lahore to meet with Jinnah and reiterated Messervy's points; Jinnah ultimately rescinded his order, but remained outraged with the situation.[37]

Auchinleck held his last meeting with the CinCs of both India and Pakistan, as well as with senior members of the Supreme Command, on 15 November. The senior commanders discussed the possibility of future outright war between the two Dominions; Auchinleck was not optimistic, and considered that there was no hope of reconciliation between the two states.[38]

As he made final preparations to depart office, Field Marshal Auchinleck refused to accept a peerage or any other award for which Lord Mountbatten had nominated him; he felt that he had failed in his mission and was quite low in spirits.[39] He advised Mountbatten, however, that there were others on his staff whom he believed were deserving of recognition for their hard work.

On 26 November 1947, Auchinleck left his residence in New Delhi and, with more than forty years of service in the Indian Army, ended his military career. Gen. Savory spoke on behalf of many officers, Indian and British, those who had remained in the Indian and Pakistan Armies as well as those who had retired or transferred service to the British Army, when he said 'Now he has gone. The flag no longer flies over his house.

---

[37] Telegram from Auchinleck to Chiefs of Staff, London, 28 Oct., 1947, No. 1275, Auchinleck Papers, University of Manchester. See also Hamid's entry for 28 October, in *Disastrous*, pp. 278–9.

[38] Hamid, *Disastrous*, p. 282.

[39] See letter from Mountbatten to Auchinleck, 8 Nov. 1947, reproduced *ibid.*, pp. 281–2.

The sentries have gone and he has gone. One of the best friends India ever had. And one on whom, at the last moment, the Indians turned. Sad. A great man who has done more for India than any living English-man and yet who during his last few months of office was misrepresented by the Indians for their own ends.'[40]

I witnessed the last, and perhaps the most fitting, tributes to Auchin-leck during a research visit to Pakistan and India in 2000. During a visit to Peshawar cantonment, a senior Pakistan general insisted on showing me personally what he considered the highlight of the tour. This was a monument to Field Marshal Auchinleck, erected at the heart of the cantonment, thanking him for all that he had done for the Pakistan Army. Later, in New Delhi, I had scheduled a meeting with a senior Indian Army general, one who had links to one of the cavalry regiments that I profiled in *Phoenix from the Ashes*. The general took me into the old CinCI office specifically to show me the room and desk where Auchinleck had worked during the Second World War and through to independence. He was immensely proud to be getting the desk in the near future, on the occasion of his promotion to full general.

Concluding comments

The final years of the Raj constituted one of the most trying periods in the history of the British and Indian interaction. The Indian Army was simultaneously vilified and expected to fill multiple political and security gaps as the pace of British withdrawal accelerated and the lack of a clear strategy became ever more apparent. The political leadership on both sides of the political divide – nationalists and HMG – failed to grasp the potential impact of many of their 'tactical' decisions, particularly those which involved the army. Ultimately, both groups expected the impos-sible from an army that became, in many places, the only line of defence against a communal holocaust that was exploding across northern India.

Other issues weighed heavily on the minds of many within the Indian Army during the summer of 1947. They watched as the nationalist political leadership aided and defended members of the INA and used them as a counterweight to the Indian Army. They watched as political parties enflamed communal violence in selected areas of the country for short-term gain. They watched as the Indian civil service and the Indian Police effectively ceased to function in northern India during the height of the civil war, leaving them 'holding the bag'. They watched as unimaginable horrors of violence committed against neighbours rose to

[40] 26 Nov. 1947, reproduced *ibid.*, pp. 284–5.

unheard-of levels in 1946 and 1947. Many of the army's professional soldiers lost family members and friends, and some of them, perhaps understandably, began to question what they were doing to protect the lives of others. The bitterest irony in all of this was the accusations by some nationalist leaders that the army was not doing enough to stop the violence. The strange request, in the summer of 1947, for the army to use maximum force to stop the violence, was for most of its members yet another example of the lack of understanding and the hypocrisy that to them characterised both sides of the political discourse.

HMG decided to use the Indian Army in the traditional role of Imperial Reserve for operations in post-Second World War Asia. In doing so, they failed to recognise not only the colossal hypocrisy of this position – the use of Indian troops to re-impose imperial rule in non-British colonies – but also the political impact of this decision in India. This policy also made it manifestly obvious that HMG considered the deaths of Indian *jawan*s a more acceptable political cost than the lives of British conscripts who were in the process of demobilisation. In the face of this reality, it becomes all the more amazing that the Indian units and formations sent to French Indo-China and the Netherlands East Indies carried out their duties with professionalism.

The military leadership of the Indian Army bears the responsibility of not recognising the complete perceptual shift of the post-war period, particularly in terms of how the emerging states of India and Pakistan viewed their military resources. Auchinleck, in an attempt to deal with the INA as an institution, did not recognise the political impact of his decision to have the trials take place at the Red Fort in Delhi. Many senior commanders wanted above all to keep the army secure from any infection of communalism and politics, foreseeing its crucial role as the last bulwark against the rise of violence in 1946 and 1947.

The Indian Army's military leadership was fighting a losing battle, as became apparent by August 1947. The pressure of nationalism, communalism, and nationalist leadership narratives began to seep into the battle-hardened veteran formations as they looked towards their mutual – and separate – futures. While loyalty to the regiment was still important, there was now an unprecedented political change on the horizon, and it caused confusion and distress for soldiers, NCOs, VCOs, and officers. The difficulties in undertaking the division of the army, especially between Field Marshal Auchinleck and Lt Gen. Tuker, highlighted tensions among the senior leadership and officers about the Indian Army's future.[41]

---

[41] Among the middle part of the officer corps, there were those who were slow to accept the realities of partition. A future Pakistani officer, Maj. Ishaq Mohammed, commented to a

Close to a century of planning, assessment, and action had forged the Indian Army into a veteran force that was above whatever political disputes raged beyond its ranks. For the most part, the British Raj had succeeded in keeping it cocooned from the contentious politics of the day. However, the expansion of the army during the Second World War – and its subsequent contraction – had left behind a huge number of demobilised – and, in many cases, disenfranchised – and trained personnel, at a loose end in a fragmenting society. As a result of high-level policy decisions, the professionals who remained in the army had, as the political situation deteriorated, to contend with politicised and lethally skilled security forces who used their military training to take communal violence to unforeseen levels of organisation and ferocity.

Even in the face of this untenable situation, the Indian Army's experiences in the Second World War proved important. Its record of service in the war – its professionalism in the face of initial defeats; its willingness to assess, reform, and learn; its transformation into an integrated and nationally representative force; and its effective and ultimately victorious action – had created a lasting bond of *esprit de corps* among all ranks and ethnicities. This bond provided a firm foundation for the army to refer and hold on to, even in this most testing period of its history.

Contrary to what is asserted in many simplistic descriptions of the period,[42] the Indian Army as an institution did not collapse. There were incidents of subunits showing a lack of discipline. Considered against the whole spectrum of events, these are amazingly few, and mainly serve to point the larger question: what army in the world, then or now, could have done a more professional job under the circumstances, and held together as well overall? The Indian Army did *not* fall apart, and this alone is a considerable achievement. It is more so when considering that virtually all of India's civil institutions in northern India *did* fall apart in the run-up to independence and partition and, without the Indian Army holding fast in the final days of the Raj, the death rate and violence could easily have been multiplied many times over. It is a testament to the army that it stood its ground and did what it could do in the midst of a civil war, among its own people, and its members did not resort to widespread violence themselves.

---

fellow British officer not long before independence became official, 'If we get Pakistan, as I hope we will, we must ensure that we keep one united Indian Army' (author's correspondence with John Grigor Taylor and mentioned in other interviews as well).

[42] See comments by Kirpal Singh in *Partition of the Punjab*, p. xxviii, as an example: 'Some of the most gruesome tragedies were enacted in the area entrusted to it [PBF] by its own units because the military force under General Rees was infected with communalism.' The evidence does not support such a forthright statement.

As stated in the Introduction, Maj. Gen. J. C. Bruce, the commander of Lahore area, speaking at a press conference on 3 June 1947, may still provide the best and most succinct summary of the Indian Army's position, responsibilities, and beliefs during this period:

The Army is not an inferior organization, we do not take sides, we do not fight for one community against another. Unfortunately in all countries and amongst all communities there are wicked and selfish men who are only too ready to stir up trouble and to seek personal gain from the misery of others ... [T]he enemies against which we have now to be prepared to operate, are, therefore, brutality and chaos in whatever form these threats may present themselves and I am confident that all ranks will not only recognize their clear duty in this respect, but will be proud to show once again that forces of goodwill and sound commonsense always prevail ... [W]hen you see fellow countrymen, perhaps even your own friends or relations, either the victims of brutal assaults, or else, guided by thoughtless or evil agitation into unworthy acts or violence, you must not give way to your personal feeling for one moment. You must remember that you are on the spot as the impartial instrument of justice and truth ... You must restrain the evil doers. You must protect and secure those who have suffered or are in danger. You must not be overcome by any desire for revenge ... In this way you will have shown yourself a worthy member of the great Indian Army to which you belong and will have held up the noble tradition of your unit.

The vast majority of the units in the Indian Army of this period can declare without hesitation that they upheld these proscriptions. Led by one of the most conscientious and surely the most forward-thinking CinCI that they had ever had, Field Marshal Auchinleck, the Indian Army could take pride in the fact that they did so despite pressure to act otherwise by numerous future political leaders in India and Pakistan, and lacking clear political leadership from HMG. In the final analysis, the historical record shows unequivocally that the vast majority of Indian Army soldiers, NCOs, VCOs, and officers were as loyal to one another and to the regiment as many previous generations had been, and under far more trying circumstances. Bonded by the battle experiences of the Second World War and by a shared sense of pride and professionalism that crossed ethnic, religious, and regimental boundaries, the army remained overwhelmingly cohesive and impartial, even when standing alone in the midst of the civil war that had erupted among their own villages and families. Ultimately, with only itself to rely upon, the Indian Army in the last days of the Raj was indeed a rock in an angry sea.

Bibliography

PRIMARY SOURCES

UNPUBLISHED

India Office Papers, British Library (OIOC, BL): printed archives
L/MIL/5/857 Lecture on Indianisation to the Imperial Defence College 1931
L/MIL/5/886 Chatfield Committee
L/MIL/7/5483 Reorganisation of the Indian Army 1920–1934
L/MIL/7/16968 Frontier Operations 1935
L/MIL/7/16971 Frontier Operations Waziristan 1937
L/MIL/7/19088 Reports of Officers Commanding Eight Indianised Units
L/MIL/7/19154 Indianisation
L/MIL/7/19155 Indianisation
L/MIL/7/19156 Indianisation
L/MIL/7/19157 Indianisation
L/MIL/7/19158 Indianisation
L/MIL/17/1/12/42 Report of the Committee Appointed by the Government of India to Investigate the Disturbances in the Punjab
L/MIL/17/5/531 Army Instructions 1941
L/MIL/17/5/1778 Indianisation
L/MIL/17/5/1793 Investigation of Strength and Composition of the Army in India 1931
L/MIL/17/5/1800 Indianisation of the Army 1938
L/MIL/17/5/1803 Plan for Modernisation
L/MIL/17/5/1805 Plan for the Modernisation and Re-organisation of the Army in India 1939
L/MIL/17/5/1816 Report on India Command Internal Defence Exercise 1946
L/MIL/17/5/2153 Recruitment into the Indian Army 1939–1945
L/MIL/17/5/2225 Lectures for Officers Joining the Indian Army
L/MIL/17/5/2234 Training Directives
L/MIL/17/5/2235–9 Jungle Warfare Training Pamphlets
L/MIL/17/5/2242 Army/Air Operations
L/MIL/17/5/2251 Camouflage and Concealment Pamphlet
L/MIL/17/5/2253 Military Training Pamphlet No. 11 Aid to Civil Power 1946

L/MIL/17/5/2271 Animal Transport Pamphlet

L/MIL/17/5/2330 Notes for Guidance of Commanding Officers, Staff and Regimental Officers

L/MIL/17/5/4252 Internal Security Instructions 1937

L/MIL/17/5/4267 Problems connected with Demobilization 1944

L/MIL/17/5/4276 India Command Fortnightly Intelligence Summary, nos. 1–27, 1946–1947

L/MIL/17/5/4277 Weekly Intelligence Summary, nos. 226–32, March–April 1946

L/MIL/17/7/51 Notes for Burma

L/WS/1/136 Recruitment in India 1939–1944

L/WS/1/155 Chatfield Committee

L/WS/1/261 Army in Burma Progress Reports

L/WS/1/267 Quarterly Returns of British Units in Burma 1939–1942

L/WS/1/303 Disaffection of Sikh Troops

L/WS/1/367 Military Reports 1936–1947

L/WS/1/376 Equipment and Training for British Units in Burma 1940

L/WS/1/382 Army Training Memo Burma 1938–1940

L/WS/1/394 Recruitment: New Units Raised

L/WS/1/428 Army in India: Move and Locations of Units and Formations

L/WS/1/439 Commander-in-Chief India Communication with GOC Burma 1940–1942

L/WS/1/456 Class Composition in the Indian Army

L/WS/1/475 Organisation of Indian and British Cavalry Units

L/WS/1/530 Defence of India Plan, 1941–1949

L/WS/1/566 Planning the India Base Pamphlet, 1946–1947

L/WS/1/590 Basic Order of Battle, 1944–1947

L/WS/1/597–8 and 1441 Org. of War Staff and Post War Organization

L/WS/1/610 Army in India: Recruitment

L/WS/1/616–17 Army in India: Divisional Organisations

L/WS/1/639 War Establishment: Infantry

L/WS/1/641 War Establishment: Cavalry

L/WS/1/645 War Establishment: Misc. Units

L/WS/1/650 Army in India Committee on Organisation for War Against Japan

L/WS/1/653 Director of Infantry Report 1945

L/WS/1/706 Operations in Burma

L/WS/1/707 Army Morale

L/WS/1/742 Publicity 'Reconstitution of Armed Forces'

L/WS/1/745 Intelligence Correspondence with War Office 1946–1947

L/WS/1/761–3 Training General Questions 1943–1948

L/WS/1/764–5 Director of Military Training Monthly Reports

L/WS/1/766–7 Training Liaison Letters – DMT to India Office 1945–1947

L/WS/1/768–9 Training infantry 1947

L/WS/1/770 Policy and Training D. D. Tactics and Assault Training

L/WS/1/771–2 Training Armoured Vehicles

L/WS/1/777 Training Study Period on Burma

L/WS/1/778 GHQ India Infantry Liaison Letters
L/WS/1/784 Publicity Reports of Indian Officers to UK 1944–1945
L/WS/1/789 Schools Training India 1945–1947
L/WS/1/790 Training Camberley Courses 1945–1948
L/WS/1/796 Training Notes 1940–1945
L/WS/1/797 Appointment of Indian Officers as Liaison and Instructors in UK
L/WS/1/799 Policy for the Provision of Officers of the Indian Army 1941–1947
L/WS/1/806 Imperial Defence College 1945–1948
L/WS/1/814 Training Recommendations Staff College 1946–1947
L/WS/1/824 Staff College Quetta
L/WS/1/829 Training Internal Defence 1947
L/WS/1/883 Lethbridge Mission Reports
L/WS/1/909 Monthly Raising Reorganisation and Units 1945–1946
L/WS/1/924 Post-war Officering of the Indian Army
L/WS/1/930–2 Demobilization and Releases
L/WS/1/939 India Command on Morale 1943–1948
L/WS/1/943 Prime Minister Minute on Indian Army Morale 1945
L/WS/1/944 Short Service Commissions 1946–1947
L/WS/1/945 Prime Minister's Minutes Regarding Morale
L/WS/1/948 Nationalisation of Indian Army 1946–1947
L/WS/1/964–6 Operations in Burma
L/WS/1/968 Expansion
L/WS/1/969–70 Chief of Staff Committee 1945–1946
L/WS/1/999 Reorganisation Post-war Army in India 1945
L/WS/1/1000 Plan 113 1947
L/WS/1/1001 Plan 113
L/WS/1/1002 Post War Army in India 1945–1946
L/WS/1/1008–11 Indian Political Situation 1945–1947
L/WS/1/1023–7 Future Employment of Gurkha Rifles
L/WS/1/1029–30 Willcox Committee
L/WS/1/1045 Chiefs of Staff Committee Minutes
L/WS/1/1057 Operation Madhouse 1947
L/WS/1/1058 Breakdown Plan 1946
L/WS/1/1068 War Organisation Army in India 1946–1947
L/WS/1/1069–70 Political Intelligence 1946–1947
L/WS/1/1072–4 Political Intelligence 1947–1949
L/WS/1/1088–9 Joint Intelligence Bureau 1946–1949
L/WS/1/1096–7 Chiefs of Staff 1946–1947
L/WS/1/1113 Reorganisation of the Indian Army 1947
L/WS/1/1125 Commander-in-Chief Weekly Conference 1947
L/WS/1/1134–5 Report on the PBF
L/WS/1/1137 Stand Down 1947
L/WS/1/1243–4 Operations in India 1942–1947
L/WS/1/1310 Army in India: Indian Light Division
L/WS/1/1313 Reorganisation of the Burma Army

L/WS/1/1323 Operations in Burma
L/WS/1/1333 Army in India: Organisation of A and MT Divisions
L/WS/1/1364 Formations of Training Divisions in India
L/WS/1/1365 Army in India: Re-organisation of Indian Infantry
L/WS/1/1366 Indianisation
L/WS/1/1371 Report of the Indian Infantry Committee June 1943
L/WS/1/1414 Strength Returns 1945–1948
L/WS/1/1433 Intelligence Summaries
L/WS/1/1449 Command of Staff Appointments in Indian and Pakistan Commands
L/WS/1/1471–2 Commander-in-Chief Meetings 1945–1947
L/WS/1/1488–9 Organisation of Post War Army in India 1945–1948
L/WS/1/1506 India Command Weekly Intelligence Summaries 1945–1947
L/WS/1/1511–13 Burma/Assam Operations and Despatches
L/WS/1/1519 Organisation of Army HQ and Commands in India 1945–1949
L/WS/1/1523–4 Army in India: Army Commanders Conference
L/WS/1/1576 Indian National Army
L/WS/1/1577 Indian National Army
L/WS/1/1578 India and Burma Committee Minutes
L/WS/1/1597–8 Monthly reports India 1947–1948
L/WS/1/1599–1600 Monthly reports Pakistan 1947–1948
L/WS/1/1603 Notes for Lectures by General Staff, India Office
L/WS/1/1608 Vetting of Articles Written by Ex-Indian Army Officers
L/WS/1/1619 Monthly Statistical Review of Authorised Expansion of Indian Army 1945–1946
L/WS/1/1635–7 India Command on Morale 1943–1948
L/WS/1/1653 Director of Infantry Report
L/WS/1/1666 Discipline in Pakistan Army 1948
L/WS/1/1672 Officers with Indian Army 1948
L/WS/1/1673 Officers with Pakistan Army 1948
L/WS/1/1692 Burma Operations 1942
L/WS/1/1711 INA Reports
L/WS/1/1771 Indian National Army
L/WS/2/45 History of the INA
L/WS/2/46 Indian National Army
L/WS/2/71 Morale Reports: India Command and SEAC

India Office Papers, British Library (OIOC, BL): manuscripts
Mss Eur A168 Freda Oliver
Mss Eur C235 Sir Charles Tegart
Mss Eur C282 Harold Bruce
Mss Eur C290 William Channing Pearce
Mss Eur C302 Lawrence Patrick Biggie
Mss Eur C357 5th Earl of Listowel
Mss Eur C363 William Francis Alfred Hamilton
Mss Eur C402 Leslie Rich

Mss Eur C416 Col Peter Green
Mss Eur C430 Revd John Robert De Chazal
Mss Eur C475 Lt Col Sydney Heard
Mss Eur C501 Basil Richard Emile La Bouchardiere
Mss Eur C642 Misc. Papers in the Writing of the History of the
    Indian Police
Mss Eur D807 Sir Evan Jenkins
Mss Eur D862 Richard Powell
Mss Eur D917 Lt Col R. N. P. Reynolds
Mss Eur D1003 John Morton
Mss Eur D1041 Indian Police
Mss Eur D1044 Robert Evelyn Cooper Broadbent
Mss Eur D1060 Alan Flack
Mss Eur D1065 William Harold Rich
Mss Eur D1114 Brig. Frank McCallum
Mss Eur D1225 Maj. Derek Hawes
Mss Eur D1233 Herbert William Waite
Mss Eur D1241 John Eadie Bishop
Mss Eur E323 John Adam Scroggie
Mss Eur F152 Frank Brayne
Mss Eur F161 Indian Police
Mss Eur F164 Sir Robert Francis Mudie
Mss Eur F189 Maj. John Short
Mss Eur F200 Mountbatten Papers
Mss Eur F250 Gilbert Waddell
Mss Eur F251 Ian Murray Hurrell
Mss Eur F255 Harold Charles Mitchell
Mss Eur F274 Maj. Gen. Pete Rees
Mss Eur F409 George Brander
Mss Eur Photo Eur 436 Gerald Robert Savage, Punjab Police
Mss Eur R144 Lt Col Brian Montgomery

India Office Papers, British Library (OIOC, BL): oral archives
Mss Eur T3 Field Marshal Sir Claude Auchinleck
Mss Eur T58 Lt Gen. Sir Reginald Savory
Mss Eur T95/2 Lt Gen. Harbarkash Singh
Mss Eur T102/2 Col Khushwaqt ul Mulk

National Archives, Kew (PRO)
DO 133
WO 32
WO 106
WO 169
WO 171
WO 172
WO 203
WO 204

WO 268
WO 305

Imperial War Museum (IWM)
Brig. E. A. Ardene 97/7/1
Lt Gen. Philip Christison Papers
Maj. Gen. A. C. Curtis Papers
Brig. H. K. Dimoline Papers
Lt Gen. Geoffrey Evans Papers
Lt Col W. L. Farrow 95/33/1
Lt Col John Hill 91/13/1
Maj. Gen. A. W. Holworthy 91/40/1
Maj. P. H. Gadsdon 78/6/2
Maj. H. C. Gay 88/48/1
Brig. P. R. MacNamara 77/32/1
Gen. Robert Mansergh Papers
Brig. L. R. Mizen 71/63/1
Maj. P. B. Poore
Maj. D. C. Purves 87/23/1
Maj. Gen. Denys Reid PP MCR 06 Reel 7
Maj. Gen. J. K. Shepheard 99/69/1
Col G. R. Stevens 67/31/1
Lt Gen. Sir Francis Tuker 71/21
Broadcast Tapes of BBC (Mandalay)

National Army Museum (NAM)
Gen. Sir Roy Bucher Papers
Lt Col A. J. F. Doulton
Gen. Sir Robert Lockhart Papers
Maj. H. R. MacDwyer Papers
Maj. Gen. L. E. Pert Papers
Gen. Sir Reginald Savory Papers
Army in India Training Memoranda
Intelligence Notes from Burma 1943–1945 GHQ India
Indian Military Intelligence Directorate 'Japanese in Battle' 1943
Southeast Asia Translation and Interrogation Centre Historical Bulletin nos.
    243 and 245
Diary of Anthony Bickersteth (4/8th Gurkhas)
Diary of Lt Col John Hill
ODTAA: Diary of a Major in the 4/10th Gurkhas
Diary of 5/11th Sikh 8 December 1941–15 February 1942 (Malaya)
War Diary of 8/6th Rajputana Rifles Mss
6509-14 5/2nd Punjab Malaya Ts History
7304-1-2 Jungle Warfare School at Shimoga
7707-35 Hindu–Muslim Violence
7709-64-2 2/13th FFRifles 'War History' Mss

7711-232 'With the 4th Sikhs' (4/12th FFR) Lt Col I. A. J. Edwards-Stuart Mss.
7809-3 Maj. P. H. MacDwyer
8002-68 Col J. C. Cotton
8012-63 14/13th FFRifles Ts History
8204-797 Papers relating to Maj. Gen. D. A. Wade
8303-110 IV and XXXIII Corps

Liddell Hart Centre for Military Archives
Lt Gen. Sir Frank Messervy Papers
Gen. Sir Douglas Gracey Papers
Maj. Gen. John Lethbridge Papers
Gen. Sir Richard O'Connor Papers
Lt Col Hamilton Stevenson Papers

University of Manchester
Field Marshal Sir Claude Auchinleck Papers

Interviews and correspondence
5th Probyn's Horse
Brig. R. Khan LOM MC
Brig. A. Singh
Maj. H. E. I. C. Stewart MC
Capt. J. Chiles
Capt. E. M. Halliwell
Capt. R. Jones
Honorary Capt. H. Nawaz
Risaldar A. Khan

7th Light Cavalry
Brig. H. Singh
Lt Col H. Singh
Capt. L. Dormer
Capt. F. Jemmett
Capt. H. Travis
Capt. G. A. Sipthorp

11th Prince Albert Victor's Own Cavalry (FF)
Maj. E. P. Marsden

Royal Indian Artillery
Lt Gen. K. P. Candeth PVSM

Royal Indian Engineers
Maj. Gen. B. D. Kapur
Maj. Gen. L. Singh
Brig. G. Singh

King George V's Own Bengal Sappers and Miners
    Maj. T. Le M. Spring-Smyth

Bombay Sappers and Miners
    Brig. D. A. Barker-Wyatt
    Brig. Colin Cowan CBE
    Lt Col D. L. Jones
    Lt Col W. L. Sheldon
    Maj. A. N. Fradgley MBE
    Maj. P. H. James
    Capt. John R. Moss

1st Punjab Regiment
    Maj. Gen. E. H. W. Grimshaw CB CBE DSO
    Maj. Gen. A. K. Luthera MC
    Brig. M. R. Dutt MC
    Brig. M. I. Qureshi
    Maj. J. Arthur MC
    Maj. R. C. S. Howe
    Maj. C. H. Manning
    Maj. D. Pailthorpe
    Maj. A. H. Robertson
    Capt. M. A. Kerr MBE

2nd Punjab Regiment
    Brig. C. S. Mehta
    Lt Col J. D. Montagu
    Maj. R. E. J. Mathew
    Capt. Peter Gutterridge
    Capt. A. L. de Montfort OBE
    Capt. R.T. Rowland QC
    Capt. P. L. Roy

3rd Madras Regiment
    Maj. T. A. J. Barton
    Maj. W. Brindley

4th Bombay Grenadiers
    Lt Gen. S. L. Menezes PVSM SC
    Lt Col P. Emerson OBE

6th Rajputana Rifles
    Col B. D. Bhanot
    Maj. M. C. Henstock
    Maj. F. D. Rushworth
    Capt. Tom Simpson
    Capt. H. K. Tarrant

7th Rajput Regiment
Brig. R. B. Chopra
Capt. S. Ottowell

8th Punjab Regiment
Maj. Gilbert Garrett
Capt. W. C. Hawes

9th Jat Regiment
Maj. R. Baldwin

10th Baluch Regiment
Maj. Gen. D. K. Palit VrC
Maj. Gen. S. C. S. Singha
Brig. N. K. Chatterji
Brig. M. Jan
Brig. J. Randle OBE MC
Col John Perkin
Maj. T. Bruin
Maj. R. MacLean OBE
Maj. C. Martin MC
Capt. A. D. Burnett
Capt. F. W. D. King
Lt C. R. L. Coubrough

11th Sikh Regiment
Maj. Gen. S. Singh
Col J. Brough DSO MBE MC
Lt Col W. L. Farrow
Lt Col C. H. McVean MC
Lt Col E. Rowland-Jones
Lt Col R. Schlaefli
Maj. T. Kirkwood

12th Frontier Force Regiment
Maj. J. Beazley
Maj. Gen. N. Prasad
Maj. R. Williams
Capt. P. Barrett
Capt. V. I. Murtough

13th Frontier Force Rifles
Lt Gen. K. S. Katoch PVSM
Maj. Gen. H. N. Shinjal
Lt Col M. Wilcox
Maj. P. Bailey
Maj. G. C. Coppen MC
Maj. A. Delafield MC
Maj. D. Lamond

Maj. R. F. Mummery
Maj. Peter Riches (aide-de-camp to Maj. Gen. Pete Rees)
Maj. F. W. S. Taylor
Capt. (Sir) G. Elliott
Capt. R. Guild
Capt. L. Howlett
Capt. (Dr) D. W. Jenkins
Capt. P. Pattullo
Capt. J. R. Wallis MC
Capt. D. Wright

14th Punjab Regiment
Lt Col C. E. N. Hopkins-Husson
Maj. V. L. F. Davin
Maj. Peter Gadsdon
Maj. M. G. Wilks
Capt. G. W. R. Garrett
Capt. A. C. Stanley
Capt. D. H. Vickers

16th Punjab Regiment
Lt Col Ronald Perkin

17th Dogra Regiment
Maj. Christopher Blake

18th Garhwal Rifles
Capt. W. Nichols

1st Burma Rifles
Maj. Gen. J. D. Lunt

Indian Parachute Regiment
Maj. Gen. S. C. Sinha PVSM

Sikh Light Infantry
Col J. D. Maling DSO MC
Capt. H. C. T. Routley

4th Gurkha Rifles
Lt Col J. Craig
Maj. M. R. Strivens
Maj. P. Sibree
Capt. D. Jeffrey
Capt. R. Steel
Revd D. Bevis

5th Royal Gurkha Rifles (Frontier Force)
Maj. G. E. Seppings

8th Gurkha Rifles
  Brig. P. Myers MC
  Maj. S. Gilmore
  Maj. P. Wickham
  Capt. P. Davis
  Capt. W. A. Dodd
  Capt. F. Seaman

10th Gurkha Rifles
  Lt Col M. Roberts

Royal Berkshire Regiment
  Col J. Hill MC
  Maj. J. Caldicott TD

PRIVATELY PUBLISHED, PERSONAL DIARIES, MISCELLANEOUS MSS

Anonymous, History of 7/10th Baluch Regiment in Burma. Mss 1945.
  History of the 7th Light Cavalry in Burma. 2 vols. 1944 and 1945.
  'Probyn's Newsletter'. 1944–5.
Barker-Wyatt, Brig. D. A. 'Partition of India 1947: The Memoirs and
  Experiences of a Sapper Subaltern with the 2nd Indian Airborne Division',
  10 Sep. 2005.
Blomfield-Smith, Denis, ed. *Fourth Indian Reflections.* 1987.
Clarke, S. D. *Now or Never – The Story of the 4/3rd Madras in the Burma Campaign.*
  1945.
Elliott, Sir Gerald. India a memoir. Mss 1960.
Kinloch, Maj. B. G. *A Subedar Remembers and Thirty Pieces of Silver* 1991.
Milne, Maj. B. H., ed. *An Account of Operations in Burma Carried out by Probyn's
  Horse.* 1945.
Murtough, V. I. 'Recollections of my war'. Mss 1970s.
Nichols, Bill. 'I'll say goodbye'. Mss 1947.
Roberts, Michael. Field diary dealing with operations in 1944.
Personal Accounts were found in the regimental newsletters of the 8th Gurkhas,
  Red Flash, copies seen 1992–2000 and *The Piffer* (Journal of the Punjab
  Frontier Force Association), copies with personal accounts are from the
  1990s.

PUBLISHED

INDIAN ARMY AND GOVERNMENT

Aggarwal, S. C. *History of the Supply Department: 1939–1945.* New Delhi:
  Government Publications, 1947.
Auchinleck, Field Marshal Sir Claude. *Despatch: Operations in the Indo-Burma
  Theatre Based on India from June 21, 1943, to November 15, 1943.* London:
  London Gazette, 1948.

Barstow, A. E. *Handbooks for the Indian Army: Sikhs*. Calcutta: Government of India, 1928.

Carter, Lionel, ed. *Mountbatten's Report on the Last Viceroyalty: 22 March–15 August 1947*. New Delhi: Manohar, 2003.

Cunningham, W. B. *Handbooks for the Indian Army: Dogras*. Calcutta: Government of India, 1932.

Demobilisation of the Indian Army, Adjutant General. Simla: Government of India Press, 1947.

Documents on British Policy Overseas, Series 1, Vol. I, *1945*. London: HMSO, 1984.

Evans, Geoffrey. *Tiger Kills*. London: HMSO, 1944.

Great Britain Organization of the Indian Army Committee. 'Report of the Commissioners Appointed to Inquire into the Organization of the Indian Army'. London: Eyre & Spottiswoode, 1859.

Indian Army List, 1922–46.

Kirby, S. Woodburn. *War Against Japan*, vols. I–V. London: HMSO, 1957–69.

Latham, A. *Handbooks for the Indian Army: Kumaonis*. Delhi: Government of India, 1933.

Leigh, M. S. *The Punjab and the War*. Lahore: Government of the Punjab, 1922.

Mansergh, Nicholas, ed. *The Transfer of Power, 1942–1947*, 12 vols. London: HMSO, 1970–83.

Mouat, G. E. D. *Handbooks for the Indian Army: Madras Classes*. New Delhi: Government of India, 1938.

Mountbatten, Vice-Admiral Lord Louis, Earl of Burma. *Report to the Combined Chiefs of Staff by the Supreme Allied Commander, South-East Asia, 1943–1945*. London: HMSO, 1951.

  Post Surrender Tasks: Section E of the Report to the Combined Chiefs of Staff by the Supreme Allied Commander South-East Asia, 1943–1946. London: HMSO, 1969.

Operations on the North-West Frontier of India, 1921–1935. New Delhi: Government of India, 1937.

Operations on the North-West Frontier of India, 1936–1937. New Delhi: Government of India, 1946.

Paiforce: The Official Story of the Persia and Iraq Command, 1941–1946. London: HMSO, 1948.

Philips, C. H., ed. *Select Documents on the History of India and Pakistan, IV: The Evolution of India and Pakistan, 1858–1947*. Oxford University Press, 1964.

Prasad, Bisheshwar. *Official History of the Indian Armed Forces in the Second World War* (volumes: *Retreat from Burma, 1941–1942*; *Expansion of the Armed Forces and Defence Organisation*; and *The Reconquest of Burma*, 2 vols.). New Delhi: Orient Longmans, from 1953.

Rideway, R. T. *Handbooks for the Indian Army: Pathans*. Calcutta: Government of India, 1910.

Singh, Amrik, ed. *The Partition in Retrospect*. New Delhi: Animika Publishers, 2000.

Singh, Kirpal, ed. *Select Documents on the Partition of Punjab, 1947*. New Delhi: National Book Shop, 1991.

Tiger Strikes. HMSO, 1942.

Tiger Triumphs. HMSO, 1946.

Wikeley, J. M. *Handbooks for the Indian Army: Punjabi Musalmans.* Calcutta: Government of India, 1915.

Zafar, Rukshana, ed. *Disturbances in the Punjab: 1947.* Islamabad: National Documentation Centre, 1995.

MEMOIRS

Atkins, David. *The Reluctant Major.* Pulborough: Toat Press, 1986.

The Forgotten Major. Pulborough: Toat Press, 1989.

Barnes, John, ed. *Empire at Bay: The Leo Amery Diaries, 1929–1945.* London: Hutchinson, 1988.

Bristow, R. C. B. *Memories of the British Raj: A Soldier in India.* London: Johnson, 1974.

Calvert, Michael. *Prisoners of Hope.* London: Leo Cooper, 1996.

Campbell-Johnson, Alan. *Mission with Mountbatten.* London: Robert Hale Ltd, 1951.

Cooper, K. W. *The Little Men.* London: Hale, 1985.

Cooper, Raymond. *'B' Company, 9th Battalion the Border Regiment: One Man's War in Burma.* London: Dobson, 1978.

Coubrough, C. R. L. *Memories of a Perpetual Second Lieutenant.* York: Wilton 65, 1999.

Cross, John. *In Gurkha Company.* London: Leo Cooper, 1981.

Cubitt-Smith, J. H. *Yadgari or the Memories of the Raj.* Saxlingham, Norfolk: Privately published, 1986.

Davis, Patrick. *A Child at Arms.* London: Buchan & Enright, 1985.

Evans, Geoffrey. *The Desert and the Jungle.* London: Kimber, 1959.

Fergusson, Bernard. *Beyond the Chindwin.* London: Collins, 1945.

The Wild Green Earth. London: Collins, 1946.

Forteath, G. M. *Pipes, Kukris and Nips.* London: Pentland Press, 1992.

Fraser, George MacDonald. *Quartered Safe Out Here.* London: Harvill, 1992.

Gilmore, Scott. *A Connecticut Yankee in the 8th Gurkha Rifles.* Washington, DC: Brassey's, 1995.

Grounds, Tom. *Some Letters from Burma: Story of the 25th Dragoons at War.* Tunbridge Wells, UK: Parapress, 1994.

Hamid, Maj. Gen. Shahid. *Disastrous Twilight: A Personal Record of the Partition of India.* Barnsley, UK: Leo Cooper, 1986.

Harper, Alec. *Horse and Foot.* York: Quacks, 1995.

Hastings, Robin. *An Undergraduate's War.* London: Bellhouse, 1997.

Hill, John. *China Dragons: A Rifle Company at War.* London: Blandford, 1991.

Humphreys, Roy. *To Stop a Rising Sun: Reminiscences of Wartime in India and Burma.* Stroud: Alan Sutton, 1996.

Ingall, Francis. *The Last of the Bengal Lancers.* London: Leo Cooper, 1988.

Khan, Mohammad Ayub. *Friends Not Masters: A Political Autobiography.* Oxford University Press, 1967.

Khan, Shah Nawaz. *My Memories of the INA and Its Netaji.* Delhi, 1946.

Llewellyn-Jones, Rosie, ed. 'Memories of August 1947', *Chowkidar*, 8, 2 (1997), pp. 1–3.

Lowry, M. A. *An Infantry Company in Arakan and Kohima*. Aldershot: Gale & Polden, 1950.

Lunt, James, ed. *From Sepoy to Subedar*. London: Papermac, 1988.

Mains, Tony. *The Retreat from Burma: An Intelligence Officer's Personal Story*. London: Foulsham, 1973.

Mason, Philip. *A Shaft of Sunlight*. London: Andre Deutsch, 1978.

Masters, John. *Bugles and a Tiger*. London: Michael Joseph, 1956.

The Road Past Mandalay: A Personal Narrative. London: Michael Joseph, 1961.

Moon, Penderel. *Divide and Quit: An Eye-Witness Account of the Partition of India*. London: Chatto & Windus, 1962.

ed. *Wavell: The Viceroy's Journal*. London: Oxford University Press, 1973.

Mountbatten, Vice-Admiral Lord Louis, Earl of Burma. *Personal Diary of Admiral The Lord Louis Mountbatten: Supreme Allied Commander, South-East Asia, 1943–1946*, ed. Philip Ziegler. London: Collins, 1988.

Nath, Trilok. *Forty Years of Indian Police*. New Delhi: Concept Publishing, 1981.

Norman, Dorothy, ed. *Nehru the First Sixty Years*. London: Bodley Head, 1965.

Palit, D. K. 'Indianisation: A Personal Experience', *Indo-British Review*, 16 (1989).

Pickford, John. *Destination Rangoon*. Denbigh: Gee Publishing, 1989.

Pownall, Sir Henry. *Chief of Staff: The Diaries of Lt. General Sir Henry Pownall*, vols. I–II. Ed. Brian Bond. London: Leo Cooper, 1972–4.

Prendergast, John. *Prender's Progress: A Soldier in India*. London: Cassell, 1979.

Randle, John. *Battle Tales from Burma*. Stroud: Leo Cooper, 2004.

Roberts, Field Marshal Lord Frederick. *Forty One Years in India*. London: Bentley Brothers, 1898.

Robinson-Horley, E.W. *Last Post: An Indian Army Memoir*. London: Leo Cooper, 1985.

Rose, Angus. *Who Dies Fighting*. London: J. Cape, 1944.

Rose, D. *Off the Record*. Staplehurst: Spellmount, 1996.

Ross, Ken. 'With the 2/8th Gurkhas in Iraq 1941–1942', *Red Flash*, no. 22, pp. 48–57.

Schlaefli, Robin. *Emergency Sahib*. London: Leach, 1992.

Sheil-Small, Denis. *Green Shadows*. London: Kimber, 1982.

Singh, Mohan. *Soldier's Contribution to Indian Independence*. New Delhi, 1974.

Sita, R. P. *From Sepoy to Subedar: Being the Life and Adventures of Subedar Sita Ram, a Native Officer of the Bengal Army, Written and Related by Himself*. Ed. James Lunt. London: Papermac, 1988.

Slim, Field Marshal the Viscount William. *Defeat into Victory*. London: Cassell, 1956.

Unofficial History. London: Cassell, 1959.

Smeeton, Miles. *A Change of Jungles*. London: Hart-Davis, 1962.

Smyth, John. *Before the Dawn: A Story of Two Historic Retreats*. London: Cassell, 1957.

Truong Chinh, *Primer for Revolt*. New York: Praeger, 1963.

Tuker, Lt Gen. Sir Francis. *While Memory Serves*. London: Cassell, 1950.

Wilson, Lt Gen. Sir James. *Unusual Undertakings: A Military Memoir*. Barnsley, UK: Leo Cooper, 2002.

SECONDARY SOURCES

Aiyar, Swarna. 'August Anarchy', in Low and Brasted, eds., *Freedom*, pp. 15–38; previously published as 'August Anarchy: The Partition Massacres in Punjab, 1947', *South Asia*, 18 (1995), pp. 13–36.
Alavi, Seema. *The Sepoys and the Company: Tradition and Transition in Northern India, 1770–1830*. New Delhi: Oxford University Press, 1995.
Allen, Louis. *Burma: The Longest War 1941–1945*. London: Dent, 1984.
  The End of the War in Asia. London: Hart-Davis MacGibbon, 1976.
Anglim, Simon. *Orde Wingate and the British Army, 1922–1944*. London: Pickering & Chatto, 2010.
Bamford, Lt Col P. G. *1st King George V's Own Battalion, The Sikh Regiment*. Aldershot: Gale & Polden, 1948.
Barat, Amiya. *The Bengal Native Infantry: Its Organisation and Discipline, 1796–1852*. Calcutta: Firma K. L. Mukhopadhyay, 1962.
Barkawi, Tarak. 'Culture and Combat in the Colonies: The Indian Army in the Second World War', *Journal of Contemporary History*, 41 (2006), pp. 325–55.
Barker, A. J. *The March on Delhi*. London: Faber, 1963.
Barr, Niall. *Pendulum of War: The Three Battles of El Alamein*. London: Jonathan Cape, 2004.
Barua, Pradeep. *The Army Officer Corps and Military Modernisation in Later Colonial India*. University of Hull Press, 1999.
  Gentlemen of the Raj: The Indian Army Officer Corps, 1817–1949. Westport, CT: Praeger, 2003.
Bayly, C. A. and Harper, T. N. *Forgotten Armies: The Fall of British Asia, 1941–1945*. Cambridge, MA: Belknap, 2005.
Bayly, C. A. and Stokes, Eric. *The Peasant Armed: The Indian Revolt of 1857*. Oxford University Press, 1986.
Bayly, Susan. 'Caste and Race in the Colonial Ethnography of India', in Robb, ed., *The Concept of Race in South Asia*, pp. 165–218.
Bond, Brian. *British Military Policy Between the Two World Wars*. Oxford University Press, 1980.
Booth, John. *Ninth Battalion Fourteenth Punjab Regiment*. Cardiff: Western Mail and Echo Limited, 1948.
Bose, Sugata. *His Majesty's Opponent: Subhas Chandra Bose and India's Struggle Against Empire*. Cambridge, MA: Harvard University Press, 2011.
Brecher, Michael. *Nehru: A Political Biography*. New York: Oxford University Press, 2005.
Brett-James, Antony. *Ball of Fire: The Fifth Indian Division in the Second World War*. Aldershot: Gale & Polden, 1951.
Brown, Judith. *Gandhi and Civil Disobedience: The Mahatma in Indian Politics, 1928–1934*. Cambridge University Press, 1975.
  Modern India: The Origins of an Asian Democracy, 2nd edn. Oxford University Press, 1994.
  Nehru: A Political Life. New Haven: Yale University Press, 2004.

Brown, Judith and Louis, W. M. Roger, eds. *The Oxford History of the British Empire*, vol. IV. Oxford University Press, 1999.

Butalia, Urvashi. *The Other Side of Silence: Voices from Partition*. London: C. Hurst, 2000.

Callahan, Raymond. *The East India Company and Army Reform*. Cambridge, MA: Harvard University Press, 1972.

The Worst Disaster: The Fall of Singapore. Newark: University of Delaware Press, 1977.

Burma 1942–1945. London: Davis-Poynter, 1978.

'The Indian Army, Total War, and the Dog That Didn't Bark in the Night', in Jane Hathaway, ed., *Rebellion Repression Reinvention: Mutiny in Comparative Perspective*, pp. 119–30. Westport, CT: Praeger, 2002.

'Coping with Disaster', in Daniel Marston, ed., *Pacific War Companion*, pp. 63–78. Oxford: Osprey Publishing, 2005.

'Were the Sepoy Generals Any Good? A Re-Appraisal of the British–Indian Army's High Command in the Second World War', in Roy, ed., *War and Society in Colonial India*, pp. 305–29.

Churchill's Generals. Lawrence: University of Kansas Press, 2007.

'The Great Sepoy Mutiny', in Marston and Sundaram, eds., *Military History of India and South Asia*, pp. 16–33.

Campbell, Arthur. *The Siege: A Story from Kohima*. London: Allen & Unwin, 1956.

Carew, Tim. *The Longest Retreat: The Burma Campaign 1942*. London: Hamish Hamilton, 1969.

Chatterji, Joya. *Bengal Divided: Hindu Communalism, and Partition 1932–1947*. Cambridge University Press, 1994.

The Spoils of Partition: Bengal and India, 1947–1967. Cambridge University Press, 2007.

Chester, Lucy. *On the Edge: Borders, Territory and Conflict in South Asia*. Manchester University Press, 2008.

Borders and Conflict in South Asia: The Radcliffe Boundary Commission and the Partition of Punjab. Manchester University Press, 2009.

Cohen, Stephen. 'Subhas Chandra Bose and the Indian National Army', *Pacific Affairs*, 36, 4 (Winter 1963–4), pp. 411–29.

'The Untouchable Soldier: Caste, Politics, and the Indian Army', *Journal of Asian Studies*, 28 (1969), pp. 453–68.

The Indian Army: Its Contribution to the Development of the Indian Nation. Berkeley: University of California Press, 1971.

Collett, N. A. *The Butcher of Amritsar: General Reginald Dyer*. London: Palgrave Macmillan, 2005.

Colvin, John. *Not Ordinary Men: The Story of the Battle of Kohima*. London: Leo Cooper, 1995.

Condon, W. E. H. *The Frontier Force Rifles*. Aldershot: Gale & Polden, 1953.

The Frontier Force Regiment. Aldershot: Gale & Polden, 1962.

Connell, John. *Auchinleck: A Critical Biography*. London: Cassell, 1959.

Wavell: Supreme Commander 1941–1943. London: Collins, 1969.

Copland, Ian. 'The Master and the Maharajas: The Sikh Princes and the East Punjab Massacres of 1947', *Modern Asian Studies*, 36, 3 (2002), pp. 657–704.

Corr, Gerrard. *War of the Springing Tiger*. London: Osprey, 1975.

Corrigan, G. *Sepoys in the Trenches. The Indian Corps on the Western Front: 1914–1915*. London: Spellmount, 1996.

Cross, J. P. *Jungle Warfare: Experiences and Encounters*. London: Arms and Armour, 1989.

Damododaran, Vinita. 'Bihar in the 1940s: Communities, Riots and the State', in Low and Brasted, eds., *Freedom*, pp. 175–98.

Darwin, John. *Britain and Decolonisation: The Retreat from Empire in the Post-War World*. Basingstoke: Macmillan, 1988.

Das, Suranjan. *Communal Riots in Bengal 1905–1947*. Bombay: Oxford University Press, 1991.

Datta, V. N., ed. *New Light on the Disturbances in 1919*. Simla: Indian Institute of Advanced Study, 1975.

David, Saul. *The Indian Mutiny: 1857*. London: Viking, 2002.

Dennis, Peter. *Troubled Days of Peace: Mountbatten and South East Asia Command, 1945–1946*. Manchester University Press, 1987.

Deshpande, Anirudh. 'Hopes and Disillusionment: Recruitment, Demobilization and Emergence of Discontent in the Indian Armed Forces After the Second World War', *Indian Economic and Social History Review*, Jun. 1996, pp. 175–207.

Donnison, F. S. V. *British Military Administration in the Far East, 1943–1946*. London: HMSO, 1956.

Doulton, A. J. F. *The Fighting Cock: Being the History of the 23rd Indian Division*. Aldershot: Gale & Polden, 1951.

Draper, Alfred. *Amritsar: The Massacre That Ended the Raj*. London: Cassell, 1981.

Dunn, Peter. *The First Indo-China War*. London: C. Hurst & Co., 1985.

Ellis, John. *Cassino: The Hollow Victory*. London: Andre Deutsch, 1994.

Evans, Geoffrey. *Slim as Military Commander*. London: Batsford, 1969.

Evans, Geoffrey and Brett-James, Antony. *Imphal: A Flower on Lofty Heights*. London: Macmillan, 1962.

Farrell, Brian. *Defence and Fall of Singapore*. Stroud: Tempus Publishing, 2005.

Fay, Peter Ward. *The Forgotten Army: India's Armed Struggle for Independence*. Ann Arbor: University of Michigan Press, 1993.

French, David. *Raising Churchill's Army*. Oxford University Press, 2000.

Gardner, Nikolas. *Trial by Fire: Command and Control and the British Expeditionary Force in 1914*. Westport, CT: Praeger, 2003.

Gaylor, John. *Sons of John Company*. Tunbridge Wells, UK: Spellmount, 1992.

Ghosh, K. K. *The India National Army*. New Delhi: Meenakshi Prakashan, 1969.

Giani, K. S. *Indian Independence Movement in Asia*. Lahore, 1947.

Gilmartin, David. *Empire and Islam: Punjab and the Making of Pakistan*. Berkeley: University of California Press, 1988.

Gordon, Leonard. *Brothers Against the Raj: A Biography of Indian Nationalists Sarat and Subhas Chandra Bose*. New York: Columbia University Press, 1990.

Gould, Tony. *Imperial Warriors: Britain and the Gurkhas*. London: Granta Books, 1999.

Grant, Ian Lyall. *Burma: The Turning Point: The Seven Battles on the Tiddim Road*. London: Zampi Press, 1993.

Grant, Ian Lyall and Tamayama, Kazuo. *Burma 1942: The Japanese Invasion.* London: Zampi Press, 1999.

Green, Nile. *Islam and the Army in Colonial India: Sepoy Religion in the Service of Empire.* Cambridge University Press, 2009.

Gregorian, Raffi. *The British Army, the Gurkhas and Cold War Strategy in the Far East, 1947–1954.* London: Palgrave, 2002.

Griffiths, Sir Percival. *To Guard My People: History of the Indian Police.* London: Benn Publishing, 1971.

Guha, Ranajit, ed. *Subaltern Studies: Writings on South Asian History and Society,* vol. II. New Delhi: Oxford University Press, 1983.

Gwynn, Charles. *Imperial Policing.* London: Macmillan, 1934.

Hamid, Maj. Gen. S. S. *So They Rode and Fought.* Tunbridge Wells, UK: Midas Books, 1983.

Hanley, Gerald. *Monsoon Victory.* London: Collins, 1946.

Hart, Stephen. *Montgomery and the 'Colossal Cracks': The 21st Army Group in Northwest Europe, 1944–1945.* Westport, CT: Praeger, 2000.

Hauner, Milan. *India in Axis Strategy: Germany, Japan and Indian Nationalists in the Second World War.* Stuttgart: Klett-Cotta, 1981.

Heathcote, T. A. *The Indian Army: Garrison of British Imperial India, 1822–1922.* Melbourne: Wren, 1974.

  The Military in British India: Development of British Land Forces in South Asia, 1600–1947. Manchester University Press, 1995.

Hickey, Michael. *The Unforgettable Army: Slim's XIVth Army in Burma.* London: Spellmount, 1992.

Hodson, H. V. *Great Divide: Britain, India and Pakistan.* London: Oxford University Press, 1969.

Hookway, J. D., ed. *M & R: A Regimental History of the Sikh Light Infantry, 1941–1947.* Radley, UK: Reesprint, 1999.

Hughes, Geraint. 'A "Post-War" War: The British Occupation of French Indochina, September 1945–March 1946', *Small Wars & Insurgencies,* 17, 3 (2006), pp. 263–86.

Hyam, Ronald. *Britain's Declining Empire: The Road to Decolonisation, 1918–1968.* Cambridge University Press, 2007.

Ishizu, Tomoyuki and Raymond Callahan, 'The Rising Sun Strikes', in Daniel Marston, ed., *Pacific War Companion,* pp. 47–62. Oxford: Osprey Publishing, 2005.

Jalal, Ayesha. *The Sole Spokesman: Jinnah and the Muslim League and the Demand for Pakistan.* Cambridge University Press, 1985.

  The State of Martial Rule: The Origins of Pakistan's Political Economy of Defence. Cambridge University Press, 1990.

  Self and Sovereignty: Individual and Community in South Asian Islam Since 1850. London: Routledge, 2000.

Jeffrey, Robin. 'The Punjab Boundary Force and the Problem of Order, August 1947', *Modern Asian Studies,* 8, 4 (1974), pp. 491–520.

Jeffreys, Alan. *The British Army in the Far East, 1941–1945.* Oxford: Osprey Publishing, 2005.

Jeffreys, Alan and Rose, Patrick, eds. *The Indian Army, 1939–1947.* Farnham, UK: Ashgate, 2012.

Johnson, Rob. 'The Indian Army and Internal Security: 1919–1946', in Roy, ed., *The Indian Army in the Two World Wars*, pp. 359–90.

Karaka, D. F. *With the 14th Army*. Bombay: Thacker & Co., 1944.

Kaur, Ravinder. *Since 1947: Partition Narratives Among Punjabi Migrants of Delhi*. New Delhi: Oxford University Press, 2007.

Khan, Yasmin. *The Great Partition: The Making of India and Pakistan*. New Haven: Yale University Press, 2007.

'Out of Control? Partition Violence and the State in Uttar Pradesh', in Talbot, ed., *Deadly Embrace*, pp. 36–59.

King-Clark, R. *The Battle for Kohima: The Narrative of the 2nd Manchester Regiment*. Chester, UK: Fleur de Lys, 1995.

Kudaisya, Gyanesh. '"In Aid of Civil Power": The Colonial Army in Northern India, 1919–1942', *Journal of Imperial and Commonwealth History*, 32 (Jan. 2004), pp. 41–68.

Lawford, Lt Col J. P. *Solah Punjab: The History of the 16th Punjab Regiment*. Aldershot: Gale & Polden, 1967.

Lawrence, Henry. 'Military Defence of Our Empire in the East', *Calcutta Review* 2, 3 (1844), pp. 32–72.

Lebra, Joyce. *Jungle Alliance: Japan and the Indian National Army*. Singapore: Asia Pacific Press, 1971.

Lewin, Ronald. *Slim the Standard Bearer*. London: Leo Cooper, 1976.

Lloyd, Nick. 'The Amritsar Massacre and the Minimum Force Debate', *Small Wars & Insurgencies*, 21, 2 (2010), pp. 459–75.

'The Indian Army and Civil Disorder: 1919–1922', in Roy, ed., *The Indian Army in the Two World Wars*, pp. 335–58.

Longer, V. *Red Coats to Olive Green: A History of the Indian Army, 1600–1974*. Bombay: Allied Publishers, 1974.

Low, D. A. and Brasted, Howard, eds. *Freedom, Trauma, Continuities: Northern India and Independence*. New Delhi: Sage Publications, 1998.

Lunt, James. *Hell of a Licking: The Retreat from Burma 1941–1942*. London: Collins, 1986.

McKelvie, Roy. *The War in Burma*. London: Methuen, 1948.

Mackenzie, Compton. *Eastern Epic*. London: Chatto & Windus, 1951.

McMillan, Richard. *The British Occupation of Indonesia, 1945–1946*. London: Routledge, 2005.

MacMunn, Lt Gen Sir George. *The Armies of India*. London: A&C Black, 1911.
The Martial Races of India. London: Sampson Low, 1933.
History of the Guides, 1922–1947. Aldershot: Gale & Polden, 1950.

Majdalany, Fred. *Cassino: Portrait of a Battle*, 3rd edn. London: Orion, 1999.

Malleson, G. B., ed. *Kaye's and Malleson's History of the Indian Mutiny of 1857–1858*, 6 vols. London: Allen, 1898.

Marston, Daniel. *Phoenix from the Ashes: The Indian Army in the Burma Campaign*. Westport, CT: Praeger, 2003.

'Lost and Found in the Jungle', in Hew Strachan, ed., *Big Wars and Small Wars*, pp. 96–114. London: Routledge, 2004.

'The Indian Army, Partition and the Punjab Boundary Force, 1945–1947', *War in History*, 16, 4 (2009), pp. 469–505.

Marston, Daniel and Sundaram, Chandar, eds. *A Military History of India and South Asia: From the East India Company to the Nuclear Era.* Bloomington: Indiana University Press, 2008.

Mason, Philip. *A Matter of Honour: An Account of the Indian Army, Its Officers and Men.* London: Cape, 1974.

Matthews, Geoffrey. *The Re-Conquest of Burma 1943–1945.* Aldershot: Gale & Polden, 1966.

Maule, Henry. *Spearhead General: The Epic Story of General Sir Frank Messervy.* London: Oldhams Press, 1961.

Mazumder, Rajit. *The Indian Army and the Making of the Punjab.* Bangalore: Permanent Black, 2003.

Menezes, S. L. *Fidelity and Honour: The Indian Army from the Seventeenth to the Twenty First Century.* New Delhi: Viking, 1993.

Metcalf, Thomas. *Ideologies of the Raj.* Cambridge University Press, 1995.

Moreman, Timothy. *The Army in India and the Development of Frontier Warfare.* London: Macmillan, 1998.

   The Jungle, the Japanese and the British Commonwealth Armies at War, 1941–1945: Fighting Methods, Doctrine and Training for Jungle Warfare. London: Frank Cass, 2005.

Mukherjee, Rudrangshu. *Mangal Pandy: Brave Martyr or Accidental Hero?* New Delhi: Penguin Books, 2005.

Nehru, Jawaharlal. *The Discovery of India.* London: Meridien Books, 1956.

Neville, Peter. *Britain in Vietnam: Prelude to Disaster, 1945–1946.* London: Routledge, 2007.

Omissi, David. *The Sepoy and the Raj: The Indian Army, 1860–1940.* Basingstoke: Macmillan, 1994.

   Indian Voices of the Great War: Soldiers' Letters, 1914–1918. London: Macmillan, 1999.

   'A Dismal Story? Britain, the Gurkhas and the Partition of India, 1945–1948', in Jeffreys and Rose, eds., *The Indian Army, 1939–1947*, pp. 195–214.

Owen, Frank. *The Campaign in Burma.* London: HMSO, 1946.

Owen, Nicholas. 'The Cripps Mission of 1942: A Reinterpretation', *Journal of Imperial and Commonwealth History*, 30, 1 (2002), pp. 61–98.

Palit, D. K. *Major General A. A. Rudra.* Dehra Dun: Lancer Publishing, 1993.

Palmer, J. A. B. *Mutiny Outbreak at Meerut.* Cambridge University Press, 1966.

Peers, Douglas. *Between Mars and Mammon: Colonial Armies and the Garrison State in Early 19th Century India.* London: Tauris, 1995.

   'The Martial Races and the Indian Army in the Victorian Era', in Marston and Sundaram, eds., *Military History of India and South Asia*, pp. 34–52.

Perrett, Bryan. *Tank Tracks to Rangoon.* London: Robert Hale, 1992.

Perry, F. W. *Commonwealth Armies: Manpower and Organisation in the Two World Wars.* Manchester University Press, 1988.

Philips, C. H. and Wainwright, Mary Doreen, ed. *Partition of India: Policies and Perspectives.* London: George Allen and Unwin, 1970.

Place, Timothy Harrison. *Military Training in the British Army, 1940–1944.* London: Frank Cass, 2000.

Pocock, Tom. *Fighting General: The Public and Private Campaigns of General Sir Walter Walker.* London: Collins, 1973.

Potter, David. 'Manpower Shortage and the End of Colonialism: The Case of the Indian Civil Service', *Modern Asian Studies*, 7, 1 (1973), pp. 47–73.

Pratten, Garth. *Australian Battalion Commanders in the Second World War*. Melbourne: Cambridge University Press, 2009.

Proudfoot, C. L. *We Lead: 7th Light Cavalry*. New Delhi: Lancer Publishing, 1991.

Qureshi, Maj. Mahommed Ibrahim. *The First Punjabis: History of the 1st Punjab Regiment*. Aldershot: Gale & Polden, 1958.

Raghavan, Srinath. 'Protecting the Raj: The Army in India and Internal Security, 1919–1939', *Small Wars and Insurgencies*, 16, 3 (Dec. 2005), pp. 253–79.

Robb, Peter, ed. *The Concept of Race in South Asia*. Oxford University Press, 1997.

Roberts, Michael. *Golden Arrow: The Story of the 7th Indian Division in the Second World War*. Aldershot: Gale & Polden, 1952.

Rooney, David. *Burma Victory: Imphal, Kohima and the Chindit Issue*. London: Arms and Armour, 1992.

Roy, Kaushik, ed. *War and Society in Colonial India*. New Delhi: Oxford University Press, 2006.

'The Armed Expansion of the English East India Company: 1740s–1849', in Marston and Sundaram, eds., *Military History of India and South Asia*, pp. 1–15.

'Military Loyalty in the Colonial Context: A Case Study of the Indian Army During World War II', *Journal of Military History*, 73 (Apr. 2009), pp. 497–529.

The Indian Army in the Two World Wars. Leiden: Brill, 2012.

Seaman, Harry. *The Battle at Sangshak*. London: Leo Cooper, 1989.

Sen, S. N. *Eighteen Fifty-Seven*. New Delhi: Government of India, 1957.

Settar, S. and Gupta, Indira, eds. *Pangs of Partition: The Human Dimension*. New Delhi: Manohar, 2002.

Sharma, Lt Col Gautam. *Nationalisation of the Indian Army*. New Delhi: Allied Publishers, 1996.

Singh, Gajendra. 'Breaking the Chains with which We Were Bound: The Interrogation Chamber, the Indian National Army and the Negation of Military Identities', in Roy, ed., *The Indian Army in the Two World Wars*, pp. 493–518.

Smith, E. D. *Battles for Cassino*. London: Scribner, 1975.

Spector, Ronald. 'After Hiroshima: Allied Military Occupations and the Fate of Japan's Empire, 1945–1947', *Journal of Military History*, 69, 4 (Oct. 2005), pp. 1121–36.

Springhall, John. 'Disaster in Surabaya: The Death of Brigadier Mallaby During the British Occupation of Java, 1945–1946', *Journal of Imperial and Commonwealth History*, 24, 3 (Sep. 1996), pp. 422–43.

'Kicking Out the Vietminh: How Britain Allowed France to Reoccupy South Indo-China, 1945–1946', *Journal of Contemporary History*, 40, 1 (Jan. 2005), pp. 115–30.

Stanley, Peter. *The White Mutiny: British Military Culture in India 1825–1875*. New York: C. Hurst, 1998.

Stevens, G. R. *Red Eagle: The Fourth Indian Division*. London: McLaren & Sons, 1948.

History of the 2nd King Edward VII's Own Gurkha Rifles, vol. III. Aldershot: Gale & Polden, 1952.

Streets, Heather. *Martial Races: The Military, Race, and Masculinity in the British Imperial Culture, 1857–1914.* Manchester University Press, 2004.

Sundaram, Chandar. 'Soldier Disaffection and the Creation of the Indian National Army', *Indo-British Review*, 19, 1 (1990), pp. 155–62.

'A Paper Tiger: The Indian National Army in Battle, 1944–1945', *War and Society*, 13, 1 (May 1995), pp. 35–59.

'Reviving a Dead Letter: Military Indianization and the Ideology of Anglo-India, 1885–1891', in P. S. Gupta and A. Deshpande, eds., *The British Raj and Its Armed Forces, 1857–1939*, pp. 45–97. Delhi: Oxford University Press, 2002.

'Seditious Letters and Steel Helmets: Disaffection Among Indian Troops in Singapore and Hong Kong, 1940–1941, and the Formation of the Indian National Army', in Roy, ed., *War and Society in Colonial India*, pp. 126–60.

'Grudging Concessions: The Officer Corps and Its Indianization, 1817–1940', in Marston and Sundaram, eds., *Military History of India and South Asia*, pp. 88–101.

'The Indian National Army, 1942–1946: A Circumstantial Force', in Marston and Sundaram, eds., *Military History of India and South Asia*, pp. 123–40.

Swarna, Aiyar. 'August Anarchy: The Partition Massacres in Punjab, 1947', *South Asia*, 18 (1995), pp. 13–36.

Swinson, Arthur. *Kohima.* London: Cassell, 1966.

Four Samurai: A Quartet of Japanese Army Commanders in the Second World War. London: Hutchinson, 1968.

Talbot, Ian. *Punjab and the Raj, 1849–1947.* Delhi: Oxford University Press, 1988.

Khizr Tiwana: The Punjab Unionist Party and the Partition of India. London: Curzon Press, 1996.

Divided Cities: Partition and Its Aftermath in Lahore and Amritsar, 1947–1957. Oxford University Press, 2006.

'A Tale of Two Cities: The Aftermath of Partition for Lahore and Amritsar 1947–1957', *Modern Asian Studies*, 41, 1 (2007), pp. 151–85.

'The 1947 Violence in the Punjab', in Talbot, ed., *Deadly Embrace*, pp. 1–15.

ed. *The Deadly Embrace: Religion, Politics and Violence in India and Pakistan 1947–2002.* Oxford University Press, 2007.

Talbot, Ian and Singh, Gurharpal, eds. *Region and Partition: Bengal, Punjab and the Partition of the Subcontinent.* Oxford University Press, 1999.

eds. *The Partition of India.* Cambridge University Press, 2009.

Toye, Hugh. *The Springing Tiger. A Study of a Revolutionary: Subhas Chandra Bose.* London: Cassell, 1959.

Trench, Charles Chenevix. *The Indian Army and the King's Enemies 1900–1947.* London: Thames and Hudson, 1988.

Turnbull, Patrick. *The Battle of the Box.* London: Ian Allen, 1979.

von Tunzelmann, Alex. *Indian Summer.* New York: Henry Holt, 2007.

Wainwright, Mary Doreen. 'Keeping the Peace in India, 1946–1947: The Role of Lt General Sir Francis Tuker in Eastern Command', in C. H. Philips and Wainwright, eds., *The Partition of India: Policies and Perspective, 1935–1947*, pp. 127–47. London: George Allen and Unwin, 1970.

Warner, Philip. *Auchinleck: The Lonely Soldier*. London: Buchan & Enright, 1981.

Wickremesekera, Channa. *'Best Black Troops in the World': British Perceptions and the Making of the Sepoy, 1746–1805*. New Delhi: Manohar, 2002.

Winks, Robin, ed. *The Oxford History of the British Empire*, vol. V. Oxford University Press, 1999.

Wolpert, Stanley. *Shameful Flight: The Last Years of the British Empire in India*. Oxford University Press, 2006.

Yeats-Brown, F. *Martial India*. London: Eyre & Spottiswoode, 1945.

Yong, Tan Tai. 'Punjab and the Making of Pakistan: The Roots of a Civil–Military State', in Low and Brasted, eds., *Freedom*, pp. 199–215.

The Garrison State: The Military, Government and Society in Colonial Punjab, 1849–1947. New Delhi: Sage Publications, 2005.

Index

Abell, G. E. B., 170
Aiyar, Swarna, 316, 335
Alanbrooke, Lord, 76, 166, 193, 274
Alexander of Tunis, Earl, Field Marshal,
  57, 76
Alexander, Horace, 220
Amery, Leo, 80, 91, 103, 107, 241–2
  comments on/dealings with Auchinleck,
    57, 78, 86–7, 109
  criticisms of London government, 91–2,
    109
  favourable comments on Indian troops,
    63, 96
  role in Indianisation process, 98–9
Amritsar Massacre (1919), 38, 40, 208, 210
Anderson, Perry, 1
Arakan region (Burma)
  Allied counteroffensive, 71, 73, 124
  Allied reverses in, 68–9
Ardene, E. A., Brig., 62
artillery units, development of, 32
assamis, 36
Attlee, Clement, 137, 193, 203–4, 234,
    247, 276, 285
  statement on Transfer of Power, 288–9, 295
Auchinleck, Sir Claude, Field Marshal,
    33, 84, 98, 145, 266, 273, 303, 342
  1936 reform proposals, 41–2
  acceptance/handling of partition, 258–9
  and famine relief, 109
  anti-discriminatory measures, 84, 86–7,
    90, 94
  appointment to India Command, 57, 70,
    86, 92–3
  biographical background, 41
  change of departure date, 345–6
  comments on civil–military situation,
    1946–7, 205, 217, 222, 226, 235,
    308–9, 319, 321, 323, 332
  comments on Indianisation, 121–42
  comments on loyalty/morale, 113–14, 345

concerns over occupation zones, 153,
  156–7, 165, 167, 170, 186, 193, 198
concerns over Transfer of Power
  announcement, 289–90
criticised by colleagues, 138–9, 265
criticisms of Chatfield Report, 43
dealings with Indian politicians, 1946–7,
  207
end of tenure, 343–8
fears for (post-independence) future,
  250–2, 266, 270, 343, 345, 347
final report, 344–5
handling of civil unrest (1946–7), 203
handling of demobilisation, 241, 243, 247
handling of INA trials, 119, 130–1,
  133–8, 140–2, 147–50
handling of North African campaigns, 54
handling of Punjab crisis (1947), 302,
  309, 312, 316, 321
Indian politicians' attacks on, 266, 269,
  271–2, 344, 346
Indian politicians' positive assessments
  of, 247
misjudgements of political situation, 131,
  265, 349
objections to Breakdown Plan, 233–4
opposition to division of army, 254–5,
  257–8, 265–6
opposition to release of INA prisoners,
  285–7
plans for Gurkhas, 274, 277
plans for post-war army, 94–5, 98–9, 112,
  136–7, 142, 246, 249
progressive approach, 4, 76, 351
proposals for nationalisation/division,
  248–9, 261–7, 280
recruitment policy, 78–81
refusal of peerage, 347
sense of failure/betrayal, 343–4, 346–7
Supreme Command of joint force, 267,
  269–70

375

Cambridge Studies in Indian History and Society
Other titles in the series